HANDBOOKS

ON THE

HISTORY OF RELIGIONS

EDITED BY

MORRIS JASTROW, Jr., Ph.D.

*Late Professor of Semitic Languages in the
University of Pennsylvania*

VOLUME V

LONDON : HUMPHREY MILFORD

Oxford University Press

THE RELIGION OF THE HEBREWS

BY

JOHN PUNNETT PETERS, Ph.D., Sc.D., D.D.

CAMBRIDGE

HARVARD UNIVERSITY PRESS

1932

PRINTED AT THE HARVARD UNIVERSITY PRESS
CAMBRIDGE, MASS., U. S.A.

TO MY WIFE

PREFACE

A knowledge of the religion of the Hebrews is of prime importance not only to the professed believer in religion but also to the student of civilization, for religion plays a large part in the history of civilization. Indeed, generally speaking, religion and economics are the two great elements of civilization.

In the broader sense of religion, the religion of the Hebrews was partner with the religions of Greece, Italy, and the Teutons in the creation of the religious-cultural-humane element of our civilization. In the narrower sense of religion, the religion discussed in this volume is the parent of the dominant religion of our civilization.

The religion of the Hebrews produced two great world religions, Christianity and Islam, the most vitally aggressive and the most universal of all religions, and a third, national, religion, Judaism, circumscribed in size though not in space by its racial character, but playing a part quite out of proportion to the number of its adherents. Of these the first and the last are direct descendants of the religion of the Hebrews; Islam belongs to a side line. Philosophically none of the three is thoroughly intelligible without a knowledge of the religion of the Hebrews; practically that knowledge is of great value both to the actual adherents of all and also to their spiritual descendants, who comprise, if not absolutely the greater, at least the overwhelmingly dominant part of the human race.

Considered critically, merely as a phenomenon, the religion of the Hebrews is of peculiar interest, because we are able to trace its development from the rudest beginnings to the completed form with an accuracy and precision possible in the case of no other religion. Hence it becomes practically the norm for the study of other religions, throwing light on their origins and the methods of their growth to a degree greater than they do on it or on one another.

Considered spiritually it is of absorbing interest because of the very great beauty of its flower and the surpassing virtue of its

ix

fruit, and also because of the fascinating manner in which flower and fruit developed.

This volume is the result of the special labor of over twenty years. I began the work light-heartedly, thinking that I knew my theme. It was years before I succeeded in writing the first chapter; and many a time I have been ready to lay down my pen and abandon the task as too hard for me. It is with deep humility that I present this volume as my attempt, to which I have given the very heart of my life, at the solution of a great problem.

One result of my study of the questions which confronted me in preparing some of the chapters of this work has been a number of by-products in the shape of books and articles dealing with special themes. If I seem to refer excessively and egotistically to these my own writings, it is because they are in a large sense a part of this work.

The literature on my theme is so vast that it is impossible for any one man to know or to have read it all; and even the small part with which I am familiar is too large for reference in such a volume. I have sought to make the bibliography of practical use, omitting the obsolete and obsolescent, and mentioning only that which is up-to-date and of present value. Where a number of works cover the same theme or present the same view, I have generally eliminated all but one or two. Where a good presentation of the matter is to be found in English, I have referred to the English, not the foreign, book or article.

I am indebted for much assistance and valuable suggestions, direct and indirect, to those too many to mention. To the general editor I owe thanks not only for general directions on scope and plan but also for a careful reading of manuscript and proof, and for many suggestions inscribed on their margins. To the publishers I am grateful, as for their good work as publishers, so also for their forbearance with my unbearable delays. Through them also I desire to thank the proofreader whose intelligent, accurate, and conscientious work has won my admiration.

JOHN P. PETERS

St. Michael's Church, New York

CONTENTS

ABBREVIATIONS

LXX	The Septuagint, or Greek translation of the Old Testament.
Mt.	The Masoretic, or official pointed, Hebrew text of the Old Testament.
J. B. L.	*Journal of Biblical Literature.*
A. J. S. L.	*American Journal of Semitic Languages and Literature.*
Z. A.	*Zeitschrift für Assyriologie.*
Z. A. T. W.	*Zeitschrift für alttestamentliche Wissenschaft.*

THE RELIGION OF THE HEBREWS

CHAPTER I

SOURCES AND METHODS OF STUDY

The primary and almost the sole source for the study of the religion of Israel is the books of the Old Testament.

The Old Testament is divided, according to Jewish tradition, into three main divisions: the Law, that is the Pentateuch, which is ascribed to Moses; the Prophets, that is Joshua, Judges, Samuel, and Kings, called the Former Prophets, and Isaiah, Jeremiah, Ezekiel, and the Book of the Twelve (minor prophets), called the Latter Prophets; and the Writings, or Hagiographa, consisting of Psalms, Proverbs, Job, Canticles, Ruth, Lamentations, Esther, Daniel, Ezra, Nehemiah, and Chronicles. Christian tradition, following the use of the Greek-speaking Alexandrian Jews, has arranged these books in a different order and added to them certain other writings, commonly known as the Apocrypha.

Almost all of these books are assigned by tradition, both of the Jews and of the Christians, to known authors. The Pentateuch was generally supposed to be the earliest work in point of date and to have been composed by Moses. The last book, excluding the Apocrypha, was Malachi, written perhaps in the fifth century B.C. These books were, therefore, supposed to cover a period of about nine hundred years, the major part having been composed before the Exile, and only a few — Kings, Jeremiah, Lamentations, Ezekiel, Haggai, Zechariah, Chronicles, Ezra, Nehemiah, Esther, and Malachi — dating from the Exile or later. Between Malachi and the earliest of the apocryphal books yawned a chasm of two hundred years or more. The apocryphal books covered the period

I

from the beginning of the third to the middle of the first century B.C. All of the writings of the Old Testament, including the Apocrypha according to one tradition, and excluding it according to another, were supposed to possess a peculiar and miraculous accuracy, not only for doctrine and ethics but also for history and questions of fact.

The analytical and critical study of these writings on modern lines began in the latter half of the eighteenth century, but it was not until the latter part of the nineteenth century that the results began to be generally accepted. It has become impossible to maintain the traditional view with regard to the books of the Old Testament. On the other hand, it must be acknowledged that the process of examination is not yet complete, and we are by no means certain as to the date or the historical value of not a few of the Old Testament books. In general we need to observe that the Old Testament is not a single book, but a collection of books, the literary remains of the people of Israel, constituting a religious library, consisting of histories, stories, legal codes, ritual directions, songs, proverbs, philosophy, and sermons. It stands, for instance, in striking contrast to the sacred book of Islam, in that while the Koran is the work of one man and, so far as it represents any progress in religious thought, represents only the progress and development of one man during a part of his life, the Old Testament is a collection of books by many hands and from many ages, diverse in thought as well as expression, so catholic that it includes within itself on the one side the most positive expressions of belief, and on the other utterances which approach very nearly agnosticism ; that we find side by side such broad-minded teachings as those of the book of Amos, that God cared alike for Philistines, Aramæans, and Hebrews, or the still broader utterances of that beautiful parable of Jonah, which seems to put Jew and Gentile on the same footing, and the narrow and exclusive teachings of the priest and scribe Ezra, or the bitterly anti-gentile spirit of Esther ; that you may find in one book the expression of a total lack of belief in the life after death, in another questionings as to the possibility of a life beyond the present, as in Job ; or, finally, the clear utterance in the Book of Daniel of a belief in the resurrection of the body. Again, turning to the ethical side, you find in one part the doctrine that a man's deeds are rewarded here with good or ill so interpreted (and that is the common view), that calamity is an evidence of sin, which sin it may be was a mere ritual or ceremonial transgression, and prosperity an evidence of righteousness; while in another part, in the grand Book of Job, this doctrine is categorically refuted (although in this same book there was ultimately inserted, by some defender of the older orthodoxy, a defense of the old view and a refutation of the new, namely, the speech of Elihu). The Old Testament is a catholic book; it is a nation's religious experience; the literature of a nation which has come down to us, but that literature sorted and sifted from the point of view of religious experience, so that what has survived is not the entire literature but the religious literature of the people, the secular literature appearing only in so far as it has been recast in a religious mold or brought into some relation with the religious experience of the nation. It is, moreover, the religious experience of the nation, not at one period, but throughout its life, from infancy onward. The Old Testament must inevitably, therefore, display development. That development is somewhat obscured in our ordinary English Bibles by the arrangement of the books, and somewhat also by the names which are attached to them, leading us to attribute certain books to certain authors and hence to certain periods to which they do not properly belong. In general the literature of the Old Testament is anonymous, and in general the individual books of the Old Testament represent a growth, extending sometimes over a considerable period of time.

The Hebrew methods of historical and legal composition and compilation may, perhaps, be most conveniently illustrated in general by a parallel in English history and legislation. With Alfred the Great in England begins the *Saxon Chronicle*, founded originally on the Bishops' Roll in Winchester. The latter consisted of very meager annals in Latin, concerned mainly with local affairs. Under Alfred's direction the effort was made to present history in the tongue of the people. The materials of the

Bishops' Roll were translated and to them was added fresh material, drawn from the narrative of Bede and other sources, and the history was brought down to date. But not content with this, Alfred made the effort to connect the history of England with the great world event of the Incarnation, and so the story was carried back to that point. Copies of this *Saxon Chronicle* were deposited in various monasteries. In some of these the work was continued by various hands, the continuations carrying on the story with additions and peculiarities distinctive of different localities.

At a later date Florence of Worcester composed a new historical work, combining some form or forms of this *Saxon Chronicle* with the work of Irish Marian, which latter work starts, not with the Incarnation, but with the creation of the world. Thus there was produced a composite narrative, with regard to which it is difficult, if not impossible, to say what is from one source, what from the other, and what from Florence of Worcester himself. As Sir Thomas Hardy writes:

Monastic chronicles were seldom the production of a single hand, as in the case of Malmesbury and of Beda. They grew up from period to period; each age added fresh material, and every house in which they were copied supplied fresh local information, until the tributary streams often grew more important than the original current. The motives and objects of the mediæval chronicler were different from those of the modern historian. He did not consider himself tied by those restrictions to which the latter implicitly submits. The monastic annalist was at one time a transcriber, at another time an abridger, at another an original author. . . . He epitomized or curtailed or adopted the works of his predecessors in the same path without alteration and without acknowledgement just as best suited his own purpose or that of his monastery. He did not work for himself but at the command of others. His own profit and his own vanity were not concerned in the result. It was enough if he pleased his superior. So with no feeling of individual aggrandizement or responsibility, he adopted what he thought good or worth preserving, at the same time adding or interpolating according to his individual knowledge, taste, or opportunities. And as he acted towards others, so others in succession acted towards him. Thus it was that a monastery chronicle grew like a monastic house, by the labour of different hands and different times. But of the head that planned it, of the hands that executed it, or of the exact proportion contributed by each, no satisfactory record was preserved. **The individual was lost in the community.**

Such was the growth of Hebrew historical writing. For Hebrew legislation, also, we may find a parallel in early English legislation. Going back once more to the times of good King Alfred, we find him setting forth a code of laws known as *Alfred's Dooms*. This begins with a recital of the Ten Commandments and the substance of that early Israelite legislation which we find in chapters xx–xxiii of Exodus. But the Decalogue and the succeeding Israelite legislation both undergo transpositions and adaptations to suit them to the new conditions to which they are to be applied under Alfred. Of this, however, there is not a word in *Alfred's Dooms*; he only says that "these are the dooms which the Almighty God himself spake unto Moses and commanded him to keep." Similarly he quotes the apostolic letter of Acts xv, 23–29, commanding " to forbear from worshiping idols, and from tasting blood or things strangled, and from fornication," to which he adds, without any indication that he is adding something not in the original text, " And that which ye will that other men do not unto you, do ye not that to other men." This introductory section, if it may be so called, taken from the Old and New Testaments, or rather adapted from the Old and New Testaments, without any indication that it is not literally copied, is followed by a code of laws taken from the dooms of preceding kings, of which Alfred writes:

I, then, Alfred, king, gathered these together, and commanded many of those to be written which our forefathers held, those which to me seemed good; and many of those which seemed to me not good I rejected them, by the counsel of my 'witan,' and in otherwise commanded them to be holden; for I durst not venture to set down in writing much of my own, for it was unknown to me what of it would please those who should come after us. But those things which I met with, either of the days of Ine my kinsman, or of Offa king of the Mercians, or of Aethelbryght, who first among the English race received baptism, those which seemed to me the rightest, those I have here gathered together, and rejected the others.[1]

Space will not permit us to pursue these parallels further and to point out that it is not only in English history and English law that we find such methods: that Arabia and India and Syria supply

[1] Cf. Carpenter and Battersby, *The Hexateuch*, I, 5.

us with similar parallels, showing that the results which have been obtained by the critical analysis of the books of the Old Testament are not something peculiar to the literature of Israel, but belong to it in common with many other literatures in the earlier stages of growth and development.

The best view of the results obtained by modern criticism, and of the general dates and tendencies of the different books of the Old Testament, can probably be given by a brief review of the history of Hebrew literature looked at from the standpoint primarily of the historical literature; for the Hebrews are unique among oriental peoples in this: that they displayed, almost from the commencement of their national existence, an historical sense.

The first historical writing which has come down to us in a form sufficiently well preserved to enable us to speak of it as historical writing is a narrative of the founding of the kingdom of David (2 Sam. i–v, ix–xx; 1 Kings i, ii). This narrative is nearly contemporaneous with the events narrated, written probably in the time of Solomon, and considerable sections of it have been preserved practically untouched by later hands. It is without "tendency" and is the narrative of a story-teller rather than of an historian. What interests the writer is the effectiveness of episodes; accordingly it is not a complete history, neither does it follow an exact chronological order. The struggle to throw off the Philistine yoke is almost passed over, and, on the other hand, certain striking incidents of little historical consequence are treated at great length; such as David's generosity to Saul, the friendship of David and Jonathan, the story of David and Bathsheba. The objective character of this narrative, its lack of "tendency," and especially the absence from it of religious pragmatism (that is, the attempt to make the history teach or confirm a religious doctrine), make it a very valuable document for the history of the time, religious as well as political.

At about the same period, a little earlier or a little later, were formed one or more collections of songs. One of these was entitled The Book of Yashar (i.e. Israel). From this by title there are quoted in the Old Testament three songs or parts of songs,

Joshua x, 12 ff.; 2 Samuel i, 19–27; 1 Kings viii, 13 (cf. Septuagint). Another songbook referred to in the Pentateuch is the Book of the Wars of Yahaweh, from which is quoted Numbers xxi, 14. Another songbook (or is this a quotation without title from one of the two already mentioned?) is cited simply as the "verse makers," or "proverb makers" (Num. xxi, 27 ff.).[1]

There are also a number of ancient songs for which no book or collection is named, — such as the Deborah Song, Judges v; the Lamech Song, Genesis v, 23 ff.; the Ark Song, Numbers x, 35, 36; perhaps also the Song of the Sea (Ex. xv), and the Oracles of Balaam (Num. xx, 14 ff.) in their original form, — but which may have been contained in some of the collections mentioned above, or in others not known to us by name.

There were also, as we shall see presently, stories, traditions, and laws which had already earlier assumed a definite form and some of which may have been committed to writing; but it is with the time of Solomon (ca. 933–910 B.C.) that the real literary activity of the Hebrews may be said to begin, — the writing of history, the gathering of songs into collections, and the like. It is in the times of David and Solomon, also, that we first meet with historical records — official annals, containing names of officials, revenue lists, notices of victories, wars, treaties, and, on what we may call more distinctly the religious side, temple reports, ceremonial or ritual directions, and the like.

Historical writing and the collection of songs and folk stories, having begun, progressed with a considerable degree of rapidity. The story of King David was soon followed by a narrative of his early life and exploits (1 Sam. xvi, 14–xxxi, which contains, however, in its present form two different narratives, later combined into one), and by a story of King Saul and the founding of his kingdom (1 Sam. ix; x, 1–16; xi, 1–11, 15; xiii; xiv). Like the story of King David these are simple narratives, without "tendency," delighting in picturesque and interesting episodes. They have come down to us practically unmodified, and are, therefore, sources of the first

---

[1] Both of these latter collections are cited by the Israelitic historians, not by the Judæan.

importance for the study of the life and thought of the rude but forceful times of Saul and David.

Note that precisely what happened in the writing of English history happened here also. First there were the narratives of contemporary events; then the attempt was made to utilize previous material and to form a history of what had been. So here the attention of the writers and collectors of history was next attracted to the period preceding the establishment of the kingdom. For this period there was not the same recent historical tradition; but in various localities the memory of heroic deeds and their doers had been preserved, such as the victory of Deborah and Barak in the struggle of the Israelites and Canaanites for the possession of the Plain of Esdraelon (for which we have also a contemporary document in the shape of the so-called Song of Deborah, Judges v), the story of Ehud the Benjaminite hero, of Jephthah the hero of Gilead, Gideon of Manasseh, and the others. In some of these there was considerable legendary matter intermixed, and in one of them, the story of Samson, perhaps even mythical material; but in general these stories as collected and rewritten by the historians of this period give us a faithful picture of the conditions preceding the foundation of the kingdom for a number of generations, but without consecution or chronological order.

Going back of this group of stories, we come to a period for which, when history began to be written, the tradition was already meager and comparatively colorless, — the invasion and settlement of Canaan, and the period lying between that invasion and the exodus from Egypt. Here and there a fuller tradition of special events had been preserved, as in the case of the crossing of the Jordan, the capture of Jericho, the war with Ai, and the league with the Gibeonites; but in general the tradition is not distinct, and the earliest written history of the period bears evidences of reflection and the working back into the earlier history of later situations, for lack of a fuller tradition of those periods. On the other hand, the deliverance from Egypt and the solemn adoption of a religious code and of the worship of Yahaweh stand out with great prominence, but are obscured, even in this earliest history, by a mass of miraculous stories. For the period preceding the entrance of Israel into Egypt the historians evidently found abundant material ready to their hands. The stories of the Patriarchs are told with a wealth of detail, in striking contrast with the terse and colorless account of the period succeeding the Exodus. But this material was of a different description from that employed for the later periods. Here we have evidently reached the legendary period pure and simple. The material out of which these legends were wrought is various. The main stock is ethnological traditions and speculations cast in a genealogical form. Different tribes and families had different memories, which were already embodied in legends. Some of the tribes were connected with the nomadic peoples to the south and southeast of Palestine. Others were connected with the Aramæans to the northeast. Some apparently had connections with the Canaanites. All these relations and traditions of migrations are represented in the Patriarchal legends, together with the legendary lore of various sanctuaries, recounting the origin of rites and customs prevalent there. With these may be mixed a few foreign elements, like the story of Joseph's temptation, which has a striking parallel in the Egyptian romance of the " Two Brothers." Mingled with what is early we find also later historical events recorded in the form of a personal narrative. The exodus from Egypt appears as the story of Abraham in Egypt, where his wife, Sarah, was taken by Pharaoh, whereupon God punished the Egyptians with sore boils, so that they gladly sent him forth out of the land with his wife and his goods.[1] The later deliverance of Israel from the Philistines is told in the similar story of Abraham, Sarah, and the Philistine king, who took her into his harem, only to suffer a similar fate; for Yahaweh was with the Israelites, and delivered them from the hand of the Philistines.[2] All these divers elements had been fused together to form these legends before the period of the historical

---

[1] Gen. xii, 11 ff.

[2] Gen. xx, 2 ff. The same story is told again of Isaac and Rebekah (Gen. xxiv, 7 ff.), one of the narratives coming from J and the other from E.

writers, and parts of the stories of the Patriarchs bear evidence of a long development in the mouths of story-tellers, so that they had reached a high pitch of the story-teller's art before they were finally committed to writing by the historians. What was done by the historical collectors or writers of this period was to gather together all this Patriarchal legend and form out of it a continuous history of the early period of Israel. And as to the *Saxon Chronicle* was prefixed an introduction, carrying back the history of England to the Incarnation, — in Irish Marian, to the creation of the world, — so to the stories of the Patriarchs was ultimately prefixed what may be called an introduction, carrying the history of Israel back to the beginning of the world. In this introduction, which will be found within the limits of the first twelve chapters of Genesis, we have a combination and reworking of material drawn from old Palestinian and Babylonian sources. The flood myth appears to be of Babylonian origin, but with Palestinian features and names. The same is true of the myths of creation and the origin of evil. The story of the beginning of the human race and the development of civilization is strikingly similar to Phœnician myths, fragments of which have come down to us. This series of writings belonging to one general line is represented in the Hexateuch (Genesis–Joshua) by the sections designated by modern critics as J, and their counterparts in Judges and 1 Samuel. As already stated, this work began to be composed in the time of Solomon (the tenth century B.C.). The work once commenced went on in Judah after the separation of the kingdom, reaching its completion somewhere in the ninth century B.C., if that can be called completion which was never complete. For, once composed, this work still continued to be changed, added to at the end to bring it down to later dates, and reëdited by each new possessor, somewhat after the fashion of the monastic chronicles before described. The work, for this series of writings may be called a work, — a history of the world, Israel, Judah, up to date, — was anonymous, and regarded very literally as the property of the reader, who might himself add to it or change it, the possession of a book entitling and almost requiring the possessor to be its reviser and editor also.

This Yahawist series of historical writings is a source of the first importance for the study of the religion of Israel in the period of David and Solomon. It is of almost the same value for the period of Saul and the Judges, including Samuel. The further back we go the more caution we must observe in its use. It has not, unfortunately, come down to us intact. There have been considerable changes made in uniting it with other works, resulting in omissions at some places, and a certain amount of modification in later editions, under the influence of the religious views which had then come to prevail.

The ninth century saw a marked change in the conditions of the northern kingdom, Israel. During the first generations after the separation of Judah and Israel there had been little chance for literary activity in the latter kingdom; but in the ninth century a great king, Omri, brought order out of the chaos which had prevailed since the death of Jeroboam, made a nation out of a disintegrating congeries of tribes, and established a dynasty which governed Israel for over forty years, to be overthrown and succeeded by another dynasty, that of Jehu, which held the reins of government for a century. This period was, moreover, one of religious agitation and prophetical activity from the time of Ahab (876–854) onward. Both of these elements made themselves felt in the literary activity of the northern kingdom. The comparative stability of the government, with the resultant increase of national pride and national feeling, and the improved conditions of life, stimulated intellectual and literary activity, and moved men to commit to writing the history of their state, while the religious and prophetical movement gave to this literary product a character somewhat different from the Judæan series of historical writings above considered. In a sense this Israelite work was a rival of the similar Judæan series. As the latter belonged to the southern, so the former belonged to the northern kingdom. The material used was the same, but the moral and religious point of view was different. Certain things offensive to the religious ideas of a later age are removed or modified in the Israelite work. For instance, the Aramæan forefathers are regarded as idolaters. Instead of merely narrating the events, this historian passes judgment upon the conduct of the people from a moral and religious standpoint somewhat similar to that of the prophet Hosea.

This is the work or series of works designated by the critics of the Hexateuch as E, with some similar material in the books of Judges, Samuel, and Kings. The origin and development of this work is very similar to that of the Judæan historical series; but here the earliest material is probably to be found in the Book of Judges, some of which is almost contemporary with the Judæan stories in the same book. As a whole, however, this Israelite historical series belongs to the first part of the eighth century B.C., a century later than the Judæan work.

Like the work of the Judæan historian, the Israelite work also underwent a series of what one might call unconscious editions in the hands of successive users with the same ideas but with a constantly increasing religious pragmatism. From the time of David, in addition to the stream of popular story, there existed in the Judæan kingdom, as already pointed out, official records of the succession of kings, the building of cities and fortified places, wars, the succession of priests, changes and improvements in the Temple, etc. These were made use of by successive continuators of the Judæan history, who brought down the story to their own times, adding to it probably additional facts and variant accounts of events already narrated. In the case of the northern kingdom either such records did not exist, or, at least, we have in the Israelite history no such extracts from official documents as meet us in the story of the southern kingdom; the stream of popular story was the principal reliance of the narrators and continuators.

As already pointed out, the Judæan series of historical writings incorporated in itself various songs and poems, derived in some cases from collections already in existence. The Israelite historical work did the same thing, and to it we must presumably ascribe the preservation of a number of ancient poems, including the Blessings of Jacob, Genesis xlix.[1] But in addition to songs

---

[1] The Blessings of Jacob (Gen. xlix) belongs to the ninth century. The Blessings of Moses (Deut. xxxiii) is a century or more later than this (ca. 775-750 B.C.). "It

and poems each of these historical works also incorporated in itself a code of laws. A fragment of the code incorporated in the Judæan history is preserved in Exodus xxxiv, 12–26. The code contained in the Israelite history has been preserved somewhat more fully in Exodus xxi–xxiii. These codes of laws, like the songs and poems, are earlier than the histories in which they are incorporated. Both of them are based as to their form upon the original Decalogue, which goes back to the time of Moses. This also was incorporated in the Israelite work, prefixed to the longer and later code, Exodus xxi–xxiii. We have, therefore, in the Israelite historical work a section of early laws (Exodus xx–xxiii, almost untouched in chaps. xxi–xxiii, but with considerable later material in parts of chap. xx), going back in their earliest stratum to the very foundation of the people and the religion of Israel.

Sometime toward the beginning of the eighth century there grew up in the northern kingdom a collection of stories about the great prophets of the ninth century, Micaiah ben Imlah, Elijah, and Elisha (incorporated in part in our present Book of Kings). This marks the growth of a new branch of literature, which became so popular that it was continued later by Judæan writers in the lives of the Prophets, of which we have fragments in our present books of Isaiah and Jeremiah. The literary development of the northern kingdom, once begun, was rapid. Following the beginning made by the stories of the Prophets, either the Prophets themselves or their hearers and followers began to collect and write down the prophecies which they uttered. The earliest collections which have come down to us are the two books or collections of prophecies of Amos and Hosea, dating from about the middle of the eighth century B.C. At this time Samaria, not

is not meant to assert, however, that these are necessarily the dates of composition of the various individual ' blessings.' The Blessings of Jacob especially is far from homogeneous in style or treatment. A comparison of the various ' blessings ' in Gen. xlix and Deut. xxxiii with corresponding passages in Jud. v and Gen. xxx seems to show that these tribal characterizations or ' blessings ' were of ancient origin. What was done by the authors of Gen. xlix and Deut. xxxiii was to work up such more ancient separate couplets into one complete poem, modifying and amplifying the same by those historical and political allusions which their time and standpoint suggested " (Peters, " Jacob's Blessing," *J. B. L.*, 1886).

Jerusalem, was the center of literary activity and religious progress. The relation of Samaria to Judah may be compared to that of the Eastern Empire to Rome in the Dark and early Middle Ages, and the capture of Samaria and its destruction by the Assyrians in 721 B.C. had the same effect on the intellectual and ultimately the religious life of Judæa which the destruction of Constantinople in 1453 had upon the literary, and ultimately the religious, life of the West in the fifteenth and sixteenth centuries. The fall of Samaria brought about a renaissance in Judah. Prophetic activity was transferred to Judah, and from 721 or thereabouts onward we have in Judah a succession of writings dealing professedly with the religious life, and in general from the standpoint of the reformer, which we call the prophetical books. They are written in a peculiar rhythm, for the most part, not prose and yet not quite poetry, but interspersed with lyrical outbursts, and occasionally containing fragments of old songs, or utterances based on the model of familiar poems, vintage songs, and the like. It is a long succession : Amos and Hosea, the prophets of the northern kingdom, whose works were cast in their present literary shape under Judæan influence ; then Isaiah and Micah ; in the next century Nahum, Habakkuk, and Zephaniah ; then, partly in the seventh and partly in the sixth century, Jeremiah ; in the Captivity, Ezekiel ; at the close of the same century, the sixth, Haggai and Zechariah ; and at a later date Malachi, Obadiah, and Joel. But, as in the case of the histories, the books of these writers have not come down to us precisely in the form in which they were composed. Once intrusted to writing, the prophecies, like all other writings of the time, became the property of those into whose hands they fell, and were edited and changed to apply to new conditions, and sometimes to conform to new theological ideas. In some cases, most notably in the case of Isaiah, there is a large amount of material from unknown writers and other times collected together in the book which bears the name of the known prophet. It became the tendency, as time went on, to ascribe anonymous prophetical writings to prophets with well-known names, and to the name of Isaiah was attached a peculiarly large amount of material of this description. Much more than half of the book bearing his name is now attributed to other writers, beginning before his time (Is. xv, xvi), and stretching onward through the Persian, and perhaps even into the beginning of the Greek period (Is. xxiv-xxvii). In the case of the Book of Zechariah the second half of the book belongs to other and later authors. In the Book of Jeremiah we have, along with the writings of that prophet, a quite full account of his life and work, which is of the first value as an historical source for the last years of the seventh and the first years of the sixth century B.C. The other prophetical writings are more homogeneous, but none of them are without additions and modifications. The present tendency is to analyze the prophetical books to an extreme degree and carry down much of their contents to a late period; but even if all that the most extreme critics assume with regard to these books should prove to be true, we still have a collection of contemporary writings by religious teachers, of the first value for the study of the religion of Israel, covering a period of four centuries and a half, from 750 to 300 B.C.

These prophetical writers all emphasize the ethical side of Israel's relation to its God and God's dealing with Israel. God's favor or wrath, Hosea teaches, depends upon Israel's faithfulness or unfaithfulness. This being the case, it is Israel's unfaithfulness which is the cause of its calamities. Succeeding prophets emphasize this doctrine still more, and carry it further toward its logical conclusion, until Ezekiel, in the beginning of the sixth century, passes a most sweeping judgment on the national life of Israel. All the calamities which have befallen the nation, even back to the oppression in Egypt, are due to hardness of heart and persistent and repeated apostasy. This prophetical view makes itself felt in the historical writings from the eighth century onward. It has already been pointed out that the historical writer designated as E passes moral judgment upon Israel on lines similar to those of Hosea; and continuators of both E and J show in an increasing degree the influence of this prophetic doctrine in the interpretation of history.

After the fall of Samaria (721 B.C.) all the religious and literary activity of the nation was transferred to and centered in Jerusalem.

Now began a reworking and combining of the two great historical works of Israel and Judah, under the influence of the teachings of the Prophets, like that work which Florence of Worcester did in English annals, in combining the *Saxon Chronicle* with the historical work of Irish Marian. This resulted in a new prophetical-historical work (designated by the critics, in the Hexateuch, J E), covering the period from the beginning of the world down to the fall of Samaria. In this work, completed, perhaps, toward the middle of the seventh century B.C., the two rival historical series were combined, and the history of Israel was interpreted according to the philosophy of the prophets. However, history is still the main thing; its moral teaching is prominent, but the history is not written merely for its moral.

And now we come to the period of the Reformation in the religion of Israel, with its mighty effects upon the literary as upon the religious life of the people. As the Reformation in the Christian Church was an attempt to restore the pure doctrine of Jesus Christ, rejecting the traditions and fables, the rites and superstitions which had grown up in the Middle Ages, and restoring the primitive doctrine and the primitive word, so the Reformation in Israel undertook to go back to the doctrine of Moses, the great founder of the religion of Israel. Sometime in the seventh century B.C. there was composed the Book of Deuteronomy, which undertook to set forth the true teaching of Moses. Much of it is put in the mouth of Moses, the beginning of a very large pseudepigraphical literature. It is a public instruction on the law of Israel, ordained of God, enforced by exhortation, in which use is made of the lesson of history. It insists upon the worship of Yahaweh at one place only, without image or symbol. It stands for a pure, national religion, uncontaminated with foreign rites. It condemns witchcraft and many of the public superstitions and religious practices of the people, and it teaches that the welfare of Israel is dependent upon a strict adherence to the law of Moses here laid down, and that any deviation from that law must necessarily bring calamity and punishment from God. This work, in fact, codifies the prophetic teaching which had its origin in Moses.

From this time on we find all the historical writing of the Hebrews colored by this doctrine, so that historians used it in the interpretation of the history of the past precisely as prophets applied it to the future, and history becomes, as it were, prophecy looking backward. From calamity the historians, from this time onward, argue unfaithfulness on the part of Israel. Calamity was the result of Yahaweh's wrath because of Israel's unfaithfulness, and the test of Israel's faithfulness was its observance of the doctrine of the worship of Yahaweh without image or symbol at the one temple in Jerusalem, uncontaminated by foreign rites. From the close of the seventh century B.C., therefore, the literature of Israel becomes (with one exception, Canticles) exclusively religious. After this historians no longer write history for itself, but only for the lesson it may teach. National and secular hymns, like the Song of Deborah and David's Lament for Saul and Jonathan, are no longer collected, even if composed. The new national poetry consists of exhortation and instruction, of which we have a good example in the Song of Moses, Deuteronomy xxxii. Poetry means moral lessons, lamentations, and hymns. History becomes religious instruction by example, and from this time forward all the historical writing of the Hebrews is religious in as true a sense as are the writings of the Prophets, for indeed, as already stated, it is inverted prophecy.

The first work of this Deuteronomic school of historical writing, which has come down to us, is the history of the kingdoms of Judah and Israel from the accession of Solomon and the building of the Temple onward. The predominance of the religious motive is apparent at the outset in the proportion of space given to the history of the Temple at Jerusalem. Those political events which illustrate the Deuteronomic lesson are made prominent, and, on the other hand, whole reigns are passed over without a word, if history did not here conform to the Deuteronomic doctrine. This new school of historians, in this also following the homiletic and exhortative method of Deuteronomy, makes use of speeches as an effective method of teaching the religious lesson of the history through the mouth of a contemporary, perhaps some nameless prophet. This historical work, our books of Kings, has come down to us in the form in which it was finally recast during the Exile. In this work the religious principles of the times of Josiah and the Exile are applied to the past; the kings of Judah are condemned for allowing the high places to stand, and the kings of Israel for countenancing the worship of the golden calves. At the same time former historical writings were revised more or less according to the Deuteronomic idea. The Book of Samuel has come down to us almost untouched by this recension. The Book of Judges, on the other hand, received at that time the pragmatic setting of its stories, — Israel sinned against Yahaweh, therefore Yahaweh sent such and such a punishment upon them, but when they cried unto Yahaweh, He delivered them by the hand of so-and-so. The stories themselves, however, have been preserved practically untouched, except at the beginning and ending of each, where they have been worked over to attach them to their setting. An endeavor was also made to arrange them in chronological order; and in both Judges and Kings we find an effort made to give dates and numbers. By the close of the Exile, we have a great historical work composed in the spirit of the Reformation, covering the period from the creation of the world to the Exile, in which was contained also the law-book of Deuteronomy.

Parallel with the writing of history ran the composition and codification of laws. Our earliest code of laws is the primitive Decalogue, which goes back to the time of Moses. Two recensions of the original Decalogue, with additions and explanations, have come down to us, one of them contained in the twentieth chapter of Exodus and the other in the fifth chapter of Deuteronomy. Evidently the Decalogue became the subject of comment, explanation, and expansion at a very early period. Subsequent codes, at least in their earlier strata, are founded upon this Decalogue, and are, to some extent, developments from it by the application of its principles to the experiences and needs of other times. The development is precisely like that of English legislation in the time of Alfred. Our first written codes of this character are contained, as already pointed out, in the historical works of the Judæan and Israelite historians, and are to be found, the first in the thirty-fourth chapter of Exodus, the second in chapters xxi–xxiii of the same book. The Book of Deuteronomy, composed in the latter part of the seventh century, shows us the existence at that period not only of the laws contained in those two codes, but also of a number of other laws of an ethical, social, ritual, ceremonial, and political character, which must have existed in writing before the date of the composition of that book. These laws were worked into a popular code in the Book of Deuteronomy, with the distinct object of reform in view. The Deuteronomic codifier did not, therefore, take every law which he found in existence, but in general such laws as were useful for the purposes of his reform, and which could be made intelligible to the people at large and applicable to their conditions. On the other hand, having a distinct object of reform in view, not only did he make a selection of laws, but he also modified laws already existing, and developed new laws intended to accomplish his purpose in reforming the people and bringing them back to the true doctrine of Moses.

From this time onward, and especially during and after the Exile, much activity was displayed in collecting and reworking the ancient laws of Israel, and more particularly the ritual and ceremonial laws of the Temple at Jerusalem. Ritual and ceremonial laws assumed, at this time, an importance in the estimation of the people that they had never enjoyed before. In the concluding chapters of the prophecies of Ezekiel (chaps. xl–xlviii), there is presented a sort of utopian restoration of the Temple and the nation. In these chapters we find a scheme of ritual, ceremonial, moral, and political laws, differing in many points from those contained in Deuteronomy. Closely akin to this scheme of laws in Ezekiel is a collection of laws, now generally known as the Laws of Holiness, the bulk of which is contained in Leviticus xvii–xxvi. This latter collection of laws is not, however, homogeneous. It is evident that at least two previously existing collections of laws have been worked together in this code. This code in its turn was worked into a later law-book or digest of the laws of Israel, now commonly known as the Priestly Code, which is contained, for the most part, in the books of Numbers and Leviticus. This is a very heterogeneous collection of judgments, laws, and statutes. Some of the laws incorporated in it merely state in the form of law actual practices, without theory and without " tendency." In other cases, we find a selection, adaptation, and correction of laws for a particular purpose. We have laws of an early date and laws of a very late date. The early material has, however, in most cases, been worked over from the standpoint of the later religious, ritual, and ceremonial conceptions.

This new codification or rather collection of the laws of Israel, from the standpoint of the priests of the Jerusalem Temple, was completed in Babylonia some time in the century succeeding the Exile. It has not come down to us as an independent law-book, but embedded in a later historical work, just as the earlier law-books contained in Exodus were incorporated in historical writings ; for during the Persian period a new history of Israel was written from the Creation to the settlement in Canaan. The object of this work, which was composed in Babylonia, was to relate the origin of the sacred institutions of the Jews. It seemed to the writer, with his philosophy of religion, that the sacred customs and the sacred laws of the Jews must date from the very beginning. Accordingly, in this work it is taught that the Sabbath was instituted at the Creation ; that the prohibition of the use of blood and the separation of clean and unclean animals dates from the time of Noah ; that circumcision was the seal of the covenant of Abraham ; that the ritual of the Temple was ordained at Sinai, and that the Temple ministry and the rules of that ministry originated at the same time. Advancing a step beyond the Deuteronomic writers, these post-exilic historians reasoned that the provision for one legitimate place of worship, for the mode of worship to be conducted there, and for the ministry by which that worship was to be conducted, were fundamental parts of the religion of Israel, ordained by God, and must, therefore, date from the foundation of that religion. Arguing from the later ritual practices, they developed an elaborate scheme of ritual, which they supposed to have been patterned on the construction and arrangement of the tabernacle

in the wilderness. The chronological tendencies of the Deuteronomic school are here developed into a scheme of statistics, and
everything is reduced to genealogies, dates, numbers, and measures.
In this work were contained many laws in an historical form:
under such and such circumstances, such and such a law was revealed. Finally it became the *cadre* for the great collection of
laws known as the Priestly Code, and in this form, as a combination of law-book and history, the work was introduced to the
Palestinian Jews.

During and after the Exile, along with the continuation and extension of historical works, took place also a unification of works
already in existence, until finally the various narratives of the
primeval world, the patriarchal age, the Exodus, and the whole
history of Israel down to and including the conquest of Canaan,
with the law-books which they contained, were united to form the
whole which we now know as the Hexateuch (Genesis–Joshua).
This work assumed its present form toward the close of the fifth
century B.C. The first five books of the Hexateuch were shortly
afterwards canonized, that is, made sacred books, and guarded from
change with a care which constantly increased as the ages progressed, so that from this time onward no changes of importance
were made in the text of those books.

During the Persian period, in the fifth and fourth centuries B.C.,
there developed among the Jews a new form of treatment of the
historical literature of the past, which we can best designate by the
Jewish word *midrash*. A *midrash* is an homiletic exposition, frequently in the form of a religious story, of the words of some
older writer. We find the beginnings of this midrashic treatment
of ancient history in the exilic Book of Kings (cf. 1 Kings xiii).
It finds its fuller development in our present Book of Chronicles,
a Palestinian work of the close of the fourth century B.C., which,
with our present books of Ezra and Nehemiah, constituted originally one work, comprehending in brief space the entire history
of Israel from the creation of the world to the time of writing.
The world is viewed from the standpoint of the Temple at Jerusalem and the law contained in the Pentateuch. From the attention

paid to the temple music, it would appear that the author was a Levitical musician. He ascribes the temple liturgy to David, and assumes that the ceremonies in use in his own day had been in existence through all the centuries before him. He judges the history of the people by their fidelity to the ecclesiastical and ritual system of his day. The prophetic pragmatism of the Deuteronomic school has here given place to a ritual and ecclesiastical pragmatism. Yahaweh vindicates His law, punishing His people for disobedience and rewarding them with prosperity for their obedience, but the law which He vindicates is no longer a law of ethics, but primarily a law of ritual. This theory is carried back into the history of the past. Whatever in the past seemed to contradict the theory is omitted or so modified as to assume a new shape. If a good king were punished, clearly there must have been some wickedness, hitherto unremarked, which the writer should discover; if a bad king, that is, one who disregarded the ceremonial law, were prosperous, clearly something was omitted, since he must have been punished in some manner, which this writer may discover and record. His aim was not to write a political but an ecclesiastical history. His work was based on a lost midrashic work, to which he refers variously as the "Book of the Kingdom of Israel and Judah," "Book of Samuel the Prophet," and "*Midrash* of the Book of Kings." The last title probably best describes its character.

The books of Ezra and Nehemiah, which originally formed a portion of this historical work, possess a value of another sort. Here the writer had before him certain contemporary historical material which he incorporated in his work, namely an Aramæan history (Ezra iv–vi) dealing with the period succeeding the Exile, memoirs of Nehemiah, some lists of priests and others connected with the Temple service, and tax lists of families of Judah. For the study of the times of which they profess to treat the books of Ezra and Nehemiah are valuable precisely in proportion as those original documents have come down to us untouched by the hand of the later writer. But besides these documents there is much material of the midrashic character already described, and the documents themselves are sometimes adapted to what the later historians conceived to be historical fact. The tendency toward chronological exactness, which we have seen developing in earlier works, is carried to an extreme in these writings. We have figures presented for everything, but the figures are enormous and incredible, corresponding with the writer's conception of what Israel should be. Aside from the documents referred to, this entire work — Chronicles, Ezra, Nehemiah — possesses no value as a record of political or religious facts, but is valuable to the student of religion for the insight which it gives into the religious point of view of the priests and Levites of the Jerusalem Temple at the close of the fourth century B.C.

Edifying stories of a kind similar to those found in the work of the Chronicler received a fuller development in a few independent works of fiction composed in the Persian and Greek periods. Of this character is the Book of Ruth, an historical romance — a beautiful idyl in prose — dating from the middle of the fifth century B.C. This work represents a more liberal Judaism than that of the school of Ezra and Nehemiah. Still more liberal is the Book of Jonah. This is a story or romance founded on the account of the prophet Jonah contained in our Book of Kings. It represents a universalistic point of view, in striking contrast to the particularistic legal view of the dominant school of Judaism, and, like Ruth, is valuable as a representation of the religious attitude of the minority about the close of the fifth or the beginning of the fourth century B.C.

The Book of Esther and the apocryphal books of Judith and Tobit represent the exclusive legal school of Judaism, but are later in date than the preceding. Judith and Tobit were originally written in Hebrew, the former in Palestine, the latter in Egypt, probably in the second century B.C. From the religious point of view they represent correct legal Judaism. Esther seems to have been written in the East, where the Purim feast originated, and assumed its present shape at about the same time. It ultimately became the most popular and, next to the Law, the most valued book of the Jews. Numerous translations and paraphrases of it are in existence, and in addition to the original Hebrew work, contained among our canonical books, there are considerable Greek additions to be found in the Apocrypha. This work represents the extreme narrow school of Judaism and exhibits particularly a bitter hatred of foreigners. Nevertheless, the basis of the story of Mordecai and Esther is heathen and mythological.[1]

In the Book of Daniel we have a combination of folk stories with prophetic, or rather apocalyptic, material. There had grown up a group of short stories of a folk character, in the Aramæan language, the common language of the people from the beginning of the fourth century or thereabouts onward, professing to be historical, the object of which was to celebrate the constancy of pious Jews to their faith and law in times of persecution; their nonconformity to the rites and customs of the heathen; their careful observance of the Jewish sacrament of circumcision, the stated prayers and feasts, the laws of clean and unclean, and the like. Outside of our canonical Daniel, specimens of this literature have been preserved, in a Greek translation, in the story of the Three Pages in 1 Esdras iii–iv,[2] and in two prose additions to the Book of Daniel: the History of Susanna, and Bel and the Dragon. A number of such stories gathered about the name of an old Hebrew saint and hero, Daniel. Some of these, including one about the Three Holy Children, in the original Aramaic, worked over somewhat to apply to the circumstances of the time, were gathered together into the present Book of Daniel at the time of the Antiochian persecution (165 B.C.), furnished with a Hebrew introduction, and made the basis of an apocalypse, or series of visions, also written in Hebrew. This is our Book of Daniel. It made a profound impression upon its own and succeeding times, and after this date apocalypses, the beginning of which we find in Ezekiel, and in a more developed form in Zechariah, take the place of prophecy.

---

[1] Similarly Tobit utilizes the Babylonian romance of the wise Ahikar.

[2] With the exception of this story 1 Esdras (3 Esdras of the Septuagint and Vulgate) consists of excerpts from Chronicles, Ezra, and Nehemiah, and furnishes us, in Greek, with a second text of the latter books. It was meant by the compiler to be a history of the Temple from the time of the purification of its worship under Josiah to the time of the restoration of the pure worship under Ezra and Nehemiah.

The Book of Daniel is not included among the Prophets in the Hebrew Bible, although it is so classed in our English Bible, following the use of the Greek-speaking Jews of Alexandria. Before the date of its composition, somewhere about the close of the fourth or the beginning of the third century B.C., the canon of the Prophets had been closed, which means that they had been accepted as sacred books, which might not be added to or subtracted from. This canon of the Prophets consisted of (1) the former Prophets: Joshua, Judges, Samuel, Kings; (2) the latter Prophets: Isaiah, Jeremiah, Ezekiel, the Twelve (i.e. the minor Prophets). Daniel is included in the third Hebrew canon, the Writings. This was not closed until the beginning of the second century A.D., or even later. Besides Daniel, it included Psalms, Proverbs, Job, Canticles, Ruth, Lamentations, Esther, Ezra, Nehemiah, and Chronicles. It excluded a number of works which had enjoyed at one time or another a high reputation for sanctity. A number of these continued to be reverenced in various parts of the Christian Church. Some of them have been preserved in our Apocrypha; others in translations made for individual churches, particularly the Abyssinian.

The Book of Daniel was followed by a large amount of apocalyptic literature, which is valuable to us as showing the trend of religious thought during the two centuries immediately preceding the Christian era, and particularly the development of the Messianic expectation. By far the most important of these apocalypses is the Book of Enoch, written originally in Hebrew and in Palestine, by at least five authors, between the years 200 and 64 B.C. This work, which once had a very wide circulation and exercised a great influence among both Jews and Christians, has not been preserved in Hebrew, and even the Greek translation has been, for the most part, lost. It is not contained in our Apocrypha, but was preserved by the Church of Abyssinia in an Ethiopic translation made from the Greek. It is a work of great value for the study of the religious thought of the Jews in the two centuries preceding the Christian era.

In Ethiopic, also, has been preserved the Book of Jubilees, a work partly apocalyptic and partly historical, sometimes known as

the Little Genesis. It is put in the mouth of Moses, and is full
of haggadic legends, edifying religious narratives, based on Genesis
and the first twelve chapters of Exodus. It was written in Hebrew
a century before the birth of Christ, and represents Pharisaic
doctrine at that time. The Assumption of Moses, another apocalypse put in the mouth of Moses, has come down to us in a Latin
translation only. This was written by a zealot, over a hundred
years later than the preceding. The Testaments of the Twelve
Patriarchs, supposed to have been written originally in Hebrew
by two Jewish authors somewhere between the years 109 B.C. and
10 A.D., but interpolated by successive Christian writers down to
the fourth century A.D., has been preserved in Greek and Armenian
translations. The Sibylline Oracles, which also belong to this class
of writing, contain pre-Christian material, beginning at about the
time of Daniel, but mixed with a larger amount of later material
extending down to the middle of the fourth century A.D. This
was written originally not in Hebrew, like the apocalypses already
mentioned, but in Greek hexameters.

It will be observed that these works are largely pseudepigraphical. Pseudepigraphical literature may be said to have begun with
the Book of Deuteronomy in the seventh century. It became a
common method of composition about the time of the Chronicler.
From his time onward it became the practice to compose stories
about the saints and heroes of the past, to put speeches, prayers,
and hymns in their mouths, and to compose books in their name,
as apocalypses, testaments, and the like. We have in our Apocrypha
several works of this character, such as the Prayer of Manasseh,
an apocryphal addition to 2 Chronicles xxxiii, 12–13, based on a
late Jewish story about the conversion of Manasseh; the Song
of the Three Holy Children, a poetical addition to Daniel, from
which is taken the noble Benedicite of the Christian Church; the
Book of Baruch, a pseudeponymous work of exhortation and con-
solation, written about 80 A.D., to which is attached a pseudo-
epistle of Jeremiah; 2 Esdras (4 Esdras of the Vulgate), a Christian
apocalypse of the second century A.D. A mass of literature was
composed in the two centuries immediately preceding and following

the commencement of the Christian era, in the names of Adam, Enoch,[1] Noah, Abraham, Moses, Solomon, Baruch, Ezra, and others. In general, the only value of these works for the purposes of our study is to show us the tendency of the period toward fantastic interpretations of Scripture and of history, and toward the composition of and belief in foolish and unreal legends built on the names of the saints and heroes of the past.

A different use of folk story and of fiction from that which we have in the books of Ruth and Esther, or in the apocalyptic Book of Daniel, is found in Job. A story about some real or legendary person, named Job, had existed among the Jews before the period of the Exile. The main matter of this story is preserved in the prose introduction and conclusion to the present Book of Job, comprising the first two and the last chapters of that book. On the basis of this old, popular story was built a work of a dramatic character, in the form of a discussion of the problem of evil between Job and his friends. This work is commonly assigned to the post-exilic period, but considerable uncertainty exists as to the precise part of that period to which it belongs. It cannot, presumably, be later than the latter part of the fourth century before Christ, and it may be a century or possibly two centuries earlier than this. It has not escaped retouching by hands later than those of the original author, and one very considerable section, the speeches of Elihu (chaps. xxxii–xxxvii), is from the hand of an author who did not understand or accept the arguments of the original author of the work. The form of the poetry and the mode of expression of thought in this book class it with that category of Hebrew writings known as *Chokmah*, or Wisdom Literature. This connection is most strikingly evinced in one of the later additions to the Book of Job, the Praise of Wisdom, contained in the twenty-eighth chapter, similar to the praise of wisdom which we find in the introduction to the Book of Proverbs.

---

[1] The most important of these is the Book of the Secrets of Enoch, also called the Slavonic Enoch, because preserved only in Slavonic manuscripts. This was written in Egypt in the first half of the first Christian century. As an apocalypse it is founded on Enoch. It represents the Platonic view of the soul, taught also by Philo, but shows in other respects the influence of Egyptian and Persian religious beliefs.

The fundamental thesis of the Hebrew Wisdom Literature is: " The fear of God is the beginning of wisdom." The characteristic or type-work of this literature is the Book of Proverbs. Collections of proverbs began to be made in the preëxilic period, how early we do not surely know. Later Jewish tradition ascribes them to Solomon. These collections were worked over and added to from time to time. Our present Book of Proverbs, which consists of a number of collections, with at least two introductions, bearing full evidence, therefore, of long and continuous growth, may probably be ascribed to the last years of the Persian period (ca. 350 B.C.). To the same general class of literature belongs the apocryphal Book of Ecclesiasticus, by Jesus ben Sirach, composed in the following century,[1] and translated into Greek more than a hundred years afterwards (ca. 132 B.C.) by a descendant of the author. Latterly some portions of the original Hebrew text have been recovered. The writer supports the same thesis as Proverbs with a wealth of practical illustrations and sententious sayings. The book is valuable for the study of the orthodox religious thought of the century preceding the Maccabæan revolt.

To the same period belongs the canonical Book of Ecclesiastes, or the Preacher. This is an agnostic work, and testifies to the introduction of foreign philosophical speculations into Palestine in the Greek period. The writer is impressed with the emptiness and vanity of life; there is no outcome, and yet clearly mere sensual living is unprofitable. The book has come down to us provided with a brief supplement of a somewhat more religious character. The apocryphal book known as the Wisdom of Solomon, which is also included in the general category of Wisdom Literature, presents a striking contrast to the agnosticism of Ecclesiastes. More distinctly than any other writing of the pre-Christian period it sets forth the belief in the immortality of the soul. It was written originally in Greek, toward the middle of the first century B.C., by a Hellenistic Jew of Alexandria. Like so much of the work of this

---

[1] More commonly supposed to have been composed about 180 B.C. The reference to Onias the high priest seems to me to be satisfied only by the first Onias, which would make the date of the author more nearly 280 B.C.

period it is pseudepigraphical, in the form of an address by Solomon to heathen kings, warning them of the folly of their idolatry and unbelief. It shows strongly the influence of Greek philosophy. Related to this in its combination of Greek philosophy with Jewish orthodoxy is the so-called Fourth Book of Maccabees, also written in Alexandria about the beginning of the Christian era, a brief treatise on the theme " Wisdom rules the Passions."

With the Wisdom Literature is sometimes classed Canticles, or the Song of Songs, known in our English Bible as the Song of Solomon. This work possesses a certain affinity to the Book of Job in its semidramatic character, but belongs in reality rather with lyric than with gnomic poetry. It is an anthology, or chain of love songs, secular in its character, which owes its inclusion in the canon of the Hebrew Bible to the mystical religious interpretation which it received at the hands of the interpreters. It belongs, presumably, to the beginning of the Greek period, the close of the fourth or the first part of the third century B.C., although containing older material.

Attention has already been called to the early Hebrew collections of lyrical poetry, such as the Book of Yashar, the Book of the Wars of Yahaweh, etc. From the poems which have come down to us embedded in the older historical literature, and from the allusions to and citations of vintage and harvest songs, dirges, and even satirical folk songs in the writings of the prophets, it is clear that there existed among the Hebrews, in the preëxilic period, a considerable amount of popular lyric poetry. In the Book of Numbers and in the Book of Jeremiah we find some early fragments of liturgical poetry, and it seems clear that poetry of this description was composed and used among the Hebrews at a very early date. Later Hebrew tradition ascribes to David both secular and religious lyrics, and makes him the originator of the peculiar form of liturgical poetry contained in the Psalter. It seems probable that there is some foundation for this tradition, and that some sort of a collection of liturgical hymns was made in the time of David or Solomon. There seem to be some traces of such a collection in the Psalter, and possibly also of collections made for use at the temples of Dan and Bethel; but these are all so obscured and overlaid by later reworkings that we are able to determine very little of their original content and character.

The earliest liturgical collection of poetry which has come down to us in the Hebrew Bible is a series of penitential poems, for the most part alphabetic acrostics, written during the Exile, — our Book of Lamentations. The Song of Moses, now incorporated in the Book of Deuteronomy (xxxii, 1–43), is a poem of the same character as Lamentations, although of different form — a religious lyric dealing with the calamities attending the destruction of Jerusalem and the captivity. Another liturgical lyric, of uncertain date, probably post-exilic, is contained in the third chapter of the prophetical Book of Habakkuk. But by far the greater part of the Hebrew religious lyrical poetry which has come down to us was ultimately gathered into the Book of Psalms. This collection of sacred lyrics, as we now have it, consists of five books, composed out of a variety of earlier collections. The earlier psalms are to be found in the earlier books, which probably date, as collections, from the Exile or the period shortly after the Exile. The last two books of the Psalter belong, in general, to the Persian period. A final revision of the whole work, resulting in modifications of some of the earlier hymns and the addition of entirely new material at the close of the Psalter, seems to have taken place about the middle of the second century B.C. The Psalter, therefore, as it stands, contains preëxilic material at the basis of some psalms in the first book (Ps. i–xli) and in the Korah and Asaph collections in the second and third books (xlii–l, lxxiii–lxxxiii). In the main, however, it is a work of the post-exilic Persian period, with a final revision in the Maccabæan Greek period.

There is, in general, a sharp distinction in character between the hymns of the later books, which are liturgical in character, composed in the Temple and for the Temple service, and the hymns of the earlier books, which give the impression of a more popular origin, and of a working-over and adaptation to liturgical use. At least, in general, the hymns of the earlier books do not give the impression of psalms composed in the Temple, from the standpoint of the priestly ritual and ceremonial. But in this regard different sections and different psalms differ materially, and even in the later books we have one collection of psalms, the Pilgrim Psalter (cxx–cxxxiv), which partakes of the nature of folk poetry. The whole collection is a national hymn-book and not a collection of hymns of an individualistic character, such as we find later in the Christian Church.

Psalmody did not cease with the close of the Psalter. The apocryphal books, the New Testament, and later Jewish literature testify to the unbroken continuance of psalm composition after that date ; but only one other collection of psalms has come down to us, namely, the Psalter of Solomon, a collection of Pharisaic psalms, composed in Hebrew about the middle of the first century B.C., but preserved to us only in a Greek translation. This psalm-book is valuable as revealing the trend of Jewish thought in the century immediately preceding the Christian era, and especially for the light which it throws upon the development of the Messianic expectation at that time.[1]

The Maccabæan period was a time of religious and intellectual awakening in Israel, and as a consequence we have a revival of historical literature at that period. The great events which were connected with the revolt of the Maccabees found their historians, and two of these histories are included in our Apocrypha. The First Book of the Maccabees, written while the memory of the events which it describes was fresh, is an historical document of the first importance. It is without tendency or bias, and of very much the same character in this regard as the story of the foundation of the kingdom and the reign of David contained in the Second Book of Samuel and the first two chapters of the First Book of Kings. This work was written originally in Hebrew, presumably about the time of John Hyrcanus, in the latter part of the second century B.C. It has come down to us only in a Greek translation. At about the same time Jason of Cyrene wrote in Greek, in five

[1] For completeness' sake reference may also be made to the Odes of Solomon, dating probably a century later. Cf. J. Rendel Harris, *The Odes and Psalms of Solomon*, Cambridge, 1909.

books, the story of the same struggle. The Second Book of the Maccabees is an abridgment of this work, which has itself been lost. It is full of divine interventions, and views history from the standpoint of religious pragmatism. The author is more concerned with the religious lesson of the history than with the history itself.

About the same period various Greek Jews of Alexandria undertook to write a history of their people from the beginning, small fragments of some of which have been handed down to us in the church fathers Eusebius and Clement. One writer, Artapanos, attempted to combine the Bible account of the history of Israel in Egypt with Egyptian history. His work is full of fables for the greater glorification of the Jews. Other writings of the same stamp followed. Verses were fabricated, professing to be from Greek authors, to show the priority of Jewish culture and religion, and all manner of fables were invented for the same purpose. To this general class of literature — stories invented for the glorification of the Jews — belongs the letter of Aristeas, purporting to give the history of the translation of the Old Testament into Greek by the Seventy. Here may be classed, also, the Third Book of the Maccabees, a fictitious story of heathen persecution and Jewish steadfastness, rewarded by miraculous deliverance. The scene is laid in Alexandria, after the death of Ptolemy Philopator (222–204 B.C.). The work itself was composed in the first century B.C. In general, the tendency of the writers of this and the following centuries was to invent history, often in the form of pseudepigraphs, for the glorification of the Jews and the conviction of the heathen. The only writer who has left us anything of objective value is Flavius Josephus, the historian of the Roman war, in the last ten books of his *Jewish Antiquities* (93 A.D.). This work is composed for Gentile readers; accordingly, the writer omits what might excite Gentile prejudice and embellishes his material with legendary amplifications; but he makes use of various sources, no longer accessible to us, which furnish some welcome material for the political, and incidentally the religious, history of the Jews during the Persian, Greek, and Roman periods.

This synopsis of the literary remains of Israel[1] shows, in the first place, that we have for the period before David only brief fragments, whereas from his time onward there is a constantly increasing amount of contemporary material, always more varied and comprehensive in its character; in the second place, that this material is largely anonymous, and has undergone a continuous process of growth or reworking, so that neither history, laws, prophetical works, hymns, or proverbial literature can be used as they stand, but must be subjected to a careful analysis for the purpose of separating the older material from the later accretions and editions. In the historical works it is not difficult, in general, to make this separation, for the reason that the method of incorporation of the older in the newer histories is mechanical. The analysis of the laws is not so easy; but, in the main points of the analysis, of both the historical works and the laws, critics have reached a substantial agreement. This is not true, or at least to the same extent, of the analysis of the Prophets, Psalms, and Proverbs. In general I shall follow in this work the analysis agreed upon by the critics. Where there is serious disagreement among them, it will be indicated, as also, where possible, my reasons for the adoption of one or the other view. In the treatment of Prophets, Psalms, and Proverbs, where the differences between critics are more numerous and more serious, I shall follow, on the whole, the more conservative analysts and endeavor, so far as possible, not to found conclusions upon material which is still under discussion.

As the lower limit of our study I have assumed roughly and somewhat arbitrarily the commencement of the Christian era, and have consequently omitted all writers of a later date, unless, as in the case of Josephus, their works possess value for earlier periods. I have also omitted all mention of the Talmud. In that heterogeneous mass of Scriptural interpretation, legal and ceremonial

---

[1] For this synopsis I am especially indebted to Professor George F. Moore's " Historical Literature " in Cheyne's *Encyclopædia Biblica*. The manuscript notes for that article, lent to me by Professor Moore, first helped me to crystallize my own conclusions, and in general I found myself so much in agreement with his results as there set forth that I fancy considerable parts of this chapter are, at least in thought, borrowed from him.

definition and expansion, tradition and legend, there are, doubtless, mixed with material of later date, some things which may cast a little light upon the religious developments of the last pre-Christian centuries; but no analysis of that material has yet been made which renders it safely available for such a purpose. The upper limit of our study is in the prehistoric and pre-Mosaic period.

For the earliest and prehistoric periods of Israel's religion we have no literary remains, and from Moses to David only fragments. The close kinship of Israel with the other Semitic peoples makes their remains for these or practically for any other periods of great value in the reconstruction of the early religious history of Israel. In their nomadic condition the Hebrews were closely allied to the Arabs, and the remains of Arab heathendom are valuable in the study of the primitive rites and customs of the religion of Israel. The Canaanites whom Israel conquered, to be in turn, partially at least, conquered by their civilization, were substantially the same in their culture as the Phœnicians, and such slight Phœnician remains as we have are useful in the study of the laws and customs adopted by the Hebrews after their entrance into Canaan, as well as for their mythical and legendary lore. For this latter, and to a considerable extent for religious and ceremonial customs and uses also, the discoveries in Assyria and Babylonia are of prime importance. Babylonia was at a very early period in close contact with Canaan, upon the culture of which country it exerted a great and lasting influence. At a much later date the Hebrews came directly into contact, first, with the Assyrians, and afterwards, at the period of the Exile, with the Babylonians. Consequently, Babylonian and Assyrian remains are of value in the explanation both of the early legendary, mythical, legal, and even ritual conceptions and practices of the Hebrews, and also of some later developments in their culture and religion. Fortunately the amount of material which we have from Babylonia and Assyria is large. Aramæan influences also made themselves felt in the life of Israel from the earliest time onward, but the amount of information which we possess with regard to Aramæan civilization and religion is still meager. From Moab, a nation most closely allied to Israel in race, language, and originally religion, we have one monumental inscription of the ninth century B.C., the Mesha stone. Egypt, with which traditionally Israel was so closely connected, has yielded in its inscriptions some material for the history of Palestine before the Hebrew conquest, but nothing for later dates. For the period of the Hebrew occupation of Palestine we have, it is true, the Aramaic papyri of the Jewish military colony at Yeb (Elephantine), which throw a little much-needed light on the conditions of the Persian period. But these papyri, like the Egyptian-Jewish writings mentioned above, are not in any proper sense Egyptian, although discovered in Egypt.

Of Hebrew monuments and inscriptions from Palestine itself we have almost nothing. In general the sites excavated, like Lachish, Gath, Maresha, Gezer, Beth Shemesh, Jericho, Taanach, and Megiddo, have thrown light on pre-Israelite, non-Israelite, or post-Israelite conditions, and only incidentally and inferentially on the conditions of Israelite life and religion during the historic period. The excavations in thoroughly Hebrew sites, like Jerusalem and Samaria, have yielded but small results, outside of tunnels, walls, and buildings. Of inscriptions all told there are the Siloah stone, a few seals and jar handles, potsherds from the commissary department of Ahab's palace at Samaria, — all of these principally valuable for the divine names used in composition, — and a Greek inscription from Herod's temple.

This is the sum of the archæological material available to supplement the literary remains of the Jews. Of accounts of the Jews and their religion, or references to their practices and beliefs in the literature of other peoples, there are none which need be considered.

CHAPTER II

LAND AND PEOPLE

I

The land of Israel, commonly known as Palestine, extends from Dan on the north to Beersheba on the south (31° 15' to 33° 20' north latitude). On the west it is bounded by the Mediterranean Sea, and on the east by the Arabian Desert. In length it is about 150 miles; in breadth at its northern end about 70, and at its southern 100 miles. This difference in breadth is confined to the region west of the Jordan valley. That valley runs north and south, but the Mediterranean coast line runs northeast and southwest. At its sources the Jordan is only 25 miles from the Mediterranean; at the southern end of the Dead Sea the distance is more than 75 miles. Both plain and mountain are broader here than in the north.

Palestine is a part of the great Syrian mountain chain, which extends from the Taurus southwestward, parallel with the shore of the Mediterranean Sea, reaching its highest point in the Lebanon Mountains and in the southern spur of the Anti-Lebanon, Mount Hermon. The peculiar feature of a double chain, which is presented in the Lebanon region by the Lebanon and Anti-Lebanon mountains, divided by the valley of the *Beka'*, is continued in Palestine, where a unique gorge, formed by the waters of the Jordan and its lakes, separates the eastern from the western highlands, and divides the whole territory into two sections, the East and West Jordan lands.

Beginning at the foot of Mount Hermon and the roots of Lebanon, the Jordan descends for some 12 miles through a valley 5 miles or thereabouts in width, bordered by hills 2000 feet in height, to the reed and marsh lands of Lake Huleh, 7 feet above the level of the Mediterranean. From this point it descends rapidly,

36

a little more than 12 miles in a straight line, to the lyre-shaped Sea
of Galilee, a basin of water 12½ miles long and 6 miles in width.
This sea is 682 feet below the level of the Mediterranean. On its
eastern side cliffs rise abruptly to the height of 1500 feet; on the
west, somewhat more gently and leaving in places a strip of fertile
soil between them and the lake, the hills of Lower Galilee rise to
about the same height. From the Sea of Galilee to the Dead Sea
the distance in a direct line is 65 miles, but so numerous are the
windings of the Jordan that its actual length in this, the longer part
of its journey, may be three times as much. In this part of its
course it receives three important tributaries : the Yarmuk, a stream
of considerable volume, almost equal to the Jordan itself, empties
into it from the eastward, not many miles below its exit from the
Sea of Galilee; the Jalud, flowing out of the Valley of Jezreel, joins
it from the westward, 10 miles further down; and the Jabbok,
coming out of the hills of Gilead on the east, unites with it after
it has covered almost two thirds of its course to the Dead Sea. The
greater part of the valley of the Jordan is and always has been
uncultivated, if not uncultivable. The valley itself varies in breadth
from 14 miles at Jericho to 5 miles at its narrowest or middle
portion. On either side rise abruptly steep limestone hills, almost
entirely without verdure. The course of the stream is rapid. It
descends more than 600 feet between the Sea of Galilee and the
Dead Sea. The river itself occupies a deep, narrow bed at the very
bottom of the valley. There is no overflow, and in most parts of
the valley irrigation by canalization is impracticable. At a few favored
spots, especially in the neighborhood of Jericho, near the extreme
southern end of the valley, where there are springs and the soil is
irrigated, the valley of the Jordan displays a phenomenal fertility.

At the southern end of the Jordan lies the Dead Sea, 1290 feet
below the level of the Mediterranean, 50 miles in length and 10
in breadth, its waters so impregnated with salts that no creature
can live in it. On either side rise abruptly verdureless cliffs, reaching at some places an elevation of 4000 feet above its surface. Only
at one or two spots along the shore, where fresh water springs enter
the Dead Sea, like En-Gedi, about midway of its western side, is

there any vegetation; but there the growth is tropical both in character and luxuriance. At the extreme southern end the sea is very shallow, losing itself at last in salt-marshes, to the west of which rises a mountain of salt. The evaporation from the Dead Sea, shut up, as it were, in a deep caldron, far down in the bowels of the earth, with white and glaring sides reflecting back upon the surface of the sea all the rays of the sun which they collect, is stupendous, reaching, it is estimated, the amount of 6,000,000 tons a day. There is in all the world no more strange and awe-inspiring gorge than this huge canal which separates the eastern part of the land of Israel from the western.

Eastward of the Jordan, stretching from Mt. Hermon southward, the mountain range consists for the most part of a high plateau, passing over at an undefined point eastward into the Arabian Desert. This table-land is divided into three great sections:

1. The northern section, from Mt. Hermon southward to the southern end of the Sea of Galilee, with the Yarmuk, bending to the southeast, as its southern boundary. From Hermon southward stretch lines of extinct volcanoes, and in general the limestone throughout this section is overlaid with black volcanic deposit. At places the country seems to be half covered by blocks of black basaltic stone. This is Bashan, a region for the most part immensely fertile, the granary of Syria at the present day, famous in antiquity for both its corn and its cattle. On the east it is bordered in its northern part by the barren Leja or Trachonitis, bad lands, consisting of a solid overflow of lava 18 miles in breadth and 27 miles in extreme length, fissured and full of chasms, a proper refuge for fugitives and criminals, but incapable of cultivation or improvement. The southeastern part of Bashan, where the Yarmuk bends to the south, is the region of the Hauran, the richest and most fertile portion of the land. The eastward boundary of this section, which stretches southward some 25 miles below a line parallel with the southern edge of the Sea of Galilee, is the mountains of the Hauran, called now, after their latest occupants, Jebel-Druze, a series of extinct volcanoes, full of fertile valleys. To the eastward of the Leja and the Hauran mountains lies the Arabian Desert.

2. The central part of the East Jordan land, extending from the Yarmuk almost to the northern end of the Dead Sea, is for a distance of 20 miles back from the Jordan broken up into mountains and valleys, and fairly well wooded. This was Gilead, a land of shepherds, but possessing also rich and fertile valleys and abundant water-springs. Back of this is a plateau, merging imperceptibly into the Arabian Desert. This section is itself divided into two unequal parts by the deep valley of the Jabbok.

3. South of Gilead, stretching along the shore of the Dead Sea from north to south, lies the high table-land of Moab, furrowed here and there by deep cañons, through which streams descend to the Dead Sea, the most notable being the cañon of the Arnon, the traditional southern boundary of Israel east of the Jordan, about midway of the length of the Dead Sea. In Gilead, with its woods and mountains, there are springs and streams. In Moab there are almost no springs or streams, except those flowing in deep cañons westward to the Dead Sea. As in Bashan and the plain of the Hauran, water must be gathered in wells and cisterns during the rainy season. The soil is rich and lends itself to cultivation where watered. Eastward the Moabite plateau merges imperceptibly into the Arabian Desert.

Westward of the Jordan the mountain range which stretches from Lebanon southward, and which forms the backbone of the land, is divided into five main divisions:

1. The land of Galilee, from the river Litany on the north to the Plain of Esdraelon, or Jezreel, on the south. Here the mountain is broken up into numerous cross ridges, among which are fertile valleys and plateaus, especially in Lower Galilee, westward of the sea of that name. In Upper Galilee are found the highest elevations west of the Jordan; Lower Galilee is a rich and goodly land, capable of very high cultivation.

2. Jezreel. Southward of Galilee the Plain of Jezreel stretches from the mountains near the Jordan on the east to the foot of Carmel on the west, watered by the stream of the Kishon, which sluggishly meanders through its whole extent from the foot of Gilboa to the Mediterranean Sea, while from its southwest side

the rich valley of the Jalud descends to the Jordan. This plain is the only complete break in the mountain chain that stretches from north to south, and hence it forms the natural highway between east and west. It is triangular in shape, with the base of the triangle to the east, stretching from Engannim (Jenin) on the south to Mt. Tabor on the north, a distance of some 17 miles. Its length from this base to the apex at the foot of Mt. Carmel is about 20 miles. It is a region of the greatest fertility; its underlying stratum is a bed of lava.

3. Samaria and Mt. Ephraim. Southward of Esdraelon the mountain begins once more, with plains thrusting in here and there from the fertile valley on the north. Toward the northwest stretches out along the side of that valley a spur of hills, a cross range, low near its junction with the mountains, so that the passage from the Plain of Esdraelon to the coast plain (the Plain of Sharon) is easy, but rising as it approaches the sea into a more pronounced chain of hills, some 1500 feet in height, always forest-clad, ending in a bold point close to the Mediterranean, but with a strip of level land between it and the sea. This cross range is Mt. Carmel. As one goes southward through Samaria and into Mt. Ephraim, the mountain becomes less broken, the valleys more seldom, until at last we come to a definite high ridge, forming a broad, much broken plateau, which passes over into the mountain country of Judæa.

4. Judæa consists of a barren limestone mountain ridge, some 2500 feet above sea level, falling abruptly to the eastward, where the lower Jordan valley and the Dead Sea lie almost 4000 feet beneath its greatest elevation, but descending more gently toward the west. Fountains and springs are rare and streams do not exist. Here and there are a few fertile oases, like Bethlehem and Hebron. Valleys capable of cultivation occur more often as one descends westward toward the foothills, but on the east, toward the Jordan and the Dead Sea, is the wilderness of Judæa, where the land is almost barren, capable only of supporting at certain seasons flocks of sheep. Here the mountain, without verdure, divides into numberless sharp ridges, separated one from another by deep

gorges, through which pour for a brief time in the winter season short-lived mountain torrents.

5. Negeb. Southward of Hebron the mountain of Judæa, which has been broadening out more and more, descends toward the southern wilderness in a succession of high steppes, fit only for pasturage, known to the Jews as Negeb, rendered "South" in our English Bible.

Between this central range of mountains and the Mediterranean Sea stretches a strip of plain-land, very narrow in the north, but growing broader southward. At the city of Tyre and for twelve miles or so to the south of that, this coast plain varies from two to six miles in breadth. At this point the mountains thrust a promontory into the sea, known as Ras-en-Nakurah, or in older times the "Ladder of Tyre." Southward of the Ladder of Tyre, as far as Mt. Carmel, is a broader plain, with many valleys running up among the hills of Galilee, and connecting to the southeast with the Plain of Esdraelon. All of this plain from Tyre southward to Mt. Carmel, and northward along the Lebanon, was the country of Phœnicia.

South of Mt. Carmel, very narrow at its northern apex but soon growing broader, was the rich Plain of Sharon, some 10 to 15 miles in breadth, rising gradually with soft foothills into the mountain country of Samaria. A little north of the 32d parallel of latitude, at Joppa, this plain rises slightly to a sort of ridge, which runs southeasterly and melts into a low chain of hills that bend around parallel to the mountains of Judæa. These are the so-called Shephelah, the disputed borderland between the Philistines and the Israelites. Between them and the hills of Judæa runs a low but fairly well-marked depression. It is uncertain whether the Shephelah belongs to the mountain range behind or to the level plain before. Between it and the Mediterranean stretches the broad and fertile Philistine plain, 20 miles in breadth, not possessed of streams, but abundantly watered, as is also the Plain of Sharon, by wells reaching the underlying water, which is here at all points abundant. Southward this plain grows sandy, until beyond Gaza it degenerates into a desert which extends to the Egyptian frontier.

Such in its main physical features was the land of Israel. Going from the west toward the east we find four zones :

1. The coast plain, narrow at the north, broad at the south, extremely fertile, dotted with rich cities ; above Mt. Carmel provided with harbors adapted for commerce, below Mt. Carmel a straight, sandy line, absolutely without harbors, useless for commerce ; the northern portion, from Tyre to Carmel, but especially that part between Tyre and the Ladder of Tyre, too narrow to be valuable for agriculture, the southern part broad and fertile, adapted to an agricultural people.

2. The central mountain region west of the Jordan, divided at one point by a rich plain, the Plain of Esdraelon ; fertile and adapted to agriculture in the northern part, especially in Lower Galilee and Upper Samaria,— the portions bordering on the Plain of Esdraelon,— more rugged and barren as one proceeds southward ; in the southern part, from Mt. Ephraim onward, a land in itself not desirable, inaccessible and easy to defend against assault.

3. East of this central mountain range, the deep gorge of the Jordan, fertile in all its upper part, but below the Sea of Galilee only at oases, like those of Bethshan, Jericho, Shittim, and En-Gedi. Between the eastern and the western portions of the land, this great gulf was fixed. It seemed as though these two parts were intended by nature to be separated, one from the other. Only in the neighborhood of the Sea of Galilee, north and south of the same, is there any practicable means of communication between them — through the Plain of Esdraelon and the valley of the Yarmuk, or along the northern border of the Sea of Galilee and so eastward.

4. East of the Jordan, the fourth and last zone, Bashan and the Hauran, the mountain country of Gilead, and the upland plains of Moab, all open eastward toward the desert and the inroads of the restless Bedawin.

II

As a natural result of the great difference in altitude of the various portions of Palestine, there is also a singular diversity of climate. On the coast plain it is subtropical, with a mean temperature of 70°. In average temperature the foothills of Samaria and

Judæa resemble the French Riviera. When the summit plateau of the central mountain ridge is reached, one has entered the temperate zone. The average temperature of Jerusalem is 62°, and during the winter season snow falls, although it seldom lies for any length of time. Going still eastward, in half a day one may descend from the temperate climate of Jerusalem to a tropical temperature in the Jordan valley. There the thermometer ranges from 77° to 118°. Across the Jordan valley, on the uplands of Moab, Gilead and Bashan, the climate is similar to that of the Judæan highlands, but somewhat colder and drier.

On the coast plain the climate is equable, with no great annual or diurnal changes of temperature. In the mountains of the West Jordan land, and still more on the uplands east of the Jordan, the changes of temperature are sudden and extreme. One may find frost on the mountains of Gilead in the early morning, while at noon the thermometer will register 80°. The nights are cold, the days hot. Similarly the annual mean difference of temperature is large. Owing partly to this difference of summer and winter temperature, and the sudden daily variations, the climate of the central region west of the Jordan, and of the East Jordan highlands, is bracing, tending to produce hardihood and energy. From most parts of the highlands, both east and west of the Jordan, Mt. Hermon is visible in the north, towering to the height of 9383 feet, and covered with snow fields, even in midsummer. About the Sea of Galilee, in full view of these snow fields, the climate is almost tropical, while in the lower Jordan valley it is most depressing, both to the physical and moral nature, owing not merely to the tropical heat but even more, apparently, to the great weight of the atmosphere. An Arab tribe descending from the invigorating uplands of Gilead or Moab to the Jordan valley, near Jericho, speedily loses both physical stamina and moral fiber.

The year is divided into a rainy and a dry season throughout the whole land, as in tropical regions. The rains begin to fall toward the end of October; these are the early or " former " rains, which prepare the earth for sowing. With the end of November the rains increase; December, January, and February are the true rainy months. In March the rains abate, and by the middle or end of April the dry season sets in. The showers of March and April are designated in the Bible as the "latter rains," and on them depends especially the success or failure of the crops. Should the rains fail, the crops fail. From April until October there is no rain, with the exception, sometimes, of a few light showers in the month of May. To some extent the place of rain is supplied during the summer by the vapors which the west wind brings from the Mediterranean, and by the heavy dews; but in general the summer months are a period of drought, during which everything seems parched and burned. With the first rains of October, as though by magic, all nature puts on at once a mantle of green. This lasts until May. From May onward the hills and fields are bare and brown. The country is exposed to droughts. The grasshopper pest is also a frequent one.

Palestine is peculiarly dependent on its winds. The proximity of the country to the desert exposes it to the sirocco, or *sherkiyeh*, the east or southeast wind, which brings with it a mist of fine sand, "scorching vegetation and bringing languor and fever to men." [1] This wind blows more particularly in the spring. The prevailing summer wind is from the northwest. In the winter come the west and southwest winds bringing moisture from the sea.

The central range was mainly a country of wine and olive culture. Even in barren Judæa the hills were capable of being terraced, and the soil was peculiarly adapted to the culture of the vine. Next to his vineyards the most important possession of the Judæan peasant was his flocks of sheep and goats. In the fertile valleys of northern Samaria and Galilee a more extensive agriculture was possible. These countries, and especially Galilee, were in their days of peace and prosperity veritable gardens of olives, figs, and fruits, with valleys full of grain. The coast plain and the Plain of Esdraelon were extremely fertile, and especially adapted to the raising of grain. The oases of the Jordan valley yielded tropical fruits. East of the Jordan, the Hauran was, and is to this day, a famous granary. The upland plains of Moab were also capable of

[1] G. A. Smith, *The Historical Geography of the Holy Land*, p. 167.

grain raising, but were more favorable for the pasturage of sheep and cattle. Gilead was a country of shepherds, with cultivated valleys and bottoms.

In ancient times Gilead and parts of Bashan, Galilee, and Samaria (including Carmel) were wooded. Carmel is still covered with woods, and oak forests exist in Gilead and southeastern Galilee. The oaks of these forests are, however, generally stone oaks, small and gnarled, not suitable for lumber. The " forests," of which we read in the Bible, in other parts of Palestine were, as a rule, rather what we should call " bush." They covered more territory than to-day, but at all times Palestine was in general an unwooded country.

There were no metals in Palestine and there was no natural commerce, whether by sea or land. In general it was a land capable of supporting a fairly large population in comfort but not in luxury, in labor but not in idleness. It could care for its own, but had little to export.

Palestine lay between Asia and Africa, between the civilization of the Euphrates and that of the Nile, partly dividing, partly connecting them. It occupied the narrow strip between the sea and the desert, which was of necessity the highway of intercourse between the culture lands of Asia — Phœnicia, Syria, Mesopotamia, Assyria, and Babylonia — on the one hand, and those of south Arabia and the Nile valley on the other. The two natural roads connecting these regions were, the one, east of the Jordan, in the general neighborhood of the present Haj route to Mecca, on the extreme eastern edge of Palestine ; and the other, either through Phœnicia and along the coast plain, or else across the plateau of Bashan, through the Plain of Esdraelon, reaching the coast plain in the neighborhood of Mt. Carmel, and so through Sharon and the Philistine lowlands to Egypt. From the earliest times onward Palestine was a bone of contention between Asia and Africa. Babylonians and Egyptians, Hittites and the men of the Nile, Assyrian Great Kings and Pharaohs, Nebuchadrezzar and Necho, Seleucids and Ptolemies, Damascus and Cairo, Sultan and Khedive, have overrun its fertile fields and valleys, and fought their battles on Esdraelon or the coast plain.

On the other hand, Palestine separated the culture lands to the north from those to the south. Its central mountain range was inaccessible and easily defended. It offered to the invader hard blows and small spoils. The same, to a less extent, was true of the mountains of Gilead, east of the Jordan. These regions were difficult of conquest and stood threateningly by the side of both the roads already mentioned, making each of them in the end nothing but a *road* which must be fortified and defended. Lying thus on the highway of communication, and yet by their character isolated, the highlands of Judæa and Mt. Ephraim, together with Gilead on the east of the Jordan,— those regions which constituted the real and permanent home of Israel,— occupied a singular position, in the midst of the world and yet cloistered from it.

III

Palestine as a whole was never occupied by the Israelites. The coast plain from Carmel northward, with an indefinite "hinterland," was Phœnician territory. Below the Ladder of Tyre, along the gulf of Acre, Israelites were mixed among the Phœnicians and at times were partially dominant. Above the Ladder of Tyre the coast plain was exclusively Phœnician. From Joppa southward, and from the Mediterranean to and sometimes including the foothills, extended the country of the Philistines. The foothills, the Shephelah, were debatable ground. The Plain of Sharon, from Joppa to Carmel, remained in the hands of the Canaanites during the greater part of Israel's history. The Plain of Esdraelon, dividing the mountains of Galilee from the mountain of Samaria, was not conquered by the Israelites until a late date. They were, in the earlier period, mixed in among the Canaanites and subject to them. Later they became the dominant race. This region was always open to inroads and invasions, and with the decay of the power of Israel passed again out of its hands.

Following the central ridge we find the hill country of Upper and Lower Galilee early occupied by the Israelites, but, especially in the western parts, towards Phœnicia, with a strong admixture of Canaanite elements, which gave it the name of Galilee, or *borderland*.

With the fall of Samaria, Galilee ceased for several centuries to be a part of Israel, but in the Greek period it was once more populated by Jews, and became in the Roman era one of the great centers of Jewish population and life.

The stronghold of Israel from the outset was the mountain south of the Plain of Esdraelon. With the exception of a few Canaanite oases, this early came into the possession of Israel. To the south of Judah it was open to inroads of the Amalekites, Ishmaelites, and kindred peoples. Some of these, such as the Kenites and Kenizzites, similar in civilization and origin to the Israelites themselves, mingled with and were incorporated in the tribe of Judah. East of the Jordan Aramæans occupied Bashan and the Hauran and disputed sometimes with Israel the possession of northern Gilead. East of the southern part of Gilead lay the kingdom of the Ammonites, between Gilead and the desert. Sometimes Israel encroached upon the Ammonite territory, and at other times the Ammonites encroached upon Israel, occupying part of southern Gilead. The same was true of Moab, which occupied the uplands east of the Salt Sea. The northern boundary of the Moabites, according to Israelite tradition, should have been the Arnon, but during the greater period of Israel's history they occupied the whole of the uplands bordering the Dead Sea, and at times extended even somewhat further north. All this territory east of the Jordan, like the south of Judah, was subject to inroads of Bedawin. These regions were the training ground in which Bedawin tribes passed over, in slow stages, from the nomadic to the settled life, to be ultimately incorporated in Israel or the other settled nations about it. The borders of the settled land to the east and to the south were indefinite, depending at each given period on the strength of the then rulers of Palestine.

Inside of itself, the region occupied by the Israelites was not a unit. It was, in the first place, separated into two parts, never capable of thoroughly coöperating, by the great canal of the Jordan valley. The Israelites to the east of this remained from the outset more closely connected with the desert and nomad life than their kinsmen to the west of the Jordan, and maintained more primitive conditions.

The central mountain range itself was separated into two parts
by the Plain of Esdraelon, so that Galilee always enjoyed a semi-
independence, and developed a civilization which was at all periods
somewhat different from that of the Israelites south of Esdraelon.
It was less isolated and more affected by the outside world. In the
central region of Mt. Ephraim and Judæa communication was not
easy. The only line of communication which existed was the rough
and difficult road along the summit of the mountain. The tendency
of the natural conditions was to develop individual, family, or clan
life, rather than national life. Agricultural conditions tended in the
same direction. There was no great river on which all alike depended and which all must unite in controlling for the common
good, as in Babylonia, or still more in Egypt. In Palestine each
wrought for himself, depending, not on the joint labor of his brethren or of the state for the success of his efforts, but on the rains
which heaven might send or withhold.

IV

There are, scattered throughout Palestine, and more particularly
east of the Jordan, remains of prehistoric peoples — menhirs,
cromlechs, dolmens, cairns, and the like. In northern Gilead and
the Hauran, as well as in the eastern foothills of Judah, there are
also rock-cut dwellings belonging, in their origin, to the prehistoric
period. Building upon these various remains, Hebrew tradition, as
it has come down to us in the Bible, tells of giants who inhabited
the land in early days. As the Israelites found the country, this
population had already vanished or been overlaid by another
stratum. At that time the country was occupied in all its central
portion by Canaanites, divided into numerous petty states, well advanced in civilization. The Canaanites were Semites in language,
and in both language and culture practically identical with the
Phœnicians. They are mentioned in the Old Testament under
numerous names, some general, like "Amorites," and some particular, like "Jebusites." Hebrew tradition also tells of Hittites in-
habiting certain parts of the land. The proper seat of Hittite power
and influence lay further northward. The Hittites, a non-Semitic

people from the north, had, some centuries before the Israelite conquest, overrun and conquered the Canaanites north of Palestine, between the Euphrates and the sea, becoming in the process strongly Semitized. The main seat of their power was Kadesh on the Orontes. But Palestine itself was at times the scene of contests for supremacy between Hittites and Egyptians. The Hittites occupied northern Bashan, and outposts pushed further into Palestine. These latter, at the time of the Israelite conquest, had, for all intents and purposes, been incorporated into the Canaanites and adopted their language and religious customs.

For our knowledge of the conditions of Palestine previous to the conquest, we are indebted, aside from the Bible and the excavations in Palestine, to a slight extent to the Babylonian, but chiefly to the Egyptian, inscriptions, and especially to the Tel el-Amarna tablets. This correspondence on clay tablets between Egyptian viceroys and subject rulers in Palestine and their suzerains, the Pharaohs of Egypt, in the fifteenth century B.C. and thereabouts, was discovered at Tel el-Amarna in 1888. These tablets reveal, along with a high civilization in Palestine, an amazing lack of political development. Cities abound, but there is no organization and no national life. All is disintegration and disunion, but without independence. These letters show also that at that time nomadic hordes were pressing into the Canaanite territory from the east and south, just as we find them doing in later history, whenever the central power was weak. These nomadic hordes were kindred in race and culture with the Israelites of the period of the conquest. A couple of centuries later, at the time of the conquest, we find, belonging to the same group of nations as the Israelites but more advanced in civilization than they, the twelve tribes of Edom south and southwest of the Dead Sea, and the people of Moab and Ammon eastward and northeastward of the same. Between the Moabites and Ammonites, and north of both of them, we find again Amorites or Canaanites overlying earlier prehistoric populations. North of these again, to the east and northeast of the Sea of Galilee, were Hittites, probably already beginning to give way to Aramæans. Northwest of the Canaanite territory, along the seacoast, lay the Phœnician cities, which, Canaanite in origin, had developed beyond their compeers a true national life and religion. Northward and northeastward of these the Aramæans were over-running the Hittite states, as the latter had overrun the former Canaanite inhabitants.

At about the same time at which the Israelites entered Canaan from the east, the Philistines invaded it from the west. They came, according to tradition, from Caphtor (either Crete, or the southern shore of Asia Minor, or both) and established themselves on the coast south of Joppa. To a large extent they adopted Canaanite customs and the Canaanite religion, as well as the Canaanite language. In other regards, as in the matter of circumcision, they remained separate and distinct, and were as truly alien to the Canaanites as the Israelites felt themselves to be. Partly the Philistines drove out the Canaanite inhabitants of the territory which they occupied, partly they mingled with them. The coast line was, when Israel came in contact with them, entirely in their possession, and at that time they already constituted a nation, with the five confederate cities of Gaza, Ashdod, Askelon, Ekron, and Gath, the first four on the coast plain, close to the sea, the last in the Shephelah. In the foothills the Canaanites still main-tained themselves in part at the period of the Israelite conquest, and for a time formed a sort of bulwark between Israel and the Philistines, which prevented these from coming into direct and hostile contact.

It has been said that Palestine was, from the outset, a bone of contention between Asia and Africa. Babylonian inscriptions, discovered at Nippur, Tello, and elsewhere, show us that as early as the beginning of the third millennium Babylonian kings overran Palestine, and some of the names of localities which have come down to us in the Bible, as well as Baby-lonian myths and legends borrowed by the Hebrews from the Canaanites and preserved in the narratives of Genesis, prove that Babylonian influence upon the land was lasting. Even the Tel el-Amarna tablets, written at the close of the period of Egyptian supremacy, are in the Babylonian language, proving this to have become well established as an official language before the Egyptian conquest.[1]

About the eighteenth century B.C. Babylonian gave way to Egyptian supremacy, which, yielding to Hittite supremacy in northern Syria, continued in Palestine until shortly before the Israelite conquest. Then follows a period of general disintegration.[2] In the west race movements were overturning the ancient Mycenæan or Ægean civilization, and causing whole nations, leaving their ancient homes, to descend upon the Mediterranean coasts of Africa and Syria, and also to pour down from Asia Minor by land in great hordes, bringing their women and children with them to seek new homes. On the Tigris and the lower Euphrates Assyria and Babylonia were struggling with one another and with invaders, who pressed in from all sides. The Aramæans occupied Mesopotamia and contested with the Hittites, broken and discouraged by the invasions from the north, the supremacy of northern Syria. Egypt was disintegrated and at war with itself, and the petty states and nations of Palestine were left to themselves. It was during this period, from the middle of the thirteenth to the middle of the twelfth century B.C., that the Israelite invasion of Canaan took place.

V

The Israelites designate themselves in the period before the Captivity *Benê Israel*, "Sons of Israel," or simply *Israel*. They are designated by others *Hebrews*, or "people from the other side," that is, apparently, the other side of the Jordan. After the Exile, when little was left of the nation except the tribe of Judah, the name *Judæans* or *Jews* came into use both at home and abroad. The Israelites belong to the Semitic peoples. These peoples are distributed almost in a circle about the Syrian, or Arabian, desert. To the south of this, including also the nomads who to-day roam

---

[1] Latterly there has been a tendency on the part of some Assyriologists to reverse the ordinarily accepted view of the relations of Babylonia and Syria, and to regard the latter as having been the original home of Semitic culture. (Cf. Clay, *Amurru, the Home of the Northern Semites*.)

[2] Cf. Peters, *Archæological History of Hither Asia*, Universal Anthology, Vol. XXXII.

over it, were the southern Semites, Arabs, Sabæans, Minæans, and
Ethiopians, the last-named of whom also crossed the straits of
Bab-el-Mandeb to Abyssinia in Africa.

Constituting the northern Semites, we have :

1. In the lower valley of the Tigris and Euphrates, the Babylonian peoples, with their offshoot, the Assyrians, along the Tigris
to the north. In the earliest period to which we can go back these
Semites possessed settled homes and an advanced civilization.

2. To the northeast of the Arabian desert, the Canaanites.
These also possess, at the earliest period with which we are acquainted, settled habitations and an advanced civilization. They
occupied all of Palestine and, originally, also the country much
further northward along the Syrian mountains. At a period antedating the commencement of the history of Israel the Hittites had
pushed into the Canaanite territory to the north, and occupied a
large part of it, stretching even into Palestine. In the process of
conquering this Canaanite territory they themselves became strongly
Semitized, and the Hittite spurs which were thrust into Palestine
appear to have adopted Canaanite language and customs, so as to
have been, to all intents and purposes, indistinguishable from the
general mass of Perizzites, Jebusites, Hivites, etc., constituting the
Canaanites or Amorites.

3. Aramæans. Besides the Canaanites, the land of Palestine was
occupied at the time of the Hebrew invasion by certain nations
close of kin to the Hebrews, speaking the same language with the
Canaanites, and yet different from them. These peoples were the
Ammonites, Moabites, and Edomites. The two former had largely
displaced the Canaanites, or Amorites, west of the Jordan from the
Yarmuk southward. The Edomites occupied the territory south of
Canaan, to the southeast and south of the Dead Sea. The latter,
with a few smaller tribes still in a nomadic condition and occupying
the territory adjacent to Edom, were closest of kin to the Hebrews.
Edom was, according to the Israelite ethnological tradition, Esau,
the elder brother of Jacob, who was Israel. Next most closely related were some of the nomadic peoples in the neighborhood of Edom,
who, according to tradition, were descended directly from Abraham.

Among some of these latter we find the custom of the twelvefold tribal division, which prevailed in Israel and Edom. Moab and Ammon were also close of kin, descended from Lot, the nephew of Abraham, Israel's grandfather. All these nations as we know them, and the Hebrews likewise, spoke the Canaanitish language, but the steadfast tradition of the Israelites was that they were Aramæans by origin, a tradition observed even in their ritual use (cf. Deut. xxvi, 5). They were the pioneers of the great Aramæan migration. They came in as nomads, overran sections of Amorite, or Canaanite, territory, and adopted the language of the people whom they had conquered. At the time of David we find that the Aramæans had largely displaced the Hittites to the north and established a number of kingdoms, the most southerly of which was Damascus. The center of Aramæan strength at that period was, however, Mesopotamia, and to Mesopotamia, and particularly to Harran in Mesopotamia, Hebrew tradition looked as the ancestral home.[1]

Hebrew tradition, as recorded in the Bible, tells of three successive patriarchs, ancestors of the Hebrew race and of Israel,—Abraham, Isaac, and Jacob,—who wandered back and forth through parts of Canaan, very much as nomad tribes do to-day and have done at most periods of the history of that country. Jacob, in these traditions, was particularly connected with Bethel and the region northward of that, occupied later by the tribes of Joseph and Benjamin. Abraham was located more particularly in the neighborhood of Hebron, later the center of the tribe of Judah; while Isaac is connected particularly with Beersheba, on the extreme southern limit of Judah. In what sense we are to understand the traditions of this early wandering in Canaan, to what extent it is a reflection backward from later times of the legends of the sanctuaries of Canaan, to what extent it is the adoption of race names and traditions of the peoples whom they supplanted and in part amalgamated, to what extent there was a true recollection of a previous

---

[1] At the time of the Tel el-Amarna letters, ca. 1400 B.C., Mesopotamia seems to have been inhabited by a non-Semitic people, the Mitanni, who were displaced by the Aramæan invasion.

wandering in that country, is not altogether certain. So far as the conditions of life go, such an occupation of Canaan by nomadic tribes was certainly not an impossible one. On the other hand, the names Jacob-el and Joseph-el for parts of Palestine or its population in the pre-Israelite period, occurring in Egyptian inscriptions, suggest that Israel borrowed these names and the traditions of their residence in Palestine from earlier inhabitants into whose land and birthright they entered. Israel was identified with Jacob, because Israel occupied the land of Jacob; and Ephraim and Manasseh became sons of Joseph, because they fell heir to the territory of Joseph.

Continuing in the genealogical form, Hebrew story ascribes the origin of the twelve tribes to the twelve sons of the patriarch Jacob, and here, in the diverse origin of those sons, it indicates at once the diversity of elements which entered into the national life of Israel.

Jacob had two wives: Leah, the first; and Rachel, the beloved, the second. By Leah he had, first of all, four sons: Reuben, the first born, then Simeon, Levi, and Judah (Gen. xxxix). Turning to the history of Israel, we find that to Reuben was ascribed, theoretically, the territory first occupied by Israel east of the Jordan, the original home of the nation in Palestine, from the Arnon northward to Gilead. But in the historic period this territory had passed again out of the hands of the Israelites and was in the possession of the Moabites. Reuben had, even at the time of the Deborah Song, practically ceased to exist as an element of Israel.

The second son, Simeon, was located southward of Judah, on the border of the desert, close to the nomadic kindred of Israel. He also vanishes from history at an early time. Levi, as a tribe, vanishes, how or where we do not know, but in close connection with Simeon.[1] The Levi which we meet later is a priestly caste.

Judah, the youngest of the first four sons of Leah, also occupied the southern country, and, as we learn, absorbed at various dates

---

[1] The story which we find in Genesis xxxiv of the treacherous attack on Shechem, and the allusion in Genesis xlix to the cruelty of these two tribes and their scattering in Israel, has suggested an original attempt to occupy the central hill country, afterwards occupied by Ephraim and Manasseh, which failed, resulting in the disruption of these two tribes. This would also account for the curious break in the historical period between the Leah tribes, Reuben and Judah on the south, and Zebulun and Issachar on the north.

kindred nomadic peoples — the Kenites, Kenizzites, etc. He was separated from the tribes of the north by an enclave of Canaanites, Gibeonites, and Jebusites, and hence isolated from the outset from the rest of Israel. There seems in this tradition of the seniority of these four sons of Leah, who are separated from all the rest, to be a recognition of the actual historic fact of possession and settlement. These four tribes of the south constituted one group in closer relationship with the nomads and perhaps earlier in occupation than the rest of Israel. Later were born to Leah, Issachar and Zebulun. In historic times we find these tribes no longer in connection with the older tribes of the south, but separated from them, occupying southern Galilee. The later birth suggests very naturally a later occupation.

To Rachel was born first, Joseph. With him especially is connected the story of the long sojourn in Egypt. From him later were derived the two tribes, Manasseh and Ephraim,[1] which, at the time of the conquest of the West Jordan land, played the main part and occupied the center of the territory. Closely connected with Manasseh and Ephraim, as a son of Rachel, but born later in Canaan, and not bearing the same relation as Joseph to the Egyptian sojourn, was Benjamin, son of the south land, that is, the land to the south of his older brother, Joseph.

Four tribes are represented as of inferior birth, born of concubines who were handmaidens, namely, Gad and Asher, children of Leah's handmaiden, and Dan and Naphtali, children of Rachel's handmaiden. In the historical period we find no differences between these tribes and the rest, and no special connection of the members of the two pairs, Gad and Asher being far separated one from another, the one east of the Jordan and the other west. At the beginning of the historical period Dan and Naphtali were also widely separated, the one being in the south and the other in the north, but later Dan migrated to a position adjoining Naphtali to the north. In the historic period these four tribes were on the borders of the

[1] The suggestion from the Egyptian name Joseph-el, found attached in the prehistoric period to the region afterwards occupied by Manasseh and Ephraim, is that those two tribes became the sons of Joseph because they occupied the ancient territory of Joseph.

Israelite territory, and, as a consequence of their situation, strongly mixed with foreign elements. It might be supposed that this is represented in the story of their unequal birth, but this does not account for the peculiar connections of these tribes with the Leah and Rachel tribes indicated in the tradition.[1]

Passing on from the tribal traditions of the twelve patriarchs, we come to a more recent tradition of a sojourn in Egypt. Israel became a denizen of the land of Goshen, the borderland of Egypt toward the Arabian wilderness, which belongs rather to the latter than to the former, and which always has been a roaming-ground of nomadic tribes. In the Orient, civilized peoples, whose borders nomadic tribes often occupy in a similar manner to this day, endeavor, where they are strong enough, to assimilate the nomads, compelling them to submit to their laws and become settled inhabitants of the land, yielding laborers for their works and soldiers for

---

[1] In the Egyptian inscriptions of the pre-Israelite period we find a people named Asher occupying approximately the region later occupied by Asher. It is suggested that this people was adopted into the Israelite confederacy. If this be so, then the same is probably true also of the other concubine tribes. We should thus, perhaps, find an explanation for the old heathen god name, Gad. On this supposition Dan is a Canaanite people, driven out of its first home by the invasion of the Philistines. We find also in this an explanation of the positions of these four tribes and their relations to Leah and Rachel respectively. The names and personal relations of the tribe fathers as given in Genesis suggest that the land of Canaan was first occupied by the sons of Leah, Reuben on the south, east of the Jordan, Simeon and Levi with their sister Dinah in the center about Shechem, then Judah in the west land to the south. Then followed Issachar and Zebulun to the north. To these were added the concubine tribes, Gad, an appanage of Reuben beyond Jordan, and Asher, of Zebulun and Issachar on the northwest. Reuben as a tribe was lost, partly through nomadization, partly through the encroachments of Moab. Simeon and Levi were largely blotted out, Levi, the special name son of Leah and the holder of the sanctuary of Shechem, continuing to exist only as a religious clan, and what was left of Simeon being nominally attached to Judah on the south, in the Beersheba region. In Shechem, however, was left a circumcised people sistered (Dinah) to Israel. Issachar and Zebulun bowed down among the Canaanites. Then came the sons of Rachel, Joseph and Benjamin. The former was divided, the older, Manasseh, lying east of Jordan, the younger, Ephraim, which later became the first-born, occupying the already half kindred land of Joseph-el, in the central mountain. To them was added a little later a new tribe, Benjamin, southward of Ephraim, and a concubine or Canaanitish adjunct, Dan. In the wars with the Philistines what part of the latter was not destroyed or subdued removed to the extreme north, at the sources of the Jordan. Later, as Israelite power grew, the region south of this new Dan, between it and Issachar and Zebulun, was wrung from the heathen as another concubine tribe of Rachel, Naphtali,

their armies — efforts which the nomads resist to the best of their power. There is a constant contest of this kind between the Turkish authorities and the Arabian nomads on the borders of Turkish territory. The Turks attempt to enforce conscription and taxation, and to assert state or individual ownership of land. All of these things are obnoxious to the nomads. They resist when they can, or, if practicable, flee into more inaccessible regions. The latter was the course finally taken by Israel, which fled from the enforced labor of the Egyptians back to the desert.

There are a few scholars who deny the historical character of this whole tradition, but they are in a small minority. Others regard the story of the Egyptian sojourn, recounted by tradition, as applicable, historically, only to Joseph, that is, Ephraim and Manasseh. However that may be, it is a fact that, according to this tradition, the relation of Joseph to Egypt was longer and more intimate than that of his brethren, the other tribes.

In the Sinaitic peninsula and the region northward was formed the nation of Israel. In this region Israel wandered for " forty years," a period used in the Bible sometimes for a generation, sometimes for an indefinite period of years. Their headquarters and sanctuary during part, at least, of this period were Kadesh Barnea, that is, the sanctuary of Barnea. Close of kin to Edom and the still older Ammonites and Moabites, but inferior to those in civilization, the Israelites were at this period, according to their own tradition, preparing to pass from the nomadic to the settled life. Finally they moved eastward and northward around Edom and Moab. There they happened on an Amorite, that is, Canaanite, kingdom, which had established itself between Moab and Ammon, with Heshbon as its capital, in a region conquered, or rather re-conquered, from those two nations. Overthrowing this kingdom, the Israelites took possession of the upland plateau between the Arnon and Gilead, and the rich lands in the Jordan valley beneath. Then they stretched northward over Gilead and into Bashan. It was in this region that they began to enter upon the settled life. From here they pushed across the Jordan to Jericho and Gilgal, which latter was for a time their center in the West Jordan land.

Thence they gradually pushed westward into the mountains. The story of the conquest of Canaan is told in historical form in Judges i, 1–3, 5–7, 11–17, 20–36. The various tribes acted, in general, upon their own responsibility. The bond of union which had been formed in the wilderness was soon loosed. Ephraim and Manasseh secured the central portion of the West Jordan territory, with a settlement in Gilead east of the Jordan. Benjamin was south of these. Judah occupied the region further southward, in close touch with the kindred nomads of the Negeb, by an amalgamation with some of whom it became a great and powerful tribe, and ultimately a nation. The country that was conquered at the outset was, with the exception of the Jordan valley, entirely mountainous. The Israelites were unable to contend with the chariots of the Canaanites on the plain. Little by little they occupied more territory, sometimes driving out the inhabitants, more often absorbing them and in the process adopting many of their customs and manners; but to the last they differentiated themselves from the Canaanites whom they found in the country, maintaining the tradition of their Aramæan origin. This is well shown in the relationship ascribed to Canaan with Ham, that is, Egypt, with which the Canaanites, as we know, had been in close connection before the Hebrew period, while they themselves were descendants of Shem. The conquest of Canaan was not completed until the time of David, and it is his kingdom which constitutes the norm of the theoretical land of Israel which we find in the Biblical tradition. In his day the Hebrews actually possessed and occupied the central mountain with its foothills from Beersheba on the south to Dan on the north. In the Plain of Esdraelon, however, the Canaanites continued to dwell among the Israelites in subject cities or mixed with the conquering people. On the coast plain conditions were different. The Philistines were made tributary, but not absorbed or amalgamated; Phœnicia, with its " hinterland," was an ally on equal terms with Israel. In Sharon the conditions were like those in Esdraelon. On the east of the Jordan, in David's time, the southern limit of the Hebrews was probably northward of the Arnon, and the northern limit in Bashan

somewhat north of the Yarmuk. The Edomites, Moabites, and
Ammonites, and the Aramæans and Hittites in Bashan were made
tributary but were not absorbed into Israel. The territory actually
occupied by the Israelites in David's day was, then, from Beersheba on the south to Dan on the north, including the coast south
of Carmel and north of Joppa, and on the east of the Jordan a
strip of land some twenty miles or so in breadth, extending from
about the head of the Dead Sea on the south to a point a little
further north than the southern end of the Sea of Galilee. Within
this region there still remained a number of Canaanite cities,
especially on the plains of Esdraelon and Sharon, along the foothills of the central range, and on the Galilean borders, which were
never really occupied by the Israelites, although included within
their territory.

In addition to the region occupied by the Israelites in David's
time, a number of the surrounding kingdoms and states were made
tributary — Philistia, Edom, Moab, Ammon, Damascus, and others,
so that his kingdom may be said to have extended from the borders
of Egypt on the south, to northern Syria beyond Aleppo on the
north, and from the Mediterranean on the west to the Euphrates
and the Syrian desert on the east.

After his death, most of the subject kingdoms soon fell away,
and the children of Israel were shortly limited to their own territory, with a few tributary states and cities, including the kindred
Edom and Moab.

In the ninth century the pressure of Aramæans from the north
began to be felt in Palestine, and in the eighth century the land
actually occupied by the Israelites began to be very perceptibly
diminished, first by Aramæan and later by Assyrian aggression.
At the close of that century, after the destruction of Samaria by
the Assyrians, the Israelites were confined to a small strip of territory in the central mountain region, extending from a point seven
miles north of Jerusalem southward to the borders of Edom, a
region about 45 miles in length by 25 or 30 in average breadth.
To the northward of this was the mixed population — Israelite
peasants with deported natives of Babylonian cities — out of which

grew, ultimately, the Samaritans. After the Exile, at the close of the sixth century, the Edomites are found in possession of the southern portion of Judah, including Hebron and the Shephelah. The Jews were limited to an area about Jerusalem less than 20 miles in length and the same in breadth. Gradually they stretched out from this center, and in the Maccabæan and Herodian periods we find them occupying in addition the lower Jordan valley, the greater part of Gilead across the Jordan and of Galilee, while a considerable population of Jews was mixed with the Greeks and Syrians in Bashan. On the south they had circumcised the Edomites, and incorporated that nation with themselves. Westward they had occupied a portion of the Philistine territory, and, from Joppa northward, a great part of the Plain of Sharon, the mountains of Ephraim and Samaria being held by their hated kinsmen, the Samaritans. But in all these regions they were more or less mixed with other peoples and affected by foreign influences. Only in Judæa were they complete masters and possessors of the land. Along the seacoast, through the Plain of Esdraelon to the Jordan, on the Sea of Galilee, in Bashan and the northern edge of Gilead, and in Ammon and Moab, were Greek or Græcized Syrian cities. The common language of the country had long before this been Aramaicized, and even in Judæa the ordinary language of the people, since the beginning of the fifth century, had come to be Aramæan or Syrian.

CHAPTER III

PRIMITIVE RELIGION OF THE HEBREWS

The Semitic languages are far more closely allied with one another than the languages of the Indo-European stock. Their relation to one another is more nearly like the relations of sub-families in the Indo-European family, for example, French, Italian, Spanish, Portuguese, and Roumanian, which together constitute the Latin languages of the Indo-European family. What is true of languages is true also of customs and religious use. The Semitic peoples are more closely related in their religious conceptions, their ritual practices, and their theological phraseology than the peoples of Indo-European stock. There are not only certain general religious ideas which belong to all the Semitic peoples, but these ideas are expressed by the same terms. The name *El*, as a designation of divinity in general, is common to them all. In a few special cases among Aramæans, and possibly also among Hebrews, it is used as the name of God; but this is only a local variation of the universal use of the word as a designation of divinity. Further than this we find throughout the Semitic world a designation of God by words denoting his power or possessor-ship, as *Adoni* or *Adonis*, "Lord"; *Malak, Malik,* or *Melech,* "King"; *Mar* or *Marna,* "Sir" or "Lord"; *Rabb,* "Master"; *Baal* or *Bel,* "Lord" or "Owner." These titles may be applied to any god, and, on the other hand, they are developed in special cases as the proper name of a divinity. Corresponding to this method of designating the gods is the designation of the adherents of those gods as servant or slave.

But behind this designation of the gods as rulers, lords, masters, and the like, lies an earlier conception of them as kinsmen. This conception shows itself in a class of names which occurs through-out the whole Semitic world, but particularly among the Himyaritic

Arabs, names which designate the bearer as related to the divinity. Among the Hebrews names of this class belong to the earliest period, antedating even the names compounded with *Adoni*, *Bel*, etc.[1] Of this formation are such names as *Abram*, "father is exalted," or *Abiram*, "my father is exalted," *Ahiram*, "my brother is exalted," *Amram*, "uncle is exalted," etc. These names must be put with a multitude of other evidences which go to show that the type of religion founded on kinship, in which the deity and his worshipers are supposed to be united by a bond of blood, was the original Semitic type of religion.[2] There was a blood relationship between the god and his worshipers, and the worshipers were related among themselves by the same bond of blood. This was the primitive Semitic conception. How distinct this idea of blood relationship among the worshipers was is shown by the manner in which they designated their relationship with one another. It is not only in Israel that the history of the race presents itself in the form of a genealogical table; we find the same conception in Arabia and elsewhere in the Semitic world. Each tribe was descended from one ancestor. The members of the tribe were his children, in whose veins his blood flowed. In a literal sense it was not, of course, the case that the tribe was descended from one individual and that one blood flowed in all veins. Outsiders were admitted into the tribal relationship; but by virtue of that admission they were conceived of as entering into the blood relationship, and indeed they were at times initiated by some ceremony of blood brotherhood. The one thing which bound the family, clan, or tribe together was the relation of blood, actual or assumed. The one great obligation upon all the members of a tribe or clan was to avenge the shedding of the blood of any member of that tribe or clan.

The same thing which united the members of the tribe or clan to one another united them to their god. Out of this patriarchal relation of the god to his worshipers was developed in course of time the conception of lordship or kinship, in the same way and through the same causes which led to the development in their

[1] Cf. G. Buchanan Gray, *Studies in Hebrew Proper Names*, pp. 252 f.
[2] W. Robertson Smith, *The Religion of the Semites*, p. 51.

relations to one another of lords, rulers, and kings out of the simpler clan relationships of the patriarchal community. As clans united with clans to form tribes, and tribes with tribes to form peoples, the head of the clan, the chief of the tribe, passed over into the lord or ruler of the people, and *pari passu* the god who was a father, brother, or uncle became a lord, an owner, or a king, and the people his servants. The fact that both of these conceptions, that of fatherhood and that of lordship, prevailed throughout the entire Semitic world, shows us that the second stage was reached at an early time, when all the Semitic peoples were still substantially one. The conception of lordship was naturally more highly developed in proportion as the political organization was more highly developed. The simpler the organization and the more closely it maintained the patriarchal form, the better it preserved the more primitive idea of blood relationship with the god. The more elaborate the social and political organization became, the more the idea of lordship and service between the god and his people tended to become dominant. Comparing the ancient Arabian customs and uses with those of the settled and more highly cultivated peoples of Babylonia and Canaan, we find that the conception of lordship is more prominent in the latter, that of kinship in the former.

Now the Hebrews before the time of Moses were nomads. Their political organization was merely the loose patriarchal connection of clans and tribes. A priori, therefore, we should expect to find the primitive religion of Israel more closely akin to that of the nomadic Arabs than to that of the more civilized and highly organized Phœnicians and Canaanites or Babylonians, and in point of fact, in studying the pre-Mosaic religion of Israel, we find ourselves compelled to turn for our comparisons to Arabia rather than to the more cultivated and developed religions of the settled Semitic peoples. Late, chronologically, as is our information with regard to the religion of the heathen Arabians, in point of development we find that religion much closer to the religion of Israel in its earlier stages than the latter was to the contemporary religions of Babylonia and Phœnicia.

The Arabs paid particular honor to stones.[1] At every sanctuary one or more stones were set up. These were generally unworked, occasionally they were rudely hewn. They were altars, and at the same time they represented the god — not in the sense that the stone was an image of the god, but that the god was supposed to dwell in the stone or to be, in some way, peculiarly connected with it. A sacred place might be determined by the presence of a spring or a tree or a mountain, but whatever the nature of the sacred place or the cause of its sanctity, the altar and the representative of deity was one or more stones, a *nuṣb*, or, in the collective form, *manṣab*.

We find the same practices prevailing among the Hebrews in the earliest period. In connection with every sanctuary there was a sacred stone, called *mazzebah*. The word is identical in root and composition with the Arabic form *manṣab*, and from the earliest references it is clear that the *mazzebah*, like the *manṣab*, was a rude stone, not an image, and that, at the outset at least, it was used like the Arabic *manṣab* for an altar and also to represent the presence of the deity. So Saul erects a stone at which the animals may be killed and on or by which their blood may be poured out, and his doing so is described as the building of an altar to Yahaweh: "it was the first altar that he built unto Yahaweh." [2]

The original sanctuary of Israel, west of the Jordan, was, according to the Book of Joshua, a *gilgal*, that is, a circle of rude stones, and this remained an important sanctuary at least until the middle of the eighth century B.C. (Hos. iv, 13 ; Amos iv, 4). In the same book we are told of an altar of unhewn stones erected on Mt. Ebal, in the mountain country of Ephraim (Josh. viii, 30 f.), and we read of at least one *gilgal* west of the Jordan, besides the one near Jericho. A similar *gilgal*, called also *mazzebah*,[3] or collection of stones, existed in Gilead, erected, according to tradition, by Jacob, at which he sacrificed, and where he made a covenant with Laban

---

[1] For the comparisons in this chapter compare in general Wellhausen, *Reste arabischen Heidentums* (Berlin, 1887), and W. R. Smith, *The Religion of the Semites*, 2d ed., and *Kinship and Marriage in Early Arabia*.

[2] 1 Sam. xiv, 32–35.

[3] The two different words are commonly supposed to be due to a combination of two narratives. Cf. Addis, *Documents of the Hexateuch*, I, 62.

(Gen. xxxi, 45–54). The form of covenant in connection with these stones may have been similar in principle to the Arabic covenant described by Herodotus (III, 8), where seven stones were set up, the hands of the covenanting parties cut with a sharp stone, and then, with threads drawn from their respective garments, the blood from their hands put upon the stones and the deity invoked to witness the covenant between them. The Hebrew expression for making a covenant was *karath berith*, " cut a covenant."

There was a *mazzebah* at Bethel which was reputed to have been erected by Jacob (Gen. xxviii, 13 ; xxxv, 14),[1] and great stones, similar to the one which Saul used as an altar, are mentioned as existing at various places, such as Shechem, Mizpah, Gibeon, and En-Rogel. Indeed, as we shall have occasion to notice later, *mazzebah* were found until the time of Josiah in connection with every shrine, as the Prophets testify. But in the later time they are, as among the Canaanites, in most cases no longer altars, but mere adjuncts to a sanctuary, representing in some vague way the presence of the deity. Among the early Hebrews, as among the Arabs, they were altars as well as representatives of the deity (if indeed the two ideas were originally quite distinct). It was in the former capacity that blood was poured out at or on the stone by Arab and primitive Hebrew alike ; it was in the latter capacity that the Arab stroked the stone. As among the Arabs a suppliant aims to come into physical contact with the great man whose protection he supplicates, so in stroking the stone the suppliant sought to come in contact with the deity which it represented. The word used by the Arabs to denote this ritual stroking of a sacred stone was *mashach*. The same word is used in Genesis xxxi, 13, to indicate Jacob's ritual treatment of the *mazzebah* at Bethel.[2]

[1] See the author's paper in *Studies in the History of Religion*, presented to C. H. Toy (New York, 1912), p. 231.

[2] Elsewhere in Hebrew this root means " to rub " something, as with paint (Is. xxii, 14) or oil (Is. xxi, 5) ; then, commonly, " to anoint." Addis, *Documents of the Hexateuch*, I, 52, says the stone was " anointed by the worshipper, who by this act anointed the god, just as the host anointed his guest at a feast. Such 'anointed stones' were familiar to all Semitic nations." Cf. the Arabic practice of anointing the head of the *nuṣub* with blood. Cf. also Macalister, *The Excavation of Gezer*, II, 388.

In the early Arabic use the altar was not a hearth and there were no burnt offerings. The part of the animal offered to God was the blood, which was poured on the stone or into a hole beneath the stone, where such a hole existed. The animals which might be sacrificed were the domestic or tame animals of the flocks and herds, that is, camel, oxen, and sheep. Gazelles and other wild creatures were not acceptable for purposes of sacrifice. The sacrifice consisted in pouring out the blood, which was the god's part; this done, the worshipers feasted on the creature sacrificed. All killing of animals for food was a sacrifice, and the word used, and still used to-day among the Mohammedan Arabs, to express this killing was *zebach*. In connection with the sacrifice there was a cry of praise, called *tahlil*, from the verb *hillal*. Even in the case of the killing of wild animals, such as gazelles, the sacrificial idea was present and a *tahlil* was uttered; in this case, however, the blood was not offered to God by pouring on the stone, but was poured out upon the ground. Whoever killed an animal made a sacrifice to God, and he who partook of it partook of the sacrifice to that god. Even to-day an Arab may not partake of an animal slain by an unbeliever, because in doing so he would take part in a sacrifice to the god of that unbeliever. The blood was the life. It was the bond of union between the members of the tribe and between the tribe and its god. Sacrifice was a renewal of covenant, a strengthening of the blood union between the god and his worshipers and between the members of the tribe. One who was not by birth a member of the tribe might be received into it by a covenant of blood. A man might enter into a covenant of blood with a member of any tribe, exchanging blood with him literally or figuratively, and both of them mingling their blood with that of the god by smearing it upon a stone, as in the form of covenant above described. For the actual blood of the persons making the covenant there was substituted more commonly, particularly in the later time, the blood of animals. The hands of the two covenanting parties might be dipped in a bowl of the blood of animals. Sometimes the blood was applied by sprinkling. The underlying principle in all these forms was that of blood relationship;[1] that the relation of members of a tribe with

1 Trumbull, *The Blood Covenant*, 2d ed.

one another was a relation of blood, that the same relation existed between the tribe and its god, and that by the transfusion of blood, first physically and then metaphorically, a blood relationship might be established or confirmed between individual men, or between men and God. Sacrifice among the Arabs was feasting together and with God on the part of the members of a tribe or family, and by this feast the blood relation was reëstablished or confirmed.

We find substantially all these practices prevalent among the Hebrews in the earlier periods. In the passage already referred to (1 Sam. xiv, 32–35), when the Hebrews are killing sheep to eat, without any religious ceremony, Saul causes a large stone to be set up and bids them pour out the blood at this stone. The blood is thus given to God and the eating of the animals is a sacrifice. It was a shocking thing, contrary to the fundamental ideas of religion, that animals should be killed and eaten without this sacrificial rite. There was no fire and no burning of a part of the animal for God. To Him was given only the blood. Even in the later ritual great stress is laid on the fact that the blood is the life. It is forbidden to eat the blood.[1] In certain sacrifices the blood is sprinkled upon the altar.[2] Again it is poured out at the foot of the altar.[3] In both cases the meaning of the ritual is that the blood, that is, the life, is given to God, and the altar stands for Him as did the primitive *nuṣub*.

But in certain peculiar cases among the Hebrews the blood was, metaphorically at least, consumed by the people. This is the meaning of the ritual of the covenant sacrifice, described in Exodus xxiv, where half of the blood was sprinkled on the altar, and half on the people.[4] In the case of the Passover the blood was communicated to the people by being smeared upon the doorposts. In both cases the idea is the same, that of a very special covenant with God, in which God and His worshipers are made of one blood, or their blood kinship renewed, by partaking of the same blood. The last use is parallel to the Arabic custom of sprinkling fresh blood upon the tents.[5] The entire Passover ritual of the Hebrews is extremely

---

[1] Cf., among other passages, Lev. vii, 27 ; xvii, 10–12.

[2] Lev. i, 5 ; iii, 13, etc.   [3] Lev. iv, 7.

[4] Cf. also the application of blood in the consecration of priests (Lev. viii, 23) and the purification of lepers (xiv, 14).

[5] Cf. W. Robertson Smith, *The Religion of the Semites*, p. 326.

primitive. The paschal lamb or goat was to be wholly eaten, head, entrails, and all, and in haste (Ex. xii, 8–10), like the ancient Arabic sacrifice of the camel; and the very prohibition of eating it raw suggests an earlier stage in which, like the Arabic camel sacrifice described by Nilus,[1] it was eaten entire, and the blood, instead of being symbolically consumed by the people by being struck upon their doorposts, was actually and literally drunk by them.

The animals which might be sacrificed among the Hebrews were the domestic animals — the flocks and the herds. Here there is a difference in detail between Hebrew and Arab use, which, however, strengthens the resemblance in principle. The camel was not a sacrificial animal with the Hebrews, because it did not constitute a part of their domestic herds. The animals on which they depended for food, at least in the earlier days, were the ox, the sheep, and the goat, and they only were sacrificial animals.[2] As over against Assyrian use, Hebrew use forbade the sacrifice of gazelles and wild creatures. Only domestic cattle and domestic fowl might be offered as sacrifice. The domestic animals constituted, as it were, a part of the clan, of the same blood as the god and his worshipers. To give their blood to the god was to give him the blood of the clan, and thus to reunite the god and his worshipers in the blood of a common life. In this it was substantially at one with the Arabic custom; nevertheless among both all killing was so far a sacrifice that the blood of gazelles and wild creatures must be poured out, and, furthermore, must be covered up that it might not be regarded as a sacrifice to some other god or to the demons of the field.[3] A creature whose blood was not thus poured out might not be eaten, among either Hebrews or Arabs; for to eat it was to ally oneself with some strange god, who had received the unoffered blood. On the same principle the Hebrews forbade the eating of an animal killed by wild beasts;[4] the blood had become a sacrifice to a demon, and to partake of the flesh was to become

---

[1] *Nili opera quaedam nondum edita*, Paris, 1639, p. 27.
[2] The use of domestic fowl, the dove and the pigeon (cf. Lev. i, 14–17), for sacrificial purposes seems to be somewhat later, but follows the same general principle.
[3] Cf. Lev. xvii, 15.
[4] Ex. xxii, 31.

united by blood with that demon. The Hebrews used for ' killing '
the same word which the Arab also used, — *zebach*, " sacrifice," —
for all killing for food had in it a sacrificial character ; and, like the
Arabs, the Hebrews used a cry of praise in connection with the
sacrifice, *tehillah* in Hebrew, *tahlil* in Arabic, from the root *h-l-l.*
In later times the *tehillah* became a psalm.

The Hebrews at an early period had, like the Arabs, developed
the ritual of blood by substitution. For the blood of human beings
the blood of animals was substituted, as in making a blood covenant. Still more symbolically the Hebrews substituted wine for
blood.[1] Among the Hebrews, also, fat and then oil were deemed
to have in regard to life the same property as blood ; hence the
use of oil in certain cases where the Arabs used blood, as in anointing (*mashach*) a stone, and hence the prohibition of the consumption
of the fat of a sacrificial animal by the worshipers.

In Arabic literature we find some references to human sacrifice,
as though at one time human rather than animal sacrifices were
offered to the gods, or as though human sacrifice were preferred
by the gods ; but on more careful consideration these seem to indicate the later development of a theory of sacrifice, and the application to that theory of the observed use of blood in establishing a
covenant relation, rather than a primitive practice. The same is
true of such references to human sacrifice in Hebrew literature as
we find in Genesis xxii, the sacrifice of Isaac ; as also of the provisions of the Hebrew codes with regard to the substitution of a
sheep or a goat for the first-born.[2] We find notices among the
Arabs, it is true, of vows to sacrifice a son or the like, which are
similar in principle to the vow of Jephthah (Jud. xi, 30–40) ; but
these were certainly exceptional, and are connected not so much
with the special Arabic and Hebrew idea of sacrifice as with a very
general idea, liable to crop out among any people, of the demand
which the god makes for the dearest possession of men. The Arabs
did, however, at times sacrifice captives taken in war. This sacrifice
consisted merely in slaying the captives. Their blood was not poured

---

[1] W. Robertson Smith, *The Religion of the Semites*, pp. 213 f.
[2] Ex. xxii, 29 ; xxxiv, 20.

out on or by a sacred stone, and the flesh was not eaten, nevertheless it was counted a sacrifice. The Hebrews put captives to
death in the same manner, as a religious rite, in accordance with
a vow, or by the direction of God. This offering of captives to God
by killing them was called *haram*, a word of the same root as the
Arabic *ihram*, "vow," an etymological connection which helps to
show the connection in thought. It should be added that the idea
and practice of human sacrifice were much more developed among
other Semites than among Hebrews and Arabs, with whom it was
not only exceptional but also rudimentary and undeveloped.

But while human sacrifice was thus exceptional and undeveloped,
the offering of a part of the body, such as a little blood or the hair,
was common among the Arabs. The latter practice was preserved
among the Hebrews to the latest times in the Nazarite vow
(Num. vi, 18); the former seems to have lingered only in the initiation ceremony of circumcision. In the times of Arabic heathenism
circumcision was a ceremony of initiation into manhood, in which
blood from the male organ was given to the deity. There are traces
of the same use among the Hebrews at an early period; [1] but in
historical times circumcision was a rite of admission into the nation,
administered at an early age, and the blood rite or blood offering
connected with it was, at the best, very vaguely remembered.

In addition to the animal sacrifices we find other offerings made
by the Arabs, but these were not deemed equally acceptable to the
gods. Meal or other food might be thrown into the hole (*ghubghub*)
by the sacred stone, and in fact any object of any sort might be
made an offering. Offerings of the latter class were *anathemata*,
things which were suspended on sacred trees, or upon or by the
sacred stone, or in some way brought into connection with the
gods. Swords were especially offered in this manner, and, above
all, swords or other weapons taken from the enemy. The sanctification of the object for such a purpose was designated by the root
nazar. The same word appears in classical Hebrew use, in connection with the consecration of the hair, in the well-known Nazarite
vow, already mentioned. We have also examples of *anathemata*

[1] Cf. Ex. iv, 25; Josh. v, 2 ff.; cf. also Gen. xxx.

among the Hebrews, and especially the consecration to God of swords taken in battle, as in the case of the sword of Goliath, kept behind the ephod in the sanctuary at Nob (cf. 1 Sam. xv, 9).

The story of the sacrifice of Cain and Abel (Gen. iv) exhibits the same sentiment with regard to animal sacrifices, as over against the sacrifice of meal or vegetable offerings, which existed among the Arabs. The whole story is full of the idea, which one finds everywhere among nomadic peoples, of the superior dignity of the wandering to the sedentary life. The bedawi looks down upon the *ma'dan*, or village Arab, as an inferior being. In the story of Cain and Abel, the herdsman, the bedawi, Abel, stands upon the higher plane, and it is his offering, the animal offering, which is acceptable to God. Cain, the *ma'dan*, the tiller of the ground, is an object of aversion, and his sacrifice, from the fruit of the fields, does not win a blessing.

Among the Arabs, while the tribes wandered from place to place, the sanctuaries, as a rule, remained stationary. A well, a grove or a solitary tree, an imposing mountain or height, were likely to become holy places. Originally within the territory of some tribe, that tribe moving to other localities would continue to make pilgrimages to its old sanctuary; or some sanctuary having become for any reason especially famous, the members of tribes not historically connected with it might make pilgrimages thither. A shrine peculiar by its location, as a lofty mountain or an especially fertile spring, might acquire a reputation which would overshadow the reputation of other local shrines and lead many tribes to resort to it; or a shrine might obtain particular sanctity, not because of its natural advantages, but from the importance of the tribe whose sanctuary it was or had been, or through events connected or supposed to be connected with it.

We have seen that the shrines at these sacred places consisted primarily of stones and heaps of stones. Such shrines or holy places were readily created, and the old habit of making holy places has lingered on to this day throughout Arabia, Syria, and Mesopotamia, furnishing us abundant examples of the way in which holy places grew and the causes which led to their growth. A man might, because of some personal — even subjective — experience, establish a shrine at any given point, setting up a stone there. The appearance of that stone would indicate to others the existence of a shrine, a place of the manifestation of deity, and lead them to worship there, and perhaps to add other stones, without inquiring about the reason for the sanctity of the place. Ultimately stories would spring up to explain the sanctuary. Tombs lent, and still lend, themselves readily to such purposes; not that there was a direct worship of ancestors, but there was a special sentiment connected with their tombs; moreover, these were prominent constructions or memorials, the possession of the tribe and a record of its experiences and heroes. Anything like a temple or house for the gods at these shrines was rare. Portable houses or arks we do not find among the Arabs, but certain sacred things representing the tribal god were at times carried into battle. On such occasions the god might be represented by a maiden mounted on a camel, by a mare, or by a banner. These were rather emblems of the deity than portable sanctuaries. The god was regarded as having a local abode, but he might go forth by emblem to march with the tribe.

It is plain from the Bible narrative that customs very similar to these prevailed among the early Hebrews. We find the same inclination to attach sanctity to any place where there was some representation of the divinity, whether it were a tomb or a pillar or whatever it may have been.[1] It was for this reason that, when they entered Palestine, the Hebrews adopted as their own the sacred cities and shrines which they found in existence.[2] There is an inclination to reverence springs and groves and heights. The sources of the Jordan were regarded as especially sacred, and there was located the temple of Dan, at which served the descendants of Moses.[3] To use the words of the Book of Kings (1 Kings xiv, 23), they "built them high places and set up *mazzeboth* and *asherim* on every high hill and under every green tree" where the nations who preceded them had worshiped. At the same time they maintained, at least in the earlier periods of their history, a

---

[1] Cf. Bethel (Gen. xxviii) or Rachel's Pillar (Gen. xxxv).
[2] Kedesh, Beth Shemesh, Anathoth, etc.   [3] Jud. xviii.

close connection with the holy places of the region from which they had come. In the Song of Deborah (Jud. v, 4, 5), Yahaweh is spoken of as having his abode in Seir or Horeb-Sinai, and coming thence to assist the Hebrews in battle; and in the story of Elijah (1 Kings, xix), we find that prophet making a pilgrimage to Horeb as the abode of Yahaweh. More frequent mention is made of Beersheba, on the northern border of the same southern region, the region of the nomadic life, as an hereditary shrine,[1] held in peculiar reverence, to which pilgrimages were made as late certainly as the middle of the eighth century B.C.

In Arabic use we have, in connection with pilgrimages to the shrines of deities, the word *haj.* This word seems to have connected itself especially with the practice of going around, or encircling, the sacred stone or stones of the sanctuary. Another common usage among the Arabs in connection with this encircling of the sacred place, or in connection with the sacred place in general, was the obligatory change of garments. In some cases men threw away their garments and went about the sacred stones naked; more often they received other garments to use in or at the sanctuary. The Hebrews used the same word *haj* for festival pilgrimages to shrines. The period of pilgrimage in the early Hebrew use was the season of the autumnal feast. This was *the haj.*[2] There are some hints also that in Hebrew use a remnant of the practice of encircling the holy place lingered on in the form of dances:[3] while the obligatory change of clothes meets us both in the primitive and also in the later Hebrew ritual.[4]

The Arabic year began in the autumn, and was divided into two parts. The second half of the year began at the vernal equinox. Each of the two sections commenced with a feast and a festival season. The *haj* took place at the commencement of the year; it was at this time that the Arabs made their pilgrimages to distant shrines, a custom which Islam has inherited in the *haj,* or pilgrimage, to Mecca. This was the holy season.

1 Gen. xxi, 33; xxvi, 24; xlvi, 1; Amos v, 5; viii, 14
2 1 Kings viii, 2, 65; xii, 32; Lev. xxiii, 39; Jud. xxi, 19; Is. xxx, 29; Zech. xiv,18.
3 Ex. xxxii, 5, 19; 1 Kings xix, 26.
4 Gen. xxxv, 2; 2 Kings x, 22.

At the beginning of spring occurred the *ragab* festival. This was the time when camels and sheep calved. At this feast the firstlings of the flocks were offered, and the month in which it fell, *Ragab*, was called a holy month. This feast was celebrated, not by a pilgrimage to a distant shrine, but either at home or at some local shrine.

The ancient Hebrew year was divided into two halves, precisely like the Arabic year, an arrangement which has been retained in the sacred, or religious, year of the Jews. The year began in the autumn, with the month Tisri. In that month was held the *haj*, a festival connected with a pilgrimage to a sanctuary. The connection of this festival with their nomadic existence was observed in later times by the Hebrews in the custom of living in booths or tents during the feast. In the spring, at the beginning of the second half of the year, occurred the Hebrew feast of the Passover. This, like the Arabic *ragab* feast, was in its origin rather a home feast than the occasion of a pilgrimage to a distant shrine. By tradition it was connected with the sacrifice of the firstlings and fell at the time of the calving of the flocks. In the historical period it was joined with the *mazzoth*, or feast of unleavened, and was to be observed as a *haj* at some sanctuary.

The sacrificer among the Arabs was not, primarily, the priest, but the head of the clan or family. There were priests among them, and in certain cases they acted as sacrificers, but their primary function was to guard the sanctuary and to give oracles. Such sacrificing as the priest did was in connection with the sanctuary of which he was the guardian. In certain families the office of priest was hereditary. Priests were connected with certain shrines or sacred places, and the priesthood passed down in those families without regard to the tribe in whose territory the sanctuary existed. The important function of the priest, aside from the guardianship of the sanctuary, was to give oracles. These were determined by lot. Before undertaking any great enterprise, and particularly before going to battle, the lots (*ksm*) were consulted by the priest.

Besides the priests there were also seers (*kahin*). These possessed a peculiar individual relation to the divine beings. They told the whereabouts of what was lost or revealed other mysteries, not by means of lots, but by oracles out of their own mouths. These men affected certain peculiarities and in general much mystery. One common peculiarity was the use of the veil. Originally, apparently, the functions of priest and seer were identical, and the *kahin* combined in himself the post of seer and priest; later the two functions were divided as above indicated. In the most primitive Hebrew times we find much the same customs prevailing. A priestly caste did not exist. David made his sons priests.[1] Micah made his son a priest at the shrine which he built.[2] Saul, Samuel, and others sacrificed, and indeed every head of a family may be said to have been a sacrificer.[3] The term used by the Hebrews for "priest" was *kohen*, a word of the same root and formation as the Arabic *kahin*. We find the priests acting as guardians of the shrines, as in the case of Micah's shrine, above referred to, and also as the givers of the sacred oracles,[4] by means of lots, for which the same word *ksm* was used as in the Arabic. In the Septuagint version of 1 Samuel xiv, 41,[5] we have a statement of the way in which these lots were cast. Both Saul and David consulted the oracles through the priest before going into battle, and while we find no mention of the priests who accompanied them acting as sacrificers, their function of lot casters is prominent.[6] The Hebrew priests might also be seers or diviners,[7] as in the case of Samuel and Moses, and in the story of the latter we meet with the veil,[8] so familiar among the Arabs.

There is further a striking resemblance between the Arabic and Hebrew cults in the use of a number of individual words besides those already noticed, such as *thr*, "clean," and *tma*, "unclean." Sometimes the difference of use is itself an evidence of original identity. So the Arabs performed the sacrifice with the *hrbh*; in Hebrew the same word is used for the implement with which children were circumcised. The word *'athr* is used in Arabic for "offerings," but

---

[1] 2 Sam. viii, 18.   [2] Jud. xvii, 5.

[3] 1 Sam. xiii, 9; xiv, 35; xvi, 2 f.; xx, 29.   [4] Deut. xxxiii, 8.

[5] "If this sin be in me or in Jonathan my son, Yahaweh, God of Israel, give *urim*; but if it be in thy people Israel, give *thummim*."

[6] 1 Sam. xiv, 18 f., 36 ff.; xxii, 10; xxiii, 9 ff.; xxx, 7; 2 Sam. ii, 1; v, 19, 23. Cf. also Ex. xxii, 8.

[7] But see, for a distinction between seer and diviner, Jastrow, *J.B.L.*, XXXVIII, 45.

[8] Ex. xxxiv, 33 ff.

especially for the offerings of the holy month at the beginning of the year. In classical Hebrew the same word is used for " prayer," suggesting an original use in the same sense as the Arabic, out of which the later significance was derived, just as in the case of the *ḥrbh*, which, used originally for sacrificial purposes in general, survived in the historical period only as the implement for circumcision.

There are also other resemblances in points of detail, which must impress any student. In Arabic the rainbow was the weapon of the god *Kuzah*, which he hung up in the heavens, reminding us of the manner in which, in the ninth chapter of Genesis, Yahaweh is said to have hung the rainbow in the sky as a sign that He would no more drown the earth. In the use at sacrificial feasts among the Arabs, the flesh of the animals sacrificed might be preserved only a definite short time, with which compare the Hebrew ritual regulations for the speedy consumption of sacrifices.[1] Again, among the Arabs a portion of the sacrifice, the so-called *lavija*, was set aside for a specially honored guest, as in 1 Samuel ix, 23, where Samuel had set aside the shoulder for Saul as a specially honored guest. Again, among the Arabs, the land was conceived of as the possession of the god. It is the Baal's land or the Athtar's land. Or we hear of the *baal land*, land which the *Baal* waters, that is, land which is not artificially watered by a system of irrigation, but is watered by God either through rain or by springs. The same conception of the land as a possession of the deity and of that deity as the *baal*, or owner, of the land existed from the outset among the Hebrews;[2] while in the Jewish traditional law land naturally watered was called *baal*, or more fully "house of Baal."[3]

---

1 Cf. Lev. vii, 16 ff.

2 So when David is driven out of the land of Israel, he is driven out of the possession of Yahaweh into the possession of another God (1 Sam. xxvi, 19). For the use of the word *baal*, cf. Hos. ii, 16 f. A similar conception and a similar use of words existed among the Canaanites. The comparison with Arabic use is for the purpose of showing that the Hebrews did not derive their ideas in this regard from the Canaanites, after they had settled in their country, but brought them with them from their nomadic state; that they were a part of their primitive religion. The same is true of not a few other matters touched upon in this chapter. They were not peculiar to the Hebrews and Arabs only, but the comparison has been confined to Hebrew and Arab use for the purpose of showing what religious conceptions the Hebrews had in their nomadic state.   3 W. Robertson Smith, *The Religion of the Semites*, p. 95.

The Arabs believed in the existence, besides the gods, of spirits or demons. In each serpent was a spirit either good or bad. Other objects might be inhabited permanently or temporarily by similar spirits. Sickness was caused by them. Ruin sites were haunted by evil spirits. The same beliefs existed among the Hebrews.[1]

Among the Babylonians, Aramæans, Canaanites, and Phœnicians we find, side by side with the male deities, female deities, and, in connection with the worship of the latter, grossly sensual practices. There was a worship of the power of reproduction as it showed itself in all nature, which was especially connected with the worship of female deities. Little or nothing of this is to be found among the Arabs. One or two traces there are which seem to indicate, in connection with the *mazzebah*, something of this sort, but they are faint, and in general it may be said that nature worship in a gross form did not exist among them. There are, it is true, female deities, but they do ·not stand in the same relation to the male deities as do the goddesses of Babylonia and Palestine. There every Bel has his Beltis. Ishtar and Ashtoreth, as female deities, play an important part. But among the southern Arabs, Ishtar or Ashtoreth appears, not as the name of a goddess, but of a god, Athtar.[2] The Hebrews stood in this regard on the same plane as the Arabs. There is no indication of the existence among them in the earliest times of that gross sexual worship of goddesses which prevailed among the Babylonians and Canaanites.

In its conception of deity Arab heathenism was polytheistic. Each tribe had its god, with whom it stood in a special blood relation. A god might manifest himself anywhere, but his chosen haunts or places of manifestation were mountain tops, springs, and groves. These were the dwelling places of local gods, but the fame and worship of these local gods might spread far beyond the territory

---

[1] For the special sanctity among the Hebrews of the serpent, as inhabited by a spirit, one may compare the story of the serpent in Gen. iii, or the image of the serpent which was an object of veneration in the Temple at Jerusalem up to the time of Hezekiah, 2 Kings xviii, 4 ; Num. xxi, 9. For the belief in spirits or demons, cf. Lev. xvi, 8 ff. ; xvii, 7 ; for their special relation to places formerly inhabited but now deserted, cf. Is. xiii, 21 ; xxxiv, 14 ff.

[2] See Barton, *Semitic Origins*, pp. 86 f.

of the surrounding tribe. There was no disloyalty to the tribe in going to some such noted shrine and worshiping there. The attachment to locality on the part of the god and the tendency to wander on the part of the tribes might lead of itself to a relationship on the part of a tribe to several gods. In the same way several tribes might worship one god, at least at the great pilgrimage festival, where they would meet together at his shrine. Behind these separate gods lay, in the Arabic mind, a conception of godhood. The Arabs never speak of the gods in the sense of the Greek θεοί or the Latin *dii*. Individual gods are spoken of commonly as *rabbi* or *rabbuna*, "my Lord," "our Lord," or as the *Baal* of such and such a place, or simply as *Allah*. In the pre-Islamic period individual names of God are rare. *Allah*, the general term for " God," is, on the other hand, in common use. Mohammed says of the Arabs of his time that when the heathen were in extreme peril or need they turned, not to the gods, but always to Allah; which is a testimony to·the dominance of the idea of God beyond and above the gods. It was this which rendered it possible for Mohammed to make of the Arabs monotheists, worshiping Allah as the sole and solitary deity.

The primitive Hebrew conception of deity was similar to that of the Arabs. In general, the primitive religion of the Hebrews was an unformulated polytheism. There was a general conception of divinity, as *El*, manifesting itself in various places and under various forms and names. But while there was this almost monotheistic idea of a general divine nature, there was an actual polytheism in the conception of God as the Baal of this place or that, or as the special divinity of some sacred locality or of some clan or tribe.[1] These were separate and different gods and were so conceived of. That they had, in some cases at least, individual names seems probable, if not absolutely proved. Two of the Hebrew tribes, Gad and Asher, bear the names of divinities, and perhaps divine names are to be recognized in the case of some of the other eponymous ancestors of the Hebrews. But these individual names play a comparatively insignificant part. They are dominated

[1] Cf. against this view Baethgen, *Beiträge zur semitischen Religionsgeschichte.*

and displaced by the designation *El* or *Elohim*. The latter is a plural of the same root as the Arabic *Allah*, the plural of majesty or might being substituted for the singular, a common use in all the Semitic languages. As Mohammed said of the heathen Arabs of his time that they turned to Allah in need or distress rather than to one of their special or local divinities, so it might be said of the Hebrews that whatever local divinity they worshiped, with whatever special name, they all worshiped *Elohim* and turned to him in special need or distress.

One famous student of Hebrew history endeavored to establish the thesis that monotheism is a natural instinct of the Semitic peoples.[1] This is clearly contradicted by the facts, but it is true that the great monotheistic religions of the world, Judaism, Christianity, and Mohammedanism, have sprung from the Semitic peoples, and that the Semites from whom these monotheistic religions have sprung are the Hebrews and Arabs. One cannot study the primitive religion of these two peoples without perceiving their close relationship and that there is in both of them, in the midst of their polytheism, a monotheistic potentiality. The conception of God seems ever and anon to overrule or shine through their polytheistic practices.

The conception of the blood relationship between the god and his worshipers, developing out of clan relations into those of tribe and nation, with the god as lord or king, holds in itself the possibility of the exclusion of other manifestations of divinity in favor of that one god who is *par excellence* the god of the tribe or nation which acknowledges him as lord above all. Mohammed found the Arabs, in spite of their polytheism, prepared to accept the monotheism to which he introduced them. He took the *Allah* — which is the same word as the Hebrew *Eloah* or *Elohim* — who was in process of becoming a general god of the Arabs, and made of him a sole god.

We have seen that the religious practices and religious views of the Arabs of Mohammed's time were strikingly similar to those of

[1] Renan, *Histoire générale des langues sémitiques* (5th ed., Paris 1878), Vol. I, chap. i, and elsewhere in Renan's writings.

the Hebrews in the time of Moses, and we shall see in the following chapter that what Mohammed did for Arabia in substituting Allah for the gods of the different localities, clans, and tribes, Moses did for Israel, uniting them into one people by the same religious motive of the worship of one god by which Mohammed bound the Arabs of different tribes into one religious and national whole. Only the method pursued was different. In the one case monotheism was immediate, by the elimination of special names and the adoption of the general designation of deity as the personal name of God. In the other case it was gradual, by the adoption of a special name for the one great national god, who, established as the god of the nation, thus became the one and only God.

CHAPTER IV

THE RELIGION OF MOSES

The traditional view of the religion of Israel represented Moses as the giver of an ethical and ritual law, of a highly developed and complex nature, centuries in advance of his time — a law so high in its ethical character that, for the most part, it is applicable to-day, in spite of the wonderful advance in morals since Moses' time ; a ritual law so complicated that, even after the nation turned into a church, in the period following the exile, there were still portions of that ritual which were impracticable of execution. In sharpest contrast to the traditional view stands what, for want of a better word, I may call the critical view of to-day, which denies to Moses the authorship, not merely of the law as a whole, but practically of any part of it, even of the Ten Commandments, and makes his principal religious function to have been to teach the Israelites the worship of Yahaweh, who was thus made God of Israel, in the sense in which, for instance, Chemosh was god of Moab ; which does not admit that Moses taught a monotheism, or even a henotheism.

Budde [1] says :

It is, therefore, in the highest degree improbable that Yahweh demanded at Sinai the exclusive veneration of His own godhead. . . . Not that I would deny that Yahweh was the only God of the nation Israel. As long as the nation Israel has existed Yahweh has been its only God, and as long as it continues to exist He will so remain. But in antiquity there were not only national gods, but also clan, family, and household gods. Every social unit had its special god, nor was any association formed between men which was not dedicated to a special deity and placed under his protection.

It is clear to Budde that the modern critical view is radically at fault in that it makes no provision, in its account of Moses' work,

[1] *Religion of Israel to the Exile*, p. 59.

for the ethical impulse on which the whole wonderful development of the history of Israel depends, and which clearly must be ascribed to Moses. He endeavors to make good that defect,[1] by the following curious theory:

Yahaweh was the god of the Kenites, the tribe of Moses' father-in-law. Under Moses' leading the Israelites adopted this god as their god, and " Israel's covenant with Yahweh and Yahweh's with Israel " was " an alliance of Israel with the nomad tribe of the Kenites at Sinai, which had as its self-evident condition the adoption of their religion, Yahweh worship. . . . This is the oldest known example of transition, or conversion, of a people to another religion." [2] " Israel needed a God mighty in war, and found Him here." " Israel's religion became ethical because it was a religion of choice and not nature, because it rested on a voluntary decision which established an ethical relation between the people and its God for all time." " All attempts to find the germ of the ethical development of the Yahweh religion in the material content of the conception of God as represented by Moses, have completely failed."

The ethical germ does not lie in anything that Moses did or taught or revealed, but in the fact that, breaking with all traditions of the past, the people, under Moses' leadership, made a choice of the god of another people as their God. That god was no more ethical than any other god. It was the fact of a choice, establishing a voluntary relation with the deity, instead of the " natural relation " conceived of as existing among all other peoples, which constituted the ethical germ.

But Budde does make this clear: that it is absolutely necessary, if one is to study the history of the religion of Israel intelligently, to find a satisfactory ethical foundation on which to rest the wonderful structure of this religion; and that this ethical foundation must be sought, if not in the teaching of Moses, then in some acts or events connected with him. The error in the critical view, if I may use such a term, seems to me to have been, in general, that, reacting from the impossible traditional picture, Moses has been reduced to the ranks, and made not only a creature of his time and age, but one who had no outlook beyond that of the commonest men and women among whom he lived and moved.

---

1 Following substantially the lead of Stade of Giessen.
2 This and the following quotations are from Lecture I, " The Origin of the Yahweh Religion."

We must recognize in the history of human institutions the peculiar and individual factor due to the peculiar and individual character of the man or men to whom they owe their origin. This is especially true in the case of systems of religious thought which are due to one man. They possess, like the man himself, an element not explicable either by environment or heredity. This must be recognized in dealing with such peculiar modern religious manifestations as Mormonism, or the Shaker religion of the Puget Sound Indians, or Christian Science. It is true also of the great ancient religions of Zoroaster, Gautama, Confucius, Mohammed, etc. It must be equally recognized in dealing with the religion of Moses. But here it seems to me that there has been a tendency on the part of the critics to stand so straight that, as it were, they lean backward. The same methods should be applied in the study of the religion of Moses as are applied in the study of the religions of Zoroaster, Gautama, Confucius, Mohammed, etc. Reacting against the false exception formerly made by Jewish and Christian religious teachers in dealing with the religion of Moses, the tendency of modern critical students has been to apply the doctrine of evolution and environment to an extent which eliminates the personal factor altogether. The personal equation of Moses must be sought in the same way in which we seek the personal equations of the other great religious founders, and by the same tests; and, as in their cases, so in his it must be recognized that it is because he was *sui generis*, towering above his race and time, that he was able to found, among a primitive and barbarous people, a religion capable of such wonderful development. We must recognize the influence of preëxisting hereditary religious ideas in the creation, and the modifying and conditioning effects of environment in the development, of the religion of Israel; but in doing so we must not fail to recognize the immense importance of the personal factor of the founder of that religion — a man spiritually and mentally in advance of those about him.

Moses was the founder of the religion of Israel in very much the same sense that Jesus Christ was the founder of Christianity, and Mohammed of Mohammedanism, Zoroaster of Zoroastrianism, and Gautama Siddhartha, the Buddha, of Buddhism. He was a unique man, towering above his time, anticipating future ages, reaching out beyond his own. We do not ordinarily call the religion of Israel Mosaism; and yet it would perhaps be as correct to do so as it is to use the names Christianity, Mohammedanism, and the like. The reformers and thinkers of all succeeding ages in Israel refer their reforms and their interpretations of the nature and commands of God back to Moses for their justification; and the more advanced the development of the religion of Israel, the greater was the inclination to hark back to Moses as the first source and the standard for comparison, precisely as in Christianity to-day men hark back to Jesus as the founder. Perhaps, however, the failure to designate in common parlance the religion of Israel by the title Mosaism may be justified and explained by the fact that our actual information with regard to his work and teaching is less than in the case of any of the other great religion-founders mentioned. He lived in a more remote age and under conditions less civilized and less adapted to the exact transmission of tradition than any of the others.

Of all religion-founders Moses may probably best be compared with Jesus and Mohammed; but the differences are almost as striking as are the resemblances. Jesus left no writings of any description, no code of law, no form of theology; but He impressed himself upon a band of disciples, who later endeavored to record both His sayings and His life for the benefit of posterity. Moses had no such disciples, and the actual tradition of his life and teaching which has come down to us is from a much later period, and is strongly mixed with legendary and traditional elements; it is connected also with a great mass of legislation, which is clearly of a later growth, however much it may be founded upon his teachings. His work was to impress himself upon a people; to make of a number of tribes a nation united by the bond of religion. In this national aspect of his work he resembles Mohammed. Like the latter he established cohesion among independent tribes by means of a religious bond. Like him also he gave to his people, if not a theoretical, at least a practical, monotheism; and like him he raised the religion of his compatriots to an ethical level, or introduced into it ethical elements previously wanting.

The story of Moses in the earliest form in which it has come down to us, in the Judæan and Israelite narratives (JE), contained in the books of Exodus and Numbers, dates from a time three centuries or thereabouts after his death. In its main features this story is as follows: Moses was the son of a Levite woman, born in the land of Goshen, where the Israelites were suffering under the oppression of the Egyptians. He was exposed by his mother in a pitch-smeared bulrush box on the Nile. He was found by the Pharoah's daughter, and given by her the name Moses, "drawn out of the water." She gave him to his Israelite mother to be suckled, not knowing that she was his mother. So he grew up under the protection of the Egyptian princess, but himself conscious of his Israelite origin. When he was grown he saw one day an Egyptian smiting a Hebrew, and, fired with indignation, he killed the Egyptian. Finding this in danger of becoming known, he fled from Egypt to Midian. There he attached himself to a priest of the country, named, according to one tradition, Reuel, or Hobab son of Reuel, and according to another, Jethro, and married one of his daughters. Later, at the call of Yahaweh, who declared himself to be the god of the Hebrews, he returned to Egypt to demand at first permission for his Israelite brethren to go and serve their God in the wilderness, and afterward their release. Assisted by his brother Aaron, he was instrumental in bringing a number of plagues upon Egypt, ending with the destruction of the first-born of the Egyptians, through the power of Yahaweh. Then at last the Pharaoh consented to let the Israelites go out of Egypt; but after they had started he changed his mind and pursued them. By Yahaweh's order Moses led the people to the shore of an arm of the Red Sea, and when the Egyptians pressed upon them from behind Yahaweh opened a way through the sea, and they escaped by night. The next day the Egyptians attempted to follow them, but were overwhelmed in the sea. For forty years Moses led the people about in the wilderness, undergoing various hardships. Their objective point was Canaan, but they were not strong enough to force their way into it from the south, although for a long time their headquarters were at Kadesh Barnea, not far from the southern border of what was afterward the land of Judah. During this period Yahaweh gave His people a law through Moses. According to one tradition this law was given at Horeb, and according to the other, at Sinai. This law consisted of two tables of stone, with five "Words" on each table, written by Yahaweh himself; but besides these there were judgments and statutes emanating from Moses by the command of God. The two tables with the Ten Words upon them were placed in a box, or Ark, with a tent to cover it. This constituted the shrine, or sanctuary, of the Israelites, and was carried before them wherever they went. Finally, under the lead of Moses, the Israelites passed to the south of Edom, and then northward, east of Edom and Moab, until they came to an Amorite kingdom, which had intruded itself between Ammon and Moab. This they conquered, and took possession of the country east of the Jordan from the Arnon northward, and there Moses died.

How much is historical in this tradition? There is no reason to doubt that the tribes of Israel, or at least a section of them, were oppressed by the Egyptians in Goshen, that borderland of Egypt inhabited by nomadic or semi-nomadic peoples. The oppression consisted largely, if not altogether, of conscription for enforced labor. Against this the Israelites rebelled, and fled into the wilderness. Their flight was connected with circumstances that impressed themselves as special providences, bringing them into a peculiar relation with the deity. Moses was their leader in the flight and the interpreter of God's action toward them. In the wilderness of Sinai and Horeb the Israelites found kindred tribes, either some of the tribes known later as the twelve tribes of Israel, which had not participated in the sojourn in Egypt and the oppression there, or kindred peoples readily capable of amalgamation with the tribes of Israel, such as the Kenites and Kenizzites. Moses was connected with one of these tribes and with its priesthood. The dwelling place of this tribe was in the Horeb-Sinai wilderness. So much is generally admitted.

Further, it is clear that Moses united the tribes of Israel by a religious bond, and that this bond connected them with the wilderness

southward and southeastward of Judah. This is shown by one of
the earliest fragments of Hebrew poetry which has come down to
us, the Song of Deborah (Jud. v). This poem, if not written by
Deborah, was at least contemporary with her and with the events
which it narrates, and probably originated not later than a generation or two after the time of Moses. The tribes of Israel are there
represented as a united people, who are bound to stand by one
another and to fight together the battles of Yahaweh.[1] Yahaweh
is their leader, who has the right to claim the allegiance and the
aid of all the tribes. It is He that fights. The tribes of Israel are
His followers, bound to come to His aid, " to the aid of Yahaweh
like heroes." How strong the bond of brotherhood among the
Israelites was, and how binding was the obligation to come to the
aid of Yahaweh, is shown by the curse invoked upon the inhabitants of Meroz, because they failed to assist their brethren in this
war.[2] But while the Song of Deborah thus testifies to a religious
bond which united Israel under the leadership of its supreme king
and ruler, Yahaweh, His dwelling place is not in Palestine, but southward, at Horeb-Sinai, in the wilderness of Seir, Israel's former
home. Thence He comes to fight for them (v, 4).

The next question which we have to ask ourselves is, What was
the nature of this bond by which the tribes of Israel were united
to Yahaweh and to one another? It consisted in the recognition of
one God as the God of all Israel, throughout all its tribes, clans,
and families, to whom it owed a special allegiance, and to whom it
stood in a peculiar relation, a blood relationship which affected all.
Now the primitive conception of a god depends upon his name;

[1] The same view is presented in the Song of Miriam, Ex. xv, which McCurdy, in
his *History, Prophecy, and the Monuments*, § 890, argues is, in its original form,
contemporaneous with Moses.

[2] It should be observed that not all the twelve or thirteen tribes of Israel are
mentioned in this poem. Those that are mentioned are, first, the Josephites and
Rachelites, Ephraim, Benjamin, and Machir, which is Manasseh, then Zebulun,
Issachar, and Naphtali, the tribes especially concerned in this war. These are all
united under Deborah and Barak. Further, we have reproaches addressed to
Reuben, Gilead, that is Gad, Dan, and Asher, because they failed to come to the
assistance of their brethren and to the aid of Yahaweh. Judah, Simeon, and Levi
are omitted entirely.

he cannot exist without a name, and, in a sense, the name makes the god. How true this was of Arabian heathenism appears plainly in the history of Islam, where Mohammed takes the name *Allah* and makes it the peculiar and special name of the god of Islam. Did Moses do the same thing?

That he did so certainly to some extent is clear, among other things, from the Song of Deborah, which has just been cited, where the God who claims the allegiance of the tribes of Israel is Yahaweh. But that Moses was the founder of " Yahwism," that the one thing which he taught was the name *Yahaweh* as the God of Israel, is clearly disproved by the evidence of Israelite proper names. It is a well-established fact that among Semitic peoples the proper names of the deities worshiped will appear in the names of the worshipers, especially the priests of the shrines and the kings and governing aristocracy. Now an analysis of Hebrew proper names shows us this peculiar fact: that, while in the earlier stages of the history of Israel we have names denoting relationship to God, that He is father, uncle, brother, etc., names denoting the government of God, that He is king, lord, master, owner, etc., and names containing the general designation of divinity, namely *El*, names compounded with *Yahaweh* are almost, if not altogether, lacking. Before the time of the kingdom, there are few, if any, such names well attested. With the establishment of the kingdom, names compounded with *Yahaweh* begin to appear in the reigning family and in the court circle. After the separation of the kingdom, such names, although continuing in Judah, are lacking in Israel, or Samaria, until the time of the prophet Elijah and the family of Ahab. It is clear that in the earlier period the father, uncle, brother, master (*baal*), king (*melek*), lord (*adon*), referred to in proper names bearing those words, is the God of Israel.[1] This God is frequently designated as *El* or *Elohim*. Now *El* is the universal Semitic designation of divinity, a sort of ideograph, which might be added to any name to make it the name of a god, or to declare that it was a divine name. *Elohim* is the plural of *Eloah*, a word recognized by the Hebrews as an ancient designation of the deity, although seldom actually

---

1 Cf. especially Gray, *Hebrew Proper Names.*

found in the more ancient documents. *Eloah* is identical with the Arabic *Allah*, the universal Arabic name for deity, which Mohammed made *the* name of God.[1] Moses does not seem to have followed quite the same method as Mohammed. He recognized but one El, or Elohim, for all Israel, whether designated as father, brother, uncle, master, king, lord, or whatever other title might be used; but from the evidence of the Song of Deborah and other early documents it would appear that he taught further the name *Yahaweh* as the special name of the God who belonged alike to all Israelites, not, however, to the exclusion of these other names or titles.

But whence was the name *Yahaweh*[2] derived? In regard to this, tradition seems to be conflicting. Passages may be cited from the

[1] The name *Eloah*, or *Elohim*, does not appear as a component in Hebrew proper names at any period (although *Allah* was so used among the Arabs); but for what reason is not altogether clear.

[2] The etymology of *Yahaweh* is uncertain. The traditional etymology connects it (Ex. iii, 14) with the root " to be," or, rather, " to become " (*hayah*). Others make it a causative of the same root. Others connect it with *hawah*, supposed to have meant originally in Hebrew, as in Arabic, " to fall," and interpret it as meaning " the one who causes (rain or lightning) to fall," etc. Cf. Brown-Driver-Briggs-Robinson, *Hebrew Lexicon*, p. 218. In composition, at the end of a word, the form *yah* or *iah* is used, and the same form occurs independently in poetical use, apparently rather late. In composition, at the beginning of a word, the contracted form *Yo* (*Jo*) is used. *Yah* appears to be an undeclined form of which the nominative is *Yahu*, which form occurs independently in the proper name written in English " Jehu." These forms are commonly regarded as abbreviations of *Yahaweh*. On the other hand, *Yahaweh* may be a secondary or specialized form from an original *Yah*, with the fuller nominative form *Yahu*. The papyri discovered at Elephantine use *Yahu*, not *Yahaweh*, evidence for the former as the original form. It is uncertain whether the name occurs in the Assyrian-Babylonian inscriptions. The trend of opinion at present seems to be in favor of such occurrence; my own opinion is that it does not occur, except in composition in names which may be attributed to Hebrew influence. The vocalization of the consonants *YHWH* (*JHVH*), which compose the sacred name, is not quite certain. Wherever this ineffable name occurred in the text of scriptures, the later Jews substituted in pronunciation *a(ĕ)donai*, " lord." When they wrote the text with vowels, therefore, they wrote with the consonants of one word the vowels of the other. Our *Jehovah* is a combination of the consonants *Y h w h* with the vowels of *adonai*. Presumably, the true vowel of the first syllable was *a*, of the second a slurred sound, such as we give in English to any vowel in an unaccented middle syllable, and of the third, perhaps, an *e* (Italian sound). The name thus vocalized is variously written as *Jahveh*, *Yahweh*, *Yahvé*, etc. These transliterations, however, fail to give any idea of the trisyllabic character of the word. I have preferred the less common transliteration, *Yahaweh*, used by Robertson in his Gifford Lectures on the *Religion of Israel*, as more correctly representing the supposed pronunciation of the word.

Judæan historical compilation which would seem to show that, according to early tradition, *Yahaweh* [1] was an ancient name of God known to the forefathers of Israel. Again, passages may be cited from the Israelite historical compilation which seem to show that, according to tradition, Yahaweh was a new God, first revealed to Israel by Moses.[2] Tradition does, however, make this clear : that the original habitat of Yahaweh was Horeb-Sinai. Horeb and Sinai, as used in the Old Testament, are clearly not some particular and individual mountain well known to later times, but a general locality. The Song of Deborah uses, to describe the same location, "Seir and the land of Edom," which use is imitated at times in later literature, as, for instance, in Habakkuk iii, 3, where the same region is called "Teman and Mount Paran." [3] The region indicated is the mountainous territory to the south or southeast of Palestine, the wilderness out of which Israel came into Palestine.[4]

According to the tradition of Moses above narrated, the first manifestation to him of Yahaweh as the God of Israel occurred in that same mountain wilderness region. According to this tradition also, Moses was connected by marriage with a priestly family, having its home in that country. Now gods were ascribed in heathen Arabia to certain localities ; and in many cases various tribes made pilgrimages to a shrine outside of their own boundaries, the god of which belonged, not to the tribe in whose boundaries his home was, but rather to the locality. In such cases it seems clear that the worship of the god by the various tribes which made pilgrimages to the shrine is to be ascribed to previously existing conditions ; that there was an earlier connection with the locality and with one another on the part of the tribes which worshiped there, or of some of their number, through their forefathers. If, in the case

[1] Cf. the use of *Yahaweh* in the Judæan document in Genesis.

[2] Cf. Ex. iii, 14.

[3] Cf. also Deut. xxxiii, 2 ; Ps. lxviii, 7 ff.

[4] Horeb is, properly speaking, the mountainous territory at the southern extremity of the Edomite country, east of the ' Aqabah. Sinai is the mountainous peninsula west of the ' Aqabah. According to the Judæan tradition, which is followed by the later Priestly narrative, Sinai was the mountain of God. According to the Israelite tradition, which is followed by the Deuteronomist and Habakkuk, Horeb, or the southern mountain region of Edom, was the mountain of God. Cf. also 1 Kings xix.

of such a sanctuary, the guardianship of the shrine was vested in a family not of the tribe occupying the land in which the shrine was situated, it is probable that the latter tribe had come to occupy land formerly in the possession of some of the tribes making pilgrimage to that shrine. It worshiped the god because he was the god of the land, whom it found in possession; but he was not, primarily, its own god. Considering these facts, it is not necessary for us to assume that Israel consciously adopted the god of a foreign tribe, the Kenites. It was because the Israelites entered into the land of Yahaweh, His sacred mountain, Horeb-Sinai, that the god of the land became their god.

The tradition that Moses, Israel's leader, was connected by marriage or adoption with priests of that land, and, therefore, presumably of Yahaweh, seems altogether credible, for without such a connection he could scarcely have established the worship of Yahaweh as an effective bond of union among the tribes of Israel. He would have been himself an outsider to the worship of Yahaweh. But, further, some at least of the Israelites were closely connected with the tribes of the southern wilderness. In part, at least, Judah belonged to that region, and, probably, Simeon also. In that case Yahaweh may have been their God. That this was the case is suggested by the difference between the Israelite and Judæan traditions. According to the former (Ex. iii, 14), the name *Yahaweh* was first revealed to Moses at Horeb. According to the latter,[1] the name *Yahaweh* was used by the patriarchs from time immemorial.[2] But whatever the connection of a part of the Hebrews with Yahaweh

---

[1] Cf. the two documents of the Hexateuch known to critics as E and J, in Driver's *Introduction to the Literature of the Old Testament*, Addis' *The Documents of the Hexateuch*, etc.

[2] It may be noted, further, that it is in the tribe of Judah that names compounded with the divine name *Yah* (for *Yahaweh*) first become prominent. They do not appear among the middle and northern tribes, with the exception of Saul's family and court, until the time of Ahab and Elijah. This suggests an earlier connection of Judah with Yahaweh. In northern Syria there was a people called Jaudi, or Judæans, and in that region also we meet with names apparently compounded with *Yah*. The Aramæan of this region, as shown by the inscriptions from Zingirli and its neighborhood, closely resembles Hebrew. It is possible that this indicates a god Yahu, worshiped by a section of the Aramæans in their original home, and carried by the van of the Aramæan immigrants to the regions which they respectively occupied,

before the time of Moses, it is clear that it was through him that *Yahaweh* became the name of the god of Israel, and apparently because of Yahaweh's connection with the land of Horeb-Sinai, in which Israel was organized under his leadership.

The earliest Hebrew tradition ascribes to Moses a representation of the presence of the deity in the shape of an Ark, or box, by which the God of Israel might accompany His people wherever they went. When the Israelites entered Canaan, the Ark of Yahaweh of Hosts was carried with them, and located in the tribe of Ephraim.[1] Where this Ark was, there was Yahaweh.[2] There has been handed down an old ritual formula, connecting itself with the time when the Ark was a movable, not a stationary, sanctuary: " Rise up, Yahaweh, and let Thine enemies be scattered, and let them that hate Thee flee before Thee " ; and its counterpart: " Return, Yahaweh, unto the ten thousands of the thousands of Israel."[3] Even after the Ark became a part of a sanctuary, first at Shiloh, and later, in David's time, at Jerusalem, it was still, at least on special occasions, carried out to battle, with the belief that with it went the presence of Yahaweh.[4]

It is clear that we have in the Ark the shrine of a god who accompanies Israel in all his movements, and it is also clear that this God is Yahaweh. Furthermore, there is no question that the Ark is to be traced back to the Mosaic period of Israel's history, and was brought with him out of the wilderness.

This idea of Yahaweh present in the Ark and accompanying Israel from place to place, or going forth to battle with his armies, does not seem consistent with the localization of Yahaweh in Horeb-Sinai, and, apparently, did not originally belong to the religion of Yahaweh of Sinai. We have in the representation of the presence of Yahaweh by the Ark and the representation of Yahaweh as dwelling at Horeb-Sinai two different conceptions, which have been blended together.[5]

---

[1] 1 Sam. iii, 1 ff.; iv, 4.   [3] Num. x, 35 f.

[2] 1 Sam. v, 6; 2 Sam. vi, 10–23.   [4] 1 Sam. iv, 4 ff.; 2 Sam. xi, 11.

[5] Cf. Ex. xxiii, 20; xxxii, 34. It may have been the sense of this inconsistency which led to the development of a view which we find represented in the traditions of the ninth century, contained in E, that it was not Yahaweh himself who went with Israel through the wilderness into Canaan, but the angel of Yahaweh.

Through the Ark the Israelites carried their God with them, that He might be ever present. Nevertheless, Horeb-Sinai continued to be, in a special sense, the residence or dwelling place of Yahaweh. It was there that He first became known; there Israel acknowledged Him as his God. From the ethical standpoint, the conception of Yahaweh accompanying Israel by means of the Ark is an advance over the conception of Yahaweh as localized in Horeb-Sinai. The importance of this new conception in the religious development of Israel becomes more apparent when we consider the consequences of the contact of Israel with the civilization and the religion of Canaan. Without the presence of Yahaweh, Israel must inevitably have lost his religion. Had his God been connected irrevocably and inseparably with Horeb-Sinai, then Israel, settling in Canaan, must ultimately have abandoned Him in favor of the gods of the land into which he entered. By means of the Ark, Yahaweh accompanied His people whithersoever they went, the special deity of Israel, always in the midst of them.[1]

The holy tent, which we find mentioned in the ninth-century writings JE, belongs also to the externals established, or at least adopted, by Moses. It is represented as an ordinary tent, which Moses sets up outside of the camp as a tent of revelation, where Yahaweh appears to him and grants him oracles.[2] Joshua, Moses' successor, is mentioned as the guardian of this tent, which suggests that it had some content. The most natural content would seem to have been the Ark; but it must be confessed that the relation of these two, one to another, is not clear.[3]

But whence was the Ark derived? The shrines of the heathen Arabs, to whom we must in general look for an interpretation of the religious conditions of pre-Mosaic Israel, were local; they did not conceive of the god as moving with his people from place to place, but as localized in some given spot. A similar belief seems to have prevailed in Canaan, where the *baal* was thought to be

[1] Cf. Peters, *The Old Testament and the New Scholarship*, chap. xiv.

[2] Ex. xxxiii, 7.

[3] In the later Priestly Code the tent is an elaborate tabernacle, and it is clearly stated that its most sacred content was the Ark of the Covenant, Ex. xxv, 10 ff.; xxvi, 34.

attached to the land, a view which the Israelites themselves shared after their settlement in Canaan.[1] Moreover, although the Arabians revered stones as the representatives or abiding places of the god, those stones could not be transported from place to place. It was the stone and the place together which constituted the shrine. The nearest approach to a transportation of the god that we find in heathen Arabia is the representation of his presence in battle by a sacred banner, or by a mare, or a maiden mounted on a mare. But this is very far removed from the conception of a god dwelling in the midst of his people in an Ark, or box, not only going forth to battle with them, but also traveling with them from one country to another. Apparently neither the Canaanites nor any of the surrounding peoples kindred to the Hebrews — Ammonites, Moabites, Edomites — had anything resembling the Ark, or any custom resembling the Israelite custom of carrying the presence of god about in, or by means of, an Ark. The nearest analogy to the Ark that has been found is the use of a boat, in Babylonia and Egypt, to transport the gods from one shrine to another, or to take a god in solemn procession through or about his land.[2] That this was not a common Semitic practice is clear from the fact that we find no similar use in Arabia or among the Syrians or Phœnicians. It seems, therefore, that we cannot, arguing from the Babylonian use of god-ships, suppose the Ark to have been a part of the ancestral pre-Mosaic religion of the Hebrews, either as an original Semitic use or as one derived from the Babylonians, in consequence of their earlier connection with the west land; for in that case we should have found the same use among some of the Hebrew or Canaanite peoples outside of Israel. Hebrew tradition itself assigns the origin of the Ark to Moses, and apparently with right. Was the Ark, then, a modification of the Egyptian god-ship, or is it in any sense due to the influence of the Egyptian use of ships to convey the images of the gods from place to place? It seems to me probable that we should recognize here Egyptian

---

[1] 1 Sam. xxvi, 19.

[2] Jastrow, *Religion of Babylonia and Assyria*, pp. 653 ff.; Erman, *Aegypten und aegyptisches Leben*, I, 373 f.

influence, and that the Egyptian ship became among the Hebrews a box, very much as in the Hebrew flood story the Babylonian ship became a box.[1]

The next question with which we have to deal is the contents of the Ark. Clearly an Ark has a purpose and an object only as the receptacle for something which it contains. An empty wooden chest cannot, like a block of wood, be a sanctuary. Since the Ark was regarded as containing the divinity, the stone contained therein must have been regarded as the " house of the divinity." [2] Such is the general verdict of scholars to-day; but, on the other hand, many, if not most, modern critical scholars, while accepting tradition up to the point of an Ark containing a sacred stone or stones, discard the tradition that the contents were two written tables of stone. They admit the Ark and the stone, but suppose the latter to have been a rude stone, perhaps meteoric, of the nature of a fetish. There is no documentary or traditional evidence for this supposition, nor even any incidental allusion which can be referred to in support of it. The main, if not the only, reason for this view is that the Decalogue seems to them too advanced to be ascribed to so early a period, and that the conception of an ethical code of laws as the representative of the presence of God, in place of an image or a fetish, is unique, and out of the line of development, at least in that age. Further than this, there is the general fact that rude stones, and especially meteoric stones, were throughout Arabia, Syria, and Palestine worshiped as representations of deity. On the other hand, there is no slightest allusion or reference in any writing which can be made to suggest a consciousness that at any time the contents of the Ark had been a rude, unlettered stone or stones, while from a very early period contemporary writers state its contents to have been two inscribed stones.

[1] In support of this proposed connection with Egypt may be cited the supposed Egyptian derivation of the name of Moses, from the time of the LXX Greek translation onward. Cf. Dillmann on Ex. vi, 20. Some have further supposed the names of Miriam, Aaron, and Phinehas, the grandson of Aaron, to be of Egyptian origin. Cf., on the last, Dillman on Ex. vi, 25. In the center of the Egyptian boat was the box, or ark, which constituted the tabernacle proper. We have also representations and specimens of this ark quite separate from the boat, identical with the Hebrew use.

[2] Benzinger, *Hebräische Archäologie*, p. 369.

The earliest writings which have come down to us, writings practically contemporary with David and Solomon, mention the Ark as "the Ark of the covenant of God," or "of Yahaweh." Similarly, in the earliest portions of the Pentateuch, JE, we find the title "Ark of the covenant" or "Ark of the covenant of Yahaweh." In the seventh century the "Ark of the covenant of Yahaweh" is the name in common use.[1] The Book of Deuteronomy (chap. x) states the contents of the Ark to have been two tables of stone containing the Decalogue, placed there by Moses. A similar statement is made in the Book of Kings (1 Kings viii, 9, 21). It is evident that from the seventh century onward the contents of the Ark were the Decalogue, and that this was then understood to be the covenant from which the Ark took its name, "Ark of the covenant of Yahaweh," as the passages referred to in JE and Samuel show. But a part of this title, namely, "Ark of the covenant," is as old as the tenth century. Moreover, it seems clear that the writer of Deuteronomy derived his information as to the contents of the Ark from the earlier writing JE, and that in the original form of the Judæan historical document of the ninth century (Ex. xxxiv) it was stated that the contents of the Ark were two tables of stone containing the Decalogue.[2] Combining these historical statements, and the names of the Ark found in the earliest documents, one may safely say that as early as the time of David the contents of the Ark were two tables of stone, containing the Decalogue, and regarded as a covenant from

---

[1] Jer. iii, 16. The use of the terms "Ark of the covenant," "Ark of the covenant of Yahaweh," "Ark of the covenant of God," etc., in the earliest strata of Samuel and the Hexateuch, side by side with the terms "the Ark," "Ark of Yahaweh," "Ark of God," is too frequent to admit of explanation by interpolation. In his *Exodus* Bacon at times assumes that the words "of the covenant," etc., are a later addition; but this is not done systematically, and, even accepting his emended text, we still have numerous cases of this use. In fact, in both JE and the earliest document in Samuel the addition "Ark of the covenant" is too common to be explained on the ground of interpolation. Moreover, some of the terms used, such as "Ark of the covenant," "Ark of the covenant of God," "Ark of the covenant of Yahaweh of Hosts," "Ark of the covenant of the God of Israel," are not names which we find used by the later writers. In Deuteronomy the name "Ark of the covenant of Yahaweh" becomes almost a *terminus technicus* for the Ark. The same name is used once in Jeremiah. The Priestly Code has its own peculiar designation, "Ark of the testimony." The Chronicler uses various names taken from the earlier books, the "Ark of God" and the "Ark of the covenant of Yahaweh" being the most frequent, and adds one name of his own, the "holy Ark."   [2] Cf. Driver, *Deuteronomy*, x, 1-5.

or with Yahaweh. In other words, we can trace back to David's time the presence in the Ark of two stones inscribed with the ten "Words." That any change should have been made between the time of Moses and that of David in the contents of the Ark, by the substitution of written tablets for a rude stone or fetish, is so improbable, in view of the unethical character of that period, that the possibility need not be considered. In fact, no one has ventured to attribute the invention of the Decalogue, and its substitution in the Ark for a rude stone or fetish, to the time of the Judges. So far as those who hold to such a substitution have defined their position at all, they suppose the substitution to have been made, or at least the Decalogue to have been composed, in the early prophetical period; a theory altogether subjective, and directly contradicted by the objective evidence set forth above.

The Decalogue of the two tables may be restored with a fair degree of accuracy by a comparison of Exodus xx and Deuteronomy v, as follows:

Table I. 1. Thou shalt have none other gods before Me.
      2. Thou shalt not make unto thee a graven image.
      3. Thou shalt not take the name of Yahaweh, thy God, in vain.
      4. Remember the sabbath day to keep it holy.
      5. Honor thy father and thy mother.
Table II. 1. Thou shalt not murder.
      2. Thou shalt not commit adultery.
      3. Thou shalt not steal.
      4. Thou shalt not bear false witness against thy neighbor.
      5. Thou shalt not covet.[1]

These Ten Words lie at the foundation, in both form and content, of all later legislation.[2]

---

[1] Possibly: "Thou shalt not oppress." Cf. *J. B. L.*, June, 1886, pp. 140 ff. For the primitive Mosaic character of the Decalogue, and its original form, cf. Briggs, *The Higher Criticism of the Hexateuch*, and especially pp. 181 f. I have followed here Briggs' arrangement, but with much hesitation. It seems to me not improbable that the first three Words were: 1. I am Yahaweh, thy God, who brought thee out of the land of Egypt. 2. Thou shalt have none other gods before Me. 3. Thou shalt not take the name of Yahaweh, thy God, in vain. In this case the provision "Thou shalt not make unto thee a graven image" is an early expansion or application of the second Word.

[2] Outside of the Decalogue, the earliest code of Hebrew laws which has come down to us is the fragmentary code, in Exodus xxxiv, from J, parallel to which we

But it has been contended that to ascribe to Moses any such teaching as that contained in the Ten Commandments would be to leave nothing for the Prophets.[1] It is, however, universally recognized that with Moses begins the ethical content of the religion of Israel, and that it is impossible to understand the later religious development without accounting in some way for the ethical element which was introduced into it at the time of Moses. Writers who have denied the Mosaic authorship of the Decalogue have, in point of fact, reduced Moses to a nonentity, and offered no explanation of the ethical impulse given by him; or else found it in the adoption by the Israelites of a foreign god, an altogether

---

have, in Exodus xxi–xxiii, a fuller code, from E. The Commandments, or Laws, in Exodus xxxiv, are almost identical with those in xxiii, 10–19, which constitute a code of feasts and offerings. This code in Exodus xxiii occurs at the conclusion of a collection of words, statutes and judgments, consisting largely of decads. Before this collection comes a brief and very primitive code forbidding images and altars of hewn stone. Before this whole mass of ritual and legal material was placed the Decalogue, as something still more fundamental. It seems to me probable that the decad in Exodus xxxiv was similarly part of a larger code bearing a similar relation to the Decalogue. The concluding words in Exodus xxxiv, 27, 28, "and Yahaweh said to Moses: 'Write these words, for according to these words have I cut with thee a covenant, and with Israel.' And he was there with Yahaweh forty days and forty nights. Bread he ate not, and water he drank not. And he wrote on the tablets the words of the covenant, ten the words," on which has been based the statement that the Decalogue of J was the laws of Exodus xxxiv, 17–26, are accordingly to be referred, not to the immediately preceding decad, but to the whole code, of which this was but a part; and the Ten Words there referred to are not the fragments of two or three pentads, which have been retained out of J, but the well-known Decalogue. That this is so is shown further by a comparison of Deuteronomy x, for it seems impossible to suppose that the writer of Deuteronomy, having JE, and probably also J and E before him, could have blundered in so fundamental a point. We have, then, in their present forms, the Book of the Covenant, Exodus xxi–xxiii, and the Deuteronomic code, both prefaced by the Decalogue, as though it were something recognized as fundamental; and apparently the same was true of the code of which we have fragments in Exodus xxxiv. In further evidence that the Decalogue once preceded the code of laws of which we have a fragment in Exodus xxxiv may be cited, as it seems to me, the fact that we have the Ten Words in Exodus xx in a Yahawistic setting, or with a Yahawistic preface: "I am Yahaweh, thy God," etc. Moreover, the additions to the Words, as Carpenter and Battersby point out, have affinities with J, as well as with E and D. The actual Words themselves find certain parallels or resemblances in both Books of the Covenant (Ex. xxi–xxiii, xxxiv), which seems to me to establish, as far as we can expect it to be established by such means, the dependence of both those codes on the Decalogue, or rather the preëxistence and the recognition of the latter (Carpenter and Battersby, *The Hexateuch*, II, 111).

[1] Cf. Budde, *Religion of Israel to the Exile*, p. 32.

inadequate cause for the remarkable ethical development which resulted from the impulse then imparted. It is necessary, as already said, to recognize that Moses towered above his time and people, precisely as did Zoroaster, or Jesus, or Mohammed; and that we must ascribe to him a rôle of very great importance, and an ethical conception in advance of his surroundings.

But the Decalogue is not in itself without connection with previously existing ideas and practices; nor is it a step in advance so enormous as to be incredible. The Decalogue was a practical code of fundamental laws concerning the relations of Israel to his God, and of Israelites to one another. It contains, it is true, grand possibilities, and put side by side with the later prophetic teaching, and interpreted in connection with that teaching, it becomes a code of ethics and of conduct universal in its character; but that was not its primary sense.

The First Commandment, "Thou shalt have none other gods before me," was an assertion of the fact underlying the union of the tribes in one people, that Israel has one god, who has become his special god, supplanting the tribal and family deities. This was in fact the necessary condition of union. The Israelites did not attain to monotheism until a much later period, nor is the command in itself monotheistic. In fact, the words of this commandment imply a belief in the existence of other gods. That this commandment was effective from the outset, and that this one god, whose peculiar personal name was Yahaweh, was the bond of union for Israel, is shown by the Song of Deborah, by the story of Gideon, by a study of the proper names of Israelites, and, in fact, by the history of Israel in general from the beginning onward.

The Second Commandment presents a difficulty, inasmuch as from the outset it seems to be disregarded. In the time of the Judges we find images used in the worship of Yahaweh, such as the ephod which was made by Gideon out of the spoils of the Midianites (Judges viii, 24 ff.), or the ephod and teraphim set up by Micah in his private temple (xvii, 5). In David's time, also, teraphim were in use, household deities, sometimes clearly of considerable size, and made after the human form (1 Sam. xix, 12 ff.).

These teraphim continued to be used as late certainly as the middle of the eighth century, as we see from the reference to them in Hosea (iii, 4), and from the story of Rachel's concealment of the teraphim, in the narrative of E (Gen. xxxi, 19), although probably before that time they had already begun to come under condemnation as foreign idolatry (cf. Gen. xxxv, 2–4, also from E). The worship of Yahaweh under the form of the golden calf in Israel, which began, according to the historical narrative in Kings, under Jeroboam, in the tenth century, was the most conspicuous form, however, of the authorized national use of an image. This calf image may be closely akin to the cherubim of the Temple at Jerusalem ; but the latter, even though they symbolized the presence of Yahaweh, were not, apparently, conspicuously presented to the eye as objects of worship. The cherubim were merely adjuncts to the Ark, which latter was the special representation of Yahaweh in the Jerusalem Temple. The calves, on the other hand, seem to have been openly displayed to the people as the representatives of Yahaweh, the objects of His indwelling, and hence they were *images* in a sense in which the cherubim, even granting that the latter may have been bull-shaped, were not. Neither Elijah and Elisha, nor yet Amos, condemned the calf, or rather small bull, images, although the latter so strenuously castigated the moral transgressions of Israel and its substitution of ritual for moral righteousness. Among the Prophets, it is Hosea who first denounces the calf-worship and the worship of " graven images "(xi, 2 ; viii, 5 ff.), about the middle of the eighth century. The same prophet, however, seems to consider the *mazzebah*, the ephod, and the teraphim necessary adjuncts of the worship of Yahaweh (cf. iii, 4). But before this time we find a condemnation of the calf-worship, under the form of historical narrative, in the Israelite document E, and still earlier than this in J, the latter taking us back certainly to the ninth century. Toward the close of the eighth century, as we learn from the Book of Kings (2 Kings xviii, 4), a brazen serpent was one of the objects of worship in the Temple. Now it is worthy of note that the Israelite document E, which condemns the worship of the golden bull, did not condemn the worship of the brazen serpent, but, on the other hand, commends it as of Mosaic origin, and a means of miraculous healing (Num. xxi, 4 ff.). Presumably Isaiah was in sympathy with the reform which abolished the brazen serpent, although neither that nor any idol or image in the Temple is mentioned by him. One gathers, rather, from his prophecies, that the images and idols which he denounced were extraneous to the Temple worship, and were connected with the worship of other gods or demons. He mentions *asherim* and " sun-images " (xvii, 8), he speaks of " graven images and molten images " (xxx, 22), and says that " the land is full of idols " (ii, 8), which he contrasts with the worship of Yahaweh. He also condemns the worship of oaks or terebinths (i, 29); but, on the other hand, like Hosea, he regards the *mazzebah* as a necessary adjunct of the worship of Yahaweh (xix, 19). There is no strong polemic against idol-worship in his prophecies, as there is in those of Jeremiah or Deutero-Isaiah; and in his general idea of what constitutes an image he has not advanced to the position of the reformers of the seventh century. It is in the reign of Josiah, toward the close of the seventh century, that we first meet with the effective and comprehensive condemnation of images of every sort, including the *mazzebah*, in the books of Deuteronomy and Jeremiah, and in the action of the king, with the counsel of prophets and priests (2 Kings xxiii). The struggle between the iconoclasts and the iconodules was not, however, ended in a day; it went on during the Exile, as is evidenced by Ezekiel and Deutero-Isaiah, and the victory of the iconoclasts was not secure until the post-exilic period.

What was the relation of the Second Commandment to that struggle? Was it an outgrowth of the struggle?[1]

The argument for this position is in part one from silence, in part one from the positive disregard of, and disobedience to, the

[1] This is the view represented by Wellhausen, Kuenen, Stade, Addis, and others. Bacon, in his *Exodus*, marks this commandment as *Rd.*, that is, " an addition to E," to which he ascribes all the other commandments but the Fifth and Tenth (which, according to him, are also *Rd.*), " a harmonistic adjustment of JE, or Deuteronomic expansion, later than 722 BC." This seems to be approximately the opinion of Carpenter and Battersby (*The Hexateuch*, II, 111), who, discussing the commandments as a whole, " conjecture that they took shape between the first collection of laws and narratives in J and E, and the later reproduction of ancient *torah* in D."

commandment in practice. But supposing that we consider the Second Commandment as the product of the period between Isaiah and Jeremiah, what are we to do with the commandments in E (Ex. xx, 23) and J (xxxiv, 17) which prohibit the making of gods of silver and gold, and of molten gods? They were a part of the law of God in Israel and Judah as early as the close of the ninth century in the latter case, and the first half of the eighth in the former. According to the theory of the above-mentioned scholars, the latter of these commandments, " Thou shalt make thee no molten gods," was included in the " Ten Words " of J. But it is precisely during the century following these " Ten Words," with their prohibition of " molten gods " or " gods of silver and gold," that the use of images was, as far as we can judge from the information at hand, most common, so that even the Prophets themselves could not conceive of the worship of God without some sort of image.

As for the argument from silence, it certainly seems to me that the references of Hosea to our commandment, and indeed to the Decalogue as a whole, unless we emend him out of all recognition, are as clear as those of Jeremiah, who confessedly had the Decalogue before him in Deuteronomy as " the sole legislation of Horeb," God's word in a peculiar sense, and the foundation of the entire law of God. The second table is referred to in Hosea iv, 2, in the same phraseology as in Jeremiah vii, 9, as " killing, stealing, and committing adultery," or, rather, Hosea is more explicit in his reference than Jeremiah, since he mentions also " false swearing." Neither mentions coveting. No other Prophets but these two make an explicit reference to the commands of the Decalogue, to however late a period one descends. Now it will scarcely be contended that one pentad of the Decalogue was in existence without the other. The general evidence of Hebrew laws of itself makes us demand two full pentads, and the existence of one pentad of the Decalogue is in so far an evidence of the other. But this negative evidence of Hosea's acquaintance with the first table finds positive support, not merely in his denunciation of the calf-worship but also in his denunciation of " graven images " (xi, 2). The First Commandment, or at least the idea which it expresses, lies at the basis

of all the teaching of Hosea and the following Prophets, but is nowhere quoted by any of them. The Fourth Commandment must
have been known to Hosea, for it appears in both " Books of the
Covenant" (Ex. xxxiv, 21, and xxiii, 12), but it is not quoted or
referred to by him, while from the words of his successor, Isaiah
(i, 13), one might well suppose that no such commandment was
known in his time. Hosea certainly had the two " Books of the
Covenant" behind him, with the larger mass of laws of which they
were but a part, all put forth as of divine authority (viii, 12). In
that mass of laws, and included, under any understanding of their
contents, among the "Ten Words," was a prohibition of images;
nevertheless, that prohibition was not effective, and did not become
so until the close of the seventh century. After that time, while the
Decalogue was recognized as the word of God, and the teaching of
historians, prophets, psalmists, and wisdom writers was in accord with
its teachings, we observe a singular lack of direct citations from, or
references to, it, and the laws of the Priestly Code are quite as independent of it as the " Books of the Covenant" are claimed to be.

There is a feature of the iconoclasm of the reformation under
Josiah which has been generally overlooked or underemphasized,
but which is of some importance for the study of the history of the
Second Commandment. That reform went far beyond the letter of
the commandment. The letter of the commandment was at that
time antiquated. It specified merely "graven images"; the reform
condemned the *mazzebah*. Isaiah, who had gone beyond graven
images to condemn grove worship and *asherim*, had accepted the
mazzebah; Jeremiah and the men of his time stretched the idea of
the commandment to condemn the *mazzebah* also. Even the commentary on, or expansion of, this commandment in Deuteronomy,
which, from its appearance also in Exodus xx, may be assumed to
be at least somewhat older than the main book of Deuteronomy,
does not cover the *mazzebah*.

This application of the commandment, by a process of gradual
evolution, to things and conditions to which its words do not properly apply seems to me suggestive of the real history of the commandment, its interpretation, neglect, and application. That history,

as I conceive it, is as follows: Moses gave the Israelites a god,
Yahaweh, as their god, throughout all their tribes. The representation of this god to them was the Ark. By this Ark, and not
by some "graven image," such as was used in Egypt, was God,
Yahaweh, to be represented to them. Technically, the wording of
the commandment does not prohibit the *mazzebah*, and the rude
stones, trees, and the like, which constituted the representations of
God in the primitive nomadic life. It was intended as a supplement to the First Commandment, to secure the service of Yahaweh
as the God of Israel, in the sense already explained, by furnishing
a symbol or representation of Him. As the Ark was thus the representation of Yahaweh, graven images would have represented some
other deity, and in fact did represent the deities of Egypt, and
were hence forbidden. With the entrance into Canaan and the
adoption of Canaanite shrines, ritual, etc., came the inclination to
adopt the Canaanite representations of deity. So long as these
were adopted as representations of Yahaweh, and not of some
other god, this did not so much matter, and did not seem to be a
breach of the commandment. The situation is parallel with that
which we find in the history of the Christian Church. In each case
a practically imageless church, having among its first principles a
condemnation of images, comes in contact with image-worshiping
peoples. The Christians, while condemning those images as idols,
when worshiped as the representations of other gods, did not regard them in the same light when adopted as representations of
their own god or their saints. There seems to have been no consciousness on their part of a breach of the Second Commandment
in doing this; and they both adopted images from other religions
and also made new ones of their own. The onus of the commandment, as they understood it, was against heathen idol-worship.
Ultimately they developed a practical polytheism. Then came the
struggle of the iconodules and iconoclasts, and finally the Reformation, with the triumph (in the northern and western lands of Christendom only, thus far) of the iconoclasts. The history of Israel
was similar. It is with Elijah, the Wycliffe or Huss of Israel, that
we meet the first mutterings of reform. His is the battle against

the introduction of a foreign religion, against the substitution of Baal for Yahaweh. At first there is no denunciation of image-worship; that is not, or is not perceived to be, an issue in the struggle. Running parallel with this struggle for the national god is the writing of the story of Israel, the telling of its deeds and achievements in the past, which awakened or renewed a patriotic spirit in the people. In this story we begin to hear the call back to primitive things, and to the primitive religion of Israel, which is so strongly developed in Amos and Hosea. But before the time of those prophets this national religious movement had already led to a renaissance of Mosaism, the condemnation of strange gods in the narrative of E, referred to above, and the condemnation in both J and E of the golden calf. The golden calf was a later introduction, a substitute for the original Ark, a "graven image" put in the place of the true and original representation of God given by Moses, namely, the Ark. This was a period of close contact with other nations, and a time of free borrowing in things religious. The result was that a contest was joined between the nationalists and the foreignizers. The conflict between the opposing views grew constantly more defined, and in this conflict the Second Commandment gradually came to have a new and independent significance, as was the case in the history of the Christian Church, until at last things were condemned which at first had been accepted on the basis of tradition as necessary adjuncts of the service of Yahaweh. The Second Commandment itself was explained, and interpreted, and applied, until there grew up about it a definitely fixed commentary, which has come down to us in Exodus xx and Deuteronomy v, attached to the original commandment. Finally, at the close of the seventh century B.C., the reformers extended the scope of the commandment, even beyond the words of the commentary, to include the *mazzebah*, and every symbol of the presence of deity except the Ark itself.[1]

---

[1] If the other arrangement of the Ten Words be adopted, and with Bacon and others the words " Thou shalt not make unto thee a graven image " be regarded as an expansion or application of later date, it is at least very early, as is shown by the similar commandments in the earliest legislation of J and E. Possibly it may have been connected with the erection by Jeroboam of the golden calves, which are so emphatically condemned as leading the people astray after false gods in both J and E.

The Third Commandment prohibits a false oath by the name of Yahaweh, and is a practical assertion of the sanctity to the Israelite of the name of Yahaweh as the name of his God, to whom he stands in a peculiar relation. Not that false oaths by other gods or other names of God were allowed, but that there is a peculiar wickedness in the Israelite's making a false oath by the holy personal name of *his* God. To-day, in Moslem lands, a man who will swear falsely by Allah, or Mohammed, or even by Ali, will not do so by the shrine of the local saints; and similar conditions are vouched for by travelers in Spain and other Christian countries. This does not mean that the Moslem of those regions does not believe in Allah, Mohammed, or Ali, or the Christian in God, Christ, or the Virgin, but that his special god, who takes direct cognizance of his affairs, and whom to offend is dangerous, is the saint of that shrine. The Third Commandment ascribes that function, so far as the Israelite is concerned, to Yahaweh; and it is thus closely related in thought and purpose to the two preceding commandments. Indeed, these three are supplementary or complementary to one another.

The Fourth Commandment deals with an institution, an ancient sacred custom. It enjoins the keeping of the Sabbath as something already well known. The later additions to the Sabbath law, or the interpretations of its meaning or origin, which connect it with agricultural life, have in themselves nothing to do with the original Sabbath law.[1] The Sabbath, as Jastrow has pointed out,[2] was not originally a day of rest, and had nothing to do with agriculture. That is part of the later application and interpretation of this commandment, but is not contained in the original "Word." The Sabbath was, in fact, an antique observance, as was the division of the week into seven days, and, apparently, a primitive Semitic

[1] Such criticisms as that of Addis are quite beside the point, and depend on a misunderstanding of the origin and original purpose of the commandment. Addis says (*Documents of the Hexateuch*, I, 139): "The Sabbath implies the settled life of agriculture. An agriculturist needs rest and can rest from tillage. A nomad's life is usually so idle that no day of rest is needed, while, on the other hand, such work as the nomad does, driving cattle, milking them, etc., cannot be remitted on one day recurring every week."

[2] *American Journal of Theology*, April, 1898.

conception, although no trace of it among the Arabs has yet been discovered. This commandment simply recognizes its existence, and makes it an essential feature of the Hebrew sacred law.

The Fifth Commandment asserts the reverence and obedience due to a parent, in true primitive fashion, placing this reverence almost on a plane with the duty towards God. It is not ancestor-worship, and, in fact, the Hebrews never developed ancestor-worship; but it is the exaltation of the parent to a position near to that of God.

The commandments of the second table, the second pentad of the Decalogue, are more distinctly ethical, in our sense of the word, than those of the first table, and it is particularly against this pentad that the protest has been raised that they were impossible at the time of Moses.[1] The code is, in fact, capable of the broadest ethical interpretation, and under the Prophets it began to receive such an interpretation. But in its literal sense it constitutes no more than the foundation, the groundwork, of the ethical structure which was developed later. All concerns of life, in the Arabian conception, as in the early Hebrew, were governed by religion. What a man should eat, his relations to his wife, to his children, the relations of guest, of friendship, the common affairs of greeting and of etiquette, were included in the sphere of religion. Everything had its origin and its sanction from the god. This was true, also, of the ethical relation of members of a family or clan toward one another, — that they were not to murder, commit adultery, steal, bear false witness, or covet, within the limits of their own family or clan, because those things were contrary to the will of the god with whom they were all united in a bloody bond, and through whom they were united with one another in the same bond. This common clan or tribal law is made, in the second pentad of the Decalogue, the law of all Israelites toward one another, because all are become the servants or worshipers of the one God, under or in whom all are united in one tribe.

In view of the fact that we have traced an apparent connection between the Ark of Moses and the god-ship of the Egyptians, and

---

[1] Budde, *Religion of Israel to the Exile*, p. 33.

a probable acquaintance on Moses' part with at least one of the most striking features of Egyptian religious observance, it is worthy of notice that the commandments of the second pentad of the Decalogue may all be paralleled from the Egyptian sacred law. In the 125th chapter of the *Book of the Dead* we have the negative confession,[1] in which the soul of the dead is made to vindicate himself before Osiris, averring, among other things, that he has not stolen, murdered, etc. From this negative confession we can restore the Egyptian sacred law, which, by the way, underwent a continual growth and development. This law was regarded as divine, and supposed to have been written by the divine scribe Thoth.[2] It may be, therefore, that Moses derived a suggestion not only of an Ark but also of a sacred law from Egypt.

The remarkable feature of the Decalogue, and that which exalts it to a place apart, rendering it universal and permanent in its character, is that it selects precisely the fundamental and ethical relations, and lays the stress upon them. It is this which makes it essentially an ethical law, and it is this which gives to the religion of Israel that ethical character which distinguishes it at the outset from other religions, and renders it capable of the further development which it received. The Decalogue sets forth an ethical conception of the God of Israel as one to whom murder, adultery, theft, and the like are especially offensive. This does not mean that the ethical relation is the only relation in which God is viewed, nor does it mean that at the outset God is viewed as one who condemns the slaughter or robbery of the enemies of Israel. Yahaweh is the God of Israel, and as such the enemy of the enemies of Israel; toward them He has no law. He must cast out and destroy the gods and their peoples before himself and His people Israel.

He is represented in the earlier writings as manifesting himself in the storm; lightning is His weapon, the thunder is His voice. This has been misinterpreted as meaning that He is a nature-god, a god of the storms. Again He is spoken of as a warrior, and

---

[1] Cf. Wiedemann, *The Religion of the Ancient Egyptians.*
[2] Erman, *Aegypten und aegyptisches Leben,* I, 204.

hence some modern writers have interpreted Him as a god of battles. In the Song of Deborah, we find Him pictured as the giver of rain (Jud. v, 5). He is not really a god of a special attribute, or the representation to the Israelites of natural phenomena. He is Yahaweh, the God of Israel, who fights for Israel, who manifests himself in natural phenomena; but He is not, therefore, limited to those. He covers the whole field alike.

In the early days of Islam, the characteristic feature of Allah seemed to be that he gave the victory to his followers. He seemed like a god of battle, because the special business of Islam was to fight; and the same is true at the outset of Israel and Israel's God. On his entrance into Canaan, Israel's special business was to fight for the acquisition of territory and possessions; and, in general, the business of any people in the transition from the barbarous stage is to fight battles. During that period Yahaweh was a god of war, because war was the special function of His people. So, also, under primitive conditions, the most striking manifestation of divine power is the thunder storm, and hence, particularly, the thunder storm manifests Yahaweh. In the Deborah Song, already referred to, we see another form of manifestation, the useful and practical, becoming more pronounced as the people advance toward the settled state as cultivators of the soil.

To turn from the conception of God, and His relation to His people, to the rites by which a relation with God was established or maintained, we find circumcision taking the most prominent place. In the later period circumcision and the Sabbath become, in fact, the peculiar characteristics of the Jews. Circumcision was customary in early times not only among the Hebrews but also among the Phœnicians and Canaanites, the Arabs and the Egyptians; in fact, all the people in the immediate neighborhood of the Hebrews, with the exception of the Philistines, practiced this rite. It is not, apparently, an original Semitic practice, since we do not find it among the Babylonians and Assyrians. It may have been introduced into Phœnicia, Palestine, and Arabia from Egypt. The Hebrews apparently inherited it from their forefathers in those regions. A curious reference in one of the oldest passages of the

Pentateuch (Ex. iv, 24–26) connects Moses with circumcision, and suggests that in some manner or other circumcision assumed a new shape at his time. Possibly the change was the transfer in age, so that instead of circumcising on the entrance into manhood, which seems to have been the original form of the rite, it was transferred to infancy, as we find it among the Israelites during the entire historical period. Circumcision was connected with the blood covenant, as is shown by the passage referred to. It is clear, also, from 1 Samuel xviii, that in the time of Saul and David it was a part of the holiness regulation, that is, of the peculiar relation of the Israelite to his God, so that there was a special stigma attaching to peoples who did not practice this rite. The same view is set forth in the oldest history of the earlier days (Josh. v, 2–3, 8–9), where circumcision is regarded as the condition of the covenant relation of Israel with its God. But here the rite seems to be connected in time with the entrance into Canaan, as though first adopted as a national rite on the entrance into that country.

In general, so far as rites and ceremonies were concerned, it seems probable that Moses left them, with little change, as he found them. If we ask after the position which Moses claims for himself, we find him represented as a priest rather than a warrior, the founder of a cult, connecting itself closely with a special symbol of divinity, the Ark, and its contents, the Decalogue. Later, we find a priesthood hereditary in his family, the priests of the temple of Dan deriving their origin from him (Jud. xvii–xviii). On the other hand, it is clear that he did not regard himself as a priest in any exclusive sense, or found a priesthood hereditary only in his family, or even assume for himself or for his family the guardianship of the Ark. That position was assigned by him, according to what sounds like a reliable tradition, to an Ephraimite, Joshua (Ex. xxxiii, 11), and the later priestly caste was derived by tradition not from Moses, but from his brother Aaron. Moses' own special function as priest seems to have been the interpretation of the oracles of God.

CHAPTER V

THE RELIGION OF CANAAN AND ITS INFLUENCE
ON THE HEBREWS

With the conquest of Canaan the Israelite nomads became a peasant population, a change which affected their entire being. The life of the peasant is different from that of the nomad. The peasant has a settled habitation. Between him and his land exists the firmest of all bonds — the love of home. His life is richer and more varied, if less free, than that of the nomad. The need of labor is more apparent, and its results are more manifest and more permanent. With the farm and peasant life come profit and possession, and the consequent social development. The greater wealth of life, its more manifold character and increased individuality, lays upon the farmer social obligations and responsibilities, and opens to him higher moral possibilities.

As different as the peasant is from the nomad, so different is his god. The god of the agriculturist can give more and refuse more; he is more present in the daily life. Man feels more constantly his dependence on him, and therefore the connection which binds him to his god is more intimate. In the desert there was neither barley nor wheat, neither wine nor oil, for which man should thank God. The Canaanites, on the other hand, enjoyed these blessings of heaven, and thanked their gods for them at the various holy places where their fathers before them had worshiped and which hence possessed an ancestral sanctity and a traditional ritual.

The conquest and settlement of Canaan, with the consequent passage from the nomadic to the agricultural life, meant a mighty step forward for the religion of Israel. But, on the other hand, the change was fraught with the gravest danger. The language of the Israelites was the same as that of the Canaanites. Canaanites and Israelites were ethnologically akin, and possessed many similar or identical customs and ideas. It was from this kindred people, speaking the same language, but further advanced in civilization, that the Israelites must learn the art of agriculture; and from them they must adopt the customs of settled life. How much of the religion of the Canaanites would they appropriate at the same time?

Our knowledge of the religion of Canaan is derived in part from the notices contained in the Old Testament, in part from the accounts in classical writers of the religion of the Syrians, in part from the rather scanty discoveries in recent excavations, and in part from the still much more scanty Phœnician and Aramæan inscriptions; for we may assume that, in principle at least, the religion of Canaan was identical with that of Phœnicia and Syria. We have only one original Canaanite document, the Moabite stone, and that comes from the east, not from the west, of the Jordan. From these sources we are able to reconstruct only in the most general way the outlines of the religion of Canaan at the time of the Hebrew invasion.

The Canaanite religion was the nature-worship of an agricultural population. Baal gave grain, oil, and wine. For this his worshipers prayed to him and for this they thanked him. Baal was identified with nature. Its yearly revival and death were a revival and death of the god. In this revival and death his worshipers took part. In connection with the latter it was their religion to mourn and mutilate themselves; in connection with the former, to give themselves over to the most unbridled merrymaking. Baal was the giver of all life, but he was also the destroyer of life. As the latter, men sought to appease his wrath by offerings, even of their children; as the former, men reveled in his bounty with the wildest orgies. The life of nature appearing to them to rest on a mystical process of generation, sexual immorality was a feature of their worship of the gods.

Each city had a Baal[1] as its chief god, and in consequence of the likeness of the life of the various cities, there was no great difference between these various Baals. They were distinguished,

---

[1] Less common than the name of Baal is that of Melek, "King." We find also *Adoni* or *Adon*, "Lord." With this latter name was connected more particularly the wild and foul Adonis, or Tammuz, worship.

in general, by adding the name of the city or place in which they were worshiped, and usually the province of a Baal was the city to which he belonged or the territory immediately surrounding his habitation. They were represented often by symbols taken from the animal world, bulls and lions, cows, doves and birds of prey, in which the generative force or the consuming ardor of the sun were represented. Various symbols, also, from the vegetable world represented the power which generates life in nature.

Along with the Baal was worshiped a Baalat, or corresponding goddess. Throughout the religion of the settled Semites, as we find it in Babylonia, Canaan, and among the settled Aramæans, there was a duality of sex and a tendency to worship the goddess with immoral rites.[1] At her shrines and in her name sexual license was permitted or commanded, and sometimes the sacrifice of female chastity was required in her service. At places strange and unnatural lust formed part of her worship; and both female and male prostitutes inhabited her temples and served at her shrines.[2]

---

[1] W. Robertson Smith, *Religion of the Semites*, pp. 58-59:

Divine motherhood, like the kinship of men and gods in general, was to the heathen Semites a physical fact, and the development of the corresponding cults and myths laid more stress on the physical than on the ethical side of maternity, and gave a prominence to sexual ideas which was never edifying, and often repulsive. Especially was this the case when the change in the law of kinship deprived the mother of her old preëminence in the family, and transferred to the father the greater part of her authority and dignity. This change, as we know, went hand in hand with the abolition of the old polyandry; and as women lost the right to choose their own partners at will, the wife became subject to her husband's lordship, and her freedom of action was restrained by his jealousy, at the same time that her children became, for all purposes of inheritance and all duties of blood, members of his and not of her kin. So far as religion kept pace with the new laws of social morality due to this development, the independent divine mother necessarily became the subordinate partner of a male deity; and so the old polyandrous Ishtar reappears in Canaan and elsewhere as Astarte, the wife of the supreme Baal. Or if the supremacy of the goddess was too well established to be thus undermined, she might change her sex, as in Southern Arabia, where Ishtar is transformed into the masculine Athtar. But not seldom religious tradition refused to move forward with the progress of society; the goddess retained her old character as a mother who was not a wife, bound to fidelity to her husband, and at her sanctuary she protected, under the name of religion, the sexual licence of savage society, or even demanded of the daughters of her worshippers a shameful sacrifice of their chastity, before they were permitted to bind themselves for the rest of their lives to that conjugal fidelity which their goddess despised. The emotional side of Semitic heathenism was always very much connected with the worship of female deities, partly through the associations of maternity, which appealed to the purest and tenderest feelings, and partly through other associations connected with woman, which too often appealed to the sensuality so strongly developed in the Semitic race.

[2] One is inclined to ask whether possibly the transfer from the feminine to the masculine, Ishtar to Athtar, was not connected with sodomy.

The Canaanite cults corresponded to their gross conceptions of the gods, overstepping very little primitive nature ideas. The gods were worshiped as the rulers of nature, who, on the one side, showed their activities in the life-giving and destroying powers of heaven, the sun, rain, storm, and lightning, and on the other side in the marvelous generation of life in the animal, and its germination in the plant world, or in the mysterious origin and wonderful life-giving powers of springs of water. Everything comes through the creative power of the god of the land; all belongs to him, and therefore the firstlings and the best of everything are his due. But the gods are in no wise always kindly disposed towards men. They bring drought and famine, cattle plague, flies to torment, and mice to destroy the fruits of the field. Men must take care to make them favorably disposed at the proper times and to omit nothing of that which is their proper due, for they are jealous and vengeful. Hence Canaanite places of worship were set up and offerings presented everywhere, on mountains and hills, by stones, in groves and under green trees, and at springs and wells. In the location of their places of worship, and in the character of the places and objects which they held sacred as the means by which the gods manifested themselves, the Canaanites differed in no respect from the Arabians and the primitive Hebrews. But besides the rude stones, or *mazzebah*, which represented the god in Arabian use, Canaanite places of worship required, to render them complete, an altar.[1] This was the central feature of the sanctuary, by which stood the *asherah*, or sacred tree, the sacred stone, or *mazzebah*, and generally an image or some representation of the divinity. This greater complexity of ritual need involved commonly, also, a structure of some description for the accommodation of the god or of the priests and attendants.

The central feature of the worship of the gods at these various altars was, of course, sacrifice. In the Phœnician inscriptions, which give us, in this respect, presumably, a fair view of Canaanite worship

---

1 It is not clear, however, that there was a separate altar at Gezer, where we have the *mazzebah*, the sacred cave, and apparently the *asherah*, with the obscene worship condemned in the Prophets. Macalister, *The Excavation of Gezer.*

also, three kinds of offerings in common use are distinguished: the whole burnt offering, the votive and thank offering, and the peace offering. In the old Arabian sacrifices the only part of the offering which was directly given to the gods was the blood, and the object of the sacrifice was to establish or renew the blood relationship. In Canaanite sacrifices we find a development corresponding in general to the development in civilization. The most essential feature of the offering is still the blood, which, above all, is given to the deity, for in the blood is the life; but flesh, oil, wine, and vegetable offerings, the latter commonly prepared in cakes and the like, as for the use of men, also constitute the material of sacrifice. The offering has become food for the god, by which he is to be placated and which, as the giver of all things, he exacts as his portion. And with the increased requirements of man in the conditions of civilized life, the requirements of the gods have increased likewise. They require flesh to eat, and with each flesh offering its proper provision of corn and wine and oil, as in the meals of men. The whole burnt offering, the god received entire. If the offering were not a whole offering the sacrificer received a portion of it. With the peace offering there was connected commonly a joyful festival.

With the development of the altar and of sacrifice among the Canaanites had gone hand in hand the development of ritual and of a priesthood. It is provided in the Phœnician tariff of temple dues, above mentioned, that a certain portion of the creature offered shall belong to the priest of the sanctuary where it is offered or a payment made in place thereof. Among the Canaanites the priests were in general the sacrificers, and the Israelites found at the sanctuaries of Canaan an organized priestly system with the *kohenim* as the sacrificers for the people, entitled to certain fees and perquisites in compensation for their services.

A system of sacrificial feasts also had been developed among the Canaanites. These feasts were connected, in part, with the moon, the new moon being always a feast day, and in part with the harvest season. There was in the springtime a seven-day festival, with gifts of the firstlings to the deity. There was, further, an autumnal festival, and, presumably, a third festival, between these two, connected with the wheat harvest. These sacrificial feasts were accompanied by music and dancing, and especially was this true of the great autumnal festival, in which the whole population took part.

Besides the priests we find among the Canaanites *nebiim*, "prophets." These were sometimes gathered together in schools or cloisters; sometimes, apparently, they exercised their office separately. They resorted to extravagant means to excite themselves, and produced ecstasy or trances by music, dancing, and cutting and gashing themselves. They were regarded as exponents of the will of the gods, and occupied toward the priesthood and the shrines very much the same relation which, in modern Islam, the dervishes occupy toward the mosques and the *Ulema*, or regularly taught and constituted interpreters of the law and directors of the religious services. In fact, the dervishes of to-day may be said to be the lineal descendants of the *nebiim*, and their organization, their rites and ceremonies are, in many respects, strikingly similar to those which the Hebrews found in existence among the *nebiim* in Canaan.

Such, in brief, are the characteristic features of the religion of Canaan as it differed from the religion of the primitive Hebrews and Arabians. It was, to all outward appearance, more similar to than dissimilar from the latter. That which constituted the striking point of difference was its relation to agriculture and a settled life.

The Hebrew conquest of Canaan was a slow and long-continued process, and cannot be said to have been completed until the time of David and Solomon; but even after the Israelites had become masters of the whole territory, there still seem to have remained enclaves of Canaanites, and in many places certainly the Hebrews had so united with the Canaanites that it would be difficult to say to which nationality they should properly be ascribed. The conquest was not by any means always by force of arms, and while in some places the Hebrews doubtless drove out or exterminated the former inhabitants, in other places they intermarried or united with them, or the two dwelt side by side, and in some regions we are told that the Israelites were subject to the Canaanites.

Turning to the earliest Hebrew laws concerning rites and codes which have come down to us, dating, in their present form, from the ninth century or possibly the tenth century B.C., we find that the Hebrews had already at that time adopted the use of the Canaanite ritual, so far as festivals are concerned. In Exodus xxxiv, 17–26, from J, and xxiii, 10–19, from E, we have a decad, or decalogue, of feasts and offerings. Three feasts are prescribed, all of which are agricultural — the feast of unleavened bread, the feast of the first fruits of the wheat harvest, and the feast of "ingathering at the year's revolution."

This earliest legislation with regard to festivals shows us clearly that, in the transition from the nomadic to the agricultural stage, the Hebrews adopted from the Canaanites the festivals of the latter. As we see by a comparison with Exodus xii, Leviticus xxiii, etc., the agricultural feast of unleavened bread was ultimately connected with the earlier spring festival of the Hebrews at the time of the casting of the flocks, and both of them with the historical event of the deliverance of Israel from Egypt,[1] the whole constituting the Passover, while the feast of the ingathering at the revolution of the year was connected with the original autumnal feast of the Hebrews, as is indicated by the persistence of the use of the booths or tents at that festival.

These codes show us further the application of the agricultural idea to the Hebrew Sabbath Day custom. With the Canaanite agricultural festivals the Israelites have also, according to the testimony of these codes, adopted the Canaanite law of firstlings. The first-born male belongs to God, and if not capable, according to the ritual rules, of being sacrificed in the ordinary manner, then it must either be redeemed by a sacrificial animal or killed, which killing is itself a sacrifice.

It is clear, from the references in the earliest historical writings, that by this period and even earlier the Hebrews had adopted, in

---

[1] This tendency to add new meanings to feasts and fasts, and especially to connect them with historical events, is well illustrated by the history of the Feast of Weeks. Quite without historical connection or the suggestion of such connection in the Bible, in post-Biblical times it was connected with the giving of the Law at Sinai ; and it is to-day observed in the synagogues as the commemoration of that great event.

general, the Canaanite shrines and sacred places. We find high places mentioned as existing everywhere, on hills and mountains, under green trees, at springs and the like, and among the Hebrew cities of refuge and the Levitical cities of the later legislation we find not a few, the names of which indicate at once that they were ancient Canaanite or even pre-Canaanite shrines which had been taken over by the Israelites as holy places. So also the legends of the Patriarchs, as they have come down to us in JE, connect Abraham, Isaac, and Jacob with ancient Canaanite shrines and the rites and worship of those shrines.

With the ancient sanctuaries it was to be expected that the Hebrews would adopt, to a large extent at least, the rites and ceremonies practiced at those shrines. In a former chapter attention has been called to traces, in the time of Saul and later, of the primitive Hebrew idea of sacrifice, where a rude stone was at once altar and representative of deity, and the sacrifice consisted in pouring out the blood on or by this stone, the flesh being consumed by the people; but there are only lingering traces of this older use. The Hebrews in general adopted the Canaanite method and theory of sacrifice. There is an altar [1] and in connection with the altar a *mazzebah* and commonly, also, an *asherah*. A comparison of the Hebrew list of sacrificial animals and the Hebrew offerings of the earlier period with the Phœnician tariff of temple dues, to which reference has already been made, exhibits the method of adoption of the Canaanite ritual of sacrifice, namely, its adoption in principle with certain divergencies in detail which are, in most cases, the persistence of earlier Hebrew use. On the other hand, we find in the Hebrew ritual, as among the Canaanites, three main classes of sacrifice — whole burnt offerings, votive and thank offerings, and peace offerings; to which were added later [sin and guilt offerings. The Hebrews also follow the Canaanites in making the sacrifice a feast of God, in which, besides the blood, God receives certain portions

---

[1] Exodus xx, 25, shows us a period of transition. The altar seems to have become fairly well established as a necessity of the ritual, but we are still in the stage where that altar, if it be made of stone at all, shall be made of rough, unhewn stone, that is, shall be practically a collection of *mazzebahs*.

of the animal offered and, as in the meals of men, wine and oil and grain, the latter cooked in various manners, as for the meals of men. Along with God the priest also receives his portion of the sacrifice.[1]

In the earlier part of David's reign the priest's chief function still seems to be to expound the lots, as in the primitive Hebrew and Arabic use. From the code in Exodus xxi–xxiii it is clear that the priests continued at that time to exercise their function as interpreters of the will of God, presumably by lot, as in the matter of suspicion of theft, trespass, and the like (Ex. xxii, 8–9), and the sacred lots, Urim and Thummim, were until a late date a priestly emblem of office. On the other hand, at sanctuaries like Shiloh, as appears from 1 Samuel ii, the priests were from an early time sacrificers, receiving a part of the animal sacrificed as their fee. This was the use in Solomon's temple from the outset, and in general, we may suppose, at all well-equipped sanctuaries. In other words, along with the Canaanite altars the Hebrews adopted also the Canaanite practice of priests to sacrifice at those altars. These priests they designated by the Canaanite name *kohenim*, the same root (*k-h-n*) which, as we have already seen, served among the Arabs to designate the seer. But the seer among the Arabs was, presumably, originally the guardian of, or attached to, a sacred place,[2] and we may presume that among the primitive Hebrews the same idea of guardian of a sacred place, and interpreter of the oracles at that place, was attached to this word. The identity of the word in use among the Hebrews to indicate the guardian of the sanctuary and the caster of the sacred lots with the Canaanite word for a sacrificing priest doubtless helped to bring about an amalgamation of functions.[3]

---

[1] For Hebrew sacrificial use cf. especially Lev. i ff.

[2] Cf. Wellhausen, *Skizzen*, III, 132 f.; also chap. vii.

[3] From the few inscriptions which have come down to us it would seem that the Aramæan name for priest was *komer* or *kamar*, and the indications are that at least in the north this title was in common use. Neo-Punic inscriptions suggest that it was also in use among the Phœnicians. In the Hebrew scriptures the word is rare, however, and only used of priests of false worship. By the time of the Reformation, if not earlier, the name seems to have become a reproach, like the Baal worship with which the *kemarim* were connected. Cf. 2 Kings xxiii, 5; Zeph. i, 4; perhaps also Hos. x, 5; and iv, 4 (corrected text).

The same identity of words assisted in the identification of
Yahaweh with Baal, and consequently in the adoption of Baal
worship and Baal theology, if we may use such a phrase, as the
worship and theology of Yahaweh. In each Canaanite city the
Israelites found a *baal*, the lord of that region, the very name
which was used among them as one, perhaps the most common,
designation of their own deity Yahaweh. It was easy to confuse
the god and the name and to take over the conceptions connected
with the worship of the *baals* among the Canaanites, the more so
after Israel came to recognize Yahaweh as *the* Baal, that is, the
owner or lord of Palestine. The idea of the connection of a god
with a particular locality was, as we have already seen, universal in
the Semitic world. It existed among the primitive Hebrews and
Arabs as well as among their more settled and civilized kindred
in Babylonia and Canaan. Among the Hebrews the Ark, as a
movable representative of the divinity of Yahaweh, served, to some
extent, to break up this conception of locality; but in spite of the
Ark, by which the divinity of Yahaweh was to be carried with
Israel wherever it went, the local connection of Yahaweh with
Horeb-Sinai still persisted, so that, while He was conceived of as
the god of Israel who fought its battles against the Canaanites, He
was still localized, in the generation following Moses, in Horeb-
Sinai — at least, presumably, by the bulk of the people.[1] Later, as
we see, for instance, from 1 Samuel xxvi, 19, and 2 Kings v, 17,
he came to be localized in Canaan and conceived of as the god,
the *baal* or possessor, of that land, and as such he was identified,
certainly by the people at large, with the *baal* of this place or that
place, a process quite similar to that by which, when Christianity
made its way into heathen countries, the Virgin or the saints of
Christianity were identified with the goddesses and local gods,
adopting their shrines and, to some extent, the peculiarities of their
worship. This was, of course, perilously close to polytheism, and
there was always danger lest the local manifestation and the local
cult should altogether usurp the place of the El, or Yahaweh, the
God of Israel. Images and animal representations of deity appear

1 Cf. Jud. v, Ps. lxviii; also 1 Kings xix.

also among the Hebrews after the conquest, taken over from the Canaanites much as Christianity took over in some places the images of the heathen. So, ephods,[1] or images, are mentioned in connection with the shrines of Gideon and Micah (Jud. viii, 27 ; xvii, 4, 5) ; we have the bull at Ephraim and Dan, and the brazen serpent in the Temple at Jerusalem.

With the sacred places of the Canaanites, their festivals, their ritual, and their priesthood, the Israelites adopted also the Canaanite *nebiim*, or prophets. According to the naïve story of Saul and Samuel (1 Sam. ix), at the time of Saul there still existed the older class of seers, *ro'eh*, such as existed also among the Arabs, who were able to tell the place of that which was lost and the like ; but these were giving way to the new order of prophets, *nebiim*, banded together in schools or troops, making use of music and dancing, exciting themselves to ecstasy, trances, and the like. By the time of Ahab and Jehoshaphat, in the middle of the ninth century B.C., these prophets are, according to the Book of Kings,[2] very numerous and constitute an important feature of the religion of Yahaweh. No great enterprise is undertaken without consulting them ; that is to say, the Canaanite order of prophets had been incorporated in the religion of Israel.

It has been pointed out that the Canaanite religion was a nature worship, often gross and sensual in its manifestations ;[3] that along with the *baal* existed the *baalat*, and that her service especially tended toward license and sexual immorality. To what extent did the Hebrews adopt into their religion this nature worship and its immoralities ? The lack of goddesses in the primitive Hebrew religion has already been pointed out, and this original lack of the idea of "goddess" was, to some extent, a safeguard against the adoption of the *baalats* in Canaan and their worship. There was a sound moral sense among the people which protested against the immoralities of the *baalat* worship, and which could be appealed to by the Prophets. But this did not prevent a very serious corruption

---

[1] Foote presents a strong argument to show that the ephod was properly the receptacle to hold the sacred lots. *J. B. L.*, Vol. XXI.　　[2] Cf. 1 Kings xxii.

[3] Cf., for instance, the numerous phalli found at the sanctuary at Gezer.

of the morality of the Hebrews, under the name of religion, by the adoption of the ideas and uses of Canaanitish nature worship, and especially the worship of the *baalat*. The Prophets of the eighth and seventh centuries protest vehemently against the abominations which are committed in the name of religion under every green tree, and in doing so testify to the adoption into the common religion of the period of all that was objectionable in the nature worship of the Canaanites. Nor was the official religion free from those abominations. The *asherahs* certainly, and in some cases probably the *mazzebahs* also, were, among the Canaanites, connected with the ideas and usages of this immoral nature worship; and it was impossible to separate them from those ideas and usages, even where a goddess, or *baalat*, was not formally worshiped. So in the Temple of Yahaweh in Jerusalem we find, as late as the latter part of the seventh century, the *asherah* with its foul surroundings[1] of " Sodomites "[2] and prostitutes, although it is not clear that the *baalat* was there worshiped as a goddess. What was true of the *asherah* in the Jerusalem Temple was true probably, in a degree, of the *asherahs* at other shrines. Apparently, from the references in the books of Kings and in the Prophets, *asherahs* and *mazzebahs* were regular adjuncts of Hebrew shrines through almost the entire period of the kings.

By the time of the first writing prophets, in the middle of the eighth century B.C., the religion of Canaan had been superimposed upon the religion of the Hebrews. The Hebrews, changing from a nomadic to a peasant population, had adopted the Canaanite places of worship with their altars and accessories, the Canaanite feasts, the conception of God as the *baal* of the land, the giver of its increase, to whom belong first fruits and firstlings, the Canaanite sacrificial practices, and the Canaanite priests and prophets. But along with those Canaanite elements which were practically necessary in the progress from the nomadic to the settled stage,

---

[1] Cf. 2 Kings xxiii, 7, 8.

[2] How prevalent sodomy was, and how strenuously it had to be fought, is shown by such narratives as Gen. xix, Jud. xxx, the frequent prohibitions in the legal codes, the description of the worship in the Temple at Jerusalem, prophetic denunciations, and the like.

they had adopted in form, if not in theory, Canaanite polytheism and idolatry, and Canaanite nature worship with its immoral practices. In part the superimposition of the religion of Canaan upon their own religion was in the line of progress; in part it was a source of corruption and moral perversion. In part the Canaanite elements were permanently incorporated in the religion of Israel, modifying both its forms and its conceptions; in part they were sloughed off after a fierce battle, which left its marks in a certain puritan and exclusive tendency of that religion. But besides the public, or official, religion, partly in close connection with it, partly existing as a sort of secret cult, the Canaanites had also a great number of superstitious arts and usages, witchcraft, necromancy, and their ilk. The beliefs underlying these connect themselves with animism, fetishism, totemism, and the like, and in so far are common to all primitive peoples. These beliefs we may assume existed, in part at least, among the Hebrews before they entered Canaan; but the expression of those beliefs in the conjuration of the dead, ventriloquism, the consultation of ghosts, the lot castings, and the various forms of witchcraft, to which we find occasional references in the historical books, and which are so often denounced by the earlier prophets, was derived not from the religion of the wilderness but from the Canaanites. While it was similarity of superstition and of fundamental animistic beliefs which led the Israelites to adopt these practices of the Canaanites, nevertheless the actual practice of witchcraft, necromancy, and the like, the semi-secret cults which we find forming part of the popular religion of the Hebrews in the tenth and following centuries, were borrowed from the Canaanites.

After the manner of preachers, and indeed after the manner of its own prophets, one is tempted to compare Israel in its experience with the religions of Canaan with an unsophisticated youth from the desert plunged suddenly into the vortex of city life, with its confinement and civilization, its allurements and dissipations, who at first yields to the latter and goes astray, but finally, accepting the civilization and the culture of the city, returns with almost fanatical fierceness to a moral standard higher than that with which he had begun. Seeking a historical comparison, we may fairly liken

Israel's relation to the religions of Canaan to that of Christianity to the religions of heathen Europe. In form, if not in theory, Christianity adopted at first the idolatry and polytheism of the religions it overran. Those it later sloughed off, at least in part; but besides this temporary element, which it finally rejected after a fierce struggle, Christianity received a permanent contribution from heathenism not only in matters of externals, feasts, ritual, and the like, but also in matters of doctrine and belief. So it was in the relation of the religion of Israel to the religions of the Canaanites.

CHAPTER VI

THE MOLDING EFFECT OF NATIONAL EXPERIENCES

Even the most casual student of the religious history of Israel must realize the great part played in the development of that religion by national experiences and conditions. In the earliest Israelite traditions which have come down to us, and in the earliest poetry, reference is made to the wonderful deliverance of Israel from Egypt in the passage of the Red Sea. This is the substance of an ancient song of triumph contained in the first few verses of the fifteenth chapter of Exodus. This song has been much added to and is, in its present shape, of relatively late origin; but the basis of the song is very ancient, antedating the earliest prose record contained in J. This prose narrative, as pointed out in the first chapter, was probably committed to writing not long after the time of David and Solomon. The tradition was at that time, evidently, firmly established. It appears also in the parallel narrative of E; and the first Prophets whose writings have come down to us refer to the deliverance from Egypt as creating an epoch in the history of Israel. After the fashion of folklore the tradition of the deliverance from Egypt at the cost of the Egyptians has found place also in the story of Abraham, the ancestor of the race. He went down to Egypt, and his wife was taken by Pharaoh. But Yahaweh plagued Egypt, and the Egyptians sent Abraham away with his wife and all that he had.[1]

A deliverance of some sort at the Red Sea, in connection with the Exodus from Egypt, had impressed itself most forcibly on the thought of the whole people. This deliverance was connected in their belief with the direct interference of Yahaweh, who, by His miraculous power, delivered them from the overwhelming forces of

---

[1] Gen. xii. The narrative is from J.

Egypt. If we are unable to restore the literal details of the event which made so deep an impression upon the minds of the Israelites, we need not, nevertheless, doubt that there was a deliverance of so remarkable a character that it was naturally attributed to divine agency. That divine agency was believed by Israel to be the God of Moses, namely, Yahaweh. Moses himself believed that Israel was delivered by the signal interposition of Yahaweh, and so interpreted to his people that deliverance. Naturally, as time went on, details were added to the story of the deliverance, and the extent of that deliverance was, presumably, magnified. It played an ever greater part in the story of Israel, lending itself finally to the most mythical interpretations. But all this is only a further evidence of the importance of the event to Israel. One can scarcely exaggerate the effect of the deliverance from Egypt in molding the religious life of Israel. At the outset it gave precisely the prestige which was necessary to enable Moses to establish Yahaweh as the God of all Israel, and to unite all the tribes under one God. Yahaweh had proved himself a God of infinite might, a God capable of contending with the ancient and powerful gods of Egypt, a God able to control the elements and make nature work to help His chosen people. This God, whom they had scarcely known as their own up to that time, had stepped in to deliver them, making it manifest that they were His choice. This God was their God forever and ever, and they were His own peculiar people, whom He had chosen for himself and brought up out of a strange land with a mighty hand and an outstretched arm.

The next great national experience was the conquest of Canaan. The Book of Joshua records a series of victories by the Israelites, which reminds us most singularly of the records of the early Mohammedan successes, when the Arabs, pouring out of the Arabian desert, overran the civilized and cultivated regions of Syria. A more sober narrative, contained in the first chapter of the Book of Judges, shows us that the conquest was not completed at once, as the narrative in Joshua might suggest, but was a slow process continuing through a couple of centuries, and not complete until the time of David. This does not, however, discredit the story of

striking successes against the Canaanites on the part of the Israelites both east and west of the Jordan. They contended with men
better armed than themselves, living in cities walled up to heaven,
and won striking victories. These they did not know how to follow up at the beginning so as to make a full conquest of the country, nor were they as yet capable of occupying it and organizing
a government, nor could they permanently maintain themselves on
the plains. Nevertheless, their victories were brilliant and striking and such as must have seemed both to their opponents and
themselves, with the beliefs of those times, due to divine agency.
They fought their battles in the name of Yahaweh,[1] and the victories which they won were another proof of the might of their
God, Yahaweh, and of His signal favor toward them. Their victories at first were brilliant, but as they passed over from the
nomadic into the peasant stage they lost some of their fighting
qualities. Moreover they were separated into tribes and clans, occupying different localities, and no longer easily brought together.
Mixed among the peoples of the land whom they had conquered
or among whom they had settled, they were no longer a body of
conquering warriors, but a peasant people occupying many scattered towns and villages. At this stage of the conquest they in
their turn were attacked by a conquering invader.

The Philistines entered Palestine at about the same time as the
Israelites, but from a different direction. They conquered the plain
country between the Judæan hills and the sea and established themselves as city dwellers, with organized and civilized states, at a time
when the Israelites, still rude barbarians, were struggling with the
Canaanites of the mountains. The double invasion had the effect
of weakening the Canaanites, and at the outset Philistines and Israelites were, therefore, helpful one to the other. But this did not
long continue. The two invaders, having each conquered and occupied a portion of the land, came into contact and inevitably
into conflict also. The Philistines were city dwellers, better organized and further advanced in civilization than the Hebrews, and at
the outset they were in general successful. They overran a good

---

[1] Cf., for instance, the Song of Deborah, Jud. v.

part of the country, defeated the Israelites, and even captured the
Ark of their God. The story of the battle in which the Ark was
lost (I Sam. iv) belongs to the earliest historical records, so near
the source that it may be considered as a historical document of
the first character. Yahaweh was considered a great God, for the
tradition of the wonderful things which He had done for Israel had
spread beyond the borders of Israel, so that the Philistines also
looked with dread upon the Ark. All this was changed by the defeat of the Israelites and the capture of the Ark. The Israelites
were conquered, their God, Yahaweh, had not the power which they
had attributed to Him; the religious bond which united them was
broken, and for a time the Ark passes out of sight and is forgotten.

Finally under Samuel and Saul a struggle for freedom begins.
Saul is for a time successful, and establishes a kingdom, but the
struggle ends in disaster. Saul and Jonathan are slain, and all
Israel is again overrun by the Philistines. This Philistine oppression stamped itself on the popular mind only less strongly than
the Egyptian. Like the story of the Egyptian oppression and the
deliverance therefrom, the story of the Philistine conquest and the
final deliverance from the Philistine yoke also found its way into
the stories of the Patriarchs, and under the very same figure, — the
wife of the Hebrew taken by the foreigner (here the Philistine
king, Abimelech of Gerar), and the foreigner afflicted by Yahaweh
until he is compelled to let the Hebrew woman go free. Of this
story we have duplicate narratives, the one connecting it with
Abraham and Sarah, the other with Isaac and Rebecca.[1]

The Philistine oppression and the final deliverance from the
Philistine yoke molded Israel into one nation. The work begun
by Moses, when he loosely united the tribes together by a bond
of religion, was completed by David when, fighting in the name of
Yahaweh, he turned defeat into triumph and won for Israel the
victory not only over the Philistines, who, from that time on never
again appear as rivals of the Israelites in power, but also over all
the neighboring peoples. He realized in his kingdom that greatness

---

[1] Cf. Gen. xx, xxvi. These are referred by the critics to JE, which means that
each of them originally appeared in each of the two sources.

of which Israel began to dream when it first met the civilized Canaanites in successful battle. He had established a great power; the period of calamity was forgotten; it was manifest that Yahaweh was indeed a great God, more powerful than the gods of any of the nations about. His Ark was replaced as the central sanctuary, the dwelling place *par excellence* of Yahaweh, and so this new manifestation of His might was connected directly with the victories under Moses and Joshua, when the Ark of Yahaweh led the people to victory.

As already stated, next to the deliverance from Egypt, it is the deliverance from the Philistines and the establishment of the kingdom of David which made the most lasting impression on the national and religious life of Israel. The career of the nation up to this time had been, on the whole, one of phenomenal success. A handful of nomads, slaves in Egypt, they had been delivered by the power of Yahaweh. Through Him they had won the victory over the civilized peoples of Canaan, dwelling in fortified cities; over the powerful Philistine confederacy, which had up to that time pursued a career of conquest; over Moabites, Ammonites, Edomites, Aramæans, and Hittites, until at length they had become the mightiest nation of the earth. David's kingdom was the acme of Israel's national career, and that kingdom gave Israel a conception of its own possibilities, which developed, finally, into a theory of the purpose of God regarding it. In the midst of all the pettiness of its succeeding national career, it constantly dreamed of a world-kingdom, like David's, and even greater, until, little by little, the dream of a world-kingdom was converted from a national into a spiritual theory.

David's kingdom did not last long, — through his time and that of his son Solomon, — but long enough to establish firmly in the minds of the people a conception of their own greatness. With the division of the kingdom under Solomon's son Rehoboam passed away forever the possibility of the realization of the dream of national greatness. Israel was relegated to the condition of petty statehood, common to Syria and the surrounding regions. To all outward appearance Israel and Judah were no different from the kingdoms of Moab and Edom, of Hamath, Damascus, Ascalon, Tyre, etc., except that in point of power they were inferior to not a few of these; but in the hearts of the Israelites remained the remembrance of the deliverance from Egypt, of the deliverance from the oppression of the Philistines, and of the glorious kingdom of David, the mightiest kingdom of its day, breeding hope, developing ultimately into belief, that their God, Yahaweh, who had wrought for them such wonders in the past, would some day interfere again to restore to them a kingdom as of yore.

Slowly Assyria conquered all the small states of the West and ground them in its cruel mill. Piece after piece was torn from Israel, fragment after fragment of the people was deported, until Samaria itself was captured and the better part of its population carried into captivity. Only Judah remained; but the hope of deliverance, by the might of Yahaweh, and the restoration of a mighty kingdom, like the kingdom of David, had not died out. One strange deliverance, when Sennacherib seemed to have the city in his grasp and to be about to destroy it utterly, helped to raise the hopes of people and Prophets alike. It was an evidence that Yahaweh could intervene when He would, and that He would not allow His city and His temple to be violated. But why did He not intervene more fully to deliver them from all their foes and to restore the kingdom of David?

The Prophets sought the explanation of the failure of Yahaweh to intervene more effectively for His people in the wickedness of the people itself; so that the period of calamity and pettiness served, by the interpretation which they put upon it, to develop a constantly higher ethical sense, until, in the time of King Josiah, in the latter part of the seventh century, we have an attempt at a reformation and the restoration of the pure religion of Moses. Inspired with a belief that Yahaweh would now intervene, and interpreting the fall of Assyria as indicating His intervention for the deliverance of His people, Josiah even ventured to oppose himself to the army of the Egyptian Pharaoh, who was seeking to seize the heritage of Assyria west of the Euphrates. He falls in battle. Then comes a period of turbulence and disorder, Egypt and Babylon struggling for the mastery, Jerusalem subject first to one and then to the other, rebelling over and over again because of the firm conviction which seems to have taken possession of the whole people, with the exception of one or two prophets, like Jeremiah and Uriah, that now Yahaweh will surely intervene to deliver His people from bondage and to reëstablish the kingdom of David. It had been a time of strange events, and those events had had their effect in impressing the minds of the people with the idea that the time for divine intervention had arrived. Wild Scythian hordes, sweeping in from the northeast, had overrun Asia Minor and Syria, established themselves at Beisan on the Jordan, and marched along the seacoast through Philistia to the borders of Egypt, ravaging and destroying everywhere. Men felt that there was no longer any great power to hold the nations in check. Assyria was in the throes of a life-and-death struggle. Finally, in 606 B.C., she was destroyed by the armies of the Medes and Babylonians, never to be restored. The kingdom which for centuries had governed the world, resistance to which had seemed hopeless, had utterly disappeared. A new order had begun. Three or four new empires were struggling to rise on the ruins of Assyria, each one striving to grasp the largest possible part of its mighty heritage, but none of these had the prestige, and none seemed to have a tithe of the ruthless might, of Assyria.

These were the conditions at the close of the seventh and the beginning of the sixth century B.C., immediately preceding the destruction of Jerusalem by the Babylonians, which helped to fan the flames of revolt in the doomed city, inspired by a fanatical belief, founded in part on the deliverance in the time of Sennacherib, in its own inviolability. Contact with the nations and experience in her struggles with the world power had taught Israel something of the solidarity of man. On the one side this displayed itself in a syncretism which borrowed the gods and the cults of the conquering or successful peoples; on the other side it showed itself in the broader and higher conception of the relation of Yahaweh to the nations, that He moved and governed all. This prophetic conception, in view of the overwhelming disaster that had befallen the centuries-long irresistible oppressor, Assyria, and the mighty upheaval of the world which seemed to be in progress, took possession of the people. Surely it was the work of Yahaweh. He was casting down the mighty from their seat. He was lord of all the earth. Surely He would save His kingdom. Time after time the Jews rose in rebellion, and even after the city had been once captured by Nebuchadrezzar and the chiefs of the people carried into captivity, in Babylonia itself they preached and planned rebellion, convinced that Yahaweh would intervene on their behalf. At last Jerusalem was captured by Nebuchadrezzar a second time, and the city, the Temple, and the nation were destroyed; and with the destruction of city, Temple, and nation the life of Israel seemed to have been brought to an end.

I have endeavored to trace historical events in building up Israel's conception of the meaning of its own existence, and its belief in the greatness of its destiny. It is not within the scope of this chapter to point out what other forces had been at work to produce the belief in the relation of the nation to Yahaweh and in the character of Yahaweh himself, as the one and only God, which enabled a remnant to remain true, through the period of the Babylonian captivity, to their faith in Yahaweh and in the ultimate victory of His people. The restoration of city and Temple and, to a certain degree, of the national life after the Babylonian captivity, by justifying this faith, solidified and strengthened that remnant in its convictions. It formed a rallying point about which others also gathered, until Jerusalem and its Temple became the center of a large population, dwelling not in Palestine only but in many lands, and cherishing a belief in the peculiar mission of the race to which they belonged, because of the peculiar choice made of Israel by its god, the only God, Yahaweh.

During the Persian and Greek periods the Jews multiplied exceedingly, both in and out of Palestine. They showed a remarkable capacity for business and commerce, and the wealth which they amassed gave them a position of peculiar importance. United by a bond of religion, they formed a nation among nations. For the first time in the history of the world a people had come into existence, united neither by the bond of locality nor that of nationality, but solely by the bond of religion, by the belief that they were the chosen people of Almighty God, whose purpose cannot fail. This belief received its seal and confirmation in the Maccabæan revolt.

Like the Jews the Greeks were everywhere cosmopolitans, with a genius alike for commerce, art, and philosophy, if not religion. Their rule, unlike that of Babylonia or of Persia, was the rule of mind rather than of force. Greek genius rather than Greek arms conquered the peoples with a conquest of civilization. The Jews, who had stubbornly resisted Babylonia and Persia, and maintained their religion and their nationality intact, were for a time in great danger of being conquered not by Greek armies, but by Greek thought and Greek civilization, and incorporated as an integral part in the great Greek world which had come into being, and in which all the nations about had been, or were being, absorbed. Then, in the nick of time, came the attempt of Antiochus Epiphanes to make them Greeks by force, and the Jewish exclusivists underwent a religious persecution, almost the first in the world's history, to compel them to abandon circumcision and their other peculiar customs and to sacrifice to the great Zeus. Mattathias and his sons, Judas first, and afterwards Jonathan and Simon, raised the standard of revolt against the Syrian king. The wonderful success of this insurrection, which resulted in the establishment of Jewish independence and a Jewish kingdom comparable in power with the kingdom of the olden time, reassured the people of the truth of their religion and convinced them that Yahaweh was not a nullity, but a reality; that He had indeed power to intervene, and when He saw fit would exercise that power to overthrow kingdoms and thrones for the sake of His chosen people Israel, and that they were a people apart from the world, separated by peculiar laws and rites, on the maintenance of which depended their singular relation to God.

Further than this we need not follow the external history of Israel for our present purpose. The great events which stand out in that history and which were interpreted by the Hebrews as the evidence of their peculiar relation to their God, Yahaweh, and of His power, and, finally, by the Jews of their peculiar relation to God

Almighty, the God of all the earth, whose chosen people they are, were: (*a*) the deliverance from Egypt in a manner so remarkable as to convince the people of its miraculous character, namely, that it was due to the direct interposition of Deity; (*b*) the conquest of Canaan, culminating in the overthrow of the Philistines and the establishment of the great kingdom of David, which was a triumph of Yahaweh over the gods of the Philistines and all the gods of the countries roundabout, a convincing proof that He was a god more powerful than any of those gods, and an evidence of His purpose regarding Israel, that He, for the sake of His own glory, would make His people the most powerful of all nations; (*c*) the wonderful deliverance of Jerusalem from the Assyrians under Sennacherib, an evidence of His power when roused to wrath by an attack upon His sacred dwelling place, and the consequent belief in the inviolability of Jerusalem; (*d*) the capture and destruction of Jerusalem and its Temple by the Babylonians, and the consequent extinction of the national life of Israel, and the interpretation of this, with reference to the past history of the people, as an evidence not of the powerlessness but of the wrath of God, Yahaweh; (*e*) the restoration of the Temple and the city after a long period of desolation, and the gradual rehabilitation of the Jews, an evidence of the undying character of God, Yahaweh, and consequently of His people; (*f*) the overthrow of the king who undertook to persecute the worshipers of God, Yahaweh, and the reëstablishment of a powerful Jewish kingdom, an evidence that God had not forgotten His people and could intervene to save against any power, however great, for He is God Almighty, and the Jews are His chosen people.

CHAPTER VII

DEVELOPMENT OF THE PRIESTHOOD

Priesthood among the primitive Hebrews, as pointed out in the third chapter, consisted primarily in the guardianship of a shrine and of its sacred contents. It has also been pointed out that, in addition to this, the primitive priests were seers,[1] or oracle men. Moses seems to have accepted these functions of the priesthood, which he found already in existence. The center of religious worship was the Ark, the representation of deity. It was a function of the priests to guard this Ark, but not the only function. Moses, himself a priest, was not the guardian of the Ark. This duty was assigned to Joshua. Our earliest historical documents show us the Ark, after the occupation of Canaan, housed in a sanctuary at Shiloh. But although having thus a local habitation, it continued, at least until the time of Solomon, to go out to battle with the Israelites, and on such occasions its guardian went with it. The guardian priests of the Ark, after the settlement in Canaan, were Eli and his sons, descendants of Phinehas, the son of Aaron (1 Sam. i ff.). But the guardianship of the Ark was not confined to this one family. Samuel, an Ephraimite, when dedicated by his mother to the service of God, is admitted, like Joshua, into the circle of the guardians of the Ark, and sleeps in the sanctuary (1 Sam. iii). When the Ark comes to Kiriath-jearim, after its sojourn in the country of the Philistines, a guardian from the people

---

[1] Among the Arabians the word *kahin*, Hebrew *kohen*, designates not a priest, but a seer, or diviner. As Wellhausen has pointed out, however, in the primitive conception both priest and seer were included under the *kahin*. Later, among the Arabians, a differentiation took place and the term *kahin* was applied only to the seer. We may, therefore, assume that the Hebrew *kohen* primarily corresponded in sense as in form to the Arabic *kahin*, and indicated both the guardian of the shrine, that is, the priest, and also the seer, or diviner; or, in other words, that the primitive priest combined in himself both functions.

of that place is at once set apart, or dedicated, for the service of
the Ark (1 Sam. vii). At the outset the Ark was the sole sanctuary of
the Israelites, and its guardians were, therefore, the priests *par excellence.* But with the occupation of Canaan other sanctuaries sprang
up or were adopted by the Israelites from the Canaanites, and here
and there an ephod was established. Wherever such a sanctuary or
ephod existed, we find guardians of the shrine and interpreters of
the oracles. So, in the story of Micah (Jud. xvii), when he has
made himself an ephod, and a house of God, or shrine, to contain
this ephod, he makes one of his sons a priest as the guardian of
the shrine and its ephod. Later the post is assigned to a Levite
whose "hand he fills," a technical designation for the appointment
of a priest.[1] At Nob we find (1 Sam. xxi–xxii) an ephod guarded
not by a single priest or guardian, as in the case of Micah's house
of God, but by a guild of priests, sons of Eli, the same who had
guarded the Ark at Shiloh.

The words which in ritualistic use came to designate the service
of the priests and Levites, namely, *shereth*, " to serve," and *shamar*,
" to guard," are in themselves evidences of this original conception
connected with the office of priest in the earlier ritual.

But in addition to the guardianship of the sanctuary, the office of
the priest, as indicated in the story of Micah and his priest, and in
the account of the destruction of the priests of Nob, was, further,
to consult the oracles, and to give *torah*, " the decision." This was
the especial function of Moses. In the early Israelite narrative,
E (Ex. xviii), the people are represented as coming to Moses to
inquire of God. The same function of the priest is represented in
the first law code (Ex. xxii, 7 ff.): "If a man deliver unto his
neighbor money or stuff to keep, and it be stolen out of the man's
house, . . . then the master of the house shall come near unto God to
see whether he have not put his hand unto his neighbor's goods."[2]

---

[1] Kings xiii, 33; Lev. viii, 33.

[2] There are similar provisions in the Code of Hammurapi for appeal to the god or
gods in cases where evidence cannot be obtained or is conflicting. Cf. for example
§§ 9, 23, 107. This appeal to the deity for decision in case of lack of evidence is in
principle one with the representation in both the Hebrew and Babylonian legal codes
of the deity as the original giver of the law. So in Hebrew Moses is represented as

In any case of trespass, if there is a dispute, both parties shall come before God, and he whom God condemns shall pay double unto his neighbor. The priest was the interpreter of God to the people in questions of dispute between neighbors, to determine suspected cases of theft, when a man was at a loss what course to pursue, whether to undertake an enterprise, etc.[1] It was also his function to give the instruction, or *torah*, of God in cases of larger importance, affecting the people as a whole; as, for instance, to determine the cause of some calamity which had befallen the people,[2] to point out what offense had been committed against the deity and how the deity might be appeased. In this function of the priest lay the possibility of both ethical and ritual development: of the latter, in so far as the offense committed might be conceived of as the neglect of duties or obligations towards the deity in the line of ritual observance; of the former, in so far as the offense might be conceived of as consisting in a breach of moral law.

The priest was consulted, or rather through the priest God was consulted, in regard to the choice of a king (1 Sam. x, 17 ff.). The earliest historical documents which have come down to us, in the Book of Samuel, show us Saul inquiring of God through the priest, before the Ark, to determine whether he should join battle with the Philistines or not (1 Sam. xiv, 18). David was accompanied by a priest, Abiathar, whose function it was to cast lots before Yahaweh to determine whether the result of the enterprise to be undertaken or of the battle to be fought would be favorable or not.[3] These lots were designated Urim and Thummim.[4] They might be cast only by the priest, who alone had the power of consulting Yahaweh in this manner. At times no answer was given.[5]

That this function of the priest was primitive, antedating the period of Moses, we may assume from comparison with Arabian

going to God in Sinai and receiving from Him tables of laws; and on the great stele containing Hammurapi's code Hammurapi is similarly represented as standing before Shamash to receive his guidance in giving a law unto his people. See also the epilogue, where he speaks of Shamash as endowing him with justice.

[1] 1 Sam. xxii, 10.   [2] 1 Sam. xiv, 41 ff.

[3] 1 Sam. xxiii, 9 ff.; xxx, 7 ff.; 2 Sam. ii, 1.

[4] Deut. xxxiii, 8. For the method of use of these sacred lots, consult 1 Sam. xiv, 41, text emended after LXX.   [5] 1 Sam. xxviii, 6.

antiquity. There also we have a consultation of lots, for which the word used is *istiḳsam*, the same root which appears in the Hebrew *ḳesem*, "lot." [1] In classical Hebrew, however, this word is used not for the priestly consultation of the lots, but in reference to magic, an evidence of the moral development among the Hebrews, which ultimately relegated the lot-casting, once the function of the priest, to the illicit practices of the magicians.

But lot-casting was not the only method in which the priest gave *torah*. The lots, Urim and Thummim, were used to give an answer in cases of doubt for which no precedent existed, such as the determination of the outcome of an expedition or the result of a battle, the whereabouts of stolen goods, the cause of calamity befalling the nation or the individual. But in the nature of the case, as a result of experience and practice, a tradition would tend to become established regarding those things, for instance, which produce calamity or welfare, which excite the wrath or the favor of the deity; so that ultimately the questions would be answered not by lot, but in accordance with certain laws or principles which were the tradition of the sanctuary and its priests. The declaration and explanation of these laws and principles becomes *torah*, which it is the priest's function to give to the people who come to inquire of him. This form of *torah* was known technically in Hebrew use as judgments (*mishpaṭim*), the decision of new cases according to principles and traditions which had become established. Besides the *mishpaṭim* there were also statutes (*huḳḳim*), written laws, like the Decalogue, and later the Book of the Covenant (Ex. xxi–xxiii, xxxiv) and other similar legislation. These statutes were, at the outset at least, the work of priests, who were also, to a great extent certainly, their conservators and expounders. The statutes were in their turn the foundation of further judgments, and they of new statutes, until we get the mass of legislation, ritual and moral, which constitutes the *torah* of the post-exilic period, the latest part of which is to-day commonly designated as the Priestly Code. [2]

---

[1] See above, p. 74.

[2] The history of Babylonian legislation is similar. So Johns says:

The Code of Hammurabi is also a compilation. He did not invent his laws. Phrases found in them appear in contracts before his time. Doubtless he did enact some fresh laws.

It has already been said that in Israel priests, guardians of shrines, were not at the outset chosen from one family only, and the same is true of priests, the expounders of the *torah*. In the seventeenth chapter of Judges we have the story of the Ephraimite, Micah, who built a house of God and put in it an ephod and *teraphim*. He appointed his own son to be the priest in this shrine and to give the *torah* by casting lots by the ephod. Similarly David appointed his own sons as priests,[1] and Solomon appointed the son of the prophet Nathan.[2] But while priests might be thus chosen from any family or tribe, from the outset the Levites were regarded as having a peculiar capacity for the exercise of the priestly function. In the story referred to above, Micah, when a wandering Levite from Judah comes to him, "fills his hand" that he may become priest in his house of God instead of his own son. The Levite has an hereditary claim upon the priesthood, although not an exclusive claim, so that where the Levite may be obtained he is preferred. He, better than any other, can consult God and give His *torah*. So when the Danites find that a Levite, the grandson of Moses, is officiating in Micah's shrine, they are eager to secure him for their priest, and he becomes the ancestor of the Levitical priesthood of the temple of Dan.

But who were these Levites who possessed some sort of hereditary claim to the priesthood, and for what reason did they possess such a claim? In the earliest accounts which have come down to us the Levites are reckoned as one of the tribes of Israel, and Levi, their tribal father, is represented as one of the twelve sons of Jacob. In the thirty-fourth chapter of Genesis, Levi and Simeon are represented as taking a cruel and treacherous vengeance on the inhabitants of Shechem because of the treatment of their sister Dinah by the prince of that place. In the ancient poem, the Blessings of Jacob, in the forty-ninth chapter of Genesis, Simeon

---

But he built for the most part on other men's foundations. The decisions already passed by the judges had made men ready to accept as "right" what was now made "law." But the question is only carried back a stage further. Did not these judges decide according to law? In some cases we know they did, for we have the law before them. (*Babylonian and Assyrian Laws, Contracts and Letters*, p. 40.)

[1] 2 Sam. viii, 18.
[2] 1 Kings iv, 5.

and Levi are represented as guilty of violence and outrages abhorrent to the conscience of Israel as a whole, as a result of which they were divided in Jacob and scattered in Israel. These two allusions to Simeon and Levi are generally brought into connection, and it is supposed that it was in some way owing to their treachery and violence toward the Canaanites that they lost their existence as tribes.[1]

But however we explain Genesis xxxiv, it is evident from Genesis xlix that, according to the tradition prevalent in the ninth century B.C., Levi had once existed as a tribe, closely allied to Simeon, of the same character as the other tribes of Israel, and that some cruel and treacherous action of the two tribes, apparently in the wars of conquest, had resulted in their destruction as tribes.

At a later date we find the word "Levite" used as the designation of a priest. This is the use of the word in the poem commonly known as the Song of Moses (Deut. xxxiii), where the Levites are the priest tribe, distinguished by the Urim and Thummim. In the seventh century, as we learn from the main body of the book of Deuteronomy, "Levites" and "priests" were synonymous terms, and by a comparison of the books of Kings and Deuteronomy we learn that, at that time, "Levites" was the term applied both to the priests officiating at the Temple of Yahaweh at Jerusalem and also to the priests officiating at the various high places and shrines throughout the country.[2] We may, perhaps, find in the story of Micah's Levite a link between the two uses of the word "Levite," namely, as the designation of a tribe of Israel, and as the designation of priests in general. This Levite was a grandson of Moses.[3] Now

[1] According to an interpretation proposed by some writers, we have in the thirty-fourth chapter of Genesis a tradition of the first attempt of the Israelites to occupy Canaan west of the Jordan. Simeon and Levi, with the sub-tribe Dinah, were the first invaders, but owing to some peculiarly treacherous and cruel dealing toward the Canaanites of Shechem, the people of the land rose against them and destroyed them. Cf. Peters, *Early Hebrew Story*, pp. 66 ff.

[2] In Ex. iv, 14, a passage of uncertain date, probably later than JE and earlier than P, "the Levite," applied to Aaron, is generally regarded as equal to "the priest." It is worthy of notice that the special function of the priest in the passage of JE in which these verses are inserted is to impart instruction in the ways of Yahaweh, so that the priest ought to be eloquent.

[3] Jud. xviii, 30.

Moses and his brother Aaron are represented in the earliest narratives as Levites. Moses was adopted by marriage into the family of Jethro, an hereditary priestly family such as existed here and there among the Arabs, and later his brother Aaron was incorporated into the priestly guild,[1] if one may use such an expression. Thus Levites became the priests of Yahaweh's shrine, and a priestly family in whom was supposed to inhere a peculiar capacity for interpreting the oracles, that is, the *torah* of Yahaweh. Later, the tribe of Levi as such having ceased to exist, the name attached itself only to this family, or guild, of priests; they were the Levites. At the outset the priests of Yahaweh officiated in connection with the Ark only, and the service of the Ark, the special shrine of Israel, was in the charge of the Levites. Into the service of the Ark were admitted, as we have seen, non-Levites, like Samuel, and in Saul's time the number of the "sons of Eli" is reported as eighty-six or eighty-seven priests.[2] But whether these priests were, in the literal sense, sons of Eli, Levites by blood, or not, they were all of his family in a real and proper sense, whether by blood or marriage or adoption.

After entering Palestine, the Hebrews, as we have seen, adopted many of the holy places and shrines of the country and also created new shrines of their own, like the shrine of Micah so often referred to, and the shrine of the tribe of Dan. All these required priests. Where Levites, members of the family of Moses, Aaron, and their kinsmen, could be obtained, these, as already pointed out, seem to have been preferred, as supposed to possess a peculiar capacity for interpreting the oracles of God. But it is also clear, from the story of Micah, that Levites could not always, or probably even generally, be obtained. Others must, therefore, be appointed priests, and, in view of the manner in which the Hebrews adopted Canaanite rites and forms in connection with the worship of their sanctuaries, we may fairly assume not only that in some cases they set up as priests non-Levitical Hebrews but also that they adopted the Canaanite priests of the shrines together with the shrines at which they served. Of the latter, however, we have no direct evidence. With its capture by the Philistines, the Ark sank

---

[1] Ex. xviii, 12. [2] 1 Sam. xxii, 18 f.

for a time into insignificance, and the sons of Eli set up at Nob an ephod, by which they cast the sacred lots and gave *torah*. But with the establishment of the kingdom of David the Ark became again the special shrine and sanctuary of Israel and its priests *the* priests of Yahaweh. These priests, as we have seen, were of the family of Levi,[1] and the importance of the Levite priests of the Temple of Yahaweh at Jerusalem and the desire to imitate or adopt the usages of that Temple, together with the traditional importance of the Levites in the foundation of the religion of Israel and the Ark worship from Moses to Eli, resulting in the preference, already pointed out, for Levites as priests, wherever they could be obtained, seems to have led to the adoption of the term " Levite " as a general designation of the priesthood of Yahaweh. Accordingly "priests" (*kohenim*) and " Levites " became synonymous terms, and are so used in the Book of Deuteronomy in the seventh century B.C.[2]

The assumption above made that foreign elements were early incorporated in the Levitical priesthood is in principle supported by the later history of the Levites. The attendants and servants in the Temple of Solomon were slaves or the descendants of slaves given for that purpose (*nethinim*); even the singers and guards were not Levites.[3]

Until the Captivity the Levite priests in the Temple of Yahaweh at Jerusalem were the teachers of the *torah* and the sacrificers, having under them, for the service of the Temple, slaves and descendants of slaves, foreign guards, musicians, singing women, and the like, who were non-Levites. At the time of the return from the Captivity, we still find the *nethinim* and singers distinguished

---

1 According to J, Levites were recognized as having an exclusive right to the priesthood of the Ark (Ex. xxxii, 25-29; Deut. xxxiii, 8-10). Bacon plausibly suggests that in Numbers xvi there is in the narrative of J a reflection of a contest between the *nethinim*, or foreign guards, and the Levites, in which the prerogative of the latter is asserted. The priestly narrative in that chapter represents the contest as one between Aaron the priest and the Levites.

2 In the main this is the view of the origin of the Levites maintained by Nowack (*Hebräische Archäologie*) and other recent writers. De Lagarde held that the Levites were originally Egyptians who attached (*Levi* = "attached" or "bound") themselves to the Hebrews, like Moses or Aaron, and who were by their training better fitted than native Hebrews to lead an ignorant and barbarous people.

3 Cf. Josh. ix, 22-27.

from the Levites.[1] At this period the name "priest" (*kohen*) was confined to the descendants of the priests of the Temple of Yahaweh at Jerusalem. These were Levites by descent; but there were also Levites who were not priests, namely, the descendants of the priests who had served at "high places," that is, at shrines to Yahaweh other than the Temple at Jerusalem. These had a quasi-priestly character which entitled them to be connected with the sanctuary and to perform certain functions there. At a later period Levites, singers, and *nethinim* were all united, and all who served in the Temple in any capacity, whatever their descent or origin, came to be reckoned as Levites, as part of whom and yet distinct from whom, alone entitled to sacrifice, stood out the *kohenim*, or priests, descendants of the priests of the preëxilic Jerusalem Temple, of the family of Zadok, the descendant of Aaron.

As already stated, the Israelite shrine *par excellence* was, from the outset, the Ark, whose priests were Levites, although after the occupation of Canaan other shrines were adopted or sprang up in various parts of the country. The Ark was for some time located in a house, or temple, at Shiloh. Finally, in the time of Eli and Samuel, it was captured and carried off by the Philistines. This seems to have destroyed for the moment its prestige, and although, according to the account in the Book of Samuel, it was restored by the Philistines to the Israelites, it was allowed to remain comparatively neglected and forgotten at Kiriath-jearim during the whole of the reign of Saul. When David finally succeeded in uniting all Israel in one kingdom, with Jerusalem as its capital, he sought out once more the ancient shrine, which had been the symbol and the means of religious unity in the past. With pomp and merrymaking he brought the Ark to Jerusalem and set it up as a national shrine. Before this henceforward his priests were to cast their lots and inquire the will of Yahaweh. With this re-establishment of the Ark as the royal and national shrine went hand in hand the organization of a priesthood for that shrine. It was desirable that the service of the Ark should correspond to the dignity of the kingdom and its king. The priests of this shrine

[1] Ezra ii, 58, 70; vii, 7; etc.

were officers of the court and are recorded as such in the lists.[1]
We find mentioned as priests in David's lists Abiathar, son of
Ahimelech, a descendant of Eli and therefore a Levite; Zadok,
who was certainly not a descendant of Eli; and the sons of David.
David himself also exercised certain priestly functions, or at least
functions which were later considered priestly. In Solomon's first
list the priests are Zadok, Abiathar, and Zabud, son of Nathan, the
latter of whom is described as a sort of private chaplain to the king.
Solomon also himself exercised priestly functions, blessing the people
and sacrificing,[2] apparently as part of his royal prerogative.

But Solomon advanced much further than his father in the
organization both of the kingdom and of the priesthood. The construction of a royal temple, connected with the royal residence,
involved both a more elaborate ritual and also a larger and better
organized priesthood. The necessary tendency of such an organization was toward the creation of a hierarchy with one head, and
grades of priests according to the requirements and functions of
the service, as in the civil organization of the kingdom; and with
Solomon we come in fact to the beginning of the hierarchy.
Abiathar was early deposed from his position as coördinate priest,
and Zadok recognized as *the* priest, the head of the Temple system. As already pointed out, it was his descendants only (understanding descendants presumably in the same sense in which we
have understood descendants of the Levitical families of Moses
and Aaron) who, at a later time, were recognized as priests of
Yahaweh's Temple at Jerusalem. Later we find the head priest of
the Temple at Jerusalem designated as the High Priest,[3] but it is
not until the post-exilic period that we find the elaborate hierarchical system in its full development, with a careful assignment in
written law of the functions of each of its members.

The erection of the Ark and its shrine in Jerusalem under David
and still more the building of the Temple under Solomon were steps
of great importance toward the centralization of worship; but that
end was still far from being attained under Solomon or his successors for three centuries and more. Numerous shrines, high places,

---

[1] 2 Sam. viii; 1 Kings iv.   [2] 1 Kings viii.   [3] 2 Kings xxii, 8.

and the like continued to exist throughout the country, some of them, like Shechem, Bethel, Dan, and Beersheba, possessing more than a local sanctity, so that people from great distances made pilgrimages thither for the annual feast. As it was with the question of centralization, so it was with the organization of the priesthood and the acquisition of exclusive claims by the priesthood of the Jerusalem Temple. So long as these other shrines continued to be legitimate places of worship, so long the priests of those shrines must continue to be regarded as legitimate priests, however inferior in wealth and prestige to the priesthood of the Temple at Jerusalem.

Attention has already been called to the fact that the priests of the Temple at Jerusalem were court appointees. As such they enjoyed peculiar rights and privileges, but on the other hand they were subject in a peculiar sense to the king's orders. The king was the head of the hierarchy, and when present, at least on great occasions, officiated as the sacrificer.[1] The priests were subject to his orders, even in the matter of ritual.[2] So we find King Ahaz (734 B.C.) commanding that the old altar should be removed and a new one put in its place, patterned after an Assyrian altar which he had seen at Damascus.[3] But not only this, the kings even introduced foreign cults into the Temple at their pleasure.[4] But with all the arbitrary power which they possessed and exercised, they never interfered with the succession of the priesthood established by Solomon in the house of Zadok, and this permanency of tenure, which gradually crystallized into dogma, was a very important factor in the development of a powerful priesthood in the Temple of Yahaweh at Jerusalem. Nor, while exercising the priestly functions of blessing and sacrificing, do the kings seem ever to have encroached upon the more primitive priestly prerogatives of casting the lots before Yahaweh and giving *torah*, although with the development of the civil organization much of the law-making and law-interpreting function of necessity passed into their hands

---

[1] 2 Kings xvi, 12 f.
[2] Similar conditions evidently prevailed at the temple at Bethel, in Israel (cf. Amos vii, 13).
[3] 2 Kings xvi, 10 ff.
[4] 2 Kings xviii, 4 ; xxi, 5 ; xxiii, 4 ff.

or that of their secular appointees. What part the priesthood played in the political life of the state, or on occasion in casting out foreign cults in favor of the worship of Yahaweh, we see in the story of the overthrow of Athaliah, or in the reforms of Josiah.[1]

Now the tendency of a priesthood is to gather into its own hands constantly more privileges, and the more firmly the priesthood is established, the greater its claims are likely to become. The priesthood of the Jerusalem Temple was no exception to this rule, and, in the matter of sacrifice, which ultimately became the especial function of the priesthood, we can trace a steady growth of privileges and prerogatives on the part of the priests as over against the people, however subservient they may have been to the king as supreme head of church and state alike.[2]

At the outset sacrifice was not a priestly function, or at least not an exclusively priestly function. Among the heathen Arabs, it is true, there were certain occasions on which a priest sacrificed, and it may perhaps be said that the beginning of sacrifice as a priestly function may on that ground be traced to the pre-Mosaic era. But these beginnings seem to have received no further development until after the occupation of Canaan. On their entrance into Canaan the Hebrews found, in some places certainly, an organized priesthood in possession of established local shrines, performing sacrifice in connection with the worship of the deity at those shrines. Sacrifice among the Canaanites, at least as a rule, no longer consisted merely in killing the animal, offering the blood to God, and then feasting upon the remainder. A portion of the

---

[1] 2 Kings xi, xxiii.

[2] 2 Chronicles xxvi, 16 ff., records a conflict between King Uzziah (750 B.C.) and the priests. The king goes into the sanctuary to burn incense, and is withstood by the priests, who claim the sole right to enter the sanctuary. In consequence of this impiety the king is smitten with leprosy. This does not, apparently, represent a true tradition of a conflict between king and priests, but is an attempt to find an explanation for the fact, recorded in 2 Kings xv, 5, that Uzziah, there described as a good king, became a leper. Leprosy was a punishment from God for some heinous wickedness, and characteristically the Chronicler looks for the cause of the punishment in a breach of the ritual law affecting the sanctuary. The suggestion for the particular form of breach of ritual law was given by the narrative in the Priestly Code (Num. xvi), which enforces the doctrine of the exclusively priestly character of the function of burning incense before the Lord.

animal offered was given to the gods, and the priests received a share of the flesh of the sacrifice.

As the Hebrews adopted the Canaanite shrines, so, as already pointed out, they also adopted much of the Canaanite ritual and the Canaanite sacrificial practices, and from the account of the sanctuary at Shiloh in the early days and the feasts and sacrifices connected with it, described in 1 Samuel i, 11, we see that priests soon began to be especially connected, at that shrine at least, with sacrifice, and to receive their portion of the animal sacrificed, outside of the general meal of which the man's family and friends partook. In the controversy between the sons of Eli and the people regarding the portion of the sacrifice which should belong to the priest, we see the assumption by the priesthood of more privileges and the beginning of the development of an unorganized into an organized system. But while at this early date we find the priests claiming special rights in relation to sacrifice, it is clear that for a long time after the conquest of Canaan, and even after the establishment of the Temple at Jerusalem, with its organized priesthood, they were not the only sacrificers. In the Book of Judges various heroes sacrifice; in the books of Samuel and Kings, Saul, David, Adonijah, and Solomon offer sacrifices, and there are, further, family sacrifices [1] at which, apparently, the head of the family was the sacrificer. Even in the post-exilic period we have in the Passover a remnant of the earlier use, according to which any man, but especially the family head, might sacrifice.

But little by little the priests arrogated to themselves the right to sacrifice, until it became first a priestly function and finally *the* priestly function, the perquisites connected with which, as carefully prescribed in the Priestly Code in Leviticus and Numbers, are in striking contrast with the modest portion assigned to the priest in the early days of Shiloh. This development of the priestly function of sacrifice (with which may be mentioned in this connection the prerogatives of burning incense, blessing the people, and finally of access to the most sacred precincts) was greatly facilitated first by the adoption of Canaanite ideas and Canaanite uses; secondly by

[1] 1 Sam. xx, 29.

the establishment of settled sanctuaries and the organization of a priesthood to minister at those sanctuaries, and especially by the establishment of the Temple at Jerusalem and the organization of its priesthood, a process which went hand in hand with the social and civil development of the people. At such shrines, and especially at the royal temples, it was impossible that there should be the same spontaneous, independent action as had characterized the earlier times. It was necessary to regulate and define the action of the people and to delegate special officers to perform, under fixed rules, that which had originally been done by anyone without rule. As sacrifice was the essential feature of worship, it was inevitable that it should become the especial subject of regulation, and ultimately be taken entirely into their own hands by the appointed officers, that is, the priests. Finally, the substitution for the numerous shrines scattered throughout the country of one shrine at Jerusalem, in which all worship was to be centered, completed, or almost completed, the process of transferring sacrifice from family and clan heads to the priesthood, making the latter the sole sacrificers, and by that fact making sacrifice *the* function of the priesthood, as we find it in the Priestly Code.

But while priests thus became the sacrificers and sacrifice became ever a more important function of the priesthood, until finally it became *the* function of that priesthood, to the end of the preëxilic period the priests continued to be interpreters of the *torah* and as such were regarded as the moral leaders of the people. So Hosea (iv, 1 ff.) mentions them as the instructors in a *torah* which forbids lying, stealing, murder, and adultery. A little later Micah rebukes them for imparting the *torah* to the people only for money (Mic. iii, 11). A century later Jeremiah still speaks of moral instruction as a fundamental function of the priesthood (Jer. xviii, 18), and even in the exilic period the same view finds expression (Ezek. vii, 26; Lam. ii, 9).

To sum up the history and the functions of the priesthood in the preëxilic period: At the outset the priests were guardians of the shrines, and the especial and highest function of the priesthood was the interpretation of God to the people. This interpretation was partly by the casting of lots before the Ark or by an ephod, partly by the conservation and interpretation of statutes (such as the original Decalogue, at a later date the Book of the Covenant, Deuteronomy, etc.), precedents, usages, and customs. The first function, that of guarding the shrines, particularly the Temple of Yahaweh at Jerusalem, was in time intrusted to menials, and ultimately, in the post-exilic period, to a secondary and inferior order, known as Levites, in distinction from the priests proper, or *kohenim*. The interpretation of God to the people remained, up to the Exile, a function of the priesthood; but the interpretation by oracles, the Urim and Thummim, which had been at the outset regarded as the most especial and characteristic function of the priesthood, gradually fell into abeyance, the interpretation in the form which we more especially know as *torah* — by statutes, judgments, and the like — taking its place. But while this interpretation of God continued to be a function of the priesthood, with the development of an organized civil system, with judges and courts, the province of that interpretation became more limited. The Prophets also, from the ninth century on, usurped a considerable part of the priestly function of interpreting God to the people, as that interpretation affected the moral law. They became especially the exponents of moral righteousness to the people. The priests, on the other hand, were becoming more and more the exponents of the ceremonial law, — the usages, customs, ceremonies, and external obligations, — this development going hand in hand with the increasing recognition of sacrifice as the priestly function. Beginning with the adoption of settled shrines after the occupation of Canaan, and the development of an organized priesthood, the duty and right of sacrifice fell more and more to the priesthood, until finally, with the abolition of local shrines, in the reformation of King Josiah toward the close of the seventh century B.C., and the centralization of all sacrifice at the Temple at Jerusalem, the Levitical priests became the only sacrificers, and sacrifice the characteristic function of the priesthood.

CHAPTER VIII

DEVELOPMENT OF RITUAL

The history of ritual runs parallel with the history of the priesthood. The two are bound together. In the later period priests developed the ritual, but at the outset it was ritual which developed the priesthood. Priests came into existence because there was a ritual which required some one to carry it on and to interpret it.

Ritual is primarily the etiquette of man in his relation to deity, but since all things are governed and controlled by deity, the etiquette of man in his dealings with his fellow men, or rather the etiquette which he observes in the transaction of all the concerns of his life, constitutes a part of the ritual which the deity requires of him, and upon the observance of which depends his welfare or calamity. In its broader sense, therefore, ritual concerns not merely the direct worship of God, but all man's actions. A man may offend the deity by the neglect of the proper forms in the ordinary everyday affairs of his life, as a huntsman or a herdsman, in his agricultural pursuits, in his domestic relations, and even in the minute personal affairs of the satisfaction of the needs and requirements of his body. That he has so offended the deity is evinced by the calamity which befalls him, the direct result of the wrath of God. His method of transacting his daily avocations becomes, therefore, a part of the man's relation to the deity and is governed by ritual rules. This is best seen in the later development of Jewish legalism ; it is manifested to a lesser extent in the legislation of the Priestly Code ; but something of it we see at every stage of the development of the religion of Israel. Some such ritual existed in the most primitive times, but apparently in an unformulated, undeveloped condition, and it is not easy to determine what the Hebrews brought with them into Canaan and what was borrowed or developed there. We shall in this chapter discuss, in general, ritual in its primary sense only, as the etiquette governing the direct worship and service of God.

There was at the very outset a ritual of feasts, since, as we have seen in a former chapter, the Hebrews in the desert period certainly celebrated a spring and an autumnal feast. There was a ritual for consulting the oracles of God; there was a ritual governing the relations of men with the evil spirits about them, — the ritual which expresses itself ultimately in magical rites, — and above all there was a ritual of sacrifice. But everything was loose and unformulated, and we can find only traces of this primitive ritual in certain general foundation principles affecting the later development, with here and there some survival of detail. The real development of what we commonly understand as ritual, formulated ritual, commenced after the occupation of Canaan by the Israelites.

Now ritual was, above all, connected with sacrifice, because sacrifice was the very kernel of religion. The earliest form of sacrifice, as pointed out in a former chapter, consisted of the pouring out of the blood to the deity, the sacrificer with his family and friends consuming the flesh, the object of the sacrifice being to establish or reëstablish blood relationship. But in Canaan another stage of sacrificial use had been reached — the offering of a gift to the deity just as a gift was offered to a king or great man. The god was entitled to tribute. Commonly this sacrificial tribute, or gift, was combined with the other idea of a feasting with the deity; but, whereas in the primitive Hebrew use the blood only was given to the god, here a portion of the sacrificial food was given to the god to be consumed by fire on his altar. Since this idea of tribute was connected with the idea of the sacrificial feast, the gift to the god consisted of flesh, blood, oil, and wine, which men used in their feasts. The Hebrews adopted this new conception and method of sacrifice, as also the sacrificial materials derived from agricultural life; but to the end the old primitive idea of sacrifice was retained, in that the giving of the blood to God continued to be the central act of sacrifice, and animal sacrifice the perfect sacrifice, bread, oil, and wine being subsidiary only. Attention has already been called to the survival, as late as the time of Saul, of the primitive form of sacrifice — the pouring out of the blood of the animal slain on or by a stone, which stone was the representative of deity.[1] Similar in conception to this pouring out of blood on or by the stone was the anointing of a stone with oil, which we found in the tradition of the sanctuary at Bethel in the story of Jacob (Gen. xxiii, 18). Here the stone, or *mazzebah*, anointed with oil, was the representative of deity, with whom the worshiper sought to enter into the blood relationship. In another place (Gen. xxxv, 14) we have, with the same significance, the pouring of wine upon the stone. The use of oil in consecration was a modification, under agricultural conditions, of the primitive use of blood. Next to the blood the fat was the most sacred part of the animal, as representing peculiarly the life. So in Canaan, in the sacrificial use, from the earliest times onward, we find the fat not eaten by the worshipers, but given as the portion of the deity, to be consumed in fire upon the altar. Oil, as vegetable fat, came to have the same general significance.[2]

But while we find, in the traditions of the sanctuary at Bethel, indications of the separate use of oil and wine as substitutes for blood in the *mazzebah* cult, in the regular ritual, as we are able to trace it in the Biblical records, neither wine nor oil was used independently. Oil was used in the anointing of persons as an instrument of consecration, a use connected with the older sacrificial anointing of the stone; but in what we ordinarily understand under the term "sacrifice," it was used only as mixed with meal in the making of bread and cakes. Wine is used as a libation, constituting a part of the feast, but not as a separate offering.

In the early documents in the Book of Samuel there are two instances of a libation of water constituting a sacrifice to the deity, namely, 1 Samuel vii, 6, and 2 Samuel xxiii, 16. The principle here was the same as in the libations of blood, oil, and wine, the consecration to the deity of something which represented life. Water is the

---

[1] Cf. 1 Sam. xiv, 32 ff.

[2] For burning of fat at the very earliest times, cf. 1 Sam. ii. For later use, cf. the Priestly Code. For the relation of blood and wine, cf. not merely the expression "blood of the grapes," which is frequent, but also Ps. xvi. 4 "their drink offerings of blood," etc.

life-giving element which brings life to the ground, having a character similar to blood and, therefore, constituting a proper sacrifice to the deity. Of this use of libations of water we find no trace in the later ritual codes contained in the Bible, but from the Talmud we learn that it continued to constitute, even after the commencement of the Christian era, a feature in the celebration of the Feast of Tabernacles.[1] These various instances of libations of blood, wine, oil, and water constitute satisfactory evidence that, in the earlier period, after the occupation of Canaan, this form of sacrifice continued in common use. It would seem also that its use was continued in Israel after it ceased to be customary in Judah. At what period it gave way altogether to the idea of a feasting with God, in which the deity should receive a part of the flesh, bread, etc. of the feast offered by fire upon the altar, we cannot certainly say. The idea of feasting as a part of the sacrifice was, as already pointed out, primitive.

That which is new in the sacrificial customs which began to formulate themselves in Canaan was the conception of a gift, or tribute, to God in connection with this feasting. The names used for sacrifice, *minchah* and *korban*, indicate clearly this conception of a gift to God, or tribute. This food tribute to God was prepared as for the use of men. So the meat offerings were accompanied by meal offerings, not presented to God raw, but cooked, being roasted, boiled, or baked with oil, in the form of bread or cakes.[2] In Deuteronomy sacrifice is still called a making-merry or an eating and drinking before Yahaweh, and even in the Priestly Code (Lev. iii, 11) the fact that God partook of the feast with His worshipers is recognized in the name "food of Yahaweh."

The early ritual in Canaan was simple and largely unformulated. We have in the first few chapters of Samuel a picture of the ritual practices at the national shrine at Shiloh, where Yahaweh was worshiped in the Ark. Once in the year it was the custom to make *haj*, or pilgrimage, to this shrine. The priests of the shrine killed

---

[1] John vii, 37, seems to be a corroboration from the New Testament of the Talmudic statement of the use of libations of water on the last day of the Feast of Tabernacles.   [2] Cf. Lev. ii. The ritual of this code is in its essence old.

the victims, and poured out the blood, presumably at or on the *mazzebah*. The fat was burned on the altar as Yahaweh's portion, and the remainder of the flesh was put in the pot to be boiled for the feast of the sacrificer and his party. While it was boiling, the priest's servant came with a three-pronged fleshhook and plunged it into the pot; what he brought up was the priest's perquisite. The remainder was eaten by the sacrificer and his party with much merrymaking. Wine and meal were furnished also for the sacrificial meal, and apparently part of these was offered to Yahaweh. There was dancing, not infrequently drunkenness, and sometimes licentiousness in connection with these sacrificial feasts. So much we gather from the earliest accounts of the annual festivals at Shiloh.[1] The offerings presented at this feast were of a twofold character, the regular tribute, or payment to Yahaweh of the increase of flocks and herds, and the special sacrifices in fulfillment of vows, for deliverance from sickness or danger, for children, etc. The primitive narrative in 1 Samuel ii shows us a development of priestly prerogative corresponding with a development of ritual details. For the chance thrust into the pot is soon substituted the allotment to the priest of a certain specified portion of the sacrificial victim as soon as it is slain. This is condemned by the writer as an innovation on the older Israelite use practiced at Shiloh.

Besides these offerings at the national sanctuary, there were occasional sacrifices on various occasions and for various purposes at numerous shrines and holy places, under trees, at rocks and high places, at springs and wells, in fulfillment of vows and the like.[2] Inasmuch as all flesh eating was connected with sacrifice, it was inevitable that the people should have such shrines. In the early literature we have abundant evidence of the existence of such shrines and such methods of sacrifice. So Gideon sacrifices under a tree, and Manoah, the father of Samson, on a rock.[3] These are sacrifices without priests. The sacrifice of Saul, already referred to, shows us that all flesh eating was sacrificial, but that such sacrifices required neither priest nor shrine. Any man might set up a stone and pour out to Yahaweh, at that as his altar, the blood of

[1] 1 Sam. i–ii; Jud. xx.   [2] 2 Sam. xv, 7 ff.   [3] Jud. vi, 19; xiii, 19.

the victim, after which it was permissible to eat the flesh. Samuel's feast at the high place at Ramah, at which Saul was an honored guest, receiving the choicest portion, the shoulder (at a later date the shoulder became the portion of the priest), which had been set aside, shows us the custom of the common, or communal, meal on the occasion of a sacrifice.[1] Again, Samuel's sacrifice of a sucking lamb is an example of the whole burnt sacrifice made in the same simple, unritual and unformulated fashion.[2] The burnt offering is perhaps a development of the idea of the peace offering, of which a portion was offered to God by fire, the rest being eaten by the worshipers. Where there were several victims to be offered, one might well be burned whole for Yahaweh's part. But, on the other hand, the idea of the giving of a precious thing, a thing of value to Yahaweh, something which was His only and in which none other might share, was also present in the burnt offering. Sin and trespass offerings, as known in the later ritual, we do not find, but the rudiments of both appear at an early period. The former of these sacrifices was offered, among other things, to appease God for an unknown or secret sin, the commission of such a sin having revealed itself through some calamity sent by God in punishment. The sin which caused that calamity may become known through an oracle or otherwise, or it may remain hidden, but in either event it is necessary to appease God by a special sacrifice. Such a sacrifice was that made by David on the threshing floor of Araunah because of the plague which had resulted from the numbering of the people.[3] The trespass offering was rather in the nature of compensation for an injury which could be rated at a value, and for which payment must be made to God as to an injured party. So the Philistines give trespass offerings to Yahaweh (1 Sam. vi, 3 ff.), which are, however, in the nature of *anathemata*. Later we find money payments to the Temple mentioned in connection with both sin and guilt, or trespass, offerings.[4] There was also the *herem*, that is, the devotion of persons and objects entire to Yahaweh, inanimate objects being burned and animate slain. This was especially practiced in war, with captives and spoil which

---

[1] 1 Sam. ix, 19 ff.   [2] 1 Sam. vii, 9.   [3] 2 Sam. xxiv.   [4] 2 Kings xii, 17.

for certain reasons the victor would devote to Yahaweh entire. Such sacrifices are referred to frequently in the earliest writings. Two well-known examples of this are the sacrifice of Zebah and Zalmunna by Gideon and of Agag by Saul.[1]

In the material of the sacrifice we find the Israelites on the same footing at the outset of their Canaanitic life as in the times of the completed Priestly Code — oxen, sheep, goats, and doves the only sacrificial animals, with offerings of meal mixed with oil into cakes, and wine, the materials of a primitive meal. But this is the same material of sacrifice which we find in the Marseilles sacrificial tablet, and apparently was the sacrificial rule among Phœnicians and Canaanites.

To sacrifice, at least on the occasion of the great festival sacrifices, one must be clean, that is, holy ; otherwise a man might not partake of the sacred things.[2] He must abstain from women for a certain period preceding contact with the holy food,[3] and he must put off, change, or wash his clothes. In part the same provisions applied to the warrior — evidence of the peculiar holiness of war.

Everywhere, as pointed out above, the Israelites appropriated shrines already existing, sacred times, feasts, methods of sacrifice, and so forth. For the ordinary sacrifices, or for village sanctuaries, a sacred tree or stone might well suffice to represent God to the worshiper ; but if the shrine were more elaborate or important, the tendency was to provide a further representation of God, following out in this, apparently, Canaanite use. At Shiloh Yahaweh was represented by the Ark. Elsewhere we find sacred objects in connection with which the ephods were used for giving lots. So at Nob there was an ephod, which Abiathar carried with him in his flight to David.[4] Gideon set up an ephod at Ophrah, and Micah one in his shrine on Mt. Ephraim.[5] Along with the ephod of Yahaweh this latter shrine contained *teraphim*, that is, household or family gods,[6] which were worshiped along with Yahaweh. The *teraphim* differed much in size and appearance, as

[1] Jud. viii, 18 ff. ; 1 Sam. xv, 32–33.
[2] 1 Sam. xx, 26.
[3] 1 Sam. xxi, 5–6.

[4] 1 Sam. xi, 9 ; xxiii, 6.
[5] Jud. viii, 27 ; xvii, 5.
[6] Gen. xxxi, 19 ff.

is clear from the different descriptions of them. It is also clear that they were a part of the furniture of a well-ordered house.[1] With this family or clan worship was connected a certain cult of graves or tombs, similar to that which we find over so large a part of the Mohammedan, and, for that matter, the Christian, East to-day. So we have the tomb of Deborah in connection with a sacred tree at Bethel;[2] the tomb of Rachel with a sacred stone or pillar at or near Bethlehem;[3] and the tombs of the Patriarchs by the sacred tree or trees in Hebron.[4] With this cult of the dead were connected necromancy and witchcraft, which we are told Saul banished from the land.[5] There were demons or hostile spirits which needed to be propitiated or guarded against, and apparently these especially lurked in the neighborhood of sacred places or watched for an opportunity to make entrance on critical or private occasions in life. All entrances, and therefore especially thresholds, needed to be guarded against them. Blood of a creature slain in the hunt must be covered with earth that it might not be drunk by a demon or spirit, which could thus as his blood-god obtain power over the killer of the beast. Amulets and charms were used as protections against these demons and evil spirits, which perpetuated themselves in the later formal ritual in tassels, talismans, etc.

With the clan or family cult were connected special family sacrifices and feasts, at which the members of the family came together and renewed their relationship with God and with one another, either at the appointed feasts or at some time of their own.[6] The new moon was a feast of importance. In the story of Saul it is reported to have been observed as a sacrificial feast at which all the court, if we may so designate Saul's rude entourage, were expected to partake together.[7] Three times in the year all males were expected to appear before Yahaweh, — that is, at some shrine, — namely, at Passover, which had been united with the spring feast of first fruits; at wheat harvest, the Feast of Weeks; and at the autumn festival, or Tabernacles. The last was the great *haj* festival, at which men

---

[1] 1 Sam. xix, 13.
[2] Gen. xxxv, 8.
[3] Gen. xxxv, 19 f.
[4] Gen. xxiii, 17 ff.; xxv, 9; etc.

[5] 1 Sam. xxv, 3 ff.
[6] 1 Sam. xxv, 29.
[7] 1 Sam. xx, 18 ff.

gathered in great numbers at shrines like Shiloh. For the other feasts they would seem to have sought some neighboring shrine.

That the Hebrews adopted shrines previously in existence has been pointed out above, as also that before their time those shrines were already provided with traditions and a ritual. Where the shrine had become one of importance, occasional sacrifice had given place to regular sacrifice, and occasional meals of God and men to a regular or permanent meal. This is represented by the shew bread always standing on a table in the sanctuary, and the regular evening, or, in more luxurious and developed form, the morning and evening sacrifice. The daily evening sacrifice, with its idea of daily flesh eating, meant a considerable advance in luxury, and points to the development of a relatively wealthy class or a court in the community. Shew bread we find mentioned in connection with the sanctuary at Nob;[1] but the daily flesh sacrifice in Hebrew worship is not vouched for so early.

The establishment by David of a kingdom and a national center for Israel exercised naturally an enormous influence in formulating and developing a common ritual and ultimately in giving it a distinctive national character or tendency, which it would seem to have lost almost altogether after the occupation of Canaan. His restoration of the Ark, and its settlement at Jerusalem, was the natural sequence of his establishment of a kingdom of all Israel with Jerusalem as its capital. He set up the Ark in a tent, apparently in the citadel, at the very top of the hill, on the threshing floor which he had bought from Araunah, thus giving to the ancient national symbol of Yahaweh prominence as the special and peculiar palladium of his kingdom. In the account of the installation of the Ark (2 Sam. vi) we find that there was a feast with sacrifices, music, and dancing, features which formed part of the ritual of all feasts in the early times. David, casting aside his common clothes, dances naked, as presumably did all the others, or bound about the loins with a strip of linen, the primitive priestly garment. They made a joyful noise before the Lord with musical instruments, as was the custom in connection with sacrifice down to the latest times.

[1] 1 Sam. xxi, 4 ff.

Later tradition ascribes to David the development of the musical side of the ritual, both instrumental and vocal. From the most primitive time, as was noted in the discussion of the pre-Mosaic religion, the *tehillah*, or shout of praise, formed an essential part of the ritual of sacrifice. There was the moment of silence, awaiting the coming of the deity, and then the *tehillah*, or burst of praise.[1] What the substance of the sacrificial *tehillah* was at a later date we learn from the Book of Jeremiah (xxxiii, 11): "Praise Yahaweh Zabaoth, for Yahaweh is good; for his mercy endureth for ever"; and we have a number of Psalms developed on this theme.

But while David restored the Ark to its old prestige as a national palladium, carried forth to battle as the presence of Yahaweh, resting at other times in a tent in the citadel at Jerusalem, he did not build a house for it, nor was it the only sanctuary, even in Jerusalem, in his time. So, in the intrigue to secure the succession, Adonijah and his party made their sacrificial feast at the stone of Zoheleth by the fountain of Rogel (Absalom at the time of his rebellion had made his similar feast at Hebron), and Solomon his at Gihon.[2] Later Solomon favored Gibeon, which is described as the great high place at that time.[3]

It is with the erection of the Temple of Solomon, which was an outcome of the autocratic and luxurious organization of his kingdom on the lines of oriental despotism, that we reach the beginning of a more peculiar development of Hebrew ritual. Up to this time we have simple sanctuaries and a simple ritual, in general the sanctuaries and the ritual of the former inhabitants, with the addition of some features brought in by the Hebrews. Yahaweh had been identified with the baals of various localities, and had become so far identified with the country, like the local baals, that David is represented as complaining that Saul, in driving him out of the country, is compelling him to worship other gods, since Yahaweh may be worshiped only on the soil of which he is the baal.[4] An evidence of this identification of Yahaweh with the local deities,

---

[1] Cf. Zeph. i, 7; Hab. ii, 20; Zech. ii, 13; and observe how the silence of Hab. ii, 20, is followed by the *tehillah*, or psalm, of Hab. iii.

[2] 1 Kings i. [3] 1 Kings iii, 4. [4] 1 Sam. xxvi, 19.

and of the consequent local differentiations of Yahaweh which had
taken place, we find in the names of certain shrines which have
been handed down: Yahaweh Yireh,[1] Yahaweh Nissi,[2] Yahaweh
Shalom,[3] reminding us irresistibly of our lady of such and such a
place, black virgins, etc., which we find in later Christian times, as the
result of similar identifications and differentiations. But the peculiar
representation of Yahaweh about which clustered whatever there
was of national and special traditions and uses in Israel, the Ark,
had been preserved and made by David the palladium of his kingdom. This it was about which Solomon built, as it were, his Temple,
a temple which was peculiarly Israelitic only through its possession
of the Ark with its traditions and uses.

The Temple was a higher representation of power, magnificence,
and ritual than anything theretofore known in Canaan, just as
Solomon's kingdom surpassed in wealth, splendor, and organization any of the petty states theretofore occupying Canaan. It was
organized after the method of the temples of the great and wealthy
cities of Phœnicia and Syria, which again resembled closely those
of Babylonia. On the top of a hill, it was itself an artificial mountain, rising terrace on terrace to the dark Holy of Holies, in which
dwelt Yahaweh in his Ark. By the Ark stood colossal winged figures, the cherubim, further representing the presence of Yahaweh.
From the eighteenth Psalm and other similar passages it would
seem that the cherubim symbolized the wind, or the storm or wind
clouds which Yahaweh inhabited or on which he rode, and the dark
Holy of Holies itself symbolized the darkness behind or between
those clouds in which Yahaweh dwelt, the thunder His voice, and
the bolts of lightning His weapons or the gleamings of the brightness of His presence.[4] In a chamber before this, somewhat less

---

[1] Gen. xxii, 14.   [2] Ex. xvii, 15.

[3] Jud. vi, 24. Cf. also similar uses of *El*, as the El of Bethel (Gen. xxxv, 7), the
El of Dan (Amos viii, 14), El Olam of Beersheba (Gen. xxi, 33), El-Elohe Israel of
Shechem (Gen. xxxiii, 20).

[4] Cf. also Ez. i, Is. vi, Ps. xxix, and many other passages. The LXX (2 Kings viii,
54) preserves from the Book of Yashar a fragment of Solomon's dedication ode in
which he says:

> The sun Yahaweh appointed in heaven;
> He declared that He would dwell in darkness.
> I have built Thee an house to abide in,
> A dwelling for Thy habitation forever.

sacred than the Holy of Holies or oracle, stood the altar of incense
— for the point had already been reached when the participation
of the deity in sacrifices had come to be connected with the somewhat finer and more spiritual sense of smell[1] — and the table on
which the bread, the so-called shew bread, stood ever ready before
the Lord. In the court without, on the right, or north, side of the
porch, stood the altar on which were offered daily the morning and
evening sacrifices, the portion of Yahaweh hallowing the meat which
was prepared daily for the king's table. On the other side of the
porch stood the great sea, resting on twelve bulls. This, it has
been shrewdly suggested, represented the *tehom*[2] of Babylonian
and Canaanite cosmogony, the great deep beneath the earth. For
further provision of water there were ten cars supporting jars.
These had about them cherubim, lions, and bulls, reminding one
strongly of Ezekiel's representation of the cherubim clouds on
which Yahaweh rode, and justifying their symbolic interpretation
as clouds.[3] The winged cherubic figures, the lions and bulls, appear
in Assyrian temples. Apparently all this imagery was borrowed
from the Phœnicians or Syrians, from whom it may be traced back
to Babylonian sources. Between the altar and the sea, before the
entrance of the sanctuary, stood two columns, Yachin and Boaz,
the same two columns which stood before all Phœnician and Syrian
temples. They were apparently connected with phallic worship,
although here, as in many cases, the original phallic resemblance
had been clothed over beyond recognition in the progress of culture. Whether these represented the more primitive *mazzebahs*, or
whether in addition to these there were *mazzebahs* in the temple,
is not clear. Later references show us that there were also in the
temple *asherahs*, the trees or poles which represented the feminine
element, perhaps marking the sacred limits. The sexual intention
of these emblems, and the general symbolization of the power of
fertilization, expressed in clouds and sexual emblems, is brought
out still more clearly by the profuse use everywhere of palms as

[1] So we have Yahaweh represented as partaking of the burnt offerings by smell-
ing, Gen. viii, 21 ; 1 Sam. xxvi, 19.
[2] See article "Cosmogony (Hebrew)" in Hastings' *Encyclopædia of Religion and
Ethics*.   [3] So Kosters and W. R. Smith. Cf. Gen. i and xlix, 25.

decorations. The duality of sex of palm trees, and the artificial fructification of the female by sprinkling upon it the pollen of the male, made the palm everywhere in the Semitic East the symbol of sexual fructification and worship of the sexual powers.

The writers of our present Book of Kings report that, besides Yahaweh, Solomon worshiped Ashtoreth and other strange gods.[1] The account of the reform of the Temple worship in the time of Josiah shows us that, as in the Babylonian temples around the central shrine of the god of the temple were grouped, for the greater honor of that god, shrines of a goddess, or Beltis, and of other gods, so here around the sanctuary of Yahaweh, in the courts of His Temple, stood the shrines of other gods, and especially of Ashtoreth with its hierodules and prostitutes.[2] Allowing for all that may have been introduced by later kings, it seems clear that from the outset shrines of other gods, or sacred symbols like the brazen serpent, the horses of the sun, etc., were set up in connection with the Temple of Yahaweh at Jerusalem, and that recognition and countenance were given to the sexual cult, which was especially connected with the name of Ashtoreth.

We have, then, a temple patterned in its symbolism — pillars, altars, cherubim, bulls, lions, seas, clouds, palms, *asherahs*, etc. — after the temples of Phœnicia and Syria, and, to judge from such comparisons as we are able to make, the ritual of sacrifice and the like was substantially the same here as there. The same creatures were sacrificial, the blood was poured at the altar and touched to its horns, the fat burned, the flesh eaten, in the same manner in one place as in the other. There were whole burnt offerings. There were stated morning and evening sacrifices, and more numerous sacrifices on festivals; there were rules of clean and unclean, provisions regarding vows, prescriptions regulating the priesthood, and rules making it the intermediary between the people and God, not only in the giving of oracles but also in sacrificing, which increased continually its prerogatives and its perquisites. The ritual language was taken from that in use among Phœnicians and Canaanites, which had been, in part at least, borrowed from or

[1] 1 Kings xi.   [2] 2 Kings xxiii.

influenced by the Babylonians during their long domination of the West land. How early any of the ritual rules were put in writing, whether there were hung up in the Temple any tablets of sacrificial or other prescriptions, such as have been found at Marseilles, Carthage, and Gortyna in Crete, we do not know. As it reaches us ultimately in the Priestly Code, after the Exile, the ritual has been much developed and modified, so that while there are portions, like the prescriptions for burnt, meal, and peace offerings in the first three chapters of Leviticus, which belong in their essence if not in their entirety to the early days of the Temple, there is much which is of later and even theoretical origin.

The ritual of the *tehillah*, the sacrificial praise songs, has a somewhat similar history. The Psalter was the ultimate praise ritual of the Jerusalem Temple, but as it has come down to us it is very late. The first book of the Psalter contains, probably in a developed and worked-over form, the praise ritual of the earlier Temple.[1]

The relation of the king to the priesthood of the Temple has been already noticed. The king was in a sense the head of the priesthood; he sacrificed, and he so far controlled the ritual that he set up and tore down altars and introduced new cults.[2] The relation of the Temple to the king, of whose house at the outset it may be said to have formed a part, and the consequent splendor of its equipment and service and the organization of its personnel, while it had the effect of making it more the place of the gatherings before the Lord and of the offerings of the people, had also the effect of changing the religious practices of the people, and of making Yahaweh more remote and awful to them. His symbol, whether a stone, the Ark, or an image, was no longer visible to them. Yahaweh dwelt in a grand temple, in a dark, mysterious inner room which they were not permitted to approach. When they would make an offering to Him they stood at a distance, and priests and servitors sacrificed, returning to them a portion to be eaten with their friends in some of the chambers about the courts. And their sacrifice was a very insignificant thing in comparison with the great

---

[1] Cf. Peters, *The Old Testament and the New Scholarship*, Part III.
[2] 2 Kings xvi, 10 ff.; xxiii, 11 f.

sacrifices constantly being offered to Him. It could not count for much with Him. All the more they were impressed with His greatness and His power. They were impressed, too, by the fact that sacrifice was continually being offered to Him by the king for himself and the nation, maintaining a constant relation with Him in which they all shared, and in which both out of pride and out of selfish interest they would wish to participate through their feasts and their vows. In this way the Temple became an object of intense reverence and affection, weaning them to a large extent from all other places of sacrifice, an effect much furthered by the nature of the country.

With all its foreign ritual it should never be forgotten that the Temple of Solomon had an Israelite core. In the midst of all this pomp of costly buildings and gorgeous rites was housed the old national symbol of their Deity, the Ark, with its tent and its vessels. That the meaning of these, their relation to the past history of Israel and its God was kept alive in the priesthood of the Temple, is manifest from the later ritual. The pictures of the Tabernacle and its ritual, from which the Temple and its ritual were developed, are no mere fictions of later times, but the exaggerated reflection of the traditions which lingered about the Ark and its covering, which traced everything back to its founder, Moses, and to the days of its construction in the remote past of the wilderness. This exercised a profound influence on the course of the development of the ritual of the Temple, and an influence potent in nationalizing that cult.

One more important influence of the Temple should be noticed here, namely, its influence in making prominent the special name *Yahaweh* as the name of Israel's God. It is with the establishment of the kingdom under Saul that this special or personal name of Israel's God begins to become prominent in personal names, as over against *Ab*, *Am*, *Adon*, *Melek*, and more particularly *El*, — "father," "uncle," "lord," "king," "god." With David and the restoration of the Ark, *Yahaweh* (*Yah*) becomes a characteristic part of names of the royal family and its supporters; it takes the place of *El* and *Elohim* as the designation of God in ordinary use, in altars, etc. ; and this *Yahaweh* is connected above all with the Ark, which ceases to be called even the Ark of God, and becomes finally the Ark of Yahaweh, or ultimately of Yahaweh of Sabaoth. This fact, the peculiar prominence of Yahaweh in connection with the Temple at Jerusalem and its central sanctuary, plays a part of some importance in the religious development of Israel.

But it is probable that all that was national would speedily have been lost had the foreign, "oriental" movement of Solomon's reign continued long unchecked. We have seen that the Temple with its ritual was in general a reproduction of the temples of the wealthy cities of Phœnicia and Syria, and especially the former. But at least it was in its central shrine a Temple of Yahaweh. As a result of his political alliances, however, Solomon directly introduced, or at least permitted, the alien cults of allied and subject peoples in separate shrines at Jerusalem,[1] Ashtoreth of Zidon, Milcom, or Melech, of Ammon, and Chemosh of Moab. The inevitable result of this must have been a pantheon similar to that of Babylon or Damascus or Zidon, and indeed the whole tendency of Solomon's national as of his religious policy was to put Jerusalem on a level with such states.

[1] 1 Kings xi.

CHAPTER IX

EFFECTS OF THE NATIONAL SCHISM

The rebellion under Jeroboam was a revolt against the autocratic rule of the king of the tribe of Judah, and his exploitation of Israel. It was also a revolt against foreign methods, the methods of the oriental great powers; a declaration of freedom and a demand for a return to more primitive and more national ways. Its effects were quite as profound in the religious as in the political field.

In Judah it checked abruptly the advance of foreign influence by cutting off the connection with foreign powers; it reduced Jerusalem from the position of the capital of a great power to that of the capital of a poor and petty principality. It did not, however, reduce the size of the Temple, which became, as it were, greater in proportion to the State than before, thus giving greater prominence in Judah to the name of Yahaweh and His cult. It would seem, also, that something of the same hostility to foreign ways and foreign cults was aroused in Judah which we find in Israel. Certainly the Judæan narrative of the Pentateuch, which we must place at no great length of time after Rehoboam, condemns foreign worship, foreign gods, and molten images in most explicit terms.[1] From the narrative of the Book of Kings it would seem that this anti-foreign spirit influenced the religious policy of Asa in the close of the tenth, and still more strongly that of Jehoshaphat in the first half of the ninth, century.

In Israel, as it was impossible to return to the simpler tribal conditions of the older time, a new kingdom was established, and, as it was equally impossible to return to the earlier conditions of unformulated local worship at all the shrines of the land, two national or royal temples were established. These were not,

[1] Cf. for instance Ex. xxxiv, 11–17.

however, new temples without history and without tradition, but two ancient and famous shrines, Bethel and Dan, the priests of the latter of which claimed descent from Moses.[1] We have in so far conditions tending toward religious centralization and uniformity in Israel as in Judah, but there were centrifugal forces, elements of freedom and independence in Israel, which were not to be found in Judah. The latter was a kingdom of one city, the royal residence, in which was centered such wealth as the land possessed, and which consequently dominated and unified the whole country in politics as in religion. The former, relatively a wealthy country, was much more diversified in its interests, no one city dominated the land, and the royal residence was not connected with the national temples. In Judah the interests of the royal family and of the hereditary priesthood of the Temple of Yahaweh were bound up with one another ; in Israel there was no such close connection.

Apparently the ritual practices of the temples of Dan and Bethel were simpler and more primitive than those of the Temple at Jerusalem, less rigid, more popular, closer in some respects to primitive Hebrew use, in others to the use of the ordinary sanctuaries of Canaan, in so far as the latter had already become a part of the Israelite heritage. There is no indication of the existence of such expensive or extensive structures, nor of such elaborate symbolism as in the Temple at Jerusalem. God was not so far removed from His worshipers. He was not hidden in a dark inner room, but was visible to their sight in the symbol of the calf or small bull, which seems to have had a traditional meaning in Israel.[2] The ancient sacred stone was a prominent feature in Bethel. An early ordinance, evidently polemic in its character, directs that altars

[1] These were both natural holy places, one indicated as such by the great spring from which the main branch of the Jordan originated, and the other by the huge stone columns, looking like the work of some giant race, in reality the result of erosion, standing near the summit of the land. The worship at both these shrines was apparently, in the main at least, an out-of-door worship, in which again we see evidence of the meaning of Jeroboam's revolt as a recall to primitive conditions. Cf. Peters, *Early Hebrew Story*, pp. 110 ff.

[2] The name *Ephraim* may be a derivation from, or a play upon, the word for bull. Cf. Hos. xiv, 2 ; Deut. xxxiii, 17 ; Gen. xlix, 22. Peters, "Jacob's Blessing," *J. B. L.*, 1886. The bull also played a part, it should be noted, in the symbolism of the Jerusalem Temple.

shall be of earth or of unhewn stones.[1] The names of the pillars and altar also are characteristic: El-Elohe-Israel, El-Bethel.[2]

The name *Yahaweh* does not play the same part in Israel as in Judah. The general name *el*, which we find in the name *Israel*, in *Bethel*, and apparently originally also in *Jacob-el* and *Joseph-el*, is used in composition, and the deity is commonly designated as the *el* of Bethel or of Dan; local deities are commonly known as *baals*, and *Elohim* is commonly used in place of *Yahaweh* as the specific name of God. This latter use is clearly marked in the literature which has come down to us, where, as in the Pentateuch, we have the Elohistic narrative from Israel and the Yahawistic from Judah. There is a similar division in the Psalter, and, apparently, as the first book of Psalms is the descendant or outcome of the psalmody of the Yahaweh Temple at Jerusalem, so the second and third books of the Psalter are the descendants of Israelite collections of hymns.[3]

The sexual worship so rife among the Canaanites, as among all the north Semitic peoples, which had made itself felt in the Solomonic Temple, which shows itself in the Judæan narrative in the oath with the hand upon the seat of life,[4] and which is testified to by later legislation and by the references of the Prophets, seems to have affected the Israelitic cult even more strongly than the Judæan, owing to the more intimate connection with the numerous local tree shrines, and probably also owing to the wealthier and more agricultural conditions of Israel in comparison with the more pastoral and poorer conditions of Judah.

The differences between the ritual of Judah and that of Israel, which a Judæan writer notices in the Book of Kings,[5] are the temples at Dan and Bethel, non-Levitical priests, the calves, and a different date for the Feast of Tabernacles — in the eighth instead of the seventh month. A comparison of the early Judæan code contained in Exodus xxxiv, 17 ff., with the similar Israelite code contained in

---

[1] Ex. xx, 24 ff.   [2] Gen. xxxiii, 20; xxxv, 7.

[3] There are, I think, indications in some of the Korah Psalms of an original connection with the temple of Dan and in some of the Asaph Psalms of an original connection with Bethel. Cf. Peters, "The Sons of Korah," in *Essays in Modern Theology and Related Subjects*, Scribner, 1911.

[4] Gen. xxiv, 9.   [5] 1 Kings xii, 28 ff.

Exodus xxiii, 14 ff., shows us a substantial agreement in the main points of ritual — the three great feasts at which all males should appear before Yahaweh, the offering of firstlings and first fruits to Yahaweh as the owner or lord of the land, the primitive prohibition of the use of leaven in sacrifice, the Sabbath rest, even the direction that a kid should not be boiled in its mother's milk. Similarly, circumcision was a condition in both Israel and Judah of admission to sacrificial, and consequently to national, fellowship.

In the period immediately following the great schism, as the result of the impetus given by the court of David and Solomon, of the wealth and culture accumulated in Jerusalem, and especially of the grand Temple of Yahaweh, religious as well as literary culture seemed to be confined to Judah. It was there that the first histories were composed, the traditions of the ancestors collected, and the like. But Judah was living on its accumulated capital, and in the very nature of the case it was inevitable that the superior natural wealth, the greater diversity of population and interests, and the more advantageous position of Israel for contact with the world should in time reverse these conditions. It is with the dynasty of Omri, in the ninth century, that Israel becomes the leader, first in power, wealth, and culture, and then in religious development, — a position which it held until the fall of Samaria in 721 B.C.

CHAPTER X

BEGINNING OF PROPHECY

Among Semitic institutions, along with the priest we find the prophet as an interpreter of God, from the earliest to the latest times. In Arabian antiquity the person, man or woman, who felt a special call to give a message to the people, would manifest his inspiration and give proof of divine authority by physical and mental disorders, or by strange acts contrary to the ordinary conventions and even decencies of life, throwing off his clothes and appearing naked, and the like. Such practices were common among the Hebrew prophets at the best period of their history. So we find Isaiah throwing off his clothes and walking naked through Jerusalem for the space of three years as a sign.[1] Precisely the same thing may be seen in the Turkish empire at this day. The madness and outrageousness of a man's conduct is the evidence of possession by a supernatural agency. This is, however, not a Semitic peculiarity, but rather a universal religious phenomenon. What is peculiarly Semitic is the development or formulation of this conception of supernatural possession or inspiration, especially in associations, guilds, or organizations, the *nebiim*, or prophets, of Phœnicia, Syria, and Canaan, the fakirs and dervishes of modern Islam. The modern dervishes are as nearly as possible identical with the prophets of these older nations and religions. They represent the idea of direct communication with and possession by the deity, without the usual ritual laws and accompaniments. They seek that communion and inspiration by physical excitement, dancing, shouting, music, floggings, cuttings, unnatural positions, trances; they express it in startling and outrageous actions, through strange and uncouth dress and manners, by

[1] Is. xx.

utterances, sometimes wild and grotesque, sometimes forceful and commanding. With instinctive conservatism, in the midst of a settled and civilized community they cling to a barbarism closely akin to the primitive nomadic life. As over against the ritual and formal conservatism of the priesthood and of organized religion and organized society, on the other hand, they are radical and subversive in their ideas as well as in their actions. They tend to form guilds or schools, having a common home and special rules and practices, which are often of a secret, or esoteric, character; but such organizations are apt to be loose. They come and go, now wandering in groups and pairs, now living singly, now united in one domicile. They have novitiates, friends and supporters, more or less initiated into their ways and manners, taking part at times in their wild ceremonies and excesses, and sharing their ecstasies and trances, but for the rest living the normal life, wearing the normal dress, and practicing the ordinary ritual of the religion about them. Their relation to the organized religion, as it expresses itself in the *ulema*, the lawyers and priests of Islam, is in general antipathetic and sometimes even hostile, but not always or necessarily so. The white-turbaned *ulema* are often seen at dervish ceremonies, and sometimes as novitiates or participants; and in times of excitement, especially against infidels, the two combine as leaders or instigators of the people. The dervishes, on the other hand, are often seen taking part in the services of the mosques or frequenting the mosque courts, and sometimes they become the guardians of shrines, the so-called welis or ziarets, thus entering what we may call the ranks of the regular priesthood. By the community at large the dervishes are regarded with a curious mixture of reverence and contempt. The common people are apt to revere them highly, the more educated and the official classes to view them with contempt or distrust, mixed, however, with dread or a superstitious veneration. In times of war they play a part of special importance as zealots for the faith. Their religious influence is partly good and partly evil; good because of the aspiration after an inward communion with God, which, with all their excesses and eccentricities, they represent and foster, and good, further, because they break down the mere outward formalism of ritual and dogma, and recall men constantly to first principles and fundamentals; evil because of their false pretenses, their emotional and physical excesses, their opposition to progress and civilization, their narrowness and ignorance.

What the dervishes are to-day, that the bands and schools of prophets were in Israel. The conception of prophecy as a possession by the deity, a frenzy and ecstasy, a direct utterance from God, the Hebrews probably brought with them into Canaan. There they found bands, or guilds, of prophets, under the influence or through the example of which similar prophetic bands came into existence in Israel.[1] The same story which gives us our first information of the existence of such bands in Israel, the story of Saul,[2] contains a curious antiquarian note according to which the prophets, or *nebiim*, were the successors of a more ancient class of seers, who told the whereabouts of things lost, foretold the future, and the like. Samuel is described as a seer of this order. But he exercised also, according to the earlier narrative, priestly functions; and he was likewise a leader of the people in their fight against Philistine aggression, preaching a holy war. In all these regards he resembled Moses, and both of them in the later narrative are called prophets. A similar title is also given to Miriam and Deborah, who, according to the narrative, aroused the people to fight for Yahaweh, and celebrated the victories of Yahaweh with song and dance. Apparently from the time of Saul onward all these manifestations of divine inspiration were included under the name of prophecy, whether the persons so inspired were included in the bands of *nebiim* and followed their methods or not.

It is worthy of note that we meet with these bands of *nebiim* first at a time when Israel is threatened with destruction by the Philistines, and that Saul, who becomes the leader of Israel against the Philistines, falls under their influence. At a later date we find the *nebiim* spurring on king and people to war against the Syrians.[3]

[1] The consciousness of the essential identity of the prophets of the surrounding nations and the prophets of Israel shows itself in such a story as that of Balaam, Num. xxi–xxiv.   [2] 1 Sam. ix, x.

[3] 1 Kings xx, 13, 28, 35 ff.; xxii, 6 ff.; 2 Kings vi, 8 ff., 31 ff.; xiii, 14 ff.

At a still later date it is the prophets of Judah who urge king and people into rebellion against Nebuchadrezzar,[1] and even instigate the Jews deported to Babylonia to revolt.[2] Throughout they are the preachers of war in the name of Yahaweh both against the external enemies of Israel and also against foreign ways and foreign influences within the state. Moreover they peculiarly use and exalt the special name, *Yahaweh*, of Israel's God.[3] Saul joins a band of these *nebiim*, who excite themselves with music, and " prophesies " with them.[4] On another occasion he is said, under the prophetic ecstasy inspired by such a band of *nebiim*, to have stripped off his clothes, " prophesied," and lain down " naked all that day and all that night."[5] A later proverb, which is recorded in connection with this, " Is Saul also among the prophets ? " helps to explain the meaning of this " prophesying," and to show that " mad man " and " prophet " were words almost synonymous, and that the " prophesying " here described as practiced by these bands of *nebiim* consisted, in large part certainly, of frenzied cries and acts by which they worked themselves into an ecstatic, or trance, state.

In the story of David we hear nothing of bands of *nebiim*, but among his attendants and the officials of his court are mentioned two prophets, Nathan and Gad, whose business seems to have been to announce to him the utterances of Yahaweh, as Abiathar and Zadok, the priests, interpreted the oracles of Yahaweh by lot through the ephod or before the Ark. It was Gad who denounced the punishment of pestilence because of the census, and bade David build an altar on the threshing floor of Araunah to stay the plague.[6] Nathan's famous denunciation of David for his adultery with Bathsheba and murder of Uriah,[7] reminding one forcibly of Elijah's denunciation of Ahab for the murder of Naboth and the seizure of his vineyard, shows us a moral side of prophecy. This narrative

---

[1] Jer. xxviii.   [2] Jer. xxix.

[3] It is worthy of note that with the children of Saul, who was closely connected with these *nebiim*, we begin to find *Yahaweh* used in composition in proper names. It is perhaps worthy of note that modern dervishes excite and sanctify themselves by repeated shoutings of the name of Allah, somewhat as the old prophets seem to have done by the use of the sacred name *Yahaweh* or *Yahu*.

[4] 1 Sam. x, 10.   [6] 2 Sam. xxiv, 11 ff.

[5] 1 Sam. xix, 24.   [7] 2 Sam. xii.

likewise presents the prophet as a privileged person who dares to beard the king and in the name of Yahaweh denounce his unrighteous deeds. The idea of the prophet as a foreteller, like the seer of old, shows itself in the story of Nathan's prediction to David, which itself, however, belongs to the later additions to the David story.[1] Perhaps also Nathan's objection to the Temple and Gad's to the census may be regarded as historical in origin, representing that clinging to the simple and primitive which characterizes prophecy throughout. The militant attitude of the Prophets towards foreign innovations is represented in Ahijah, in the time of Solomon, who incites Jeroboam to revolt.[2] After that for three quarters of a century we have almost no records. The literary activity which had begun in the times of David and Solomon was continued in Judah in the historical compilation which we know as J, which must have helped to rouse somewhat the national religious sense; and we have a brief notice of a movement in the time of Asa (ca. 917–876 B.C.) against some of the grosser expressions of the sexual cult. In Israel this was a period of confusion, in which the prophets of Yahaweh seem to have played an important and perhaps somewhat turbulent part, denouncing the kings whose policy did not please them, and thus assisting their downfall[3] in no small degree. Finally a strong king, Omri, ascended the throne about 887 B.C. He and his more famous son, Ahab, organized the kingdom, formed an alliance with Tyre, brought Moab into subjection, put an end to the long hostilities with Judah, and entered into a matrimonial alliance with Jehoshaphat, who became a subject ally of the Israelite king. Israel became a strong and wealthy kingdom, able successfully to resist the encroachment of the powerful Syrian kingdom of Damascus, which was reaching out after the hegemony of the West land.[4] The contact of Israel with the surrounding countries became intimate. There was a Syrian khan, or quarter, for Damascene merchants in Samaria,[5] and a similar khan, or quarter, for Israelite merchants in Damascus. But worst of all, Ahab's wife was Jezebel ("woman of Baal"), daughter of Ethbaal ("man of

---

[1] 2 Sam. vii.   [3] 1 Kings xvi, 2 f.   [5] 1 Kings xx, 34.
[2] 1 Kings xi, 25 ff.   [4] 1 Kings xiv, 10; xvi, 7.

Baal "), the usurping priest-king of Tyre, a woman of remarkable character and strong influence, who seems to have been a genuine devotee of Baal. At his residence city, Samaria, Ahab built a temple to her god, in precisely the same way in which Solomon had built in Jerusalem temples to the gods of the lands with which he had entered into alliance, matrimonial or otherwise, and the cult of the Tyrian Baal with its priests and prophets was introduced in Israel. The religious policy of Ahab was practically identical with that of Solomon. He recognized Yahaweh as the special god of Israel, as we learn among other things from the use of that name in composition in the names of all his children.[1] But while giving that name a prominence which it had not possessed in the royal houses of Israel before that time, he did not sympathize with that henotheism which recognized no other god in Israel but Yahaweh. Like Solomon he strove to make Israel equal in power and culture to the neighboring Phœnician and Aramæan kingdoms. To do so he must enter into alliances with those kingdoms, an essential feature of which was sacrifice to their gods. More particularly was this the case where the alliance was sealed by marriage. In that case the wife must bring her god with her. We have interesting examples of this in the history of Egypt, as also of the opposition of the native priesthood there to the cult of the foreign gods. This feeling showed itself still more strongly in Israel, and the leaders in the national movement against the foreignizing policy of Ahab were the prophets, the *nebiim*. The leader in this struggle is one of the commanding characters of Israelite history, — a "Titanic figure," as he has been well called, — Elijah the Tishbite, from the country of Gilead, where the conditions were relatively more primitive, and from the point of culture as well as of geography men stood nearer the desert. Gilead was also the battle ground in the great struggle between Damascus and Samaria, the disputed region where the God of Israel was battling for existence against the gods

---

[1] It is curious to observe that after Solomon's time the name *Yah* in composition in royal names does not appear again until the time of Asa in Judah and Ahab in Israel. With the children of these two monarchs it reappears, and from that time onward is an almost constant factor in the royal names of both kingdoms.

of the Aramæans. Elijah does not appear to have belonged to the bands of the *nebiim*, the " sons of the prophets," as they were then called, or if he did, his connection with those bands was not a prominent feature of his life and mission, as it was with Elisha. On the other hand, he was one of them in his methods and ideas, his garments, his symbolic actions, his wild life, his close relation to desert conditions and the nomadic existence. The relation of the civilized court of Ahab to men of this ilk was the same as that of the court of the caliphs of Damascus or Baghdad to men of a similar description in the earlier political and religious history of Islam. Into the council of the mighty caliph in his civilized and luxurious capital would stride a rough captain, a wild dervish or preacher, a free son of the desert, asserting a democratic equality strangely in contrast with the apparent autocracy, a simplicity in apparently irreconcilable conflict with the luxury, of city and court. To the face of the monarch such a man would utter his word with unhesitating directness, quite the opposite of the obedience of the official or the flattery of the courtier. In that way the people spoke and made its voice felt in the councils of the caliph. Islam was strongly conscious of its origin and its mission, and rudely determined to assert its inherent simplicity and sternness as over against the enervating softness of foreign ways and city habits. So Israel preserved in the midst of increasing luxury and civilization a keen consciousness of its desert origin, its native and democratic simplicity. The heart of the people at large responded to the man who asserted that simplicity and plainness in the face of the king and court. One of the striking incidents related in connection with Elijah is his denunciation of Ahab for the murder of Naboth, where he voices the outraged moral sense of a free and democratic people against the methods of the oriental despot. By such actions and utterances the early prophets appealed to and quickened the moral sense of the community, and asserted in the name of Yahaweh the prime importance of morality in religion as over against forms and cults.

But the great mission of Elijah was the denunciation of foreign cults, especially of the Tyrian Baal, and his assertion that Yahaweh alone was the god of Israel, a jealous god, who would tolerate no strange god beside Him. His name, " God (or my God) is Yaha-weh," is itself the declaration and epitome of his message. He has nothing to say against or about ritual forms, about the bull wor-ship of Bethel, against the teraphim, the tree worship with its sex-ual cult, all which had been adopted into the worship of Yahaweh; his fight, according to the tradition which has come down to us, was against the worship of the Tyrian Baal, which had been intro-duced. Were not the personal picture so sharply reproduced in the stories of the next generations, one might be tempted to sup-pose that this prophet with the typical name was merely the type figure in the battle of Israelite " prophetism " against the invasion of foreign cults. The nature of the struggle and its importance in the religious history of the nation are brought out the more clearly by those legendary accretions which obscure the details of the con-flict. Most picturesque and most famous is the contest between Elijah and the prophets of Baal on the eastern height of Carmel, and the dramatic triumph of Elijah.[1] But the story as a whole makes it clear that Elijah did not succeed in his immediate purpose of expelling the cult of the Tyrian Baal; on the other hand, he won a real and substantial victory, as later generations recognized, in setting in motion those forces which finally not merely expelled the cult of the Tyrian Baal but also purged Israel from that native Canaanite *baal* cult which had become combined with the worship of Yahaweh.

The story of this contest and the history of Israel for a little over a century, from the time of Ahab to the time of Jeroboam II, is known to us chiefly through the Tales of the Prophets, which were utilized by the compilers of the Book of Kings. The very existence of such a literature shows us what a part the Prophets played in that period, while that literature itself gives us a very good picture of the activities of these earlier prophets. It was a period of life-and-death struggle with Damascus. At times the whole land was overrun by the Syrians, and the capital reduced to the last straits; at times it was a struggle for the possession of Gilead. Alliance with Tyre seemed an absolute political necessity. We have

[1] 1 Kings xviii.

seen the attitude of the Prophets, and especially of Elijah, towards
the Baal cult, which was a necessary part of that alliance. On the
other hand, as has been pointed out, the Prophets, like the modern
dervishes of Islam, were ever ready to encourage king and people
in the war against the Syrians. The king was surrounded by a host
of prophets ready to promise victory in the name of Yahaweh;[1]
the army was pervaded by prophets urging the people to victory,
and preaching the utter extinction of their foes.[2] There were
naturally intervals of peace in these long Syrian wars, and we
catch glimpses of the relations of Israelites and Syrians which
show us that there was a close resemblance between them in at
least the outer expressions of religion, as well as in their civilization
and culture in general. As in the story of Balaam a foreigner, a
Syrian or an Edomite, it is not altogether certain which, is recognized as a true prophet, so in the story of Elisha the Syrians recognize the Israelite prophets.[3] In the story of Elisha and Naaman
we find Yahaweh regarded as the God of the land of Israel, who
can only be worshiped on that land, so that if Naaman would
worship him in Damascus it is necessary that he should carry
thither some of the land of Israel.[4] The same story emphasizes
strongly the exclusive attitude of the Yahaweh prophets. Even
the Syrians ought to carry with them some of the soil of Israel
that they may be able to worship Yahaweh. But while we thus
have the recognition of Yahaweh's peculiar relation to the land of
Israel, so that He and the land are become as it were inseparable,
on the other hand Israel has not lost its conception of its relation
to Yahaweh in the southern wilderness. Beersheba to the south
of Judah was a favorite place of holy pilgrimage, even in the times
of Amos and Hosea, and when Elijah in his distress would seek
Yahaweh he goes not only to Beersheba but even on beyond to His
primal home in Horeb. There Yahaweh dwells, and there He manifests himself in a way in which He never manifests himself in Israel.[5]

The story of Elijah's visit to Horeb gives us a very simple, and
at the same time lofty and spiritual, picture of the method of

[1] 1 Kings xxii.   [3] 2 Kings v; viii, 7 ff.   [5] 1 Kings xix.
[2] 1 Kings xx, 35 ff.   [4] 2 Kings v, 17.

Yahaweh's revelation of himself in the still, small voice that speaks to the prophet.[1] Striking also is the representation, so opposed to the later somewhat dualistic conception of the agency of Satan, of the method of prophetic inspiration through the spirits sent forth from Yahaweh, in the story of Micaiah.[2] Yahaweh alone is recognized as the source from whom come the utterances of all prophets, whether true or false, through the spirits which are His servants to do good and to do evil.

The prophetic antagonism to the house of Ahab finally culminated in the murder of his son Joram, of Jezebel, and of the whole house of Ahab by Jehu at the instigation of the Prophets of Yahaweh.[3] The name *Jehu*, it should be noted, is *Yahu*, the form of *Yahaweh* which we find in composition. The remainder of the name has been lost, and the name by which this king has been handed down to us is the name of the Deity, which he made the watchword of a fanatical campaign against everything foreign, having in this the approval and support of the Prophets. Among his allies in rooting out the worship of Baal, characteristic of the extent to which the prophetic movement had affected the people, we find the Nazarite sect, or guild, of Jehonadab, the son of Rechab, which would neither drink wine nor dwell in houses, but, in their zeal for the ancient and primitive, had eschewed these expressions of civilization, which Israel had adopted from the Canaanites.[4] This is the extreme expression of that zeal for the ancient and primitive conditions fostered by prophetism, the triumph of which was represented in the downfall of the dynasty of Ahab, and the ruthless massacre, in the name of Yahaweh, of the prophets, servants, priests, and worshipers of the Tyrian Baal. The same movement made itself felt a little later in Judah, when, after the overthrow of Athaliah, Jehoiada dedicated the people to Yahaweh, destroyed the temple of Baal in Jerusalem, and slew his priest, Mattan.[5]

By the middle of the next century this anti-foreign prophetic movement made itself felt in the condemnation of the native Canaanite cults, and especially of the sexual immorality which was authorized

---

[1] 1 Kings xix, 11 ff. [3] 2 Kings ix. [5] 2 Kings xi, 17 f.
[2] 1 Kings xxii. [4] 2 Kings x, 15 ; Jer. xxxv.

and fostered by those cults. It was no longer the Tyrian Baal against which the prophets thundered, but the native Canaanitic *baalim*, with which Yahaweh had been identified. This conflict belongs, however, not to this first stage of Hebrew prophetism, but to the second or literary stage, the first representatives of which are Amos and Hosea. By their time the guilds of *nebiim* had done their work, and come into more or less disrepute because of their excesses. So we find Amos somewhat scornfully denying that he was a prophet or the son of a prophet,[1] a member, that is, of a prophetic guild. Hosea speaks in a divided tone of the prophets of his day. Apparently, however, they were, in his judgment, better than the priests. This period, the reign of Jeroboam II, was one of wealth, prosperity, and apparent power. The kingdom was more highly organized, more civilized, and more luxurious than it had ever been before. There was not the same opportunity for the activities of the primitive *nebiim* as during the Syrian wars, and the increase of culture and luxury on the part of the mass of the people discredited their barbarous and primitive ways and manners at the same time that it corrupted them. Their work had been done, and they made way for the later type of prophet.

This does not mean to say, however, that guilds of *nebiim* ceased to exist. We find evidences of their existence, their use of the old coarse, rough garments, and the physical stimulants to excitement, including the gashing of the body, very late in the post-exilic[2] period. All later prophetism shows its descent from these *nebiim* and much that was characteristic of the earlier days of their activities, the strange actions and garments, symbolic and wild gestures and deeds, continued to be found among the Prophets in a greater or less degree to the end. The great mass of prophets of the later time retained, further, much of that warlike and almost fanatical attitude towards all things foreign, and that close connection with the primitive and even the uncivilized past, which distinguished the earlier *nebiim*. The peculiar zeal also for the name *Yahaweh* continued to make itself felt through the entire period of the writing prophets.

[1] Amos vii, 14.   [2] Zech. xiii, 2 ff

CHAPTER XI

THE EARLIEST WRITINGS

Before we proceed to consider the new prophecy which commences with Amos and Hosea, we must go back and note the study and interpretation of history, and the formulation and codification of laws, which preceded those first writing prophets. As was pointed out in Chapter I, historical writings began in Judah at or shortly after the time of David, with the story of the life of that monarch. This was followed by the history of Saul, and this by the story of the period preceding, until at length the history was carried back to the Creation. At the same time it was continued forward to cover the reigns of succeeding monarchs, but after Solomon in the form of brief, dry chronicles. Later a similar work was composed in Israel. When Amos and Hosea prophesied, at or before the middle of the eighth century, these two collections were in existence, and considerable portions of them, embedded in the later historical works, the Pentateuch, Joshua, Judges, Samuel, and Kings, have come down to us.[1] A study of these early compositions shows us the development in some circles of a higher, more spiritual life than that which was expressed either in the ritual or in that earlier prophetical movement of the *nebiim* which we have just traced. The latter movement, in fact, while it influenced the thought of the writers or compilers of these collections, was in general the medium through which certain of the doctrines or ideas of these higher thinkers were communicated

---

[1] They are known in the critical analysis as J and E, and earlier and later strata are often designated by further differentiations as J¹, J², etc. They may be read separately in such works as Addis' *The Documents of the Hexateuch*, Bacon's *Genesis* and *Exodus*, and the different volumes of the Polychrome Bible, edited by Paul Haupt. The analysis will be found in Kautsch, Driver, or any good modern introduction, or in modern commentaries on the separate books.

to, or made effective on, the mass of the people, and the people prepared for that higher movement based on these ideas which commences with Amos and Hosea.

For the story of creation, of the development of civilization, agriculture, and the arts, of the division of men into different nations with different languages, and the like, the original material of the Judæan narrative is evidently the myths, legends, and traditions which the Israelites found among the Canaanites. These the Canaanites on their part had borrowed from the Babylonians, probably during the long period of Babylonian domination of the West land, and the old Babylonian material is clearly recognizable in the Hebrew narratives. So it is eastward, in Eden, that man takes his origin; it is at Babel that the speech of man is confounded and different languages originate. The connection of the Hebrew flood story with the Babylonian is clear to the most casual observer, and it is plain that the Hebrew idea of the heavens, and of the water above and the water below the earth, are identical with the Babylonian. The sacred tree and the tempting serpent appear in old Babylonian art, and the man who must consort with the beasts before a helpmeet is found for him recalls Engidu,[1] the primitive man in the Gilgamesh epic, who satisfies his passion with the beasts until Ishtar sends him a woman from her devotees.[2] The comparison of this last-named story with the sweet, wholesome, and beautiful picture of the relation between man and woman in the Judæan narrative brings out a characteristic feature of Hebrew religion as here represented, its freedom from the sexual idea. We have already noticed the prominent part played by Ishtar or Astarte in Babylonia, Phœnicia, Syria, and Palestine, and the importance of her cult, the worship in kind of that great mysterious life-bearing power, to which is attributable so much of the joy and happiness, as well as the sorrow and pain, of life and without which the world must speedily come to an end. In the Hebrew there is no Ishtar; her life-giving functions have been assigned to Yahaweh, and the

---

[1] Formerly read Eabani.

[2] Gen. ii, 18 ff. Cf. Jastrow, *A. J. S. L.*, XV, 207 f.; Barton, *Sketch of Semitic Origins*, p. 43; Peters, *Early Hebrew Story*, chap. v.

sex feature has been eliminated. In the story of the temptation we find a view of the carnal relation of man and woman which seems in some regards almost monastic. It is through this relation that the eyes of man and woman are opened, the sense of decency in clothing is developed, innocence is lost, God is in some way offended, man estranged from Him, banished from His presence,[1] and condemned to a life of toil and pain. It is true that we have passages, like the story of Judah and Tamar,[2] in which the consecrated harlot, or *kedeshah*, appears. This particular story belongs not to that part of the narrative derived from the ancient myths, but to the folklore history of the tribes, and narrates the mixture by intermarriage of Judah with the native Canaanites. It was in precisely such intermarriage with its resultant combination of gods and cults that the danger of Israel lay. That the religion of Israel was affected by its contact with Canaan in this regard, and that certain immoral practices were introduced in the cult of the temples and high places, has already been pointed out. This is testified to not only by such stories as that of Judah and Tamar but also by categorical statements of both the Judæan and Israelite[3] narratives; but it is also clear that this did not meet the approval of the better minds, and that such practices were never regarded by them as an integral part of their religion. It is presumably true that certain ideas and practices, not considered immoral at the outset but so considered later, were glossed and eliminated by succeeding writers; but, making all due allowance for this, it remains a fact of the greatest significance that the thinkers of Israel, having such myths as their material and surrounded by such licentious practices sanctioned and required by religion, should have developed a product so spiritual and so void of immorality.

It is noteworthy also that these myths, which in their original form are grossly polytheistic, become in Hebrew monolatrous and

---

[1] Cf. with this the rule which forbade a man to partake of holy things within a certain period after cohabitation, 1 Sam. xxi, 4 f.

[2] Gen. xxxviii, 21. Evidently certain usages, immoral in their nature and inconsistent with the general principles represented by J, were accepted as facts, after a manner familiar in the history of all religions.

[3] Cf. Jud. ii, 13; iii, 5 f.

almost monotheistic. It is Yahaweh who creates earth and heaven, man and the beasts, who drives man out of Eden because of his transgression, and sends a flood to drown men because they were become corrupt. We find a few slight indications of the polytheistic sources from which the material was drawn, such as the remnant of a story about the offspring of the " sons of god" (or the gods) and the " daughters of men " ;[1] but such remnants only make more clear the monotheistic character of the Hebrew version of these ancient myths and legends, and emphasize the fact that the Hebrews deliberately blotted out all other gods, recognizing no god beside Yahaweh.

There is also in general a strong moral element pervading the Hebrew tales. So in the flood story it is the wickedness of man which causes Yahaweh to send destruction upon him, not, as in the Babylonian tale, the mere caprice of the gods or a sort of fate which compels the gods themselves. There is a moral purpose in Yahaweh's government of the universe and His dealings with men. This is not, it is true, carried out consistently, and in some cases the motives ascribed to Yahaweh are those of caprice or favoritism or jealousy. It is the smell of the sweet fragrance of sacrifice, so long absent, which leads Yahaweh to say in His heart that He will not again curse the ground because of man.[2] It is jealousy of man's power and independence which causes Yahaweh to drive him out of Eden[3] and to confound his speech at Babel.[4] But while we have such representations, similar in principle to the representations of the sources from which the compilers of these tales drew their material, yet in general Yahaweh is represented as acting on moral grounds, and as showing loving-kindness and mercy toward men.

The stories of the Patriarchs, beginning with the twelfth chapter of Genesis, are of a different origin. One important element is local folklore and especially the tales of the local sanctuaries which were adopted by the Hebrews. The story of Abraham in the Judæan narrative connects itself with Mamre or Hebron and with a tomb, or *ziara*, of Abraham at that place. It is evident from the story

[1] Gen. vi, 2 ff.   [2] Gen. viii, 21.   [3] Gen. iii, 22.   [4] Gen. xi, 6 f.

that the sanctity of this place antedated the Hebrew occupation. This sanctity was taken over by the Hebrews, with its local traditions. With these local traditions were combined by the Hebrews their own ethnic traditions, so that Abraham becomes in a sense the impersonation of the Hebrew people. Even the great historical event of the deliverance of the Hebrews from Egypt appears, as already pointed out, in the Judæan narrative of Abraham. The Israelite, or Elohistic, narrative connects the name of Abraham with the region further southward, about Beersheba, a favorite place of pilgrimage for Israelites. With this latter region, and especially with the shrine of Beersheba, were connected also the name and the traditions of Isaac.

The name of Jacob was associated with the ancient sanctuary of Bethel. This was conquered by the Israelites, who, according to the early and evidently historical narrative in Judges,[1] destroyed the inhabitants. But clearly also they took over the ancient sanctuary, so that in the same narrative we read that "the messenger of Yahaweh went up from Gilgal to Bethel; and they offered sacrifice there to Yahaweh."[2] With the sanctity of the place were taken over its cult and its traditions, the great *mazzebah* which Jacob set up, and the natural high place, rising in terraces, like steps, or a *ziggurat*, heavenward. With the local traditions of the ancient shrine were combined the folklore of Israel, and the native Jacob was identified with the conquering Israel. As in the case of Abraham, so here, also, the descent into, and the return from, Egypt were woven into the story, until the folklore connected primarily with the sanctuary of Bethel became a compendium of the national legends and traditions.

Somewhat similarly, with Shechem was associated Joseph, who becomes the parent of the great central tribes of Manasseh and Ephraim.

As these stories have come down to us, they have been brought into connection with one another and with the worship of Yahaweh. He has displaced the local divinities, and these are His shrines consecrated by those honored fathers, the Patriarchs, who, after

---

[1] I, 22 ff.   [2] Jud. ii, 1, 5.

a method common in other religions, have been brought into a genealogical relation.

Other shrines and cults were more local in their influence. In the story of Jephthah [1] an historical event of Israel's history has been brought into connection with a cult in Gilead in which the maidens lamented " four days in the year for the daughter of Jephthah." In the story of Samson [2] we have, apparently, combined with historical events of a struggle with the Philistines, mythical elements connected with the neighboring Beth Shemesh, the sanctuary of the sun-god Shamash. Here we have also a strange and primitive combination of the Nazarite and the consecrated harlot. Both of these stories, like that of Judah and Tamar, already noticed, bring us into connection with the obscene sexual worship evidently so common in Canaan. It is probable that other stories of a similar character existed in the earlier period, and that those tales which have come down to us contained gross elements which were later glossed over or eliminated. Considering their origin in the cult and myths of the native shrines, this is at least what we should expect. The remarkable fact is that these grosser elements should have been so effaced, and at such an early date, that the earliest Judæan and Israelite collections contain only such feeble traces of them as are noted above. [3]

The lore of most of the sanctuaries perished, or was preserved in small fragments mingled with later history or with the great stream of popular story which connected itself with Bethel, Mamre, and Beersheba. So popular on the other hand did the tales connected with these sanctuaries become that Abraham, Isaac, and Jacob assumed a national existence, dissociated to some extent from locality, and connected with the people as a whole. These stories, as their content shows, the historical references interwoven

---

[1] Jud. viii.　　　　　　　　[2] Jud. xiii–xvi.

[3] It is worthy of note that the stories of Jephthah and Samson belong to the concubine tribes of Gad and Dan, which we have reason to suppose were of Canaanite origin. These stories may, therefore, be connected with their ancient worship. In the case of Dan the myths or legends of Beth Shemesh are mingled with the historical struggle against the Philistines. All the more remarkable becomes the monotheistic transformation which they underwent in the crucible of Israelite folklore.

with the earlier myths and legends, had assumed form before the time of David, as a part of the lore of the nation. They were utilized later as history by the early historical writers of Judah and Israel, and underwent more or less modification and probably also spiritualization at the hands of those writers. But the gist and the bent of these tales were presumably settled long before the time of those writers or compilers.

As a whole this patriarchal lore presents a pure and spiritual, if naïve and childlike, conception of mingled religion and morality. Especially is this the case with the story of Abraham, whose character is depicted as wonderfully grand and beautiful. He becomes a type of that unworldly goodness rooted in faith which the later prophets preach. At the divine command he leaves his home to seek a foreign land which God promises to give him. His wife is barren, and God promises that his seed shall inherit the land. At God's command he prepares to offer up his only son. He goes through life listening for the true teaching of God, which is not shut up in formal precepts.[1] He is hospitable, merciful, compassionate.

The story of Jacob does not present so high a model, and that of Isaac is shadowy compared with the others, but all alike exhibit a clear conception of the difference between Israel and other peoples, more particularly the Canaanites, and their racial and religious antagonism to the latter. Israel is the people of Yahaweh, whom He has chosen from among all peoples, and to whom He has given the land of Canaan. Abraham, Isaac, and Jacob are their ancestors, strangers to the Canaanites among whom they dwelt, to whom Yahaweh promised children and heirs, which they are. Their relation to Yahaweh is a moral one, or rather He is a moral God who abhors and punishes sensuality and crime. So He destroys Sodom and Gomorrah with fire and brimstone because of their unnatural lust, from which, as it would seem, Moab and Ammon as well as Israel were free. How prevalent this unnatural lust was, and that it was sanctioned by religion, is made clear by the later history and legislation of Israel. How abhorrent it was to the better consciences in Israel, and yet how great a danger to the

---

[1] Cf. article "Abraham," in *Encyclopædia Biblica.*

people, is shown not only by the story of Sodom and Gomorrah [1] but also by the ancient and gruesome story of the crime of Gibeah,[2] which is evidently in its main features historical. Another of the abominations, not only of Canaan but also of the surrounding nations, was the sacrifice of first-born sons. This is condemned in the story of Abraham's would-be offering of Isaac, which recognizes the right of God to the first-born, for whom, by substitution, is to be sacrificed a ram.[3]

The deliverance from Egypt, the life in the wilderness, and the formation of the people of Israel under the law of Yahaweh, form the center of a cycle of traditions of another character, entirely Israelite in origin, centering around the person of Moses. These traditions evidently originated among the people before the time of the Judæan and Israelite collectors, by whom they were gathered together and incorporated in their histories. In these traditions Moses is represented as the founder of the nation and religion of Israel, the interpreter and mediator to it of the will of Yahaweh, who gives it a law from Yahaweh. Accordingly the laws which existed at the time when these collections were made were ascribed to Moses, who was supposed to have obtained them from Yahaweh. This cycle of traditions also makes clear the fact that the god of Israel was one, and that Israel might have no god besides Him, for He was a jealous god, who would brook no rival. Israel was a peculiar people, separated from the nations, holy to Yahaweh. Yahaweh fought for them and gave them the land of the Canaanites for an heritage.

Closely connected with this cycle are the traditions of the conquest of Canaan, which reveal the same conception of Israel's relation to Yahaweh and to the nations of Canaan. Intermarriage with them is forbidden, since it involves acceptance of their gods. The worship of those gods was connected with immoral practices abhorrent to the religion of Yahaweh.[4] Sometimes, however, we

---

1 Gen. xix.   2 Jud. xix–xxi.

3 Gen. xxii. This appears in the Israelite narrative (E) and seems to be a product of the period of reflection, when these stories were collected, rather than a part of the original Hebrew lore.

4 Cf. Num. xxv, 1 ff.

find that some foreign or even immoral practice has been condoned and has lingered on, its existence being accounted for and excused by a story like that of Rahab, the harlot of Jericho, which may have an historical foundation.[1]

Following this we have a cycle of local and tribal traditions of the vicissitudes of the occupation of the land, the struggles with Canaanites, Moabites, Ammonites, Midianites, and Philistines, material contained in our present Book of Judges, with part of Samuel. These traditions are diverse in character and some of them have connections with local shrines and cults, as already pointed out.

With the story of Saul we begin to find ourselves on more strictly historical ground, the events narrated being closer to the time of their recording, and the conditions favoring a more accurate preservation of the facts. The story of David was written almost, if not quite, by contemporaries, and from that time on we are dealing in general with history. But throughout all this mass of diverse material — Babylonian-Canaanite myths and legends, the legends of the sanctuaries, tribal and clan legends and traditions, the national traditions of Israel, the stories of its legendary and traditional heroes, its patriotic and folk songs, the records of court chroniclers and historiographers, and the stories of the Prophets — runs the same monotheistic strain, the same pure, moral tone, distinct from and antagonistic to the surrounding polytheism and religious licentiousness.

The picture of Yahaweh's religion and of Israel's relation to Yahaweh, which we obtain from these earliest writings, may be roughly described as follows: Yahaweh is a person, like man, only wiser and stronger. He walks in the garden of Eden in the cool of the day, He comes down to see what man is doing at Babel, He visits Abraham in human form. But in the later thought represented in these writings we find a movement away from this naïve anthropomorphism. He reveals himself through His messenger, He shows himself in the pillar of cloud and fire, man cannot see Him face to face, but only His hinder parts, and we even reach in the story of Elijah the thought of His manifestation not

[1] Josh. ii; vi, 22 ff.

in the cloud or the fire or the earthquake, but in the still, small voice which speaks in the heart of man. He is localized, having His abode in Horeb or Sinai, in the land of Canaan, which becomes His land, or more peculiarly in this or that sacred spot or object in which He manifests himself. He dwells in the Ark, in the cherubim, He is worshiped in the stones or pillars at or on which one pours out the blood or the oil and which one touches or strokes. He is summoned by the smell of the sacrifice, and placated and satisfied by it; He consumes it by His fire. But withal He dwells unseen, in a region and a wise beyond the ken of man, in thick darkness. This is all very crude, unphilosophical, and inconsistent; and it is inconsistent partly because it represents different stages in the development of the thought of God, partly because it is unphilosophical. They knew Yahaweh only as they came in contact with Him; beyond that, not being speculative, they did not go.

Yahaweh is clearly marked off from the forces of nature, which He controls. He is a jealous God, not tolerating any god beside himself, and therefore all supernatural agencies and effects in His land are centered in Him. He sends alike drought and rain, famine and plenty, sickness and health. Greatly to be feared is His wrath, which He displays especially towards Israel's foes, but at times also towards Israel itself when it violates His honor and sanctity. While in general Yahaweh has an ethical character and bestows His bounties or displays His wrath for moral causes, yet this is by no means always the case. The causes of His wrath are at times unethical, due to a transgression of His prerogative in some possibly unknown manner; and because His wrath is thus at times unethical, therefore also it must be satisfied by unethical and savage means, such as the sacrificial or semi-sacrificial death of innocent offenders, or members of the family of the offender.[1]

But it was not in general the wrath of God which was in the mind of the Israelite in connection with God. In its outward expression, in its feasts and its friendly relations with its God, the religion of Israel was glad and joyful, and a similar conception of

[1] Cf. the death of Saul's descendants, 2 Sam. xxi.

the relations of Israel to Yahaweh shows itself in these writings. The Israelite was proud of his God, and of His unique power and character. He delights to tell of the victories of his God over the gods of other peoples. In Egypt his God enables Moses to over-match the sorcery of the Egyptians. But in Israel's relation to Him there is neither sorcery nor magic art, in fact there is a remarkable freedom from superstition. This and the thought that Yahaweh alone was lord in Canaan led to the condemnation of sorcery and witchcraft, which, nevertheless, continued to be practiced. Clearly the common people believed in the existence of malignant spirits, whom they sought to propitiate in order to avoid their curse and win their favor, and through whom, or the spirits of the dead, they sought to obtain guidance and knowledge of the future. The higher thinkers, although not prepared to dispute the existence of such agencies, nevertheless opposed their recognition and cult as an offense against the jealousy and exclusiveness of Yahaweh, who can and does in fact himself fill this field, so that the propitiation or consultation of such spirits is really quite unnecessary.

The name *Yahaweh*, as already pointed out, while it plays in these writings a larger part probably than it did in common practice, is not even there the exclusive use. Men might, and did, call God *baal*, or *melek*, or *adon*, or " father," " uncle," " brother," etc., and in Israel there was more particularly an inclination to use the more general *el*, " deity," or *elohim*, " God." This rendered it easier at the outset to identify the God of Israel with the gods of the various local shrines, the *baal* or " god " or " father," of Mamre or Bethel or whatever else. But gradually more emphasis is laid upon the special name, *Yahaweh*, of Israel's God. This development we can trace in these writings.

And now where and under what influences were these writings composed, and what relation did they bear to the actual religion of the people in the preprophetic period?

They bore the same relation to the actual religion of the people which the works of a few spiritual-minded thinkers, chiefly monks, bore to the actual religion of the masses of the people in Italy or France or Germany or England in the Dark Ages. The name of Yahaweh, the tradition of His wonderful deliverances of His people, the belief that Israel was the people of Yahaweh, — this the people held fast in the darkest part of the dark ages of Israel. This colored their folklore. There was a remembrance also of Moses, but, one would judge, very little of his teaching or religion, except as that and the rough morality of the nomad combined to protect them somewhat against the licentiousness of the religion of Canaan, or to keep alive a protest against it. A more formal expression of Moses' religious teaching was preserved in the cult connected with the Ark, and probably also, borrowed from that, in a more or less modified form in other shrines. A more ethical recollection and understanding of the religion of the great prophet and founder was preserved by a few thinkers. With the development of the national and literary sense this was applied to the folklore which had sprung up or been borrowed in the ways above indicated, with the result of selecting what was best in that, and modifying and spiritualizing it still further.[1] The strengthening of the national sense aroused a desire to be informed of the past, and a pride in the nation's origin, achievements, and, as it were, peculiarities, which greatly reënforced the literary and religious motives. With the attempt to study their past comes inevitably a higher appreciation of the ethical aspect of the religion of Moses and a truer perception of the principles of that religion. We have here in fact the same sort of result which followed from the attempt among Christians to study the life and teachings of Jesus. This affected in its turn the folklore as embodied in the national stories which were being collected, and this again, as the culture and the national sense of the people increased, affected a constantly increasing number, but in its entirety always a relatively small minority. Religious practice did not change at all in pace with the changed conceptions of the thinking few who were most deeply affected by the spiritual and ethical literary development, until at last the latter came to be not only far in advance of but also in opposition to the common expression of religion among the people, and the ideas

[1] The Judæan story is on the whole closer to the folklore than the Israelite, which shows more of the reflective and conscious element.

connected with that expression.[1] This was the condition reached in the prophetic period, but prepared for by the school of writers and compilers whose work has come down to us in the fragments of the Judæan and Israelite collections known in the Hexateuch as J and E, with the kindred material in Judges, Samuel, and Kings.

In that period, as we shall see later, those whom we know as the Prophets, and whose sayings and writings have been passed down as such, stood, as a rule, in opposition to, or were distrusted by, the contemporary religious authorities, including the great bulk of the prophets of their day.

---

[1] For parallels in Anglo-Saxon chronicles and laws to the growth of Hebrew chronicles and legislation described in this and the succeeding chapter, cf. Carpenter-Battersby, *Hexateuch*, Vol. I, chap. i; Peters, *The Old Testament and the New Scholarship*, chap. v.

CHAPTER XII

EARLY CODES

The compilers of the Judæan and Israelite narratives found codes of laws in existence.[1] These they embodied in the story of Moses, as the great lawgiver, who had given the words and the judgments of Yahaweh to Israel.

From the Judæan compilation only a small fragment of a ritual code has come down to us. This fragment consists of "words," short utterances of command or prohibition, and may have constituted a decalogue. The "words" have, however, undergone considerable expansion, and it is not altogether clear what was their original form, nor how much of the expansion occurred in the code, and how much was due to the compiler of the narrative in which the code was embalmed. It was originally the ritual code of a Yahaweh sanctuary ; not the code of the priests, but a simple code

---

[1] For the analysis of these codes cf. Carpenter-Battersby, *Hexateuch*; Addis, *Documents of the Hexateuch*; Bacon, *Exodus*, in loc.; also Briggs, *Higher Criticism of the Hexateuch*, appendices.

The Babylonian code of Hammurapi (ca. 2000 B.C.) shows sufficient resemblance to the early Israelite code contained in Ex. xx–xxiii to suggest kinship. Hammurapi's code was formed, like that of Alfred the Great, largely of already existing material. Whether, during the period of Babylonian supremacy, Hammurapi's code affected Canaan, resulting in the development there of laws and legal principles which later passed on to the Hebrews ; or whether those laws and legal principles were derived from a common source, antedating Hammurapi, is not clear. For our purpose it is sufficient to know that the Hebrews found in Canaan laws and legal principles akin to those in the code of Hammurapi, which they took over and applied. It is perhaps worthy of note that the early Israelite code shows a less developed industrial and civil organization than that of Hammurapi, although the latter antedates the former by a thousand years. For a fuller account of the code of Hammurapi, and a comparison of Hebrew law with that code, see Harper, *The Code of Hammurabi*; Johns, *Babylonian and Assyrian Laws, Contracts and Letters*; Kent, *Israel's Laws and Legal Precedents*; Jeremias, *Moses und Hammurabi*; D. H. Müller, *Die Gesetze Hammurabis und ihr Verhältniss zur mosaischen Gesetzgebung sowie zu den xii Tafeln*; Kohler-Peiser, *Hammurabis Gesetz*.

dealing with the relations to the sanctuary of the people in general. Some of it is very primitive in tone, but as a whole it represents the conditions of settled existence, after the Hebrews had adopted, together with the village and agricultural life, some part of the ritual uses of the Canaanites (Ex. xxxiv, 14–26) : [1]

Thou shalt not bow down to another god (for Yahaweh is Jealous, His name, He is a jealous god).

A molten god thou shalt not make thee.

The feast of unleavened bread thou shalt keep. (Seven days thou shalt eat unleavened.)

All that openeth the womb is mine (namely, all thy cattle that is male, the opener of ox and sheep; and the opener of the ass thou shalt redeem with a sheep, and if thou redeem it not, thou shalt break its neck).

All firstlings of thy sons thou shalt redeem (and they shall not appear before me empty).

Six days thou shalt work, and on the seventh day thou shalt keep sabbath. (In plowing time and harvest thou shalt keep sabbath; and the feast of weeks thou shalt make, the firstlings of the wheat harvest; and the feast of ingathering, at the close of the year.)

Three times in the year shall all thy males appear before the Lord Yahaweh, the God of Israel.

Thou shalt not offer with leaven the blood of my sacrifices (and there shall not remain until morning the sacrifice of the feast of the passover).

The first of the firstlings of the ground thou shalt bring into the house of Yahaweh, thy God.

Thou shalt not cook a kid in its mother's milk.

The legislative material in the Israelite narrative [2] is more extensive and more varied, consisting of " words," statutes (*hukkîm*), and judgments (*mishpatîm*), and dealing not only with ritual but also with civil relations. At the close of this compilation we have

---

[1] A study of this code shows that in the form here given it is not all from one source; as it has come down to us it has been still further expanded by comments and explanations.

[2] Ex. xx–xxiii.

a series of ritual prescriptions almost identical with those in the second pentad of the Judæan code:

Six days thou shalt do thy work, and on the seventh day thou shalt keep sabbath.

Three times shalt thou feast to me in the year. (The feast of the unleavened thou shalt keep; and the feast of the harvest, the first fruits of thy labors which thou sowest in the field; and the feast of the ingathering, in the going out of the year, when thou gatherest in thy labors from the field. Three times in the year shall all thy males appear before Yahaweh, the God of Israel.)

Thou shalt not sacrifice with leaven the blood of my sacrifice (and there shall not remain of the fat of my feast until morning).

The first of the firstlings of the ground thou shalt bring into the house of Yahaweh, thy God.[1]

Thou shalt not cook a kid in its mother's milk.[2]

This ritual code in the Israelite compilation follows a somewhat heterogeneous mass of " words, " statutes, and judgments, which includes all but one of the provisions contained in the Judæan code, mixed in with other material.[3] Immediately preceding the ritual code above quoted is an extension of the Sabbath commandment which shows both reflection and ethical development — the provision for a sabbatical seventh year in which the land, including by an after provision vineyards and olive yards, shall lie fallow, that the poor of the people and the wild creatures may eat.

Preceding this are two pentads on the administration of justice, separated by a couple of judgments[4] enforcing the obligation of friendliness in regard to strayed beasts or beasts fallen under their burden, even though they belong to an enemy (not, as the word used shows, an alien, but a member of the community). It is, in other words, a community provision, enforcing the brotherly obligations and claims of Israelites toward one another. The pentads on the administration of justice commence with a commandment strikingly similar in form to the third commandment of

1 This ordinance and the next one are supposed by the critics to have been copied from the Judæan code by a harmonist.

2 Ex. xxiii, 12–19.   3 Ex. xxii, 18–xxiii, 11.   4 Ex. xxiii, 4–5.

the Decalogue of Moses, against false swearing. The first pentad [1] deals with the witness, and ends with the command " And the poor man thou shalt not favor in his cause." The second pentad [2] deals with the duties of the judge. It commences with a commandment against wresting " the judgment of the poor in his cause," prohibits gift taking by the judge, and closes with the commandment " A stranger thou shalt not oppress." The latter commandment, in a slightly different form, appears also in an earlier part of this same collection of laws. [3] This pentad has undergone some commentation of a hortative character.

Immediately preceding these two pentads on the administration of justice is a not altogether homogeneous group [4] of five " words," prescribing the offering to Yahaweh of the first fruits [5] of crops, vineyards, and orchards (literally, " thy fullness and thy tear "), and the first-born of sons and cattle, the latter on the eighth day. Then follows a commandment to eat no flesh torn by beasts, on the ground that the Israelites are holy to Yahaweh. This is based on the idea of the sacrificial nature of all flesh eating. Israelites, being holy to Yahaweh, that is, separated or peculiar to Him, might partake only of flesh sacrificed to Him. Preceding this pentad, mixed with judgments in regard to loans, and in part considerably expanded and commentated, is a heterogeneous pentad of " words " and statutes, scarcely constituting originally a unit : [6]

A sorceress thou shalt not let live.

Any one lying with a beast shall be put to death.

He sacrificing to a god (or the gods), except Yahaweh only, shall be devoted (that is, utterly destroyed).

(And) a stranger thou shalt not wrong (neither oppress him).

God (that is, the judges) thou shalt not revile (nor curse a ruler of the people).

The body of the so-called Book of the Covenant [7] is a mass of case laws, or judgments, with a few statutes intermingled, dealing

---

[1] Ex. xxiii, 1–3.

[2] Ex. xxiii, 6–9.

[3] Ex. xxii, 21.

[4] Ex. xxii, 29–31.

[5] A commandment to offer the first fruits probably stood originally before the prohibition to cook a kid in its mother's milk. See Bacon, *Exodus*, in loc.

[6] Ex. xxii, 18–28.

[7] Ex. xxi–xxii, 17.

in general with property relations, injuries, and so forth. These judgments are introduced by an "if," that is, ' in the case of,' and are cast as a rule in the form of pentads and double pentads. The judgments are based either on generally accepted principles or on statutes, but in only two cases do we find these quoted in connection with the judgments based on them : once in the law of injuries, where we have the *lex talionis*, or general foundation principle of retaliatory punishment, cited, " life for life, eye for eye, tooth for tooth, hand for hand, foot for foot, burning for burning, hurt for hurt, blow for blow " ; and once where we have in participial form four general rules dealing in a less primitive way with acts to be punished by the death penalty, and under one of these two judgments :

He smiting a man that he die shall be put to death (and under this two cases, [1] where the murder was not premeditated, in which case the murderer may claim the benefit of sanctuary ; [2] where the murder was premeditated, in which case sanctuary shall not protect him).

He smiting his father or his mother shall be put to death.

He stealing a man and selling him (or if he be found in his possession) shall be put to death.

He reviling his father or mother shall be put to death.

This collection of case laws has the heading " These are the judgments which thou [Moses] shalt set before them," which marks it off as an entity, a code which had grown up through decisions, and which was known and had the sanctity of prescription and religion at the time the Israelite narrative was compiled.

Preceding this collection we find a few ancient prescriptions of a ritual nature,[1] apparently not altogether homogeneous or contemporaneous in origin, concerned with the worship at Yahaweh sanctuaries, which the compiler evidently found in existence, but very likely without explanations or hortatory additions, and which are by him placed in the mouth of Moses as spoken by Yahaweh :

" Ye shall not make with me [other gods]. Gods of silver and

[1] Ex. xx, 23–26.

gold ye shall not make you. An earthen altar (or earthen altars) thou shalt make me (and thou shalt sacrifice thereon thy holocausts, and thy peace offerings, thy sheep and thine oxen ; in every place where I record my name, I will come to thee and bless thee).

" And if thou make me an altar of stones, thou shalt not build them hewn (if thou lift up thy tool upon it, thou hast profaned it). And thou shalt not go up on steps to my altar (that thy nakedness be not discovered thereon)."

The Decalogue, and the story of how Moses gave that first and fundamental law of Yahaweh to the people, has been brought into connection, in the Israelite narrative,[1] with this compilation of " words," statutes, and judgments, being placed immediately before it. It is given as an entity,[2] in which both the order of the commandments and their contents were well known and established, but receives the same explanatory and hortatory treatment, apparently from the compiler or compilers, as do the laws in the other codes. So the commandment to make no graven image is defined as meaning the likeness of anything in the three realms, and is explained and enforced by a reference to the jealousy of God. In a somewhat similar manner the Sabbath " word " and the " word " against coveting are defined and applied in detail to the existing conditions of life.

The largest single element in this compilation of laws is the collection of case laws, or judgments. These represent the settled but simple conditions of a primitive agricultural people. The right or duty of blood revenge is assumed, but it has been modified by the law of sanctuary. There is also justifiable homicide, as in the case of night robbery, in which the primitive rule of blood revenge does not apply. We find in general the same stage of civilization in regard to taking life and protecting property which prevails to-day among Arabs in the village state. As in the case of murder and theft, so in the case of adultery the fundamental law is not mentioned, since these are only judgments in cases not clear under the general rule. We have, however, a judgment in regard to fornication

---

[1] We find the same arrangement in Deuteronomy, and apparently there was a similar arrangement in the Judæan narrative.   [2] Ex. xx, 1–17.

with an unmarried woman, for which a money penalty is provided. This is based on the conception of marriage as a matter of purchase, in which the man pays the father or family of the bride, as among village Arabs to-day. Community rights and obligations are developing, as is shown by judgments regarding indirect injury. As a result of property inequality native slavery, that is, slavery of Hebrew by Hebrew, exists, but is tempered by a recognition of race relationship and brotherhood obligation, which does not exist toward outsiders. By the provision of the sabbatical year,[1] also, the Hebrew man slave had his release at the end of seven years. The Hebrew female slave or concubine was protected by a provision similar to that regarding wives. The relation toward the alien slave was different.[2] In the matter of injury he was a little better than property, but much less than a fellow Hebrew. But there are in the appendices to this code of judgments general rules of kindliness and consideration toward the stranger sojourning among them, enforced by exhortations from the compilers. In general these laws present a kindly, if rude and primitive, picture of the relations of life. In general, also, it may be supposed that the practices represented by these laws were borrowed from the Canaanites. On the other hand, they make clear the sharp distinction existing between Hebrew and non-Hebrew. The recommendation of kindness toward the stranger, almost as much as the difference in the provisions regarding Hebrew and alien slaves, makes clear the fact that the Hebrew was " holy unto Yahaweh," and that the law of the Hebrew did not apply to the alien.

The source of these laws and the method of their development are well explained in the form of a narrative, the story of the advice of Jethro, Moses' father-in-law, in the Israelite compilation.[3] " Be thou for the people to Godward, and bring thou the causes unto God;

---

1 It is not clear whether this was a special Hebrew development.

2 The danger from and temptation to man stealing, owing to the universal demand for slaves among the surrounding nations, are shown by the statute against man stealing.

3 Ex. xviii, 19 ff. This is sometimes regarded as literally historical. It seems to me rather in the nature of an explanation of later conditions, of which it gives presumably a true picture.

and thou shalt teach them the statutes and the laws. . . . Moreover thou shalt provide out of all the people able men, such as fear God, men of truth, hating unjust gain, and place such over them . . . and let them judge the people at all seasons ; . . . every great matter they shall bring unto thee, but every small matter they shall judge themselves." The primary source of the law was God, and His *torah*, or instruction, the sanctuary priests gave to the people. To them the people always turned for interpretations or decisions in cases of doubt or difficulty. So in the Book of the Covenant it is provided that in the case of a question as to trespass or loss of property the parties in dispute shall come before God, that is, to the sanctuary, for decision. Similarly, when a Hebrew slave elected to remain with his master instead of claiming his release in the seventh year, he was to be brought before God and his ear bored through against the doorpost of the sanctuary in witness and pledge of his perpetual servitude. In a statute in the appendices of the Book of the Covenant, God, that is, the sanctuary priests or judges, and rulers are joined together on the same plane. This legislation represents primarily the agency of the priests and sanctuaries, — and presumably also the Prophets, as special interpreters of God's oracles, — in the development of Hebrew civilization and Hebrew religion, as interpreters of the law of God.[1] But besides the sanctuaries there were also civil courts in which the village or town elders, or judges appointed by the king, or the king himself, not only executed sentence but also gave judgment and promulgated statutes. So David makes a decision regarding the division of the spoils, which has the force of statute henceforth.[2] In general, David kept in close connection with priestly decisions or prophetic utterances, the interpretations of the will of God either by lots cast by Abiathar before the Ark or by the oracles of Gad and Nathan. Solomon is represented as holding court and executing sentence.[3] In the story of Ahab and Naboth[4] it is the elders and nobles who act as judges. Some of

---

[1] There was, besides the laws which have come down to us in these codes, a mass of laws and customs to which we find allusions or which are assumed in the early narrative, but which we do not find formulated until a later period, — levirate marriage, divorce, circumcision, laws of clean and unclean marriage relations, etc.

[2] Sam. xxx, 24-25.   [3] 1 Kings iii, 16-28.   [4] 2 Kings xxi.

the judgments and statutes contained in this compilation emanate from such tribunals, but up to the time of the destruction of Samaria it is plain, from the references of the early prophets, that in Israel the priests of the sanctuaries or the Prophets, as interpreters of the *torah* of God, continued to exercise practically legislative functions. It was their part to interpret in doubtful cases, and to decide questions of the application of generally accepted law or custom to new cases, all law or custom being held to originate from God. The elders or the king and his officers could enforce penalties, try cases, or proclaim statutes.[1]

There are two statutes in these collections which recall historical events in such a manner as to suggest a connection between statute and event: "A sorceress thou shalt not let live," which recalls the statement that Saul had cut off the witches from the land;[2] and " He sacrificing to a god, except Yahaweh only, shall be devoted," which represents so precisely the attitude of King Jehu[3] that it may well have taken this particular form at that period.

It has been pointed out that some of the individual laws in both the Judæan and Israelite compilations, as also the codes as a whole, are provided with explanatory and hortatory comments. These represent the prophetic tendencies of the compilers, the preaching and moralizing tendencies. In the Israelite narrative a conflict between prophetic and priestly elements makes itself felt; there is no such conflict in the Judæan narrative. The latter represents more closely, especially in its older strata, the best and most spiritual side of folklore. There is also in the Judæan narrative a sympathetic touch with the Temple of Yahaweh at Jerusalem, where the Ark was the special object of veneration as the representative of Yahaweh. The two stories of the making of the golden calf in the wilderness illustrate the difference of attitude of the two narratives towards the

---

1 In Judah there was presumably more centralization, more of regal and less of popular government, than in Israel, where, to the last, local sanctuaries and town elders continued to play the chief part. The story of the organization of justice by Jehoshaphat (2 Chron. xix, 5–8), however, is chiefly, if not altogether, a midrash on his name, *Jehoshaphat,* " Yahaweh hath judged."

2 1 Sam. xxviii, 9.

3 2 Kings x, 15–28.

priests, and explain to some extent the reasons of that difference.[1] In the Judæan narrative the people, in Moses' absence on the mount, set up a golden calf. The Levites show themselves to be on Yahaweh's side, and for their faithfulness to Yahaweh are consecrated as the guardians of Yahaweh's proper sanctuary, the Ark with its tables of stone. This is a reflection backwards, into the story of Moses, of the great apostasy in the days of Rehoboam and Jeroboam, and the setting up of the golden calves in Israel in opposition to the ancient cult of the Ark handed down in the Temple of Yahaweh at Jerusalem. A similar attitude toward the Levites is shown in the Blessing of Moses,[2] where Levi is described as the bearer of the Urim and Thummim.

The Israelite narrative is more distinctly "prophetic" in its character and shows an inclination to interpret folklore from the ethical standpoint of "prophetism." In Israel the attitude of priests and prophets, or perhaps rather the attitude of the Prophets, toward the worship of the officially recognized shrines was quite different from that existing in Judah. As advocates of the national religion, the religion founded by Moses, it was inevitable that the Prophets should object to the cult of the golden calves as a defection from the ancient cult of the Ark of the Covenant, established by him. When this attitude was definitely assumed is not clear, perhaps not until after the time of Elijah; but at least the Israelite narrative of the golden calf makes it clear that the worship of the golden calf was condemned by the compilers of the Israelite document known as the Elohist, before the time of Amos and Hosea. In that narrative Moses, the prophet, is the founder of the true religion, and Aaron, the priest, panders to or misleads the people by setting up the golden calf. In another passage Aaron, the priest, and Miriam, the singing women of the sanctuary, contend with Moses, the prophet, saying, " Has Yahaweh indeed spoken with Moses only ? "[3] But in spite of this condemnation of the priesthood,

---

[1] Ex. xxxii. Cf. Bacon, *Exodus*; Addis, *Documents of the Hexateuch*; or any modern commentary for the analysis of this chapter, in its present form a composite of J and E.

[2] Deut. xxxiii, 8. Written about, or before, the middle of the eighth century.

[3] Num. xii, 2.

as misleading and pandering to the people in the worship of the calf, and this exaltation of prophetism as over against ritual, the divine place and mission of the priesthood, Aaron, is recognized, and the *torah*, emanating primarily from the sanctuaries, has been incorporated in the prophetic narrative.

The ritual codes contained in both the Judæan and the Israelite narrative reveal a monolatrous and practically monotheistic conception of Yahaweh, the God of Israel, corresponding to the conception exhibited in the treatment of the early myths, the patriarchal legends, and the national traditions of Israel. Him only may Israelites worship. He is the Creator of mankind. He chose out for himself the ancestors of Israel, brought them out of distant lands, guided and guarded them in all their wanderings. Because of Israel He visited the Egyptians with plagues, and delivered Israel from the land of Egypt. He controlled the powers of nature for their benefit, revealed His law in clouds and lightning and thunder, led them through the wilderness, brought them into Canaan, and gave them the land in possession, casting out the Canaanites before them. The agent of their deliverance was Moses, through whose mouth He taught them in His holy mountain His law and His religion. Both narratives emphasize the might, the wisdom, and the love of this God.

Both codes denounce image worship. In the matter of feasts and sanctuaries, sacrifice and common ritual observance, both codes, agreeing with the general representations of the narratives, show us the adoption of the holy places and the common usages of the country, and the combination with those usages of earlier Hebrew customs and traditions.

The narratives of J and E represent what we may call the prophetic, the codes embodied in them the priestly, point of view, the latter being earlier than the former. In general they are in agreement, both representing a high ethical standard; only toward the end of the period of this joint development do we find the beginnings of the conflict between the prophetic and the priestly point of view.

CHAPTER XIII

WRITING PROPHETS AND THEIR NEW DOCTRINES

With the writing prophets commences an epoch in the development of the religion of Israel, so modern in its conception of God and of man's relation to God, so advanced and apparently so clearly marked off from what precedes, that not a few modern writers have been led to assume this as the real commencement of the spiritual development of Israel's religion and to regard the writing prophets as the actual founders of that religion. In reality their work is rather like the visible superstructure of a building. From this point on the building is, as it were, apparent to our eyes. What was done before, in spite of its great importance, does not impress the imagination, because it is underground; but in reality the superstructure depends upon the foundation.

The practical monotheism with which the writing prophets begin, and on which they lay so great an emphasis, was already a tenet, as we have seen, of the spiritually minded thinkers in Israel. The conception of an ethical God, requiring ethical righteousness, so characteristic of the writing prophets, was no new thing. It appears in the Yahawistic and Elohistic narratives, and in the legislative codes embodied in those narratives; and even that identification of the ritual practiced by the Israelites as heathen and Canaanitish, which is so emphasized, for instance, in the prophecies of Hosea, was no new thing. The Prophets assumed for themselves and demanded for the people a direct personal relation to God, but in doing this they really did no more than the narrator of the story of Abraham had done in his picture of the relation of that patriarch to his God and their God, or the composer of the story of Elijah in his account of Elijah's communion with God at Horeb.

The way of the writing prophets had been prepared by the schools of the prophets, with their Israelitic chauvinism, and especially by the great prophetic movement headed by Elijah, with his call back to Yahaweh from the foreign Baal[1] and his stern and fearless denunciation of the moral evils of the oriental despotism which Ahab and Jezebel sought to establish in Israel. The way for the writing prophets had been prepared by the spiritual and monotheistic treatment and interpretation of the ancient myths, legends, and stories of Israel and Judah, which we find in the Judæan and Israelite narratives, and by the awakening, through those writings, of the interest of the people in its own past and the furtherance of the study of that past; necessarily resulting in a comparison of the religion of the present with the religion of Moses, to whom, and to the Patriarchs before him, with whom God made a covenant of promise, the whole life of the people was attributed. And finally the way for the writing prophets was prepared by the codes of legislation contained in those histories, which claimed to go back to Moses, regarding his teaching and his statutes as the foundation on which the whole superstructure rested, and thus referring the origin of their law and their religion to a period and a source antedating and different from their present Canaanitish environment.[2]

But while the superstructure which the first prophets commenced[3] to erect was founded on well-built and comprehensive foundations and could not have come into existence without them, none the

[1] The story of the destruction of the prophets of Baal by Elijah at Carmel may be an incorporation in the story of Elijah of the actual destruction of the foreign Baal worship by Jehu.

[2] Cf. such passages as the curse of Canaan for his shameless disregard of even the decencies of immorality, Gen. ix, 20 ff., with which cf. also Amos ii, 7 f.

[3] From Amos' style — the new prophetic diction which meets us full-grown in his book — it seems clear that the writing prophets in outward form also were founded upon predecessors whose works have vanished. It is not, however, necessary to suppose that the prophecies of these predecessors were, to any considerable extent certainly, written prophecies. It may well be that the schools of the prophets developed in their utterances this particular form of diction without committing those utterances to writing. But with Amos and Hosea we reach an age of considerable advancement in literary development, an age where those things can be written down which aforetime were only spoken; hence, while the utterances of Elijah, Elisha, and their ilk formed the style and prepared the way for the writing prophets of the middle of the eighth century B.C., it was not until the latter date that prophecies began to be preserved in written form, either by those who uttered them or by their friends and pupils, with a view to reaching a larger audience and even future generations.

less, precisely because with that work the superstructure does begin, the commencement of written prophecy marks a great epoch in the development of the history of the religion of Israel.

To understand those prophecies and why, at precisely this point, we should find such prophets and such prophecies, we must consider briefly the political and economic condition of Israel and Judah. Toward the middle of the ninth century, after a long period of quiescence, the Assyrians undertook the conquest of the West land, and finally, in 854 B.C., fought a great battle at Karkar with a Syrian and Palestinian alliance, of which Ahab of Israel was a part. As a result of that battle Shalmaneser III claims to have received tribute from those princes; but the Assyrian advance appears to have been checked.

Damascus was at that time the greatest and most aggressive of the western states, and Ahab and his successors fought against its aggression, sometimes for existence itself. The especial bone of contention between the two was the possession of Gilead.[1] To help him in these struggles, Ahab made an alliance with Tyre, which, with its consequence of the introduction of foreign worship, was denounced by the Prophets. Finally, as the result largely of prophetic opposition to the policy of foreign alliance of the house of Omri, sometimes with Tyre, sometimes with Damascus, the house of Omri was overthrown and Jehu usurped the throne, pledged to fight to the death against the foreigner and foreign gods. It was especially alliances with the neighboring nations, the Phœnicians, Syrians, and the like, with their temptations to the adoption of other gods beside Yahaweh, which seem to have been objectionable to the prophetic party of that day. Relations to a more distant nation, like Assyria, did not involve the same danger of foreignization. Hence we find Jehu in 842 B.C. paying tribute to Shalmaneser III, who was at that time engaged in war with Hazael of Damascus. For a time the Assyrian war, which Jehu thus furthered, held Damascus in check. But troubles in other quarters soon caused the withdrawal of the Assyrian armies from the West land, and enabled Hazael to turn his whole force against Israel. The war

[1] Cf. Gen. xxxi, 43 ff.

was à *outrance*,[1] and Israel suffered terribly. At length, however, under Shalmaneser's grandson, Adad-Nirari IV, the Assyrians resumed their advance upon Damascus, besieging and capturing it in 803 B.C. This enabled Jehu's grandson, Jehoash, to recover the ground lost by his predecessors. Thirty years later the Assyrians again overthrew Damascus. With its chief opponent crippled by this long struggle against the empire of the east, Israel was able to set itself free from foreign dominion altogether and, under Jeroboam II, to extend its dominion from Hamath on the north to the Dead Sea on the south, or, including the territory of its subject ally, Judah, from Hamath on the north to the Red Sea on the south. The joint dominion of Israel and Judah was, therefore, at this period, almost as extensive as at the time of David and Solomon.[2] This political eminence involved a similar economic eminence, and there was a consequent remarkable and very rapid advance in prosperity. Israel and Judah controlled the roads of commerce east and west, north and south. As a natural result of the commercial development which ensued, the cities of the country increased in number, wealth, and luxury. Agriculture ceased to be the only or even the chief source of national wealth. Fortunes were rapidly made, and, seeing that fortunes were to be made in the cities, the young and enterprising were attracted thither out of the fields and pastures; the old holdings of agricultural land were bought up by city dwellers, who had enriched themselves through commercial enterprises, and farm workers became, to a considerable extent, tenants and practically serfs of the townspeople. With this increase of wealth, so rapidly and readily gotten, developed a corresponding luxury and extravagance, in connection with which the slave trade flourished inordinately.

It was such conditions that awakened the consciences of the first writing prophets. The very prosperity which seemed to the people

---

1 Amos i, 3 ff.; 2 Kings xiii, 7.

2 The conditions of this period, the prosperity of the country, especially of the dominant Joseph, the friendly relations toward Judah, and the respect paid to the religion of Yahaweh and the Levites, as the officials sacrificing at his shrines, are reflected in the Blessings of Moses, Deut. xxxiii, an Israelite composition, with which compare, for an earlier period and a different political and religious point of view, the Blessings of Jacob, Gen. xlix.

at large an evidence of their own righteousness and the favor of God toward them aroused in the mind of the prophet a sense of indignation and wrath. That because of wealth they should pervert the ways of the fathers, the good old things which had come down from the past, was in itself an abomination. For, from the outset to the end of prophecy, as has been already pointed out, the prophet was in this a conservative: he stood close to the wilderness and primitive things; and therefore modern improvements, the refinements and luxuries of civilization, were offensive to him. But in this case there were also moral perversion and corruption, an effeminacy and immorality, which are, apparently, an inevitable concomitant of the sudden increase in wealth of a community or nation. These stirred the soul of a man like Amos to its very depths.[1]

It is evident, from Amos' prophecies, that he seized a particular occasion for prophesying, when the whole community was alarmed by certain great disasters. A pestilence,[2] an eclipse of the sun,[3] an earthquake[4] and a famine,[5] the latter caused by or connected with terrible devastations by locusts[6] and drought,[7] are mentioned in his prophecies. To the people these were evidences of the wrath of God. To Amos they were warnings which it was his part to interpret to the people; and the people, on their side, disturbed by such phenomena, were prepared to listen to the prophet who claimed to explain their meaning. It is to these peculiar circumstances that we may be said to owe the prophecies of Amos and their preservation; because through them he was led to prophesy, and through them he secured a hearing for his prophecies.[8]

[1] The conditions of Israel at this period have been aptly compared with those of England in the fourteenth century, which called forth Langland's *Vision of Piers Plowman*. See G. A. Smith, *The Twelve Prophets*, I, 42.

[2] iv, 10.

[3] v, 8, 18 ff.; viii, 9.

[4] i, 1; iv, 11.

[5] iv, 6; viii, 11.

[6] iv, 9.

[7] iv, 7; viii, 11.

[8] It is possible, through these events, to obtain an approximate date for the prophecies of Amos. From the Assyrian records we learn that there was a pestilence in 765 and an eclipse of the sun in 763. There seems every reason to assume that these are the pestilence and eclipse to which Amos makes reference. The earthquake, drought, and locust plague cannot be vouched for by similar evidence, but presumably they occurred at about the same time. The entire period of Amos' prophetic activity would seem to have been not more than a couple of years at the outside, commencing about, or shortly after, 763 B.C.

Amos resembles Elijah much more than the men of the prophetic schools, like Elisha. As he himself tells us, he was not a prophet by training and profession, but a herdsman and a gatherer of a poor grade of figs at Tekoa,[1] on the border of the Judæan wilderness. Israel, not Judah, was at this time the leader in religion and culture as well as in power, and Bethel was its religious capital. Moreover, to a man like Amos the out-of-door temple of Bethel, with its primitive and simple worship, was probably more congenial, or at least less uncongenial, than the more elaborate form of temple, on the Phœnician model, which Solomon had erected at Jerusalem. Apparently Amos came to Bethel primarily to seek and to worship God. Profoundly affected by the great phenomena of earthquake, eclipse, pestilence, locusts, drought, and famine, he instinctively sought a means to propitiate God and turn aside His wrath. But what he saw and experienced of the religion practiced at Bethel filled him with indignation; and the herdsman who had come to seek God at Bethel became a prophet to denounce God's wrath on the religion of Bethel. It may be added that Bethel, crowded on the occasion of the great festivals with pilgrims from all Israel, afforded an admirable opportunity to deliver his message effectively to the whole people, a vastly better opportunity than was offered by Jerusalem, the capital and shrine of the smaller Judæan state.

Preëminently Amos is a prophet of righteousness and wrath. First and foremost he is concerned in denouncing evil and threatening the punishment of God on evil-doing:

Ye that turn justice to wormwood;
And righteousness they throw to the earth.[2]
Oppressors of the righteous, takers of bribes,
Who have perverted justice from the needy.[3]
Ye have turned justice to gall,
The fruit of righteousness to wormwood.[4]

---

[1] vii, 14. The passage shows the distrust of those prophetic bands which existed among the most thoughtful and spiritual of Israel's leaders. The reaction against that form of prophetism and what it had come to stand for is perhaps still better evidenced by Hosea's condemnation of Jehu, who was the anointed of the "sons of the prophets" of his day.   [2] v, 7.   [3] v, 12.   [4] vi, 12.

The fact that, while doing such things, they supposed that their sacrifices and festivals and pilgrimages and gifts would be acceptable to God, seems to Amos especially outrageous and leads to the sternest denunciation of those things as evil, because, so far as he sees, they promote evil instead of preventing it. So he says:

Hear this, ye that grasp at the needy, to destroy the lowly of the earth; saying, When will the new moon be past, that we may sell grain? and the sabbath, that we may offer corn? And corn-chaff will we sell; making small the ephah, making large the shekel, making crooked the false weights, buying for silver the poor, and the needy for a pair of shoes.[1]

Or again, addressing himself on the occasion of some festival to the pilgrim crowds who have come to feast at Bethel:

I hate, I scorn your feasts;
I will not smell sacrifice in your solemn assemblies.
Though ye offer unto Me offerings of flesh and offerings of fruits, I am not pleased;
And the thank-offerings of your firstlings I regard not.
Put away from Me the noise of thy songs;
And the music of thy harps I hear not.
But let justice flow like waters,
And righteousness like an ever-flowing stream.[2]

It is with intense sarcasm that he makes mock of their religious ceremonies, sacrifices, etc.[3] These are the luxuries of religion, which are as offensive to him as the personal luxury of the rich men and women at which he scoffs in bitter songs.[4] This luxury and self-indulgence, won at the expense of justice and virtue, as the result of oppression and extortion, and this ritual, with its feasts and holy days, its tithes and sacrifices, an expression of that same luxury in another form, and an effort to make God a partner in their crimes, are equally damnable. Both alike are abhorrent to God, and for both God's judgment shall fall upon Israel.

In one striking passage Amos announces that famine, drought, pestilence, and earthquake have been sent to turn the people from

---

[1] viii, 4–6. [2] v, 21–24. [3] Cf. iv, 5; v, 4–7.
[4] Cf. iv, 1–3; vi, 1–8. These are almost, if not quite, lyrical, and may well have been sung or chanted. Later we find Isaiah making use of street and folk songs in his prophecies (Is. iii, 16; v, i), while Jeremiah mingles psalms, pæans, and dirges with his other more prosaic utterances.

their sin.[1] In another the famine becomes the text of a prophecy of the abandonment of the people by their God.[2] In another the eclipse of the sun forebodes dire affliction, like " the mourning for an only one." [3] At first Amos evidently expected the divine punishment to take the form of calamities which should not be final. " Yahaweh, God of Hosts, will peradventure show mercy upon Joseph's remnant." [4] " As the shepherd rescueth from the lion's mouth two shank-bones, or an ear-tip, so shall the sons of Israel be rescued, that dwell in Samaria, on the corner of a couch, on the damask of a divan." [5] As he finds that his words produce no effect, or as he himself develops in earnestness, conditions appear more terrible and the wrath of God more inexorable, until finally he prophesies the utter destruction of Israel, as a result of its sin. " Fallen, not to rise again, is the virgin of Israel; stretched upon the ground, none raiseth her." [6] The method in which this final destruction is to be wrought also becomes plain to him. It is not by earthquakes or pestilence or famine. Yahaweh will raise against the house of Israel a nation that shall afflict it " from the entrance of Hamath to the brook of the Arabah." [7] There is to be an adversary and besieger, who shall bring down the strength of the people, plunder its palaces, smite winter houses and summer houses,[8] etc. Jeroboam himself shall die by the sword,[9] Israel shall surely be led away captive out of the land.[10]

It is, of course, the Assyrian great power which is in Amos' mind, and, to the reader of the present day, it seems more or less a matter of surprise that the people at large should not have been more awake to the danger from this source than they seem to have been. Partly the cause of this confidence is made plain in Amos' prophecies. They counted themselves as having a peculiar relation to Yahaweh. He was their God and they His people, whom He could not desert. He had given evidence of His power in the past. He had brought them out of Egypt; He had driven out the Amorites before them; He had overthrown the Philistines; and more recently He had delivered them from the power of Damascus

---

1 iv, 6–13.	3 viii, 9 f.	5 iii, 12.	7 vi, 14.	9 vii, 9.
2 viii, 11.	4 v, 15.	6 v, 2.	8 iii, 12 ff.	10 vii, 17.

and given them their present prosperity. As He had overcome the gods of the nations in the past, so He would do in the future. They looked confidently to the " Day of Yahaweh," when He would intervene to conquer all their foes and give them even greater wealth than at the present time. We have here an expression of the simplest form of that Messianic hope which grounded itself in the events of the past, and in the Jewish kingdom more particularly in the great and glorious reign of David,[1] and which was to lead the Jews over and over again to revolt against their conquerors, where there would have seemed to others to be no chance whatsoever of success. Amos scoffs at this belief, declaring that the Day of Yahaweh, instead of an interference on their behalf for the punishment of the nations, would be a visitation in wrath upon them for their sins. " Woe unto you that desire the Day of Yahaweh! What would ye with the Day of Yahaweh? It is darkness and not light. For the Day of Yahaweh shall be to you as though a man fled from a lion, and a bear met him ; or as though he took refuge in the house, and rested his hand on the wall, and a serpent stung him. Is not the Day of Yahaweh darkness and not light, gloom and no brightness in it ? "[2]

As a natural consequence of this view of the dealings of Yahaweh with His people and His attitude toward them in connection with the world about, we find Amos placing Israel on a plane with the surrounding nations in the general denunciation of woe which he pronounces on them in common with Damascus, Gaza, Tyre, Edom, Ammon, and Moab.[3] As God will punish those nations for their moral ill-doing, so will He punish Israel for selling " the righteous for silver, the needy for a pair of shoes " ; for that land hunger which makes them grasp at the dust of the earth on the heads of the poor, and for that immorality which exhibits itself at the very sanctuary, where " father and son go in unto one damsel," where the worshipers stretch themselves on pawned clothes and drink debtor's wine in the house of their god.[4] More definitely

---

[1] There is a section in the last chapter of Amos' prophecies (ix, 11 ff.) which would seem to show that he also entertained the view of a restoration of Israel under a king of David's line ; but this is now generally regarded by scholars as an addition of a later period.   [2] v, 18 ff.   [3] i–ii.   [4] ii, 6 ff.

he sets forth the same point of view when, in answer to the claim of the people that they stand in a particular relation to God, who brought them up out of Egypt by His mighty power, he says that they differ in no respect from the nations about, for in the same way in which Yahaweh brought Israel from Egypt He brought the Philistines from Caphtor and the Syrians from Kir;[1] and in the same way in which Calneh, Hamath, and Gath have perished, Israel also shall perish off the earth.[2]

It should be said that here, as in the prophecy of the final destruction of Israel, Amos seems to work up to this extreme utterance as a result of opposition. The general tenor of his book shows that in practice he does not altogether place the Israelites on the same plane as the nations about them, just as in fact he does not really look to a final destruction, in spite of his extreme utterances to the contrary.[3] Indeed, his very denunciations of Israel are based upon his conception of their peculiar relation to God. " You only have I known of all the families of the earth: therefore upon you first I will visit all your iniquities."[4] In the same way, while some of his utterances seem to show a theoretical monotheism, — it is Yahaweh who has made all things in heaven and earth,[5] it is Yahaweh, and not some other god who rules the nations, and even makes them His tool for His judgment upon Israel, — yet the general tone of the book renders it probable that in fact this monotheism was practical rather than intellectual; that is, while exalting Yahaweh, as the god powerful over all, and regarding him as the one whom alone Israel should worship, Amos was not a philosophical monotheist; he had not reached the attitude of intellectual belief in the nonexistence of the gods.

In general Amos was a prophet of righteousness, denouncing the wrath of God — for Yahaweh is God — on all evil-doing, setting forth God as the righteous and mighty judge, concerned not with ritual, but with life, a God of morality. His religion may be described as emphatically a religion of morality, in which God is a great and awful power of righteousness, or rather righteousness personified. Of course Amos views the people as a whole; he is

---

[1] ix, 7.   [2] vi, 2.   [3] ix, 3 f.   [4] iii, 2.   [5] iv, 13 ff.; ix, 1 ff.

concerned with the nation rather than with the individual; he preaches national righteousness. Toward modern things and modern ways, the life of the city and the pleasures and luxuries which come with it, he is intolerant, as he is toward the wealth of ritual and the development of the sacrificial life. He is a man of the desert, who calls the people back to their desert ways and desert life.[1] He would have them do now what they did in the old times, of which he has heard and read, when God brought them out of the land of Egypt and they wandered forty years in the wilderness. They had then no altars for sacrifice to Yahaweh; those are the later inventions of their Canaanite life; and these sacrifices which they now offer on those altars are not really offered to Yahaweh, but to false gods. Therefore as once Yahaweh took them out of Egypt to wander in the wilderness, that He might teach them His way, so shall He take them again, with their star-gods and their images which they have made, and carry them captive beyond Damascus.[2] Amos is an enthusiast for Yahaweh, and one is even reminded by his utterances of the descendants of Jonadab, the son of Rechab, who assisted Jehu in extirpating the Baal worship.

Amos makes a vast advance on the teachings of the spiritual thinkers who had preceded him, as expressed in the Yahawistic and Elohistic narratives and the legislative codes embodied in them. For while, as already pointed out, they teach a personal relation with Yahaweh, and while they teach a practical monotheism and a high standard of moral righteousness, yet these teachings are combined in their narratives, and in the legislation contained in those narratives, with other material of a lower character. The Israelite may worship Yahaweh only, but Yahaweh is confined to

---

[1] Amos' training for prophecy, like his preaching, reminds one of John the Baptist. Amos was also, like John Baptist, no illiterate, in spite of his shepherd life. He knew the substance, at least, of the national writings, as his references to them show, and the very loneliness of his life led him to ponder on them, and on what he heard of the world about him, of the events occurring in that world and in the world of nature about and above him, — the stars, the seasons, bears and lions, famine, pestilence, and earthquake, — to see them in the large, freed from the pettiness of everyday life and the everyday religion of forms and ceremonies.

[2] v, 25 ff,

the land of Israel. He who passes the border of that land passes beyond the realm of Yahaweh's influence and might. Their morality is a morality which, on the whole, confines itself to Israel and the relations of Israelite to Israelite. So again Yahaweh is connected with certain places and shrines, where He has manifested himself, and the relation of the people to Him is conditioned by those shrines and the worship connected with them. And so, furthermore, while the moral code of those documents is a high one, yet its moral prescriptions are combined with ritual prescriptions, directions as to feasts, sacrifices, altars, and the like, the two things being set practically upon the same plane; and even the older Decalogue of Moses, on which both codes are primarily based and which they recognize as possessing a peculiar sanctity, is not itself entirely moral, but places the observance of the Sabbath, a ritual or ceremonial act, on the same footing with the worship of one God and the prohibition of murder, adultery, and the like.

Amos absolutely separates the moral from the ritual, and indeed even reacts to an extreme attitude regarding ritual; denouncing it altogether because of its practical exaltation above, or at the expense of, the moral law by his compatriots. His religion consists only of morality. He knows of no appearance of God in one place more than another, and in fact the very places in which, according to the Elohistic narrative, God especially showed himself to the fathers, became to him particularly abhorrent for the same reason that the ritual was abhorrent. Bethel is a curse. Instead of finding their God in Bethel, there Israel shall meet the punishment of God, and, so far from God being confined to Israel, God has manifested himself in the history of other nations, just as He has manifested himself in Israel. Israel believed in a special covenant between God and Israel, which established a peculiar relation of Israel to God, somewhat similar to the relation with their tutelary divinities claimed by the natives about them, only purer and more spiritual, at least in the conception of the higher thinkers. Their conception was a development of the common belief in a natural relation of the god to his people. They regarded the relation of Israel to the divinity as a preëminent relation, because of the greater power of their God, Yahaweh, and because of the peculiarly moral character of their God. Amos does not so far separate himself from the thought of his contemporaries as to deny this peculiar relation, but he bases the preëminence of Israel entirely on moral grounds. God has exhibited His favor to Israel by revealing His will to Israel through the Prophets.[1] The privilege of Israel is a greater enlightenment in the knowledge of God. Precisely in proportion to Israel's greater opportunity of knowing God a greater righteousness is demanded of him, and the punishment of a failure to exhibit that righteousness becomes the more terrible.

In many ways in striking contrast to Amos is the other great prophet of Israel, Hosea, whose prophecies come slightly later than those of Amos, toward the end of the same period of prosperity. Unlike Amos, he was a native of the land, one used to the ways of civilization and not offended by city life and its natural concomitants of comforts and luxuries as such. The introductory chapters of the book of prophecies bearing his name seem to contain, woven in, the history of his own life, which suggests both the cause of his prophetic activity and the thought foundation on which his prophecies rest. It was not outer conditions of war, pestilence, and the like which led him to prophesy, but first and foremost the condition of his own domestic affairs, by the experience of which he interpreted the relations of Yahaweh and Israel. He appears to have married a wife who proved false to him.[2] The children borne by her he did not regard as his own.[3] Ultimately leaving him or cast off by him, she descended to the condition of a fallen woman and sold herself or was sold into slavery as such.[4] Finally he found her and repurchased her and ultimately brought her back to himself.[5] This

---

[1] Am. iii, 7.

[2] Presumably this infidelity was in connection with the immoral Baal worship, in which prostitution of the person became an act of service to the god.

[3] After a common method, which we find also in Isaiah, the prophet gives his children significant names. The first, his own child, he names *Jezreel*. The second is *Lo-ruhamah*, "unpitied." The third, whom he repudiates utterly, is *Lo-ammi*, "not-my-kin"; and these children, their names, and the occasion of their birth he makes the vehicles of prophecy, precisely as Isaiah does with his children a little later. Hos. i, 6 ff. Cf. Is. vii, 3; viii, 1.

[4] Perhaps as a professional prostitute attached to a shrine.   [5] Hos. iii.

experience of her sin, his own continuing, yearning love toward her, and her ultimate redemption and restoration became to him an allegory of the relation of Yahaweh to Israel.

Elijah had put himself at the head of the battle against the introduction of the foreign Baal worship. The Yahawistic and Elohistic narratives show that from that time onward there was an increasing perception of the differentiation of Israel not only from the outside heathen but also from the Canaanites within their borders, and a differentiation of their own religion from the cults of the Canaanite sanctuaries, many of which, with their rites and practices, Israel had adopted, practically identifying Yahaweh with the various Baals of the land. Attention has already been called to the similarity of these conditions in Israel to those prevailing in Christendom in the Dark and Middle Ages. As then the gods, demigods, and heroes of the various heathen populations were either adopted bodily as Christian saints, or else their attributes, rites, and customs attached to some Christian saint or to God himself, so that, while nominally continuing to believe in one god, for all practical purposes the Christian Church became polytheistic,[1] so now Israel was really polytheistic, and, while claiming to serve one god, yet by serving him as the Baal of this or the Baal of that place, with the ritual and sacrifices formerly pertaining to the gods of those places, they were in fact worshiping so many separate gods. But there was one element in the heathenism of Canaan, practically nonexistent in the heathenism of Europe, which differentiated the religious conditions of Israel from those of Christianity, namely, the worship of the life-giving power, represented by the Baals, with sexual rites. It was this characteristic of Canaanitic worship, introduced into the cult of Yahaweh as expressed at the Canaanite shrines, which gives

---

[1] This experience was by no means peculiar to Christianity or to Israel; Islam and Buddhism both have made, or rather are making, the same experience. This is indeed a common fact of religious history, the survival of the primitive, popular religion, under and through the superimposed higher and more spiritual religions. Palestine itself furnishes even to-day one of the best illustrations of this. One may still find Jew, Christian, and Moslem worshiping together at the same shrine, under the same or different names, a saint, who is really a prehistoric god, with rites, and even sacrifices, which have been handed down from pre-Israelite times. Cf. Curtiss, *Primitive Semitic Religion*, chap. vii.

occasion for the continual use in the Hebrew prophets of terms and phrases which are not pleasant to modern ears, the characterization of the worship by Israel of other gods than Yahaweh as prostitution, often with much offensive detail. In point of fact that worship was apt to be prostitution in a very literal sense. While, as stated, the protest against the identification of Yahaweh with the Canaanite Baals began to be voiced in the Yahawistic and Elohistic narratives and legislation, it is Hosea who first makes this protest emphatic and distinct. As Elijah's mission was to protest against the introduction of the Tyrian Baal, or any other foreign god, and to affirm that Yahaweh alone was God of Israel; so Hosea's mission was to protest against the identification of the Baals of Canaan with Yahaweh, and the adoption of their cult into His cult. His experience with his own wife, and her faithlessness and final prostitution, which had presumably grown out of the immoral worship of the day, gives special occasion for and meaning to his protests against that immoral worship of Yahaweh as the Baals, and to his designation of that worship as harlotry. He declares that the worship which they profess to render to Yahaweh is in reality a worship of Baal. Yahaweh, who is their God, who has given them all the blessings which they possess, cannot recognize this worship as directed toward Him. They are worshiping Baal. " Israel knoweth not that I gave her the corn, and the wine and the oil, and multiplied her silver and her gold, wherewith they made a Baal ? " [1] And again : " I will lay waste her vines and her fig trees, whereof she hath said, These are my hire that my lovers, the Baals, have given me," [2] or " I will visit upon her the days of the Baals, unto which she burned incense ; when she decked herself with her nose-rings and her jewels, and went after her lovers ; but Me she forgat, saith Yahaweh." [3] The general theme of the first three chapters is a protest against the adulteries of Israel with the Baals, for whom she has deserted the husband [4] of her youth, Yahaweh, with a

[1] ii, 8.   [2] ii, 12.   [3] ii, 13.

[4] The word *Baal* means "husband." The Baal was the husband of his land, and the land cared for by the Baal was *Beulah*, or ".married." Henceforth that name is to be banned in Israel, and the husband relation of Yahaweh to Israel is to be indicated by another word, *Ishi*, " my man " (ii, 16).

prediction of purging and purification, after which she shall be brought back to her first love.

In some of his later prophecies Hosea makes use of the history of Israel under the figure of the relation of father to son:

> When Israel was young, I loved him;
> Out of Egypt I called My son.
> Others called them so they left Me;
> They sacrifice to Baals, and to images burn incense.
> Yet I taught Ephraim to walk, I dandled them in Mine arms.
> But they know now that I healed them.[1]

Like Amos, Hosea uses the earlier historical narratives and legislative codes, showing on the whole, however, a greater dependence on and familiarity with written sources than the former prophet. Especially he builds on the story of the captivity in Egypt and the deliverance therefrom, drawing from the past a lesson for the future. Captivity and the desert life are to be once more a purgative and curative power, to cleanse Israel of its corruptions and to restore it to a true relation with Yahaweh. Yahaweh will allure Israel and bring her into the wilderness, and she shall prove docile there, as in the days of her youth and as in the day when she came up from the land of Egypt; and as then He made a covenant with her, so now He will renew His covenant, and part of that covenant now, as of old, shall be His name, Yahaweh, for which He will put the name of the Baals out of her mouth that there be no more mention of their name. And Israel shall say, " I will arise and return to my first husband, Yahaweh, for then it was better for me than now." [2] As later events make more plain the Assyrian peril, and the danger of deportation as a result of Assyrian conquest becomes imminent, the place and character of the new captivity are specified, at the same time that the reference to the ancient captivity is retained. So we read:

> Ephraim shall return to Egypt,
> In Assyria shall they eat the unclean,[3]

where the Egypt meant is Assyria.

---

[1] xi, 1-3.   [2] ii, 7-17.   [3] xi, 5. Cf. also ix, 4; viii, 13.

Amos had predicted the captivity of Israel and evidently looked to the Assyrian empire as the source of that judgment of God which he foresaw. The greater part of Hosea's prophecies were delivered after a change in political conditions which made the approach of that judgment more certain. Tiglath-Pileser IV, who ascended the Assyrian throne in 745 B.C., undertook with new energy and increased power the conquest of Syria. With him also Assyria entered on a new policy. Heretofore her conquests had been little more than plundering raids. The conquered cities had been compelled to pay an indemnity and to promise tribute for the future, but allowed to retain their autonomy. Tiglath-Pileser inaugurated the imperial policy of annexing, as rapidly as possible, conquered states as provinces, making them integral portions of the Assyrian empire; and as part of that policy he deported a large portion of the population of the better class from the cities which he conquered to other regions, settling in their place the inhabitants of some other cities. Assyrian conquest, therefore, meant henceforth the utter destruction of national existence. After Jeroboam's death (ca. 740 B.C.) political disintegration followed rapidly in Israel. Usurper succeeded usurper. As the Assyrians advanced westward and southward, Israel was also drawn into the vortex of the conflict with that great power. Alternately her rulers paid tribute to, or entered into alliance against, Assyria. Egypt, just beginning to consolidate after the disintegration following the Libyan conquest, also appears upon the horizon as a possible balance to Assyria, and Israel vacillates between tribute to Assyria and alliance with Egypt. The conditions of internal disturbance and political intrigue of this period are graphically reflected in Hosea's prophecies; in fact these conditions not only furnish many of his figures but are also the occasion of his prophecies, for, like Amos, he is concerned primarily with the nation, and views the individual only as part of the nation. Now Israel calls to Egypt, now it turns to Assyria. They are " like a simple, senseless dove." [1] Again " Ephraim saw his sickness " and he went to Assyria, but Assyria could not heal him; for after all it is Yahaweh himself who is behind all that befalls him. He is like

[1] vii, 11. Cf. also xii, 1-4.

the lion to Ephraim. It is He that rends and carries off, and none rescueth.[1] But precisely because of this, therefore, the end of His judgments is not destruction, but reform. Hosea never loses sight of this altogether, as Amos seems to do. While some of the so-called Messianic passages attributed to him may be later additions, since the whole conception of his prophecies is of a restoration of Israel under better and happier conditions, those additions themselves may be regarded as merely developments or continuations of his genuine prophecies. Apparently, however, Hosea does not expect this restoration to be connected with the reign of a king of David's line, or with any king whatever. He was an Israelite, not a Judæan. His general point of view with regard to kings is that of Samuel xii. The establishment of the kingdom was in fact a departure from the true conception of Israel's relation to God. Hosea is, therefore, out of harmony with the political organization of the state, a position which he may well have reached as a result of the usurpations and misrule of the kings of those latter days.[2] He emphasizes the direct personal relation of the people to God. That was the condition of Israel in the good old times under Moses and Joshua, the religious millennium of the past, if one may so express it; and he expects a similar condition in the millennium of the future.[3] In this direct personal relation of Israel to a loving God, who cannot cast them off because of His love, lies the essence of his prophecies: " I desire love and not sacrifice, and knowledge of God more than burnt offerings." [4]

As might be expected from their different temper and different antecedents Hosea does not denounce sacrifice and ritual with the same violence as Amos. He is a prophet, and in so far a spiritual descendant of the schools of the prophets of the past that he seeks a direct mystical union with God, and that the acts of religion are relatively indifferent to him if not more than indifferent. He holds in reverence the prophets of the past,[5] except that he appears to condemn that fierce and cruel fanaticism which expressed

---

[1] v, 13-15.   [2] v, 1 ff.; viii, 4; x, 15; xiii, 9-12.

[3] The Judah passages and those passages which promise a king of David's line are generally regarded by scholars of the present time as later Jewish additions.

[4] vi, 6.   [5] vi, 5.

itself in the accession of Jehu and the crimes incident thereto, whose punishment, or curse, he finds in existing conditions.[1] But with him that mystic union consists not in ecstatic states, but more nearly in what we should call moral oneness with God. Like Amos, he is a descendant and a developer of that moral line of prophetism which found its incipient expression in the Elohists. To him moral, not ritual, acts constitute the essence of religion. Hence his condemnations of the sacrificial religion of his day. " Ephraim hath multiplied altars to sin; for sin his altars serve him." [2] But, in general, Hosea is not concerned so much with ritual as with those who stand behind the ritual. He condemns the priests, not for their sacrifices, but because they fail to teach and expound the moral code which has been intrusted to them, and are guilty of lawless and immoral conduct.[3] Sacrifice itself, with its accompaniment of altars, ephods, teraphim, and *mazzeboth* he conceives of as the natural if not necessary concomitants of the worship of Yahaweh.[4] In general, he recognizes and builds on the religious conceptions of the more spiritual thinkers of the preceding age, embodied in the Elohistic narrative, the legislative codes, the Tales of the Prophets, and the like. To him, as to them, Israel is Yahaweh's land, where alone He may be worshiped. All other lands are unclean, and in them Yahaweh may not be found. Exile, therefore, involves separation from Yahaweh.[5] Unlike Amos, who sweepingly condemns the worship of Israel as a whole, Hosea differentiates in his condemnation the Baal worship which has crept into the worship of Yahaweh. As part of that worship he denounces the idols or images,[6] of which, on the other hand, Amos makes no mention, because they are mere details of the general worship which he condemns as a whole. Evidently images were at that time in use, worshiped by the people as representations of the God of Israel, but really derived from

[1] i, 4.   [2] viii, 11.   [3] vi, 8–10.   [4] iii, 4–5.

[5] ix, 4–6. Even Amos, with all his universalism, it should be added, cannot quite emancipate himself from this idea. Cf. Amos vii, 17.

[6] Although, as already noted, he does not condemn *mazzeboth*, teraphim, and ephods, which he appears to count as part of the ancient worship of Israel, following in this the Elohists.

the worship at the Canaanite sanctuaries of the Baals of the land. They are innovations on the ancient worship of Israel and are in Hosea's view really part of the Baal worship which he condemns. On the same ground, following here, also, the earlier writers, but with much greater emphasis, he denounces the bull worship of Bethel[1] and Dan.

Hosea, as already suggested, was much more dependent on and much more closely connected with preceding thought and writing than Amos. The covenant of Israel with Yahaweh recorded in the earlier writings is an essential element, in his conception, of the relation of God to Israel. He refers to written codes of laws, even making a direct reference, in one passage, to the Decalogue,[2] and apparently regards the ritual as well as the ethical portions of those laws as of divine origin.[3] His references to the story of Israel as contained in those earlier writings are frequent and essential, and it is out of that story, as already pointed out, that he draws the suggestion of Yahaweh's future dealing with Israel, namely, that He will bring her into a new Egypt and a new wilderness.

Hosea profoundly affected later thought in minor matters, as, for example, the prohibition of the name *Baal*, resulting in the revision of some of the earlier writings and the substitution of *bosheth*, "shameful thing," for *Baal* wherever the latter name occurred; and also in the broader field of the general view of the relation of Israel to God in the past and in the present. His views in this regard were practically embodied in such pre-Deuteronomic additions to the stories of Joshua and Samuel as the final speeches assigned to those two heroes (Josh. xxiv, Sam. xii), and the whole Deuteronomic movement of the succeeding century shows his influence. He very profoundly affected, also, the Messianic hope.

Both Amos and Hosea, and the same is true of practically all the Prophets, represented a minority. They were the only, or almost the only, prophets of their day who prophesied not a Day of Yahaweh which should be the overthrow of Israel's enemies, but a Day of Yahaweh which should be the fall of Samaria. This

[1] viii, 5-6.   [2] iv, 2.   [3] viii, 11-13.

gave their prophecies at the moment special prominence, and later, when their utterances found fulfillment in fact, led to the preservation of those prophecies; so that while the utterances and writings of their contemporaries have perished, their writings were handed down to later generations as worthy of veneration. It must be remembered in general, in dealing with the prophetic utterances contained in the Biblical books, that they represent not the prevailing sentiments of their time, but the very exceptional sentiments of men of singular spiritual insight and boldness, who, during their lifetime, stood almost alone, and whose influence was almost always felt much more strongly after their death in molding the thought of future generations than during their lifetime in affecting the religious beliefs or practices of their contemporaries.

CHAPTER XIV

THE FALL OF ISRAEL AND THE RENAISSANCE IN JUDAH

As already pointed out, Judæa was, intellectually and spiritually as well as politically and economically, behind Israel. It was in Israel first, therefore, that the higher prophetic movement made itself felt. But Judah profited by the same conditions by which Israel profited during the first sixty years or so of the eighth century. It increased in power and wealth; it secured a port on the Red Sea and renewed commercial relations with Arabia and the south. These conditions of increased prosperity and wealth had the same effect in Judah as in Israel; owing to its more protected position in relation to the Assyrians, they also lasted longer; indeed, Judah profited politically and commercially as well as intellectually and spiritually by the conditions which brought about the downfall of Samaria. Written prophecy commences in Judah just at the time when it comes to an end in Samaria. The internal and external embroilments which presaged and prepared the downfall of Samaria began to drive out of Israel into Judah the literary and the spiritually minded men who had heretofore found a more congenial atmosphere for their labors in the former kingdom. Much as the fall of Constantinople in 1453 affected western Christendom, resulting first in the Renaissance, and then contributing, as a development of the Renaissance, to the Reformation, so the fall of Samaria affected Jerusalem and Judah. Art, literature, and religion were transferred from Samaria to Jerusalem. This process began, as stated, shortly after the death of Jeroboam II, with the conditions of anarchy and confusion, internecine war and foreign invasion, which then ensued, resulting in the destruction of Samaria and the deportation of its inhabitants in 721 B.C. It reached its climax as a renaissance under King Hezekiah in the quarter of a century or so succeeding the

latter event. Of the literary activities of that period we get a suggestion in the Book of Proverbs (xxv, 1), where the " men of Hezekiah " are said to have transcribed proverbs of Solomon. While
this verse may be in itself late, it represents a true tradition of the
literary activity of that period, an activity which preserved for us
the literature of Israel, — the Elohistic narrative of the Pentateuch,
with much later historical material embodied in our present books
of Judges, Samuel, and Kings; laws and decisions; songs and
psalms; the Tales of the Prophets; the books of Amos and Hosea, — and, stimulated by these writings, sought also to preserve and
develop the literature of Judah. The religious effect of this literary
revival made itself felt at once in the reawakening of prophecy in
Judah, and it is worthy of note that the first great prophet of Judah,
Isaiah, is master of a style which may be said to be the classic of
Hebrew literature.

When we begin to study the Judæan prophets we observe at
once the different attitude which they take toward state and church,
as a result of the difference of environment. In Judah there was
but one city of importance. The land in general was barren and
sparsely populated, and Jerusalem played a part in relation to the
land which no single city of Israel played in relation to Israel.
Jerusalem was Judah, in the view of Isaiah and of a very considerable part of his contemporaries and successors. In Jerusalem,
also, the Temple of Yahaweh occupied a unique position, unlike
that of any shrine in Israel. While not the only shrine of Yahaweh,
it possessed in the eyes of the people a peculiar sanctity and claimed
to be in a special sense the abode of Yahaweh. Accordingly, one
does not hear, in the Judæan narratives, of pilgrimages to Beersheba and Horeb-Sinai, as in the Israelitic tale. To the Israelite
those places represented the ancient home of his race and his
religion, as they did not to the Jew.

These divergent conditions are reflected in the writings of the
great prophets of Judah. There the priests of Yahaweh's Temple
were the leaders in reform. Isaiah, if not himself a priest, stood
in close and sympathetic relations with the chief priest of his time,
while his great successors, Jeremiah and Ezekiel, were themselves

priests, the former certainly of high rank. It was the priesthood, moreover, which originated the Deuteronomic reform. The Temple of Yahaweh was the scene and source of the inspiration of the greatest prophets of Judah; for in the Holy of Holies of His Temple at Jerusalem rested the Ark, the ancient palladium of Israel's faith, which dated back to the time of Moses, the founder. The priests who served this shrine claimed descent from Aaron, the brother of Moses, the original priest of the Ark. The guardians of that Ark were of necessity the special champions of the ancient worship. The very conditions which had, up to that time, militated against prophetic activity in Judah, had increased the importance of the priests of the Ark, both as interpreters of *torah* and as champions of Yahaweh. It was the priests of Yahaweh's Temple who, a hundred years before, had headed the movement against the Tyrian Baal worship and saved and restored to the throne the native David dynasty.

The existence, moreover, of a stable dynasty in Judah played a part of no small importance in its religious development. The fact that the dynasty had endured three hundred years, while the dynasties of other kingdoms, including Israel, had changed many times in that period, not only rooted much more firmly the affections of the people toward their rulers; it made those rulers seem to be in a special sense of divine appointment. Their permanence was the result of divine interference, a conviction which was confirmed by the strange deliverance of the dynasty by the help of the priests of Yahaweh in the time of Athaliah. Moreover this dynasty inherited the glamour of the kingdom of David and Solomon, and in and through this dynasty the Judæan saw himself the heir of a glorious past, which Israel could not claim, certainly in the same degree; for David was a Judæan, and the kingdom of David and of Solomon was the kingdom of Judah. That kingdom shed a glamour over the whole history of Judah, and the Jew, looking back to it, beheld it not only as a glory of the past, which made him potentially greater than anybody else around him, but also gradually translated that potentiality of greatness into the expectation of the return of that glory under a new David, an expectation precisely similar to that which made Britain look for the return of Arthur, Germany for the return of Charlemagne, and Portugal for the return of Sebastian.

Isaiah's prophecies are so closely connected with the political history of this period that they cannot be rightly understood without some knowledge of that history. Indeed, it was his effective treatment of the political events of the time and his interpretation of the purpose of Yahaweh in those events, which gave him his preëminence and power in Judæan prophecy. He was evidently a man of family and importance, of high social or official rank, *hoffähig*, to use the German expression, having the *entré* of the palace and able to speak to the king in relations of comparative equality, not merely from the religious but also from the social and official standpoint. We find him at one time denouncing the grand vizier and demanding his removal.[1] At another time he appears as the honored counselor of Hezekiah;[2] and even Ahaz treated him with marked deference.[3]

Politically, the history of this period is briefly as follows: After the death of Jeroboam, there ensued a period dangerously approaching anarchy in Israel. Usurpers seized the throne. There were both internecine war and foreign war. The Assyrians had now advanced so close that it was manifestly necessary for Israel to take part with Damascus and the surviving Syrian states in contesting that advance for the sake of its own existence. To some extent Judah was involved with Israel, being regarded, apparently, as a tributary ally of the latter. The refusal of Ahaz to join the alliance against Assyria led to the attempt to put another king in his place, and the invasion of Judah by the allies; as a result of which Judah lost Edom and its port on the Red Sea, and its tributary Philistine cities. It found safety by becoming tributary to Assyria, which speedily gained the upper hand over the allies. Damascus was captured in 732, Gilead and Galilee were overrun and their inhabitants deported, and Samaria was only saved from destruction by accepting an Assyrian partisan as king and paying a heavy ransom. From that time on until 721 Samaria remained nominally in

---

[1] Is. xxii, 15. [2] Is. xxxvi ff. [3] Is. vii, 10 f.

allegiance to Assyria, but perpetually intriguing with the neighboring states and with Egypt to throw off the Assyrian yoke, until at last Shalmaneser V resolved to destroy it and deport the population; which was accomplished by his successor, Sargon, in 721 after a three years' siege. During this period and until 705, Judah seems to have remained reasonably true to its allegiance and to have enjoyed on the whole special peace and prosperity, advancing continually in wealth and in prestige in relation to the surrounding countries. These conditions of prosperity and ease and the evils consequent upon them are reflected in general throughout the prophecies of Isaiah and Micah.

During this period Egypt loomed on the horizon as a possible counterpoise to the Assyrian power. While still divided into numerous states, which only began to come under the control of one head, the king of Ethiopia, toward the close of the century, it was at least vastly more powerful than any of the west Asiatic states; and accordingly all who looked to throwing off the Assyrian yoke sought its intervention. There were various risings, in none of which, however, did Judah take part. Egypt encouraged and probably even subsidized these revolts, but never actually sent an army into Asia until the great revolt of 705, on the death of Sargon and the accession of Sennacherib. At that time both east and west rose against the Assyrian master, under the instigation chiefly of the indefatigable Merodach-Baladan, king of Chaldæa, who had succeeded in establishing himself in Babylon. The outcome was, after a long struggle, a complete victory for Sennacherib. First he conquered the eastern rebels, and then, in 701, invaded Syria and Palestine, where Hezekiah of Judah was the soul of the rebellion. The Assyrians overran the whole country, receiving the submission of all the allies, including Hezekiah himself. The latter paid a heavy tribute, surrendering even his wives and children to the conqueror. But the Assyrians were not satisfied with mere submission. To avert future insurrections it seemed necessary to destroy the fortress of Jerusalem, or to make it an integral part of the empire, garrisoned with Assyrian troops. Hezekiah refused to surrender the city, and the Assyrians undertook to reduce it by siege or blockade, in the meantime devastating Judah, destroying its fortresses and deporting the population. An Egyptian or Ethiopian army, which was tardily sent out to help the western states in their resistance, was defeated and the fall of Jerusalem seemed imminent. But just at this moment, when Sennacherib's attention was also distracted by new disturbances in the east, his western army was crippled by the breaking out of pestilence. The result was that Assyria was obliged to content herself for the time with the punishment already inflicted, and withdraw her forces from the west. Jerusalem remained uncaptured and was allowed to maintain her independence, only paying tribute to Assyria as before.[1]

Isaiah's call to prophesy, as recorded in the sixth chapter of his book, connects itself with the Temple. Worshiping in its courts, he sees in vision, within the dark Holy of Holies, Yahaweh himself, surrounded by the seraphim chanting the ritual hymn: "Holy, holy, holy, Yahaweh Sabaoth." The vision reveals a man full of faith in the special sanctity of the Temple as the abode of Yahaweh, and finding in that Temple and its ritual his spiritual inspiration. It is not, therefore, to be wondered at that, throughout his prophecies, we find him maintaining the idea of the inviolability of the Temple. Samaria may be destroyed, Judah may be laid waste and its people carried into captivity, but Jerusalem cannot be taken, because the Temple is the dwelling place of Yahaweh, which no power is able to destroy. When Pekah of Israel and Rezin of Damascus, failing to persuade or coerce Ahaz to join them in an alliance against Assyria, sought to dethrone him and put Tabeel in his place, and laid siege to Jerusalem, Isaiah, in spite of the very much superior force of the allies, prophesied that they would not succeed, and urged Ahaz, in the name of Yahaweh, not only to oppose them but to do so single-handed, not calling on Assyria for aid.[2] Fourteen years later, when Samaria was captured by Sargon, while Isaiah used the destruction of Israel as a warning of divine punishment to the wicked rulers and nobles of Jerusalem,[3] he does not regard it as a presage of the fall of that city. Jerusalem, from his point of view, is altogether different from Samaria. In fact the very destruction of

[1] 2 Kings xviii f.; Is. xxxvi f.   [2] Is. vii–viii.   [3] Is. xxviii.

the northern kingdom is in a sense a preparation for the blessedness that is to be; for the new kingdom is to be Judæan, under a
king of David's line. So also earlier, when Tiglath-Pileser overran
Gilead and Galilee and detached them from the kingdom of Israel,
Isaiah, so far from seeing in this a presage of the destruction of
Jerusalem, as Amos would have done, made it the basis of a prophecy of the advent of the glorious kingdom of David.[1] Finally when,
in spite of all Isaiah's protests, Hezekiah having entered into league
with Merodach-Baladan and others to throw off the Assyrian yoke,
Sennacherib invaded the country, took all its fortified towns and
besieged Jerusalem itself, Isaiah encouraged him to resist and promised him victory in the name of Yahaweh. He had opposed the
revolt against Assyria, he had protested against the alliance with
the neighboring states and trust in Egypt for help against Assyria,
and he had announced the devastation of the land as a punishment
for these deeds and the faithlessness which they implied; but when
it came to the siege of Jerusalem, he at once became the leader and
the inspiration of those who were ready to resist to the death, because of his firm conviction of the inviolability of the city of the
Great King and of His holy sanctuary therein.[2]

As a natural consequence of his belief in the special sanctity of
Jerusalem, Isaiah emphasized also the idea of holiness unto Yahaweh.
The people of Israel, more particularly as represented in the tribe
of Judah and the citizens of Jerusalem, are set apart to Yahaweh,
holy to Him. To a certain extent this idea of the holiness of the
land to Yahaweh was a general Israelitic conception. So in the
early narrative of David, when David flees into the Philistine
country he can no longer sacrifice to Yahaweh. Similarly, in the
tales of the prophets, Naaman, the Syrian, asks for two mules'
burden of earth, that in Damascus he may have as it were an
enclave of holy land on which to sacrifice to Yahaweh. Hosea[3]
voices this general belief when he says that, carried into captivity,
the Israelites cannot offer sacrifices, because the land of their captivity will be unclean, that is, not holy or not belonging to Yahaweh.
Even Amos reflects this belief when he prophesies that the priest

1 Is. ix.   2 Is. xxx–xxxi, xxxvi–xxxvii.   3 Hos. iii, 4–5.

of Bethel shall eat unclean or unholy food in a land that is unclean. This idea of holiness seems to have received special emphasis in the ritual of the Yahaweh temple at Jerusalem, and out of that ritual comes on the outward side Isaiah's call to prophecy. He naturally, therefore, emphasized very strongly the conception of the holiness of land and people to Yahaweh; but he also introduces for the first time a spiritual element into that conception. Although within the holy land and even within the precincts of the Temple itself, although belonging to the holy people and conformed to the outward laws of holiness, he feels himself altogether unclean in the presence of Yahaweh, because of his inward sinfulness. His lips must be purged with the burning coal taken by the seraphim from the altar of Yahaweh, before he may utter the message of Yahaweh to his people.[1] Similarly the people must be purged as by fire that they may be inwardly holy to Yahaweh. While they are indefeasibly Yahaweh's people, consecrated to Him, holy unto Him, yet that holiness is mixed with and corrupted by sin, which must be purged by punishment. The fire of Yahaweh's wrath shall burn out their sin. The means of this purging is the Assyrians. They are God's instrument[2] to purge away the evil, that the people may become holy in the new moral sense which Isaiah is giving to the word, and which is one of his contributions to the development of the religion of Israel. But whatever befall there shall still be a holy remnant.[3] Indeed, that is the object of all the calamities which Yahaweh sends upon them: not to destroy them, but to purge away their sin, leaving only a holy remnant. So Isaiah names one of his sons Shear-Yashub, " a remnant returneth." So also he predicts that, as a result of Ahaz's failure to follow his advice and trust in Yahaweh instead of making alliances against the Assyrians, the latter shall sweep over the land like a flood. Judah shall be laid waste; its gardens and vineyards shall be turned into a wilderness of thorns and briars; but out of the agony of these birth pangs the virgin[4] daughter of Jerusalem shall give birth

---

[1] Is. vi.   [2] Is. x, 5.   [3] Is. vi, 13; x, 20.
[4] Is. vii, 14, Greek text. Cf. Peters, *J. B. L.*, 1892; *The Old Testament and the New Scholarship*, Appendix.

to Emmanuel ("God with us"), the people which is really holy, with whom God does actually dwell. As a natural result of his point of view he foresees also the continuance of the Davidic dynasty. A stock from Jesse's root shall reign over the purified and holy Israel.[1] "If ye do not believe, ye shall not be established,"[2] is his consistent attitude. Convinced of the almighty power of Yahaweh and of the certainty that He will not let His people be ultimately destroyed, he demands a similar faith in others. Contrary to the teachings of ordinary prudence and of political common sense, he bids Ahaz refuse all foreign alliances — for such alliances are offensive to Yahaweh, both because they involve a recognition of other gods, which offends His uniqueness and His sanctity, and also because they imply a lack of belief in His power and good will. Ahaz must trust Him and Him alone. Later, when Hezekiah, reduced to the lowest extremity, is offered terms on condition of the surrender of Jerusalem, which involves the profanation of the Temple, Isaiah bids him to persist in his resistance, not trusting, however, in the Egyptian alliance or in any power of man. It is the sword of Yahaweh which will destroy the Assyrians.[3]

When, through pestilence or some other calamity, the Assyrian army was finally forced to retreat, although Judæa had suffered terribly and the Assyrians had carried off an enormous booty in slaves, cattle, and treasure, yet the deliverance of Jerusalem from capture appeared to prove the truth of Isaiah's contention that Jerusalem was inviolable because it was the seat of the Temple, the abode of Yahaweh, whose power is almighty. The very afflictions which had befallen Judah were themselves an evidence of the truth of his prophecies. Precisely that which he foretold had come to pass. The land had been scourged, but Jerusalem had not fallen. Yahaweh had vindicated His power, punishing the people for their sins, but preserving a remnant.[4] But while Isaiah's religious conceptions were so profoundly affected by the Temple, and while his prophetic utterances connected themselves so largely with political events, he was also a true descendant of the prophetic tradition in his attitude toward form and luxury alike in the domestic

[1] Is. xi.   [2] Is. vii, 9.   [3] Is. xxxi, 3.   [4] Is. xxxvii.

and the religious life. His denunciations of the vices of luxurious wealth, and the rude symbolic actions by which at times he
reinforced his utterances, connect him with Amos and Elijah. In
spite of his high social rank, he retained a close touch with the
primitive barbarism of prophecy. So, when Sargon was chastising
Ashdod and the Philistine coast, Isaiah, we are told, went about
for a long period naked, as a sign and a symbol.[1] His appearance
before Ahaz, preceding the attack on Jerusalem of Pekah and Rezin,
and the tone of his address, remind one of Elijah's appearances to
Ahab. His rebuke of Shebna, the grand vizier, is as fierce as Amos'
curse on the priest of Bethel. Like Hosea he gave his children names
with meanings, living out his prophecies in his domestic life.

While we are not told of schools of the prophets in Jerusalem
at that time, we find in connection with Isaiah a little group of
followers, pupils or close friends, who might perhaps fairly be
called his school. With these he devotes himself to the study of
torah and testimony, evidence of the veneration felt toward the early
writings, especially the Yahawist and Elohist and the law codes contained in them.[2] In large part, in fact, Isaiah's reverence for the
Temple and the priesthood was connected with the Law. As in
his prophet-making vision it was the Holy of Holies, the shrine of
the Ark of the Covenant, which was the center of his thought, so in
his relation to the priesthood it was the function of the priests as
interpreters of the *torah*, not as sacrificers, which he valued. The
attempt to establish a relation with Yahaweh by elaborate ritual and
sacrifice was as abhorrent to him as to the other prophets. In
comparison with ethical righteousness, all sacrifices, festivals, and
outward forms were nothing. His attitude toward the Temple and
its sacrifice on the one hand, and the moral law on the other,
may be compared with the attitude of Jesus according to the traditional representation in the Gospels. Jesus attended the feasts;
He loved the Temple courts. The sacrifice and ritual of the
Temple were not abhorrent to Him, and were in fact accepted

[1] Is. xx.

[2] Is. viii, 16 ff. *Torah*, or teaching, and testimony, or tradition, appear to refer
not only to the writings mentioned above, but also to the teachings and traditions
which had been handed down in the Jerusalem priesthood.

by Him as the normal and ordinary service; but they possessed for Him no essential importance, and wherever they appeared to interfere with moral comprehension He denounced them as dangerous and misleading.

Isaiah takes the same attitude. Although the whole scheme and conception of his prophecies may be said to center around the Temple, nevertheless he denounces, in the strongest language, the sacrificial and ritual practices. "What is to Me the multitude of your sacrifices? saith Yahaweh. I am full of the burnt offerings of rams, and the fat of fed beasts; and in the blood of bullocks, and lambs, and he-goats, I delight not. When ye come to see My face (who hath required this at your hand, to trample My courts?) bring no more vain oblations; incense is an abomination unto Me; new moon and sabbath, the calling of assemblies, I cannot endure; yea, the solemn meeting is iniquity; your new moons and appointed feasts I hate; they are a cumbrance unto Me. I am weary of forgiving; and when ye spread forth your hands, I will hide Mine eyes from you; yea, though ye make many prayers, I will not hear; your hands are full of blood. Wash you, make you clean; put away the evil of your doings from before Mine eyes; cease to do evil; learn to do well; seek justice, relieve the oppressed, judge the fatherless, plead for the widow." [1]

Isaiah was very keenly alive to the evil about him; and he gives us a dismal picture of the moral condition of Jerusalem in his time. It must be remembered, however, that prophets paint only one side of the picture. While he denounces so bitterly and in such extreme language the ritual and sacrifice, it is yet evident from his own acts and writings that the Temple and its services played a great part in his life and thought, and that he recognized in practice spiritual possibilities and spiritual good in the very ritual which he denounced. So also there must have been a fair amount of virtue in Judah, otherwise he could not have obtained a hearing for his denunciations of vice. His prophecies evidently appealed to the consciences of a fair part of his contemporaries. From the evils which he denounces it would seem that, in addition

[1] Is. i, 11 ff.

to the ordinary vices resulting from the increase of wealth and luxury, there was in Jerusalem a great deal of idolatry, that is, the worship of God or the gods under the form of images ; and also much practice of witchcraft and sorcery. Contemporary accounts show further that in the Temple itself there was worship of a sort which we of to-day should consider immoral, hierodules and sacred prostitutes connected with some shrine or shrines within the Temple enclosure. Strangely, as it seems at first sight, Isaiah himself makes no clear allusion to this, and neither is there in his writings that stress upon sexual immorality in connection with false worship which we find later in Jeremiah and earlier in Hosea. The *mazzebah*, which in its essential conception represented a sexual cult, although perhaps at that time so conventionalized that this was not evident, clearly gave him no offense, for he speaks of it as a natural and essential part of the worship of Yahaweh, in a passage which,[1] for its conception of the relation of Yahaweh to the peoples about, is worthy of comparison with the writings of Amos. Amos speaks of Yahaweh as dealing with the other nations precisely as with Israel. Isaiah looks for the time when, as now the gods of Assyria or Egypt are recognized in Jerusalem, so Yahaweh shall be recognized in Assyria and in Egypt, and in those lands people shall set up an altar and a *mazzebah* to His name. As Amos concerned himself in his prophecies with the nations about Israel as well as with Israel itself, so Isaiah uttered or wrote prophecies about the surrounding nations.[2] Amos seems to place those nations on the same plane with Israel and denounces punishment on all alike for moral evil. Isaiah regards them rather as tools in Yahaweh's hands to accomplish His purpose concerning His own people. It is not for kidnaping or cruelty or the like that they are to be punished ; it is only as a part of Yahaweh's plan regarding Israel. He is a practical monotheist, so far at least as Israel is concerned, and indeed he invents for other gods than Yahaweh the mocking title " not gods " (*elilim*); and yet he is farther away from a philosophical monotheism than either Amos or Hosea.

[1] Is. **xix**, 19.　　　　[2] Is. xiii–xxiii.

Isaiah's position in relation to the throne rendered it possible for him to make his ideas effective in practical reforms in a way in which Amos and Hosea could not. We find Ahaz, it is true, rejecting his counsel, offering up his son,[1] making alliance with the Assyrians, and, as a result of that alliance, introducing an altar built on the Assyrian pattern and presumably also sacrificing in the Temple to the Assyrian gods.[2] But with Hezekiah Isaiah's counsel was more effective, and a religious reform was undertaken somewhat along the lines of his prophecies. Some of the heathenish images in the Temple and in the shrines outside were cleared out, including the brazen serpent, a very ancient emblem of an original serpent worship,[3] later converted, apparently, into an emblem of Yahaweh — the explanation given being that Yahaweh, when in the wilderness the people were bitten by poisonous serpents, ordered Moses to set up a brazen serpent on a rod, by the sight of which those bitten were healed.[4] It is difficult to determine precisely how far these reforms went. It is clear that in making them recognition was given not only to Isaiah's words but also to the prophetic narratives and the codes of ritual and moral legislation which had been incorporated with them, to which Isaiah also makes reference in his writings, more particularly using very effectively, as Amos and Hosea had done, the wonderful deliverance from Egypt in the past.[5] It is clear also that Hezekiah's attitude toward Isaiah and his readiness to put the latter's teaching in practice affected in its turn Isaiah's prophecies, increasing his natural inclination to connect the expected millennium with a king of David's line. Apparently it developed an optimism in his prophetic visions, leading him to expect that kingdom very shortly, perhaps under Hezekiah himself.

Like all prophets Isaiah was a mystic, but his mysticism was of a different order from that of Hosea. He was the type of mystic who uses and even loves outward symbols, forms, and ceremonies, and yet counts them as worthless because he beholds so clearly the something behind them; the sort of mystic who, in a temple full of unworthy and even impure worship, can keep his gaze fixed on

[1] 2 Kings xvi, 3.   [3] 2 Kings xviii, 4.   [5] Cf. Is. xi, 16.
[2] 2 Kings xvi, 10 ff.   [4] Num. xxi, 4 ff.

the holiness and purity of God. But his mysticism does not bring about that tender, personal relation with God which we find in Hosea. God to him is rather a wonderful and terrible king, full of fear, but adorable for His might and for the goodness which He has showed toward the children of Israel.

As a complement to the picture of the religion of the time which we obtain from Isaiah, we have the writings of another prophet, Micah, from the small town of Maresha on the Philistine border. His different surroundings and different view-point make themselves manifest especially in his attitude regarding Jerusalem. To him the Temple does not have the same sanctity which it possesses for Isaiah, who had spent his life in it, nor is Jerusalem inviolable as the dwelling-place of Yahaweh. Micah interprets the Assyrian advance in the same general manner as Isaiah. The Assyrians shall overrun and destroy the land, and that destruction is a punishment from Yahaweh for the sins of the nation, precisely as it had been interpreted by Isaiah. Micah also agrees with Isaiah that this destruction shall not be final, and that after a drastic purging and purification a new Judah shall come into existence. He further agrees with Isaiah in his view of the permanence of the Davidic dynasty and his reverence for that dynasty, as a consequence especially of David's greatness and David's fame. It is out of Bethlehem, that is, out of David's line, that the king who is to initiate the new conditions shall arise.[1] But while Isaiah declared that Jerusalem, the city of the Great King, could not be captured, Micah expected it to be destroyed together with the rest of Judah. Using the same figure which Isaiah had used, of the travailing woman whose birth-pangs are the calamities of the Assyrian invasion, he predicts that she is to be deported, and led into captivity ; there she shall give birth to her child.[2] Afterward the new Israel shall be brought back. His attitude toward Jerusalem may fairly be described as hostile.[3] Like a true provincial he saw the wickedness of the capital through a magnifying glass.

Hear this, ye heads of the house of Jacob, and judges of the house of Israel, that abhor justice, and pervert all equity; who build up Zion with

---

[1] Mic. v, 2.　　　[2] Mic. iv, 10.　　　[3] Mic. i, 5.

blood, and Jerusalem with iniquities; its rulers judge for reward, and its priests teach for hire, and its prophets divine for money; yet would they lean upon Yahaweh and say, Is not Yahaweh among us? no evil shall befall us:

> Therefore, because of you,
> Zion like a field is plowed,
> Jerusalem becometh heaps,
> The temple-mount forest heights.[1]

Like Isaiah, Micah testifies to the prevalence of worship at the shrines of the dead, witchcraft, and image worship;[2] and unlike Isaiah he makes note of the immoral *asherah* worship and human sacrifices.[3] His moral attitude was similar to that of the greater prophet. He depicts conditions of evil-doing consequent upon the development of wealth in the smaller towns, much as Isaiah had noted them in Jerusalem. He denounces especially the wickedness of the rulers:

Hear now, ye heads of Jacob, and judges of the house of Israel: Is it not your part to know justice? Haters of good, and lovers of evil; that pluck the skin of my people from off them, and their flesh from their bones! And because they ate the flesh of My people, and flayed their skin from off them, and brake their bones, and chopped them in pieces, as for the pot, and as flesh in the caldron; therefore shall they cry unto Yahaweh, and He will not answer them, but will hide His face from them at that time, according as they have wrought evil.[4]

Evidently Micah was not the only prophet in Maresha in his day, and evidently he was in a very small minority in the interpretation of the events of his time. His denunciation of his mercenary fellow prophets gives a graphic presentation of their functions and of the prevailing conception of the relation of the prophet to God:

Thus saith Yahaweh concerning the prophets that lead My people astray; when one giveth them to gnaw, they cry, Peace; but whoso putteth not into their mouths, against him they prophesy war: Therefore shall night befall you, that ye have no vision; and darkness come upon you, that ye divine not; and the sun shall go down upon the prophets, and the day be black over them. And the seer shall be ashamed, and the diviners confounded; and they all shall cover their lips; for there is no answer from God.[5]

---

[1] Mic. iii, 9 ff.　　[3] Mic. vi, 7.　　[5] Mic. iii, 8 ff.
[2] Mic. v, 13.　　[4] Mic. iii, 1 ff.

Divining was the prophet's function, for which he received a gift from the person who sought his divination, just as the priest was paid for teaching. For at the local shrines, as at Jerusalem, it would appear that the special function of the priest was still to give *torah*. He was, also, however, a sacrificer, a function which seems to make no appeal to Micah. Micah's attitude toward sacrificial religion, which is substantially the same as that of Amos and Hosea, is set forth in a passage of great moral elevation in the form of an impleading of Israel, with the everlasting hills of Judah, which towered above him eastward, as the witnesses or assessors of Yahaweh's suit.

Hear, O ye mountains, Yahaweh's suit, and ye enduring foundations of the earth; for Yahaweh hath a suit with His people, and He will plead with Israel.

(Yahaweh.) O My people, what have I done unto thee? and wherein have I wearied thee? testify against Me. For I brought thee up out of the land of Egypt, and redeemed thee from the house of bondmen; and I sent before thee Moses, Aaron, and Miriam.

(Israel.) Wherewith shall I come before Yahaweh, and bow myself before God on high? shall I come before Him with whole burnt offerings, yearling calves? Will Yahaweh be appeased by thousands of rams, ten thousands of rivers of oil? Shall I give my first born for my transgression, the fruit of my body for the sin of my soul?[1]

He hath shewed thee, O man, what is good; and what doth Yahaweh require of thee but to do justly, and love mercy, and walk humbly with thy God?[2]

[1] Incidental evidence of the prevalence of human sacrifice at this time, and of the high rank which it held in the popular religion.

[2] Mic. vi, 1–4, 6–8.

CHAPTER XV

THE REACTION AND FOREIGN CULTS

The year 701 saw Isaiah at the height of his influence. He enjoyed great prestige as a true prophet, because of the deliverance of Jerusalem and the calamity which befell the Assyrian army through the interference of Yahaweh. He seemed to have imbued king and people with his own belief in a righteous and holy God and with his own expectation of the establishment of a glorious kingdom ruled over by a king of David's line, and his influence with the king had led to reforms looking toward the abolition of images and the worship of Yahaweh only. Then came a reaction. We cannot say precisely when it commenced, for with the close of the eighth century we plunge into a period of darkness, there being almost no records of any sort for the next three quarters of a century; but it appears to have become effective with the accession of Manasseh (ca. 686 B.C.). Hezekiah had undertaken to force the worship of one God, Yahaweh; and to some extent, probably, to concentrate that worship in the Temple at Jerusalem. A favorable opportunity for these reforms had been afforded by the Assyrian invasion, which doubtless destroyed numerous local shrines and which by that fact afforded apparent proof that Yahaweh was indifferent, if not hostile, to those local shrines. Hezekiah caused also the destruction of *Nehushtan*, the brazen serpent, and apparently of other image forms, under which Yahaweh was worshiped, and did away with some of the immoral practises connected with His worship.[1] These reforms were a serious interference with the popular religion of the people, as well, probably, as with the vested rights of a considerable body of priests who served at these shrines or were connected with these rites. In these reforms Hezekiah was

[1] 2 Kings xviii, 4.

in league with the Yahaweh priesthood of the Jerusalem Temple. Manasseh appears to have stood in friendly relations with the other party, the party of the popular religion. He undertook to restore the old rites which Hezekiah had abolished;[1] and, precisely as in Egypt, 700 years earlier, the reaction following Amenophis' monotheistic[2] reform resulted in violence and bloodshed, so did the reaction in Judah in Manasseh's time. Tradition says that Manasseh put Isaiah himself to death, and Jeremiah's writings[3] testify to the use of violence against the Yahaweh prophets, the followers of Isaiah and of his school.

There were various causes working with considerable effect at this time toward a change of popular sentiment. That very study of the past and collection of its literary remains which in the case of Isaiah had tended toward spiritual development and been an incentive to prophecy, led others into infidelity and heathenism. As in Italy, in the fifteenth century A.D., on the one side the art and letters brought in by the Greeks promoted a new study of the Scriptures, and developed new spiritual conceptions, which were to result in the Reformation, while on the other side they developed an intellectual and profligate heathenism which affected the high officials of the Church, popes and cardinals becoming infidels and practically heathen for the nonce; so in Judah in the seventh century B.C. similar causes produced a similar result. It must be remembered that the literary remains of Israel which have come down to us have been worked over and over by spiritually minded men whose interest in them was religious, and whose object was to convey by means of them religious truth. These remains, as they have come down to us, constitute only a part of the original whole. It has been pointed out elsewhere to what extent Israel's

---

[1] 2 Kings xxi.

[2] Cf. Breasted, *Development of Religion and Thought in Ancient Egypt*, Lectures ix, x. One may also to some extent compare the reforms of Hezekiah and the resulting reaction with the reforms of Nabonidus in Babylon in the following century. There the centralizing policy and the abolition of ancient uses aroused a bitterness of feeling and an organized opposition which helped to bring about the Persian conquest.

[3] Jer. ii, 30: "Your own sword hath destroyed your prophets like a destroying lion." Cf. also xix, 4.

myths and legends, customs and laws, were derived from heathen sources. They have come down to us purified of their grosser elements, and made monotheistic by the translation of gods and goddesses into the one god Yahaweh. But in Isaiah's time many of those older traditions and much of that older material out of which the Elohistic and the Yahawistic narratives were created, many hymns and songs full of heathenism, out of some of which, by a similar process of purging and reforming, the Psalms of the Psalter were created, were still in existence; and the study of these tended to produce heathenism rather than an ethical monotheism.

Moreover, the world had been opened to this isolated mountain people. For a time it had passed out of its insignificance. It had been a tributary of Assyria. It had been a leader in alliances against Assyria; it had exchanged embassies with Nineveh, Babylon, and Egypt, not to speak of numerous minor states and kingdoms. This contact with foreign countries had not only stimulated thought and increased knowledge, it had also brought Judah into contact with the religious practices of those countries. Men heard of their wonderful temples, of the statues of their gods, of the pomp and splendor of their ritual, of their different beliefs, and their different methods of winning the favor of the gods. But especially the failure of those alliances against Assyria made thinking men more conscious of the great power of that kingdom, and led them to ask themselves whether it was not because of the greater power of the gods of Assyria, or because the Assyrians knew the right method in which to worship those gods, that they won their victories, destroying the kingdoms and the peoples of other gods through all the world.

The political events of this period were certainly calculated to aid greatly in bringing about a change in the popular sentiment toward Yahaweh-monotheism and the reforms of Hezekiah and Isaiah. The very optimism of Isaiah's prophecies helped to produce this change. When it was seen that, in spite of the reforms which Hezekiah had introduced in accordance with Isaiah's teaching, the kingdom of the king of Jesse's stock, which Isaiah had depicted as so close at hand, was not ushered in, but that conditions grew more distressful; when it was seen that the Assyrians, whom men had for a time thought overwhelmed by the power of Isaiah's God, and who according to Isaiah's prophecies were merely the tool, whom Yahaweh Sabaoth would shortly punish and destroy, grew ever stronger and stronger, — it was natural for men to say: These prophecies are not fulfilled. The service of Yahaweh has not brought what was promised. Let us turn back again to the old conditions and let us seek the gods who will bring us prosperity and power. It was natural that a king in Manasseh's place should seek to win favor with the gods, with his subjects, and with his overlords, by punishing the men who had been instrumental in abolishing the old cults, by restoring those cults, and by introducing in addition the worship of the gods of Assyria. These then were some of the promoting causes of the reaction which took place in his reign.

To realize precisely what this reaction meant in practice we must turn back a little to consider the history of the Temple. David brought to Jerusalem the Ark of the Covenant, which, with its contents of the two tables of the Ten Words, had been the palladium of Israel in the heroic days of the conquest. He made it again Israel's palladium, carrying it forth or sending it out to battle in cases of great need, and providing for it a tent or tabernacle at Jerusalem. Its priests and prophets were among his chief advisers, and in their number were even men of royal blood. This did not mean that in David's day or afterwards the Ark was the only place of worship. It was the central, peculiar palladium of Israel. But Yahaweh, Israel's god, might be and was worshiped also in many other places and under varying forms — teraphim and brazen serpents, green trees, springs, strange rocks, and much more besides. He had already been brought into connection with the gods of the land, and their worship and their names combined with His. He was El, Baal, Adonis, and Melek. The *mazzebah* and the *asherah*, the male and female emblems of fertility, were used at His shrines, and the immoral practices which grew out of and were connected with the worship of the mystery of life were appropriated to Him.

Solomon placed the Ark in the Holy of Holies of the Temple, which he built largely after Phœnician models; and in so far glorified the Ark and the worship of Yahaweh connected with it. He reorganized the priesthood of the Ark, and gave it new and increased importance; but while he thus enriched and glorified the shrine of the Ark of Yahaweh, he also, as a result of his alliances and his marriages with foreign princesses, introduced into Jerusalem foreign cults as such. According to the Book of Kings, he " went after Ashtoreth the goddess of the Zidonians, and after Milcom the abomination of the Ammonites," he built " an high place for Chemosh, the abomination of Moab," and " for Melek (Molech), the abomination of the children of Ammon." [1] The first of these implies an immoral cult, and the last child sacrifice. Some of these shrines are described as built on the hill before Jerusalem; probably, also, such shrines were introduced into the Temple, set up in and about its courts, after the manner of foreign worship, where the honor of the god of the central cult was supposed to be increased by having chapels or shrines of other divinities about his central shrine. Rehoboam, Solomon's son, is said to have erected *mazzeboth* and *asherim* throughout the land, " on every hill and under every green tree"; and, in addition to prostitution, sodomy also is mentioned in the Bible account as connected with the worship of his time.[2] These immoral rites, however, do not necessarily imply the conscious worship of foreign gods, for such rites and practices might be adopted into the Yahaweh worship. Asa is reported to have put away out of the land the sodomites and " removed all the idols that his father had made," and also to have cut down the " abominable image for an *asherah* " of his mother Maacah.[3] Jehoshaphat, his son, is reported to have carried this reform further, putting away " the rest of the sodomites who were left from the day of his father." [4] This is the period of the introduction into the northern kingdom, Israel, by Ahab and his wife Jezebel, of the distinctly foreign cult of the Tyrian Baal, and it is also the period of the great Yahaweh movement under Elijah, which undertook to get rid of all foreign cults, asserting that there was only one god of Israel, Yahaweh. Both these movements were felt in Judah. Jehoshaphat's alliance with

[1] 1 Kings xi, 1–8.
[2] 1 Kings xiv, 23.
[3] 1 Kings xv, 11 ff.
[4] 1 Kings xxii, 46.

Ahab was consolidated by a marriage of his son Joram with Ahab's daughter Athaliah. The latter brought with her the worship of the Tyrian Baal, to whom a temple or a shrine was built in Jerusalem, perhaps in the courts of the Temple.[1] In the very nature of the case the priests of the Ark were opposed not only to the introduction of foreign worship, but also to the development of cults or forms which might interfere with or detract from the worship of their own shrine. Their shrine was imageless. The setting up of images was to a certain extent a discrediting of their shrine, and interfered with their profits and prerogatives. Morally, also, the existence of such a representation of deity as the tables of the Ten Words, inclosed in the Ark, must have had some effect on the priests of the Ark, tending to raise them above their surroundings. It was the obligation and duty of priests everywhere to give *torah*, to interpret the will of God to those who came to ask, by lot, sacrifice, or whatever means. The existence of such a law must have made itself felt to some extent in their *torah*. That the priests of the Ark of the Yahaweh temple enjoyed also a special position in regard to royalty,[2] a natural result of the fact that they were guardians of the palladium of Israel, the central, initial shrine of the Temple, has been already pointed out. It was owing to this that King Joram's daughter married the priest's son, an alliance which led to the saving of the Davidic dynasty after Athaliah's massacre of the royal brood, and to the restoration of that dynasty to power; a natural result of which, again, was the abolition of the

[1] 2 Kings xi, 18.

[2] Suggestion has already been made of the possibility of the connection of the tribal name *Yehudah* with the original form of the divine name *Yahu*. Certainly it would seem that the first Judæan king, although not himself bearing the divine name in composition, recognized a peculiar personal and dynastic relation to Yahaweh. This may be indicated in the emphasis laid on the personal relation of David and Solomon to Yahaweh, as "my" or "thy" god (cf. especially 1 Kings i, 36). It is marked also by the use of *Yahu* in composition in the names of the kings of David's dynasty, in striking contrast with the dynasties of the kingdom of Israel. After Rehoboam all the Judæan kings, with the exception of the two kings of the anti-Yahawistic reaction, Manasseh and Amon, and possibly Asa (Ahaz's full name was Jehoahaz; and similarly Asa's full name may have contained *Yah*) bear names containing *Yahu* in composition. On the other hand, in Israel the name appears first in Ahab's children; but even after that names without Yahu are more numerous than those with it.

foreign Tyrian cult under Jehoash. We are not told in so many words that the other foreign cults were banished at this time, but it seems to be implied in the narrative in Kings. This period in Israel was to such an extent marked by the abolition of distinctly foreign cults that the tendency in Jerusalem also may be supposed to have been in the same direction. This would not imply, however, that the point had been reached of abolishing the immoral worship of Yahaweh, or the sacrifice of children to him as Melek. In the mind of the people at large those things were not foreign worship of strange deities, but were conceived to be pleasing to Yahaweh. They had appropriated to Him the rites and the worship and even the names of their gods.

With King Ahaz and the period of the renaissance, we come to different conditions. Ahaz's alliance with Assyria meant the recognition of foreign gods; and the very thing which led him to recognize the Assyrian gods led him, apparently, to recognize the gods of the peoples about him. He seems to have been a man of intense religiosity, and as such he resorted to religious practices of every sort and description. He " made his son to pass through the fire," he worshiped at all the shrines throughout the land, or, as the Book of Kings says, he " sacrificed and burned incense in the high places, and on the hills, and under every green tree." [1] From the prophecies of Isaiah it would appear that necromancers and diviners of every description flourished in his time, and idols, that is, images, whether of Yahaweh or of some foreign god, were everywhere in use. In the Temple itself Ahaz modified the Yahawistic worship so as to make it more closely resemble Assyrian practice, substituting an altar of Assyrian pattern for the one formerly in use. [2] What the worship of Manasseh's time consisted of we may determine partly by the account of his own reign [3] and of Josiah's reformation [4] in the Book of Kings, partly by references in Deuteronomy to the abuses which were to be corrected, and

[1] 2 Kings xvi, 3 f.

[2] 2 Kings xvi, 10 ff. This would seem naturally to have been Assyrian, on account of the relation of dependence and alliance of Ahaz to Assyria; not Syrian, as the Chronicler interprets it, 2 Chron. xxviii, 23.

[3] 2 Kings xxi.   [4] 2 Kings xxiii.

partly from the statements of Jeremiah, Zephaniah, and Ezekiel as to conditions existing in their time. Images were largely used, in spite of the denunciations of the Prophets and the prohibitions of the prophetic codes of legislation. The *Nehushtan*, or brazen serpent, had been destroyed by Hezekiah and could not be restored; presumably, however, other objects of similar character, representations of animals and the like, were in use, if not in Jerusalem, at least at some of the local shrines. Besides these there were images in human form, smaller and larger, the *teraphim* especially serving as household gods. Images of both these descriptions had come down from antiquity; they had long ceased to be connected in the thought of the people with foreign worship as such, and were regarded as a natural and proper part of the worship of Yahaweh. Besides these actual figures, there were sacred trees, stones, fountains, and the like, which were regarded as the places of the indwelling of the divinity, the divinity indwelling in them being, in the popular thought and religion, loosely identified with Yahaweh. There were also the *asherim* and *mazzeboth*, which were a component part of the native Canaanite religion, from which they had been adopted by the Israelites. These, as already stated, were connected with the sexual cult. The original conception of that cult was the worship of the mystery of life, in connection with which prostitution was practiced as an act of worship, the proceeds of such act being regarded as an especially acceptable offering to the deity. This cult naturally developed a gross immorality and, passing out of its original conception, came to include unnatural lust, so that from a relatively early period there were both hierodules and prostitutes connected with the shrines of Yahaweh. This is shown not only by repeated references in the Book of Kings and in the Prophets, but also by the legislation of the Book of Deuteronomy: " There shall be no harlot of the daughters of Israel, neither shall there be a sodomite of the sons of Israel. Thou shalt not bring the hire of a whore, or the wages of a dog, into the house of Yahaweh thy God for any vow : for even both these are an abomination unto Yahaweh thy God." [1]

[1] Deut. xxiii, 17 f.

The sacrifice of children was also adopted into the cult of Yahaweh, he receiving in connection with that special cult the title of Melek, king.[1] The conception behind this is an ancient and primitive one : the idea of giving to the divinity that which is dearest, namely, one's own children, and the belief that God demands such sacrifice. Ahaz had given this horrible cult official sanction, sacrificing, according to the writer of Kings, his own son in the fire. From the references in the Book of Micah it seems to have persisted through Hezekiah's reign. Under Manasseh it was a cult of considerable prominence.[2] It must be regarded, as already pointed out, not as a foreign cult, but as a development in the Yahaweh cult of Canaanitish use.

Isaiah protests loudly against the necromantic practices of his day. Men consulted witches and wizards, and especially did they seek to know the future through consultation of the dead. The legislation in the Book of Deuteronomy shows the prevalence of these practices in Manasseh's reign.[3] Here we have again a native rather than a foreign cult, although doubtless new methods of divination, omen interpretation and the like, were introduced from the neighboring peoples. There had always been an inclination toward the worship of the spirits of the dead and the effort to communicate with them in order to ascertain the plans of the gods concerning the future. This was a very important part of the actual popular religion, which believed in spirits everywhere and in everything. That which we have to consider at the moment is the revival of this cult and its practical authorization by the attitude of the court and the leaders of the people during the reaction. It should be added that divination did not appear to the ordinary man to be so far removed from prophecy. We have seen that Micah speaks of the office of the prophet as that of a diviner. Men went to him to be informed with regard to what was lost

---

[1] According to the writer of the Book of Kings, this cult was also practiced by men of Sepharvaim whom Sargon settled in Samaria, the gods to whom the children were offered being Adar Melek and Anah Melek (2 Kings xvii, 31), from which it would appear as though the appellation *Melek* were in some special way connected with the cult of child sacrifice, being applied to a given god as he was worshiped in this manner. Hence the later Hebrew objection to this appellation of divinity, and the substitution for it of *bosheth*.　　[2] 2 Kings xxi, 6.　　[3] See also 2 Kings xxi, 6.

and paid him for this divination.[1] To the ordinary man it made little difference how the divination was wrought, whether by a prophet or a conjurer of spirits.

Ezekiel testifies to the existence of animal worship,[2] a form of totemism, which found a home even in the Temple, and the names [3] which meet us in the records of the period following Manasseh are, taken in connection with other facts, evidence of the widespread revival of shamanistic and magical conceptions under Manasseh.

But, besides these idolatrous, immoral, cruel, and superstitious practices which throve and flourished under Manasseh as part of the religion of Yahaweh, there were also distinctly foreign cults which were introduced in his time. Jeremiah tells us how popular in his day was the worship of Ishtar. "Children gather wood, and the fathers kindle the fire, and the women knead dough, to make cakes to the queen of heaven." [4] Ezekiel gives a graphic picture of sun worship, as conducted in the precincts of the Temple of Yahaweh, where men turned their backs on the holy place, the abode of Yahaweh, and faced eastward toward the rising sun to worship; [5] and the Deuteronomic law-book felt it necessary especially to condemn the worship of the sun, the moon, and the stars.[6] The Book of Kings tells us that there was a movable throne of Shamash, the sun god, in the temple of Yahaweh during this period, and that there were altars on the roofs of the chambers and in the courts of the Temple for offering sacrifices and burning incense to the heavenly host, as well as private altars on the houses of individuals in Jerusalem.[7] It must be remembered that the cult of Shamash was the especially popular cult in Assyria at this time, and that next to this in popularity stood the cult of Ishtar. Star worship, or rather the worship of the deities behind the stars, and the worship of the signs of the zodiac, or the deities who control the divisions of the heavens, was also characteristic of the Assyrian-Babylonian religion. The worship of the "host of heaven" was

1 Sam. ix, 6–9.
2 Ezek. viii, 7 ff.
3 As, for instance, *Shaphan*, " rock-rabbit."
4 Jer. vii, 18 ; xliv, 15 ff.

5 Ezek. viii, 16.
6 Deut. xvii, 3.
7 2 Kings xxiii, 5, 11 f.

one which, in itself considered, made a strong appeal to the imagination; moreover these were the gods of the victorious Assyrians, through whose power they had won their victories. Men could not readily worship Ashur, who was a local god, but these gods were gods whom anyone might worship and whose favor anyone might win, as the Assyrians had done. The name of Manasseh's son and successor, Amon, suggests also a religious connection with Egypt.

Yahaweh was the national and local god. Probably the great bulk of the people served Him and Him alone. The service that was rendered to Him, however, was not that imageless and moral worship which the prophets demanded, but a worship similar to that offered to the gods of the surrounding countries, or to the old Canaanite divinities, a service of ritual and of sacrifice, stained with cruelty and lust. In court circles, as a consequence of the relation of the court to the surrounding nations, the worship of foreign divinities had become fashionable, and from them this worship had spread to a certain section of the natives of Jerusalem, the foreign cult particularly favored being the Assyrian cult of sun and stars. Yahaweh was only one among many gods, their local god, who, however, had shown himself less powerful than these other gods, and whose cult seemed to them less intellectual, as well as less profitable on the whole, than that of the foreign divinities. All alike, court and people, consulted omen diviners and the spirits of the dead; while totemistic cults, more or less secret and degrading in their character, had established themselves within and without the precincts of the Temple. High places and shrines for the different public cults had been created within and without Jerusalem, the most notable in the Temple itself. As the Temple was in a sense the royal chapel, it was natural that the cults favored by the king should be recognized in its courts, but the central shrine of the Temple remained to the end the shrine of Yahaweh.

Manasseh's reaction and introduction of foreign cults did not mean an attempt to suppress the Yahaweh cult, nor was his persecution a persecution of the worshipers of Yahaweh. It was a reaction against the attempt to make the Yahaweh cult the only cult and to abolish the images and the immoral practices which, derived from Canaanite sources, had connected themselves with that cult. The men on whom his persecuting hand fell were those who had led the movement to abolish the local shrines, the images, and the like ; men like Isaiah. In the very nature of the case the men of Isaiah's way of thinking and the priests of the Ark were natural allies. The introduction of foreign cults, the increase of local shrines, witchcraft, divination, necromancy, and all the rest of it, interfered with their prerogatives, and, viewed from the temporal as well as from the spiritual standpoint, threatened the supremacy of the priests of the Ark if not their very existence.

CHAPTER XVI

THE REFORMATION

It must not be supposed that the whole people followed Manasseh in the polytheism which he introduced, or in the immoral and cruel practices, connected with the worship of Yahaweh, which were revived under his reign. Presumably the great bulk of the people remained worshipers of their national god, and there was a considerable number, the nucleus of which consisted of the priests of the Ark and the followers of Isaiah and other prophets, who adhered to the imageless worship of Yahaweh. These men devoted themselves also to the collection, study, and propagation of the prophetic and other writings which taught and advocated such a method of worship. The writings of the Yahawist and Elohist, with the older legislative codes, had already been united into one book (JE). The teaching of this book, the legislation and the doctrine of which professed to go back to Moses, was directly opposed to the method of worship of Yahaweh prevalent under Manasseh, and much more to the foreign cults introduced by him. This book inculcated hatred of the Canaanites. Their shamelessness and immorality were held up to reprobation;[1] intermarriage with them was represented as abhorrent to the sense of the forefathers, so that neither Abraham nor Isaac would take wives for their children from among the Canaanites, but sought a connection with the Syrians beyond the river.[2] On the other hand, the friendly relation and close kinship with Arabia and Midian were emphasized in these narratives.[3] Both narratives, as well as the codes contained in them, forbade the worship of strange gods, and the story of Bethel[4] connected the Israelite adoption of that shrine with the

---

[1] Gen. ix, 22; xix; xxiv, 3.   [3] Gen. xvi; xxi; Ex. iii.
[2] Gen. xxiv; xxviii f.   [4] Gen. xxxv, 2.

destruction of the former inhabitants and of the strange gods. No other god than Yahaweh might be worshiped,[1] images were prohibited,[2] and the bull worship of Israel was reprobated as the chief cause of Yahaweh's indignation with Israel, which had led to its destruction.[3]

The Yahawist particularly emphasized this; indeed, according to this narrative it was the zeal of the Levites in opposing the bull worship which caused them to be chosen as the ministers of the Ark. Child sacrifice was condemned by the Elohist in the beautiful story of Abraham's sacrifice of a ram instead of his son, Isaac.[4] Sorcery was prohibited by the Elohistic[5] code. If this writing, the Yahawist-Elohist, was to be accepted as representing the true religion of Israel, which had been handed down from Moses, then, manifestly, the nation was sinning most grievously and would surely incur the curses which the preceding prophets had denounced against such sins.

So we read in the Second Book of Kings that because Manasseh, king of Judah, had done these abominations and had made Judah sin with his idols, "therefore, thus saith Yahaweh, the God of Israel; Behold, I bring such evil upon Jerusalem and Judah, that whosoever heareth of it, both his ears shall tingle. And I will stretch over Jerusalem the line of Samaria, and the plummet of the house of Ahab; and I will wipe Jerusalem as a man wipeth a dish, wiping it and turning it upside down. And I will cast off the remnant of Mine inheritance, and deliver them into the hand of their enemies; and they shall become a prey and a spoil to all their enemies; because they have done evil in My sight, and have provoked Me to anger, since the day their fathers came forth out of Egypt, even unto this day."[6]

There was a condition of sharp conflict between Manasseh on the one side and the more fanatical or more rigid adherents of the imageless Yahaweh worship on the other side. With the latter were doubtless the sympathies of the priesthood of the Ark and those less radical or less violent Yahawists who expressed their faith rather

[1] Ex. xx, 3; xxii, 20. [3] Ex. xxxii. [5] Ex. xxii, 18.
[2] Ex. xxiii, 24; xxxiv, 17. [4] Gen. xxii. [6] 2 Kings xxi, 12–15.

in worship, the study of the ancient writings, and the development of the doctrines contained in those writings, than in violent opposition.

Esarhaddon's reign was the period of the greatest development of the Assyrian empire. Egypt was conquered and Assyria became a world power. In the reign of Esarhaddon's son, Ashurbanipal, falls the great rebellion of the latter's brother, Shamash-shum-ukin, whom his father had made overlord of Babylon. This stirred the whole empire, east and west. Manasseh appears to have been among those suspected of sympathizing with the rebellion, if we may believe the Chronicler,[1] and to have been brought a prisoner to Babylon to answer to Ashurbanipal for his supposed faithlessness. This, according to the Chronicler, was the cause of a change of policy on Manasseh's part, which did not, however, lead to an abandonment of all the foreign, superstitious, and immoral worship which he had fostered. What is historical in this statement in the Book of Chronicles it is difficult to say. The fact that Manasseh's son, who succeeded him, was named Amon, would suggest that Manasseh was coquetting with the Egyptians and had introduced the worship of Egyptian gods, perhaps in the hope of finding assistance against the Assyrians. Whether as a result of the failure of his foreign policy, which led to the humiliation recorded in the Book of Chronicles, or because of dissatisfaction with his religious policy, fostered by the agitation of the Yahaweh prophets, the party of opposition gained the ascendant shortly after his death, his son Amon, who followed his religious policy, was dethroned and murdered, and his grandson, Josiah, a boy of six, put upon the throne.

Up to this point it must be said that our reconstruction of religious conditions and movements is somewhat conjectural, but about this time we begin once more to find written sources. To this period belong the prophecies of Nahum and Habakkuk, directed against Assyria, which are somewhat variously dated at different points between the middle and the close of the seventh century B.C.

One of the causes of the reaction under Manasseh had been the apparent failure of fulfillment of the prophecies of Isaiah with regard to the punishment of the Assyrians and the establishment of

[1] 2 Chron. xxxiii.

the great kingdom of Israel under a king of David's line. The success of the Assyrians had seemed to falsify his predictions and prove the truth of the Assyrian claim that their gods were the mightiest of all gods. Now Assyria was tottering to her fall and prophets of Yahaweh were announcing that this was the work of Yahaweh's hands; that those things which He had promised He was now fulfilling. While these prophecies contain nothing new for the history of religious development, they were of great importance in preparing the way for a practical reformation and the overthrow of foreign worship in Judah.

Somewhere after 625 came the great Scythian invasions. Scythian hordes overran the whole of Asia. The Assyrian power was utterly unable to stem the current. A condition of chaos resulted. There was no overlord. Each small kingdom struggled to save itself as best it might. Judah itself seems to have escaped devastation and destruction on account of its favorable position on the hills, but the Scythians overran the Philistine plain, capturing the Philistine cities and advancing to the very gates of Egypt, where they were bought off by a ransom. They overran the Esdraelon plain also and settled themselves permanently at Bethshan, which, as a result of their invasion, later came to be known as Scythopolis. These events produced, naturally, a profound impression on the Judæan community, which was voiced especially by two prophets, Zephaniah and Jeremiah. Zephaniah takes up Amos' doctrine of the Day of Yahaweh, evidence of that study of the former prophets which had been going on, and applies it to the present occasion. This is that Day of Yahaweh, which Amos had declared should be darkness, not light. Yahaweh's judgment has at last come: " Be still before the Lord Yahaweh; for the Day of Yahaweh is at hand. For Yahaweh hath prepared a sacrifice, He hath sanctified His guests. And it shall come to pass in the day of Yahaweh's sacrifice, that I will punish the princes, and the king's sons, and all such as are clothed with foreign apparel. . . . And in that day, saith Yahaweh, there shall be the noise of a cry from the fish gate, and an howling from the second quarter, and a great crashing from the hills. . . . The great Day of Yahaweh is near, near and hasting greatly, — the voice of the Day of Yahaweh; bitterly crieth the mighty man then. A day of wrath is that day, a day of trouble and distress, a day of wasting and desolation, a day of darkness and gloom, a day of clouds and blackness, a day of trumpet and alarm, against the fenced cities, and against the high battlements. And I will distress men, that they shall walk like the blind, because they have sinned against Yahaweh; and their blood shall be poured out like dust, and their flesh like dung. Neither their silver nor their gold can save them in the day of Yahaweh's wrath. And all the land shall be devoured by the fire of His jealousy, for He maketh a speedy riddance of all them that dwell in the land." [1]

Jeremiah derives his motive rather from Hosea: " Go, and cry in the ears of Jerusalem, saying, Thus saith Yahaweh: I remember the affection of thy youth, the love of thine espousals, when thou wentest after Me in the wilderness, in a land that was not sown. . . . What evil did your fathers find in Me, that they went far from Me, and walked after vanity, and became vain? Neither said they, Where is Yahaweh that brought us up out of the land of Egypt; that led us through the wilderness, through a land of deserts and pits, through a land of drought and shadow, through a land that none passed through, where no man dwelt? And I brought you into a land of gardens to eat their fruit and goodness, but ye entered and defiled My land, and made Mine heritage an abomination. The priests said not, Where is Yahaweh? and they that handle the law knew Me not; and the rulers transgressed against Me, and the prophets prophesied by Baal, and walked after things that profit not." [2] He also sees in the invasion of the Scythians the punishment of God, Yahaweh, because the people have forsaken Him and gone after strange gods: " Thus saith Yahaweh: Behold, a people cometh from the north country ; and a great nation is stirred up from the uttermost parts of the earth. Bow and spear they grasp; cruel are they, and have no mercy; their voice roareth like the sea; on horses they ride; like men arrayed for battle are they arrayed against thee, daughter of Zion. . . . O daughter of My people, gird thee with sackcloth, and wallow in ashes. Put on thee

[1] Zeph. i, 7–18.   [2] Jer. ii, 2–8.

mourning for an only son. Bitter be the lamentation. Suddenly cometh the spoiler upon us."[1] "Go ye up upon her walls, and destroy; . . . tear away her branches; for they are not Yahaweh's. For the house of Israel and the house of Judah have dealt very treacherously against Me, saith Yahaweh. They have denied Yahaweh and said, It is not He, and evil shall not come upon us, neither shall we see sword nor famine. . . . Lo, I bring upon you a nation from far, O house of Israel, saith Yahaweh. It is an everlasting nation, it is an ancient nation, a nation whose language thou knowest not, neither understandest what it saith. Its quiver is an open sepulcher; they are all mighty men. And it shall eat thine harvest, and thy bread; it shall eat thy flocks and thine herds; it shall eat thy vines and thy fig-trees; it shall destroy thy fenced cities, wherein thou trustest, with the sword. And it shall come to pass, when ye shall say, Wherefore hath Yahaweh our God done all these things unto us? then shalt thou say to them: Like as ye have forsaken Me, and served strange gods in your land, so shall ye serve strangers in a land that is not yours."[2]

According to the Chronicler,[3] Josiah early showed himself inclined to return to the methods of Hezekiah and to change the policy of his father and grandfather, Amon and Manasseh. Later events would seem to show that he stood in friendly relations with the priests of the Ark and with the Yahaweh prophets; but he does not seem to have undertaken any actual reformation, in the sense of abolishing the foreign worship, putting down child sacrifice and the like, until 621. In that year, according to the account in the Book of Kings,[4] Hilkiah the priest found in the Temple a law-book, and when the king sent his representative Shaphan to the Temple to receive the regular revenues and attend to repairs, Hilkiah gave the book to Shaphan, who brought it to the king and read it before him. Dismayed by its contents, the king rent his clothes and sent an embassy, at the head of which was Hilkiah, the priest of the Temple, to inquire of the Lord for him, for the people, and for all Judah. They addressed their inquiries to a certain Huldah, a prophetess, whose answer was quite in line with

[1] Jer. vi, 22, 23, 26.   [2] Jer. v, 10–19.   [3] 2 Chron. xxxiv, 3.   [4] 2 Kings xxii.

the prophecies of Zephaniah and Jeremiah already referred to, denouncing evil " upon this place and upon the inhabitants thereof, . . . because they have forsaken Me and have burned incense unto other gods that they might provoke Me to anger with all the work of their hands." [1] Thereupon the king gathered together all the elders of Judah and Jerusalem and went up to the house of Yahaweh. Here the book which had been found was read in the ears of all the people gathered in the courts of the Temple, and the king took a solemn oath to walk after Yahaweh, to keep His commandments and His testimonies and His statutes, with all his heart and with all his soul, and to perform the words of the law that were written in the book ; and the people stood to this covenant. The first practical result was that all the vessels made for Baal and for the *asherah* and for all the host of heaven were taken out of the Temple and burned without Jerusalem in the fields of Kidron. The *asherah* itself was burned at the brook Kidron and stamped to small powder, and the powder cast upon the graves of the common people. The male and female prostitutes were driven out of the Temple and their houses broken down. The movable throne of Shemesh was burned and his horses removed from the Temple. The altars to the host of heaven were similarly destroyed. Outside of Jerusalem, not only was Tophet defiled, in the valley of Hinnom, that no man might make his son or daughter to pass through the fire thenceforth, and the places of worship of Ashtoreth, Chemosh, etc. cut down, but also all the high places. The shrines for the worship of Yahaweh himself at the gates of Jerusalem and throughout Judah were destroyed ; and the *asherim* and the *mazzeboth*, which had been heretofore connected with every shrine for the worship of Yahaweh, as for the worship of any other god, were broken in pieces and cut down wherever found. According to the account in Kings, Josiah extended his reform even across the borders of Judah to Bethel, where he broke down the altar, burned the *asherah*, and defiled the whole site. Then the king ordered that those who had familiar spirits, and the wizards and teraphim and the idols and all the abominations in the land of

---

[1] 2 Kings xxii, 16–17.

Judah, should be put away, and directed that a passover should be held, as it is written in the Book of the Covenant.

The reforms described in this account make it clear at once that the Book of the Covenant found was Deuteronomy, or at least the greater part of our present Book of Deuteronomy : the legal section (xii–xxvi), with the introduction (iv, 44–xi), and the curses contained in chapter xxviii. The reforms were in accordance with the provisions of that book. The question at once arises : How did the book come into existence? There seems no reason to doubt that it was found as described. An analysis of the legal sections of Deuteronomy shows that it is founded on the laws which are to be found in the Book of the Covenant in the Elohistic narrative (Ex. xxii ff.), and on a collection of laws, on which later the author of the holiness code in Leviticus [1] drew. This latter work was, as we shall see later, closely connected with the Jerusalem Temple, in fact had its origin in the legislation and ritual of the Jerusalem Temple.

We have already seen what great stress Isaiah laid on the idea of holiness, and that he derived that idea primarily from the worship and ritual of the Jerusalem Temple. The Book of Deuteronomy may be said to have been a development of that combination of priestly and prophetic elements which we have seen working in the Temple of Jerusalem since the time of Isaiah, and which indeed began before his time, influencing to some extent certainly the Yahawistic narrative. This is the work of those followers of Isaiah on whom he had urged especially the study of the law of Yahaweh, and whom he imbued with that same reverence and devotion for the Temple courts which he himself had shown.[2] His followers, as the result of the conditions which they found, went farther than their master, developing his doctrines to their logical conclusions. So Deuteronomy, while founded on the combined Yahawistic and Elohistic narratives and the laws contained in them, pushed the principles there set forth much further. To the composers of this book it had become clear not only that the worship of the Canaanites was immoral and demoralizing, but that there was no way of

[1] Lev. xvii ff.   [2] Is. viii, 16.

avoiding the corruption of Yahaweh worship by Canaanitish abominations except by rooting out the Canaanites. Therefore, not only are all marriages with Canaanites forbidden in the Book of Deuteronomy, but the Canaanites are to be devoted; Israel is to blot them out utterly.[1] Similarly, the writers of Deuteronomy advanced to the conclusion that even the *mazzebah*,[2] which had seemed to Isaiah[3] a natural if not an absolutely essential concomitant of worship, is idolatrous. No images, no representations of Yahaweh of any sort are to be tolerated.[4] The Ark, which had come down from the days of the wilderness, and the cherubim which stood with it in the shrine of the Yahaweh temple, these and these alone are the representatives of Yahaweh. Furthermore, Yahaweh might not be worshiped in any other place except the Temple at Jerusalem.[5] This was a natural and logical outcome of the attitude taken by Isaiah and those connected [with him, adherents, if we may so put it, of the Ark, the shrine of Yahaweh in the Temple at Jerusalem. It was also the logical outcome of the attempt to get rid of the abominations and immoralities which had grown up or been handed down in connection with the worship of Yahaweh. They were not essential parts of the Ark worship. They seemed to be essential parts of the worship of Yahaweh in every other place. If a clean, ethical worship was to be established, it was absolutely necessary that all these places, all other shrines except the Ark shrine, should be abolished. That was also a logical development of the teaching contained in the Yahawist and Elohist narratives, which referred all law and religious development to Moses. The call now was "back to Moses." Emphasis was laid upon the great deliverance from Egypt, and the wonderful power which Yahaweh had shown in delivering His people at that time, leading them through the wilderness and giving them the land of Canaan. The Yahawist and Elohist had emphasized the goodness of those old times and the nearness of the people in those days to Yahaweh. Amos and Hosea had taken up this cry, and, protesting against the abuses which had crept into civil and religious life alike, demanded a return to the

1 Deut. vii, 1–3; **xx**, 17.   3 Is. xix, 19.   5 Deut. xii, 1–16.
2 Deut. xii, 3.   4 Deut. xvi, 21 f.

wilderness; but one condition of the wilderness life was the central sanctuary of the Ark, at which God had revealed himself to Moses. To that one central sanctuary they must return, if they would win the favor of God as set forth by the teaching of the Prophets. Therefore, all other sanctuaries must be destroyed.[1] No sacrifices might be offered elsewhere. Only in the Temple at Jerusalem could Israel worship God; there they must celebrate their feasts to Him, and especially that great feast, the Passover, which signalized and commemorated the deliverance from Egypt.

It was, of course, necessary to make special provision to carry this out, and some of the peculiar legislation of Deuteronomy is that legislation which endeavors to provide for these changes of conditions. So it was specified that priests of other Yahaweh sanctuaries, Levites (for, in the terminology of Deuteronomy, priest and Levite are identical), should be provided for at the Temple at Jerusalem; that is to say, all the priests of Yahaweh in the land were to be gathered together at Jerusalem and were to share with the priests of that temple.[2] Similarly it was necessary to provide, in order that the people might be able to eat flesh, that the killing of an animal should no longer in itself be accounted sacrifice; that men might kill animals and eat them where they would, without any sacrificial rites other than pouring out the blood.[3]

Interesting are the provisions which aim to make the people holy unto Yahaweh on the physical side, the camp regulations and the like.[4] The provisions for clean and unclean are substantially those which had always been handed down in the Temple, and are practically identical with those afterwards adopted in the Priestly Code,[5] evidence that they were derived from the Temple use.

Attention has been called to the fact that in the Yahawist and Elohist narratives the writers consistently separate Israel from the Canaanites, claiming relation with the Syrians. So in the ritual prescribed in Deuteronomy the Israelite who makes an offering is to say: " A wandering Syrian was my father." [6] The whole legislation is practically made to depend upon the Decalogue of Moses,

---

[1] Deut. xii, 1–16; xvi, 21 f.   [3] Deut. xii, 15 ff; 20 ff.   [5] Deut. xii, 1–21.
[2] Deut. xviii, 6 ff.   [4] Deut. xxiii, 9 ff.   [6] Deut. xxvi, 5.

which appears in Deuteronomy in a form different from that in which we have it in JE,[1] representing perhaps the *torah* (that is, the explanation and interpretation of the Ten Words) traditional in the Jerusalem Temple, as against that which had developed in northern Israel. In some respects, however, Deuteronomy follows the Israelite rather than the Judæan tradition. So it is Horeb,[2] not Sinai, which is the place of revelation. The spirit of the northern prophet Hosea also has strongly affected the spiritual conceptions of the writers or compilers of Deuteronomy.[3]

[1] Deut. v, 6–21.   [2] Deut. xviii, 16.

[3] Attention has been called in a previous chapter to the fact that prior to the fall of Samaria it was Israel and not Judah which was the intellectual and spiritual as well as the political leader, and that it was the destruction of Samaria which brought about an intellectual and later a spiritual revival in Jerusalem and Judah, precisely as the fall of Constantinople resulted in the Italian renaissance and later in the Reformation of the West. Deuteronomy is the final, Calvinistic development, if we may so put it, of the fall of Samaria. As stated above, spiritually Deuteronomy shows the influence of the great Israelite prophet Hosea in its permeating doctrine of loving-kindness. Its great practical doctrine of mono-Yahawism is also Hoseanic. Elijah had fought the fight against the foreign baals: Yahaweh is God. Hosea fought against that sort of identification of Yahaweh with Baal which resulted in a poly-Yahawism, the identification of Yahaweh with the baals of the various shrines, so that there was a Yahaweh-Baal of this place, worshiped in this way, and a Yahaweh-Baal of that place, with such attributes and properties. Yahaweh was not Baal, and Yahaweh was one. This is the substance of the Creed of Deuteronomy: " Hear, Israel, Yahaweh our God is one Yahaweh " (vi, 4). As stated above, also, Deuteronomy follows the Israelite tradition and takes the Israelite attitude with reference to Horeb rather than Sinai, similarly in reference to Aaron (ix, 20), to Solomon (xvii, 16), the Ammonite, Moabite, and Edomite (xxiii, 3–8), and the Syrian ancestry (xxvi). The emphasis on the name Elohim and the repetitiousness of its combination or equation with Yahaweh are Israelitic (cf. for instance vi, 5 ; vii, 9 ; iv, 1 ff.). The poetry attached to the original Deuteronomy is Israelitic in its origin (xxxii–xxxiii). More specifically we find the Josephite tradition predominant, as in the Blessings of Moses (xxxiii), in the great emphasis upon and frequent reference to the Egyptian Captivity, especially in the admonition to remember that they were slaves in Egypt and hence to do or not to do so and so. Above all we have the distinct local reference to Gerizim and Ebal as the mountains of the blessing and the curse (xi, 29 ; xxvii), identifying the famous old Josephite shrine of Shechem as the original home of the original Israelitic composition behind Deuteronomy. The actual Deuteronomy was developed out of this Shechemite document in the hands of the mono-Yahawistic priests of the Ark shrine in the Temple at Jerusalem and the followers of Isaiah (cf. Is. viii, 16) by a combination with it of material from JE and of the traditional laws, ritual, and use of the Ark shrine, with a prophetic interpretation of the same. It remained a theory, the theory of the true religion given from God by Moses, and through the reigns of Manasseh and Amon a secret theory, to be brought to light by the priests of the Ark shrine in 621, a half-century perhaps after its compilation.

In accordance with the methods which had been pursued already in earlier codes of law, this new law-book was ascribed to Moses. It was written in his name, a fact which makes plain the idea and intention of those who compiled the book. They believed that they were returning to the primitive faith of Israel. They sought to restore and they believed that they were restoring the religion of Moses.

More important, perhaps, than the legal portion of Deuteronomy is the spiritual or exhortative part. The whole book is permeated with a spirit of mercy and loving-kindness. The laws which are adopted from the previous legislation are modified in the direction of mercy and loving-kindness. Old institutions, like the Sabbath, are interpreted in this new sense.[1] Even the relation to prisoners and captives is made to partake of the same spirit.[2] But, while instilling kindliness toward captives and toward foreigners sojourning in the land, the book is meant for the Israelite. His salvation depends upon his separation from the abominations of the nations round about. All foreign practices and customs are to be abolished, and all relation with those who use those things and who might by means of them corrupt Israel is to be cut off.[3] Theologically Deuteronomy advances beyond the monotheism which we have heretofore found in the prophetic writings. God is one God, the God of all the earth, in a sense beyond that which even Amos had reached.

The reformation was made effective, as stated, in 621. All that was prescribed in Deuteronomy was not accomplished, it is true. It was provided there that the priests of the high places should become priests of the Jerusalem Temple. But the priests of the Jerusalem Temple objected to sharing their position with outsiders, and the result was that the latter, so far as they were admitted to any position in the Temple, became a lower grade of priesthood, the origin of the later Levites.[4] So far as the people at large were concerned, a good deal of the reform was doubtless perfunctory and consisted merely in the observance of outward rites. Later events make it clear also that a great deal of the sorcery and

---

[1] Deut. v, 15.　　[2] Deut. xxiv, 17, 21.　　[3] Deut. xiii.　　[4] 2 Kings xxiii, 9

witchcraft, the secret rites, the immoral worship, and the foreign cults which Manasseh had introduced, continued to be practiced in secret. Nevertheless, the period from 621 to 606 was in general a period of religious purity. It was also a period of political independence. Assyria, in its death throes, was not able to compel tribute from its distant vassals. The Scythians, who overran the rest of the world, spared Judah. Men came to conceive that these things were a reward from God for the fulfillment of His law, and to expect a still further fulfillment of the prophecies of good of the prophets of the past. In 606 Nineveh was finally captured and destroyed by the united force of the Medes and Babylonians, and Cyaxares and Nabopolassar proceeded to divide up the Assyrian empire between them. But a new power had arisen in Egypt. Psammetichus, the Libyan, with the aid of Greek mercenaries, had united Egypt into one kingdom. His son Necho, seeing that the Assyrian power had fallen and that for the moment no one had appeared to lay claim to the Syrian provinces of that empire, undertook to extend over the region west of the Euphrates the sovereignty formerly exercised there by the Thothmes. But this would interfere with the establishment of the great kingdom of David which Josiah and his coreligionists at Jerusalem expected. There had sprung up in Judah that same half fanatical, half splendid expectation of a great deliverance through the power of God Almighty which one finds at various periods in the history of Israel, sometimes inciting to wonderful deeds of heroism, sometimes resulting in disastrous and selfish turbulence and rebellion. As the result of the religious reform which had been inaugurated men looked for the restoration of David's kingdom, promised by Isaiah and the other prophets. And so, in the belief that Yahaweh would fight with his army against the Egyptians as in the good old times glorified by the Prophets, Josiah with his inferior might faced Pharaoh Necho at Megiddo, at the entrance of the plain of Esdraelon, the natural point for defending the land of Israel from invasion. His hope of divine intervention proved futile. The Judæans were defeated and Josiah himself slain.[1]

[1] 2 Kings xxiii, 29 f.

CHAPTER XVII

THE FALL OF JERUSALEM AND THE PROPHECIES OF THAT PERIOD

The defeat and death of Josiah at Megiddo resulted shortly in the complete surrender of Judah, which became a vassal kingdom of Egypt. Shallum, the son of Josiah, who had taken the throne under the name of Jehoahaz, was deposed and his brother Eliakim was made king by the Pharaoh under the name of Jehoiakim. For three years Judah continued a vassal state of Egypt. But Syria was a portion of the region which, in the division of the Assyrian spoils between the Medes and the Babylonians, was allotted to the latter. Nineveh captured, Nabopolassar laid claim to this heritage. In 604 his son Nebuchadrezzar defeated Pharaoh Necho at Carchemish on the Euphrates, a battle celebrated by Jeremiah in a dirge,[1] and all Syria shortly fell into his hands. Jehoiakim made submission and was allowed to retain his kingdom. Three years later, however, he joined with others in an attempt to throw off the Babylonian yoke with the aid of the Egyptian Pharaoh, who in the meantime had had an opportunity to repair his losses and return to Syria with a new army. This army Nebuchadrezzar defeated so completely that the king of Egypt "came no more out of his own land."[2] In the campaign Nebuchadrezzar made his headquarters at Riblah. He seems to have made use of irregular bands of Chaldæans, Syrians, Moabites, and Ammonites to assist him in bringing the whole region into subjection. Finally, in 597, three months after Jehoiakim had been succeeded by his son Jehoiachin, Nebuchadrezzar advanced against Jerusalem and besieged it; whereupon Jehoiachin capitulated and was carried away captive to Babylonia, with "all the princes and all

[1] Jer. xlvi.   [2] 2 Kings xxiv f.

the mighty men of valor, and all the craftsmen and smiths, ten thousand captives." [1] None remained save the poorest people of the land. However, the kingdom of Judah was allowed to continue, and another son of Josiah, own brother of Jehoahaz, Mattaniah, was made king under the name of Zedekiah. He seems to have been a weak man in the hands of turbulent advisers and an unruly populace, who forced him, against his will, to break the solemn covenant which he had made to serve Nebuchadrezzar. Once he was summoned to Babylon on suspicion, but apparently succeeded in justifying himself and returned to Jerusalem. Finally, trusting in the assistance of the Egyptian king, the people rebelled and the Babylonian army laid siege to Jerusalem. The siege was raised on the rumor that an Egyptian army was approaching, and there was much rejoicing, the people supposing that Yahaweh had interfered to save the city as He interfered to save it in the days of Hezekiah. [2] The siege was soon resumed, however, and although the people fought desperately, the city was captured, in 586, and utterly destroyed. A portion of the remaining population was deported to Babylonia. Judah was incorporated as a province in the Babylonian empire under a Jewish governor named Gedaliah.

There still remained armed guerilla bands, Jews who had not surrendered to Nebuchadrezzar. At the instigation of the Ammonite king the leader of one of these bands, a man of royal extraction, under pretense of accepting the amnesty granted by the Babylonians, slew Gedaliah by treachery, but was in his turn defeated by another guerilla leader. The latter, fearing the vengeance of the Babylonians because of the murder of the governor appointed by them, which they might rightly regard as an evidence of the turbulent and rebellious spirit of the country at large, fled into Egypt with a considerable body of followers against the advice of Jeremiah, taking the prophet with him by force.

These are the events of the closing years of the first Jerusalem, which are most graphically recorded in the book of Jeremiah; [3] and for the religious views and the religious development of that

---

[1] 2 Kings xxiv, 14.   [2] Jer. xxxiv; xxxvii.   [3] Chaps. xxxvii–xliv.

period we are particularly indebted to this book and to the prophet Jeremiah, whose name it bears.

The book itself is a combination of prophecy and narrative. According to the account contained in chapter xxxvi, it was not until the year 604, twenty-three years after he had begun to prophesy, that Jeremiah wrote down any of his prophecies. At that time he dictated the prophecies to Baruch. These were read in the ears of all the people in the court of the Temple on the occasion of a great fast. The book was destroyed by the king, Jeremiah escaping the royal vengeance only by concealing himself at the advice of his friends. Then he rewrote the book, adding further prophecies. After that, from time to time, he appears to have written down other prophecies. The kernel of the book thus described is to be found in chapters i–xii. The remainder of the book narrates events, and gives us prophecies from the period succeeding 604. The prophecies of the book contained in the first twelve chapters deal with events anywhere from 627 B.C., when Jeremiah was prophesying about the Scythians, on to 604 B.C., when he was denouncing judgment upon Jehoiakim and prophesying the destruction of Jerusalem by the Chaldæans. Various events and various stages of prophetic development are combined in this section. So, for instance, we find put side by side in the seventh chapter the sins of the men of Jehoiakim's time, who failed to keep the covenant made with Yahaweh by king and people in the reformation in 621, and the abominations of a preceding period when the people burned incense to Baalim or worshiped other gods.

The thought and style of Jeremiah's writings are both closely akin to those of Deuteronomy.[1] Jeremiah was himself actively concerned in the promotion of the reforms of Josiah's reign. He was evidently in close sympathy with the reformers and with the whole Deuteronomic movement.[2] Following the publication of that book there had been a renewal of the study of the ancient writings and of the history of Israel on the lines of the Deuteronomic reform. The point of view of this school was that the punishments which

[1] Cf. Jer. iv, 4 and Deut. x, 16.   [2] Cf. Jer. xi; xxxiv, 8 ff.; xxxi, 31.

Yahaweh had inflicted upon Israel in the past were due to the evil doings of the people. Yahaweh rewarded their well-doing with good and their evil-doing with evil. Accordingly the Book of Judges was rewritten, or recast, in substantially its present form, from this point of view: the calamities which came upon the people were due to their evil-doing; the deliverances with which Yahaweh favored them were because of their repentances. Jeremiah is thoroughly imbued with this Deuteronomic point of view, and it is largely that which renders him, from the period of Jehoiakim onwards, a prophet of doom and disaster.[1] He had himself seen the conditions of heathen and immoral worship prevailing under Manasseh.[2] From the history of his people, as he read it, it was clear to him that they had been guilty of apostasy almost from the outset.[3] It was inevitable that a great penalty should fall upon them for this. In the ardor of his youth he had hoped that the reforms instituted by Josiah would constitute a repentance sufficient to turn away the wrath of Yahaweh. The fall of Josiah and the threatening advance of the Babylonian power convinced him of his error. For sins committed for so many generations such repentance was not sufficient. They must be wiped out by a much greater punishment.

We have seen that Jeremiah was strongly influenced by Hosea. From him he borrowed the symbol of the wifely relation of Israel to Yahaweh.[4] From him, also, he borrows some of his interpretations of the relation of Israel to Yahaweh, and apparently also some of his phraseology, as, for instance, his constant reference to the service of Baalim. As Hosea had declared that the faithless wife must suffer the penalty of banishment, so Jeremiah takes the same point of view, and, from 604 on to the end of his activity, he is the prophet of woe and gloom, convinced that there is no other outcome possible than the fall of Jerusalem, the destruction of the Temple, and the banishment of the people. This exile shall last for a period of indefinite length (seventy years).[5] A generation (forty

---

1 Jer. i, 10.   4 Cf. Jer. iii, 20 ; xiii, 26 ff.
2 Jer. xv, 4.   5 Jer. xx, 10 ; xxv, 12 ; xxix, 10.
3 Jer. xxviii, 8, 9 ; x ; cf. also xxxii, 30 ff.

years) in the wilderness had been enough to prepare Israel for the
occupancy of Canaan, but more than that is needed to purge Israel
from the sins which it has committed in Canaan, and to prepare it
for the reoccupancy of the land.

It is notable that Jeremiah's prophecies are not confined to
Judah. This is due in part, doubtless, to his sympathetic relations
to Hosea, the prophet of Israel. But still more it is due to the
study of the history of the past in the writings to which we have
already referred. That history dealt with twelve tribes. These had
from the outset constituted the children of Israel, and, in spite of
the destruction of the kingdom of Israel and the deportation of the
ten tribes, the men of Jeremiah's time (Ezekiel also shared this
view) looked to a restoration which should affect not Judah only,
but Israel also. It was for this reason that Josiah's reformation
did not confine itself exclusively to Judah. He undertook to purify
Bethel as well as Jerusalem, and the battle in which he lost his life
was fought, apparently, in the effort to protect the land of Israel
against invasion by the Egyptians. He evidently laid claim to that
land as his own and, indeed, the Samaritan [1] Israelites were worshipers of Yahaweh, of the same religion as their Jewish compatriots.

Jeremiah's call to prophecy, as described in the first chapter of
his book, is interesting as exhibiting the conditions with which he
had to deal. The political confusion was like a seething caldron,
the mouth of which opened toward Jerusalem. From the north he
saw the nations pouring out a stream of devastation and destruction on Syria and Palestine. [2] There is in his call to prophecy no
such simple inspired vision as we find in Isaiah. The basis of his
call was not devotion to the Temple, nor was his spiritual inspiration derived from the Holy of Holies. He pictures this call as
an inward struggle. He is, if we may so define it, the Low Church
prophet, the one whose inspiration and whose teachings are quite
detached from outward forms and ceremonies. This may be connected with the fact, mentioned in the book bearing his name, that
while he was a priest of Yahaweh, and apparently a man of rank

---

[1] For the attitude of at least some Israelites or Samaritans toward the Jerusalem
temple at this period cf. Jer. xli, 5.   [2] Jer. i, 13.

and means, by residence he was a countryman from Anathoth.[1] At the same time it must be said that Jeremiah displays familiarity with, and influence by, the Temple liturgies. We have seen that in his call to prophecy Isaiah makes use of one of these liturgies in the song of the seraphim, " Holy, Holy, Holy, Lord God of Hosts." Jeremiah makes a larger use of liturgical formulæ,[2] and there are also contained in his writings several psalms, based on Temple models, some of which are singularly like the minatory psalms of the Psalter[3] both in tone and form. But sacrifices and the conception connected with them in the minds of the worshipers, the belief that Yahaweh could be appeased or that His favor and help were to be won by them, were peculiarly abhorrent to him, more so than to any of the preceding prophets except, possibly, Amos. Accordingly his denunciations of ritual religion go in principle far beyond those of Isaiah. The worship of the Temple became offensive to him. It was false worship, because it was based on the idea that by the service rendered in the Temple men could win the favor of God Almighty, something which could be done in fact only by observing the moral law.

Near the beginning of the reign of Jehoiakim Jeremiah took his stand at the Temple gate and prophesied to those who were entering in, as follows : " Hear the word of Yahaweh, all Judah, that enter in at these gates to worship Yahaweh. Thus saith Yahaweh of Hosts, the God of Israel : Amend your ways and your works, and I will cause you to dwell in this place. Trust not in lying words, saying, The Temple of Yahaweh, the Temple of Yahaweh, the Temple of Yahaweh, are these. For if ye thoroughly amend your ways and your works ; if ye thoroughly execute judgment between a man and his neighbor ; if ye oppress not the stranger, the fatherless, and the widow, and shed not innocent blood in this place, and walk not after other gods : then will I cause you to dwell in this place, in the land that I gave to your fathers, from

---

1 Jer. i, 1.

2 Cf. Jer. xxxiii, 11, the sacrificial chant (cf. 1 Chron. xvi, 34), used as the basis of a number of the later Psalms, " Give thanks to the Lord," etc.

3 Cf. Jer. xv, 15 ff. ; xviii, 19 ff. ; xx, 7-13 (the following poem, xx, 14-18, is like Job iii, 3 ff.) ; xlv.

everlasting unto everlasting. Behold, ye trust in lying words, that cannot profit. Will ye steal, murder, and commit adultery, and swear falsely, and burn incense unto Baal, and walk after other gods whom ye know not, and come and stand before Me in this house, which is called by My name, and say, We have been rescued in order again to do all these abominations? Is this house, which is called by My name, become a den of robbers in your eyes? Yea, behold, I have seen it, saith Yahaweh. Go ye unto My place in Shiloh, where I caused My name to dwell at first, and see what I did to it for the wickedness of My people Israel. And now, because ye have done all these things, saith Yahaweh, and I spake unto you, rising up early and speaking, but ye heard not; and I called you, but ye answered not; therefore will I do unto the house which is called by My name, wherein ye trust, and unto the place which I gave to you and to your fathers, as I did to Shiloh. And I will cast you away from Me, as I have cast away all your brethren, the whole seed of Ephraim."[1]

He was at once seized and came near losing his life. It is interesting to find that it was the priests of the Temple and the prophets in alliance with them who would have put him to death.[2] The civil officials and the laymen protected him, manifesting that respect for any man who professed himself to be a prophet, with a message from God, which is as characteristic of Islam to-day as it was of Israel of old.

Since the time of Isaiah the priests and prophets had maintained the inviolability of the Temple as the abode of Yahaweh and of Jerusalem as the seat of the Temple, a truth which they believed had been confirmed by the destruction of the Assyrian army under Sennacherib. The contemporary prophecy of the country prophet, Micah, that Zion should be ploughed like a field, "Jerusalem become heaps and the temple mount forest heights,"[3] had been, apparently, quite forgotten, albeit the book of prophecies of Micah had been preserved. Now that prophecy was recalled, and by it as a precedent Jeremiah's life was saved. At the same time another prophet, Uriah, who ventured to utter the same prediction, was

[1] Jer. vii.   [2] Jer. xxvi.   [3] Mic. iii.

forced to flee for his life, pursued, brought back from Egypt, and put to death.[1]

One might suppose that the defeat and death of Josiah would have been regarded as an evidence that his reforms did not have the divine approval, and that the Jews would, therefore, have sought to go back to the worship in vogue before the reformation. This does not seem to have been the case. The account of this experience of Jeremiah, at the very outset of Jehoiakim's reign, is evidence that, in spite of the defeat of Josiah, the covenant with Yahaweh established in his reign was not annulled. Even the names of the kings who succeeded him are themselves evidence of the prevalent Yahawism. Each king bore the name of Yahaweh in his name. This seemed to be regarded as essential, and in one case the king's name was changed to make it comply with this rule. The king of Judah must be a servant of Yahaweh and must acknowledge that service by bearing the name of Yahaweh in his name. Ezekiel does, indeed, represent all sorts of abominations as existing in the Temple after the deportation of the captives under Jehoiakim, but from the Book of Kings and from the Book of Jeremiah it would seem that we are not to interpret his prophetic pictures as a literal representation of conditions formally and officially allowed. There were doubtless a number who secretly practiced the cults which had been condemned, and not a few believed that the reforms of Josiah had been offensive to the divine powers. This is made clear by Jeremiah's experiences, after the final abandonment of Judæa, with the women who worshiped the host of heaven;[2] but the very account there given is itself evidence that the people did not apostatize from the covenant of Josiah's reign so far as the worship of Yahaweh was concerned. Court and people both seem to have been dominated by the priests of Yahaweh's Temple and His prophets. But both priests and prophets viewed the covenant from a different standpoint from that of Jeremiah. To them the worship of Yahaweh was the main point; to Jeremiah the observance of the moral law was the main point; or rather that was the essential feature of the worship of Yahaweh,

[1] Jer. xxvi, 20 ff.   [2] Jer. xliv, 15 ff.

and any other worship of Him was false and must involve the destruction of Jerusalem and the Temple. This view finally brought him into conflict with the civil authorities [1] and the populace, as it had from the outset with the priests and prophets. Against the latter, his peers and confrères, Jeremiah stood almost alone, at least during the later years of his prophetic activity. They were continually prophesying to the people the deliverance of Yahaweh; that He was more mighty than all the gods of the heathen; that His abode was in the Temple at Jerusalem; that they were His people, with whom He had made a covenant; that He would interfere against the armies of their foes, however powerful they were, for their deliverance. And with the prophets were closely united the priests of the Temple. Their temporary and pecuniary advantage lay with the magnificent maintenance of the worship at that temple, while spiritually they were in sympathy with anything that exalted the shrine which they served, the abode, in their belief, of Yahaweh himself. Jeremiah was thrown into the stocks. [2] Several times he narrowly escaped death. During a good part of the final siege of the city he was a prisoner, with sentence suspended, as one may say; that is, had the siege been raised, he would have been put to death as a false prophet. But superstitious reverence prevented the king and the rulers from resorting to extreme measures, and the weak Zedekiah, turning in his extremity first to one side and then to another, consulted more than once with the Prophet who prophesied his downfall. [3]

Jeremiah's prophecies contain not only denunciations of the prophets and priests but denunciations of kings and rulers, and in each case woe is denounced for moral iniquity. Like his great predecessor Isaiah, Jeremiah concerned himself with political events. Like Isaiah, he opposed alliances with foreign nations. Like Isaiah he made use, at times, of what we of to-day would call dramatic and sensational methods of presenting his views, after the manner of ancient prophecy. So on one occasion, when embassies of various neighboring states were seeking to engage Zedekiah in the conspiracy to throw off the Babylonian yoke, Jeremiah appeared

[1] Jer. xxxvii.   [2] Jer. xx.   [3] Jer. xxxviii.

in the courts of the Temple wearing a yoke on his own neck and bringing similar yokes for the ambassadors, by this object lesson proclaiming the will of Yahaweh that they should wear the Babylonian yoke. A certain prophet, Hananiah, however, seized Jeremiah's yoke and broke it, declaring that as he broke the yoke from Jeremiah's neck, so Yahaweh would break the Babylonian yoke from off the neck of Judah. A few days later Jeremiah appeared with an iron yoke instead of the wooden one which had been broken, announcing as the word of Yahaweh that for any attempt to break the Babylonian yoke a still harder yoke, even a yoke of iron, which was unbreakable, should be laid upon them.[1]

Unlike Isaiah, when Jerusalem was besieged, Jeremiah, far from giving help and inspiration to the besieged, urged king and people to surrender the city and go forth and trust to the Babylonians. He had no expectation that they would be saved from captivity, but at least in this way their lives would be spared and so the national existence continued.[2] Such an attitude certainly seemed lacking in patriotism, and naturally the Jews regarded him as practically an ally of the Babylonians, while the Babylonians on their part not only spared his life when the city was captured, but set him free and gave him his choice of going to Babylonia and holding there a position of honor, or remaining behind in Judah.[3]

Like Isaiah and Amos, Jeremiah in his prophecies deals with the neighboring nations,[4] but his point of view with regard to the power and the province of Yahaweh shows a marked advance over his predecessors, his doctrine of the restoration of the neighboring nations surpassing in its universalism the prophecies of Amos. Phœnicia, Philistia, Ammon, Moab, Edom, and Egypt are to meet the same fate as Israel and Judah. They are all to be carried captive, and in course of time they are all to be restored again. In this connection Jeremiah introduces a figure which becomes common later, the figure of the cup which Yahaweh gives the nations to drink.[5] Judah and its neighbors are to drink it first; afterwards Babylon also is to drink it. There is never any question in his mind

---

1 Jer. xxviii. 3 Jer. xxxix, xl. 5 Jer. xxv, 15.
2 Jer. xxxviii. 4 Jer. xlvi–li.

as to the restoration of both Israel and Judah, and we find a vivid illustration of that confidence in his purchase from his cousin, while captive in the Temple in the latter part of the final siege, of certain family lands at Anathoth, a place at that time in the possession of the Babylonians.[1] Indeed, Jeremiah makes this purchase the text of a prophecy of the future restoration of those lands to Israel. Following the line of the former prophets, he connects this restoration, which is to take place only after a long period of purging through captivity, with the Davidic dynasty, but he appears to lay much less stress upon the Davidic stock of the Messiah than did Isaiah.[2] Indeed, he has relatively little to say about the conditions of the restoration, being much more concerned in prophesying the calamities that shall befall the state and their cause. Again, while looking for the restoration of the Jewish state, he seems to have largely freed himself from that conception of the connection of Yahaweh with the land of Israel which we have met in some of his predecessors. Conversely he seems to have no feeling that a foreign land is in itself unclean, so that the people cannot worship Yahaweh there. To compare the Jews carried away by Nebuchadrezzar to Babylonia in 597 with those left behind in Judah he uses the figure of the two baskets of figs. The good figs are in the basket taken to Babylonia; the bad figs are those that are left behind in Judah.[3] When the Jews in Babylonia became restive through sympathy with that element in Jerusalem which was conspiring against Nebuchadrezzar, Jeremiah wrote to them urging them to build houses, to till the ground, and to make themselves homes in Babylonia, for it was the will of God that they should dwell there.[4] He does not represent the foreign land as cursed, or speak of them as eating unclean food in an unclean land, as Amos and Isaiah had done. They were to continue to conduct themselves in Babylonia as they would have done had they been in Judah. At the same time Jeremiah does expect that ultimately, after seventy years (that is, an indefinitely long period of time), their descendants

---

[1] Jer. xxxii.

[2] Jer. xxiii, xxxiii, xxx, 9. The two latter passages are under deep suspicion of coming from a later hand, but the first is unquestionably genuine.

[3] Jer. xxiv.   [4] Jer. xxix.

shall be restored to Judah, and so when he is given his choice of living in comfort and honor in Babylonia, or remaining in Judah in the uncertain and disturbed conditions which followed the Babylonian conquest, he chooses the latter, in order that he may do what he can to prepare the way in Judah for the coming of the kingdom of the future, for which he looks.[1]

Jeremiah is often spoken of as the purest exemplar of Israelitish prophetism, in whom prophecy attained its highest and ablest development,[2] and, on the practical side, there can be no question of the immense influence which he exerted on later generations. Partly this was due to conditions succeeding his prophecies. Practically alone, against all the religious teachers of Jerusalem, he announced the destruction of Jerusalem and the exile of its inhabitants as a punishment for their sins. With equal positiveness he declared that the nation could not and should not be destroyed and that in due time God would restore them to their land, purged and purified by a long punishment. His utterances, while in line with those of former prophets, were much more distinct, and much less involved in poetic fancies. The fact that precisely that which he and he alone had foretold, both as to the captivity and the restoration, came to pass, gave his utterances in regard to other matters an altogether peculiar importance.

Further, there was something singularly appealing in the love which Jeremiah showed for his people and his land. Accused of treason, reviled, punished, in constant danger of death, he never lost that love. Finally he fell a martyr to it, and that martyrdom made of him to later ages, who saw from the event that his was the true patriotism, a popular hero. Perhaps, in part at least, it was because of this love that while Jeremiah was a thorough-going monotheist, believing in Yahaweh not merely as the only God of Israel but as the only God of all the world, he had also a profound faith in the special and eternal relation of this God to His people Israel.[3] In the main, however, his belief in this regard was an

[1] Jer. xli, xlii.
[2] Cf. for example Cornill, *Introduction to the Canonical Books of the Old Testament.*
[3] Bade (" Hebrew Moral Development," *University of California Chronicle*, XIII, 1; " Der Monojahwismus des Deuteronomiums," *Zeitschrift für die alttestamentliche*

inheritance through the Prophets from an earlier henotheism; but whatever its origin, the justification of this peculiar faith by the fulfillment of his predictions was profoundly influential in commending that faith to his people. The very fact that his life ended in apparent failure, the last we hear of him being his protest against the worship of the "queen of heaven" by his compatriots in Egypt, gave a peculiar and dramatic emphasis to his doctrine in view of later events. He was right, they were wrong. This was such proof as appealed to the imagination and understanding of the common man.

It must be understood, of course, that Jeremiah was not the only monotheist of his time. The Book of Deuteronomy and the Book of Lamentations show us that the spiritual leaders of that day had in general attained to the same position. God was no longer to them the God of Israel only, but the God of all the world; albeit Israel was His special, chosen people. Accordingly, when Jerusalem was destroyed, the authors of the Lamentations refer all that has befallen them, including the triumph of their enemies, to God, who is wroth with them for their sins. These sins, however, they supposed were, to a large extent certainly, the sins of their fathers. "Our fathers have sinned and are not, and we have borne their iniquities."[1] "The fathers have eaten sour grapes and the children's teeth are set on edge."[2] Jeremiah's higher ethical perception led him to detect the fallacy of such argument. His prophetic hatred of forms and ceremonies had arrayed him against those men (and it was they especially who took this view) who sought to make up to Yahaweh for the misdeeds of their fathers by an increased observance of ritual acts and an increased emphasis on external laws. Their very effort to appease God by these things, revealing as it did their lack of perception of the higher moral truth, brought home

---

Wissenschaft, 30. Jahrgang, 1910) maintains that Deuteronomy is not monotheistic, but only *mono-Yahawistic*. As already pointed out, it is based on an Israelitic mono-Yahawistic composition, its immediate practical aim is the abolition not only of all worship alien to Yahaweh but also of all shrines of Yahaweh but one, and its creed, "Hear, Israel, Yahaweh our God is one Yahaweh" (vi, 4), is mono-Yahawistic; but on the other hand there are various statements and allusions scattered through the book which show that the author believed that Yahaweh the God of Israel was also lord of all the earth, maker of all things, beside whom there is no God (cf. iv, 19, 28; x, 14–17).   [1] Lam. v, 7.   [2] Jer. xxxi, 29.

to him the conviction of the guilt of his own age. The enormities of the past were great and must incur punishment, but the wickedness of the present was equally great. His own isolation from the nation tended also to develop in him a new perception of the relation of the individual soul to God.[1] All the Prophets, his predecessors, had been conscious, it is true, of a peculiar, personal relation to God, but with him first this relation began to assume the form of individualism. The problem of evil, the same problem which was later discussed in the Book of Job, occupies his mind. The explanation that God's punishments were given because of the iniquity of the people does not seem altogether to satisfy the conditions as he sees them. Are all so bound together that each individual, good or bad, must suffer for the evil-doing of every other? It cannot be said that he finds a satisfactory solution of the question, but it is interesting and important to observe that he begins to suggest the separation of the individual from the nation in his relation to God. Imperfect as his solution of the problem was, he laid in it the foundation of the later religion which was developed in and after the Exile, and was thereby a powerful factor in preventing the absorption of Israel in the surrounding nations as a result of its political death. It is true that his light regard of the Temple as such and his attitude of universalism in respect to heathen lands was effective in leading the Jews in Egypt to building there temples to Yahaweh, and, to that extent, tended toward disintegration of the people by loss of a local center. On the other hand, by leading the way toward a worship of God and a relation to God of a personal and individual character, separate from forms, not depending on locality, he helped to hold the people together in the worship of Yahaweh in heathen lands and to prevent them from becoming worshipers of the gods of those lands.

It was in line with that same prophetic development of which he was the outcome, and instinctive, if one may so say, in that individualism in religion toward which he was reaching, that he sought to transmute the outer into an inner law. To some extent the prophetical law-book of Deuteronomy had done this, as, for

[1] Jer. xv; xxi, 29.

example, with the ancient rite of circumcision,[1] which it makes symbolic of the inward reality of circumcision of the heart. Jeremiah, who was, as has been already noted, a child of the Deuteronomic movement, would fain convert the whole covenant of the outward law, entered into by the nation with such solemnity in the time of King Josiah, into a new covenant, the laws of which should be written in the heart and life of the people.[2]

But in this Jeremiah was not to modern perception altogether consistent. It was impossible for him to free himself entirely from the outward forms and laws. Precisely as, with all his universalism, he still, illogically and inconsistently if you please, preserved his belief in a peculiar relation of God to Israel, so, with all his disregard in other respects of outward law, he still placed great emphasis on the observance of the Sabbath.[3] That part of the law set forth in Deuteronomy which appealed to him was the moral law. His mind was led away from the laws dealing with clean and unclean, and the like, to those laws which dealt with the real moral facts of man's heart and man's inner relation to God. Now morally the Decalogue stood out above everything else, and his use of the moral law of the Decalogue in the book of his prophecies[4] shows the impression which that code made

[1] Cf. Deut. x.   [2] Cf. Jer. xxxi, 32 ff. Cf. also Jer. iv, 4.

[3] Cf. Jer. xxii, 19 ff. Modern critics have very largely denied the Jeremianic authorship of this passage on subjective grounds. They admit that its linguistic usage and phraseology are Jeremianic, but contend that its contents are in "palpable and sharp opposition to the prophetic theology of Jeremiah" (Cornhill, *Introduction*, p. 303) because of the very great importance ascribed by him, who elsewhere denies the value of outward forms, to this, which they consider an outward form. This is to judge men rather by a logical theory than by the actual facts of known experience. Perhaps the best answer to their argument is to point out that precisely the same attitude was adopted by Scotch Presbyterianism. Jeremiah's attitude appealed forcibly to the conscience and intelligence of the old Scotch Presbyterian leaders, who were, in fact, Jeremianic in their entire view of religion. They were as unaware of any conflict between the principle of their doctrine and their sabbatic dogma as was Jeremiah, and they laid quite as much stress on Sabbath observance as an essential feature of spiritual religion as did Jeremiah himself. It may be added that, to a large extent, this is true to-day of English-speaking Protestants in general. The argument from the language and phraseology of this passage seems conclusive as to its authorship; and, in an historic study of the development of the Sabbath idea among the Jews, Jeremiah's teaching seems a necessary link in the chain.

[4] Cf. chap. vii.

upon his mind as a divine revelation.[1] But a part of that Decalogue was the law of the Sabbath Day. By its very position in the Decalogue, therefore, and its consequent connection with the lofty morality of the laws of the Decalogue, this became to him an essential element of religion, on the observance of which, as a part of the moral law, depended that restoration to which he looked forward. Whatever we of to-day may think of this attitude from the moral standpoint, it must be said that in its influence in preserving the religion of Israel in foreign lands Jeremiah's attitude in this respect was one of profound significance and importance.[2]

---

1 It should be remembered that the Ten Words, as the contents of the Ark, and at this period certainly regarded as in a special sense the commandments of God, given on tables of stone to Moses, enjoyed a peculiar position which might well lead even a Jeremiah to hold them in special reverence as sacrosanct, which is precisely the manner in which they have been treated by the Christian Church. While rejecting the Law as a whole, the Christian Church has accepted the Decalogue with an unquestioning and almost unreasonable faith.

2 The Book of Jeremiah has come down to us in a double redaction, in the Hebrew and the Greek, the latter preserving the shorter form. There are very few additions in the Septuagint, but many omissions of words and passages occurring in the Hebrew text, so that the Greek version of Jeremiah is smaller by about 2700 words, or one eighth of the whole, than the Hebrew. In general the Septuagint preserves presumably a more primitive form, and in the references to the Book of Jeremiah in this chapter no emphasis has been placed upon any passages not contained in the Septuagint, all passages appearing in the Hebrew only being (to say the least) under serious suspicion in regard to their genuineness.

CHAPTER XVIII

EZEKIEL THE THEOLOGIAN

It is very difficult for men of the twentieth-century West to realize the small part which the individual as such played in the national and religious conception of the ancient eastern world. It was the family, the clan, the nation, which counted. The life or death of the individual was in itself insignificant. There was no belief in personal immortality as we understand it. A man lived on in his children, and there was therefore no greater misfortune which could befall anyone than to die childless. Each tribe or clan had its god with whom it was connected by a blood relation, and, so far certainly as popular belief was concerned, the Hebrews developed their monotheism out of this idea of their special relation to their god, Yahaweh, with whom they were one in blood. For His honor he must avenge anything done to a member of His tribe. On the other hand, the extinction of the tribe would mean His own destruction.

Immediately before the Exile the more thoughtful and more ethical element among the Jews had come to conceive of their tribal god as the one and only God and to entertain a very lofty conception of His individuality or holiness. They nevertheless still continued to think of Him as a tribal or national god. The breaking up and destruction of the Hebrew nation had very much to do with developing the idea of an individual, personal relation to God and an individual, personal religion, and finally a conception of individual immortality, as over against the conception of race immortality, a race religion, and a race relation to God.

The first distinct expression of the conception of this relation of the individual to God is found, as already pointed out, in the prophetic teaching of Jeremiah, largely because Jeremiah prophesied at the period of national disintegration. The commentary to the Second Commandment (which at that period had become an essential part of the original commandment or *word* itself, as the practically identical forms in Exodus xx and Deuteronomy v show), " I, Yahaweh, am a jealous god and visit the sins of the fathers upon the children unto the third and fourth generation of them that hate me," expressed the attitude of the men of Jeremiah's day. This was a doctrine or dogma of the Jewish religion of that time. It expressed that conception of family and tribal relationship already described. There was no escape for the children, to the third and fourth generation, from the punishment of the sins of their ancestors. To a certain extent Jeremiah and Ezekiel adopted this view. Jeremiah held that the sins of the fathers had been so great and so long continued that a generation of punishment was not sufficient, but that the nation must go into captivity for an indefinite period, seventy years. But the more the reasoning sense of the people increased with the development of experience and civilization, the less ready they were to accept on authority what had come down from the fathers. On the other side, as the national and tribal spirit decreased, so the doctrine of family solidarity, as expressed in such teaching as that of the suffering of the children for the sins of their ancestors, tended to become an enervating and demoralizing force in the life of the individual and of the people. When calamities came and the Prophets preached reform and pronounced punishment, the people answered: " It is not our fault. These punishments have come upon us for the sins of our fathers." The old national-tribal sense of loyalty, which would have made men hesitate to put the guilt upon their fathers, was weakened ; the old national solidarity was disappearing, — and as yet no sense of personal responsibility had been developed to take its place. Why should they try to reform, when they believed that they were suffering not for their own sins but for what their ancestors had done ?

This was the condition which the Jews had reached in the latter part of the seventh century and the beginning of the sixth century B.C., and it is to this condition that, as already pointed out, Jeremiah in part addressed himself in such words as these : " In those days they shall say no more, The fathers have eaten sour grapes and the children's teeth are set on edge; but each shall die for his own iniquity. Whoso eateth sour grapes, his teeth shall be set on edge." [1] But this teaching is only, as it were, incidental to his main message, nor is it altogether consistent with his doctrine of the punishment, which must be so much the greater because the sins of the fathers had been so long continued and so great. It remained for Ezekiel to develop this doctrine more fully and more logically and to make it an essential part of his message, drawn from the conditions of the Exile.

Ezekiel belonged to the priesthood [2] of the Jerusalem Temple, which, by the method in which the reformation of Josiah on the basis of Deuteronomy was carried out, had become a temple of the aristocracy. While still a young man he was carried off from Jerusalem to Babylonia by Nebuchadrezzar, in 598. His fellow captives constituted the nobles, the priests, and the men of wealth of Judah, in general the aristocracy, the plain people being left behind in the land. [3] Ezekiel, with a number of other captives, was settled at an old ruin site called Tel-Abib, by the Canal Chebar, in Babylonia. [4] The Jews of the Captivity were not poor men, as is evinced by the fact that they early began to play an important rôle in the commercial life of Babylonia. They regarded themselves also as being the true Jewish people, looking down upon those who had been left behind by Nebuchadrezzar as the offscourings of the people. [5] On the whole they seem to have retained the expectation of a restoration to Jerusalem and of a divine interference for that purpose. They do not seem to have been conscious of evil-doing on their own part, and believed that what had befallen them was the result of the evil-doing of their ancestors. They were inclined to take part in any movement for the overthrow of Nebuchadrezzar, and maintained an attitude of restlessness up to the period of the final destruction of Jerusalem in 586. [6]

With that destruction the situation changes. Their hope of restoration had been connected with the preservation of Jerusalem

---

[1] Jer. xxxi, 29. Cf. also Ezek. xviii, 2 ff.   [2] Ezek. i, 3.   [3] 2 Kings xxiv, 14 f.
[4] Ezek. i, 3; iii, 15.   [5] Ezek. xi.   [6] Jer. xxix; xxiv, 1-3; Ezek. xi, 14-21.

and the Temple.[1] With the destruction of the Temple their religion and their nationality were at once annihilated and a new situation was created.

The book of Ezekiel's prophecies is divided into two almost entirely distinct parts by this event, which entirely changed the conditions of his constituency.[2] While thoroughly a Jew and a priest of the Jerusalem Temple, Ezekiel was profoundly affected by the religion of Babylonia. Its ritual and its imagery appealed to him, as they did to the men, of the same type of priestly training, who at that time and later recodified the ritual and the religious laws of Israel. Ezekiel was also a student not only of the past history of Israel, but more especially of its earlier religious and ritual customs, legends, and traditions.[3] According to his conception, — and in this he differed radically from the mass of his contemporaries in Babylonia, — when Jerusalem was captured for the first time by Nebuchadrezzar and the holy vessels carried off along with the leaders of the priesthood and the élite of the people,[4] Yahaweh deserted His temple and returned to His heavenly tabernacle on the mountain of the north. From this mountain, which reminds one, on the one side, of Babylonian mythology, and on the other of certain of the old Hebrew legends like the Flood story, Ezekiel sees Yahaweh

---

[1] It would appear from Ezekiel's prophecies (xx, 27 ff.), however, that, in the earlier part of the Exile at least, there was a tendency to follow pre-reformation practices, just as among the Jews in Egypt, and that the colony at Tel-Abib, like the colony at Elephantine, established a shrine or temple of Yahaweh for sacrificial purposes.

[2] Ezekiel's task in the second part of his book, xxxiv-xlviii, is out of the grave of the nation Israel to resurrect the congregation Israel. He was a pastor of souls. The nation was dead, the individuals were alive. Out of them he must reconstruct a new sort of an Israel. He had to face a tendency to think God overcome, or that He had forsaken his people, an inclination to dwell on the hopelessness of their sins, which could not be atoned for, and for which they were dead (xviii, 2 ; xxxiii, 10 ; xxxvii, 11). To those who felt God was unjust, punishing them for the sins of their fathers, he must preach contrition ; to those who felt the justice of their punishment and were overwhelmed with the hopelessness of their guilt he must preach hope.

[3] As the student, and also probably under the influence, of Babylonian recordism, Ezekiel, while uttering prophecies and using symbolic forms and acts like his predecessors, commonly uses writing, not speech, as his vehicle of expression. In this, also, he differs from his immediate predecessors : while their names had *Yah* in composition, his had *El* : a premonition of that sanctity of the *Name* which was ultimately to prohibit the very utterance of *Yahaweh*.   [4] 2 Kings xxiv, 10 ff.

come, in the vision which constitutes his call to prophecy, in flaming brightness, only partly distinguishable in form, borne on a wonderful chariot, surrounded and supported by cherubim, which consist of winged men, eagles, bulls, and lions, precisely the symbols which we find on old monuments and monumental representations.[1] But while there is an evident Babylonian coloring in this picture, there is also a still more distinct representation of the conditions of the Temple worship, where Yahaweh dwelt in the mysterious dark inner shrine,[2] and of the conception which that embodied of the brilliancy of the divine presence, lightnings flashing forth from the dark tabernacle of the clouds.[3]

Although Ezekiel disowned Jerusalem and the Temple, as they existed under the control of the mob that was left behind, polluted, as he asserted, by every vile form of false worship,[4] he never for one instant forgot the Temple itself. It was the center of his conception of religion, nor did he ever forget his priestly office. The ritual of the Temple he cherished most lovingly, and one essential part of his work was the adaptation of that ritual, purified from certain of its grosser elements, to the new Temple and the new Jerusalem, which he devoutly believed and insistently taught should be restored.

Another function of the priesthood which he exercised, and which practically constituted his prophetic message, was the old function of interpreting *torah*. The people were in the habit of coming to him to consult him and ask the word of the Law.[5] The prophetic call is associated indissolubly in his mind with his priestly function. His is not the distinctly personal relation to God which we find in the other prophets. With Ezekiel the personal relation comes as a result of his official station. He is a priest. God has set him apart officially for that work and this is an obligation arising out of his priestly office. He has been set to watch over the people.[6] His obligation is to tell the sinners of his people of their sin, to warn them of the destruction that will come because of that sin.[7]

---

[1] Ezek. i.   [3] Cf. also Ps. xviii.   [5] Ezek. xiv, 1; xx, 1.
[2] 1 Kings viii, 12.   [4] Ezek. viii; ix; x; xiv, 22 ff.   [6] Ezek. iii, 17 ff.; xxxiii.
[7] Ezek. xxii. It should be said that in the definition of their sins his emphasis falls on false worship and idolatry rather than on immorality.

If, after he has done this, they still persist in their sin, he is free from culpability ; but if for any cause whatsoever he fail to fulfill his function, if through fear or favor or carelessness he do not warn them, their blood shall be visited upon his head. His conception of his relation to them is a part of that individualism [1] which he teaches in a more definite and precise manner than Jeremiah had.

Like Jeremiah in Jerusalem, Ezekiel in Babylonia stood alone, or practically alone, against the great mass of the prophets among his countrymen.[2] They were advocates of rebellion against Nebuchadrezzar, dervishes who preached a holy war. He steadfastly opposed this rebellion, and indeed he seems to have entertained a fairly good opinion of Nebuchadrezzar, who, according to his teaching, was a tool of Yahaweh,[3] to execute his purpose not only against Jerusalem but against the nations at large. One curious prophecy, in fact, seems to condole with Nebuchadrezzar for his failure to capture Tyre and promises to him Egypt as a recompense instead of it.[4] He is as unpatriotic, from the point of view of the ordinary Jew of that day, as Jeremiah.[5] Up to the time of the final capture of the city and the destruction of the Temple, his prophecies consist in denunciations of punishment.[6] He supports

---

1 For individualism note the watchman and his responsibility, Ezek. iii, 16 ff.: the mark on the forehead, ix ; the punishment of the individual for the worship of idols, the good cannot save the bad, xiv ; exposition of the doctrine, and catalogue of sins, xviii ; salvation or punishment not for past good or evil deeds but for present, xxxiii.

2 Ezek. xii ; xiii ; xiv ; xxii, 25.

3 Ezek. xxx, 24.

4 Ezek. xxix, 18 ff. In his prophecies about the nations, xxv–xxxii, Ezekiel takes a very different attitude from Jeremiah. Yahaweh will destroy or grievously punish the nations to evince and vindicate His holiness. They are to be punished for their treatment of Israel. After their humiliation Yahaweh will gather His people again in their land and sanctify them in the sight of the nations. In these chapters we find on the one side old Hebrew legends woven in, like the Garden of Eden (xxvi–xxviii, xxxi), and on the other references to the most recent history (xxv, xxxv).

5 In addition to his opposition to rebellion and his friendly attitude toward Nebuchadrezzar, cf. also his designation of Jerusalem as the daughter of Amorites and Hittites (Ezek. xiv), utterly depraved, a harlot and worse, and his parables and histories of Israel and Judah, setting forth their innate wickedness, and representing Judah as the worse of the two (xix–xxiii). Like Jeremiah he condemns unsparingly the breach of covenant with Babylon (xvii).

6 Even in these, however, he does not look for the utter destruction of Israel. Jerusalem, it is true, is to be utterly destroyed (Ezek. xxi), and for those left behind

his prophecies by symbolic acts, which are sometimes curiously fantastic and sometimes curiously prosaic. Once he takes an un-baked brick, makes a picture of Jerusalem on it, lays siege against it, builds a fort and sets a camp against it with battering rams. Then he sets an iron pan between himself and the brick, to picture the way in which, when Jerusalem is besieged by the Chaldæans and the people pray to Yahaweh, they shall pray in vain, for He has shut himself off from His people as with a wall of iron.[1] He cuts off his hair, a sign of mourning, then weighs what he has cut off in weights, scatters some of it to the wind, burns some in the fire, and hacks some in pieces with a sword, a representation of the way in which Yahaweh will treat the Jews of Jerusalem.[2] He gathers all his household goods together and prepares them for removal. Then, when evening is come, he takes a load, breaks a hole in the wall of his house, and staggers through in darkness — a picture, as he tells the people, of what was about to befall Jeru-salem, the way that the Jews of Jerusalem should be carried into captivity through the breaches in the walls of their city, loaded with their own goods, as slaves of others, their eyes blinded, after the cruel fashion of treating captives.[3] After the news of the capture is received, his prophecies take a new turn.[4] His object from that time on is to reconstruct the nation. To this section belong his prophecies of the restoration of David's kingdom, in-cluding both Israel and Judah.[5] " I will set up one shepherd over them and he shall feed them." " My servant David, he shall feed them and he shall be their shepherd." But this new kingdom exists because of their peculiar and special relation to Yahaweh. He is their real king and David but a prince under him. " I the Lord will be their God and my servant David prince among

in Judah he holds out no hope. The land is to be laid waste. The people are to be carried away into captivity. As once they were captives in Egypt (a figure familiar in earlier prophets), so now they are to be carried into a new wilderness, and there to make a new covenant; after which they shall be brought back to Jerusalem (xx).   [1] Ezek. iv.   [2] Ezek. v.   [3] Ezek. xii.

[4] Ezek. xxxiii, 21. In the first part he dealt with the past and the present, and his prophecies are in general prophecies of judgment. In the last part he deals with the future, and his prophecies are prophecies of hope.

[5] Ezek. xxxiv.

them." [1] It is this conception which lies at the basis of his whole picture, contained in the last nine chapters, xl to xlviii, of the new state, with the Temple in its center. [2] The important thing is the relation of Israel to God, and the fundamental law is the law which governs that relation. Ritual, therefore, holds a place as important as what we commonly call morality or ethics.

One of the most famous and most characteristic of his prophecies is that of the prophecy of the dry bones. [3] His fellow exiles, overwhelmed by the destruction of Jerusalem and the Temple, were crying out: "Israel is dead. How can life come to a nation that is dead and not even buried in a tomb, whose bones lie scattered on the hills?" "Behold, O my people, I will open your graves and cause you to come out of your graves and bring you into the land of Israel." The wind of Yahaweh comes from the four quarters of the earth and breathes upon the slain that they may live, and the breath comes into their body and they live and stand on their feet, an exceeding great army.

Closely connected with his view of the restoration is his eschatological doctrine, expressed in the famous prophecy of Gog and Magog, in which he pictures the overthrow of all the heathen foes. [4] The development of this prophecy out of the prophecies of his predecessors is an interesting one. The great Scythian upheaval, which played so large a part in the prophecies of Zephaniah and the earlier prophecies of Jeremiah, has colored the particular form in which he sees the great world-movement of the Day of Yahaweh. His own curious predilection for details and figures, in which again

---

[1] So also Ezek. xxxvii, 15 ff., where the two sticks of Judah and Israel are to be united, and there is to be one king over them, David, with an everlasting covenant of peace. His ideal new state involves the restoration of all the twelve traditional tribes, xlviii.

[2] This is a picture of the Kingdom of God as Eden restored. It is a Messianic prophecy. It was the ideal that had much to do with molding the policy of succeeding ages in Jewry, as Augustine's *Civitas Dei* did in Christianity.

[3] Ezek. xxxvii.

[4] Ezek. xxxviii, xxxix. They are brought up in a great host to the land of Israel and there destroyed for the vindication of Yahaweh's holiness, who is jealous of His name. He will show Israel and the nations that the captivity was His act, because of Israel's transgressions; then He will hide His face no more, but pour out His spirit on Israel.

he shows the influence of Babylonian recordism, expresses itself in this prophecy most markedly in the details of the massacre of the foes of Yahaweh.

Ezekiel exercised probably a more profound influence upon the later developments of Judaism than any other one man. As Jeremiah in Jerusalem stood alone against all the other prophets in proclaiming the coming destruction of the city, so did Ezekiel in Babylonia. When that which he had prophesied came to pass, it tended naturally to give him an enormous prestige. Unlike Jeremiah, Ezekiel gave the people something very precise and definite as his message, something which they could understand and which was concrete in its character. Ezekiel was a " pastor of souls." [1] But to him the exiles are representatives of a larger Israel. He was pastor to those of the captivity, and at the same time he was a prophet to the whole mass of Israel.[2] This idea of the extension of his words to an audience not present appears in his discourse to those left on the mountains of Israel,[3] and in the allegories of the religious history.[4] Ezekiel gave definite expression to great religious truths, the presuppositions of earlier prophecies, which had not up to that time found a definite and concrete expression. As a natural result of this attempt to give definite expression, he carries their doctrines to their logical conclusions and sometimes beyond. Going further than Jeremiah, he condemns the past of Israel and Judah entirely. They had always been wicked from their birth onward. Looking backward, he could see only a long course of sin ; which is the logical result of his applying the Deuteronomic covenant to the past. From the day of Moses, to whom he ascribes Deuteronomy, they had violated that covenant. There had been false worship, and the evident need of rectifying this develops ritualism. Again, following out Deuteronomy to its logical conclusion, he judges the virtue of past kings by their success, since God required virtue and punished sin. Therefore, as

[1] Ezek. iii, 17 ; xviii, 23 ; xxxiii, 1, 12. This was the beginning of the Synagogue. On another side the individual, concrete teaching finds its fullest expression in the Wisdom Literature.　　　　[2] Ezek. ii, 3 ; iii, 4, 11.

[3] Ezek. vi ; xxxvi.

[4] Ezek. xvi ; xxiii.

David's reign was glorious, David's reign must be virtuous. Emphasis now lies not on immorality, as with the former prophets, but on false worship. In his interpretation of the history of the past and in his emphasis upon the Jerusalem Temple and proper ritual observance in that temple,[1] Ezekiel may be regarded as the prototype of the priests of the Exile.

Special importance was given to the priests of Yahaweh's Temple by the Deuteronomic reform, and the condition of the priests of that Temple in the Exile gave a peculiar priestly tendency to the development of thought among the exiles. This is especially exemplified in Ezekiel,[2] and it was his great influence which, to a large extent, caused this tendency to develop into doctrine in later Judaism. He also exhibits in another way the effect of Babylonian conditions upon the priestly exiles. The example of Babylonian recordism had its effect upon them. They were led to record and codify traditions, ritual practices, history, legends, as they had never done before. So Ezekiel becomes a theologian, in a sense in which no preceding prophet had been a theologian. He combines the great religious truths which were the presuppositions of earlier prophets into something approaching a theological system. He gives a peculiar direction to the Messianic Hope, making it a practical idea in the life of the nation and a starting-point for a new religious development; and, in connection with this, he may be said to be the father of Jewish eschatology.

For the sake of the vindication of His own holiness before the nations,[3] Yahaweh must restore Israel and finally overthrow the united heathen powers. This logical conclusion from the presuppositions of the earlier prophets Ezekiel formulates, and it becomes fundamental in the later Messianic doctrines. But this conception of Yahaweh's necessity of self-vindication is connected with Ezekiel's

---

[1] Ezek. xl–xliii; xlvi; xlvii. The Temple is the place from which the life-giving river flows, making the land a new Eden.

[2] Ezek. xliv, the sons of Zadok are the priests and judges; the Levites are ministers, and no others are to be admitted to service in the Temple. In the allotment of land the priests take precedence over the prince, who is thus separated from immediate contact with the Temple, xlv.

[3] Ezek. xxxvi, 21 ff.; xxxix, 25. Cf. in the later Psalms the frequent phrase "for His name's sake."

doctrine of His holiness, which is also intimately associated with His transcendency. The activity of Yahaweh is self-centered, and the supreme motive of all His dealings is the manifestation of His godhead: " They shall know that I am Yahaweh." [1] This exhibits itself in ways which at first sight are rather unexpected. It was because Israel was bad from the beginning that God chose him to manifest the glory of His name to the nations; but as God has chosen him to manifest the glory of His name to the nations,[2] so God must restore Israel in order to vindicate His glory. This salvation depends on the sovereign grace of God, not on the virtue of Israel; but inasmuch as Israel cannot be virtuous, and therefore vindicate the glory of Yahaweh without some radical change from conditions of the past, therefore God will bestow upon Israel a new spirit.[3]

Practically, as a result of this transcendency, Ezekiel teaches the removal of God from direct contact with man. He manifests himself through cherubim and angels; [4] He is too terrible for man to see; He addresses Ezekiel as the " son of man," [5] — doctrines which are more fully developed in later writers, but which are first clearly formulated in Ezekiel. Because of this transcendency of God, His exaltation out of all things human, a sense of sin is developed in connection with certain relations of the past belonging to a more direct and physical relation with God. So such things as the *bamoth* (high places), the connection of the Temple and the palace, the secular assumption of priestly office, are condemned by Ezekiel as transgressions of divine law. In the organization which he plans to make the people holy,[6] so as to prepare it for its part in God's vindication of His holiness, he provides for a very careful

---

[1] Ezek. xxxix, 28.

[2] The world exists for the glory of Yahaweh. Alike the judgment on the nations and the restoration of Israel have it as their object to vindicate His honor.

[3] Ezek. xxxvi, 26 f.

[4] Ezek. i, 5; ix. But Ezekiel does not altogether free himself from the old anthropomorphic conceptions. God is in human form, and to some extent acts directly, as by the hand which lifts Ezekiel (viii, 3). We have not yet reached fully the representation of His presence by the Shechinah, or of His action by the wind. So also He is localized in an earthly dwelling, although knowing and seeing all things.

[5] Ezek. ii, 1.

[6] Ezek. xl–xlviii.

separation between religious and profane, something which is still
further developed later in the Priestly Code. And here comes in
the practical sense of Ezekiel. Such a doctrine of the transcendency
of God, of His choice of Israel, etc., would seem theoretically to
do away with all free will, and therefore to develop a tendency
toward immorality; but in practice Ezekiel asserts the free will and
the moral responsibility of the people. Side by side with that extreme view of the action of Yahaweh by which Israel is to be restored to its land, the heathen overthrown, a new spirit put in
Israel, etc., he provides an organization by which Israel may coöperate, and throughout his prophecies he emphasizes the doctrine
of an individual relation of each Israelite to God, which involves
the punishment or the reward of the individual according to his
own individual merits.

CHAPTER XIX

HOLINESS

Contemporary with Ezekiel in the Babylonian exile and in close touch with him, at least so far as thought was concerned, were certain priests who seem to have devoted themselves to a codification and explanation of the holiness laws of the Jews, and especially of the Jerusalem Temple, with which those laws were connected. The holiness laws thus codified were later embodied in the Priestly Code, and are contained in Leviticus, chapters xvii–xxvi. This holiness legislation is so important in the study of the development of the religion of Israel that it is desirable here to analyze the growth of the idea of holiness, which finds expression in those laws.

The Semitic peoples in general used words of the root *ḳds*, "holy," to denote a peculiar property of deity, or of persons or things consecrated to deity, or of customs governing the relations of men to the deity. So the Phœnicians spoke of the "holy gods," and we find among the Syrians persons consecrated to the gods, designated as "holy ones." Holiness was that which especially belonged to a god, his divinity, which not only differentiated the deity from man, but differentiated one deity from another. It is this peculiarity of each deity, his individuality, in which his holiness consists. In order to have relations with the deity, a man must take into consideration this holiness of the deity. A violation of the rules of this holiness, whether voluntary or involuntary, is liable to be followed by dire consequences to the unfortunate individual who has violated these rules. To have communication with any given deity, a man must not only put away the common things of his relations with other men and put on that which is holy, which belongs to deity in general, but he must also put on that which

belongs to the special holiness of this deity and is in accordance
with his peculiar laws. Holiness on the part of men or things, for
things follow the same laws as men in their relation to the deity,
is a consecration to the service of that particular deity. Primarily
there is nothing ethical in this holiness, and indeed it may even be
distinctly immoral, as in the case of the holiness of the hierodules
of the Canaanitish, Israelite, and Jewish shrines.

The first mention chronologically of the holiness idea in Hebrew
literature is in 1 Samuel vi, 20. The Ark of Yahaweh had been left
at Beth Shemesh. Because the men of that place violated in some
way the holiness of the Ark, therefore they were smitten with a
great slaughter, and the men of Beth Shemesh said: " Who is able
to stand before Yahaweh, this holy God? " In their ignorance of
the ritual of the Ark they had infringed upon the holiness of God,
and He exhibited His holiness in the slaughter which ensued.

The earliest mention of holiness in the legislation of the Hebrews
occurs in the Book of the Covenant.[1] The Israelites are to be holy
men unto God; therefore they shall not eat any flesh that is torn of
beasts in the field. Here holiness is connected not with a distinctly
moral idea, but with what seems to modern thought a mere provision of physical cleanness. To the ancient there was, however, something more in such a provision. Just as in Leviticus, chapter xvii,
it is prescribed that the blood of wild animals slain in the hunt shall
be covered up with earth, so that it may not become an offering to
the demons of the field, so to eat the flesh of animals killed by wild
beasts was to partake involuntarily in the worship of other gods by
feasting on creatures sacrificed to them. The Israelite might eat
only of that of which the blood had been given to Yahaweh. To
the Hebrew, therefore, this law was not primarily a law of physical
cleanness, but a law intended to prevent any relation on his part
with demons and evil spirits. Amos testifies to the common conception of the land of Israel as holy to Yahaweh when he pronounces
upon Amaziah, priest of Bethel, the punishment of death in a land
that is unclean.[2] This is only a statement on the positive side of
that which is stated on the negative side in the early narrative of

1 Ex. xxii, 31.   2 Amos vii, 16 f.

David, contained in the book of Samuel,[1] where David is made
to complain that by being driven out of the land of Israel he is
compelled to serve other gods. Similarly, in the prophetic narrative
of Elisha,[2] Naaman is made to ask for two mules' burden of earth
that he might offer sacrifice unto Yahaweh thereafter in Syria, instead of to the Syrian gods. He could offer such sacrifice only
upon land holy to Yahaweh, that is, the land of Israel.

Similarly Hosea calls the land of Israel Yahaweh's land.[3] All
other lands, together with the things which they contain, are
unclean, and one of the horrors of the exile which he foresees
is the compulsion to eat unclean food in a land not holy. Only in
Yahaweh's land can food be consecrated to Yahaweh, and only
such food is clean. The food in other lands is holy to the gods of
those lands and therefore unclean to the people of Yahaweh.

But while this idea of holiness was common in Israel, it received
a peculiar emphasis and a peculiar development in connection with
the Yahaweh cult in the Jerusalem Temple. From the account of
the vision of Isaiah[4] by which he was called to be a prophet, we
learn incidentally the burden of a ritual song of the Jerusalem
Temple—" Holy, holy, holy is Yahaweh Sabaoth "—which Isaiah,
in his vision, puts in the mouth of the seraphim, and which becomes to him the special message from Yahaweh. It is with his
writings that we begin to find the word "holy" emphasized and the
idea connected with it developed into a new and more ethical conception. " The Holy One of Israel " is with him a common designation of the divinity.[5] But this holiness has not merely the sense
of exclusiveness, that which relates alone to the individual divinity;
it expresses rather that moral something which constitutes the very
essence of Yahaweh and which distinguishes Him from all else.
To Isaiah the essence, the nature, of Yahaweh is morality, consequently the holiness of Yahaweh must consist in moral attributes.
This is well shown in the first passage in which the phrase " Holy
One of Israel " occurs, namely Isaiah i, 4: The people have
" forsaken Yahaweh. They have despised the Holy One of Israel."

---

[1] 1 Sam. xxvi, 19. [3] Hos. ix, 3. [5] Cf. Is. i, 4; v, 19.
[2] 2 Kings v, 1 f. [4] vi, 3.

They are " a seed of evil-doers, children that deal corruptly." There has been no lack of sacrifice, of burnt offerings of rams and bullocks. The new moon, the Sabbath and appointed feasts, have been celebrated, prayers and ceremonies have not been wanting. But they have offended the holiness of God, because they have been guilty of immoral abominations.

The Book of Deuteronomy, which was also closely connected with the Temple of Jerusalem, makes a similar free use of the word *holy*; but, while an ethical element is not lacking in the Deuteronomic idea of holiness, the stress is laid not, as with Isaiah, on the ethical, but rather on the external or ceremonial side. So the Israelites are forbidden to cut themselves or "make any baldness between their eyes for the dead ";[1] because Israel is a holy people unto Yahaweh, for Yahaweh has chosen Israel to be a peculiar people unto himself out of all the peoples that are on the face of the earth. While this command lays the stress on ceremonial observance, there is, however, the same thought underlying the prescription as in the case, noted above, of the legislation with regard to pouring out of blood or eating of animals torn by wild beasts. Cutting themselves and making a " baldness between their eyes for the dead " are forbidden, because these are connected with the worship of other gods and are hence a violation of the holiness — that is, the exclusiveness — of the worship of Yahaweh.

On the same principle the Deuteronomist forbids magic, which is in reality the service of demons, or the worship of Yahaweh at high places. The worship at those high places, as Hosea taught, although nominally Yahaweh worship, was yet inextricably connected with the worship of the *baalim*,[2] the ancient gods of the land; hence those high places were an infringement of the holiness of Yahaweh.

The same principle underlies the laws of clean and unclean food in Deuteronomy,[3] which are of course the ancient custom of the

---

[1] Deut. xiv, 1 f.   [2] Hos. ii, 16 f.

[3] Deut. xiv. Not all the creatures prohibited to be eaten were originally prohibited because they were holy to other gods or demons. Some were naturally unclean because of their appearance, their habits and associations, or even their utility. In the lists in Deuteronomy and Leviticus we find an attempt at classification of clean and

Jew codified, expounded, and made authoritative by Deuteronomy. The fundamental principle is not that of physical cleanness or of hygiene, but of the exclusive worship, the holiness, of Yahaweh. For an Israelite to partake of certain animals was to connect himself with the worship of other gods or of demons, and thus offend the holiness of Yahaweh. For the same reason, while " the stranger that is within his gates " or the foreigner may partake of that which " dieth of itself," the Israelite may not, since the manner of its death may connect it with some demon or some divinity other than Yahaweh.

These ceremonial rules in Deuteronomy have no distinctly moral character. They do, however, make for monotheism, the sole worship of Yahaweh. This is clearly set forth in what may be called the motto of Deuteronomy : " Hear, oh Israel ! Yahaweh our god is one Yahaweh and thou shalt love Yahaweh thy god with all thy heart and with all thy soul and with all thy mind." [1] The twenty-sixth chapter, which ends the legislation of Deuteronomy, closes with the statement of the peculiar relation of Yahaweh to His people, a relation of holiness or exclusiveness. These are Yahaweh's statutes and judgments. Israel has avouched Yahaweh as its god and hence has accepted these statutes and judgments, and Yahaweh has chosen Israel to be a peculiar people, holy unto himself.

Jeremiah does not make the same use of the term holy as his predecessor Isaiah did, or as the Deuteronomist did. He is distinctly anti-ritualistic. His concern is only with the moral side of things. Nevertheless, like Deuteronomy, he recognized the need of holiness, that is exclusiveness, as regards the place of worship. The worship and ritual of the high places, although nominally directed toward Yahaweh, has been in reality a worship of the *baalim*, an offense against the holiness of Yahaweh ; and so it is that Jeremiah declares that Israel has polluted the land holy to Yahaweh by following after *baalim*.[2] So long has this offense

---

unclean by certain characteristics ; an attempt which itself shows that such characteristics were not the real cause of the distinction. Whatever the original cause, however, the whole system, as the lists and their connections show, was finally based on the principle of holiness.

[1] Deut. iv, 5. [2] Jer. ii, 23.

against the holiness of Yahaweh's land continued that it can be cured not in one generation, but only by the land lying entirely waste for an indefinite period of years. There is in all these conceptions of holiness, it will be observed, the idea of exclusiveness, and the closer the approximation to monotheism, the more exclusive this sense of holiness must necessarily become.

It is this idea of holiness as exclusiveness which is peculiarly developed in the holiness legislation of Leviticus. This, as already noted, is a code of laws of earlier date than the Priestly Code, into which it was later incorporated. In its incorporation into the great law-book it has undergone some changes, involving excisions, additions, and rearrangements, and some fragments of the original holiness laws are to be found elsewhere in Leviticus, Exodus, and Numbers; but the bulk of the code is contained in Leviticus xvii–xxvi. This code is, however, itself based upon earlier codes, some of which, at least, were in the form of decalogues, and some of which were expansions and applications of the original Decalogue of Moses.

We have in the law of holiness a final codification of traditions and usages of the Jerusalem Temple, moral, ritual, and ecclesiastical, going back to a very early date, modified by comparison with other similar codes from other sources, and codified finally in the exilic period. This code lays the greatest " stress on ritual correctness and endeavors, with anxious care, to secure the ceremonial purity of the Israelites." [1] From the point of view of that code this is holiness. It must not be understood that moral laws are wanting in the holiness code. Moral, ceremonial, and ecclesiastical laws are here combined in one whole, but all are placed on the same footing and regarded from the same point of view, namely, the holiness, that is, the exclusiveness, of Yahaweh. He alone may be worshiped, and in accordance only with those methods and rites which belong to Him. Individual laws or minor sections of the code are prefaced or closed by the exhortation to the people to be holy, because " I, Yahaweh, your God, am holy." [2] " Ye shall be holy unto Me, for I, Yahaweh, am holy and have separated you

[1] Addis, *Documents of the Hexateuch*, II, 173.   [2] Lev. xix, 2.

from the nations, that ye should be Mine." [1] The priest shall be holy unto the people, because he offers the bread of God and God is holy.[2] Over and over again occurs the phrase " I am Yahaweh, who maketh you holy." Moral and ritual laws are placed on the same footing, and any breach of any of these laws of any description is counted a profanation of the name of Yahaweh, a phrase now coming into increased use in the effort, as it were, to remove Yahaweh far off, in order that His very peculiar holiness should not be impinged upon. So the sacrifice of children to Molech is spoken of as a profanation of the name of Yahaweh ; [3] but the same language is used with regard to physical and even accidental contact with holy things.[4] As already pointed out, Ezekiel treats the holiness of God in a similar spirit. To him the land of Israel is a land holy — that is, peculiar — to Yahaweh. All other lands are unclean. There is only one land and only one people which is holy to Him. He only may be worshiped by the Jews, and only according to the laws and rites peculiar to Him. Violations of moral laws and violations of ceremonial laws were alike a profanation of His holiness. This doctrine of holiness Ezekiel applies to the history of Israel. Israel had profaned Yahaweh's holy land consistently and persistently by its idolatry ; [5] for to worship any other god upon the soil of Israel, which was holy to Yahaweh, was to profane that soil, and, like Jeremiah and practically the Deuteronomist, Ezekiel regards all worship of Yahaweh at high places as in fact worship of other gods. So long as Yahaweh had remained in the land of Israel and dwelt in the Holy of Holies, in the midst of His holy city, that city and its temple were inviolable, because God is almighty. In fact, while there is only one land and one people which is holy to Yahaweh, yet, according to Ezekiel, Yahaweh alone is God and therefore is of necessity almighty because He is without rivals or opponents. But with the first capture of the Temple, in 597, Yahaweh left the land which had been so wickedly profaned, and withdrew from His earthly abode to the mountain of the north. The Temple was destroyed not because the Babylonian gods were stronger, for they

[1] Lev. xx, 26. [3] Lev. xviii, 21. [5] Ezek. vi, 3–5.
[2] Lev. xxi, 8. [4] Lev. xxii, 2.

were not gods, but because Yahaweh no longer dwelt there. For the same reason the land which was once holy was laid waste and the people carried captive. By the removal of His people and the fallowness of His land, Yahaweh will finally purify it of its uncleanness. Then Yahaweh will manifest His holiness in delivering a purified remnant of His people and restoring them to His holy land. It is necessary that He and He only shall be worshiped in that land, in the one place which He has appointed and in the special manner which He has ordained; and to secure that result Ezekiel, as already pointed out, closed his book with a picture of the temple that is to be and the ritual of that temple, together with the relation to the Temple of priests, prince, and people.

Ezekiel and the holiness law in its final form are practically contemporary. They came out of the same stratum of the exiles in Babylonia, the priests of the Jerusalem Temple. While both recognize the moral exaltation of Yahaweh, both lay stress in the matter of holiness on the outward or ceremonial rather than on the moral side. Both emphasize the idea of exclusiveness as the holiness of Yahaweh, but Ezekiel makes prominent also the conception of might, which may be said to follow logically from the connection of exclusivism and monotheism already pointed out. If there be but one God, who is the maker and ruler of all things, then His is the power and might over all things. But the manner in which Ezekiel represents Yahaweh as manifesting that might is closely connected with the idea of holiness as the exclusion and consequent destruction of all sin and uncleanness. Yahaweh manifests His holiness in punishing sin and destroying sinners, and in delivering His sanctified people from all their enemies. This idea of the holiness of Yahaweh in the destruction of all the enemies of Israel and the purification of His land, Ezekiel appears to carry even beyond the point of morality in his picture of the destruction of Gog.[1] It should be said that the same conception of the holiness of God may be traced backward to an early period, but the special element of holiness receives at this date a new emphasis. It is because of this holiness that He destroys the heathen, according to various hymns

[1] Ezek. xxxviii, 16, 23.

and psalms of this period and later.[1] Holiness may be said to receive at this period peculiar stress. It was the thought to conjure with, the popular conception or phrase of the moment. It was not, consequently, limited to the school to which Ezekiel and the priestly codifiers of the holiness laws belonged.

It has already been noted that Isaiah, taking the phraseology and partly the thought of holiness out of the liturgy and ritual of the Temple in the time of Hezekiah, gave it a peculiarly moral meaning, and that he is indeed the first writer whose writings have come down to us to make a free use of the word. That use of the word and idea became characteristic of a school of prophetic writers who may be said to be the spiritual descendants of Isaiah, and whose writings, from various times, now bound up with his, constitute one volume called Isaiah, which we might perhaps fairly describe as the writings of Isaiah and the school of Isaiah.

Most prominent, and most characteristic in the use of the word and the conception of holiness, is that group of writers of the post-exilic period, the authors of chapters xl–lxvi, sometimes called Deutero-Isaiah. In the usage of these writers the holiness of Yahaweh is closely connected with that same thought of His omnipotence and of His deliverance of Israel from its enemies which Ezekiel emphasizes. His holiness does not show itself, as in the prophecies of Isaiah of Jerusalem, in His moral purity and exaltation, His abhorrence and punishment of sin, but rather in His omnipotence as displayed in the redemption of Israel, and His wonderful love toward his people. " To whom, then, will ye liken me, that I should be equal to him ? saith the Holy One."[2] " Thus saith Yahaweh, the Redeemer of Israel, his Holy One, to him whom man despiseth, to him whom the nation abhorreth, to the servant of rulers : Kings shall see and arise and they shall worship because of Yahaweh that is faithful, even the Holy One of Israel, who hath chosen thee."[3]

In three of the Psalms we find the exact phraseology of the Isaianic school, " the Holy One of Israel," used ; and this title is connected in two cases with that same idea of the deliverance of Israel which we find in these post-exilic prophecies.[4] In the third

[1] Cf. Ex. xv, 11.   [2] Is. xl, 25.   [3] Is. xlix, 7.   [4] Ps. lxxi, 22 ; lxxxix, 18.

case[1] the use is more like that which we observed in the Isaiah of Jerusalem. The Holy One is provoked by the sins of Israel. Elsewhere in the Psalter we find the holiness idea prominent, but without the exact phraseology of the Isaianic school.[2] The holiness exhibits itself rather in the great and terrible power of God, reminding us in part of the earlier use of the term "holiness" referred to above (1 Sam. vi, 20), and in part of the semi-ethical, semi-ceremonial holiness of Ezekiel and the Holiness Code, only with the ethical side more clearly expressed. God establishes righteousness, and pleasing to Him are those who observe His testimonies and His statutes.

From the time of the Exile on, holiness becomes an essential and a very prominent element in the expression of religion and religious thought. It is found in the Wisdom Literature, as well as in the Psalter. In Job we have "the Holy One" used as the name of God,[3] as in the writings of the Isaianic school, the conception seeming to be the ethical one, of the God who is too holy to endure sin and who must hence punish the evil-doer. In Proverbs we have the same ethical use of the term ;[4] but in general throughout the later literature the exclusive idea rather than the ethical idea is prominent. This exclusive element shows itself even in the later chapters of the volume of Isaianic literature, where the Jews are spoken of as the "holy people,"[5] and their cities are called holy cities.[6] Naturally it shows itself above all in the later legal literature and in the writings depending upon that legalism, where the Jews are conceived of as absolutely separate from all the rest of the world.[7]

There is only one Holy One in the world, and He has but one holy people, and so Israel is exalted over all the peoples of the world, and it is the duty of Israel to maintain itself as the people

---

1 Ps. lxxviii, 44.

2 The best example is Ps. xcix, par excellence the holiness Psalm, where we have three stanzas, the first two closing with the refrain "Holy is He" and the last with the longer variant "for Yahaweh our God is holy."   3 Job vi, 10.

4 Prov. ix, 10. For the first time the plural is used instead of the singular.

5 Is. lxii, 12.   6 Is. lxiv, 9.

7 Cf. Ezra ix, 2, "The holy seed have mingled themselves with the peoples of the lands," Dan. vii, 18, where we read of the "holy ones of the most high," that is, faithful Jews, and Dan. viii, 24 and xii, 7, where the Jews are called the "holy people."

of the only true God, the Holy One of Israel, making itself holy by excluding and avoiding everything that is unholy. This is the attitude of the Priestly Code, that codification of moral, ceremonial, and ecclesiastical laws which included within itself, as already stated, the laws of holiness (Lev. xvii–xxvi). As a code this is the work of the priestly scribes of the exilic and post-exilic periods, based, of course, on older material, and taking its final form, for all practical purposes at least, toward the close of the fifth century B.C. Ezekiel, in his representation of the ideal Israel (chaps. xl–xlviii), had made the sharp distinction of holy and common an essential element of that ideal. Ezra's law-book carries that conception farther, if possible ; certainly into much greater detail. I cannot better explain the view of holy and common therein contained than by a quotation from Dr. Cheyne :

To understand Ezra's law-book it is necessary to realize its object. This was not to cultivate a lofty type of personal piety, but to guard against a recurrence of the great national calamity of the past. The old religion of Israel, with all its attractive variety of local and family rites, had proved itself inadequate. The presence of the divine king among his people had been continually interrupted. Tyrants had often usurped the dominion, for how could a God be said to rule in a conquered or even in a tributary land ? and there had also been a permanent obscuration of the theocracy by the institution of a human royalty. Hence the necessity of a perfect divine law to which priests and laymen, rich and poor, should be equally subject — a law which should take into account the huge difference between God and man, and should spare no pains in determining the points in which a super-natural God would be necessarily offended — i.e., in marking the limits between the holy and the unholy, the sacred and the profane. And since the primitive confusion of the material and the ethical was not yet over-come and since it was vastly easier to deal with material than with ethical violations of the divine sanctity, it came to pass that the main subject of the Jewish as well as of the Zoroastrian law was the distinction between clean and unclean, and the manner in which lost ceremonial purity could be recovered. It was only those who were technically clean who could appear before God, and the object of the elaborate sacrificial system was not to produce peace of mind for the individual, but to unify the community on a sound religious basis, maintaining its consecrated character unimpaired. The individual who voluntarily or involuntarily transgressed any precept of the law injured the sanctity of the community. As long, therefore, as his transgression was unatoned for, he was a source of danger to that organic whole of which he was a member. It mattered not whether the precept were moral or ritual, the divine holiness had been wronged, and satisfaction had to be given, either by ceremonial means or by the cutting off of the offending branch from the parent stem.[1]

There is, of course, a high moral character in this code; but, on the other hand, the ceremonial enactments appear to stand (and in the interpretation of the Law they ultimately came to stand) on the same footing as the moral. Sin, and God's abhorrence of sin and the sinfulness of men, are emphasized; but we find that sin is not always the result of intention on man's part. The inadvertent touching of an unclean thing, something of which he is not himself conscious, may render him unholy, provoke the wrath of God, and bring calamity upon him, or even upon the whole nation.[2]

The later development of Judaism was along these same lines, with an ever-increasing externalism and ceremonialism for the sake of ceremony. Holiness tended more and more to become a thing of the proper observance of forms. The ceremonialism of the earlier laws had, as we have seen, an ethical basis. The laws of clean and unclean, the prohibition of tattooing, hair-cutting in mourning for the dead, and the like, were not in their origin mere ceremonial laws. They were intended to prevent polytheism and a false worship which was to no small extent immoral and debasing. To assure the holiness of Israel, Israel must be made to refrain from these things. Hence the laws forbidding such practices. But the day came when the danger of polytheism was past forever, when the reason for the prohibition of the swine and the mouse, of tattooing and hair-cutting, no longer existed, and even the cause why these things were forbidden had been forgotten. But the laws still continued to be observed, and even to be sharpened and strengthened. There was no longer any reason for their existence. Their ethical value in the promotion of true holiness had vanished. Henceforth they were without meaning in themselves, and their "holiness" was a hollow formalism. That is the condition which was reached by later Judaism. Ceremonial laws, which had long since lost their real significance, were maintained and developed

1 Cheyne, *Jewish Religious Life after the Exile*, pp. 73-74.   2 Lev. iv-v.

into a constantly more elaborate and artificial system in the interests of what had become a selfish exclusivism. Holiness came to mean the observance of this system and the maintenance of this exclusivism. It is true, nevertheless, that physical cleanliness, in the ritual, not the actual sense, was regarded mystically as a representation, or even as a *sacrament*, of spiritual holiness; and there were also individuals who interpreted holiness in the high ethical sense of an Isaiah, and understood the law in its highest and most spiritual significance; but we are speaking of the system as a whole, and of what holiness commonly meant, let us say at the commencement of the Christian era.

Such, in brief, is the history of the holiness idea from its origination in the belief in the peculiar nature of the god or gods, common to the Hebrews with the nations about them, to its culmination in the conception of one God, righteous and omnipotent, and its decline in later Judaism to a system of ceremonialism.

CHAPTER XX

THE EXILE

The destruction of Jerusalem and the Temple and the accompanying breaking up of the nation produced a most profound impression upon the religious development of Israel. It marks an epoch in Israel's religious life. To appreciate the full meaning of the Exile, it is desirable at this point to take a glance backward and resume in their entirety the effects which led up to the Exile and the immediate results of the Exile itself.

From the ninth century onward the great power within the Israelitic horizon had been Assyria. Slowly and seemingly irresistibly it had expanded, conquering nation after nation. From the time of Amos onward, it had been clear to the best thinkers of Israel that it was bound to extend still further and involve Israel and Judah in its advance. Its irresistible might impressed itself strongly upon their minds. They, of course, regarded this as a part of the divine plan. In point of fact, like all the neighboring kingdoms, both Israel and Judah became vassal states of Assyria in the eighth century B.C. They both were involved in various attempts to throw off the Assyrian yoke, the issue of which only proved more conclusively the irresistible power of the Assyrian empire and confirmed the Prophets in their attitude of opposition to such movements. As a result of the insurgency of the northern kingdom, it was stripped little by little of its outlying provinces, and finally, in 721, the capital was destroyed and the kingdom of Israel apparently incorporated as a province of the Assyrian empire. The fact that Jerusalem, in spite of its continued insurgency, was not taken by the Assyrians, although Judah itself was severely punished, became, as interpreted by the Prophet Isaiah, a ground for the later Mono-Yahawistic development. The destruction of

Samaria and the devastation of Judah, with the consequent over-throw of numerous shrines, led to the belief that the true home of Yahaweh, the god of Israel, was in Jerusalem, and to the new development of the power and prestige of the Jerusalem Temple at the expense of local shrines.

By the middle of the succeeding century, the seventh century B.C., the Assyrian power had established itself still more securely in the West. Egypt had been subdued, Assyrian garrisons were placed in such towns as Gezer,[1] and by the close of Manasseh's reign it seemed as though all hope of resistance to the Assyrian power was thereafter at an end.[2] To the ordinary observer it appeared that the Assyrian empire was now a world power in the sense that there was nothing anywhere which could compete with it. Its stability seemed to have been tested by the long continuance of its empire, and men in general accepted it as one of the great facts of the universe.

The last thirty years of the seventh century saw a break-up of the Assyrian power so sudden that it seemed like a cataclysm; and not only was the Assyrian power broken up, but the whole world seemed to be in movement. From the south Ethiopians overran Egypt, with whom soon hordes of Libyans from the region westward of Egypt were contending for supremacy in the Nile valley. The Greek regeneration had been accomplished, and Grecian colonists, invaders and adventurers, were stirring and moving through the whole Mediterranean basin, upsetting the former order and introducing new elements and new national activities to the experience and the ken of the Hebrew. In Asia Minor new states were springing into existence as a result of the same world-wide movement, and especially the great Lydian kingdom. Eastward Media had arisen, but in arising had let loose the Scythian hordes of the northeast, who swept over all western Asia, a scourge of God, as later the Huns became to Europe. It was this movement above all which gave the effect of catastrophe, of a shaking

---

[1] Macalister, *The Excavation of Gezer*, I, 22.

[2] The evil effect of this on the religious development of the period has been already traced in a preceding chapter.

of the whole earth, of a vast upheaval, reviving in a somewhat new
form and with great vividness the old belief which the Prophet
Amos denounced, but which he and the other prophets, his successors, utilized in a new form in their teaching of the divine government of the world, of the Day of Yahaweh, the great day when
He should hold judgment upon the earth and overthrow the powers
of the nations. This made itself felt in the literature of the time,
as has already been pointed out, and became from that day an
important factor in the prophetic and apocalyptic teaching, as
well as in the popular belief, playing a great part in the development of eschatological hopes and doctrines among the Jews. This
great world movement helped largely to render possible the Deuteronomic reform of religion and cult in Jerusalem. Yahaweh had
now manifested and was manifesting His great power, precisely
as the former prophets had promised. Their discredited doctrines
proved to be the truth. Yahaweh was mighty, and the dwelling
place of this mighty Yahaweh was Jerusalem and the Temple.
The other Yahawehs of the local shrines had proved themselves
useless. They were not really Yahawehs; it was only in Jerusalem that Yahaweh really dwelt. That reform made emphatic
the doctrine "Yahaweh, our god, is one Yahaweh," not many;
dwelling in Jerusalem only, and there only to be worshiped. The
prophets in general were at one with this doctrine. Even the great
minority prophet, Jeremiah, of the school of the ethical prophets,
descended in the line of Amos, Hosea, Isaiah, and Micah, was in
sympathy with this doctrine, as putting an end to the Baal worship
under the name of Yahaweh worship which had existed in the high
places, and to the foreign and unethical worship which existed in the
Temple at Jerusalem itself. With the doctrine of the inviolability of
Jerusalem and the teaching that it was the dwelling-place of Yahaweh, in the sense of the Deuteronomic reformers, as with the ritual
paraphernalia and the emphasis on sacrifice, he was not in sympathy.
He believed that the Babylonian empire was established to take the
same place and to do the same work which the Assyrian empire had
done in the past, and advocated the same attitude with regard to it
which former prophets had advocated with regard to Assyria.

As a result of the Jewish rebellion against Babylonia he looked forward to a period of indefinite captivity, an evidence of his belief in the stability of the Babylonian empire. There were enough indications of instability, however, to give certainly a show of plausibility to the arguments of his opponents, and to fill the rebels with hope of ultimate success through the downfall of the Babylonian empire. Not only was the Babylonian empire a new one; it had inherited only a part of the Assyrian inheritance. Eastward and northeastward there was the important empire of Media, soon to give way to Persia; in Asia Minor, Lydia, while the movements in the Mediterranean basin and in Egypt could not but make the Hebrews conscious of the existence of great influences and great movements beyond the sphere of Babylonian power. At any moment, through some of these agencies, might come a great overturning, similar to that wrought by the Scythians. Who knew what was in store, in Yahaweh's plan, and how He might overthrow His enemies? As we have seen, even the capture of Jerusalem by Nebuchadrezzar and the deportation of the heads of the nation, religion, and society to Babylonia did not destroy this hope. It centered in the Temple at Jerusalem, the dwelling-place of Yahaweh. So long as that was intact, Yahaweh might interfere to save His people. The destruction of the Temple put an end, for the time, to those hopes. What it meant to the men of Judah everywhere is well set forth in the Book of Lamentations. It was a numbing, deadening blow, which seemed for the moment to destroy the life of the nation. In reality the destruction of Jerusalem and the Temple was only a final point in a dispersion of Israel which had been going on for centuries. Not to speak of the slave trade, through which Israelites had been stolen to be sold into distant lands, certainly since the days of Amos,[1] the Assyrian conquerors had deported from time to time large numbers of Israelites and Jews, settling them in different parts of the Assyrian empire. What became of all these exiles, and what part if any they took in the future resurrection of Israel, is not clear; but from the course of history it would seem that one result of the continual

[1] Amos ii, 6; Jer. ii, 14; Joel iii, 6.

invasions and deportations was to change the Jews from an agricultural to a commercial nation. We have seen the strong cityward movement which took place among both Israelites and Jews in the eighth century, as testified to by the prophets of that period, and the development of commerce at that time, accompanied by the reduction of the country population to a condition approaching serfdom. The deportation of city-dwellers, as a result of the capture of the various Israelite and Jewish cities, scattered through Assyria and Babylonia precisely that element of the population which had already become commercial; and at least in the latter country, as we know from the recent discoveries in Babylonia, they speedily became an important commercial force. Although we cannot show that the same was true of Jews who had been deported to other regions at an earlier date, we may, from the analogy of the Babylonian Captivity, argue that the deported Israelites and Jews engaging in commercial pursuits would have had some relation and intercourse with their former country, tending to develop still further commercial life in Israel and Judah.

Certain it is that with the Captivity itself a change of far-reaching importance was effected in the conversion of the Jews from an agricultural to a commercial people. It must be said, however, that those who remained in Judæa after the destruction of Jerusalem were primarily agriculturists and almost entirely of the poorer and poorest classes of the community. The Jews of the commercial element were deported or driven into exile, to become in their places of adoption still more commercial, and ultimately to exert such an influence upon the homeland itself, directly and indirectly, as to make that also commercial.

Our information with regard to the Jews who remained in Judæa after the destruction of Jerusalem or who returned to the land is very meager, our direct knowledge being confined to the account contained in the Book of Jeremiah of the murder of Gedaliah and the migration of Jews to Egypt (xli). That account shows us that there were numerous Jews who had taken refuge in the surrounding regions at the time of the destruction, and who, as soon as the Babylonian armies had retired, began to return to their own homes.

Some of the nations around Judah had assisted the Babylonians in the final overthrow of Jerusalem. This was especially true of the Edomites, toward whom, from that period on, Jewish writers show a particular bitterness. So Edom becomes the synonym of the treacherous, unrelenting foe, who never forgives and who therefore never can be forgiven.[1] He is the typical hater of Yahaweh, whose punishment means the punishment of all sin. Others of the surrounding peoples were more sympathetic, and in the Samaritans the Jews had a brother race, kindred to them not only in blood but also in faith, as worshipers with them of Yahaweh. What the attitude of the Jews and Samaritans was toward one another is shown not only by occasional references to Samaritans worshiping at Jerusalem, but also by the attitude of the prophetic writers of this and the following period, who look to a restoration of Israel which shall include Samaritan and Jew alike. The fact of the existence of this Samaritan state and the continuance there of the worship of Yahaweh after the fall of Samaria throws light upon the conditions which may be supposed to have existed in Judæa after the fall of Jerusalem and the final flight of the Jews with Jeremiah to Egypt. There was a population left which was Jewish in faith and nationality, and which continued to worship Yahaweh as in the natural order of events the god of its land, because, in fact, if it wished to worship any other god it had none to worship. It was a people which inherited the Deuteronomic reformation as its faith, and which was practically compelled to continue in that worship and doctrine, however much it might have lost confidence in the great promises and hopes contained in the prophetic teaching. It was a poor and petty remnant, which, as events showed, was not able to occupy or to retain even the whole of the Judæan state, small as that had been. It centered about Jerusalem, and its sacred place was still the site of the old Temple. It formed the nucleus to which, from time to time, Jews returned from other regions; and constituted the kernel from which later a new Jewish people and religion was to be created. The Jews who fled to Egypt, with presumably many more who had, for one reason and

---

[1] Jer. xlix, 17; Ezek. xxxvi; Obadiah.

another, migrated thither before the destruction of Jerusalem, constituted ultimately a very large body and an important section of the Jewish people, which remained faithful to the belief of their fathers, but whose development, especially during the first part of the centuries preceding the Maccabæan reformation, followed a course peculiar to itself.

The Jews of whose flight to Egypt we are informed in the Book of Jeremiah took with them that prophet. They were to a certain extent his followers; and while some of them, as that account shows, reverted to the heathen practices which Jeremiah had so emphatically denounced, the bulk of the Jews in Egypt, as is clear from later history, continued to remain worshipers of Yahaweh — very much on the lines, however, on which He was worshiped in an earlier period, as their chief god, their special god, with whose worship might be combined reverence for the gods of the land. In another respect, also, the Egyptian refugees differed from their Babylonian compatriots. They made Egypt, in fact, their home. They not only settled there, but they built there temples to Yahaweh for their worship.[1] The attitude of the Babylonian Jews was very different. They were, from the outset, captives. They so regarded themselves, and the Captivity (*galutha*) continued to be their special name from the time of the original deportation on into the Middle Ages. As has already been pointed out, they were different in class from the refugees in Egypt or the Jews who remained behind in Palestine. They represented especially the official element, the nobility and the clergy. From the outset their attitude was that they were the true Israel, and the man who became their mouthpiece, the priest-prophet Ezekiel, taught that with their removal Yahaweh had forsaken Jerusalem and His temple. The people who were left in the land and the refugees in Egypt were not, from their point of view, in the legitimate descent. They had the faith. It was theirs to formulate and develop that faith.

---

[1] We know of at least two Jewish temples in Egypt: (1) at Yeb (Elephantine), in existence in the fifth century B.C., and probably founded before the time of Jeremiah (cf. Sachau, *Aramäische Papyrus u. Ostraka aus Elephantine*); (2) at Leontopolis (Josephus, *Antiquities*, xiii, 3; *Jewish War*, i, 1; vii, 10), commonly supposed to have been founded at a much later date, probably in the second century B.C.

The part which Ezekiel played in turning this remnant into a congregation has already been referred to. What became of the Babylonian captivity, and its later relation to the developed form of the Jewish religion, we shall see in future chapters. At present let us follow the line of the Judæan development.

CHAPTER XXI

THE RESTORATION

The duration of the Babylonian empire proved to be short. Stability had not yet been reached. The world-shaking process still continued. In the east Media gave way to Persia, and soon Lydia and Babylonia also fell before the Persian empire. New hope was aroused among the Jews. It began to be clear that the end was not yet. The remarkable nature of Cyrus' conquests, the rapid overthrow of Media and Lydia, and the imminent catastrophe hanging over the new Babylonian empire established by Nebuchadrezzar, called forth new prophecies of the great day of the Lord, which concerned themselves particularly with the coming downfall of Babylon. These prophecies are especially valuable in the history of religious development as showing us the continuance of the ancient belief in the Day of Yahaweh and its capacity of adapting itself continually to new surroundings; the vitality of the faith of the Jews in the power of Yahaweh and His peculiar relation to them, which must make Him the avenger of their wrongs on those who oppress them.

After his conquest of Babylon, in 538 B.C., Cyrus set free all conquered peoples, the Jews included, not only giving them permission to return to their own countries, but encouraging them to return and reëstablish their nationality and their religion.[1] His attitude, as shown by the inscriptions, was not that of a devoted Zoroastrian. He was quite ready to worship the god of any place where he might be, and to support and honor such worship. The permission to return and the encouragement to reëstablish the state and the religion of the Jews did not, however, result in

[1] Ezra i, 1–4, 7, 8, 11 b. Confirmed by Cyrus' own inscriptions (Peters, *Scriptures, Hebrew and Christian*, II, 45).

the immediate return of any large number of Jews from Babylonia. To return meant a long, perilous, and expensive journey,
the abandonment of home and comfort and means of support; a
dangerous, difficult, and uncertain enterprise. The account of the
return which later Jewish tradition developed is to-day generally
accepted as exaggeration, and not a few scholars are inclined to
deny that there was any return whatsoever. The course of events
would seem to show, however, that this was not the case, and it
would be almost impossible that there should not have been some
men of sufficient patriotism and religious zeal and devotion to accept the opportunity to return to what they still counted the holy
land and the holy city.[1]

Our first unquestioned record of conditions in Palestine after
the Persian conquest of Babylonia and the release of the Jews
from captivity, that is, from compulsory residence in Babylonia, is
the prophecies of Haggai and Zechariah, beginning in the year
520 B.C., eighteen years after Cyrus' conquest of Babylon. At that
period we find a Jewish settlement in Judæa, with Jerusalem as its
center, governed by a prince of the Davidic line, Zerubbabel, son
of Shealtiel, and having as its religious head a chief priest, Joshua,
the son of Jozadak.[2] The prophecies of these two prophets also
give us some information with regard to religious conditions existing up to that time. Worship had been carried on in the ruins of
the Temple, but it had been, if we may so express it, a religion of
fasting and mourning. Ritually its most essential elements seemed
to be numerous fasts on days commemorating various events connected with the fall and destruction of the Temple. It was, so to
speak, the Book of Lamentations[3] put in practice — a belief in
Yahaweh along Deuteronomic and Jeremianic lines, but without
much hope or outlook, devoted to looking backward rather than
forward. There was a friendly relation with Samaritans, who came
to Jerusalem to worship, and Jews from Babylonia and also from

---

[1] In this matter, and in general in the treatment of Ezra and Nehemiah, I take the
middle position represented by Batten in his commentary in the International series.

[2] Ezra iii, 8; Hag. ii, 4.

[3] Were the Lamentations intended for ritual use like the Sumerian liturgies of
national calamities? Cf. Langdon, *Sumerian Liturgies.*

other countries seem to have paid visits of a religious character, pilgrimages to the ruins of the ancient shrine of Yahaweh at Jerusalem.[1]

With these prophets, however, a new era begins. While Cyrus' permission to return to Jerusalem had been in itself a hopeful sign, on the other hand the tremendous success of his career had offered little hope of the development of an independent national life, or the realization of that expectation of divine interposition in the great Day of Yahaweh which former political conditions had encouraged. He had overthrown Media, Babylonia, Lydia, and his son Cambyses overran Egypt. Cambyses' empire was far greater than that of Assyria at its greatest; but with the death of Cambyses new conditions arose. Darius was compelled to face rebellions in every part of his empire. During the first two years of his reign it seemed as though the Persian empire must inevitably be rent in sunder. The earthquakes had been resumed with double vigor. It was in this disturbed condition of the Persian empire that Haggai took up the old prophetic message. He is full of zeal for the Temple as the dwelling-place of Yahaweh. His message is, on the whole, a very simple one. It is a call to Zerubbabel, Joshua, and the people, to come together and build the Temple: an assurance that if they will do so Yahaweh will help them; that He will shake all nations and bring the wealth of all nations to Judah.[2] Following the Deuteronomic method of interpretation of good fortune and misfortune, but connecting it precisely with the Temple, he assures the people that their lack of prosperity is their own fault, because of their failure to build the Temple of Yahaweh. They had looked for prosperity, supposing apparently that with Cyrus' release of the captives and with the recognized reëstablishment of Judah, with a prince of David's line as its ruler and with a legitimate high priest by his side, a new era of prosperity was to begin; and they had been bitterly disappointed.[3] The fault lay with themselves.

The period covered by Haggai's few prophecies was very short, only about a year, but his prophecies fell on willing ears. The

---

[1] Zech. vii, 2 f.　　　[2] Hag. ii, 6 f.　　　[3] Hag. i, 2 ff.

time was ripe. He said things which his compatriots understood, interpreted the disturbances which were taking place and their own local conditions quite in accordance with the line of teaching which was their inheritance from the past. He was supported by at least one other prophet, whose writings, covering a broader range and a longer period of time, have come down to us; namely, Zechariah the son of Berechiah. The latter's prophecies throw somewhat more light than Haggai's on the political condition of the Jews. He clearly expected at the outset that the time had come for the restoration of the king of David's line, predicted by former prophets, and most recently by Ezekiel in Babylonia. Zerubbabel was to realize this very ancient hope, which connected itself with the Davidic kingdom;[1] but by the end of two years Darius had overthrown the rebels who threatened his rule on every side, and established his power on a firm basis. The latter prophecies of Zechariah accordingly take on a new aspect. The hope of the Davidic restoration in Zerubbabel had vanished. Apparently Zerubbabel himself had vanished, displaced by a Persian governor, after a policy inaugurated by Darius for the unification and better administration of his great empire.[2] This does not, however, mean a loss on Zechariah's part of his belief in the future of Jerusalem. The most hopeful and beautiful part of the whole book is the last chapter,[3] in which he pictures the prosperity that shall be. At the time of this prophecy Jerusalem was wall-less because of its poverty and because of its subjection to the Persians, who would not allow it to be walled. In Zechariah's vision it should be unwalled not because of poverty or powerlessness, but because of its greatness and its power. Its population should be too large to live within walls and its power too great to need them. For the king of David's line with whom Zechariah had connected the hopes held out in his earlier prophecies he now substitutes the personal rule of Yahaweh, their God. Both Haggai and Zechariah are optimistic to the last degree. Their message

---

[1] Zech. iv, 9. [2] Zech. vi, 11 ff.

[3] Zech. viii. The remaining chapters of our present book belong to a later date and a different author.

is one of hope and rejoicing, couched in promises which seem extravagant. Zechariah, in answer to messengers who come from Samaria to ask whether they shall continue to observe the fasts of the fifth, seventh, and tenth months, teaches them to turn all fasts into feasts.[1] The occasion of a pilgrimage from Babylonia, with gifts for the Temple, he turns into a prophecy of the great new kingdom. These distant Jews have come bearing the tribute which, unknown to themselves, is the crown of the new king.[2] Like Haggai, Zechariah may be regarded as in general a successor of the line of prophecy represented by Jeremiah, and of the Deuteronomic school. There are, however, some points in his book which suggest that he is a priest and is more in sympathy with the ordinary priestly view than was Jeremiah. In his use of apocalypses he shows touch with Ezekielian thought, going, however, much further in the development of the apocalyptic method than that prophet had done. He is here falling in with a method of presentation, in its origin perhaps extra-Judæan, which was admirably adapted for conveying teaching without incurring responsibility. His apocalypses are largely political in character. He is dealing with the conditions of the Persian empire, the possibilities of its overthrow. To have spoken in direct words would not only have involved himself in danger, but very likely brought disaster upon the whole people. Like Ezekiel, also, he is influenced by the thought of the Day of Yahaweh, the day of judgment upon the foes of Yahaweh and of Israel; but he does not take the exclusive view which belongs to Ezekiel and which was later still more definitely connected with the Babylonian Jewish school of thought. He not only pictures the Jews living over all the world making their pilgrimages (and incidentally this is an evidence of the fact that such Jews were making pilgrimages to the Temple); but the Jew is to become the agent, through his very dispersion, to bring all nations of the earth to worship Yahaweh: "Ten men out of all nations of the earth shall take hold of the skirt of him that is a Jew."[3] But the place of worship is to be Jerusalem and the Temple of Yahaweh in Jerusalem.

[1] Zech. viii, 19.   [2] Zech. vi, 11.   [3] Zech. viii, 23.

The greatest prophet of this new school of Judæan prophecy, and the one whose utterances mark the highest range of Old Testament prophecy, was an unknown writer or series of writers whose utterances, as they have come down to us, are now included in the Book of Isaiah, chapters xl–lxvi. Haggai *uttered* his prophecies, which were occasional — that is, utterances for a particular purpose, and connecting themselves with events and conditions of the moment. In part Zechariah did the same. More largely his prophecies were *written*, after the manner of a large part of the Book of Ezekiel. The utterances of this unknown prophet are all written, but, so far from being prosaic like the greater part of the prophecies and writings of Ezekiel and of Haggai and Zechariah, they are in the highest degree poetic, frequently passing over into lyrical poetry. From the literary as well as the spiritual side they are very beautiful, representing scholarship and culture as well as spiritual insight. They are not occasional utterances. There are very few references to current events. They are the work of the scholar and the mystic, who interpreted the literature of his people and the history of his people, not merely to a present generation or a local audience, but, in his dreams, to a vast multitude of Jews everywhere and at all times. He evinces a thorough acquaintance with the history and literature of Israel in the past, the line of his tradition being the Yahawistic-Elohistic narrative and the former prophets, especially Isaiah, whom he most resembles in style and choice of words and phrase, and Jeremiah, who most profoundly, both by his personal experiences and his teaching, affected his conception of the meaning of Israel's history, the mission of Israel, and the hope of its future. He has the same message of hope which is to be found in Haggai, and at times almost in the same words. Yahaweh will shake all nations and bring the wealth of all nations, and make his land once more glorious.[1] But the ruler who shall rule over the new Israel is not a prince of David's line, but, as in the latter prophecies of Zechariah, Yahaweh himself, the Holy One of Israel, as this writer so frequently calls Him, following the use which first became noticeable

[1] Hag. ii, 7; Is. lx, 9.

in Isaiah of Jerusalem at least 200 years earlier. In considering the history of Israel he is brought face to face with the problem of calamity, in his view of which he is akin to the writer of the Book of Job. Like that writer, he adopts an explanation quite different from the explanation given by the Deuteronomic school, which was at that time finding a further development in the teaching of the legal school of the Babylonian captivity. And this is one of this writer's greatest contributions not merely to the religious development of the Jews, but to the religious development of the world; for he must be reckoned as one of the world's greatest religious teachers. It is clear to him, although he reaches his conclusions and expresses his results, not in the more logical manner of the Wisdom school, but rather in the mystical and poetical method, that calamity is not an evidence of guilt. Israel had not sinned above other peoples. The terrible punishments which it had received did not mean a greater degree of guilt. If they were expressions of the wrath of God because of their sins, that is now put behind them.[1] If God had been wroth, it had been but for a moment.[2] The relation of God to Israel was one of love,[3] as Hosea had taught, and the relation was an ineffaceable one, so that Yahaweh could never forget his people Israel.[4] God's punishment would purge the dross away. It was done in mercy and loving kindness, that He might bring Israel back to himself; and so great was His love for Israel that for His own sake He must forgive Israel's transgressions.[5] But Israel's calamities had a further purpose, and here the writer steps most markedly beyond anything which any former prophet or poet of Israel, of whom we have knowledge, had ventured.

Amos, it is true, interpreted God's plan as one that concerns the whole earth. The bringing up of Israel out of Egypt was a no more special thing than the bringing up of the Syrians out of Kir.[6] This book carries out that idea further and in a somewhat different way. Yahaweh rules the whole world, but He has a special relation to Israel. The destruction of Jerusalem and the scattering

---

[1] Is. xl, 2; xlvii, 6.   [3] Is. liv, 8.   [5] Is. xliii, 25.
[2] Is. xliii, 4.   [4] Is. xliv, 21; xlix, 15.   [6] Amos ix, 7.

of Israel to the four quarters of the earth is a part of the plan by which He would give His people Israel a vastly greater place and fame than they could have in any kingdom confined by the limits of their own land, like the Davidic kingdom of prophetic dreams.[1] Such a mission is too small for them. Their mission is to the whole earth, so that the suffering which they had borne and by which they are purged shall become the means of redeeming the world.[2] That redemption is thought of in terms of Palestine, and we have pictures which connect us with the language and thoughts of earlier prophets, both Jews and Israelites; for, like Haggai and Zechariah, his vision of the Holy Land and of the chosen people covers Samaria as well as Judæa.[3] They are brought back to the chosen land from all corners of the earth by Egyptians, Babylonians, and Greeks alike, but their relation to these is not that of hostility or conquest, but rather of union in the worship of Yahaweh, with the Jew as the elder brother, serving and helping rather than ruling.[4] This doctrine of service is developed in the finest passages of this book. Israel is the servant[5] of Yahaweh, and as the servant of Yahaweh the servant also of his fellow men. His service to Yahaweh is the redemption of the world, and his sufferings are a part of his service, a new form of sacrifice, by which he bears the burdens of mankind. The writer was not only profoundly influenced by Jeremiah's writings; he was also evidently profoundly influenced by the story of the life of the man who so selflessly and so thanklessly loved his people, and who was so deeply and so sorrowfully sensible of their wickedness. He shared in their guilt (i.e. the consequences of their sins), not protestingly, but willingly and more than willingly bearing with and for his people the consequences of those sins; abused by those he loved and sought to serve; misunderstood, despised, and hated as a false Jew by the people for whose good he was ready to lay down his life; dying ultimately amid the ruins of his nation, with the apparent failure of all for which he stood, at the hands of his own countrymen, to have them afterwards perceive that he was truly a man

[1] Is. xlii, 1, 6. [3] Is. lxv, 9 f. [5] Is. xliv, 1.
[2] Is. xlix.   [4] Is. lxvi, 18 ff.

of God, the true patriot, the true prophet. He was to this writer a pattern of the true Israelite, the true conception of the servant of Yahaweh; only, of course, idealized in his thought.[1]

It is his *working out* of this ideal picture of the servant who is the very essence of Israel, through whom not only Israel but the world shall be redeemed, which results in the great picture presented in the fifty-third chapter, as follows:

> Behold, My servant shall prosper; he shall be high and exalted, and lofty exceedingly. As many were amazed at thee (so marred was his visage from that of man, and his form from that of the sons of men), so shall he dazzle many nations. Kings shall stop their mouths at him; for what was not told them they have seen; and what they heard not, they have understood.
>
> Who believed our report? and to whom was the arm of Yahaweh revealed? He hath no form nor comeliness, that we should see him, no beauty that we should desire him. Despised, and forsaken of men; a man of sorrows, acquainted with grief; as one from whom men hide their face, despised, and we esteemed him not.
>
> Surely our griefs he bore, and our sorrows he carried them; and we esteemed him stricken, smitten of God, and afflicted. But he was wounded for our transgressions, bruised for our iniquities; the chastisement of our peace was upon him; and by his stripes we are healed. All we like sheep went astray; each turned his own way; and Yahaweh made to light on him the iniquity of us all.

[1] Jeremiah, "under the shadow of the exile," set forth three great religious truths "which are of prime importance. These are theoretical monotheism, or the recognition that the gods of the heathen are figments of the imagination (x, 15; xiv, 22), the perception that God is as willing to welcome penitent Gentiles as penitent Jews to His worship (xvi, 19–21), and the fact of individual responsibility in morals" (xxxi, 29 f.). These doctrines Deutero-Isaiah enlarged and developed. Brooding " over the reason why the leaders of his people had been torn from their homes and the independence of his land destroyed, he saw in these events the fulfillment of a divine mission. Like Jeremiah he believed that Yahaweh would welcome the coming of the heathen to himself, but he went beyond Jeremiah in believing that God had chosen Israel to be His missionary, and the sufferings involved in the uprooting of the people, which had marred the nation's beauty and left only the unlovely stump of her peasant population in the dry ground, were in part vicarious. Israel had suffered at the Lord's hand double for all her sins (Is. xl, 2). The half of this was for the sins of the nations. Later (lii, 15) he pictures the kings of these nations as standing astonished at Israel's sufferings, and then in a flash of insight perceiving that ' he hath borne our griefs and carried our sorrows' (liii, 4 ff.) " (G. A. Barton, *The Biblical World*, June, 1911).

He was oppressed, and was humbled, not opening his mouth; as a lamb that is led to the slaughter, and as a sheep that before her shearers is dumb. By false judgment was he taken away; and his posterity who shall recount? for he was cut off from the land of the living; for the transgression of My people was he stricken. And they made his grave with the wicked, and with prisoners his tomb; although he had done no violence, nor was any deceit in his mouth. But it pleased Yahaweh to bruise him; to put him to grief.

Though he give his life a guilt offering, he shall see his posterity; he shall prolong his days, and the pleasure of Yahaweh shall prosper in his hand. He shall see of the travail of his soul, and be filled; by his knowledge My servant justifieth many, bearing their iniquities. Therefore will I give him a portion with the great, and he shall divide the spoil with the strong; because he poured out his life unto death, and was numbered with the transgressors. But he bare the sins of many, and maketh intercession for transgressors.[1]

In the teaching of Deutero-Isaiah we find a full and complete expression of monotheism. Mono-Yahawism and monolatry alike are left behind. In the most unmistakable language he sets forth a full and complete belief in Yahaweh as God alone, the maker of all things, bad as well as good.[2] His writings are full of reiterations of this teaching, frequently in the form of polemics, suggesting that here he is teaching something which has by no means met with full acceptance either in profession or in practice. Evidently there was not only idolatry among the nations about, but among his own people and in his own land there were those who, while claiming to be followers of Yahaweh, yet along with Yahaweh worshiped other deities. In the later chapters we find glimpses of the conditions among his own people which necessitated such arguments, the continuance of the old folk-religion and of many of the old idolatrous practices.[8] In the denunciations of ritual[4] and the emphasis on morality[5] we get both the old prophetic note and also an indication of the prevalence of the old false conceptions of religion. In general, however, the writer is concerned with such broad and great things that the matters of the immediate local

---

[1] Is. lii, 13–liii, 12.
[2] Is. xliii, 10; xliv, 6; xlv, 7.
[8] Is. lxv, 6–12.

[4] Sacrifice, Is. lxvi, 3; fasting, lviii.
[5] Is. lix.

environment seem to slip out of sight as too small. His references
show thorough accord with the emphasis which had come to be
laid upon the Sabbath,[1] the importance of circumcision, general
sympathy with the laws of clean and unclean, and the like;[2] but,
on the other hand, he belongs to what we may call the broad
school of Hebrew thought. He would not exclude those who
desire to come into the Judæan community as worshipers of
Yahaweh. The stranger and the eunuch should be admitted.[3]
Yahaweh is to him the great source of living water in the world,
to which all are to be freely invited.[4] The very breadth of his
teaching and the greatness of his thought, speaking for all times
rather than for special occasions, makes analysis of his work somewhat difficult. It was not all produced at one time. The prophecies
overlap one another, and no completely satisfactory arrangement
in separate chapters or poems has ever been proposed, for the reason that they seem to have been worked over and over, the same
theme with variations being treated numerous times and then reworked again; so that ultimately the chapters have come to constitute one whole, whether originally from the hand of one author or
of several taking up and developing in close sympathy one another's
work. One thing seems fairly clear: that they cover a considerable interval of time, a lifetime or more. The earlier prophecies
begin not very long after the commencement of the building of
the temple, in 520. The book as a whole may be dated probably
somewhere between that and the middle of the following century.[5]

---

[1] Is. lvi, 2; lviii, 13.   [2] Is. lii, 1.   [3] Is. lvi, 3 f.   [4] Is. lv.

[5] The prevailing view is that this book, as a whole, is Judæan, not Babylonian;
although there are still not a few who hold the older view, that it was composed in
Babylonia. Still others have assigned different parts to the two different localities
and divided them into Deutero-Isaiah, Trito-Isaiah, etc. To me it seems that the
book is a unit, the product of a school by which an original work was continued,
revised, and recast. There are in the earlier chapters very evident marks of a close
acquaintance with Babylonia, and of the enthusiasm awaked by Cyrus' favor to the
Jews, in the light of which his conquests and his religion are interpreted. He is a
Messiah, one specially favored by the Holy One of Israel, in all respects a contrast
to the idolatrous Babylonian oppressors (xlv). On the other hand, even in the
earlier chapters there are allusions which one would expect only from one writing
in Judæa. In the latter part of the book these increase in number, and gradually we
find ourselves in an environment which closely resembles that of Malachi. The book,
in fact, connects at one end with Haggai and Zechariah and at the other with Malachi.

In tracing the Judæan development after the Exile our last document is the anonymous book of prophecies known as the Book of the Prophet Malachi. This book deals directly with the problems of the Judæan community shortly before the reforms of Nehemiah, somewhere toward or after the middle of the fifth century B.C. In Deutero-Isaiah we find frequent reference to the poor, the needy, the meek-spirited, the humble,[1] etc., as representing that element of the people which was in sympathy with the ideal servant. This element appears under a somewhat different form in Malachi; but now these poor and needy are a very actual and literal fact. The conditions which he sees resemble, to some extent, those which Micah had depicted — wealth gathered in the hands of a few, the body of the people poor and oppressed. The ruling classes and the priests were selfish and regardless of their responsibilities. The priests had lost zeal for the Temple service. The glorious hopes of the former prophets, Haggai, Zechariah, and Deutero-Isaiah, had not been fulfilled, and Malachi, like Haggai, finds that the trouble lies with the people themselves. Partly the evils are ritual, partly they are moral.[2] Dishonesty in sacrifice is a part of the evil conditions which he denounces, and only by remedying which can the promises be fulfilled.[3] The tone of the book is one of discouragement with present conditions, an attitude which reminds one in general of the attitude of Isaiah as expressed in the eighth chapter of the book of that name. In the midst of prevailing corruption and evil there are still a godly few remaining who confer with one another and hope and look for Yahaweh.[4] In its earnest desire for reformation the book seems

The presumption is, as it seems to me, that the great beginner of this book was one of those who returned from Babylon to Judæa, and that the first completed prophecy was closely connected with the rebuilding of the Temple. As in the case of the Book of Job, there is a sense of incompleteness about the latter part of the book. Two great cycles of prophecies and poems were thoroughly worked out; the latter part is incomplete, a continuation of the preceding in spirit, it is true, but inferior in thought, and both inferior and incomplete in form, giving evidence also in its teachings and allusions of a change of conditions in the community as in the writers.

[1] Is. xli, 17; lxi, 1.
[2] Mal. ii, 14 ff.; iii, 5 ff. Cf. also, however, Is. lxv, 3, 4, 11.
[3] Mal. i, 6–14; iii, 8–14.
[4] Mal. iii, 16.

almost like a preparation for the reforms of Nehemiah, which were in fact so close at hand.

Eschatologically Malachi adds an interesting doctrine, by a transference from the history of the past into the history of the future. The writer's hope for a strong reformer connects itself with the history of Elijah's reform, and leads to a prophecy of the coming of a new Elijah to prepare the way for the great and terrible Day of Yahaweh.[1] In regard to this latter doctrine of the Day of Yahaweh, Malachi is in close touch and sympathy with that line of prophets, commencing with the Scythian invasion, who interpreted the old popular doctrine in relation to the great folk-movements which were disturbing the earth. Some trace of the continuance of those movements is felt in Malachi,[2] as in the contemporary prophecy of Obadiah. Apparently as a sequel of or in connection with the great folk-movement which had been shaking the whole civilized world, there commenced a northward movement out of Arabia, the beginning of the great Arabic migration. The forerunners of this movement, the Nabatheans, overran ancient Edom and drove the Edomites out of their original territory, forcing them upward into the south and the southwest of Judah in the neighborhood of Hebron and the Shephelah.[3] This was interpreted by both of these prophets as a foretaste and precursor of the great Day of Yahaweh. Edom was the especial representative of the foes of Yahaweh, and Yahaweh's punishment of Edom was the beginning of a general judgment of the wicked, His foes and the foes of His people.[4]

---

[1] Mal. iv, 5.   [2] Mal. iv, 1.   [3] Mal. i, 4.   [4] Ob. 15. Cf. also Is. lxiii.

CHAPTER XXII

THE PROBLEM OF EVIL

The problem of divine justice was forced upon the people by the experiences of the Exile. The theory of the Deuteronomist was the old popular conception, spiritualized and monotheized: that evil came upon man because of divine wrath; that good things were granted to him through divine favor. A contribution which the Deuteronomist made to the old theory of divine reward and divine punishment was the ascription of all the good which came to the Israelite to Yahaweh, and Him alone, and all the evil likewise. Evil did not come from some other god, who was more powerful than Yahaweh, but from Yahaweh as the result of His displeasure. His pleasure and displeasure were primarily moral, the result of real good or ill behavior on the part of His people; but to some extent due to what we should consider unmoral causes, ritual or religious offenses — sacrificing in some other place than Jerusalem, the failure to make the right kind of sacrifice in the right manner, etc.

In the later legal developments, which express fundamentally the older popular conception of religion as over against the prophetic idea prevalent in Deuteronomy, the unmoral or ritual side assumes the greater importance, and the pleasure or displeasure of God is made more dependent upon that; without, however, at least in the official development of the religion of Israel, exclusion of the moral element. Ezekiel had contributed an individualistic element to this philosophy of evil. It seemed to the men of the Exile that Yahaweh had inflicted undeserved suffering upon His people, punishing the innocent with the guilty, making the children suffer for the sins of their fathers. Ezekiel accepted the Deuteronomic theology in its fullness, and solved the difficulty by a strict, hard logic. Yahaweh is just; He cannot punish the innocent with the guilty. He punishes or rewards men according to their deserts. The man that sins shall die; the man that does righteously shall live;[1] and naturally, reversing the thought, the man that dies has sinned, and the man that lives has done righteously. These rewards shall be, of course, in the present life. The wicked are punished by early or painful physical death, while the righteous live out the years of normal humanity. The simplicity of the theory commends itself to the average man. It found expression in the story of Job, which was widely current in Ezekiel's time, and to which he appears to refer.[2] That story, in its main features, is contained in the prose introduction, and probably, in a modified form, in the conclusion also, of our present Book of Job.[3] But even for the average man this theory seemed to require some sort of modification.

According to Ezekiel's theory, it must be observed, the final decision with regard to the good or evil doing of a man could not be reached before his death; and the same was true of the nation. Israel suffered more severely than many of the nations about. Some of those that were vastly more wicked were flourishing and thriving, while Israel was in exile and like one dead, its temple destroyed, its land laid waste, its men and women captives. But in God's good time the conditions would be reversed. In the end the nations were to be punished and destroyed, while Israel was to be restored to favor and loaded with blessings.

Ezekiel's theology, as it appeared to the average man, may be said to be found in such a Psalm as the thirty-seventh, which depicts exactly such conditions: the wicked flourish like a green bay tree, the righteous are afflicted and distressed; but in the end the wicked shall perish and his seed be cut off, while the righteous shall inherit the land; Yahaweh rescueth them from the wicked and giveth them the victory, prosperity, and peace.

Still better this theology of the average man expresses itself in the old story of Job, which is in substance the Ezekielian doctrine. Job was a rich man, whom God had blessed with children, with flocks and herds and great possessions. To test him and to prove him, at the suggestion of Satan, God caused invaders to fall upon him

---

1 Ezek. xiv; xviii.   2 Ezek. xiv, 14.   3 Job i–ii; xlii.

and destroy his flocks and herds. His children were killed, his house fell in ruins about his head. Still further to test him, at the further suggestion of Satan, God smote him with leprosy. But through it all Job preserved his integrity, believing in God and worshiping Him. At the last, because he had preserved his integrity, God rewarded him with wealth and children vastly exceeding those which had before been his.

But while this explanation of evil satisfied the average man, there were out-reaching and reflective minds to whom it failed to give satisfaction. We have seen how Deutero-Isaiah reached out beyond the Deuteronomic conception and developed, in relation to the experience of Israel, a new doctrine of the expiatory power of suffering, of suffering which might be inflicted not to test and try Israel, albeit Israel was purified in the process, but as a part of the purpose of God toward the whole world, by which the ideal servant of Yahaweh, himself innocent, might, not through the hate but in the love of God, bear the sins of many. Other thinkers of a different type were busy with the same problem, and if they did not solve it they at least offered suggestions concerning it which have been embodied in the sacred books of Israel.

The author of our present Book of Job was one of those to whom it seemed that the Deuteronomic theory, or the Ezekielian theory, did not conform to the facts. Certainly it was not true of every man who died an early or a painful death that he was a sinner above other men who lived longer, happier, and more successful lives. It was not true of everyone who died in prosperity, wealth, and happiness, that he was a good man; and as this was not true in the case of the individual, it was likewise not true in the case of nations. It was not a true explanation of the history of Israel, and, the conclusion reached in the Deuteronomic or Ezekielian teaching being invalid, it followed that their premises also were false. Israel was not altogether sinful; why had it been so long oppressed by the Gentiles? The Gentiles were not more righteous; why should they be allowed to triumph? There was a body of faithful Jews in Jerusalem in Egypt and in Babylonia who had kept the law of God and served Him with all their hearts;

why should they still be the prey of the oppressor? Must one give up the belief that God is just? These are the questions which the author of the Book of Job debates rather than answers, taking the popular story of Job as his theme. Why does God afflict the righteous?[1]

This is developed in the form of a colloquy between Job and the three friends who come to comfort him in his affliction, the representatives of tradition and philosophy. In form the work approaches the drama more closely than anything else in Hebrew literature. In thought it is a drama, but a drama of inward, not of outward action. Job may be said to represent somewhat the same thing which the servant in Deutero-Isaiah represents — the ideal Israel; or, rather than the ideal Israel, the faithful Israel in captivity and humiliation. But the writer seems also to be considering the problem of evil as it touches the individual man. Everything goes to show that Job is a sinner beyond all men, deprived

---

[1] In the form in which the old theme of Job is here presented we find the same development of angelology which makes its appearance in the Book of Zechariah. The heavenly court is conceived of somewhat after the manner of the Persian government. Yahaweh is no longer resident in the Temple at Jerusalem, but in heaven, lord of the whole earth; He directs His government by angels, somewhat as the Persian king governed his distant provinces by satraps. These go to and fro through the earth and make report to Him at assizes. A sort of inspector or detective to look for and detect the evil in these different provinces, but not confined to any one of them, is Satan. In the Book of Zechariah he appears as prosecutor in the arraignment of Joshua before the heavenly throne. In the Book of Job, when the angels appear in the Presence to report on the condition of their different provinces of the universe, Satan, the special prosecutor or agent of God to detect evil, appears among them, his business being to find flaws in the universe if he can. To the question whether he has observed Job, the upright, he replies with the insinuation that his uprightness is a mere matter of selfish calculation, and the suggestion that if he lose his property his piety will go also. Yahaweh permits him to put Job to the test. That test endured satisfactorily, he makes a second insinuation that Job cringes and professes belief, in fear that otherwise he may lose his life. If his body be touched, then he will blaspheme. But this test also Job endures, holding fast to his integrity. Possibly there is in this angelology a suggestion of another solution to the problem of evil: "the thought that, if we could see all that goes on in the divine council, we should see a reason for much that is now obscure to us in the government of the world. Among the spiritual existences there, as among men here, there may be doubt as to the reality of virtue, at least of human virtue. To prove that virtue is more than selfishness, there is no way except to send calamity upon the virtuous. It concerns mankind and angels to be convinced that there is such a thing as disinterested goodness" (H. P. Smith, Old Testament History, p. 366).

of possessions, family, home, touched by the finger of God with the incurable sickness of leprosy. On the prevailing theory the evidence is overwhelming that he is a sinner beyond all men. In this fate the writer, as an Israelite, finds himself. His people, of which he was a part, were thus afflicted : their wealth destroyed, their land made desolate, their children slain, their houses destroyed, even the very Temple of God itself, and they themselves were touched by the finger of God with the disease of death. If the old theology were correct, then he and his were guilty of wickedness and hypocrisy almost incredible ; but his conscience is clear. He knows with a certainty of inner conviction that he is not guilty of the flagrant sins which alone could call down such signal punishment, neither he nor his. The friends who represent the traditional philosophy mock his misery in their attempt to assuage it, because they have no doubt, however gently and considerately they may desire to express it, that this punishment is a punishment for sin. They show the grounds for this belief in the traditions of the ancients, confirmed by their own observations. They claim to have been taught by divine revelation concerning the divine method of dealing with men. They invite Job to repent, and promise help and restoration to life if he will follow their advice. Ultimately they proceed to make direct charges of sin against him. Their very promises of restoration in case of repentance are a mockery, which aggravate his misery and increase his perplexity. He finds no hope anywhere. The best that he can wish for is annihilation. He accuses his friends of failing him. He describes his sufferings. At last, in desperation, he expostulates with God. Why should he, so insignificant in the sight of the Almighty, be watched as though he were the rebellious ocean or the primeval dragon? Would it not be more worthy of God to forgive human failings, seeing that the divine dignity cannot be injured by the puny efforts of the creature?[1] His friends insist with greater vehemence upon their arguments, and affirm the justice of God. Job sees nothing but might. Conscious of his innocence, such an argument means to him merely that might makes right. The theory of the friends is

[1] Job vii, 12–21.

that God is in the right, because He has the power to crush opposition. But if this be so, then God is not the God in whom Job has trusted. The god of justice has disappeared and a tyrant has taken his place. Job is innocent; this he will protest to his last breath, and he could prove it to God if God would lay aside His terrors and meet him as a man in argument. If there were an umpire, who would impartially consider the evidence, before him he would gladly defend his case against God. Conscious of his right, he cannot lie even to curry favor with the Almighty and win the blessing of restoration. He must affirm the right of the creature, though the affirmation seem to be a denial of the Creator.

To the friends these words of Job are merely blasphemy. He is a monstrous sinner, and a more monstrous hypocrite, because he protests that he is innocent. They reaffirm their argument with increasing heat, until at last they accuse him to his face of impossible crimes; recalling Ezekiel's doctrine of the infamous wickedness of Israel from its birth. More and more distinctly Job sees that there is no relief for him in anything they have to say; that their theology is bankrupt. But in proportion as he is driven away from that interpretation he is driven back to God. Something of that older prophetic conception of the relation of the individual soul to God, through which prophecy itself was rendered possible, makes itself felt. The author of Job is brought back to the thought of the personal relation of the soul to God as the means through which solution of his problem is to be found.[1] The God whom he knows must be just. Why he is afflicted he does not know. It is a mystery which his philosophy does not solve; but somewhere, somehow, because God, whom he knows, is just, God will disprove the false charge brought against His servant, and he and God be made at one.

[1] Similarly in another somewhat later book of the Wisdom Literature, Ecclesiastes, while criticizing in a manner which seems frequently dangerously skeptical the order of the universe and the doctrines of life suggested by philosophy and religion alike, although the author reaches and emphasizes the conclusion that all is vanity, yet he never questions the existence, the omnipotence, and the righteousness of God. Indeed, the fundamental thought of the Wisdom Literature through all its questioning, its philosophizing, and its practical teaching is: " The fear of God is the beginning of Wisdom." It reflects and inculcates a personal faith in God.

The thought of the resurrection of Israel, of which Ezekiel had made use in the vision of dry bones,[1] seems to be in the author's mind in one passage, where he expresses a hope of vindication hereafter. The author certainly comes near to a glimpse of the solution of his problem to be found in individual immortality ;[2] but he appears to move away from this hope again, and, so far as he does finally offer any solution of his problem, that solution is the state of peace of soul, and of conscious relation to God, attained through the struggle. His Job loses his faith for the time being, but comes through his doubts and finds his God again. It is not a solution of the problem, but it is the renunciation of the popular theology, which falsely asserts that this world is administered on the scheme of temporal rewards and punishments. Observation of the facts shows not only that the righteous suffer, but that the wicked prosper. To the question : On what principles is the world governed ? no answer can be given; yet faith is not altogether taken away from us. As we look at the marvelous works of God in nature, we see that perfect wisdom is at work. We can rest in the conclusion that He who is able to carry on such a wonderful scheme will also be able to give a reason for His dealings with men. His ways are unsearchable; notwithstanding, we may trust that they are true and right.[3] To enter into such trust in God is the best that man can do.

The book is entirely free from ritualistic connections.[4] It belongs in that class of literature called *Chokhmah* (Wisdom), which may

---

[1] Ezek. xxxvii.   [2] Job xix, 23–27 ; cf. also xiv, 12 ff.
[3] Chaps. xxxviii, xxxix.

[4] The Babylonians also had a category of Wisdom literature, if we may judge from what appears to be the heading of a series of tablets found in the library of Ashurbanipal: " I will praise the Lord of Wisdom." Dr. Jastrow finds in a tablet in this series a parallel to the Book of Job. This tablet contains the lament of a sufferer who, although a faithful worshiper of and sacrificer to the gods in most correct form, finds himself mysteriously sore afflicted. In certain respects this does undoubtedly resemble the lament of Job. Apparently it was part of a ritual to be used for a sufferer under such conditions, whose sufferings could not be attributed to any lapse in his religious observances. One is inclined to ask whether the original Job was not a ritual of the same character. If it had, however, such original ritual connections, our book of Job has certainly left them far behind. (Jastrow: " Babylonian Parallel to Job," *J. B. L.*, 1906, II.)

be said to represent rather the common-sense thinker and philosopher than either the prophet or the priest. It is cast, apparently purposely, in archaic form and surroundings, consistently with the fact that the whole discussion is based on an ancient story in somewhat modern dress, representing both the traditional and the theological exposition of the meaning of God's dealing with Israel, and hence with man.[1] That the book, if it was not comprehensible to the great bulk of the men of the writer's day, made a strong appeal to some thinkers is evinced by the fact of its continued existence and of its incorporation in the canon of sacred literature. It did

[1] It should be said that the book is a very difficult one, and no altogether satisfactory explanation of all the details of its present form, or even a convincing interpretation of its entire content, has ever been presented. Largely I think this is due to a certain incompleteness of composition. The first part is well worked out, as follows: i–ii, Prose Setting; the old Job story. iii, Job's complaint; being the thesis of the drama. iv–xiv, First Cycle of Argument; the friends expound the gracious purpose of God's ways and the corrective object of affliction; but Job finds in himself no great wickedness wherefore he should be afflicted above all men. This cycle closes with the suggestion of a reservation or preservation of his existence in Sheol until God's wrath turns. xv–xxi, Second Cycle; the friends set forth the terrible punishments of the wicked, Job proves that prosperity and misfortune are not given according to guilt. In the nineteenth chapter Job goes beyond the wish of the fourteenth, that he might be preserved in Sheol, to an assertion of a belief in his resurrection and vindication. As stated in the text, as a national hope this had already been set forth in Ezekiel. The application to the individual, which at first sight seems to have been made in Job xix, did not apparently make itself thoroughly effective even to the author. At all events the remainder of this cycle and the whole of the succeeding cycle have to us moderns somewhat of the effect of an anticlimax. From this point on there is also a certain effect of incompleteness and confusion. The third cycle (xxii–xxxi), as we now have it, is not well rounded off; the final speeches are incomplete and their attribution in part apparently unsatisfactory; they are followed by the section of Elihu speeches (xxxii–xxxvii), evidently not part of the original scheme of the book, nor apparently conceived in the spirit of the original writer. This section again is followed by a series of speeches of Yahaweh of the general type of the Praise of Wisdom in Proverbs, setting forth the wonders of God in creation, His might and His wisdom, some parts of which are of great beauty, but which in their present form certainly scarcely present the solution which the argument of the earlier parts of the book would lead one to expect. Then comes the brief prose epilogue. The impression is as though the great drama had been completely worked out only through the second cycle, the remainder containing in part material from the original author, not complete, which has been developed, added to, interpolated, by successors; the whole finally put together as one book, with that lack of thorough harmonization and amalgamation which so often surprises and confounds us in the study of the Old Testament. The zoölogy and mythology of the latter chapters suggest an Egyptian connection; but whether that is true of the whole book is very uncertain.

not, however, change the prevalent and the official theology;[1] and it was even largely unintelligible to the average theologian of that and succeeding ages, as is clear from the insertion of the Elihu passages,[2] in which both Job and his friends are rebuked and the true theology expounded, namely that same Deuteronomic-Ezekielian scheme to which reference has already been made. But, while setting forth the Deuteronomic-Ezekielian scheme, the speeches of Elihu also contain new material, adding elements of moral and religious value; especially the doctrine of suffering as an instrument of education in the hand of God, a proof of the divine love, the recognition of which love in and through the suffering becomes to the sufferer a source of infinite blessing.

[1] See, for example, the later Psalms; also various passages in the New Testament, which testify that the prevailing and apparently official view at the commencement of our era was that of Ezekiel and earlier. So Jno. ix, 1; Luke xiii, 2.

[2] Chaps. xxxii–xxxvii.

CHAPTER XXIII

THE LAW

Having followed the religious development of the Jews in Palestine after the Exile, before the adoption of the Law, let us now consider the development of that Law in Babylonia. The Captivity [1] in Babylonia was composed of the more well-to-do classes, those who, in the nature of the case, were best acquainted with the history and the literature of their country. It contained, also, a strong priestly element. Such a body of men was less likely to be lost in a foreign population than an equal number of the poorer and less educated class. On the other hand, precisely in proportion as the Captivity preserved its identity in a foreign land, it was natural that it should dwell upon the traditions of its country and upon its religion, both collecting what was already written and also putting in writing traditions, laws, and usages which had not yet been written down.

Naturally that body of the exiles which had remained true to country and religion attached itself especially to the Deuteronomic reform. Its point of view of the history of the past was first of all the point of view of Deuteronomy. And so it came about that during the Exile the history of the past was largely rewritten from the Deuteronomic standpoint, so far as that had not been already done.

---

[1] The term "Captivity" is used not merely as the designation of those who were carried captive by Nebuchadrezzar, but also of their descendants who for centuries, of their own free will, continued to live in Babylonia, making up for their failure to undergo the hardships and privations involved in repatriation to Palestine by the development and punctilious practice and study of a theoretic Judaism, calling themselves the while the *Galutha* (Captivity), bemoaning their hard lot, and persuading themselves and others that they were afflicted and oppressed. Claiming to be the legitimate descendants and guardians of pure Judaism, they first made their claim effective on the Jews of Judæa, and through them ultimately imposed their orthodoxy on the Jewish world.

All the evil which had befallen the nation came from a violation of the laws of Yahaweh. Yahaweh and Yahaweh alone was the God of Israel, who had chosen Israel as His own peculiar people. He was more powerful than all the gods of the nations. He showed His love toward Israel by giving it a good land, success against its enemies, prosperity and wealth at home ; but when and because Israel broke His laws, He punished it by defeat of its armies, invasion by its foes, loss of its crops, pestilence, sickness, and the like.

Looking back over the history of Israel with this theological presumption, it was plain that Israel had for a time been faithful and that Yahaweh had blessed it very abundantly. Afterwards it fell away and suffered accordingly. There had been, it is true, periods of restitution to Yahaweh's favor on account of obedience to His laws, but in general the history of Israel had been one of faithlessness and disobedience, punished more and more severely, until the final destruction of Jerusalem and the Captivity.

Accordingly the Book of Judges was thrown into its present form, with moral introductions and conclusions to the various tales, narrating how Israel proved faithless, whereupon, for its sins, Yahaweh sent such and such a calamity upon it and the nation was punished so and so many years, under such and such a foreign tyrant, as a scourge of Yahaweh. Then, when the nation repented and returned to Yahaweh, He sent a deliverer, and His great power overthrew the enemy, and the land had peace and happiness for so and so many years, until the nation again rebelled and dealt wickedly.

The Book of Kings is a document of this period, and the judgment passed upon the various kings is passed upon this principle. If they were prosperous, it was clear that they had been good, and Yahaweh had rewarded the people with prosperity for their obedience to His law ; but if they had been unsuccessful, it was clear that they had been wicked and Yahaweh had punished them for their wickedness. Israel had been wicked from the outset, in that its kings had worshiped Yahaweh at shrines other than the shrine in Jerusalem which He had ordained, setting up rival sanctuaries with the golden bulls at Bethel and Dan,[1] hence its complete destruction a hundred and fifty years before Jerusalem fell. It was not only the question of observance of the ethical law, but equally or rather more the question of place and form of worship which decided whether a king or a period was bad or good. Did he magnify the one central sanctuary at Jerusalem? Was the worship free from the concomitants of *asherah* and *mazzebah*, and the sexual impurities and unnaturalnesses which Deuteronomy condemns in such strong language?

This theological point of view affected in its turn the historical presumption. If a king were good, that is to say, particularly if he abolished the high places, the prostitutes and sodomites, if he magnified the worship of Yahaweh at Jerusalem, or in proportion as he did so, he must have been successful, and history is bent according to this presumption. This makes itself especially felt in the story of the early days. As Moses and Joshua were the God-chosen leaders who founded the religion of Israel, so, on the one hand, it is manifest that their religious observances must have been in acordance with the law of Deuteronomy, and, on the other hand, that in those early days Yahaweh must have been peculiarly present with His people, giving them great and wonderful victories. Accordingly the account of the conquest of Canaan was rewritten in the form in which we have it in our present Book of Joshua.

This Deuteronomic writing of history began presumably before the Exile, but it was in the Captivity especially that the earlier writings were collected and recast.[2] Naturally, from the fact that there was so large a priestly element among the exiles, the same process was applied to ritual and to laws. From the outset *torah* (law or instruction) had been especially a function of the priest. His it was to interpret the will of Yahaweh to the people, to give *torah* or interpretation of the law. From the Book of Ezekiel we

[1] i Kings xii, 28.

[2] Haupt and others perceive a Babylonian influence even in some of the technical legal terms, such as *qorban, torah, berith, kipper,* clean place, tent of meeting, breastplate of judgment, shewbread, as also in certain legal and ritual provisions, like the caste system of the priesthood. More certain is the influence of Babylonian recordism in the development of the scribal spirit among the Jews of the Captivity.

learn that during the Exile Ezekiel continued to interpret law to the people who came to ask him the will of Yahaweh,[1] and to a large extent his prophecy was an interpretation of divine will to the people through an application of the Law and of the prophecies of his predecessors to existing conditions.

He was not the only priest who devoted himself to the interpretation of the law of the past and its development to fit present needs. There were others doing the same thing. Sacrifice was impossible in the foreign land, but they looked forward to a time when the national life should be revived and, in consequence, the Temple reconstituted. It was necessary to prepare for that day by gathering together all the laws and usages of the Temple, or which had been handed down in connection with the Temple, as an interpretation of the *torah*, so that when the time of Yahaweh's great deliverance came the people should be ready, and especially the priests, to resume in a proper way the sacrificial and ritual life interrupted by the destruction of the Temple. And because sacrifice was impossible, in the very nature of the case, all those who clung to the national hope turned more earnestly toward those customs and usages which could be practiced on foreign soil, which did not require the Temple.

A new punctiliousness developed itself regarding the Sabbath,[2] stated fasts, especially on anniversaries connected with the fall of Jerusalem, distinctions of food, formal lustrations, prayer offered toward Jerusalem,[8] and, above all, circumcision, as a sign in the flesh which set them apart from the heathen people among whom their lot was cast.

The code of Deuteronomy had undertaken to enforce by law mono-Yahawism. Its object was to abolish the high-place sanctuaries throughout Judah and to confine the sacrificial worship of Yahaweh to the Temple at Jerusalem. While theoretically the Judæans were worshipers of Yahaweh, and the gods of the high places were Yahaweh, in practice the old Baal-worship had been simply transferred to Yahaweh, and the Yahaweh of any given

---

[1] Ezek. viii, 1; xiv, 1; xx, 1.   [8] Dan. vi, 10.
[2] Ottley, *The Religion of Israel*, p. 108.

shrine was nothing more than the old Baal of that shrine, worshiped under the name of Yahaweh. The Yahaweh of this place
was different from the Yahaweh of that place, and, while the name
of Yahaweh was used, there was a real polytheism, the worship
not of one Yahaweh, but of many Yahawehs. The motto of the
Deuteronomist, contained in the prophetic introduction to the code,
may be said to be this: "Hear, O Israel! Yahaweh, our god, is
one Yahaweh." [1] To bring about this unity of Yahaweh it was a
practical necessity to confine His worship to one shrine. So the
code opens with the enunciation of the law of the single sanctuary,
in which Yahaweh alone should be worshiped, and the prohibition
of the adoption of Canaanite rites and practices — that is, of the
rites and practices of the local sanctuaries thus legislated out of
existence — in the worship of that single sanctuary.[2]

Practical provisions were made, or attempted, to counteract the
general disturbing social effects of this reform. The priests of the
sanctuaries thus abolished were given the right to go to Jerusalem
and serve there if they would, and, to some extent, maintenance
and support were provided in their home towns and villages,
partly by the regulation that certain feasts might be held in the
towns instead of in Jerusalem, and partly by exhortations to the
people to care for the Levites as a matter of religious obligation
to Yahaweh.[3] Similarly, an attempt was made to offset in some
way the loss to the poor and needy from the abolition of the festivals of the local shrines and the local sacrifices of well-to-do citizens, which had been in the past among their means of livelihood.[4]
Provision was also made for the slaughter of animals for food
without sacrificial rites.[5] The judiciary was secularized by the appointment of judges in the various towns, the sanctuary at Jerusalem, however, retaining its position, in connection with the king,
as the court of last appeal, for the determination of all new and
difficult questions[6] requiring reference to God himself. The Deuteronomist was profoundly affected by the Prophets, and the whole

---

1 Deut. vi, 4.
2 Deut. xii.
3 Deut. xii, 12, 19; xiv, 27, 29; xxvi, 11.
4 Deut. xiv, 29; xvi, 11, 14.
5 Deut. xii, 15, 20.
6 Deut. xvi, 18; xvii, 9 ff.

book is shot through with prophetic exhortation. But especially do the appended blessings and curses [1] and the introductory exhortation [2] connect the whole work with the prophetic teaching of the past, which promised Yahaweh's blessing for obedience to His law, in the shape of material prosperity, and denounced calamity upon the nation for violation of that law. Deuteronomy further evinces its prophetic ancestry by the emphasis which it lays not only on the one Yahaweh, and the necessity of serving Him and Him only at one place, free from all the abominations of the peoples about, but also on the moral nature of Yahaweh, as a god of love, requiring loving-kindness in the 'relation of man to man. This relation of brotherly kindness, it is true, is to a considerable extent limited to the relations of the Israelites to one another, and indeed it would seem at first sight as though the relation of the Israelite to the neighboring nations was one of barbarous and extreme cruelty. It must be remembered, however, that the nations which Israel was ordered to blot out were at the time of the composition of Deuteronomy practically no longer in existence. Hence these cruel prescriptions were in fact quite otiose, a mere survival of ancient history copied out of older documents or handed down by inherited tradition.[3] There are in the Deuteronomic code a few laws which appear nowhere else, such as the law of levirate marriage.[4] The marriage of a man, as proxy for his deceased brother, to the latter's childless widow to raise up issue for him, was intended to prevent the extermination of the family, and thus preserve, if we may so express it, the Israelite hope of immortality in and through the family.

In general, however, the laws of the Deuteronomic code are the same which appear in JE, modified somewhat by the growth of a century or thereabouts, and permeated with a new or at least much more highly developed ideal of loving-kindness. The body

---

[1] Deut. xxviii.   [2] Deut. v–xi.   [3] Deut. vii, 1 ff.; xxv, 17 ff.

[4] Deut. xxv. While not appearing in any other code, this was evidently an ancient use in Israel. Cf. Gen. xxxviii, also the Book of Ruth. The principle involved in the practice was not uncommon, and similar provisions are found among various ancient or primitive peoples. Probably the old Indian use, as represented in the Laws of Manu, was most nearly like the Hebrew.

of these laws may be said to be derived from the old code of
Israel as we have it preserved in Exodus xxi ff. The doctrine of
loving-kindness which pervades the Deuteronomic volume may
also be traced to Israelite sources, being especially referable to the
influence of the prophet Hosea, with his doctrine of the love of
God toward Israel and the loving personal relation of God and
Israel. In other regards also the Deuteronomic code shows, as
already pointed out, a connection with Israel rather than Judah.
But there is another element in Deuteronomy, which connects it
with the so-called Holiness laws.[1] Deuteronomy lays great stress
on the holiness of the Israelites. They are children of Yahaweh,
who may not connect themselves with other gods and who must
offer even their tithes in the one place set apart to Him. They
may not cut themselves, they may not eat " any abominable thing,"
nor " anything that dieth of itself," as do the worshipers of other
deities.[2] There must be a physical and a moral cleanness or holiness about them, by which they are, and are to be, set apart from
all other peoples as the peculiar people of Yahaweh, who is a
jealous God.

These Holiness laws were apparently derived from the *torah*
of the Jerusalem Temple, and the relation of Deuteronomy to
the Holiness laws is due especially to its connection with that
Temple.[3] To what extent those laws had been committed to writing before the Exile, to what extent they existed in the form of
decalogues, handed down by word of mouth among the priests of
the Temple, as part of the traditional *torah*, it is difficult to say.
In outward form the laws of the Holiness Code are distinctly more
primitive than those of Deuteronomy. They are, to a considerable
extent, in the pentad and decalogue form of the earlier legislation,

---

[1] Lev. xvii–xxvi.   [2] Deut. xiv.

[3] As already suggested, it would seem as though the original Deuteronomy were
the code of, or founded on the code of, the great sanctuary at Shechem. Like other
writings of the northern kingdom, it was carried to Judah by refugees or emigrants
toward the close of the eighth century, the same men who brought the other writings
of Israel, including Hosea. It was worked over by the little prophetic-priestly group
connected in Isaiah's time and later with the Yahaweh shrine of the Jerusalem Temple,
accepted by them as a work of Moses, and was finally given to Josiah as a work of
Moses in 621.

showing in general an oral origin and use, the pentad or decalogue form serving largely mnemonic purposes, and at the same time investing the content with a certain sanctity, owing to its antiquity. Accordingly the decalogue form became an evidence of the sanctity of the content.[1]

Some of the laws in the Holiness Code are a *torah*, cast in the form of decalogues and pentads, on the original Decalogue of the Ark.[2] The Holiness laws covered ordinary relations of life, administration of justice, the obligations of honesty, and the like, but more particularly are they concerned with those things which touch the Israelite in his relation to the holiness of Yahaweh. Much stress is laid upon the matter of the sexual relations, because of the purity or holiness questions there involved. It is here that we find the codes of forbidden degrees for marriage.[3] Emphatically the object of the laws in the Holiness Code is to establish the holiness of the people in relation to Yahaweh, and to one another as a part of that relation. Ethically they reach a high standard, but a standard which is primarily a standard for Israelites: " Thou shalt love thy neighbor as thyself,"[4] the neighbor being the fellow worshiper of Yahaweh; albeit, a similar relation was enjoined toward the settler permitted to sojourn among them, a provision of Deuteronomic type.[5]

In the form in which these laws have come down to us we have numerous duplicates,[6] showing a considerable working over of the same traditions by different groups, with modifications, partly intentional, partly unintentional, due to the processes of time and of transmission.[7] The holiness sought for, while it has an ethical content, is in essence ritual, as might be expected in a code of such origin.

This Holiness Code in the main was contemporary with, and somewhat older than, Ezekiel. He evidently was familiar, as a

---

[1] Cf. Paton, " The Original Form of Leviticus xvii–xix," *J. B. L.*, 1897.
[2] Lev. xix. [3] Lev. xviii, xx. [4] Lev. xix, 18. [5] Lev. xix, 34.
[6] Cf., for instance, chaps. xviii and xx.
[7] The codes of other shrines, kindred to the *torah* of the Jerusalem Temple, may be represented in these duplicates. The scribes of the exile sought to collect and collate all that had come down of law and ritual from the preëxilian period.

Jerusalem priest, with the Holiness *torah*, the statutes and judgments of the Jerusalem Temple. He makes use continually of laws which, both in content and form, are identical with those of the Holiness Code. Peculiarities of phraseology, found nowhere else, occur in Ezekiel and in that code. Ezekiel, however, was not a mere compiler of ancient laws, as were the collectors of this code. He was a prophet as well as a priest; and accordingly he presents certain developments of his own which constitute a very radical variation from the laws and usages of the Jerusalem Temple. Sometimes these are in the direction of an increased holiness, of a careful separation from outside profane things, like the exclusion of non-Israelites, slaves given by kings and princes, from service in the Temple;[1] the removal of the palace from the Temple to avoid pollution by the tombs of the dead, or the entrance into the sacred precincts of those not of priestly caste.[2] He seems also to voice the sentiments of the Jerusalem priests with regard to their exclusiveness as a caste. In Deuteronomy all Levites were priests, and as such entitled to serve at the altar of Yahaweh in Jerusalem. In the Holiness Code we have the Aaronid priests, showing the old tradition of the sanctuary of the Ark, and of a priestly descent in the family of Aaron from the earliest days. Ezekiel introduces the Zadokite priests, the descendants of Zadok, the chief or head priest of Solomon's Temple. His descendants only are to be allowed to serve as priests in the Temple. Levites not of Zadokite descent (whom Ezekiel designates by the word "Levites," the Zadokites being priests) are to take the place of the Temple slaves and servants,[3] whom Ezekiel would exclude from the sacred precincts as unholy, and are to perform the menial offices formerly intrusted to the latter, which, in Ezekiel's mind, from their relation to the Temple, are yet noble and holy services.

Here we are on the road of the peculiar development of the Captivity. The old laws of sacrifice were gathered, worked over, and codified by the priests and their descendants the Scribes in the Exile. The Jews in Babylonia, however conscious of their race and nation, how patriotically soever they dwelt on the history of the

[1] Ezek. xliv, 7 ff.   [2] Ezek. xlviii, 28.   [3] Ezek. xl, 46; xliv, 10 ff.

past or looked forward to the future, were now no longer a nation with political rights and duties, but an exclusively religious body or congregation, in which members of the priestly order were numerous out of all proportion, presumably, to the total. Israel formed a church rather than a nation, and consequently, almost insensibly to itself, it came to regard the worship of God as the chief duty of the Jewish community. The main concern was to guard against every form of impurity that might be an offense to Yahaweh, so as to prepare for the time when he should return to His Temple and they return to the Holy Land and the worship in the Temple. They could not return to the Holy Land until Yahaweh returned to His Temple.[1] On the Temple, therefore, their thoughts were centered.

According to the tradition of the Jerusalem Temple, connected particularly with the Ark, which had been its palladium from the outset, it was the descendant of the ancient worship of the wilderness, when the Ark was carried from place to place. Tradition had doubtless already dealt to some extent with those earlier conditions, magnifying and glorifying them. This tradition the priests of the Captivity took up and developed still further. Ezekiel had drawn an ideal picture of the Temple that was to be the center of the whole land, laid out with mathematical accuracy, as though it were on the flat plains of Babylonia. Others, turning their thoughts backward to what had been in the ideal days of early Israel, elaborated an equally artificial camp, transforming the simple Tent of Meeting of the olden time to a tabernacle as wonderful and impossible as Ezekiel's Temple of the future.[2] It was in both cases the glorification of the Temple as the dwelling-place of the Almighty, in the one case in the wonderful future, in the other in the wonderful past. There was a very strong element of religious " medievalism " in this new development.

Ezekiel had dreamed, on the basis of his priestly training and experience, of the new Temple that was to be ; but, from the point of view of the ordinary priest, the Temple that was to be must be a reproduction of the Temple that had been, for that was the ideal.

[1] Ezek. xliii.   [2] Ex. xxv ff.; xxxvi ff.

Just as in the legal codes the effort had been to connect with the past, and above all with the great revealer of the past, Moses, so that all laws were given as from Moses, until finally the prophetic law-book of Deuteronomy was issued as spoken by Moses himself, so now the priestly reformers sought to ascertain what had been of old, and to restore the Temple and the Temple worship as in the time of Aaron, the traditional founder of the priesthood.[1] In part the customs, laws, and tradition of the ritual and the sacrifice, which they gathered, were ancient laws. Notably is this the case with the first few chapters of the Book of Leviticus. Partly their work was novel, customs and traditions being modified, and new ritual and new laws developed on the basis of their own presuppositions of what must have been the conditions of the past. Little by little there grew up that great mass of priestly laws, regulations, and the like, which is known to-day as the Priestly Code.[2] By far the largest part of this code is devoted to the regulation of the cultus. Sacrifice was henceforth the appointed means by which Israel was to realize its special privileges, as a people admitted to communion with the Most High. Sacrifice had always been, the Prophets to the contrary notwithstanding, the special means by which the average Israelite sought to enter into communion with his God, to win the divine favor, to make propitiation for his sins. The Priestly Code sought, above all things, to regulate this sacrifice as the appointed means by which Israel was to realize its special privileges as a people admitted to communion with the Most High; but it no longer concerned itself principally with the free-will offerings of individuals or families, but with sacrifice as the solemn public service of a consecrated community. As the Temple was to be the center of the new national life, so henceforth the chief function of Israel, organized as a religious community, was to be sacrificial worship. For this reason the whole burnt offering, relatively rare in the older time, when sacrifice was a matter of the individual with his family, and formerly confined chiefly to the royal sacrifice at

---

[1] Ex. xxviii.

[2] Substantially the books of Exodus from chapter xxiv onward, Leviticus, and Numbers.

Jerusalem, was now made the principal act of daily worship by the congregation in the Temple. Every morning and every evening a spotless lamb was to be offered, around which, as a center, were grouped the prayers and praises of Israel.[1] The common sacrificial feast of the older time, where a portion of the victim was burned, a portion given to the priest, and the rest eaten by the worshiper with his family and friends, continues but loses its original importance. Piacular sacrifice has now become the distinct feature; not the feasting with God, but the making of an offering to God, as a propitiation. A sense of sin and guilt has been greatly developed. Ezekiel had emphasized the wickedness of the nation. The curses of Deuteronomy upon the land for its wickedness, repeated in the Holiness Code,[2] became in the Babylonian Exile an essential part of the thought of the exiles. They were intensely conscious of their wickedness as a nation and of the need of propitiating Yahaweh. Sin offerings and trespass offerings had always been offered. It was always possible that a man should in some unwitting manner commit a sin, first becoming conscious that he had done so because of the disease which befell him in consequence, and which was the evidence that he had committed sin. A special ritual and special offerings had been provided at an early time for this class of offenses.[3] These now assumed a new importance, and one that was bound to increase with the increase of emphasis upon ritual, upon laws of cleanness and uncleanness, and the like. Sin and guilt offerings became the especially characteristic feature of the new sacrificial system. These sacrifices were preceded by a verbal confession of guilt. The offender placed his hand on the head of the victim offered, as if to convey his personality to the creature which was to be offered for him as an atonement, to make a covering for his sin. The blood in this sacrifice was not simply to be poured out at the foot of the altar; it was sprinkled on the horns of the altar. The flesh was sacrosanct, not to be eaten. Such sin offerings might be offered for the individual or for the community, and the frequency with which such offerings were offered according to the ritual of the Priestly Code

[1] Num. xxviii. [2] Lev. xxvi. [3] Cf. Lev. iv ff.; Ps. vi.

was a kind of object lesson to Israel, awakening and deepening its consciousness of guilt.[1]

This ritual system culminated in a fast which we meet for the first time in this period, the great Day of Atonement,[2] observed on the tenth day of the seventh month, five days before the feast of Tabernacles, which summed up and interpreted the whole conception of sacrifices designed by divine appointment to gain for man access to God. The fundamental idea of the day was that the community as a whole, from the high priest downward, was defiled by sin and therefore rendered unholy, and that it needed some special and periodical purgation in order to restore it to its true position as the people of God.[3]

While according to the conception of the Priestly Code sacrifice was the chief means of cleansing the nation and the individual alike from guilt, sin, and uncleanness, in a minor degree rites of purification were to perform the same service. Accordingly we have a development of ceremonies of purification, since a man almost of necessity became impure through contact with the unholy or profane things which had been multiplied in the endeavor to secure the physical sanctity of the Israelite.

In the growth of the Priestly Code the old feasts underwent some degree of development, as was to be expected, and some modification of their meaning, to conform them to the new ideas of priestly legislators and codifiers. The Temple system also underwent modification in the line of the development of a hierarchy, and the increase of the perquisites and the dignities of the priests, especially of the higher orders. As this legislation was developed in Babylonia, free from the restraining influence of actual practice, it was naturally developed in certain directions in a theoretical manner quite impossible in practice. So, for instance, the old theory of

[1] Schürer, Div. i, Vol. I, 193 f. " In the form of a law given by God himself, the Jew was told what he had to do as a faithful servant of Jehovah, what festivals he should celebrate, what sacrifices he should offer, what tribute he should pay to the priests who conduct the services, and generally what religious ceremonies he should perform. Precision in the observance of all these prescribed rites was to be made henceforth the gauge and measure of piety."   [2] Lev. xxiii, 26 ff.

[3] While we meet this fast first in the Priestly Code, its ritual contains primitive features, evidence of a more ancient origin.

the Sabbath with its Sabbatical year was developed, with theoretical impracticability, into the year of Jubilee. After seven Sabbaths of years, there was to come a great Sabbath year, when the land should return to its original inhabitants, all sales be blotted out, and the like.[1]

As a natural result of the development of this priestly system, we find a new view of the history of Israel. Offenses against ceremonial laws take on a new importance, and, as the Temple becomes more ancient, so the priesthood and the ritual reach back into a greater antiquity. The peculiar rites and sacraments of the Jews are traced back to a pre-Israelitic period, or, as in the case of the Sabbath, to Creation itself. With the development of the legal sense, the Law assumes an essential importance as a thing existing for itself. Even God is subject to the Law which He has made; so, in creation, He must rest upon the Sabbath Day, because the Sabbath is eternally and fundamentally holy, as a part of the Law. As a result of this view the men of this legalistic school undertook a rewriting of history, and in the form in which the Law has come down to us it is embedded in or connected with such a rewritten history of Israel, extending from the creation of the world down to the building of the Temple.

One result of the movement which we have here noticed was the removal of God from immediate contact with Israel or with the world. Once He walked on earth, spoke with men, consumed the sacrifices, revealed His presence by various activities. Now He is spiritualized and transcendentalized. This difference of view is well expressed in the sacrificial system referred to above, with its greater recognition of the sinfulness of man and the holiness of God, and the removal of God farther and farther from contact with man. In connection with this we find the tendency to substitute for the old personal name *Yahaweh*, expressing the peculiar relation of God to Israel as His people, His children, and His beloved, the more formal and general names *Elohim* and *El*.[2] Similarly the old

---

[1] Lev. xxv.

[2] The Law does not actually make this substitution. In it *Elohim* is the ancient common name; *Yahaweh* is the special name revealed to Moses, the peculiar property of Israel, by the knowledge of which Israel is brought into a particular relation to God, and endued with a special power. Such a name may not be used lightly or commonly, else it and the power attached to it may become the property of all.

anthropomorphisms are banished. God is conceived of no longer
as showing himself in human form, or even as appearing through a
messenger or an angel, but as operating through a word, a breath,
a thought.[1] We have passed into the field of a pure and spiritual
monotheism. It has been noted that the practical theology of Deuteronomy was mono-Yahawism. The new law-book was more nearly
abreast of the highest prophetic teaching in its thorough monotheism,[2] albeit having lost much of that sweet touch of a personal
relation with God which belongs to the older teaching.

The development which we have here indicated was one that
took place gradually. It began with Ezekiel. It did not reach its
final goal until some two hundred years later. It was essentially an
outcome of the Babylonian Exile; not, however, the work of the
actual exiles carried captive from Jerusalem by Nebuchadrezzar.
It began among the priests of that captivity, who had served in the
Temple at Jerusalem; it was developed by the scribes of the theoretical Captivity which succeeded the restoration under Cyrus. It
was in a sense their compensation for their failure to take advantage
of that restoration. They could not or would not make the sacrifices
or undergo the hardships involved in the transfer of their domicile
from the rich and safe Babylonia to the poor and half barbarous
Judæa; they made amends by a painstaking application to, and development of, the theory of their religion. This theory their superior
education, their greater wealth, and their material support enabled
them to impress upon Judaism.

The Law was an outcome of the Captivity; but it could not
reach its completion, nor become effective as the religion of the
Jews, until it had been brought in contact with the Temple and
applied by the Jews of the Judæan homèland.

---

1 Ezekiel, while representing God as remote from direct contact with man, yet
cannot altogether avoid anthropomorphisms. With him also God manifests himself
through angels, merely one remove from anthropomorphism (similarly also 1 Kings
xxii). This is carried further in Zechariah and developed ultimately into an elaborate
angelology, which became part of the popular orthodoxy. This was both extra-legal
and post-legal. More in accordance with the legal doctrine is the development of
the Wisdom Literature, with its tendency toward the personification of properties
or attributes of God — Wisdom, Spirit, Glory, Shechinah, Word.

2 It differed from prophetism in the intense particularism which it connected with
that monotheism.

CHAPTER XXIV

THE NEW RELIGION

It is not to be supposed that there was no contact between the Jews of the Babylonian Captivity and the Jews of Jerusalem, and that each community developed in its own independent fashion. Even while the Temple lay in ruins we find mention of a pilgrimage to Jerusalem [1] from the neighboring Samaria. With the completion of the Temple such pilgrimages became more frequent.[2] The development of legalism in the Captivity tended to promote such pilgrimages.[3] Doubtless, also, there was a continual drifting of exiles to Jerusalem, both men who in maturer life went to spend their last days in the holy city of their faith, that they might be buried within sight of the walls of the Temple, and also younger men, influenced by zeal to abandon their homes and families and go and settle in the Holy Land; very much the same influences which lead pious Jews to-day, even though the Temple lies desolate, to migrate to Jerusalem. These immigrants brought with them the stricter views of Babylonian legalism.

From the Book of Nehemiah it would seem that during the century after the return the party of laxity was in control, a party which, if nominally accepting the Deuteronomic law as its code, interpreted it as permitting friendly relations, including marital intercourse, with the surrounding peoples. Indeed, this is what we might expect from the fact that the Jews of Palestine during this century were mainly the peasantry. The religion of Judah before the Exile, as we know it in the Book of Deuteronomy, had been the religion of Jerusalem. This, with its exclusivism and its worship at one sanctuary, had been imposed upon the country folk,

---

[1] Jer. xl, 1, 4 ff.   [2] Zech. vi, 9–15; vii, 1–7; viii, 18–23.
[3] Cf. Ps. cxx–cxxxiv. This Pilgrim Psalter is an evidence of the popularity and the organized character of these pilgrimages during the Persian period.

but had not yet become part of their life. More conservative than the city-dwellers, they clung more tenaciously to the older religious traditions, customs, and superstitions. Just as in the early Christian ages it was the country folk who clung to the older faith, so it was in Judah at the time of the Reformation. When Jerusalem was destroyed they had not yet caught up with the city. They were still largely adherents in practice of the pre-Deuteronomic religion, and with the destruction of Jerusalem, the incentive to progress removed, they stopped where they were, a long distance behind the religion of the Temple. That religion, and the power to progress still further, had alike been transported to Babylonia. The peasantry which remained behind was conservative in doctrine and extremely lax in use.

This party of laxity was strengthened also by a Samaritan element, the Samaritans and Jews constituting practically one community worshiping at the Temple in Jerusalem.[1] To what extent this party of laxity and liberal relations was in sympathy with the maintenance of the old order of popular semi-heathen religious customs, which, as appears from the prophetic writers of this period, still continued to exist among the people much as they had existed in the later days of the monarchy, is uncertain; at least the prophetic writers testify that those old customs still prevailed.[2]

It would appear further from the Book of Nehemiah that during the century referred to a strong party had been built up, probably as a result of the influence of Babylonian Judaism, favoring a more exclusive attitude, a stricter ritualism, and a more exact legalism.[3] The strength of this party was naturally in Jerusalem itself and

---

[1] Jer. xli ; Zech. vii.

[2] Is. lxv and lxvi refer to a variety of heathen practices as prevalent in Judæa. This, again, is what we might expect in view of the brief period intervening between the Reformation and the Captivity. There had not been time to root out the old cults. So in Jer. xlii–xliv we find the worship of the Queen of Heaven, suppressed in 621, breaking out with new vigor among the Jews who fled to Egypt after the destruction of Jerusalem in 586. Zechariah and Malachi, as well as Deutero-Isaiah, testify to the prevalence of witchcraft among the Jews of Palestine in their days.

[3] The conditions prevailing in Judæa were probably more orthodox than the conditions prevailing among the Jews in Egypt, as pictured by Jeremiah and revealed by the papyri discovered at Elephantine, but much less orthodox than the conditions required by the theories of the Babylonian legalists.

about the Temple, where the returned exiles centered. This party maintained the Ezekielian view of the superiority of the Jews of Babylonia, descendants of those aristocratic and priestly captives who had claimed in Ezekiel's time that they were the people. It was their boast that they had maintained the pure blood in Babylonia. Naturally they looked down with a certain degree of contempt and abhorrence on the Samaritans, whom they reckoned to be of mixed blood; Israelites, not Jews, to begin with, and furthermore crossed with all sorts of heathen peoples, so that even the blood of Israel was scarcely to be found among them. The essential element of the controversy between the two parties was for practical purposes exclusiveness, prohibition of intermarriage with the neighboring peoples, which involved also the question of the admission or the exclusion of the Samaritans as part of Israel.

The prophetic writers had certainly seemed to preach doctrines which would in practice mean the inclusion of the Samaritans, and in general during the first century succeeding the Exile the tendency had been toward the reëstablishment of those relations which had existed in the good old past, the union of Judah and Israel in one people. Not a prophet had raised his voice against the practical reunion which was taking place through intermarriage with the Samaritans, or even with the other peoples round about. The development of the strict legalistic party, with its exclusive attitude, tended to reawaken the old animosities of Israelite and Judæan and to cause cleavage along the old lines of jealousy and distrust between Judah and Joseph. On the part of the Samaritans there would seem to have lingered the old political suspicion of Jerusalem.[1] A strong Jerusalem meant a weakened Samaria; and the political was closely associated with the religious situation. In the past Samaria had found it necessary, in order to maintain its political supremacy, to establish places of worship which could rival Jerusalem. This necessity was certain, in any case, to make itself felt again; the more so if the Samaritans were discriminated against at Jerusalem.

[1] So the Samaritans appear to have opposed, and successfully, the attempt to rebuild the walls of Jerusalem (Ezra iv, 4–23), although offering in Darius' time help in the erection of the Temple, Ezra iv, 1–3.

While, however, this jealousy and distrust between Judah and Joseph had begun to make itself apparent before the time of Nehemiah, it did not become a matter of great practical moment from the religious side until his time. It is difficult to follow the history of the period succeeding the Restoration, or even of the adoption of the reforms recorded in the books of Ezra and Nehemiah. Those books, which are practically the only documents that we have for this period, date, in their present form, from a later time. They were incorporated in that great history of the Temple which we now know as the Book of Chronicles, composed about or a little before 300 B.C., and are under suspicion of containing much history made after the facts to support the theories of the Chronicler. They do, however, contain original documents of the first historical value, namely, the Memoirs of Nehemiah.[1] From these it appears that Jerusalem remained unfortified during the first century succeeding the Exile, such slight effort as was made to restore the walls having been frustrated by the jealous interference of the neighboring peoples, especially the Samaritans, who, with the approval and consent of the Persian authorities, broke the walls down after they were partly rebuilt.[2]

About a century after the return under Cyrus, 444 B.C., a Jew named Nehemiah held a high and well-paid position at the court of the Persian king, Artaxerxes I, at Susa.[3] Himself pious, and belonging to a pious family, he was strongly affected by the account brought by some returning pilgrims, his brother Hanani among them, of conditions in the sacred city.[4] To them and to him it

---

1 In general I have followed the conclusions of Batten (*Ezra and Nehemiah*, in the International Critical Commentary), and his analysis and arrangement of those books, as follows:

In time of Cyrus, Ezra i.
In time of Darius, Ezra ii, 70–iv, 3, iv, 24 b–vi, 18.
In time of Xerxes, Ezra iv, 4–6.
In time of Artaxerxes i, Ezra iv, 7–23 ; Neh. i, iv, vi–vii, 5, xi–xii, v, xiii, x.
In time of Artaxerxes ii, Ezra vii–x ; Neh. viii, 1–12, vi, 19–22, viii, 13–18.
Batten ascribes Neh. x to the time of Nehemiah. It is more usually ascribed to the time of Ezra.

2 Ezra iv, 23 ; Neh. i, 3.
3 Neh. i, 2 ; ii, 1. As cupbearer he is generally assumed to have been a eunuch. Cf. attitude of Deutero-Isaiah toward eunuchs, Is. lvi, 4.
4 Neh. i, 2–3.

appeared plain that any scheme of reform which would make the Temple what in their estimation it should be, could never be enforced so long as the walls of Jerusalem were in ruins.

With fear and trembling, presuming upon his position as favorite of the king, Nehemiah begs for leave of absence to go to Jerusalem, where the sepulchers of his fathers lie waste,[1] with power to rebuild the walls. Permission is granted to him, and royal authority. He knows that the restoration of the walls will be opposed as before by the surrounding peoples, the Samaritans, headed by Sanballat of Beth Horon, their governor, the Ammonites, headed by Tobiah "the slave," and other neighbors, headed by Geshem "the Arabian" — as also by the kinsfolk and friends of these men among the Jews themselves.[2] Hence it was secretly by night that he made his first inspection of the walls.[3] The other measures for the construction of the walls were similarly taken, in order to forestall, if possible, the organized opposition of Sanballat and the others.

The walls once established, Nehemiah took measures to secure a population for the city,[4] and to build up some sort of national spirit and some sense of civic responsibility. The bulk of the people were practically slaves to a small number of landholders and capitalists. Their lands had passed or were passing out of their hands, and their children had become slaves to satisfy the lust and the greed of a privileged class. Nehemiah partly persuaded, partly compelled a release of debts, a restitution of lands, a manumission of slaves, and a system of loans without interest to poor Jews.[5] In doing this he created, out of the practical necessities of the social-industrial conditions, new laws, which were later embodied in the Priestly Code.[6] The achievements of his first term as governor

---

[1] ii, 1–8.   [2] ii, 10, 19.   [3] ii, 12–16.   [4] Neh. xi.   [5] Neh. v.

[6] Both the laws of JE (Ex. xxi, 2–6) and of Deuteronomy (xv, 12–18) permitted enslaving of Hebrews; Lev. xxv, 39–41, provides that the Hebrew may never be a slave, but only temporarily held as a servant, and treated and regarded as a hired man. So the provision of the Priestly Code (Lev. xxv, 35–37) for loans without interest differs from the provisions of the earlier codes regarding the taking of interest (Ex. xxii, 25 ; Deut. xxiii, 19–20), the provision of the Priestly Code representing the actual practice introduced by Nehemiah (cf. Kent, *A History of the Jewish People*, pp. 184 f.). It seems to me that this whole chapter (Lev. xxv) bears evidence of the influence of Nehemiah's practical experience on the makers of the Priestly Code.

seem to have been essentially political and economic, the establishment of a real city, fortified, self-dependent, endued with a sense of civic brotherhood. On his departure his brother Hanani became governor in his stead. Then we hear a calamitous tale. The Samaritans and Ammonites, who had been shut out politically by the walls, locate themselves in the city, and even in the Temple itself through their marital and other relations with the priests, including the ruling hierarchy.[1] It had been expected that when once the walls were completed the Temple would be the center of life, well and freely served by all, its special servitors, the priests and Levites, dwelling in and about its courts, held in honor and abundantly provided with all things needful for themselves and for their office. In fact its service was neglected, and its half-starved ministers had been compelled to abandon Jerusalem and seek a living as farm laborers.[2] It seemed as though all Nehemiah's work would go for nothing unless the principles of the exclusive party could be put in practice. Nehemiah obtained permission to return, and reappointment as governor. His second administration of the office was marked by a practical enforcement of the principles of the exclusive Babylonian party. He drove out of the Temple precincts all foreigners, and expelled, at least from ministry in the Temple, all who had married foreign wives, or compelled them to put away their wives.[3] He enforced the Sabbath laws.[4] He brought back the Levites, making proper provision for them and for the Temple services in general, and levying a new tax for the purpose.[5]

It would appear from the account which has come down to us (Neh. x, 28–39) that Nehemiah enforced his reforms by the exaction of an oath and "a curse." The reforms were seven in number, the first three being provisions of exclusivism : abstention from

1 Neh. vi, 17–19; xiii, 4–9, 28.

2 Neh. xiii, 10.

3 Neh. xiii, 23–30; x, 28–30. This is in accordance with the instruction of Deuteronomy vii, but the citation in Nehemiah is of a different passage, not involving the real principle of Nehemiah's action, which seems to be regarded as something new. Cf. further Neh. xiii, 1–3; Deut. xxiii, 3–5; Neh. xiii, 26 f. The reason for this exclusiveness indicated in the latter passages is clearly brought out in Mal. ii, 11; and in general Malachi is an admirable supplement and commentary to Nehemiah.

4 Neh. xiii, 15–21; x, 31.   5 Neh. xiii, 11–13, 30–31; x, 32–39.

intermarriage with the heathen, and from all buying and selling on the Sabbath, and observance of the sabbatical year. The remaining four concerned the service of the Temple: payment of a poll tax; provision of wood for the sacrifices; bringing the firstlings to the Temple; delivering the tithes to the Levites. The first three are described elsewhere in the narrative, and are revivals of Deuteronomic laws, not enforced. Of the remainder, three, the poll tax, the firstlings, and the tithes (also called for by Malachi), are partly old and partly new, and all three appear later in a more developed form in the Priestly Code, for the adoption of which Nehemiah's reforms in point of fact prepared the way.[1]

In the reëstablishment of the city Nehemiah seems to have had, on the whole, the hearty support of the men of Jerusalem itself — especially of the priests and those connected with the service of the Temple — as well as of the neighboring villages. In relation to the abolition of mixed marriages and the enforcement of the Sabbath laws his party was either in general in the minority, or at least opposed by a very strong influence, well intrenched among the privileged classes and, at the other extreme, among the peasantry; so that what he accomplished was accomplished chiefly by his own energy and decision, supported by the authority of the Persian government behind him.

Nehemiah's memoirs give us a very naïve and, on the whole, pleasing picture of his character. Full of zeal, he is also full of the spirit of loving-kindness and of service toward his fellow countrymen. Materially he makes no profit for himself, but gives bountifully of his means, setting an example of generosity and good will. Although a great man, he is ready to work with his own hands

---

[1] The provision of wood in Nehemiah's reforms is referred to as prescribed "in the Law" (x, 34). It is not in the Priestly Code, however, and its only other authority is Nehemiah's order, contained in Neh. xiii, 31. Tithing of the ground is prescribed in Deut. xiv, 22–29, but not of the herd and flock. The latter is provided for in the later developments of the Priestly Code (Lev. xxvii, 30–33). The poll tax of a third of a shekel for the support of the Temple is developed to half a shekel in the Priestly Code (Ex. xxx, 11–16; xxviii, 26). Such development seems to show that these reforms belong to Nehemiah, not Ezra; on the other hand, the continual references to the Law in this passage indicate a later revision in the spirit of Ezra, or even of the Chronicler.

among the people, conscious, above all, that he and they are Jews and hence brothers of one blood, servants of one God. He is full of confidence that in proportion to the good that he does will be his reward, and he does not hesitate to lay his good deeds before God, from whom he expects that reward. Indeed, his very belief in such rewards must have had an inspiring effect upon the people with whom he worked, filling them with the same belief, which we may say was now a dogma of the Jewish faith, that faithful service to their God would be rewarded by material blessing.

In his two terms as governor, commencing in 444 B.C. and covering a period of twenty years more or less, Nehemiah rebuilt the walls of Jerusalem and made it a city, reformed social-industrial conditions, and enforced the Deuteronomic Code, with certain additions, as the law of the land ; which meant exclusive worship in the Temple at Jerusalem, strict observance of the Sabbath and circumcision, and exclusiveness as regards neighboring peoples. In doing this he naturally alienated the Samaritans, whom he treated as foreigners, not Israelites. He compelled those Jews who had married foreign wives, or at least the priests, to put them away. One of these, Manasseh, the grandson of the High Priest, Eliashib, had married the daughter of Sanballat, governor of Samaria. He preferred rather to retain his relation with his wife and with Sanballat than to obey Nehemiah's orders, and hence was compelled to leave Jerusalem. Some others in the same plight seceded with him. The result was the establishment on Mount Gerizim, at Shechem, of a Samaritan sanctuary, supported by Sanballat.[1] It was a repetition

---

[1] Neh. xiii, 28 ; Jos. *Ant.* xi, 7–8. The Elephantine papyri have fixed the date of Sanballat, whose name is indissolubly connected with the Samaritan schism. Josephus' date is manifestly incorrect by about a century. It must be remembered, however, that this was a period for which Josephus had no chronological framework from Hebrew scriptures. All that happened between the time of Nehemiah and that of Judas Maccabæus is for this reason heaped together by him in one confused mass ; which does not mean that there are no facts in that mass, but merely that chronologically they are tangled together. Putting together what we learn from Nehemiah, the Elephantine papyri, and Josephus, it would seem that the schism began with the exclusion of Manasseh and Nehemiah, about 430 B.C., and the erection of a Samaritan shrine on Gerizim, which, basing upon the Book of Deuteronomy (xxvii), the Samaritans ultimately claimed to be the one and only temple ordered in the Law. This latter stage, however, was not reached until a century later, at the commencement of

of the old schism, political and religious, of the times of Rehoboam and Jeroboam. But not only did Nehemiah's high-church reformation cause the Samaritan schism, it also aroused earnest protest on the part of some among the higher thinkers, followers of the school, if we may so call it, of Deutero-Isaiah. We have evidence of this in a little book which has come down to us from about this period, the beautiful idyl of Ruth. Probably basing on some older tale, the author of this book tells the story of a Moabite ancestress of the great and pious king, David. Now Moabites, it must be remembered, were, according to the Deuteronomic law, absolutely excluded from the congregation.[1] On the other hand, in the histories of David which have come down to us his connection with Moab is clear.[2] He had found support and refuge there in the times of his distress and need, and evidently there were some relations, apparently of a family nature, between him and the Moabite country. The writer of Ruth tells of a Jewish family which, in time of distress in Israel, wandered over to Moab, a sort of thing which was continually happening in that day among the writer's own compatriots. There they found hospitality, and the sons of the family married Moabite wives. Her husband and her two sons dying, Naomi, the Hebrew mother, longs to return to her own country. Ruth, her Moabite daughter-in-law, with filial devotion, insists upon accompanying her. Her declaration of this devotion is among the most beautiful passages in Hebrew literature : " And Ruth said, Intreat me not to leave thee, and to return from following after thee : for whither thou goest, I will go ; and where thou lodgest, I will lodge : thy people shall be my people, and thy God my God : where thou diest, will I

the Greek period, when we find the schism complete, two temples, one at Jerusalem and one on Gerizim, each claiming to be the sole and only temple, ordained of God ; and Jew and Samaritan facing one another in bitter and irreconcilable schism. The Jewish text of the chapter above referred to, it should be added, names Ebal as the place for the erection of the altar of the law (v. 4). The Samaritan names Gerizim. That the latter is correct the context of both texts proves, especially vv. 11–13, where Gerizim is named in both as the mountain of the blessing and Ebal as the mountain of the curse. The change of name in the Jewish text is a testimony to the bitterness that developed between the two sects, and of the methods to which each was ready to resort to prove its claims. [1] Deut. xxiii, 3. [2] 1 Sam. xxii, 3, 4.

die, and there will I be buried: the Lord do so to me, and more also, if aught but death part thee and me." [1]

Ruth proves herself by her deeds a devoted daughter-in-law of Naomi, and through her obedience and filial devotion it falls out that she becomes the wife of a devout and honorable son of Israel, and the ancestor of David and his royal house.

The object of the writer is to show how a Moabitish woman, by marriage with an Israelite, may become a true worshiper of Yahaweh, the God of Israel, and how Israel may gain strength by winning the adherence of members of the surrounding peoples, and thus increase the number of the servants of Yahaweh. The character of Ruth is beautifully drawn throughout, and the whole constitutes a sweet picture of simple conditions of godliness and piety, giving us a most attractive idea of the religion of Jews of this school of thought, and presenting a very favorable view, on the whole, of the moral life of the Jewish community of that period. The beauty and piety of the book are so manifest that, in spite of the fact that the view of the author and his school did not prevail, the book itself became a favorite and was ultimately incorporated in the canon of sacred literature. [2]

The books of Ezra and Nehemiah, as we now have them, give the record of a second and further reformation connected with the name of Ezra, but so confused is that record that some modern scholars have denied that Ezra was a real person, regarding him as a mere personification of the scribal schools, or a shadowy personality brought to the front by later writers to represent the doctrines and achievements of those schools. [3] A slight rearrangement of the book, placing the Ezra portions after those dealing with the reforms of Nehemiah, seems to bring order out of this confusion, as already noted. The reforms connected with Ezra's name belong not to Nehemiah's time or to the period of the first Artaxerxes, but to the time of the second Artaxerxes, half a century after Nehemiah. It was Nehemiah's reforms, his restoration of the walls, the secure political situation given to Jerusalem thereby, and the

[1] Ruth i, 16-17.   [3] Cf. Torrey, Ezra Studies, 1910.
[2] Its supposed relation to David was of course also influential in this.

reëstablishment as the law of the land of the Deuteronomic code, which rendered possible the further and fuller reforms of Ezra and the adoption of the great law-book, which included not only Deuteronomy and the earlier codes but also all the mass of legal literature which had been developed in Babylonia and which is contained in the present Pentateuch.

In its essential features the story of Ezra is true. As a result of Nehemiah's work the legalistic party secured the control. It was continually strengthened by new migrations from Babylonia. The wealth of these pilgrims, their aristocracy, and their culture, naturally made them first the leaders and then the people. The very fact that they claimed and practiced a greater strictness of law also had its influence. As the idea of Jewish exclusiveness became more prevalent, good Jews, especially priests, sought evidence to prove that they were not of mixed blood, that is, mixed with the natives of the land. The best evidence of pure Jewish race was descent from Babylonian exiles, and pretty soon we find the whole of Palestinian Judaism claiming to be descended from the Babylonian exiles and giving its genealogies accordingly: hence the lists which appear in Ezra and Nehemiah and which are developed much further in the Book of Chronicles. At last it came to pass that all were descendants of the Captivity, and it was believed that Palestine was made *tabula rasa* after the destruction of Jerusalem, and repeopled at the close of the Exile by Jews returned from Babylonia. This is the theory of the Chronicler, into which he has sought to fit the records of the activities of Ezra and Nehemiah.

A careful sifting of these records seems to show that the bulk of the Jewish population, especially of the villages, was left in the land at the time of Nebuchadrezzar's two deportations. These, the *Am ha-Arez*, or people of the land, were the kernel of the later Jewish congregation and state. But while they constituted the bulk of the Jewish population, those left in Palestine were poor, uncultured, and lacking leadership; and hence in danger of losing their racial and religious integrity. Those who returned with Sheshbazzar and Zerubbabel in the days of Cyrus and Darius, while relatively few in number, furnished the leaders who were needed to rebuild the Temple and awake the national-religious consciousness. They failed, it is true, in their attempt to restore the city, but they did prepare the way for Nehemiah's later work. The Temple, rebuilt in 520, became the center of Jewish aspiration for both Palestine and Babylonia, and the goal of pilgrimages from the latter region. The great bulk of the Jews remaining in Babylonia satisfied their piety by directing not their steps but their thoughts, their studies, and their alms to the Temple and its holy land, becoming in the process themselves continually more Jewish. Some doubtless migrated to Palestine from time to time, but, eighty years after the restoration of the Temple, Jerusalem was still a village and the bulk of the inhabitants of the land were still the poor and stunted country folk, descendants of the old Jewish peasantry. Nehemiah's achievements and influence brought about a change. He not only rebuilt and repeopled Jerusalem, he established a new attitude toward the Holy Land on the part of the Babylonian Jews. Among those fired with zeal to imitate his service was Ezra, a priest and scribe. In the reign of Artaxerxes II,[1] sometime about or after 380 B.C., he gathered a party of others like-minded and like-stationed with himself to go, with royal permission, to Jerusalem to carry thither and put in practice the true law worked out in Babylonia. What Nehemiah had done literally for the Temple and its holy place, in building a wall about it, Ezra planned to do mentally and spiritually. The details of his achievements it is difficult to follow. That he secured the enforcement of the new Babylonian priestly code of laws;[2] that there was under his lead some formal adoption of the law-book by the people, and something of the nature of a canonization of that part of the great historical work in which the Law was contained, namely the Pentateuch, seems clear. From this time onward the Pentateuch became the Bible of the Jew. But while this is true, the account of the ceremony of the adoption of the Law by the congregation, as recorded in the Book of Nehemiah,[3] can certainly not be accepted as history. It is in the last degree improbable, moreover, that the new law was from the outset carried out in the extreme manner recorded in the Book of Ezra. Ezra

---

[1] Ezra vii, viii.   [2] Ezra ix, x.   [3] Neh. viii.

and Nehemiah as historical documents recounting this reform stand toward it in very much the same position that our present Book of Joshua stands toward the actual facts of the conquest of Canaan. As there that which was spread out over centuries is recorded as occurring in a lifetime, so here the final results of Ezra's reformation are related as its immediate accomplishment.

But, if the Law did not achieve its full enforcement at once, and if Ezra did not for many generations come to his own as the second lawgiver who imposed upon the Jews the Law, it seems plain that this was his achievement; and this is the sum and substance of the record of his work contained in our books of Ezra and Nehemiah.

The Law thus imposed was something more than the Priestly Code, the development of which has already been described. That code was embodied in an historical work, commencing with Creation, and ending with the conquest of Canaan : the Hexateuch, that is, the books of Genesis, Exodus, Leviticus, Numbers, Deuteronomy, and Joshua. That work contained in itself not only the Priestly Code, but also a great mass of other legislation, the Decalogue, the early Judæan and Israelite codes of J and E, Deuteronomy, and the Holiness Laws. These were retained, with the exception of the last named, as separate codes, although to a certain extent worked over in the spirit of the Priestly Code. The object of the whole work was to preserve and present the entire religion of Moses. Whatever was supposed to have come from him, or to constitute a part of his religion, was here gathered together. The object of the new movement was to restore the ancient religion, given, as the scribes of Babylonia conceived, by Moses, as the law of the Holy Land, civil and religious ; essentially the latter, for the people in their conception constituted a congregation, dwelling in and around the Temple, as in the wilderness, in their imagination, the Israelites dwelt about the Tabernacle. It was a continuance and a development of that idea which found expression in King Josiah's time in the promulgation of Deuteronomy as the book of the religion of Moses. It was the same call back to Moses, but the book of the religion of Moses included now much more than then. The religion of Moses was now complete, and the intention of the movement of which Ezra was the expression and embodiment was to impose that religion as a finality upon Israel. The new religion was much more therefore than the adoption of the Priestly Code, it was the canonization of the work in which had been embodied the story of God's preparation of the world for the revelation, to the people whom He had prepared, of the complete and perfect religion by the hand of Moses. It was in the conception of the scribes a re-conquest of the Holy Land; but, as that which was actually essential in their conception was the religion of Moses, so in practice what followed his death, namely the book of Joshua, describing the conquest of Canaan, finally dropped out, and only the Pentateuch was canonized. This Jew and Samaritan alike adopted, and it became the law and the Bible of the temple at Gerizim, as of that at Jerusalem, which might not be changed or altered, but only interpreted, its very words and letters being sacred. This was the achievement of Ezra, which began with his promulgation of the Law, somewhere about 380 B.C., and ended in the final canonization of the Pentateuch within a period probably of about half a century. No wonder that a later age, realizing the importance of this new movement, accounted Ezra a second Moses, who had, through divine revelation, rewritten the ancient writings of Moses which had been lost. In their belief he had restored the ancient religion of Moses; in reality he had founded a new religion.

CHAPTER XXV

THE TEMPLE

In the earlier times it was Israel and not Judah which was the land of religious as well as civil progress, the land of prophets and poets, of publicists and sages. Only with the destruction of Samaria and the transference of its thought and its thinkers to Judah does the religious development of the latter really begin. In the post-exilic period precisely the opposite was the case. The religion of Samaria was merely a devitalized transplant from the religion of Jerusalem. The priesthood of Gerizim was an offshoot of the least progressive element of the Jerusalem priesthood, and its high priest an expelled member of the high-priestly family of the Temple at Jerusalem, whose connections were not with the cultured element of the Jewish people, that element which maintained relations with the Jews of Babylonia, but with the *Am ha-Arez*, the people of the land, and the neighboring Samaritans and Ammonites.

The Samaritan priesthood, like the Jewish, accepted the Pentateuch. It became the law of their religion, but absolutely unchangeable, so that to this day its text is preserved in the characters in which it was then written. Conservative as the Jewish attitude came to be with regard to the five books of the Law, anxious as they were to preserve the exact text, they still permitted a complete change of character at a later date, when the present square letters were substituted for the old form of script. The only change in the outer form of the Samaritan text which has taken place, on the other hand, is the gradual and unconscious corruption which has differentiated the Samaritan from the old Phœnician alphabet. Their treatment of the script is characteristic of their treatment of the Law in general. Moreover, the Samaritans limited themselves to the Pentateuch, as the Hebrews did not. Before the adoption of the five books of Moses as the Law, the Book of Joshua had been connected with those books to constitute a Hexateuch. Accordingly, Joshua became known to the Samaritans. It was received and held in honor among them, and in their hands was developed and expanded in a curious manner. Beyond that there was no literary activity, and there was no spiritual progress. They stopped short, for all practical purposes, with the adoption of the Pentateuch as law and Bible. Had they maintained relations with the Jews, probably the spiritual activities of the latter would have influenced the Samaritans; but, as pointed out in the preceding chapter, some time at or about the commencement of the Greek conquest those unfriendly relations which had existed from the outset reached such a point of extreme animosity as to preclude any possibility of the religious and literary developments of Jewry affecting Samaria. The Samaritans adopted from the Jews at the time of Ezra a religion complete for all practical purposes. Where they stood at that point they stand to-day. We may exclude them from further consideration in our study of the religion of the Hebrews.

The Jews, on the other hand, while they adopted the five books of Moses as a Bible, so sacred that it might not be added to or subtracted from, did not cease development at that point. Politically, those were times of quietude; but they were not, from the religious, intellectual, and literary standpoint, times of stagnation.

From the time of Nehemiah to the time of Antiochus Epiphanes, a period of over two hundred years, we possess no external history of the Jews, and secular history lends little assistance in determining the course of events. During the first half of that period, under Persian rule, the Jews were a part of what was on the whole, in relation certainly to what had gone before, a well-ordered and well-organized empire. From the time of Darius onward the policy of that empire was not the recognition, under Persian overlordship, of separate nationalities with their native princes as rulers, but the organization of the whole empire into provinces, governed by Persians, appointees of the crown, and a subdivision of those provinces into minor sections, also governed by Persian officials. While the religion of the empire was Zoroastrian and the Persian officials were worshipers of Ahura-Mazda, the various subject peoples were permitted to maintain their ancestral religions, the Persian government exercising a certain supervisory or regulative power in the appointment of officials, the erection of temples, the institution of new ritual, sacrifices, and the like.[1] Everywhere, also, the offering of sacrifices in behalf of the Persian authorities was compulsory. The result was that these various peoples became, under Persian rule, religious communities, very much like the so-called nations in Turkey to-day, whose heads were the heads of the congregation.

The head of the Jewish nation or congregation was, from the time of Darius onward, the High Priest, a functionary not known in the preëxilic age, which had recognized the king as the religious as well as the political head of the nation, the chief priest being merely a priest appointed by the king as head of the college of priests, if we may use such a term. Under the Persian empire the prince or national head was abolished, and this chief priest assumed an independent and therefore much more exalted position. His office also became hereditary; or at least when we begin to obtain reliable records we find the office hereditary, in the sense that it was confined to a certain family. Ezekiel recognized the prince in his scheme of laws but not the High Priest, and the prince appears in actual practice in the first years of the return, until the reorganization of the empire under Darius. The Priestly Code, on the other hand, conforms to the new order, and with the adoption of that code under Ezra the high priesthood became theory and doctrine as well as practice.

Not only do we now have a High Priest as the head of the community, but also, as a result of the exaltation of the Temple and of religion as constituting the entire sphere of the life of the people, there was developed a priestly aristocracy, centering about the High Priest, and constituting, as it were, his court.[2] A natural result of

---

[1] This is made clear by the Elephantine papyri.

[2] At the beginning of the post-exilic period we find the priests of the line of Zadok, that is of the old priesthood of the Jerusalem Temple, and the priests of the line of Ithamar, another branch of Aaron. Subordinate to these are the Levites, few

these conditions was a narrowing of the interests of the Palestinian Jew. In the nature of the case he could take no part in politics, and all that belongs to the life of the state. His sphere became more and more the sphere of religion only, so that even in literature that which belongs to what we call the secular side of life was gradually eliminated. Art there was none, nor interest in nature and its beauties for its own sake. Only to some extent, through their official position, did the High Priest and the priestly aristocracy maintain a certain relation with the outer world of politics ; the tendency of which, however, was not to broaden but to corrupt. The high priesthood offered the only opportunity for wealth and power, and inevitably it became a goal of ambition to worldly-minded priests.[1] The appointing power lay with the Persian government, and Persian rulers were susceptible to the arguments of money ; hence the intrigues of this period between aspirants to the office of High Priest, culminating in the murder in the Temple of a priestly rival by his own brother.[2] In general, so far as internal conditions were concerned the period of Persian rule was one of peace, the people remaining unmolested by foreign foes and having opportunity to pursue their own affairs, burdened only by the exactions and

in number, at least in comparison with the priests. Outside of these we have singers, porters, and other servers, including the *Nethinim*, or Temple slaves. By the close of our period these latter foreign elements have vanished entirely, perhaps in part done away with, but presumably in general amalgamated with the Levites, who in the Chronicler's picture have become much more numerous and important than before, and who now perform all the service of the Temple.

1 All Jews throughout the world paid a tribute to the Temple, so that great treasure was accumulated there, under the control of the priestly rulers. Individually, also, priests were members of a priestly caste, abundantly provided for financially under the Law. All meal, sin, and trespass offerings were theirs (Num. xviii, 9), with a part of every animal sacrificed (Lev. vii, 30–34) or killed for food (Deut. xviii, 3) ; to them belonged the first fruits (Deut. xxvi, 1 f.), together with the choice (*t'rumah* or " heave offering ") of the vintage, the harvest, and the oil (Num. xviii, 12), besides a tithe of the whole crop, paid to the Levites, of which the priests received a tenth (Num. xviii, 21–30). In addition the priests received from the baking of the grain into bread one loaf in each twenty-five (Num. xv, 17 f.), with the first born of all cattle, or a price for the same, and five shekels for each first-born son (Num. xv, 18 ff.) ; a share in the shearing (Deut. xv, 19) ; together with the special vows (Num. xviii, 14), and gifts of conscience (Num. v, 5–10). Cf. Bevan, *Jerusalem under the High Priests*, pp. 9–10.

2 Jos. *Ant.* xi, 7, 1.

impositions of their Persian rulers.[1] There were, however, some exceptions to this rule. In practice individual satraps sometimes made themselves almost independent sovereigns, and private wars were carried on between them or permitted in their provinces. We have incidentally in secular history a notice of one such independent satrap ruling over Syria. We have also a notice of a rebellion in that section and its severe repression by Artaxerxes III (Ochus); but to what extent this affected the Jewish community in Palestine we do not know.[2]

The conquest of Persia by Alexander and the establishment of Hellenism changed, to some extent, these conditions. Greek conquest meant, as no other conquest up to this time had meant, the diffusion of Greek methods and ideas of government, of social life, of art, of thought. In distinction from the nations and provinces of former dispensations, the unit in Greek political economy was the city, a body locally self-governing, and the city was of necessity equipped with certain social features which touched the life of every citizen — the market place, the gymnasium, the bath, the theater. All about the Judæan community sprang up Hellenistic cities, sometimes new creations, more often transformations of the older towns by the infusion of the new life. The cities of Phœnicia, Philistia, and Syria became, as we know from their monuments, Hellenistic communities, governed after the style of the Hellenic cities, provided with the same social-economic government, and imitating, as well as they knew how, Greek thought and Greek life.

In this process the ancient gods were translated into Greek divinities and the old religions Hellenized, which did not, of course,

---

[1] The Persian governor, Bagoses, punished them for seven years, according to Josephus, for the murder by the High Priest John of his brother Jaddua, referred to above ; but whether the punishment amounted to anything more than the defilement of the Temple by Bagoses' forcible entry and the exaction of an increased tribute is not clear from his account.

[2] Some scholars, including W. Robertson Smith, Cheyne, and Kent, have ascribed to this period especially Psalms lxxiv and lxxix, finding in them references to a capture and desecration or destruction of the Temple by Bagoses or Artaxerxes Ochus, and in other passages allusions to deportation. I think the Psalms named belong to the Maccabæan period, in their last revision, and that the other supposed allusions do not support this thesis. Certainly the general tenor of the literature of the period is placid, concerned with internal affairs, quite unlike the preëxilic literature, or even the literature of the Maccabæan period.

prevent a continuance of the old religious rites, beliefs, and customs among the common folk, and which did result, among the more cultured and wealthier classes, who were the Hellenizers, in the introduction of very much of the old religions into the new. Indeed, so far as thought and religion were concerned, it may be said that in Syria for the most part Hellenism was a veneer. As is almost inevitably the case in the superposition of one civilization upon another, the Orient adopted more of the vices than the virtues of Greece, combining the former also with many of its own. The result was a compound, morally repugnant to the higher ethical teaching of the Jews, from the influence of which in thought and religion the Jews in Palestine were largely protected, in the period covered in this chapter, by their moral antagonism. Such influence as Hellenism exerted upon them, as a stimulus to thought and as influencing the course of religious development, was indirect and relatively slight.

Politically the influence of the Hellenistic conquest was more immediate and direct. Perhaps to the influence of the Hellenic organization of city government we may attribute the formation of the council, composed of laymen as well as priests, which we find later, under the Greek name of Sanhedrin, standing by the side of the high priesthood to control the affairs of the people, secular as well as religious. As a city community, Jerusalem probably received a greater degree of autonomy in the administration of its own affairs, and inasmuch as through its religious relations to the dispersed Jews it was the racial religious center, the council which governed Jerusalem became the central religious synod of the whole Jewish world.

While on the whole the Greek period was one of relatively unmolested development, it was by no means so tranquil as the Persian period had been. After the death of Alexander and the division of his empire, Palestine became a football in the struggles between Syria and Egypt. During the central part of this period, from 290 to 220 B.C., it was in the possession of Egypt. At the beginning and the end it passed frequently from one to the other, being more often in possession of the Syrian than of the Egyptian rulers. Its own condition of absorption in its religious affairs and

general lack of interest in the political life about it, is finely illustrated in the way in which it was captured on a Sabbath day by
Ptolemy, the people remaining absolutely passive because it was
their holy Sabbath.[1] They asked only to be let alone, and the extent of their participation in the struggles of the two opposing
parties was in general that of a more favorable disposition toward
one side than the other, as either offered or seemed to offer more
hope of non-interference.

One result of the wars between Syria and Egypt was the deportation of large numbers of Jews, and the consequent development
of the Diaspora, or Dispersion, intensifying that commercial movement already so marked. In Egypt especially the Jews became
very numerous, and in Alexandria they constituted an important
part of the population, said to be at least one third of the total
population of the city. Upon the Jews in the Diaspora their Greek
surroundings exerted a powerful influence to be reflected back upon
Palestine. During our period, however, the Palestinian Jewish community remained agricultural as before, and in general pursued its
own course in religious development, practically uninfluenced by
Greek as it had been practically uninfluenced by Persian thought.

The general conditions of the Persian and Greek period are
reflected in the Wisdom literature and in a large number of the
Psalms. These evince, on the whole, a quiet and peaceful life.
There are outside foes and from time to time oppression at their
hands, but in general such oppression as there is comes from men of
their own nation, and their calamities are due to the forces of nature.
So, for example, the Prophet Joel, who belongs to this period, pro-
claims a fast and preaches the coming of the Day of Yahaweh,
not because Judæa is invaded by foreign foes, nor under the stimulus of world movements, but because of a plague of locusts. The
dangers of which Sirach complains (Ecclus. xli) are due to slanders
by one of his own people addressed to the king. Both Proverbs
and Ecclesiasticus concern themselves with what we may properly
call affairs of peace, the life of a small city community, " with its
commerce, its feasts, its gossip, its temptations to licentiousness,

---

[1] Jos. *Ant.* xi, 1.

its relaxation of family ties, its worship of money and its close relations with royalty." [1]

So far as the governing official class, the High Priest and his court, were concerned, the natural result of the conflicts between Syria and Egypt was to increase the possibilities of intrigue and corruption. It was in these circles also that toward the close of this period Hellenic influences began to make themselves felt. But while the Temple was the center of intrigue and corruption it was also the center of the life of the nation. The extension of Jewish relations through the Diaspora increased the wealth and the importance of the Temple. It was the center of Jewry, and because Jewry was the center of the world, therefore the Temple was the center of the world, physically as well as spiritually and intellectually. This was in a sense a development of the ideas of the later kingdom ; but the new conception of the Temple went much further than the preëxilic conception set forth in Deuteronomy. It was the Jews of Babylonia especially who had dreamed of the Temple as the nation's center, and who had crystallized that dream in the Law ; and because they had dreamed this dream and striven for this goal for over a century, the leadership of religious thought and religious activity had belonged to them. But with the realization of their dream, first in the rebuilding and restoration of the city of Jerusalem by Nehemiah, and finally in the adoption of the Law under Ezra and the resulting canonization of the Pentateuch, that leadership passed from Babylonia to Palestine. The Jews of Babylonia were more wealthy, more cultured, presumably, than those of Palestine. The study of the law continued to be pursued by them, and a large part of the later Talmud was a development of Babylonian Judaism. From the time of Ezra onward, however, it is not the Babylonian Jews who lead in religious thought and who constitute the Jewish nation, but rather the Jews of Palestine, because the heart of the nation was the Temple. That was the home of the Jews, the center of their life.

To the Jews outside of Palestine the Temple was the goal of pilgrimage. To visit it was virtue, and it was the desire of each

[1] Toy, *Proverbs*, p. xviii.

pious Israelite's heart, in whatever place he dwelt, to visit Jerusalem before his death. We have in Psalms cxx–cxxxiv a collection of pilgrim hymns, composed for the most part in Babylonia, which show us the part the Temple played in the life of the Jews in the Dispersion. But it is the Book of Chronicles, including Ezra and Nehemiah, which most clearly sets forth the importance of the Temple. That work was a history of the world, written on the theory that the Temple is the central object of the universe, and consequently of all history. The earlier part of the history consists entirely of genealogies made out of the earlier books, the object of which is to set forth Israel's favored place among the nations, and that post-exilic Israel is the descendant of old Israel, not *Am ha-Arez* [1] like the Samaritans. It is of the greatest importance to prove that the whole Temple staff is of pure Jewish blood, and to do this it must be shown that they are descended from those who were carried captive into Babylonia. The writer himself evidently belongs to the Temple staff, and from his special interest in Temple music it would seem probable that he was one of the Temple musicians. [2] He is honestly convinced that the legislation of the Pentateuch was given by Moses, put in practice at Jerusalem — especially in its priestly part — by David and Solomon, and maintained by their pious successors. This thesis being correct, the history of Israel must conform therewith. Accordingly, he rewrote the history of the whole period covered by the books of Samuel and Kings from this standpoint. History begins with David, and David was a saint of God. His saintship is proved by his relation to the Temple. The same is true of Solomon. Whatever in the earlier works would contradict this is omitted. Of the kings after Solomon, all who honor the Law and its institutions are blessed. They are victorious in their wars, while those who violate the Law are punished by calamity and invasion. And so it goes on to the end.

---

[1] This name, first applied to the plain people, the peasantry, was gradually extended to cover the mixed and impure blood and even the surrounding heathen.

[2] Cf. 1 Chron. xv, 16–24; xvi, 8–36; v, 28; xiii, 8; xvi, 5; vi, 16–47; 2 Chron. v, 12; xxix, 25.

But not only this; it was impossible that such men as David and Solomon could have been kings of a petty kingdom, or that the people of the days when the Temple stood in honor could have been few and insignificant. So the numbers of the armies of David and Solomon are multiplied and multiplied again, and the same is the case with their wealth. This is the method pursued throughout the whole history, not with any intention of falsifying, but from a devout desire to expound the glory of God as manifested in and through His Temple. One cannot read the book without being convinced of the genuine piety and sincerity of the author. The work in its present form belongs to the Hellenic period, perhaps somewhere about 300 B.C. It is in a sense a polemic, inspired by an anti-Hellenic spirit, the first of a long series of works written by pious Jews to convince, sometimes their own countrymen, sometimes foreigners also, of the greatness and might of their God, who has in the past so often shown His power to overthrow the greatest and most mighty peoples of the earth, and who can and will do so again. The value of the work is not historical, but religious, and in this field it possesses a high value. Not only does it reveal the belief of Israel, but it shows the high standard which religion had reached. There is now no possible question of polytheism. There is but one god over the whole earth, and that god is Israel's god; but while He is god of all the world, His relation may be said to be a relation only to Israel. Israel He loves; Israel He has chosen. All other peoples exist for Israel's sake. To them God has no other relation than that of using them or destroying them for Israel's sake. He and Israel are identified. And so it is that while He is the god of the whole universe, for whom heaven is too small, He yet dwells in the Temple in Jerusalem. It is for this reason that the Temple is the center of the world and of history.

The Chronicler's picture of the relation of God to Israel and of that which He requires from Israel is a very beautiful and a very lofty one.[1] That the Chronicler, in ascribing such importance to the Temple, was not speaking for himself alone, but represented

---

[1] Cf. David's instruction of Solomon, 1 Chron. xxviii, 9; and the latter's blessing or prayer before the congregation, 1 Chron. xxix, 10 f., especially verse 17. Cf. also the picture of God's omniscience in 2 Chron. xvi, 9.

the general view of the pious Jew of this period, is clear from a comparison of other writings of the time. One may open the Psalter almost at random and find a reference to the Temple, showing the part which it played in the life and thought of the people. " Out of Zion, the perfection of beauty, God shines forth."[1] " Blessed is the man " who is allowed to dwell in God's courts. It is the goodness of Yahaweh's house which brings satisfaction to His people.[2] Wisdom literature testifies to the same attitude; so to Sirach the most wonderful and beautiful thing, to which he devotes the better part of one whole chapter of his work (chap. l), is the Temple service, the center of the whole life of Israel. He depicts Simon the Just officiating in his robe of glory, with all the sons of Aaron about him, the Lord's offering in their hands, before all the congregation of Israel; and when the sons of Aaron shout and sound the trumpets, the people haste to fall down on the earth on their faces, to worship their Lord, the Almighty God most high, and to receive the blessing of the High Priest over the whole congregation of the children of Israel. For weal or woe everything centers in and about the Temple. The prophets of the period, like Joel, are full of the Temple and sacrifice and altar. Joel does not, like his predecessors of the preexilic period, rebuke the abominations connected with the Temple and the priests, but, assuming the sanctity and virtue of the Temple service and the Temple servitors, he summons the people to fast and to worship there.[3]

The sweetest and the highest development of the Temple religion was the Psalter, which belongs in its general content to this period. To be sure, its roots are ancient, the kernels of the earlier collections dating from the preëxilic period. On the other hand, it received its final revision in the Maccabæan period. The general tone of the Psalter reflects, however, the religion and the piety of the Jews of this period. As its Hebrew title *Tehillim*[4] indicates, it was the Temple hymnal, and attention has been called already to the prominence of the Temple in the Psalms. But the

---

[1] Ps. l, 2.   [2] Ps. lxv, 4.   [3] Joel ii, 15 ff.

[4] *Tehillim* is the plural of *tehillah*, the cry or song uttered at the killing of the sacrificial victim.

glory of the Psalms is that they unite in themselves various lines of thought and religious aspiration, representing in fact a catholic Judaism, in which the religion of the entire people found expression. The teaching of Deutero-Isaiah in regard to the Israelite sufferer is reflected in the solicitude for the meek, the lowly, the pure, the humble, for whom God cares.[1] In comparison with the world about, Israel is this meek, lowly, and poor one; but in Israel itself there is a contrast between the poor and righteous kernel and the rich and godless oppressors. The former are the beloved of God, the *Chasidim*, or saints. Of course the Law plays a great part in the Psalms, and the Psalter was even divided into five books to correspond with the five parts of the Law. The morality of the Psalms is, on the whole, the morality of the Law. They are orthodox in their view of righteousness as the fulfillment of the Law, as in their doctrine of the reward of righteousness and the punishment of sin. That which particularly impresses the student of the Psalms, however, is the wonderfully sweet picture which they give of the direct personal relation of the Jew to God, his confidence in God's loving-kindness toward him, God's care for him, God's willingness to help him and to forgive him his sins, and his consequent certainty of ultimate beatitude, whatever his present distress. So spiritual, so personal, and so catholic is the religion of the Psalter that at a later date this book became the hymnal of the Christian equally with the Jewish church. It is concededly the most beautiful collection of religious poetry ever composed.[2]

---

[1] Cf. Isaiah lvii, 15, and lxv, 2, with Ps. xxxiv, 18; li, 1 f.; cxlvii, 3.

[2] The first Book of Psalms, less the first two introductory Psalms (iii–xli), was in its essence the hymnal of the preëxilic Jerusalem Temple. The Psalter of the Sons of Korah (xlii–xlix) was similarly from the Temple of Dan (cf. Peters, in *Essays in Modern Theology*, 1911, "The Sons of Korah"). The Asaph Psalter (l, lxxiii–lxxxiii), was Josephite. During the exilic period these collections were sifted and worked over, like so much earlier literature, and to them was added *The Prayers of David, Son of Jesse* (li–lxxii), which show, like the Korahite and Asaphite collections, marks of Israelite descent or influence, especially in the use of Elohim instead of Yahaweh. This collection is a psalter of agony and struggle, Psalms li–lx constituting one great cry of pain and affliction, while the four succeeding psalms, although showing some relief, still represent a condition of national calamity. Toward the end of the collection, however, are a few (lxv–lxviii) joyful liturgical hymns, celebrating the deliverance from Babylonian Exile as a repetition of the deliverance from Egypt. Apparently as a collection *The Prayers of David* is exilic and early post-exilic.

These three Elohistic collections were revised to some extent by Yahawistic editors, and a small group of Yahawistic Psalms (lxxxiv–lxxxix) added in the early post-exilic period, as is shown for example by the use in lxxxix of the old Yahawistic document J and of Samuel, not of P or Chronicles. These collections, now forming the first three books of Psalms, constituted the Temple hymnal in the first century after the restoration of the Temple. To these were added in the period under consideration in this chapter Psalms xc–cxxxiv, divided by the time of the Chronicler into two books, constituting, with the preceding, five books corresponding to the five divisions of the Law. The new religion of the Law and the Temple shows itself more particularly in these latter Psalms (cf. for instance cxix, the Praise of the Law) ; but to some extent also earlier Psalms were modified under the new influence (cf. i, ix, and the second part of xix). In spite of the repeated reworkings a religious development may be traced in the books of the Psalter. In the first book, in general, sacrifice is assumed without question, the same attitude which appears in the introduction to the Book of Job, and the simple and joyful side of sacrifice is presented. In Books II and III we find the most vehement denunciations of sacrifice, and also the most anthropomorphic pictures of sacrifice, indicative of a period of change. The outcome was a certain mystical treatment and spiritualization of sacrifice, which reaches its full development in the latter books of the Psalter, where sacrifice is removed, as it were, from the everyday life of the people into an inner court, and where it has become the function of a holy priesthood. Aaron, or the priests, and the Levites, who had not been mentioned in the first three books, now appear continually as the leaders and representatives of the congregation for the sacrificial ceremonies. Similarly, the glorification of the Law meets us continually in the latter books, whereas in the earlier Psalter it occurs only in the late additions to which reference has been made. There is an advance in the spiritualizing of religion, and in the abolition of anthropomorphic and mythological references. In the earlier books, while Yahaweh or Elohim is recognized as the God of Israel, the true God and the great God, the Psalmist is never entirely able to rid himself of the idea that the other gods have an existence. The later books, on the other hand, are absolutely and completely monotheistic. It is in those books also that we find the exalted conception of creation, of God's relation to nature, and of His omniscience. They represent the attitude of the Priestly Code in the Hexateuch, as over against the conceptions of the Yahawistic and Elohistic writers. (Cf., for instance, Psalms civ and cxxxix with xviii, xxix, lxxvii, 17–30 ; lxxx, 2–4.) The treatment of the future life in the Psalter shows a similar development, or perhaps in this case a retrogression, owing to that attitude of the Temple theocracy which was in time to become Sadduceeism. But while the Psalter was the hymnal of the Temple and while in general it reflects the development of the Temple religion and the theology of that religion, the Psalms were also in use in the synagogues, and to that use probably is to be attributed the personal character which they assumed ; for they were still in flux, and while in flux they were capable of being very considerably modified by such use. The Psalter does not seem to have reached its final form until after the Maccabæan revolt. Several of the Psalms in the earlier collections, notably lxxiv and lxxix, underwent a revision at that time, and quite a body of Psalms, cxxxv–cl, were added at the close of the whole book, some of them bearing unmistakable marks of that period of struggle and stress. Here also the Synagogue played its part ; but in general the Maccabæan Psalms, like those which had preceded, bear theologically the impress of the Temple. (Cf. Peters, '' The Development of the Psalter," *The New World*, June, 1893.)

CHAPTER XXVI

THE SYNAGOGUE AND THE SCRIBES

While the Temple, as the dwelling of God, with its ritual and its sacrifices, played such a part in the religious life of the period, there developed alongside of it, destined to supersede it and yet not consciously antagonistic to it, another less mechanical, less external, less hierarchical, more intellectual, more spiritual, and more democratic place and method of worship, the Synagogue.

The Exile developed the Scribe, the man who sought to reduce to writing and thus preserve the records of the past. The first scribes were priests, like Ezekiel, whose concern was especially the preservation by their reduction to writing of Temple rules, regulations, and laws. Their tone and tendency is well exhibited in the latter chapters of Ezekiel's prophecy, which are concerned exclusively with the Temple. But there were also laymen interested in the preservation of the records of the past, and the scribal body came to include laymen concerned in the preservation of the history of the nation and hence of its literature. The Pentateuch represents the combination of the two.

The Priestly Code is especially concerned with the Temple, its history, its form and appearance (told under the guise of the tabernacle of the camp), its sacrificial rites, its hierarchy, and its rules for clean and unclean; but this Priestly Code is embedded in an historical document, which represents the effort to preserve the history of Israel. This history has been brought into close relation to the Law, which is conceived of as its most essential part. It was this combination of priestly and lay scribal work which was adopted, under the title of the Law, as the Bible of Jewry.

The Law, as understood by Ezra, aimed first and foremost at the reëstablishment of the Temple worship in its correct form and order. In the case of the Samaritans the new movement stopped there; but the Jews of Palestine were in touch with Babylonia, where, besides the Law, there had been gathered, during the Exile and the centuries succeeding it, a body of histories, prophecies, poetry — all the literary remains which belonged to or grew out of the old life of the nation, some of them fairly intact, others interpreted from the new legal standpoint. With the drawing off of the priests from Babylonia to Jerusalem under Ezra, the collection, study, and interpretation of these ancient writings fell more and more into the hands of laymen, and indeed the priests and Levites who remained in Babylonia themselves became, for all intents and purposes, laymen. They could not sacrifice, they were not part of the priestly body which administered the Temple. In practice and association they were a part of the general body of the Jews in Babylonia.

For this body of Jews remaining in Babylonia some form of common religious life became necessary. Shrines at which they might sacrifice were forbidden. There was only one practicable form of worship by which they could be united with one another and take part in the common national and religious life, namely, the reading of the Law and its interpretation and, as a part of that interpretation, the reading of those ancient books which told the story not only of the preparation for the Law and of its promulgation, but also of its application in the life of the nation, — as Joshua, Judges, Samuel, Kings, — and the records of the lives and teachings of the men who had admonished former generations of the punishment to ensue upon neglect or violation of God's law, and the rewards to follow on its observation, — that is, the Prophets. Such readings and interpretations, accompanied with prayers and hymns, constituted the only religion possible for a people keen to maintain its communal integrity, and prevented by the one Temple theory from the development of shrines for sacrifice, served by priests. The natural leaders of such worship were not priests, because there were no sacrifices to be offered, but scribes. The Diaspora increased the importance of this movement toward a form of worship without a Temple, consisting of reading, interpretation, prayer, and singing.

Babylonian influence, as we have seen, had been dominant in Palestine in the establishment of the Law; and although, after the adoption of the Law, Palestine became officially the religious leader, nevertheless Babylonian influence and Babylonian culture continued to make themselves strongly felt.[1] What had been adopted in Babylonia was pretty sure to find its reflex in Palestine. The Dispersion, which took place after the commencement of the Hellenic period, scattered the Jews who had adopted in Palestine not only the Law, but in general the Babylonian point of view. These exiles transported with them to the regions to which they went this same idea of the study and interpretation of the Law. They made pilgrimages to the Temple, but their particular means of keeping alive religious and national life was through the Sabbath-day gatherings for the study and interpretation of the Law and the other scriptures which were in process of collection. It was these gatherings which ultimately came to constitute the Synagogue. At what date we may say that the Synagogue actually began to be it is somewhat difficult to determine. Its roots are in the Exile. The character of some of the writings which were collected at that time suggests to us the existence of gatherings at which they were read, for in many cases they are of such a nature that it is clear that they were intended for reading aloud before a gathering of the people. Such are the writings of Ezekiel; and indeed the gatherings of Jews to listen to Ezekiel's preaching and to hear his instructions in the *torah* may be said to constitute the beginnings of the Synagogue. It is possible that the reference in the Book of Malachi (iii, 16) to the speaking one with another of them that feared the Lord, and their prayers to God, to which He hearkens, are an evidence of the existence of synagogue worship in Palestine in the second half of the fifth century B.C. Our first actual historical notice of the existence of a synagogue, however, is of a much later date, 242 B.C., and from a different region, namely, Egypt. At that time

[1] So Jewish tradition has it that when the Law was forgotten it was restored by Ezra; when it was forgotten a second time Hillel, the Babylonian, came and restored it; when it was forgotten a third time R. Chija came from Babylon and gave it back once more.

the institution was already well known and completely organized, with a considerable history behind it.

The Book of Chronicles shows us the development and dominance of the Temple and Temple literature during the fourth century B.C. The Synagogue comes to its own in the succeeding century. Its object was study and instruction in the Law, the Prophets, and the writings of the fathers, with praying and singing. On a large scale we may say that the Synagogues were Sabbath Schools for adults; or rather they were great Bible classes, meeting everywhere on the same day at the same time, and reading and studying the same scripture, thus uniting the Jewish world in and by the same sacred occupation, and habituating each Jew to forms of worshiping God without the concomitant of ritual or sacrifice. While the Psalter as we have it was the Temple hymnal, it also played an important part in synagogue gatherings, and through them entered most effectively into the life of the people, expressing their sentiments and becoming a method of addressing God by small groups and by individuals. It was owing to the influence of the synagogal training that the Jews became at this time a praying people, so that we find the literature of the period shot through with prayers, often of a singularly beautiful and lofty character.

The Synagogues were partly the product of the scribal movement, and in their turn they further fostered and developed that movement. The first scribes were priests, like Ezekiel, who, in the lack of opportunity for the performance of their priestly functions, gave their time to the transcription and study of sacred writings and traditions, their interpretation and transmission. As the life of the Jew became narrowed down to religion, this came to be a function of laymen as well as priests, and so the Synagogue afforded an opportunity for the layman to express himself in religion. The Synagogue was, therefore, a democratic institution. The Temple was ruled and controlled by a caste, which constituted also the governing aristocracy. The Synagogue was the property of the people. The Temple was conservative and opposed to progress. The Synagogue, because it was popular and democratic, was progressive. Theoretically the Synagogue looked with the greatest reverence to the Temple, because the Temple was based upon the Law, and the Temple worship was the fundamental doctrine of the Law. The Temple on its part in theory reverenced the Law and approved the study of the Law, and hence approved the Synagogue.

The study of the Law was the great function of the Synagogue. The leaders of the Synagogue were those who were learned in the Law, those who studied it, and those who transcribed it, the Scribes. All the literature of this period is founded upon the Law. Its place in the actual life and thought of the people is testified to by the Psalter. The first and the one hundred and nineteenth Psalms, with the latter half of the nineteenth Psalm, give the best concrete examples of the reverence in which it was held. Beginning with the words "Blessed are they that are perfect in the way," Psalm cxix continues through 176 verses, numerically arranged according to the letters of the alphabet, to set forth the praise of the Law and the reward and blessing of the man who studies it and who adheres to its precepts, in each verse mentioning the Law by some one of its titles. The good man is he "whose delight is in the Law." [1] The law of the Lord is perfect; it gives life, wisdom, joy, enlightenment, purity. [2]

This honor of the Law resulted, in the case of the ordinary Israelite, in a high code of morality in his relations to his fellow Israelite, which is well set forth in the Wisdom literature. So the ideals of Sirach, drawn from a study of the Law, included patience, courage, modesty, kindness, temperance, chastity, and prudence. [3] The character of Sirach's proverbial philosophy, expressed in Ecclesiasticus, and of that of various unnamed writers contained in the Book of Proverbs, shows that these were really the ideas inculcated in the community at large by the Law, and that Jewish legalism was indeed provocative of a high standard of workaday morality. The Law was the covenant of God with Israel, an evidence of His love toward Israel. It brought God into an everyday relation with His people, and developed in each one of them something of that relation in which the older prophets had felt that they

1 Ps. i, 2.   3 H. P. Smith, *Old Testament History*, p. 430.
2 Ps. xix, 7 ff.

stood to God, a relation of personal love and communion. While the national relation was never forgotten, the individual relation to God, with its development of personal religion, is now made prominent, and, looking backward, the religious leaders begin to interpret the old Prophets in terms of the individual. The relation toward God into which the Prophets entered is to be the relation toward God of each individual Jew, and that which the Prophets taught about the community, with regard to righteousness and unrighteousness and their rewards or punishments, is now applied to the individual.

Unfortunately this relation of brotherly kindness was confined to a Jew's relation to his fellow Jews. Precisely because God stood in this relation to the Jews He was, according to the legalistic view, removed from a similar relation to the world at large. So the hatred of the outsider, and of the sinner within Israel, goes hand in hand with lofty teachings of love toward one's neighbor in the faith.[1] The Law was made for Jews. It was their privilege and their joy. From it the rest of the world was excluded. God dealt in one way with the Jew, in another with the world outside; and as was their God's relation, so was that of His people, one of alienation from, and to an extent hostility toward, the rest of the world. This was the evil side of the legal development of this period, which worked powerfully to exalt the ethical standard within Israel itself, of Israelite toward Israelite, but in the relation of the Jews to the outside world was a prolific source of prejudice and delusion. While it guarded the Jew against much immorality and folly prevalent in the people about, it also shut his ears and his eyes to the good which they had to contribute.

The Law did undoubtedly, however, teach the ordinary Jew a high code of duty toward his fellow countrymen, and established in him a fine and exalted sense of his own relationship to God as his Father. But legalism also tended toward and developed certain prejudices within Israel itself, making a distinction between men

---

[1] Cf. Ecclus. xii with xxviii, 1–7. For the extreme development of the spirit of hatred toward the outsider cf. Esther, and note the great popularity which this book achieved.

on grounds not simply of righteousness and moral worth, but of legal knowledge and technical fulfillment of the Law. The Law was a mass of prescriptions governing ceremonial as well as moral relations. In actual bulk the ceremonial portion of the Law vastly exceeded the moral and spiritual part. Technically there was no distinction between the two, and while the better thinkers realized the greater importance of the moral element, there was a continual tendency on the part of the mass of legalists to ignore this distinction, and almost to lay the stress on ceremonial fulfillment, practically placing even above the violation of the moral precepts of the Law the violation of its ritual and ceremonial precepts.

To the modern and western mind it seems inevitable, when we consider its extraordinary details in regard to clean and unclean and the like, that the Law must have been extremely burdensome. In point of fact, a study of the literature of the period shows that this was not the case. There was, it is true, a body of strict legalists who sought painfully to attain at all times a legal purity irksome to any but the fanatic. This class developed ultimately through the *Chasidim* — a name which we begin to find in this period; that is, the beloved, the pious, or the saints — into the Separatists, or Pharisees, of the post-Maccabæan period, who separated themselves even from the mass of their own people, whom they designated as the *Am ha-Arez*, a name which, in the time of Nehemiah, applied to aliens or half-breeds, had gradually and almost insensibly been transferred to those who neglected the Law, the Law becoming, as it were, the country of the Israelite and the test of his nationality. In general, however, legalism did not bear hard on the common man, except only in the matter of tithes, tribute, and the like. It was no easy matter for the plain Judæan agriculturists to meet the exactions, often extremely heavy, of the foreign political authorities, and then pay in addition the large tax imposed for the maintenance of the Temple ritual, sacrifices, first fruits, etc., directly and indirectly enjoined by the Law.

A question which one almost inevitably asks in studying the legal development was: What was the motive for keeping the Law? and it is asked because the asker thinks of the Law as a burden. As already pointed out, that was not the point of view of the average Jew of this period. The Law was a glory and a delight. The motive for its observance was that it was the will of God, to obey which was a joy and a privilege. This is a distinct advance over the morality of the preceding period. The motive urged in the Deuteronomic Code, high as is the standard of morality of that code, was entirely selfish, eudæmonistic, for the purpose of securing a reward : material prosperity if God's commandments are kept, material calamity if they are not kept. It is true that in our period also the keeping of the Law was rewarded with blessing and its violation with calamity ; but that is not urged as the motive for keeping it. With the development of the idea of a direct personal relation to God, a new motive came in — the motive of fulfilling the will of God. The observance of the Law became the end in itself, and no longer the means to an end.

Like the Temple, the Law became the means of bringing God down to the Israelite. As God was in heaven, ruling over all, and yet dwelt in the Temple in Jerusalem, in the very midst of His people, so, by the exaltation of the Law to a divine place, He was in a sense brought down from heaven to earth, to dwell in the very lives of His people. But the Synagogue, with its study of the Law, with its prayers and hymns, in which all joined as individuals, was in its nature personal and individualistic, as against the collective and racial service of the Temple. We have already traced the development of individualism, which began with Jeremiah and was formulated by Ezekiel in the Exile. The Synagogue completed that development. By its interpretation of the Law and the prophetical writings it applied to the individual the lessons of the community. It took all that collective and national literature and interpreted it into terms of the individual life. The individual Israelite is dear to God because of God's love for Israel as a whole, and the good or evil deeds of each Israelite affect the whole, hastening or re tarding the coming of the Messianic kingdom, which all Israelites expected ultimately. Out of the belief in the coming of the Messianic kingdom and the resurrection of all Israel to life came, as individualism was logically applied, the belief in the resurrection of the righteous dead to share in the glory of the kingdom, and finally the belief in the immortality of the individual in a future heavenly life; a belief, however, only foreshadowed in the literature of the pre-Maccabæan period.

Through this individual application of the Scriptures a new theology was growing up, a theology which concerned itself with the practical everyday life of the individual man. Great stress was laid in this theology upon the practice of fasting, and that because out of the interpretation of the history of the past, as told especially by the Prophets, there had developed a strong sense of sin.

The doctrine of the evil inclination in Israel, which the early Prophets taught and which culminated in Ezekiel, had become in the individualistic development of this period the doctrine of the evil heart in each Israelite. Sin lay in the violation of any law of God, even unconsciously, but still more sin lay in the inclination of the heart. All are sinners; no man is righteous before God.[1] And not only this: because of the naturally evil heart no one could be righteous. There was a tendency, against which Ezekiel had been obliged to contend, to so interpret this as to deprive the individual of responsibility for his wickedness. But, while pushing the doctrine of the evil heart to the extreme which he did, Ezekiel had always asserted the responsibility of the individual, and his freedom to choose between good and evil; and in the individualistic development of this period we find the teachers assuming the same attitude.[2] Even Ezekiel, however, was convinced of the ultimate restoration of Israel. God for his own glory must redeem Israel, and that it might not sin hereafter He would give it a new heart. The partial fulfillment of Ezekiel's prophecy in the restoration of the Temple and of Jerusalem was naturally interpreted as showing that, to some extent certainly, this had been accomplished, that Israel had been received into favor with God, and that, at least in comparison with the outside world, Israel was counted righteous by Him. The individual, therefore, might be supposed, like the nation, to be living under new conditions toward God. Still more the conception of the relation of the nation and the individual

---

[1] Ps. cxliii, 3; Job xv, 14.   [2] Ecclus. xv, 11–17.

toward God was modified by the teaching of divine love promulgated by Deutero-Isaiah. No one can be righteous, but the loving-kindness of God prevents Him from reckoning sin when a man turns from his sin. Repentance assures forgiveness for the Israelite (Jonah makes it do the same for the non-Israelite); for God's loving-kindness, in the case at least of the Israelite, is greater than His righteousness.[1] This belief in his relation to God relieved the mind of the Israelite, although conscious of sin, from the constant apprehension of punishment. To be sure, sacrifices must be offered continually to atone for the sins of the people, his own included, and individually he must seek to overbalance his sin by deeds of righteousness.[2] Ultimately the special deed of righteousness which would atone for sins came to be almsgiving,[3] and the word "righteousness," like our word " charity," came to connote almsgiving. But this peculiar stage of development had not yet been reached in our period.[4]

As sin was so closely connected in thought with misfortune that calamity was supposed to indicate sin, it might be supposed that the calamities of both Israel and the individual Israelite would be too literally regarded as evidence of sin. That this was to some extent the case, and that it exerted a deleterious influence, is clear from various allusions in the literature of this period ;[5] but on the whole the Israelite managed to avoid the logical evil results of the dogma. For one thing, you could not tell until the end whether a man was bad, for suffering was educational and disciplinary and might be given for the purpose of purifying and bettering, as a father chasteneth his son. One must wait, therefore, and see what was the latter end of the man.[6]

While emphasis was laid upon sin, it must not be supposed, however, that the tendency of the religious development of the Synagogue was gloomy or mournful. The personal religion which became dominant especially in the third century was in general

[1] Ps. lxxxvi, 15 ; ciii, 78 ; Jonah iv, 2 ; Ecclus. iii, 3 ; iv, 14, 15, 30.
[2] Prov. x, 2 ; xi, 4.   [3] Dan. iv, 24 ; cf. Matt. vi, 1.
[4] So we find Sirach exalting honor to parents as the redeeming virtue (Ecclus. iii).
[5] Job xxxii–xxxvii ; cf. John ix, 2.
[6] Ps. xxxvii, 35–37.

joyful rather than sorrowful. The conception of a loving, personal relation to God had taken possession of the people.

In early Hebrew literature we are continually confronted with such expressions as "the Fear of Isaac"[1] as a designation of Yahaweh, and Yahaweh is represented as a terrible deity. Such stories as that of the destruction of the men who touched the Ark[2] illustrate and exalt His terror. If His wrath were kindled, yea but a little, destruction was certain.[3] Moreover He is a capricious god. Who can tell when His wrath will be aroused? "The Fear of God" remains a prominent phrase in the post-exilic period, and in the Priestly Code much stress is laid on the awful power and majesty of God. No one could see Him and live. He gave the Law with terrible accompaniment of fire and earthquake.[4] When His wrath burned against the Israelites for violation of the Law, they were destroyed in thousands by pestilence or earthquake or consuming fire.[5] In the Psalms and Proverbs we have the same picture repeated, and indeed the religion of Yahaweh is frequently designated throughout this period as "the Fear of God." But while God was still thus conceived of as terrible and His wrath beyond measure, yet He is now recognized to a much fuller extent than heretofore as a god of law; not a capricious monster whose wrath might burst out at any moment, but a god whose relations to His people Israel were governed by a law which He had given them as a covenant. "The Fear of God," therefore, takes on a new significance. It is in fact defined in Proverbs as hatred of evil,[6] and much the same definitions are found also in Ecclesiasticus and the Psalter.[7]

With this definition of the fear of God it is quite possible to combine that conception of a special relation of loving-kindness between God and Israel which is so prominent in the Psalms and, in general, in the literature of this period. Toward Israelites, as keepers of His Law, having in their hearts His Fear, which is the hatred of evil, God is full of loving-kindness; and so the special

---

[1] Gen. xxxi, 42, 53.
[2] 2 Sam. vi, 7.
[3] Ps. ii, 12; xxi, 9.
[4] Ex. xix.
[5] Num. xi; xvi.
[6] Prov. viii, 13.
[7] Ps. xcvii, 10; Ecclus. ii, 15-16.

name *Chasidim* — saints, or " men of loving-kindness " — is applied to those Israelites who are devoted to the service of His Law.[1]

To this period belong, in general, the development of what may be called the two sacraments of Israel, which, while not originating at this time or in the Synagogue, became a part of the synagogal and personal religion as distinguished from the sacrificial national religion of the Temple, namely, Circumcision and the Sabbath. Both of these were ancient, pre-Israelitic practices, of the actual origin of which we know very little.[2] Presumably circumcision was primarily a blood sacrifice, connected with manhood rites ; but, whatever its origin, it became among the Israelites in the early historical times a mark of national distinction. Israelite circumcision was administered not at the age of puberty, or at the commencement of manhood, but in very early infancy. It was thus dissociated from any relation to the processes of generation and constituted merely a national mark. With the development of the conception of exclusivism, emphasis was laid more and more upon this national mark, until circumcision became to the Jew the sacrament of initiation into the church and nation, in and by which alone he might be saved. But this sacrament was not connected with the Temple nor administered by the priesthood. It could be administered in the midst of heathen nations, and practically by any one. The great point was that the Jew should be circumcised. Such a mark of distinction was of immense importance in the maintenance of the Jews as a separate people in the midst of the nations. Without it they must have been absorbed.

Similarly the Sabbath day set off the Jew from the peoples round about, keeping his separation from them clearly before his own mind and theirs. In the synagogal development it became further the means of uniting the Jews together in and for the study of the Law. So the existence of the day of rest not only set them apart from all other peoples, but also helped to

---

[1] In general, loving-kindness takes the place of fear, wrath, and righteousness in the Psalms of this period. Cf. xcii, 2 ; ciii, 4 ; cviii, 3 ; cxix, 88.

[2] Cf. the elaborate article on Circumcision in Hastings's *Encyclopedia of Religion and Ethics* to see how little we know of the origin and early history of this widespread custom.

develop and maintain a high grade of intelligence and spirituality, raising them above the peoples among whom they lived. So clearly was this the case that the two religions which have developed out of Judaism, namely Christianity and Islam,[1] although discarding the particular day of the Sabbath, have maintained in its essence the principle of its observance.

Theologically at this period we have reached absolute monotheism. Yahaweh still remains Yahaweh, that is to say, His personal relation to Israel is prominent; but He is no longer conceived of as the one greater god among many lesser ones. Of Yahawism there is, in the nature of things, no trace. As there is only one place for the worship of Yahaweh, so there is no opportunity for different Yahawehs with different attributes, the result of different theologies. But while this personal relation of Israel to the one supreme God is manifested in the continuance of the name *Yahaweh*, in the presence of God's dwelling-place, the Temple, in the midst of His people in Jerusalem, and in His expression in His Law in the hearts and lives of His people, yet He is conceived of as transcendent, not immanent. The lack in the post-exilic Temple of any outward expression of His presence, such as the Ark, helped to increase this transcendental conception of His nature and being. He is too far removed from man, albeit man is made in His image, to manifest himself to men. The very sight of Him would mean death. With this conception of the transcendence of God comes a higher conception of His glory. His personal relation to Israel is for the purpose of showing forth His glory. The goal of history was the triumph of Israel, but that triumph was to manifest God's glory. There is at times a certain hardness and, if we may so put it, selfishness in the expression of this conception of God. So we find Psalmists crying to God for deliverance, or for the cancellation of their sins for His own name's sake.[2] To be sure this is not carried to such an extreme as to eliminate the loving-kindness of God; and so a Psalmist even combines the two thoughts thus: "Not unto us, Yahaweh, not unto us, but unto Thy name give glory for Thy

---

[1] Cf. Jastrow, *Hebrew and Babylonian Traditions*, chap. vii.
[2] Ps. xxv, 11; lxxix, 9.

loving-kindness and for Thy truth's sake."[1] There is, nevertheless, a falling away from the beautiful thought of the tender love of God for Israel which we find in Deutero-Isaiah.[2]

The overassertion of monotheism in this ultra-transcendentalism results in some respects in an actual descent from the noble philosophical conception of monotheism which we find in Deutero-Isaiah. There God was maker of good and ill. All things were of Him. He was the universe. There was no such thing as other gods in any shape. There were no intermediaries between God Almighty and the smallest as well as the largest thing in creation or life. Now there is a tendency to interpose a mediary between the individual and God, even in His relation to prophets and psalmists. He makes the winds His messengers and flames His ministers.[3] It is through His wisdom or His spirit that the inspiration comes,[4] not by the direct utterance of His voice in the prophet's heart (and here we are well along the road toward the hypostasis of wisdom and spirit). The Glory of God assumes a similar almost independent identity ; and even the Name of God becomes a reality by itself.[5] In ancient magic the name was the reality of the person, so that he who knew and could call the real and secret name could control the person attached to the name. So a man knowing the name of a god or demon could compel that god or demon to obey his commands. The development of a transcendentalism which made the Name of God a sort of intermediary of His being, and hence an independent or almost independent reality, completed the circle, bringing the Jews back in this regard to the conception of primitive magic. The name, as the essence of God, must be hidden. The emphasis on Yahaweh as the personal name of God, therefore, led finally to the loss of that name. It must not be pronounced. The holy writings in which the letters (consonants) of the name occurred might not be changed, but in their place other letters

[1] Ps. cxv, 1.

[2] Cf., for instance, Is. lxiii, 9. In a somewhat cruder form we have the same idea expressed at earlier periods ; Jud. x, 16.　　[3] Ps. civ, 4.　　[4] Ps. li, cxxxix, cxliii.

[5] Wisdom and Spirit appear more especially in the Wisdom literature ; *Shechinah*, or Glory, and Name, in the Psalter. Cf. Prov. i, 20 ; viii, 1 ; iii, 19 ; Job xxvi, 13 ; Ps. civ, 31 ; lxxii, 17 ; cxlviii, 13.

were pronounced. So the true name of the God of the Jews was hidden ; a result not completed, however, in our period, although far advanced.[1]

Sometimes God's action takes place through intermediaries of another class, namely angels. In the early writers the angel of Yahaweh is mentioned, through whom God has personal touch at times with man. But that angel was a mere passing thought, a mask for the person of Yahaweh, disappearing with the occasion for its use. Now we have real angels, who come to bring messages to the prophets, through whom God deals with the nations, and who begin to have names, indicating their permanent existence. We see the beginnings of this in Zechariah and Job, where the court of God and His administration of the world are imagined after the manner of the Persian court, with provinces ruled by subordinates through whom God transacts the affairs of those provinces, and who report to Him from time to time. The angels are brought into close relation with the stars. The gods of the heathen are also worked into this scheme. They are now no longer gods with independent power, but subordinates to the one great God, with whom Israel is so peculiarly identified. Sometimes the evil that is wrought in the world is attributed to the improper action of these satraps of the Deity, who move for their own hand, just as the governors of the Persian provinces were wont to do. This affords an explanation of certain evil conditions affecting Israel, which it was hard to ascribe to the intentional action of their God.[2]

Deutero-Isaiah had described God, Yahaweh, as the author of good and evil alike. With this removal of Him from direct contact with the affairs of earth, the tendency is to ascribe the evil to His agents, and so we find Satan introduced. It is Satan through whom calamities fall upon Job.[3] It is Satan who presents himself as an adversary against Joshua, the High Priest.[4] But the difference of view is best illustrated by a comparison of Samuel and Chronicles.

---

[1] In the last revision of the Psalter, *Adonai* was apparently substituted in a number of places for *Yahaweh*.

[2] For angelology, and the part other gods, stars, etc., play in it, cf. Montefiore, *Origin and Growth of Religion as illustrated by the Religion of the Hebrews*, p. 429.

[3] Job i-ii.   [4] Zech. iii, 1.

In the former David was tempted by God to muster Israel, an act which brought upon the nation the wrath of God.[1] In the Book of Chronicles it is Satan who put it into the heart of David to muster Israel.[2]

The question arises: to what extent was foreign influence felt in all this, and to what extent were these things a development of Hebrew thought? The general line of development was Israelitic, stimulated by Persian, Greek, and, to some extent, Babylonian ideas, but not (with a few possible exceptions) directly borrowed from these. The Persian doctrine of the judgment and the resurrection doubtless stimulated the development of similar Israelite doctrines; but in germ those doctrines were already there. The Day of Judgment is the ancient Day of Yahaweh, which was a popular doctrine before the time of Amos. The resurrection is a natural development, by the individualizing and spiritualizing methods of treatment of this period, of such doctrines of the future renovation of Israel and its restoration to national life as we find in Ezekiel's vision of the dry bones. The eschatology and the doctrine of the future life, so far as that doctrine was developed in this period, are intrinsically Jewish, modifications and adaptations of the older theology, with, in the case of the former, a considerable Babylonian element.

The angelology and demonology, which were more fully developed in the succeeding period, owe more to Persian and Babylonian influences. The angel of Yahaweh, the gods of the heathen, and the stars, conceived of as possessing an independent existence, were, as already pointed out, woven into the new transcendental monotheism to form the angelology, which finds its official expression in the writings of the second century, such as Daniel, Enoch, and Tobit. Ultimately the angel host was conceived of in popular theology as a mighty army of archangels, angels, principalities, powers, and much else besides,[3] constituting the agencies for good, so organized as to ascend in gradations from man to God. Over against these was a similar host of demoniacal agents, working harm. This was dualism, and in its completed form, as it showed

---

[1] 2 Sam. xxiv, 1. [2] 1 Chron. xxi, 1.
[3] Rom. viii, 38; Eph. i, 21; iii, 10; vi, 12; Col. i, 16; ii, 10, 15; Tit. iii, 1; Jude 5.

itself in later Judaism, it is doubtless to be ascribed to Persian influence, modified by Babylonian ; but it was rather the organization than the angels and the demons which were Persian.

That Persian dualism early made an appeal to the Jews as an explanation of the existence of evil in the world, especially in its relation to Israel, is clear from the language in which Deutero-Isaiah enounces his monotheism. His assertions that Yahaweh is the author of evil as well as good constitute a polemic against dualism, and are an evidence of the strength of the influence against which he was contending. The view which he antagonized found ultimately a modified adoption in the form of Satan, who became a partial reflex of Angra Mainyu. Etymologically, however, Satan was Semitic, not Persian ; nor does he ever assume, at least in classical Jewish theology, the position of an actually independent principle of evil. The demons, who were later associated with Satan, were a part of the ancient and popular belief of the Jews as of all other peoples, a belief which was condemned by the Prophets and the higher thinkers in general. Demonology as such found expression in the Law in the Azazel ritual of the Day of Atonement.[1] In the second century, in the books of Daniel, Enoch, and Tobit, it appears more fully developed as the opposite of angelology, a part of the dualistic conception of the contending powers of good and evil. In later popular Judaism demonology came to play a very important rôle. Considering the part which it played in the religion of the world in general, this is not to be wondered at. The remarkable thing, testifying to the exclusive force of Judaism, is that demonology should have played so small a part in the official cult of this period, making itself consciously felt only in the Azazel ritual of the Day of Atonement. Angelology and demonology, although both existed and were developed to the extent and in

---

[1] Lev. xvi. Cf. also Enoch x. The belief in demons, spirits of the dead, etc., lay behind the prohibition to pour the blood on the ground (Lev. xvii), some of the taboos of clean and unclean, the ritual of the tassels, the sacrifice of the red heifer (Num. xix), and much more. The Azazel ritual, however, is the only overt expression of this belief embodied in the Law. For the later development of demonology and magic among the Babylonian Jews see Montgomery, *Aramaic Incantation Texts from Nippur* (1913), Babylonian Expedition of the University of Pennsylvania.

the manner described, were nevertheless logically inconsistent with the spiritual, transcendental monotheism which is characteristic of this period.

As Jewish angelology and demonology felt the influence of Persian religion, so in the matter of the quasi-personification of the attributes of God, wisdom, spirit, etc., the somewhat similar personification of attributes among the Greeks may have been an exciting cause.[1] The main motive, however, was Jewish. It was a result of that transcendental movement which removed God from such direct touch with man (especially with the heart of the prophet, the singer, or the sage) as was claimed and represented in the earlier literature.

During this period a change took place in the language, which exerted some influence on the religious development. In the fifth century Nehemiah was distressed because some of the people no longer spoke Hebrew, but were conversant only with Aramaic, which had become the current language of all Syria.[2] From the following centuries we find, in the sacred literature itself, passages no longer written in Hebrew, but in Aramaic.[3] Hebrew was becoming or had become the language of religion only. As a result both the composition and the interpretation of scripture came to be more and more confined to the Scribes. This helped to eliminate all secular material from Hebrew literature, and enhanced the tendency to narrow life down to religion. The Law comprehended all knowledge. The Law was, accordingly, the special study of the Scribes. Their study was not, however, confined to the Law as such. They were also engaged in collecting and interpreting all the writings of the ancients which enforced and carried out the teachings of the Law. To this period belongs the collection of Proverbs, the wisdom of the ancients, which especially connected itself with the name of Solomon.

---

1 In the later Alexandrian Jewish literature Greek philosophy played a much more important part.

2 Neh. xii, 24. Contrast with this the conditions in the time of Isaiah, 2 Kings xviii, 26.

3 Ezra iv, 7–vi, 18, vii, 12–26, from the third or fourth, and Dan. ii, 4–vii, 28 from the second century.

This work consists of various collections of gnomic sayings, having their origin in an earlier time, which have been worked over and over until, in the form in which they have come down to us, they may be regarded as altogether a product of this period. They are not popular proverbs in the ordinary sense of the word, but rather literary proverbs, representing the wisdom of the sages, mediated through the Scribes. The whole work is prefaced by a gnomic poem describing and praising the wisdom of the Jew. But always the compilers and scribal editors remained conscious that they were dealing with ancient Hebrew literature, however much it had been modified and recast — a literature the originator of which they assumed to have been the great and wise Solomon, the builder of the Temple.

To this extent Proverbs shows Greek influence: it is conscious of the intellectual development of the Hellenic world and the charm Hellenic wisdom was beginning to exercise upon the Jews, not only in the Diaspora, but also to some extent in the homeland. Just as the Book of Chronicles sought to answer those who were looking outside of Judæa for real things, by setting forth the supreme greatness of the Temple at Jerusalem and the power and magnificence of those who were concerned in its construction as an evidence of the latent power by which the Jews could ultimately overthrow the kingdoms of the world and manifest their nation once more in the splendor of God; so the editor of Proverbs sought to show that the wisdom of the Jew, which had been handed down from the time of Solomon, was greater far than any wisdom of the world.[1] The influence of Hellenism on Proverbs is the stimulus of antagonism rather than of suggestion or imitation. Wisdom, as the author of Proverbs conceived it, was entirely different from Hellenic wisdom. Jewish wisdom is not the possession of man alone, but the attribute of God himself. This wisdom is the Fear of God; that is, the knowledge of the Law, which is the expression of God, and which belongs only to Israel. Wisdom had visited all the nations of the

---

[1] Typical of the Jew from the Exile on was his effort to prove himself not inferior to the non-Jews. His magic was greater than theirs, his wisdom than theirs, his God than theirs. Hence the various stories in canonical and non-canonical literature of the triumphs of Jews at heathen courts, and the strange discomfitures of heathen gods.

earth, but in Israel alone had she taken up her abode, given permanent form in the Law ordained by Moses. By study of this Law and by a life after its precepts all practical problems of life are solved, and it is with these practical problems that the bulk of the Book of Proverbs and the whole of the Book of Ecclesiasticus deal.

In the latter book we obtain a glimpse of the Scribes as a separate body, devoting themselves to meditation and study. Wisdom was the knowledge of the Law, and this can be acquired only by continuous study. So Sirach taught that wisdom can come only to him who, through leisure, has opportunity for study.[1] To this extent wisdom was a possession of the intellectuals, and in this intellectualism Jewish wisdom may be said to resemble Hellenism. But precisely because it was intellectualism, wisdom did not always bring satisfaction and that simple assurance of a personal relation to God, comfort in the belief that through Him all would be well, which has been described above as the property of the ordinary pious Jew of the day. It is among the intellectuals who, conscious of the movement of Hellenic wisdom, sought to develop and apply the wisdom of the Law in Israel, that we find evidences of mental disturbance and of the existence of skepticism. It is in the Book of Job, the earliest writing of the Wisdom school, that we first find an expression of skepticism, or dissent from the ordinarily received view of God's administration of the universe with the reward of good for good and evil for evil. The Book of Ecclesiastes, written at the very close of this period, but attributed, like Proverbs, to Solomon, is a still more striking example of skepticism in another form. In a series of dissertations, partly prose, partly poetry, the author sets forth the order of the world, reaching the conclusion that all is vanity. He does not deny the existence of God and he advises that man should live according to moral laws, but he is quite without hope for the future and finds no satisfaction in conditions as they are. There is no more outlook for the man than for the beast. All is vanity. But although Ecclesiastes is skeptical of the prevailing theory of his day, his work still shows the effect of the legal teaching. His morality is generally sane and wholesome,

---

[1] Ecclus. xxxviii, 24.

and, although unable to accept the views of God's government and of the personal relation to God adopted by his fellow countrymen, he still retains his belief in Him; and indeed both of the skeptical works of the Wisdom Literature give us convincing evidence of the manner in which faith in their God permeated, in all conditions and all circumstances, the life of the Jew. Like Job, Ecclesiastes was somewhat modified by more orthodox hands, the better to fit it for a place in the Canon. " Vanity of vanities, saith the preacher, all is vanity," [1] is tempered by the teaching, " Fear God and keep His Commandments, for this is the whole of man." [2]

In its ultimate developments Wisdom literature moves along the lines of what became Sadduceeism. In contrast with this stand the prophetic writings which, in certain very important particulars certainly, move along the lines of what ultimately became Phariseeism. It was with the collection and reworking of the latter that the Scribes of this period more particularly concerned themselves. Amos, Hosea, Micah, Isaiah, and Jeremiah were all worked over, and modern critical scholars suppose that a considerable part of the Messianic material contained in those prophecies belongs to this period and to the scribal rather than the original prophetic element in those books. But not only were the ancient prophecies collected and reworked; to some extent prophecy itself continued down to the end of the period with which we are now dealing, and even the ancient primitive methods of prophecy were preserved, as is manifest from such passages as Zechariah xiii, 2–6, which certainly cannot be earlier than the third century.

Of the prophetic writings of this period, one, Joel, shows distinctly the effect of the dominance of the sacrificial and the legal ideas. In the description of the calamity which has befallen the land, emphasis is laid on its effect on the Temple service. The meal offering and the drink offering are cut off from the house of Yahaweh. The priests, the Lord's ministers, mourn.[3] The calamity is to be averted, not, as in the older prophets, by moral regeneration, but rather by ritual means, by the sanctification of a fast.[4] It

---

[1] Eccles. xii, 8.   [3] Joel i, 9, 13; ii, 14.
[2] Eccles. xii, 14.   [4] Joel i, 14; ii, 15.

must be said, however, that Joel is not content with that fasting which is merely an outer form ; he insists that it shall be primarily the rending of the heart.[1]

A little apocalypse of this period, incorporated in our present Book of Isaiah (xxiv–xxvii), describes God's judgment, apparently with some reference to the legalistic standpoint, as due to the fact that the people have transgressed the Law, changed the ordinance, broken the everlasting covenant. This prophecy as a whole, however, is concerned rather with the facts of judgment and deliverance and the resurrection to life than with the causes of the judgment of the world. It is Messianic.

In general the Messianic hope expressed in the prophetic writings or the prophetic-scribal additions of this period is the simpler form of the expectation of a triumphant king of David's line, who shall restore David's kingdom in a still more glorious manner and over- throw and punish the heathen. Sometimes, however, the Messianic kingdom is to be brought about by the direct interference of God. The great Day of Yahaweh, the day of judgment on the nations, forms a part of this latter conception. The prophecy of Joel, the particular occasion of which was a plague of locusts, introduces into the picture of the Day of Judgment, as known to us before, a new and local element, namely that the judgment of Yahaweh is to take place in the valley of Jehoshaphat, which seems to be the val- ley of the Kidron.[2] In another prophecy of this period,[3] already referred to, the punishment of the Day of Yahaweh is made to affect not only the kings of the earth upon the earth, but also their astral spirits, the hosts that are on high. This prophecy also, in its beautiful description of the victory over death, shows that we are on the road toward the doctrine of the resurrection.[4] Both this prophecy and the Deutero-Zechariah, that is, Zechariah ix–xiv, are characterized by that emphasis upon the *poor* which we find so frequent in the Psalms of this period, and which met us first in Deutero-Isaiah. Yahaweh is a stronghold to the needy in distress.[5] In one passage the Messianic king himself is represented as lowly

[1] Joel ii, 13.
[2] Joel iii, 14.
[3] Is. xxiv–xxvii.
[4] Is. xxv, 6.
[5] Is. xxv, 4.

and riding upon an ass and upon a colt, the foal of an ass,[1] recalling the idea expressed in Isaiah liii.

The almost overwhelmingly dominant tendency of this period was that of the separatist. God was Israel's god, full of mercy and loving-kindness toward Israel and of wrath against the outside world, which was Israel's foe. His religion and His promises are for Israel and for Israel only. There is one law for Israel, and all the world besides is outlawed. One voice is raised in protest against this.[2] The Book of Jonah, appealing to antiquity, as we have seen was the custom of the period, argues in the line of some of the older prophets, but with a much broader liberalism, for the application of the same law to the Gentile as to the Jew. Taking an old story of a prophet of Israel, Jonah,[3] in the same way in which the author of the Book of Job had used an old story as the basis of his dramatic discussion of the problem of evil, this author works over and adapts the tale to the purposes of his argument, in the form of what we may call a religious novel. Jonah had been sent to announce destruction upon the great world capital, Nineveh. Fearful of the result of such a mission, he attempted to escape Yahaweh's jurisdiction by taking passage on a ship of Tarshish. But Yahaweh is God of the whole world, whom winds and waves obey, from whom it is impossible to hide in the depths of the sea or in the heights of heaven. He sends a great storm, and Jonah, conscious of the cause, bids his shipmates cast him overboard as the only means by which they can be saved from destruction. For this event, which in His omniscience was foreseen, God had prepared a great fish to swallow Jonah and to convey him in his belly safe to shore, upon which he was disgorged by the sea monster after three days' entombment. Thus warned even more dramatically

---

[1] Zech. ix, 9.

[2] The author of Ruth, as already pointed out, was opposed to the exclusive policy of Nehemiah and Ezra. Universalistic implications are contained also in a few prophetic utterances, such as Malachi's: " From the rising of the sun even unto the going down of the same, my name is great among the heathen ; and in every place incense and a pure oblation are offered unto my name ; for my name is great among the heathen, saith Yahaweh Zabaoth " (i, 11). Nowhere, however, since Amos is there any utterance so broad and so inclusive as the Book of Jonah.

[3] 2 Kings xiv, 25.

than Balaam of God's omnipotence and the futility of all attempts to disobey Him, Jonah proceeds to Nineveh and commences to denounce the destruction of the city because of its sins; whereupon the Ninevites repent and turn to God with fasting and prayer. Now such repentance of the Israelite would procure forgiveness of sin and avert the wrath of God. Here it has the same effect in the case of the Ninevites, to the indignation of the pious Jonah, and the story closes with God's explanation to Jonah of His lovingkindness to all mankind.

While opposed to the prevailing view, and of recent date, Jonah found a place in the canon of the Prophets because on the one side it professed to tell the story of an ancient prophet, on which account it was treated as ancient; and because on the other side it told of the triumph over the heathen of the God of the Hebrews, a theme wonderfully appealing to the Jew, and much developed in the later literature. The fact of its inclusion in the Canon is a testimony to the generally catholic spirit of the Scribes toward prophetic literature.

Somewhere, probably, toward or about the close of the third century B.C., as a result of the work of the Scribes and the influence of the Synagogue, the Prophets were added to the Bible, which since the middle of the preceding century had been the Law. The Prophets consisted of two parts, the Former Prophets, those books which we commonly class as historical, — Joshua, Judges, Samuel, and Kings, — and the Latter Prophets, Isaiah, Jeremiah, Ezekiel, and the Twelve. There is no record of a formal adoption of these books, but the literature of the immediately succeeding period shows us that they were reckoned as Bible by that time. They did not then take, nor have they ever since come to take, a position quite equal to that of the Law. Second only to that, however, they were the inspired word of God, set off from all other literature of any sort, to be treated with the greatest reverence, preserved with most scrupulous care, and studied and obeyed as the word of God.

The creation of the Canon of the Prophets was the greatest achievement of the Synagogue and the Scribes. It was the result of the Sabbath-School work of the Synagogue in the study of ancient scripture, with the Scribes as leaders of the Sabbath School in collecting and interpreting those scriptures. It was not Temple influence which created the Canon of the Prophets, but that influence which stood over against the Temple. The books of this Canon represent what may be called the Synagogal as against the Temple point of view. The Synagogue was interested in the Prophets; Wisdom, the Psalter, and Chronicles more nearly represent the views of the Temple. When it is said, however, that at this time the prophetical books were adopted as canon and became Bible, it is not meant to imply that there were not a number of other writings which enjoyed a high repute or exercised great influence; only those books could not be cited as authoritative evidence in the sense in which the Prophets could. The contents of the latter were Bible doctrine.

It should be said in conclusion that it is quite possible from the scriptures used or created during this period to adduce texts to prove almost any view, provided one confines one's self to individual passages, or even to single books. The literature must be viewed historically and as a whole, to determine the tendency and the dominant view of the period. The continued use of and reverence for the early writings always rendered possible the retention by a part of the community of divergent views, or the outcropping of ancient motives in a new form. Their very reverence for the past, and for the great men and the great teachers of the past, as peculiarly inspired by God, made it the special object and glory of the Scribes to collect and preserve their writings. As a result of the work of the Scribes in the collection of all sorts of ancient scriptures, in spite of or partly because of their additions to and revisions of those scriptures, and as the result of their exaltation of the scriptures as all of them in some sense the word of God, there arose the possibility of a babel of different doctrines. In actual practice what may be called the dominant, or orthodox, religion of the period is not difficult to discern.

CHAPTER XXVII

PERSECUTION AND NATIONAL REVIVAL

From the time of Alexander the Great onward, the Jews in Palestine were subjected increasingly to Hellenistic influence. Alexander's magnificent dream had been to found a universal empire, held together not by force but by unity of civilization. This empire should be saturated with the Hellenistic culture. Accordingly Greek colonies followed in the steps of his conquests, both new cities inhabited by Greeks and colonies of Greeks settled in the old cities. Alexander's successors continued this work, spreading Greek culture over all Hither Asia and Egypt. The Jews, as has been pointed out, resisted more effectively than any other people the progress of this culture, but the whole surrounding territory was thoroughly Hellenized until the Jews formed a very small enclave in the midst of Greek civilization. Upon this enclave, as time went on, Hellenism encroached more and more. It became necessary for the Jews to hold intercourse with the people about them, and, in order to do so, to make use of the universal language, Greek. With the acquisition of the language came, inevitably, a certain amount of Greek culture. Moreover this was on the whole a time of peace and prosperity, and precisely because of this there was the greater tendency to adopt Hellenistic manners and customs.[1]

It has already been pointed out that outside of Judæa it was the upper and more cultivated classes who were especially susceptible to Hellenic civilization. So with the Jews it was among the cultured classes, and especially the priestly aristocracy, that these Hellenistic encroachments made themselves felt. They were subject to the same law as all other aristocracies. They felt the influence of their kindred class in other communities as the simpler and

[1] According to Josephus, *Ant.* ii–iii, the Seleucids granted the Jews special privileges in their cities. They occupied also a favored position in Alexandria.

poorer part of the population did not. They were naturally brought into contact with their rulers, whether Antiochian or Ptolemid, in a manner different from that of the plain people, and their power and their preferment depended upon their adopting a certain veneer at least of this civilization. One natural result of their prosperity, and of the dependence of the priestly aristocracy upon the good will of foreign governors, was the corruption of that aristocracy. By the beginning of the second century of the Christian era we find it occupying toward the faith the same attitude which the Roman hierarchical aristocracy occupied in the days of the Renaissance. Priests competed with one another in buying the favor of the Syrian court, maintaining the while the outer form of religion with much pomp.

The influence of the Jews in Egypt, a numerous, wealthy, and important body, further favored the cause of this Hellenism. There the sacred scriptures had been translated into Greek. Greek had become the regular language of the community, and, while remaining faithful to their religion, the Jews sought intellectually to bring that religion into touch with the philosophic schemes and systems of the outside world.[1] In close intercourse with their brethren in Judæa, traveling back and forth, their influence tended to promote the movement of Hellenization going on in the priestly and aristocratic circles in Jerusalem itself.

Over against this there was the countervailing influence of Babylonia. It was from Babylonia that the impetus had come which had originally brought into being the separatist and legalistic party and created the new religion of the Law. The Judaism of Babylonia still continued to maintain the separatist attitude. There the Jews formed a large and powerful community, which did not yield to Hellenistic influence; and indeed Hellenistic influence in Babylonia was at all times much weaker than in Egypt or Syria. In Babylonia the Jews continued the study of the Law and thence pious pilgrims,

---

[1] Partly this grew out of the not-to-be-inferior attitude of the Jews, mentioned above; partly it may be due to the monotheistic consciousness. Their own God was God of all the world. Hence all good was His. Whatever spiritual good they found anywhere, therefore, they appropriated as belonging to Him.

versed in that study, made pilgrimages to Jerusalem. The commercial intercourse with Babylonia was not so close. Such intercourse as existed was religious, with that old-Jewish section of their own countrymen who continued to call themselves the *Galutha* (Captivity), and who proudly boasted descent from the aristocracy of the preëxilic period.

In Palestinian Judaism there had developed, by the end of the first quarter of the second century B.C., two parties: those friendly to the Greeks, comprising in general the priestly aristocracy and the wealthier portion of the population, who were in close communication with the outside world, and whose wealth and comfort depended upon their Hellenistic superiors and neighbors; and the Chasidim, or pious Jews, who clung to the old order of Jewish legalism, and who may be roughly said to represent the Babylonian movement, which had originally achieved its supremacy through the influence of Nehemiah and Ezra. The great bulk of the people belonged to neither the one nor the other. They were Jews. They accepted the customs, habits, and religion of their forefathers. In case their national and spiritual pride was aroused, they would undoubtedly rank themselves on the separatist side. On the other hand, if the practices of Hellenization had gone on gradually, and without a direct antagonism of Jewish race prejudices, this great mass would probably, in due course of time, have been Hellenized, like the peoples about them, or like their own fellow countrymen in Egypt. But this was not allowed to occur. In the year 175 B.C. Antiochus Epiphanes ascended the Syrian throne.[1] A fanatical Hellenist, his endeavor was to do away with all heathenish, barbarous customs and rites, establishing in their place the beautiful civilization of Greece in its entirety. His point of view and that of men like him is well expressed in Tacitus's description of his purpose. Antiochus strove to overthrow the " superstition " of the Jews and to introduce among them Greek customs, to improve the condition of " this execrable nation." [2]

So far as the Jews were concerned, Antiochus was induced to adopt this policy in part certainly by their own corrupt priestly

---

[1] 1 Macc. i, 10.   [2] History, v, 8.

aristocracy. First Jason, or Jesus, and then Menelaus bought the position of High Priest, partly by money contributions, and partly by offering to assist in Hellenizing their fellow countrymen.[1] Jason offered Antiochus money to make him High Priest and to permit him to erect a gymnasium and allow the inhabitants of Jerusalem to be enrolled as " Antiochians." Clearly this man had no conception of the real spirit of his own countrymen. It was no wonder that Antiochus should be deceived; but Jason was not alone in his point of view, as is clear from the way in which his acts were viewed and supported by the young aristocrats of Jerusalem. When a gymnasium was erected the very priests forsook the altar to take part in the games, and many sought to remove the evidence of their circumcision. Shortly Menelaus outbid Jason for the high priestly office and incidentally caused the murder of Onias, the former High Priest, who had sought sanctuary at Daphne. A little later a contest between Jason and Menelaus gave occasion for direct interference on the part of Antiochus, who massacred a number of Jews and plundered the treasures of the Temple, including the sacred vessels. This was the beginning of an actual persecution, which ultimately consolidated the whole people in a fanatical anti-Hellenism.

It is probable that if Antiochus, unhampered by Roman interference, could have carried out his plans of foreign aggression, his aversion to the Jews and their barbarous superstitions might never have found expression in actual persecution. The humiliation of his treatment by the Romans, who forbade his invasion of Egypt in 168 B.C., and compelled him to return without striking a blow, was the immediate exciting cause of the persecution. He was anxious to express his wrath in some way, and the Jews lay right in his path. He determined to Hellenize Jerusalem thoroughly, to exterminate the population which would not accept Hellenic culture and religion, and to fill their place by Greek colonists. The walls of the city were thrown down and a strong Syrian garrison placed in the old citadel, which was restored for the purpose. Orders were given to root out the Jewish religion in Jerusalem and the whole

[1] For this period cf. Jos. *Ant.* v, xii; 1 Macc. i; 2 Macc. iv ff.

country and to introduce the worship of Greek gods. An altar was built on or at the great altar of burnt offerings, and on this sacrifices were offered to the Olympic Zeus, to whom the whole Temple was rededicated. The observance of all Jewish rites, especially the Sabbath and circumcision, was forbidden under penalty of death, and all copies of the Law were ordered to be destroyed. The result was that even among the indifferent the latent spirit of national, racial, and religious feeling was aroused once more.

The Chasidim resisted passively but stubbornly the king's commands, and the martyrdom of many of their members fanned into hot flame the national and religious conscience. They expected a divine interference on their behalf. If only they religiously observed the Law, then God was sure to interfere miraculously to save and protect them ; therefore they devoted themselves still more strenuously to observe the Law in its minutest details. This spirit of legalism and martyrdom shows itself in the literature developed at this period. The Book of Daniel constitutes a history of the inner life and thought of the Chasidim at the time of the Antiochian persecution and the Maccabæan revolt. Daniel was a famous character in ancient folk-story, about whom numerous tales had grown up, going back to the Babylonian school, to which reference has already been made. These represented that separatist and legal point of view which had been developed in Babylonia and brought thence to Palestine. Growing up about the old folk-hero, Daniel, they presented him to the people as the type of legal virtue, and as illustrating God's wonderful blessings upon the strict observer of the Law. Some of these stories, long current in the mouths of the people, a genius of this period recast, touching them with a divine fervor which made them a mighty power in present distress. This little booklet, consisting of chapters ii–vii of our present book of Daniel, set forth the wisdom and the piety of that old folk-hero, telling how he was delivered in an extraordinary manner from great perils, and how he discomfited his foes, the conquerors and oppressors of the Jews. It was prefaced and closed with two visions, the dream of Nebuchadrezzar and the dream of Daniel, both foretelling clearly, although under other names, the final destruction of the oppressing

Syrian.[1] This booklet was wonderfully well calculated to inspire the Jews of that day with a belief in the power and willingness of God to intervene on behalf of His pious and oppressed people, and to fill their minds with the hope of deliverance from their present tribulation and victory over their heathen foes. While it did not directly or indirectly counsel human resistance, or predict or suggest deliverance from calamity by means of human arms, it was nevertheless admirably calculated to be the spark to kindle the flame of religious war.

It was not, however, among the Chasidim that the outbreak actually began, nor was it primarily the Law which was in question. It was a priestly family which first raised the standard of revolt; for there were priests, and those evidently not a few, who had remained faithful to the tenets of Judaism. It is perhaps worth while to remind ourselves that religious history was here repeating itself. The men of the older time, like Jeremiah, who denounced sacrificial and sacerdotal abuses most scathingly, and who advocated the most drastic reforms, were themselves priests. It was the Temple which suggested to Isaiah his vision of a people of holiness. So now it was priests who, aroused by the desecration of the Temple and the attempt to make the Jews sacrifice to heathen idols, precipitated the inevitable outbreak. To the mass of the priests religion was vitally bound up with the outward forms of the Temple sacrifices, and idol worship and the desecration of the altar of Yahaweh roused their indignation as nothing else could.

The occasion of the outbreak itself was the visit of the king's commissioners to the little town of Modin to compel the people to present the heathen sacrifice.[2] Mattathias, an elderly priest residing there, refused to obey the command of the officer to present sacrifice; and when another Jew, anxious to curry favor by obedience,

---

[1] This part of the Book of Daniel was written shortly after 168 B.C., and is in the Aramaic dialect. The second part, written in Hebrew, is a series of apocalypses of somewhat later date, 165 or 164 B.C. Afterwards the two parts were united in one book, with an introduction, also in Hebrew. Cf. Peters, *The Old Testament and the New Scholarship*, chap. xv.

[2] The authorities for the history of the revolt are the First Book of Maccabees, Josephus' *Antiquities*, and the Second Book of Maccabees, in that order.

prepared to do it in his stead, Mattathias rushed forward and killed him on the altar, afterwards slaying the king's commissioner and leveling the altar to the ground. He then fled with his five sons into the mountains, where a multitude of the Pious had already sought shelter from the persecutors. The unimpeachable legal attitude of these men was well shown by the method of their observance of the Sabbath. To them the Sabbath law of rest was fundamental. It lay in the nature of God himself. They were made for the Sabbath, not the Sabbath for them; hence they might not even resist an enemy on the Sabbath day. Accordingly, the Syrians sought them out on that day and hewed them down without resistance. This was the attitude of the Chasidim. Mattathias and his followers, however, proceeded to active resistance, subordinating the Sabbath law to the necessity of the present situation. They gathered together a body of right-minded men ready to fight for the faith, and marched up and down the country, overturning the heathen altars and succoring all who were ready to oppose the Syrian persecutors, at the same time directing their fury against those of their fellow Jews who had turned apostate, slaying all who had allied themselves with the Syrians and circumcising such children as they found uncircumcised. Their courage met with a speedy response. The great body of the people rallied to their support, and the Chasidim, abandoning the policy of passive resistance, made common cause with them. Indeed, for the moment Mattathias and his followers became the Chasidim, the pious Jews, in opposition to the priestly aristocracy and their apostate or cowardly followers, who had willingly or unwillingly Hellenized in obedience to the orders of Antiochus. It is outside the purpose of this work to narrate in detail the struggle which followed under the lead first of Judas, second son of Mattathias, who succeeded his father on his death shortly after the commencement of the revolt, then of Jonathan, and last of Simon, as one succeeded the other.

The attitude of Judas Maccabæus was that of a national rather than of a religious patriot; that is to say, he was not, like the Chasidim, solely concerned with the restoration of the religious liberties and privileges of the people. When the legitimate High Priest, Alcimus, was permitted to assume his functions, and liberty was granted to the Jews to worship according to the Law and the rites of their religion in the Temple, purified and restored to its original use, the Chasidim withdrew their support from Judas. They were not fighting for national but for religious freedom. They were zealous for the Law. It is true they looked for an ultimate kingdom of righteousness, established on the lines of the Jewish Law, excluding most rigidly the outside world, which should be subdued under them or subjected to the dire punishment of an offended God; but they expected this to be wrought through the interference of God himself, and along the line of the exact fulfillment of the Law. A part of this exact fulfillment of the Law was the supremacy of the legitimate high-priesthood. Here was their point of contact with the Zadokite office-holding aristocracy, and the explanation of their attitude of halting between the Maccabees and their high-priestly opponents, the allies of the Antiochians. As for the Zadokite office-holding aristocracy itself, as already pointed out, it was through its secularization that the trouble had begun. The high-priestly leaders had practically ceased to have any religion whatsoever in the time of Jason and Menelaus; they constituted an aristocracy pure and simple. The religious functions were a mere incident of their tenure of office, which had no real meaning for them. Hence their readiness to join with Antiochus in forcing upon the Jewish people different religious rites and practices, these being the rule of the Syrian court, to which by virtue of their aristocracy they belonged. They were quite as ready to accept these as the conditions of their tenure of power, and to enforce them, as they had been to accept and enforce the others.

The first three years of the Maccabæan revolt made it plain to the Syrian rulers that the forcible Hellenization of the Jews along the lines originally attempted by Antiochus Epiphanes was impracticable, and with the passing away of that fanatical dreamer it was possible to adopt a new policy. His successors were not, like himself, concerned with the enforcement of a uniform religious worship and the adoption of a uniform Hellenic Syrian cult, provided they could secure political submission, abundant tribute, and soldiers at need. If by granting the Jews full exercise of their religion they could make Judæa an integral and submissive part of the Syrian empire, they were quite willing to permit the free exercise of the Jewish religion. With this policy the Zadokite office-holding aristocracy of the Jews was in entire sympathy. Such a policy would naturally bring over to their side a considerable body of priests who, while not zealots for the law like the Chasidim, were yet really Jews in belief; to whom the Jewish religion was the only true one, at least for Jews, Yahaweh the only true God, and His worship in His temple the only true worship. But by the time of the restoration of Alcimus matters had gone too far to permit the carrying out of such a policy. On the one hand Judas by his successes had reawakened the old national spirit of which he and his brothers became the reincarnation. They were fighting for the restoration of the kingdom of Israel. Their successes, comparable with the successes of the original invasion of Canaan under Joshua as recounted in their sacred books, had awakened in the Jews the old national religious heroism, and a confidence that God was interfering in their behalf as He had done of old. They could not be content with an administration of their state and religion conditioned on, and hampered by, the presence and control of the Syrian idolaters. On the other hand, the Syrians and their Zadokite allies were distrustful of the Chasidim, who had made common cause with Judas, and used their restoration to power to establish themselves more securely, as they thought, by proscribing those who had been active on his side. This mistaken and stupid policy played into the hands of Judas and his followers, convincing both the Chasidim, and also that large body of the Jewish priesthood who were really Jews at heart, that there was no hope of free practice of their religious rites except by complete victory over the Syrian oppressors. It was this which finally unified the whole people under Judas' leadership, and even after his defeat and death, and through all the calamities and vicissitudes which followed, made them united followers of the Hasmonæan brothers as religious as well as national leaders.

As a leader in the war of independence Judas may not inaptly be compared to Wallace in Scotland. He fought not for his own hand, claiming kingship or high-priesthood. In fact he did not have to consider the future outcome of the struggle. He fought merely to throw off the Syrian yoke, with singleness of purpose. While a fierce and almost fanatical believer in the God of Israel and zealous for His Law, he was thoroughly sane and common-sense in his adaptation of his beliefs to the needs of the struggle. In his belief God helped those who helped themselves. He was ready to meet enormous odds in the firm belief that the God of Israel would give His people the victory, but he used every human as well as divine means to secure that victory. The Law was a good and holy thing, but when the Law said to rest on the Sabbath, it must be interpreted on the lines of common sense. Judas had no notion that God meant him to sit still on that day and let himself be massacred by the Syrians. Similarly, he was zealous to purify the Temple, to remove the Antiochian abominations and restore the sacrifices to Yahaweh. As a priest he believed in the priesthood; but he had no idea that merely because Alcimus was the legitimate high priest, therefore he should be reinstated and given an opportunity to undo all the work which he, Judas, had done as a practical man dealing with hard facts. The mere theory of the Law or the legitimacy of the high-priesthood was to him a minor consideration. Whether Judas, had he lived to bring the struggle to its conclusion, would have himself assumed the high-priesthood, it is of course impossible to say.

Jonathan, who succeeded him, seems to have possessed less of that spiritual enthusiasm and national-religious singleness of purpose which distinguished Judas. While not the leader who could have aroused the religious and national enthusiasm necessary to unite the people, he was eminently adapted to take up the work where Judas left it. He won his victories chiefly by political cunning, playing off one pretender to the Syrian throne against another, now on this side, now on that, gaining constantly greater power and independence for himself and for his nation. Simon, the eldest of the brethren, but the last to assume the reins of power, showed even greater astuteness. He was a statesman of no mean ability. The time was ripe to found a new state, a combination of the ancient monarchy of David with the hereditary priestly government which had been developed in the Persian period. The people could conceive of no other head of the State than a high priest. Not only had they been habituated to this conception during the centuries which followed the return from Babylonia, but the very war which had now given them their independence had been a religious war, and their leaders in that war had been priests, fighting in the name of Yahaweh, and primarily for the establishment of the religion of Yahaweh. The old high-priesthood had proved faithless in the struggle, and what was left of it had set up a rival temple in Egypt. There was no other practical outcome than the establishment of a new high-priesthood, and no one to assume the office of High Priest but Simon. Without opposition, therefore, he assumed that rank and title. For all intents and purposes he was also king, lacking only the title, of an independent kingdom comprising not only Judah but Galilee, a considerable part of the Trans-Jordanic territory, and the Sharon Plain from Carmel to Joppa. He coined money and otherwise exercised sovereign prerogatives. Only his own prejudices and those of his subjects prevented him from actually assuming the title of king. With the death of Simon the great era of national religious revival came to an end. The history of the dynasty which he founded illustrates the apparently inevitable result of the combination of priestly and royal power in the same hands.

John Hyrcanus, son of Simon, pursued the policy of conquest initiated by Jonathan and Simon.[1] When defeated and besieged by the Syrians, he appealed to Rome, which compelled Antiochus VII to restore the conquered territory. When, after Antiochus' death, pretenders fought for his throne, Hyrcanus utilized the opportunity to annex Moab, Samaria, and Edom, circumcising the Idumæans by force and imposing on them the whole Jewish law. In this manner he made his wars holy wars, for the glory of Yahaweh's name and the spread of His religion. But in fact his policy was a worldly

---

[1] Our only historical authority for the remainder of this period is Josephus' *Antiquities*.

one, having as its aim conquest and dominion. Like David of old he employed mercenary soldiers, and indeed he may be said to have reverted in his whole attitude, moral and political, to the period of David. His reign was brilliant and successful, and the religious stamp which he gave to his wars reconciled the people at large to his usurpations and violations of the Law. The Pious, on the other hand, the zealots for the Law, were offended by his attitude. They stood for that idea of the congregation which had been developed during the Persian and the first part of the Greek period, when there had been no really national life, but the nation had been a congregation with a High Priest at its head, and the chief business of the community to obey and develop the prescriptions of the religious law and keep themselves separate from the world. With this party, the successors of the Chasidim, now known, however, as the Pharisees, it was inevitable that such a High Priest Prince as John Hyrcanus should break. And so we find the second generation of Maccabæan rulers allied with that very element of the nation against which Judas fought, the worldly aristocracy of priestly officeholders and their adherents, now known as the Sadducees. But now, as in the time of Judas, the former rather than the latter represented more nearly the prevailing sentiment of Judaism, its theory or ideal. This became manifest under Hyrcanus' successors. Hyrcanus, in spite of the outwardly religious character of his wars, showed decidedly Hellenic leanings, as for instance in the names of his sons, Aristobulus, Antigonus, Alexander. These leanings, the same which had characterized the Zadokite aristocracy of Judas' time, were still much more pronounced in Aristobulus and his brother and successor, Alexander Jannæus or Jonathan. It is true that they gave their conquests a religious character, as John Hyrcanus had done, by compelling the conquered peoples to be circumcised and keep the Law, and by destroying the towns and cities which refused to do so ; by which process, by the end of Alexander's reign, 78 B.C., Judæa had come to include the whole of the seacoast plain from Egypt to Mount Carmel, except Ascalon, and the entire region east of the Jordan from Lake Merom to the Dead Sea. In other respects, however, they imitated their neighbors. So

Aristobulus assumed the title of king, which none should bear but a descendant of David. Alexander used Greek as well as Hebrew on his coins.

The murderous intrigues of the sons of John Hyrcanus, and their debauchery, tended further to alienate the people and to strengthen the hands of the Pharisees. The latter were offended by the neglect of the Law, especially in the matter of the sacrifices, a very tender point with the people at large. This neglect they were able to make so apparent that on one occasion, when Alexander was about to offer sacrifice, the people pelted him with citrons and cried out that he was unworthy of the office of priest. He called in his mercenaries and a massacre ensued, followed by a civil war. Alexander was finally victorious, partly because his adversaries aroused the nationalist feeling against them by an alliance with the Syrians, thus compelling the people to choose between a return to the Syrian yoke or the rule of their own prince of the Hasmonæan line. With this as an issue, even many of the Pharisees reverted to Alexander's standard; but in the end it was by force rather than by favor that he maintained his power, supported by the Sadducees, and bitterly hated by the Pharisees.

The latter had a friend and apparently an adherent in Alexandra Salome, the widow of both the brothers, Aristobulus and Alexander Jannæus, who herself succeeded the latter on the throne. In spite of their defeat by Alexander, the Pharisees were numerically much the stronger party, and had Alexander's successor endeavored to continue the policy of his father, his fate might have been similar to that of Solomon's successor, Rehoboam. By her husband's will Alexandra ascended the throne as regent, her eldest son, Hyrcanus, becoming High Priest. She showed herself a pious ruler, after the heart of the Pharisees. Josephus says that while "she had indeed the name of regent — the Pharisees had the authority." She gave legal sanction to Pharisaic ordinances abolished by her predecessors, restored and freed banished and imprisoned Pharisees, and permitted some slight reprisals upon the Sadducean advisers of Alexander. But in general the aristocracy was left unmolested, and her reign was one of peace and prosperity at home as abroad, promising apparently a long continuance of the Hasmonæan dynasty. Scarcely was she dead, however, when her two sons, Hyrcanus and Aristobulus, commenced an internecine struggle for the kingship and high-priesthood, fostered and promoted by the Idumæan Antipater, which brought about the interference of the Romans, and finally the capture of the city by Pompey and the loss of Jewish independence in 63 B.C.

It is worthy of note that when Hyrcanus and Aristobulus sent embassies to Pompey, a third embassy appeared, purporting to represent the Jewish people, and asking for the abolition of the monarchy and the restoration of the old pre-Maccabæan theocracy. In part they had their wish. Hyrcanus was made High Priest and the kingship abolished. Judæa was annexed to the Roman Empire, as part of the province of Syria. But this was only the beginning of a new era of turbulence and confusion. Judæa was swept into the field of Roman politics and became an unwilling partaker in the wars and policies which resulted in the establishment of the Roman Empire. Under Herod, son of the Idumæan Antipater, it again became a kingdom, nominally subject to Rome, but in its actual internal administration practically independent. In the estimation of the Jews Herod was a foreign rather than a native king, in spite of the fact that he had married the heiress of the Hasmonæans, that he was a Jew by the outward forms of religion, and that he restored the Temple with great magnificence. For all intents and purposes the Jews under his rule were, as in the Persian period, a theocracy, managing their own religious and local concerns by a council, the Sanhedrin, subject politically to a foreign power, the Roman, whose representative Herod was. After his death the Roman government became still more direct, and the last vestige of national independence, the kingship, was swept away. Jewish nationalism existed only in the religious organization of the congregation.

Such, briefly, was the course and outcome of the Maccabæan revolution, viewed on its external side. At first successful in reviving and restoring national life, it ended finally, with the death of Herod, in complete absorption in the Roman provincial system.

But if in the matter of political independence and self-determination the national movement inaugurated by the Maccabees ended in failure after a brief period of success, nevertheless it made a strong and enduring impression on the religious development of Judaism. It reawakened and to some extent transformed the expectation of a Messiah and a Messianic age, making this hope from that time forward a large and essential part of Jewish religion. In connection with this it created an eschatology, giving also form and substance to the hitherto vague glimmering of the hope of a resurrection from the dead.

Almost in the nature of the case it called forth a literature, consisting in part of independent writings, like Maccabees, Daniel, Enoch, Judith, Tobit, Esther, the Psalms of Solomon, and some of the later Psalms in our Psalter; in part it resulted in the revision or modification of writings already existing, particularly the Psalms. But in the end this literary awakening was choked by the spirit of legalism and scribalism, which, commencing earlier, found its full expression in this period. It was the Law, the religion and the customs of their forefathers, which this national movement sought to restore and preserve. All new things were looked at with suspicion. The scribal view of literature and religion prevailed. Hence, while this great national revival called forth a considerable literature, at the end this literature was viewed with distrust, and of the new writings composed in the second and first centuries B.C. only two books, Daniel and Esther, with a few Psalms, found their way into the canon of Jewish Scriptures, albeit the entire book of Psalms and perhaps some parts of the Prophets underwent a revision to adapt them to the new conditions of persecution and national revival.[1] The final result was to sanctify and consolidate, if it may

---

[1] The results here described were only attained gradually. The canon, as stated in the introductory chapter, was not actually completed until some time in the second century A.D. Some of the books referred to above, like Enoch, were in use and much reverenced in Palestine in the century preceding and the century succeeding the birth of Christ. The tendency of Pharisaic legalism, however, was toward the exclusion of these books, and in general against the creation of new literature other than the actual interpretation of the Law. In Egypt, on the other hand, an abundant literature was produced, the two different influences resulting in different canons: the Palestinian canon, embodied in our Massoretic Hebrew text, and the Alexandrian

be so expressed, the ancient literature, rather than to create a new one; or, perhaps better, to set the old more distinctly in a sphere of its own, forever separated from the new. So we reach that conception of the Law which gives it almost an independent existence. It was so holy that one may say that man was created for it and not it for man. To a less extent legalism and scribalism reflected this conception from the Law to the Prophets and the Psalms, which had now become very holy and sacred, secondary only to the Law and separate from all other literature. The highest and holiest life is that which is employed in the contemplation and interpretation of the Scriptures, and such interpretations possess in themselves a high degree of holiness. The Temple shares the sanctity of the Law. It also was specially created by God, designed and planned by Him from eternity, and its form prepared in Heaven.

Of necessity continued reference has been made in this chapter to the two great Jewish sects, the Sadducees and Pharisees. Our information with regard to these sects, outside of the internal evidence contained in the books of the Old Testament and the apocryphal literature above referred to, is derived from the Antiquities of Josephus, supplemented by a few allusions in the New Testament.

The Sadducees, as has been stated, constituted the Temple aristocracy, whose doctrine was received but by a few, yet those still of the greatest dignity.[1] In their religious point of view they probably differed but little from the Samaritans. Like the Samaritans, their Bible was the Law. With its adoption their progress came to a halt. Unlike the Samaritans, however, the Jewish priesthood was in constant contact with that study of the ancient scriptures for which the Synagogue stood, which doubtless had a modifying effect on their conservatism. Some of the priests were scribes and themselves engaged in such study. The dominant party among them, however, stood for conservatism against the progressive movement, which,

canon, contained in the Greek translation and handed down in the practice of the larger part of the Christian Church. This latter canon did not, however, preserve all of the literature of this period. Some of it, like Enoch, was preserved in local canons of Christian churches, but the great part failed ultimately of canonization.

[1] Jos. *Ant.* xviii, i, 4. Elsewhere he says: "The Sadducees are able to persuade none but the rich," xiii, x, 6.

toward the close of the third century, added the Prophets to the Canon of scriptures. As in the Maccabæan period the opposition between the two elements resulted in the development of Sadducees and Pharisees, and as the distinction between these became more sharp and pronounced, doubtless the conservatism of the former increased. In general they rejected the new observances delivered to the people by the Pharisees through tradition and " by succession from their fathers, which are not written in the laws of Moses. " [1] In more detail Josephus says that " they also take away the belief of the immortal duration of the soul, and the punishments and rewards in Hades " (*Bell. Jud.* ii, viii, 14), holding that " souls die with the bodies " (*Ant.* xviii, i, 4). Of their philosophy or theology he reports that " they take away fate (providence) and say there is no such thing, and that the events of human affairs are not at its disposal, but they suppose that all our actions are in our own power, so that we are ourselves the causes of what is good, and receive what is evil from our own folly " (*Ant.* xiii, v, 9).[2]

With this agree in general the statements about the Sadducees contained in the Gospels and the Book of Acts,[3] where they are represented as not believing in the resurrection, nor in spirits and angels. The literature which we are able to connect with the Temple in the Persian and Greek periods, like the Psalter, also confirms both of these latter statements.

The Pharisees were the descendants of the Chasidim, or Pious, the outcome of the scribal movement. As a sect they date from the time of John Hyrcanus, 135–104 B.C. As the Sadducees belonged to the Temple and were the representatives of the old sacrificial worship, so the Pharisees belonged to the Synagogue and the Law. Theoretically both Temple and Law were needed to make the whole religion. In practice the representatives of the Temple sacrificial idea and the representatives of the legal scribal idea constituted two sects, each emphasizing one part. The Scribes sought to gather all the traditions of the fathers. These were to be added to the Law for its interpretation and understanding. The

---

[1] *Ant.* xiii, x, 6.   [3] Cf. Matt. xxii, 23 ; Acts iv, 1 ; xxiii, 6–8.
[2] Cf. also *Bell. Jud.* as above.

Law, according to the Pharisee, was the Law plus the traditions of the fathers. Josephus emphasizes the contrast thus :

" The Pharisees have delivered to the people a great many observances by succession from their fathers, which are not written in the laws of Moses ; and for that reason it is that the Sadducees reject them, and say that we are to esteem those observances to be obligatory which are in the written word, but are not to observe such as are derived from the tradition of our forefathers." [1] He mentions also the following special doctrines of the Pharisees : that they ascribe all to fate or providence (that is to say, God), and yet allow that to do right or wrong is within the power of each individual, although fate does coöperate in his action. They believed, further, in the immortality of the soul, or at least to the extent that the souls of the good are removed into other bodies, while the souls of the wicked are subject to eternal punishment.[2] In another place Josephus says : " They believe that souls have an immortal vigor in them, and that under the earth there will be rewards or punishments, according as they have lived virtuously or viciously in this life ; and that the latter are to be detained in an everlasting prison, but that the former shall have power to revive and live again." [3]

The Pharisees were the progressives ; they were also the democrats. For both reasons they were popular with the people at large, so that in the conflict between Sadducees and Pharisees the sympathies of the populace were ordinarily with the latter sect. Certain of their beliefs, moreover, appealed peculiarly to the popular mind and were indeed parts of the popular theology, such as the belief in angels and spirits and the belief in the future life with rewards and punishments after death.

On the other hand, the sacrificial religion of the Sadducees was in touch with the very foundations of the popular religion, that element which never lost its hold on the hearts of the people as the main and essential element of religion — sacrifice. The bulk of the people, therefore, were neither Pharisees nor Sadducees, sympathizing in certain regards with the sectarian teachings of each, but

---

[1] *Ant.* xiii, x, 6.   [3] *Ant.* xviii, i, 3. Cf. also Dan. xii, 2.
[2] *Bell. Jud.* ii, viii, 14.

in closer touch and more in personal sympathy with the Pharisees than with the Sadducees. The Pharisees are the authors of modern Judaism. The Sadducees perished with the Temple.

Besides these two Josephus mentions a third sect, small in number and of relatively small importance except as showing the religious currents of the time, namely the Essenes. These lived in small communities, eschewing marriage, like the Shakers of this country in the last century. Each community had a central house, around which they dwelt and in which they assembled for their religious observances, including the common meal. In their effort at extreme purity and brotherhood they developed, in the matter of property, socialism; and in the sphere of personal religion an individualism which excluded them from the community at large. They could not associate with their fellow Jews; they could not enter the Temple, and hence took no part in the sacrifices. They impressed all with the austerity of their morality and the holiness of their character, very much as Trappist monks and similar orders of nuns impress the imagination, without producing permanent or extensive results. They may be said to be the outcome of the holiness provisions of the Law. As the Sadducees emphasized the Temple, and the Pharisees the Law with the traditions of the fathers, so the Essenes emphasized holiness.[1]

To this notice of the sects should be added, perhaps, summing up what has been said from time to time, a word about the distinction between the Alexandrian Jews and the Jews of Palestine. The latter represent in general the victory of the separatists, who originated or developed in Babylonia and whose type work of bitter hatred of the outside world, combined with a curious and ultimately unconscious appropriation of its superstitions, is Esther. The former were a combination of Judaism with Hellenism. In general the Jews of Egypt remained enthusiastic nationalists. Socially they were Jews and even fanatics in the Jewish quarters, but elsewhere hardly to be distinguished from Greeks. Politically

---

[1] Jos. *Ant.* xviii, v; *Bell. Jud.* ii, viii, 5–7. For other minor and lesser sects cf. also Schechter, *Jewish Lectures*, and G. F. Moore, *Harvard Theological Review*, vol. iv, pp. 330–377.

they were similarly duplex. They regarded Jerusalem as the sacred city and its Temple as the one place in which sacrifices should be offered.[1] On the other hand, there was a temple in Egypt, served by descendants of the old Zadokite line of the priesthood, which at Jerusalem had been displaced by the Hasmonæan priesthood. They despised the heathen world, and theoretically disregarded its opinions; but were always eager to claim its great things and great men as their own, and to convince the heathen of the greatness of their saints, inventing marvelous fables for that purpose. They maintained the faith, and that in a very highly spiritual form, as even Tacitus testifies: "The Egyptians worship various animals and images, the work of men's hands; the Jews acknowledge one God only, and conceive of him by the mind alone, condemning as impious all who, with perishable materials, wrought into the human shape, form representations of the Deity. That Being, they say, is above all, and everlasting, neither susceptible of likeness nor subject to decay. In consequence, they allow no resemblance of him in their city, much less in their temples."[2]

On the other hand, they were profoundly affected by Hellenic philosophy, and the peculiar literature which characterizes Alexandrian Judaism attempts to explain and defend Jewish scriptures and beliefs by identifying them with Greek philosophy. The great leader and representative of Alexandrian thought at about the commencement of the Christian era is Philo, who may be said to have developed a Judæan neo-Platonism. Not under the influence of either Sadducees or Pharisees, the Alexandrian Jews developed a larger religious literature than the Jews of Palestine. It was the Palestinian-Babylonian rather than the Alexandrian which was the orthodox parent of modern Judaism. Christianity, on the contrary, at least after the first generation, derived more from Alexandrian than from Palestinian Judaism.

---

[1] *Bell. Jud.* vii, x, 3.   [2] *History* v, 5.

CHAPTER XXVIII

THE MESSIANIC HOPE

The most striking and characteristic feature of the religion of Israel was the Messianic Hope: the belief in the advent of a Messiah or Christ (the anointed of God), the overthrow or annihilation of the heathen, the punishment of the wicked, and the establishment of God's kingdom on earth. The foundations of this doctrine were laid in the most ancient period of Hebrew history. In the earliest writings which have come down to us we find a firm belief in a peculiar relation of Yahaweh to Israel and Israel to Yahaweh. This is an intensification of a belief common among at least those Semitic peoples with whose religion we are acquainted, the belief in a special relation of each people to its tribal god, a relation of blood kinship, continually confirmed and reëstablished by the sacrifice of blood. Not only the honor, the very existence of the god was bound up in his people. He was honored in their honor, dishonored in their dishonor, and annihilated in their destruction. This relation was peculiarly emphasized in the religion of Israel, and, partly owing to the circumstances of Israel's history, it was to a considerable extent dissevered from the limitation of locality, which played so important a part in modifying among kindred peoples the conception of their relation to their god. Moreover, as a result apparently of their confederation through the influence of Moses into one nation, with one general God taking the place of various tribal gods, this relation to Yahaweh became a covenant relation. They had entered into covenant with one another and with Yahaweh.[1] As a part of that covenant Yahaweh gave them victory over the people of the land of Canaan and possession of their land.[2] As a result

[1] This is emphasized even by those who, like Budde and Stade, take a very different view of the covenant of Israel with Yahaweh. Cf. chap. iv.

[2] For other covenants cf. Gen. xlix; Deut. xxxiii; Gen. iii, 15; ix; xii, 3; 2 Sam. xxiii, 5.

partly of historical events and partly of the interpretation put by Moses and other leaders on those events, Israel became convinced that its God, Yahaweh, was a god of peculiar power, stronger than the gods of the peoples about them. How this came about has already been pointed out.

Yahaweh came out of the mountains of the south and led his people to victory. Yahaweh, in or through the Ark, not only guided them to Canaan, but led them in the wars against the neighboring peoples. The victories to which they went were the victories of Yahaweh. Such was the Day of Midian, or the Day of Yahaweh upon Midian. The phrase "Day of Yahaweh" was used to indicate the intervention of Yahaweh for the destruction of His foes.[1] It was continually expected that He would show His power by such intervention. He might be quiescent for a time, Israel might undergo reverses, but Yahaweh would surely intervene again. There was a continual expectation of the Day of Yahaweh, which meant, originally, nothing more than His intervention for the discomfiture of the present adversaries of Israel; to relieve Israel in times of oppression, or to give it success against its foes and ultimately the final success of a complete conquest of the promised land. The culmination of these successes in the glory of David's kingdom, David's brilliant victories, as the warrior of Yahaweh, over the neighboring nations, and his establishment of a great kingdom of consolidated Israel with suzerainty or hegemony over all the surrounding peoples from the border of Egypt to the Euphrates, was the convincing proof of the invincible might of Yahaweh and His superiority to all the gods of the neighboring nations. It was the evidence both of His power and of His will to fulfill the covenant with Israel (in accordance with which they had become His people)

[1] In the popular conception the "Day of Yahaweh" meant a deliverance by the intervention of Yahaweh because He had chosen Israel. In the prophetic conception, the sin of Yahaweh's own people and of other nations called for His intervention as the moral ruler of the world, this judgment, however, preparing for redemption. Israel should be brought back into its own land, and the other nations made subject to Israel by force or by persuasion. Cf. "Day of Midian," Is. ix, 4 ; "Day of Jezreel," Hos. i–ii ; "That Day," Am. ii, 16 ; Is. ii, 11 ; Jer. iv, 9 ; "Day of Yahaweh," Am. v, 18 ; Is. ii, 12 ; xiii, 6, 9, 13 ; xxxiv, 8 ; Lam. i, 12 ; Jer. xlvi, 10 ; Ezek. xiii, 5 ; xxx, 3 ; xxxix, 8, 11, 13, and increasingly common in later literature.

that He would give them the land of Canaan in possession. Because Israelite dominion culminated in David, because Solomon ruled for Judah only and with his son the kingdom was divided and its power diminished, never to be regained, therefore from this time onward, in combination with the doctrine of Israel's peculiar and indefeasible relation to Yahaweh and of its covenant with Him, the kingdom of David and David himself play an important part in the Messianic belief.

David and the kingdom of David became to succeeding ages what the Roman Empire and Cæsar became to Italy and then to Europe. First the name and fame of Cæsar were passed on from generation to generation of Roman rulers, becoming an integral part of the conception of the Roman Empire.[1] For this empire there was sought also a divine sanction, until finally the Emperor was deified. The tradition of this empire, and its mighty founder, who had brought a world peace and order out of confusion and chaos, continued after the fall of that empire, and the disorder and distress which succeeded that event strengthened and idealized the tradition. The greatness of that Cæsarean empire centered about Rome, its capital. The tradition of this Roman Empire and its deified head was taken over by the Christian Church. So we find, in Christian history, the Holy Roman Empire claiming to be the successor of the empire of the Cæsars. The same thing took place here which, as we shall see, took place also in the development of the idea of the Messianic kingdom : the divine and human elements were first dissevered, then the latter was made subject to and finally swallowed up in the former. In the Christian concept the Cæsar was first subordinated to the Roman Pontiff ; finally the latter came to be regarded as vicegerent of the Almighty, combining in himself as such political and religious supremacy. Here Rome played the same rôle as Jerusalem among the Jews, and Cæsar gave way to the Roman Pontiff, as, in the development of the Messianic Hope, Zerubbabel the Davidic prince gave way to Joshua the High Priest.

For the effect of the Davidic kingdom on the Messianic Hope,

---

[1] Cf. the modern use of the name *Caesar* for "emperor," as German *Kaiser*, Russian *Czar*, Hindustani *Kaisar-i-Hind*.

and particularly the popular belief in the return of David, we may also compare the Arthurian legend of the Britons, or the Charlemagne legend of the Germans.[1] Such popular hope of or belief in the return of a national hero may be analyzed as a longing for the

[1] While this belief in the return of a popular hero may not be universal, it is certainly widespread. Besides the instances mentioned above we have also among European peoples the belief of the Montenegrins in the return of Ivan the Black, who sleeps in a cave near Obod, awaiting the day when he shall wake again to lead his people in triumph against the Turks. In Germany the legend of the return of a national hero to lead his people victoriously against their foes attached itself not only to Charlemagne, but also to Frederick I (Barbarossa) and Frederick II. Like Ivan, Charlemagne sits in a cavern waiting to be called by his country's need. For about a century after his death Frederick was believed by the people still to be alive, and several impostors claimed to be Frederick returned or revived. To him also the cave legend attaches. In Portugal similar legends attached to Sebastian. Among some of our own American Indians Hiawatha plays the same rôle. Among Semitic peoples we have something of the same sort in the Mahdi. While the Moslem belief in a Mahdi, always supposed to be the reincarnation of a vanished Imam, or leader, has been doubtless strongly influenced by Jewish and Christian Messianism, there are also in it other elements common to the various European legends already mentioned, suggesting an original belief of a similar character. This belief is in the nature of the case dynastic as well as personal. In the Roman world it was Nero, as the last of the Cæsars, whose return was expected; a belief utilized by various impostors. The earliest expression of this belief in the return of a national hero, or the perpetuation of his dynasty, which I have found outside of the Bible, is that which attached itself to Nebuchadrezzar. In his Behistun inscription Darius records the fact that among the various rebels who rose against him two claimed to be Nebuchadrezzar (son of Nabunid), and these the Babylonians gladly followed. (Neissbach, Die Keilinschriften der Achaemeniden, Leipzig, 1911, pp. 22–23.) These legends in various countries assume various forms; in some they are very literal, displaying a belief in the actual return of the dead hero, of which advantage was taken by impostors, as in the case of Nebuchadrezzar, Nero, the Emperor Frederick, and Sebastian. Sometimes it is an ideal return, the restoration or revival of that for which the hero stood, his reappearance in a descendant or the like. Sometimes mystic or mythological elements have been added, especially in the legends of Charlemagne, Arthur, and Hiawatha, or these legends may even be affected by Jewish or Christian Messianic conceptions; but in all cases we have the same historic foundation; the existence of a hero whose leadership profoundly impressed his people, and whose return after death has been expected in a form partly literal, partly ideal. The basis of this belief is psychological. After an heroic age created or dominated by some hero, followed by calamities and misfortunes or even by pettiness strongly contrasting with the heroic achievements and imaginations of the age of glory, the mind goes back with longing to that past, meditating on and enhancing its glory and proportionately minimizing or decrying present conditions. Such living in the past tends to realize it and thus to create a hope in its return, which hope, developing into belief, naturally associates itself with that hero to whom those glories real and fancied are attributed, and the expectation of the return of those glories becomes an expectation of his return also.

glory of the past, metamorphosed, through much meditation in time of great distress on the glory, welfare, and happiness of that past, into the hope of its restoration in the future. David was the great king, the anointed of God in the past, to whom in later calamity, distress, and pettiness the people longingly looked back. His glory, like the glory of the Roman Cæsars, was in each new age reflected on his descendants. It is a longing for that glory of the past, driven by an utter lack of its realization in the present first to the hope, then to the belief in its restoration in the future, which we see in the expectation of the return of David. As in the Arthurian legend, this hope was not quite literal, nor yet altogether ideal. It connects itself literally with the name, the place, the family of David, and yet what it looks for is not David, but the kingdom and glory of David. Inevitably this hope idealized the actual Davidic kingdom of the past, finding in it a complete fulfillment of the covenant of Yahaweh, and in David an ideal king ruling in accordance with divine law. Indeed, the covenant idea is to some extent transferred to him. With him Yahaweh has concluded an everlasting covenant, to maintain his kingdom and his dynasty. To the people at large this conception of a restored Davidic kingdom, the simplest and crudest form of the Messianic hope, always remained the most intelligible and the most appealing form of that hope. We find it written into the historical narratives in such passages as 2 Sam. vii, 16 : " And thine house and thy kingdom shall be made sure forever before thee : thy throne shall be established forever."

Coming down from the time before the establishment of the kingdom, and connected — in the thought of later writers certainly — with the Mosaic dispensation, existed the conception of a sort of theocratic republic under Yahaweh as king.[1] In its extreme form this shows itself in a prophetic protest against the establishment of royalty as a concession to popular clamor contrary to the will of God.[2] This conception was more peculiarly Israelite. Unlike Judah, Israel had no well-established dynasty to which the people were attached by a great past. Its old traditions, as represented in Judges, pointed in the other direction. Both Israel and Judah,

---

[1] Deut. xxxiii.   [2] 1 Sam. xii; Deut. xviii, 14 ff.

however, looked theoretically to Yahaweh as their supreme ruler — a thought associated in both in different degrees with the conception that the human king reigns by right only if he reigns by commission or unction from Yahaweh.[1] The two views, that of an ideal kingdom ruled over by David or a king of David's line, and that of a kingdom of God upon earth ruled by God himself, are not incompatible. They may be reconciled somewhat as the two documents in the Book of Samuel are combined, and in point of fact, as we shall see later, both views existed side by side and sometimes both are represented by the same writer.

This is the form which the Messianic Hope had assumed by the time of the writing prophets, as vouched for both by the earlier literature which has come down to us and also by the Prophets themselves.[2] This is the material which the writing prophets used, the motives which they combine and vary, elevating them at the same time to a higher ethical and spiritual plane, and which they were able to use as the foundation of their prophecies because the people were thoroughly imbued with these hopes and ideas: the establishment of an ideal kingdom, more wonderful even than that of David; a complete fulfillment of the covenant entered into with Yahaweh, by which Israel had become His peculiar people, whom for His own sake He would not cast off nor reject; and for whose salvation He was to manifest His power by sitting in judgment on their foes and overthrowing them by His great might in a day of judgment, the Day of Yahaweh.

[1] Gen. xlix; 2 Kings ix, 6.

[2] Amos refers to the peculiar relation of Yahaweh to Israel and Israel to Yahaweh, with the accompanying covenant of blessings and curses (iii, 2): "You only have I known of all the families of the earth: therefore I will visit upon you all your iniquities." Such passages as vi, 8: "The Lord Yahaweh hath sworn by himself, saith Yahaweh, the God of hosts: I abhor his palaces: therefore will I deliver up the city with all that is therein," are an evidence of the existence of a belief in the peculiar love of God for Israel, which is contradicted in Yahaweh's name by Amos in the same way in which (v, 18: "Woe unto you that desire the Day of Yahaweh! wherefore would ye have the Day of Yahaweh? It is darkness, and not light") he contradicts their conception of the nature of the Day of Yahaweh. That contradiction is of course evidence of the general belief in his time in that great day of Yahaweh's judgment on Israel's foes. The passage in which he refers to the restoration of Israel under a king of David's line (ix, 2 ff.) is now generally regarded as a later addition.

The writings of the first of the writing Prophets, Amos, may at first sight seem anti-Messianic, but in fact they bear striking testimony to the existence of the Messianic expectation in his time, and especially to the expectation of the great Day of Yahaweh, in which Yahaweh will hold assizes, judge and overthrow the nations of their enemies, and bring about, in its completeness, the fulfillment of the covenant, the possession of the land of Canaan, flowing with milk and honey, which they shall inhabit in peace and prosperity, unmolested of all foes. Inspired by that hope, they could be blind or indifferent to the threatening disaster of the Assyrian advance. They lived, as it seemed to Amos, in a fool's paradise.

Perhaps we may say that Amos' great contribution to the development of the Messianic idea was his interpretation of this concept of the Day of Yahaweh as a judgment, first and foremost, upon themselves, a purification of the nation; and from this time onward we find, first in the prophetic expectation and ultimately in the popular conception of the Messianic period, the idea of a judgment within the nation itself so severe as to blot out the entire guilty past.

The complement to this, in the prophetic concept in general, is a final complete realization of a kingdom of God, Yahaweh, upon earth, in a regenerate nation;[1] but this is not expressed in Amos, although one studying the book carefully will observe that, while he seems to be only a prophet of wrath, he has clearly not broken with the old conception of a peculiar relation of Yahaweh to Israel, which cannot be annulled, and as a result of which there must be a final restoration.

In emphasizing Yahaweh's tender love for Israel, the wife of his youth, Hosea strengthens materially this conception of the indestructible relation of Yahaweh and His people, giving it also an ethical relation. For its sins Israel must suffer and again go into exile; but, as out of the first exile it was brought into the promised land, so after the removal of its sins the purified people shall finally

---

[1] Each prophet connects the final restoration with the removal of the sins of his own age, and the accomplishment of such a work of judgment as he sees to be required within his own kingdom.

be restored to a better kingdom, which is a realization of the conception of the rule of Yahaweh himself, of a national organization of Israel under Yahaweh, made effective through rulers reigning by commission or unction from Him.

The Messianic views of Amos and Hosea are not vivid, but they represent certain features common to all prophecy down to the close. All the prophets believe in a final restoration of the ideal kingdom, or the theocratic republic, with either Yahaweh himself as ruler, or else a human representative commissioned or anointed by Him. Each connects this final restoration, which is but the ideal fulfillment of the ancient government, with the removal of the sins of his own age as a prerequisite ; and also with the accomplishment of such a work of judgment upon the sinners within the nation and the heathen without as lies within his own horizon of vision. The book of Hosea, as it has come down to us, includes the Davidic hope and affects Judah as well as Israel ; but it is now generally agreed that the passages containing such representations belong to a later, Judæan revision. Among the Prophets it is with the great Judæan, Isaiah, that we find the earliest indisputable presentation of the Davidic hope. Isaiah, Jeremiah, and Ezekiel all look for the restoration of David, or a king of David's line, ruling over a kingdom supernaturally refined and glorified.[1] But this is not the only form in which the Messianic Hope appears in their writings. Isaiah also depicts the kingdom of supernatural peace and righteousness, without mention of an earthly king, as ruled over by Yahaweh ; and in one passage, certainly, the people itself, purged of its sins,

[1] To Amos God is righteousness ; to Hosea love. To Isaiah God is Yahaweh, the king, who has founded His kingdom in Zion, on the throne of which shall sit forever a scion of the house of David, the Prince of Peace, filled with the fullness of the Spirit of God : ix, xi. In general, the Judæan prophets of the preëxilic period connect Israel's deliverance with an ideal Davidic king, so Mic. v, 2 ; Jer. xxiii, 5–8 ; xxxiii, 14–26 ; Ezek. xxxiv, 23 ; xxxvii, 24–25 ; cf. also 2 Sam. vii, 13 f., for use of word " scion " or "branch." Cf. also Is. iv, 2, and Zech. vi, 12 (in latter passage of Zerubbabel). Isaiah's ideal king is a scion of Jesse's stock, on whom will rest the spirit of God, as the spirit of religion ; who will rule in the fear of God. He will not engage in war or conquest, but will establish justice among his people, Is. ix and xi. The people will not aspire to political greatness, Is. xxxii. This scion of Jesse will be a beacon to lead other nations to the same state. Haggai and Zachariah, on the other hand, see in him, as realized in Zerubbabel, only one who shall rebuild the Temple and rule Israel, Hag. ii, 23 ; Zech. iii, 8, vi, 12.

— that is, the remnant left after the destruction wrought upon the sinners through the foreign invaders, Syrians, Israelites, and Assyrians, by Yahaweh's judgment, — is the anointed of God, Emmanuel, " God with us." Emmanuel is the child of the Virgin of Zion, brought into the world by the birth pangs of Zion's tribulation and affliction.[1]

The same view is set forth in the contemporary provincial prophet, Micah ; only in his presentation of the theme Jerusalem is captured, and the Virgin of Judah must flee into the wilderness to meet there her travail, out of which shall be born the people of holiness.

Isaiah, as has been noted elsewhere, had a special veneration for the Temple as the dwelling-place of Yahaweh, and for Jerusalem as the city of the Temple, and he consequently brings Jerusalem into a peculiar relation to the birth of the Messianic kingdom. Attention has already been called to the effect, in confirming this doctrine of Isaiah, of the deliverance of Jerusalem from the Assyrians in the time of Sennacherib. Isaiah also makes most effective use of the theme of the Day of Yahaweh.[2] But while, both at the time of the invasion of the allied Syrians and Israelites and also in the time of the Assyrian invasion, he becomes the militant prophet of Yahaweh, calling the people to arms, urging resistance in Yahaweh's name, and promising a Day of Yahaweh upon their foes, he also emphasizes that conception of the Day of Yahaweh which Amos had made so effective, God's punishment upon the sinners within the land. It is in this spirit that he denounces woe upon the monopolists, the drunkards, those that go after magicians, wizards, false gods, those who abuse the ritual and the service of Yahaweh, using it as the end and not the means of their religion.[3]

The Scythian invasion in the last quarter of the seventh century gave, in the hands of the Prophets, a new meaning and a peculiar coloring to the doctrine of the Day of Yahaweh. This new and mysterious nation, coming from the unknown regions of the north, with its wild appearance, its strange and inhuman ways, and its

---

[1] Cf. Peters, *The Old Testament and the New Scholarship*, Appendix on " The Virgin Birth."

[2] Is. ii–iii, where it is connected with convulsions of nature.

[3] Such pictures of the Day of Yahaweh are found in chaps. i–ii, v.

irresistible onset,[1] shaking and overturning all the stable powers of the earth, became to Zephaniah [2] and Jeremiah both the fulfillment and the picture of the day of the judgment of Yahaweh. Through the Scythians was being realized upon the nations without and on the sinners within that judgment which should usher in the expected kingdom.

The adoption of the Deuteronomic Law and the reforms of Josiah, partly accompanying, partly following the Scythian catastrophe, seemed to fulfill another condition of the Messianic Hope, the reformation within the nation itself. The Day of Yahaweh had come in vengeance on the nations. The great oppressor of the world, Assyria, had fallen, the Jewish nation had purged itself of its iniquities and become the people of Yahaweh in very truth, and a vivid and present expectation of the realization of its great and ancient hope possessed the people. We have seen how Josiah was inspired by that hope to expect the fulfillment of the promises in his own person and to venture, in expectation of divine help, to oppose himself and his army to the Egyptian invaders, with the result of his defeat and death at the Battle of Megiddo.

But this hope was not quenched by that calamity. Suppressed at one point, it flared up at another, until it set all Jewry in conflagration and brought about the capture of Jerusalem and the deportation of the chiefs of the nation, both priestly and lay, by Nebuchadrezzar. But even this was not the end. The expectation of the Day of Yahaweh upon the heathen, of the intervention of their God to destroy His foes by a mighty catastrophe, thus ushering in the expected paradise, persisted, both among the deported Jews in Babylonia, leading them to attempt a revolt against the Babylonians, and also among the Jews left behind in Jerusalem, resulting in a second rebellion and the final destruction of the city.[8]

---

[1] In Isaiah xiii also it is some fierce and distant nation which is the instrument by which Yahaweh executes His judgments.

[2] Zephaniah's vision of the great day of Yahaweh's vengeance on the sinners in Israel involved also the destruction of the surrounding nations and the subsequent happiness of Zion. But in this vision no figure of the Messiah appears.

[8] The conditions are almost precisely parallel to those existing in the first century of our era, when the unrest, culminating in the great rebellion, resulted in the capture and destruction of Jerusalem by Titus ; and this unrest, after smoldering for a time,

Up to this time it is clear that in the vision of the Prophets, as well as in the belief of the common people, the Messianic kingdom was a kingdom of the not remote future, a glorified Davidic kingdom, or a glorified theocratic kingdom or republic. It is with Jeremiah that we begin to find this kingdom pushed onward into the more remote future. The captivity which he foresees is to be not one of a generation, forty years, the length of time which Israel wandered in the wilderness in the past; but a period of indefinite length, seventy years. But Jeremiah is as clear as the former prophets in his belief in the fulfillment of the Davidic ideal, the restoration of David's kingdom glorified, ruled by a king of David's line.[1] Although the realization of this ideal is postponed and the exiles are directed to make themselves at home in the land where they may be, to become part of it, to buy houses and plant fields and vineyards and the like, yet the kingdom is not so far removed but that Jeremiah buys the field on which the Babylonian army is encamped. His conception of the method of preparing for the kingdom is in one respect very practical, if not materialistic. But with the advice to the Israelite to make himself at home and till the land, wherever he may be, there is combined a very spiritual and unpractical element of faith: the Israelite is to be circumcised in his heart, and to have the law of God written there. As he fulfills that law in his life, Yahaweh himself will, in His good time, establish the kingdom.

Here Jeremiah's point of view seems to differ from that of his famous predecessor. Isaiah had encouraged his countrymen to fight: Yahaweh would assist them. Jeremiah bids them not to fight: their one business is to be righteous, to fulfill the law of God and to engrave it upon their hearts. When that is done, Yahaweh himself will usher in His kingdom.

led, half a century later, to the rebellion of Bar-Kokheba, in the time of Hadrian, and the third destruction of Jerusalem.

[1] Jeremiah foresees a succession of kings of David's line, xvii, 25; xxii, 4; xxxiii, 15, 17. The essential characteristic of his idea is a king standing in a peculiar relation to Yahaweh, reigning by His appointment, in His name and by His power, who shall do all God's will, whose rule shall be one of absolute righteousness, who will compel all men to honor the God of Israel, and who will bestow on his people perfect happiness, and peace forever.

Very much the same view is taken by Jeremiah's younger contemporary, Ezekiel, except that Ezekiel's conception of righteousness and of fulfillment of the law is different from that of Isaiah. In his prophecies, also, we see the influence of the Scythian invasion upon the idea of the Day of Yahaweh. It develops in Ezekiel into the picture of the armies of Gog,[1] a summing up of the hosts of evil, which are overwhelmed by the might of Yahaweh. With Ezekiel also we enter the field of eschatology. His views of the after times and the last days are more developed and detailed than those of his predecessors. After the Day of Yahaweh upon Gog comes the reëstablishment of the idealized kingdom. But to Ezekiel the Temple is more important than the palace. The offering of sacrifice and the observance of the laws connected with that sacrifice, with clean and unclean and the like, are more important than the civil and political laws. He cannot conceive of the kingdom without a king, but the king exists primarily that he may fulfill the divine law, which connects itself with the sacrifice and other Temple observances : and so we find, in the latter part of his book, the prince subordinated to the Temple and its priesthood.[2] Ezekiel has carried farther that which we began to see in Isaiah. Isaiah had taught the inviolability of Jerusalem because of the Temple that was in it. Ezekiel exalts the Temple still further. It is not only the center of the life of the nation, but the nation may be said to exist for the Temple. The way is being prepared for that later conception which was to make the Temple a preëxistent or almost preëxistent entity, planned by God from eternity and concealed in heaven.

With Haggai and Zechariah, after the return from the Exile, we find the old hope, with the expectation of a speedy fulfillment. With the erection of the new Temple, the new kingdom shall be ushered in. God will shake all nations and bring their treasures to Jerusalem. Haggai looks for the restoration of the old Davidic kingdom under Zerubbabel. Zechariah at first sees in Zerubbabel the prince of David's line, who has been allowed to return to Jerusalem, the king that is to be ; but in his later prophecies, after the reorganization

[1] Ezek. xxxviii f.
[2] For restoration of Levitical priesthood cf. Ezek. xliv, 15 ; xlviii, 11.

of the Persian kingdom under Darius, the High Priest takes the prince's place, and we have apparently the expectation of a priestly kingdom, somewhat on the lines of Ezekiel's later hope, except that the prince has vanished altogether and all expectation of the future is centered in the priesthood. The vision of neither of these prophets is of the highest and grandest order. Their Messianic kingdom is a relatively small thing, conformable to the pettiness of their surroundings in church and state.

In striking contrast with the pettiness and narrowness of their hope is the grandeur and catholicity of the hope of that great prophet or school of prophets whose work, for want of a better name, we designate as Deutero-Isaiah. In the vision of these writers the punishment of the sinners of Israel, predicted by the former prophets, has been fulfilled.[1] By the destruction of Jerusalem and all the suffering and distress connected with that event and with the Exile, they have been purged, they have received double for all their sins. The Day of Yahaweh has come, His judgment has already been executed upon them. Now, in the time of peace and happiness, the everlasting covenant made with David shall be kept; but the conception of the kingdom is not the petty conception of a Davidic kingdom, nor is the king who is to reign mentioned as David or one of David's line.[2] As in Jeremiah's and Ezekiel's conception, it is not by force of arms nor even by the heroism or leadership of some one man that the kingdom is to be ushered in. In the conception of Deutero-Isaiah it is the ideal people, the perfectly holy Israel, which is to be, if one may so put it, its own Messianic kingdom.[3]

[1] In the preëxilic prophets the judgment falls primarily on Israel, involving its dissolution in order to a new reconstruction (Am. iii, 2). The sinners shall be destroyed and a humble people left behind, Zeph. iii, 12; Is. ii–iii; Hos. ii, 18; xiv. With the exile, the judgment having been executed on Israel, the judgment of the Day of Yahaweh falls on the heathen world, and issues in Israel's redemption. Is. xiii; Hag.; Zech. i–viii. So also Is. xl ff.; Ps. xciii–xcix. When Israel again becomes a people the prophets once more threaten Israel with judgment, so Mal. iii, 2 ff.

[2] There is a mention of David in Is. lv, 1–5, but he seems more like a figure of speech than a reality, and his covenant seems to have been transferred to the people.

[3] In Deutero-Isaiah the salvation of mankind is the goal of history. Israel's prerogative is to suffer for the good of the whole world. Israel and not an individual is the servant of God, through whom the regeneration of mankind will be accomplished,

Jeremiah's teaching of the law written on the heart, of the wait-ing upon God's will everywhere, has achieved a profound effect; but Deutero-Isaiah goes farther. He perceives that the holy people, planted here and there and everywhere, have a peculiar relation to, and a special obligation for, those among whom they are placed, so that instead of serving only itself Israel is to serve all the nations of the world. Israel is to be brought from all the ends of the world into the final ideal kingdom in Palestine, for that old conception the author does not abandon; but the judgment by which they are to be brought is, if one may so put it, not one of destruction, but one of love. The nations, in bringing them, are to bring themselves — a concep-tion which, it is true, we find to some extent in the first Isaiah also.

The most striking contribution of the writer or writers of Deutero-Isaiah to the Messianic Hope is the conception of the perfect ser-vant, the ideal Israel, atoning for the sins of Israel by his sufferings.[1] We have here the same conception which the other prophets have set forth, of the need of a purging away of sin, a reformation so complete as to constitute a breach with the sinful past; and we have also the same conception of a purified remnant which appears in Isaiah; but the combination of conceptions produces some-thing entirely new. The servant (that is, ideal Israel) represents also in his attitude the conception set forth by Jeremiah. He does not strive nor cry out, but waits in patient obedience, submitting to the violence of external foes and the evil-doing of the sinful within the nation. As already pointed out,[2] Jeremiah's personality as well as Jeremiah's teaching made a profound impression upon this writer, and had much to do with the development of the servant idea which he sets forth. It will be observed that the idea of the ineffaceable relation of kinship, of eternal love between Yahaweh and Israel, as a result of which Yahaweh cannot cast

who will spread true religion among the nations, xlii, 1–6 ; xlix, 1–6 ; l, 4–9 ; lii, 13–liii, 12. The same picture appears also in Is. ii, 1–4 ; Mic. iv, 1–4. In Malachi, Joel, and the late apocalypse in Is. xxv–xxvii, there is also no personal Messiah. Here God, without the instrumentality of man, will redeem Israel from present misery and bring about a new era of salvation. Malachi, however, introduces a forerunner, Elijah.

[1] A representation running through the earlier chapters, and culminating in liii.
[2] Chap. xxi.

off nor desert His people, is prominent in the Deutero-Isaianic conception; but this writer represents a return of that love and affection by a holy kernel in Israel itself.

With the establishment of the Law and the commencement of the scribal period, we find no waning of the Messianic Hope. Israel, however, no longer felt itself a living nation. The tendency, therefore, was to dissever the Messianic Hope from the present and interpret it as a feature wholly new and supernatural. The interpretation of the written word now takes the place of the spoken word of the former period. Everything that had been written was gathered, examined, and interpreted. As an almost necessary result of this we have the harmonistic exegesis, which seeks to gather up every prophetic image in one grand panorama of the history of Israel and the world. But this harmonistic exegesis did not result in one consistent Messianic conception. The harmonization of the Messianic motives was very much the same kind of process as the harmonization of the different documents or works which the scribes found in existence. Just as the Yahawistic narrative and the Elohistic narrative, the Deuteronomist and the Priest Code, the Law of Holiness, and the rest were united into one glorious patchwork, so the different Messianic motives were attached to one another.

One cannot read critically the result of this scribal work without realizing the fact that the Messianic Hope had become not merely an integral part of the whole religious life, but the inspiring motive of that life. On the one side patient obedience and scrupulous fulfillment of the Law in the present: this was the means to the end; this was worth while, because, on the other side, there was the hope in the future of a wonderful deliverance and triumph.[1] The prophetic material was worked over from this standpoint, and those books which did not seem to express this hope sufficiently, such as Amos and Hosea, were revised. No message of doom and destruction could be left without the bright promise of the Messianic Hope attached to it.

The center of such national life as there was among the Jews at this time was the Temple. The Davidic dynasty had practically

[1] The beginnings of this are to be found in Joel and Zech. ix.

passed out of existence. The head of the nation was the High Priest, and the visible emblem of national life was the Temple: hence the tendency to develop still further the attitude which we have already found expressing itself in the Book of Zechariah. The final expression of this point of view is contained in the Book of Chronicles, where all emphasis is laid upon the Temple and the priests and Levites connected with it. Indeed, the Book of Chronicles is a history of the world, viewed from the Temple as the center of the world and the object for which the world exists. To the author of these chronicles the Davidic dynasty no longer seems a necessity. God may raise up Gentile monarchs to do his great works for him, like Cyrus and Darius.[1] This may be regarded, however, as the extreme view on one side. The evidence of the revision of the prophetical books, as well as of the historical narratives and the legal writings, shows that the people in general did not lose the old view of the connection of the Messianic kingdom with the Davidic dynasty.

Some of the prophecies of that period, like Zech. ix: "Rejoice greatly, O daughter of Zion, shout, O daughter of Jerusalem. Behold, thy king cometh unto thee. He is just and having salvation, holy and riding upon an ass, even upon a colt, the foal of an ass," indicate a temporary revival of national life, under conditions of which we have no exact historical knowledge. And, just as in this period of a merely ecclesiastical existence there were such revivals of national life, so in the midst of the scribalism which concerned itself with a reworking of the old there were not lacking also men who wrote new books and promulgated new ideas. Some of the latter show a curious and interesting development of the thoughts of the past. So the above passage from Deutero-Zechariah has much in common with the earlier Isaiah. The kingdom which is to be restored is the old kingdom of David, or, perhaps better, of Solomon. New conditions of life are shown by the list of hostile nations which are to be destroyed by the might of Yahaweh. His

---

[1] So also in Deutero-Isaiah (xlv, 1). Later we find Alexander in the same rôle: cf. Jos. *Ant.* xi, 8; Talmud, Yoma 67b; and various later traditions having their origin in Alexandria.

judgment rendered, a king shall reign, who reminds us of the king in Is. ix. He shall rule in peace and destroy all implements of war. He will restore peace to the nations, and his rule shall be from sea to sea and from the river to the end of the earth.

Joel develops Ezekiel's picture of the judgment of Gog into that famous vision of the judgment in the valley of Jehoshaphat, which is accompanied by convulsions of nature such as prepare for the Day of Yahaweh in Isaiah's picture of that judgment (Is. i–ii). As in the former prophets, so in Joel, this Day of Yahaweh will lead to a spiritual regeneration and bring about a state of moral perfection.[1] Whereas Deutero-Isaiah had conceived of the Day of Yahaweh as already having taken place, so far as Israel was concerned, with the restoration to a quasi-national life the prophetic writers are again conscious of the national sinfulness, and we revert to the older view of the need of judgment and punishment.

I need not call attention to the fact that the Wisdom Literature and the Psalms are likewise full of the Messianic Hope. If space permitted, it would be interesting to point out the various phases of that hope represented in the Psalms.[2] The day of Yahaweh, the direct rule of Yahaweh upon earth, the Messianic king, and the anointed priest (or, perhaps better, the nation conceived of as itself a priest through whom the salvation is to be wrought) are all to be found in the Psalms.

During this period of low or nonexistent national life there was developed also the conception of personal religion. Beginning with the individualism of Jeremiah, this received its real formulation in

[1] Joel ii, 28 f.

[2] Book i, Day of Yahaweh, vii, ix, xi.
Yahaweh will visit Israel and deliver a seed, xxii.
A king to rule through his generations forever, ii.

Books ii and iii, Day of Yahaweh, l, lxxv, lxxvii, lxxxix.
A king to rule through His covenant forever, lxi, lxxii.
Davidic covenant, lxxxix.

Books iii, iv, Day of Judgment, in general xc–c, especially xciv, xcvi, xcviii.
ci–cxix, in general, deliverance through God's power, and the establishment of His Kingdom, Israel waiting in obedience and righteousness.
In cx the nation is a priest, and God executes judgment in its behalf. cxii–cxvi, it is the pious Israel which shall be delivered.
Davidic covenant, cxxxii.

Ezekiel. It seemed almost a necessary consequence of his teaching to apply to the individual the same theories which had been heretofore applied to the nation. As the nation ceased to be important, the importance of the individual was enhanced. The individual was to be held responsible for his own sins. As he was punished for his iniquities, so he was rewarded for his righteousness. Hence the hopes and expectations which once attached to the nation began now to be transferred to the individual. Ezekiel, in that dramatic vision of the valley of the bones,[1] prophesied the resurrection of the nation. The nation should rise again from the dead. By transference this began to be interpreted also of the individual. The development of a belief in the resurrection was stimulated undoubtedly by contact with the Persians, but in its origin it was Jewish — the transference, as stated, of the teaching with regard to the nation to the individual. We see in this period further indications of the development of a belief in individual immortality, and at the same time of the influence of foreign ideas, as in the treatment given to the story of Elijah and to the story of Enoch. The translation of Elijah, told in the Tales of the Prophets as contained in our Book of Kings, is woven into the Messianic Hope. Elijah is to return, resume his old place and functions on earth, and prepare the way for the coming of the great day of Yahaweh. Enoch, who walked with God, is conceived of as hidden with God.

The astral religion, which developed from the contact of Persia with Babylonia, makes itself felt in Jewish thought in a new conception of the heavens and the things contained therein. Corresponding to the existences here are the great existences there, of which these are but the pattern. The things there are the ancient ones. They came down from above to earth. The place of the dead who win favor with God is no longer, as in the earlier lore, the parts beneath the earth, but the heavenly places. The final development of those thoughts is found in the apocalypses of the Maccabæan period, Daniel and Enoch. In Daniel is reached also the idea of a resurrection, the resurrection of the pious, who shall

[1] Ezek. xxxvii.

shine like the stars in Heaven.[1] There you see the earthly contests
as the mere pictures of the heavenly, the battles of earth as expressions among men of the struggles between the archangels of God
and the powers of evil.[2]

It is interesting to note that with that great flaming out again
of the Messianic Hope which begins to show itself in the Book of
Daniel there is no expression of the expectation of a Davidic kingdom. The one like to a son of man, to whom victory is to be
given by the power of God, is the pious among the Jews.[3] We are
here in the direct line of succession of that idea expressed in Isaiah
vii, 14 f., and passed down through the prophecies of Deutero-
Isaiah; but in other respects the Messianic hope of the Book of
Daniel is quite unlike that of Isaiah or the Deutero-Isaiah. With
the belief in a resurrection the Messianic kingdom has been transferred, in part certainly, to another sphere. It takes place on earth,
it is true, but it is connected with the resurrection of the dead. The
saints who have died are to rise against the great Day of Yahaweh,
and the Messianic kingdom follows after the Day of Yahaweh, when
He shall hold judgment upon the kingdoms of the earth. And so,
basing upon Daniel vii, the Messianic kingdom develops from the
kingdom of God into the kingdom of heaven, two phrases with
which we are very familiar in the New Testament.

---

[1] To the individual at first old age is promised, Is. lxv, 20; Zech. viii, 4. But the
abolition of death is also promised, Is. xxv, 8. Resurrection is at first the revival of
the dead nation, Hos. vi, 2; Ezek. xxxvii, 12–14; afterwards of the pious, that they
may share in national restoration. In Daniel xii, 2, both the pious and sinners shall
rise again.

[2] Dan. x, 13, 21; xii, 1.

[3] Dan. vii, 18, 22, 27. One "like unto a son of man" represents the saints of the
Most High in contrast with the earthly kingdoms represented by forms of beasts.
The language implies his existence in some extra-terrestrial region before his appearance upon earth. The preëxistent Messiah first appears clearly, however, in
Enoch xxxvii–lxxi, in the first century B.C. Here the Son of Man is an angelic being
resembling man, occupying a seat in heaven by the Ancient of Days, chosen and
hidden with God before the creation. In the Apocrypha the imagery of the Prophets
is molded into certain fixed forms and taken with a literalness not intended by the
Prophets: Ecclus. xlvii, 11; 1 Macc. ii, 57. In general, for Messianic hope in Apocryphal books see Ecclus. xxxvi, 1–17; xxxvii, 25; xlvii, 11; l, 23–24; Wisdom iii, 8;
v, 1; Bar. ii, 27–35; iv, 36; v, 5–9; Tob. xiii, 12–18; xiv, 7; 1 Macc. ii, 57; 2 Macc. ii,
18; xiv, 15.

The Antiochian persecution resulted in reviving national life under strong leaders; but it is interesting to notice the difficulties with which the Maccabees had to contend even among their own people. The Chasidim looked for a direct intervention of God. If they kept the Law, even to the extent of allowing themselves to be killed on the Sabbath Day, God would intervene to save them. The success of the Maccabees revived, over against this, the popular hope. To a considerable extent it brought the Messianic kingdom back from heaven to earth. It restored human agencies to their part in the introduction of that kingdom, and revived in the people a spirit which was finally to find its expression in the same desperate and fanatical valor that had been shown after the Reformation at the time of Josiah.

The writings of this period show apparently an almost total disappearance, for the nonce, of the Davidic expectation in Palestine. That this expectation was still latent, however, is evinced by later developments. Even at this time its disappearance was confined to Palestine; for we find the Sibylline prophecies, composed in Egypt about 140 B.C.,[1] representing the Davidic hope of the Messianic kingdom. The final disappointment[2] resulting from the tyranny and corruption of the later Hasmonæans led again to the revival of the Davidic hope.

This now became the doctrine and belief of the Pharisees, and we find in the Psalms of Solomon, of the Herodian period, the most exact expression of that hope,[3] with the use of the word "Messiah" in what may be called a definite theological sense.[4] Here we have a fusion of Pharisaism with the national religious feeling of the Maccabæan revival, claiming on the one side a leader against the Romans, and on the other deliverance from the corrupt and ungodly Sadducean aristocracy. The national hope again sets in

---

[1] iii, 194–195. A righteous king whom God shall raise up from the East. Cf. Ps. xli, 2.

[2] This is foreshadowed in Enoch xc, where the white steer, the leader of God's herd after deliverance from the heathen, stands in contrast to the inadequate sovereignty of the horned lambs, i.e. the Hasmonæans.

[3] xvii, 23. Behold, O Lord, and raise up unto them their king, the Son of David, in the time which Thou, O God, knowest.

[4] xvii, 36. For all shall be holy, and their King is the Lord Christ.

the first place the idea of kingship rather than of resurrection and individual restoration. Two sets of ideas are combined: the traditional idea of the earthly kingdom of David's line, and a new conception of the heavenly preëxistent Messiah.

The final Jewish doctrine of the Messiah, prevalent at the commencement of our era, if we can call that final which was so vague and many-formed, was the result of using all the various scriptures of various times. These scriptures might be appealed to at any time, however, and, in view of new circumstances, might even receive a new interpretation. The result was that, in addition to the view which I have just described, which may be said to be the dominant and official view of Judaism, there were at the commencement of the Christian era other views for which arguments could be and were presented. It was possible, as said, to use any of the ideas of the Messianic hope contained anywhere in the ancient scriptures. So we find references to a priestly Messiah of Levi and a Messiah Ben Joseph; and it was always possible that some strong, spiritual leader, taking one of these conceptions and adapting it to new conditions, might make it a dominant or at least a permitted Messianic view. In general, however, what was expected at the commencement of the Christian era was the appearance of a preëxistent Messiah, one conceived and hidden of God in the heavenly places, but connected with the Davidic dynasty, a sort of David restored, who was to come with judgment on the nations of the world, after the sinners of his people had been converted or purged out, and who was to rule over a new kingdom, the kingdom of heaven brought down to earth, whose center, if not its extent, was the people of Israel.

CHAPTER XXIX

FUTURE LIFE

There has existed almost everywhere, among all races, some sort of a conception of the continuance of existence after death, and of something in man, different from his body, by or in connection with which this continuance of existence is achieved. This is the life spirit, which animates the body, and yet is separate from it. It is associated with the blood, which is manifestly the principle of life, because in proportion as a man loses his blood his life departs, until finally he becomes lifeless. So also it is the ghostly bloodlessness of the corpse which is the marked feature in death. It was for this reason, because the blood is life, that those organs which are the manifest seats of blood, primarily the liver, secondarily the heart, came to be regarded as the seats of life.

It is associated with the breath, because with the departure of the breath life ceases. The invisibility of the breath led also to the conception of an invisible spirit, or wind, which could come and go, different from the blood, mobile and more spiritual, but still the principle of life.

Sleep suggested still another conception of the principle of life, for sleep is, like death, a temporary cessation of existence, yet without the loss of either blood or life. Moreover, in sleep a man may think and act, yet it is clear he does not do it with his body, which remains inert, senseless, and motionless. His dreams are out of himself, yet connected with himself, as though something went out of him and in other form or guise, in a different world and nature, lived and thought and acted. Here was a third principle of life, different from the blood or the breath, connected with the body, yet able to leave the body sleeping and live away from it.

One or all of these principles of life are recognized among all primitive peoples, and that recognition has resulted in some form

446

of belief in the continuance of individual existence after the death of the body. On the other hand, individuality is associated with the body. It is the bodily appearance of his neighbor which each man has known, and without which he is unable to visualize either his neighbor or himself. Life after death cannot be imagined without some appearance of the bodily form. It tends, therefore, to become a shadow of the earthly life, and to connect itself still with the body of the dead. It continues his mutilation or his completeness. The preservation of his body in some form, its interment in some state, provision for its continued housing and care, even to eating and drinking, become essential to the preservation of that life after death. As this is conditioned on the body, so the appearance of that body and the place where it is deposited tend to determine the condition of that life — in general a shadowy, bloodless, cheerless continuance of existence, rather than of life, beneath the surface of the ground (at least if the dead are buried), where all is dust. What the dead did and were above, that, dependent upon the condition of proper interment of their entire bodies, they do and are in a shadow below. The great, interred with honor, are great there. The beasts of the people are not worthy of consideration, and whether and what they are after death, carrion left to rot like dung or be eaten by beasts and birds, none knew clearly or considered.

It follows, also, that if the dead have such an abode and such a life they may in some way affect those here for good or ill, and, as the malevolent is uppermost in primitive thought, chiefly the latter; either from malice, because they are deprived of the joys of life, or from wrath, because they are not provided with what they need or what beseems them in the place beyond. Removed from sight, while deprived of the joys of life, they tend at the same time to be exalted to a greater power and wisdom than those on earth. Hence they are brought into connection with spiritual powers, reverenced or worshiped, their help and counsel invoked, or their anger or malice appeased by offerings and ritual.

These are the fundamental primitive conceptions regarding death and the spiritual life. All of these we find among the Hebrews, in various connections and combinations, from the outset to the close of their history. What we desire to consider is the peculiar forms and combinations assumed by these common elements, and their ultimate development into the specific Jewish doctrine or doctrines of the consequences of death.

From the very earliest times the blood was conceived of as the life, both of men and beasts. Coming from Yahaweh, to Yahaweh it must be restored. It might not be consumed like the flesh. Shed, it must be buried under the ground; else it cried out to Yahaweh, and brought His vengeance upon the shedder of blood.[1] To this extent it seems to possess an independent existence; but that independent existence was never developed further. The blood as vital principle was identified with the *nefesh*, as the soul or self of the man. The *nefesh* is sometimes said to be the blood, sometimes to be in the blood, and vice versa.[2] Apparently also the *nefesh* was in some way connected with breath. So man became a live person by the breath which Yahaweh-Elohim breathed into his nostrils.[3] *Nefesh*, or " person," may be used of the whole man, but more specifically it is used, like " blood," of the living or vital element in contrast to the flesh of both man and beast.[4] So it comes also to mean the appetites, desires, emotions,[5] in contrast to the physical and tangible parts of the man. It is also used of the person after death, especially in the legal literature.[6] *Nefesh* is the active vital element of man and beast, but not of God. The active principle in God is *ruach*, wind or spirit. In the later literature, as the spiritual kinship of man to God is emphasized, " spirit " tends to take the place of " person " as indicating the higher, immaterial element in man[7] — thought, emotion, and that intangible something which constitutes his real being; and there is also a tendency to connect that life

---

[1] Gen. iv, 10; ix, 4; Lev. xvii, 14; Deut. xii, 23; Ezek. xxxiii, 25; Job xvi, 18; Zech. ix, 11.   [2] Deut. xii, 23; Lev. xvii, 11.

[3] Gen. ii, 7; Job xxvii, 3; xxxiv, 14; Is. xlii, 5; lvii, 16.   [4] Prov. xii, 10.

[5] Deut. xii, 20; 1 Sam. ii, 16; 1 Kings xi, 37; Ezek. vii, 19; Mic. vii, 1; Ps. cvii, 9; Prov. xiii, 4; xxvii, 7; Eccles. ii, 24; iv, 8; vi, 2; vii, 28. This use increases as we descend in date.

[6] Lev. xix, 28; xxi, 1, 11; Num. v, 2; vi, 6, 11; ix, 6 ff; Zech. ix, 7; Hag. ii, 13.

[7] Gen. vi, 3; xii, 1; Num. xiv, 24; Is. xxxviii, 16; xlii, 5; Ps. civ, 29 f.; cxlvi, 4; Job x, 12; xvii, 1; xxvii, 3; xxxii, 8; xxxiii, 4; xxxiv, 14; Eccles. viii, 8; xii, 7.

essence more closely with God, as something which returns to Him after death rather than as something continuing to exist independently. Blood, person, spirit, seem in general to represent an ascending scale of spiritualization in Hebrew thought.

The early Hebrews believed in the persistence of the *nefesh*, or personality, after death. Perhaps this is best testified by the story of the appearance of Samuel at the behest of the witch (1 Sam. xxviii). The ghost of Samuel was called up from some place beneath the earth; he is a shadow of Samuel, resembling Samuel as he was before death, an old man with a cloak; he is divine (*elohim*), and possesses superhuman knowledge when brought back to life. Ghosts were called *refaim*,[1] the name also used for the vanished races, who had left colossal remains behind them, evidences of their more than normal human powers. They dwelt in Sheol, a place beneath the earth, where differences of earthly rank were continued,[2] and habitation in which depended in general on proper entombment. Although possessing godlike powers, nevertheless life in Sheol is a miserable existence at its best, to which the worst lot on earth is preferable. But, evil as the state of the dead may be in Sheol, it is still much worse not to be in Sheol at all, which is the lot of those unburied or mutilated before death.[3] Hence, partly out of piety, partly to prevent injury[4] from or to secure advantage through the dead, a son sought to give his parent a fitting tomb. While the dead rested in Sheol, he was also associated with the tomb in which his body was interred, and with that were connected, consequently, such rites and ceremonies as were intended to strengthen his power and propitiate his favor.[5]

---

[1] In earlier use an ancient people, so Gen. xiv, 5; xv, 20; Deut. ii, 11; iii, 11; Josh. xii, 4; xiii, 12; xvii, 15; 2 Sam. v, 18. In late use, especially in Wisdom Literature, ghosts: Is. xiv, 9; xxvi, 14, 19; Ps. lxxxviii, 11; Job xxvi, 5; Prov. ii, 18; ix, 18; xxi, 16.

[2] Is. xiv, 9.

[3] Is. xiv, 18 f.; Jer. xxii, 19; xxv, 33; xxxvi, 30; Josh. vii, 15, 24 f.

[4] Diseases came from the shades in Sheol. Cf. the late references to this belief in Job xviii, 12 ff; xxxiii, 22 ff. Cf. also Hos. xiii, 14. In the prophetic view, which abolished Sheol, these powers, like all powers of Sheol, are absorbed in Yahaweh; as diseases and insanity, Num. xii, 10; 1 Sam. xvi, 14: fulfillment of parental curses, Gen. ix, 25-27; xlix, 2-27; punishment of the violation of tombs, Am. ii, 1.

[5] Gen. xlvii, 30; 2 Sam. xvii, 23; xix, 37; xxi, 14.

The worship of the dead was forbidden among the Hebrews from an early period, and consequently also necromancy, but the literature and the ritual show abundant evidence of a cult of the dead and of necromancy, which continued as a part of the popular religion to a late date. Such Hebrew graves as have been found in Palestine contain deposits similar to those found in Canaanite graves (and indeed in the graves of all the neighboring nations) — food, drink, arms, tools, and the like. Also offerings to the dead are frequently mentioned.[1] The prohibitions in the Law of cuttings for the dead show us something of the ritual connected with the worship of the dead ; and the taboo of unclean is further evidence of that worship.[2] The reverence paid to or at the tombs of the ancestors, and the monuments, heaps of stones, and pillars (*mazzeboth*), in all other relations objects of religion, erected by or over them, are convincing proof of its prevalence.[3] We have, moreover, a chain of references to the invocation or consultation of the spirits of the dead, through a class of persons specially employed for that purpose.[4]

Connected with the cult of the dead was the importance of posterity. Sons conducted the cult, and offered the sacrifices without which the quasi-immortality of the dead, and their power and honor, could not continue. Hence childlessness or the destruction of children meant the loss of such joy and such life as existed after death.

Sheol, in which the dead dwelt, subject to the connection with the tomb already noted, was a hollow or pit beneath the surface

[1] Deut. xxvi, 14 ; Jer. xvi, 5 ff. ; cf. also Hos. ix, 4 ; 2 Chron. xvi, 14 ; Ps. cvi, 28. In spite of all prohibitions, offerings to the dead continued to a late date. They are mentioned not infrequently in the Apocryphal books, sometimes in commendation (Tob. iv, 17 ; Ecclus. vii, 33 ; and cf. 2 Macc. xii, 42 ff.), more often in condemnation (Ecclus. xxx, 18 ; Jer. vss. 31 f. ; Wisd. xlv, 15 ; xix, 13 ; Sib. Or. viii, 82–84 ; Jub. xxii, 17). For the custom of putting treasures etc. in the graves cf. Jos. *Ant.* xiii, viii, 4 ; xvi, vii, 1 ; *Bell. Jud.* i, ii, 5. See also Ezek. xxxii, 27.

[2] Gen. xxxvii, 34 ; Lev. xix, 28 ; xxi, 1, 11 ; Num. v, 2 ; vi, 6, 11 ; ix, 6 ff. ; Deut. xiv, 1 ; 2 Sam. iii, 31 ; cf. Lev. xxi, 10.

[3] Gen. xxxv, 20 ; 2 Sam. xviii, 17 f. Note sanctity of Hebron, burial place of patriarchs, 2 Sam. v, 3 ; xv, 7, 12 ; Josh. xx, 7 ; xxi, 11 ; of Shechem, tomb of Joseph, Gen. xii, 6 f. ; xxii, 9 ; Deut. xi, 30 ; Josh. xxiv, 26 f. ; Jud. ix, 4, 37, 46 ; the tombs of the kings, as a place of worship in connection with the Temple, Ezek. xliii, 7–9.

[4] 1 Sam. xxviii ; Is. viii, 19 ; xix, 3 ; xxviii, 15 ; xxix, 4 ; 2 Kings xxi, 6 ; xxiii, 24 ; Deut. xviii, 11 ; Lev. xix, 31 ; xx, 6, 27 ; Ezek. xxii, 18 ; Is. lvii, 9 ; lxv, 4.

of the earth, or even in and below the waters which are beneath the earth.[1] Here the dead rested in their places, according to the character not of their deeds but of their graves, only the unburied being excluded. In the earlier thought Sheol[2] was outside of the authority of Yahaweh. He was the God of the land of Israel. Other lands had their own gods. For Sheol there was no god of its own. It was in a sense godless, but, on the other hand, the spirits dwelling there were themselves divine. Yahaweh dwelt in

[1] Paton (*The Hebrew Idea of the Future Life*, p. 75, 159 ff.) expresses the opinion that the original Hebrew and Semitic belief connected the dead only with the tomb, and that Sheol is of Sumerian origin, early adopted by the Canaanites, and from them by the Hebrews. I do not think there is sufficient evidence on which to base such a conclusion. For practical purposes Sheol and the tomb appear combined from the beginning of our knowledge; and they continue to be so combined in the worship at tombs and the belief in a future life in those same regions to-day.

[2] There is considerable vagueness and uncertainty with regard to the exact character of Sheol, partly because it never was clearly defined in thought, remaining always a land of darkness and confusion (Job x, 22); partly because different writers and different periods held different views. In general it was a great pit or hollow beneath the earth to which all the dead go: Gen. xxxvii, 35; xlii, 38; xliv, 29; Deut. xxxiii, 22; 1 Kings ii, 6; Prov. xv, 24; Job vii, 9; Ps. lv, 16; lxxxviii, 4; hence also called *Bôr*, "the pit": Is. xxxviii, 18; Ezek. xxvi, 20; Lam. iii, 53; Ps. xxviii, 1; xxx, 4; xxxviii, 6; cxliii, 7; or *Shaḥath*, "cave": Is. xxxviii, 17; Ezek. xxviii, 8; Is. li, 14; Job xxxiii, 18. It stands in contrast to "heaven," to indicate the depths beneath, as the former does the heights above the earth: Am. ix, 2; Is. vii, 11; Job xi, 8; Ps. cxxxix, 8. It is immediately below the earth, so that it may be entered by a splitting or yawning of the earth: Num. xvi, 30, 33; 2 Sam. xxii, 5 f.; Prov. i, 12; Ps. lv, 15. It is conceived of as very far away: Is. lvii, 9. The entrance to Sheol is in the distant west: Enoch xxii, 1-4. It is below or beyond the waters: Job xxvi, 6; Jon. ii, 3; Lam. iii, 53 (cf. also Deut. xxx, 12 f.). It is guarded by bars: Job xvii, 16; Jon. ii, 6; and has gates: Is. xxxviii, 10; Ps. ix, 13; cvii, 18; Wisd. xvi, 13; and gatekeepers: Job xxxviii, 17 (LXX). It is divided into various chambers and divisions: Is. xiv, 15; Ezek. xxxii, 23; Prov. vii, 27; finally defined as seven in number: 2 Esdras vii, 80 ff. The ultimate place of misery was the lowest Sheol: Deut. xxxii, 22. Sheol is itself the grave: Is. xiv, 11; and dust: Is. xxix, 4; Job vii, 21. On the other hand, in Sheol are the graves of the nations: Ezek. xxxii, 17-32. In Sheol all of every sort are together: Job iii, 13-19; Is. xiv, 9; again the dead are divided according to race or religion: Ezek. xxxi, 15 ff.; xxxii, 21 ff.; buried or unburied, whole or mutilated: Is. xiv, 19; Ezek. xxxii, 23; Ps. lxiii, 9. Sheol tends to be more particularly the abode or the punishment of the wicked, or they are consigned to the lowest part of Sheol: Is. xxxiii, 18; Ps. ix, 18; xxviii, 17; xxxi, 18; xlix, 15. On the other hand, under the prophetic teaching of the utter nothingness of Sheol (Is. xxxviii, 11, 17 f.; Job xiv, 21), it may even become a welcome place of rest for the oppressed and enslaved: Job iii, 13-19; or for the righteous a place of refuge from the evils to come: Is. lvii, 1. As the place to which souls go, and as the hollow womb within the earth, it also comes to be the place where souls are formed: Ps. cxxxix, 15; so also 2 Esdras iv, 41, and Apoc. Baruch.

Sinai, in Mt. Seir, in the place where He was worshiped, in heaven, whence He beheld and whence He visited men. Sheol was beyond His vision or concern, and even when He is said to have created the world, Sheol is excluded.[1] His rewards and punishments were given on this earth, not in the world beyond.[2]

From the outset the Hebrew religious leaders, and the official religion, taught monolatry. Yahaweh was the god of Israel, and beside Him Israel could serve no god. We have seen how primitive Mosaism was modified in Canaan, taking over the Baals of the land and their shrines and cults, identifying them with Yahaweh, hallowing them by myths of His appearances and manifestations, and adapting them to its own religion and worship. What took place with the gods of the land and their cults took place, with some modifications, with regard to the shrines of the dead ancestors, their cult, and the invocation of the divine powers of the beings of the under world. The shrines of the great dead became shrines sacred to Yahaweh. Their marks and monuments were appropriated to Him,[3] together with certain of their functions. Some of the ritual connected with the worship of the dead was incorporated in His ritual ; other parts, which were incompatible with that ritual, were prohibited, together with sacrifice to, or invocation of, the dead. Sheol was made as it were a foreign land, excluded from the religion of Yahaweh like other foreign lands. The process was a long one, and the procedure was not altogether consistent. Moreover, in the popular religion the old practices and ideas persisted, prohibitions and denunciations to the contrary notwithstanding, continually affecting the thought of the leaders and the official cult of Yahaweh, and receiving from time to time in some new guise recognition or sanction.

It was inevitable that the teaching of the Prophets, with its emphasis on the moral attributes of Yahaweh and its increasing

[1] So Wisdom i, 13, formally stating the old view in opposition to the later doctrine says : " God made not death." Cf. also ii, 24.

[2] Those in the grave are beyond the remembrance and the powers of Yahaweh : Ps. lxxx, 4 ; Is. xxxviii, 10 f. So also from the side of the worshiper : Is. xxxviii, 18 f. ; Ps. v, 5. Punishment was by sudden death : 1 Sam. xvi, 8 ; or it was visited upon the family of the culprit : Ex. xx, 5.

[3] Gen. xii, 6 f. ; xxii, 9 ; xxxv, 8, 20 ; Deut. xi, 30 ; Josh. xxiv 26 f. ; Jud. ix, 4, 37, 46.

approximation to real monotheism, should make itself felt in the conception of the state and condition of the dead. To the Prophets all the gods of the heathen became not-gods, mere vanities, and what was true of them was true of the shades of the dead. They lost alike their power and their terror.

There was, in the conception of the Prophets, an intense reality in Yahaweh, as a living, present, acting God, and so thoroughly were they concerned with the present realities of His plan for living men, as to leave no place for, nor interest in, the dead; albeit they did not free themselves from many of the beliefs and feelings of the older cult, the horror of lack of burial, mutilation of the corpse, destruction of offspring, and the like. To them the relation of the children to the parents was still a means of immortality, not because of the sacrifices they might offer to or for their parents, but because of the conception of the solidarity of parents and children, which had grown up out of, and in connection with, those sacrifices. The parents still continued to live on in their children. But the Prophets were also intense nationalists. They believed in the solidarity of the nation, and so the continuance of the parents in their children became a continuance of the existence of the individual in the nation, which was indestructible because of its relation to Yahaweh. The Messianic Hope was an expression of this patriotism. The Prophets felt and taught an intense patriotism to Yahaweh, His religion, and His people, which merged self in the nation. Sheol became to them more and more a nothingness, and *Place* its denizens unreal to the point of annihilation. All life was transferred to this world and to Israel. Here and here only were the rewards of existence, connected with Israel as the people of Yahaweh. Here Yahaweh would reward His people for their faithfulness to Him with victory, health, and wealth. Faithfulness to Him meant obedience to His laws, which came to be more and more moral, until we even reach the point of denunciation of ritual and outward forms as indifferent or displeasing to Yahaweh.

With the destruction of the Hebrew state, first Israel (721 B.C.) then Judah (587 B.C.), begins the development of individualism, which expresses itself clearly first in Jeremiah, to be more definitely developed by Ezekiel.[1] The absolute rights of parents over their children were abolished,[2] and that solidarity of parent and child which visited the sins of one upon the other first questioned,[3] then denied. It was not because the fathers had eaten sour grapes that the children's teeth were set on edge (Jer. xxxi, 29 ; Ezek. xviii, 2) ; the children were punished for their own sins. But not only was the child thus separated from the father and the father from the child, the individual was separated from the nation as a whole. " The soul (person or individual) that sinneth, it shall die " (Ezek. xviii ; cf. also ix, 3–6 ; xiv, 12–20).[4] This individualism tended toward democracy, more especially in view of the destruction of royalty as a result of the captivity. The individual Israelite as such came to have a new worth, and the humble and poor began to come to the front as those who, carried into captivity, remained true under temptation ; then later as those who, unfettered by wealth and prosperity, forsook all and returned to Zion.[5] Ezekiel does not, however, lose sight of the national hope. He sees the reward of good given to the good Israelite here, and the evil to the evil. They shall be punished or rewarded here ; of future reward or punishment he knows nothing.[6] But if in his teaching he throws aside the old solidarity of generation with generation, out of which had grown the great national hope of immortality, that hope itself he does not throw aside. The nation shall rise again, its dry bones shall be clothed with flesh ; David shall once more rule over Israel ; the poor of the flock shall be shepherded, and insolent and self-serving rulers abolished ; and this can come about only through repentance and reform of the individual Israelites. Their sins prevent this consummation ; their righteousness shall establish the

---

[1] For a more detailed consideration of the results of Ezekiel's individualism cf. Charles, *Eschatology, Hebrew, Jewish, and Christian*, pp. 62 ff.

[2] Deut. xii, 31 ; xviii, 10 ; Lev. xviii, 21.　　　[3] Deut. xxiv, 16 ; 2 Kings xiv, 16.

[4] The old view continued on, however, side by side with the new : Job v, 4 ; xxvii, 14 ff. ; Ps. cix, 9–15 ; Dan. ix, 7–16 ; Tob. iii, 3 ; Jud. vii, 28 ; Bar. i, 15–21 ; Matt. xxiii, 25 ; Jno. ix, 2.

[5] These conditions are mirrored in the emphasis laid on the poor and oppressed in Deutero-Isaiah and the Psalter.

[6] Ezek. ix, 3–6 ; xiv, 12–20 ; xviii, 5–32. This continued to be the prevailing view even into the New Testament times, although opposed strenuously by the author of Job and others. Cf. Ps. xxxiv, 19 ff. ; cxlv, 20 ; Prov. iii, 33. ; Job xxxii–xxxvii ; Jno. ix, 2.

new kingdom of God upon earth. For all his individualism Ezekiel was a keen nationalist, and the joy of the expectation of the
fulfillment of the national hope was sufficient recompense for his
soul here and hereafter. But the national hope of resurrection and
future life is, because of this combination, so expressed as to carry
in itself a suggestion, bound to be developed later, of individual
resurrection and future life. Ezekiel's individualism, as touching
the relation of father and child, was very far from prevailing to the
exclusion of the old belief. Both lingered on together; just as in
fact the older view of Sheol and the life beyond continued to exist
under and alongside of the prophetic view of its nonexistence, and
the ignoring or denying of the life of the shades.

Here, as suggested, the development of monolatry into monotheism also exerted its influence. Beginning with Amos the prophets
were denying and abolishing the old view of the exclusive relation
of Yahaweh to Israel and the land of Israel. Amos proclaimed that
Yahaweh had brought the Aramæans from Kir and the Philistines
from Crete as truly as He had brought Israel from Egypt. Isaiah
saw in thought the symbols of Yahaweh worship in Egypt,[1] and
Israel united with Assyria and Egypt in His worship;[2] and, in
point of fact, at or about that time the Jews did erect a temple to
Yahaweh in Egypt. The exilic and post-exilic prophets present
the complete monotheistic view of Yahaweh as the one god of all
the earth, maker of all things, beside whom there are no gods, not
even the spirits of evil, for He is the creator of evil as well as good.[3]
This absoluteness of Yahaweh, which makes Him lord of heaven
and earth and the parts under the earth, of visible and invisible, of
good and evil, is very fully stated and enlarged upon in the Book
of Job. To such thinkers there is no longer a Sheol possible in the
older sense, nor that miserable continuation of existence remote
from the light and life of God; for all things are now in His presence, and while old words and myths may still be used, they are
mere figures of speech.[4]

---

[1] Is. xix, 19 f. [2] Is. xix, 24 f. [3] Is. xlv, 7; xliv, 25.

[4] So Yahaweh can reach the fugitives in Sheol: Am. ix, 2; the demons of Sheol
obey him: Hos. xiii, 14; His wrath reaches the lowest recesses of Sheol: Deut. xxxii,
22; Sheol is naked before him: Job xxvi, 5 f. Similarly Ps. cxxxix, 8, and Prov. xv, 11.

In the Book of Job we see also the old and new view of sin and suffering in inevitable conflict. If God be all-powerful and all-wise there can be no getting around the fact that all things come of Him, good and evil alike. He and He only punishes and rewards, and as He is a god of right and justice it must be that He gives health and wealth to the good, and sickness, misfortune, and poverty to the bad. Vice versa it must be concluded that the healthy and wealthy are good, and that the sick and stricken are bad. But clearly that is not the fact,[1] even though one wait to observe the latter days.[2] The Book of Job is the discussion of the problem of evil primarily from the national side; but the author cannot escape from the individual aspect of the question. It seems impossible to solve the problem satisfactorily from the view of this life only, and now that all the world, the parts beneath and the parts above as well as the earth, evil as well as good, are recognized as from God and in His sight, the question arises whether a solution may not be found in the hereafter.

" O that Thou couldest hide me in Sheol,
Conceal me until Thy wrath do turn,
Appoint me a time, when Thou couldest remember me.
(If man die, shall he live again?)
All the days of my warfare I would wait,
Till my release should come.
Thou shouldest call, and I would answer Thee;
Thou wouldest long toward the work of Thine own hands."[3]

" I know that my redeemer liveth,
Who shall stand up at last upon my dust;
And after this my skin is destroyed,
Without my flesh shall I see God;
Whom I shall see for myself,
Mine eyes shall behold, and not another."[4]

It is nothing but a suggestion of the restoration to life after death. It seems to carry out individually the idea which is expressed for the nation in Ezekiel xxxvii, but it appears only as a

---

1 This difficulty is recognized as early as Jeremiah. Cf. xii, 1 f.; also Hab. i, 2–4, 13–17; Ps. xxii, 1–21; xliv, 9–26; lxxiii, 1–16.

2 This was a view by which it was sought to explain the difficulty: Ps. xxxvii, 1 f., 7 f.; lxxiii, 18; Job v, 3, 18–27; xx, 4 f.   3 Job xiv, 13–15.   4 Job xix, 25–27.

suggestion, to be dropped, not pressed, as though even the one who suggested it, while not quite willing to forego the suggestion, does not himself dare to believe in its real possibility, so alien is it from all other thinking of his people.

The question arises whether any extraneous impulse is discernible in this suggestion of the Book of Job. The book affects, and perhaps actually displays, a certain foreign tone of thought and expression. Is it possible that the suggestion of immortality came from a foreign source ?

From the outset of its existence Israel had lived side by side with a nation which had a highly developed belief in a future life, in a judgment, and in rewards for good or ill done in this life ; and yet we find absolutely no trace of any influence of the Egyptian belief on the Hebrew. Apparently that was true not only of the question of the future life but also of religious influence in general. Excavations in Palestine show the great material influence of Egypt on Palestine. Politically also her influence was great; but in the matter of religion her influence, so far as it existed, was rather one of repulsion. Even in the post-exilic period, and after there had come to be a large Jewish population in Egypt, the religious and philosophical influence exerted through and by the Egyptian Jews was entirely Greek. The Book of Job quite evidently owes nothing to Eyptian sources.

Canaan, Syria, and Babylonia seem to have held much the same belief as the pre-prophetic Hebrews. The Persians, however, who had now become the masters of the world, held a doctrine of a future life which, while it contained, like the Egyptian, a judgment with reward for the righteous and punishment for the wicked, was in presentation and principle very different. Here was no underworld, no pantheon of gods and spirits, no embalming and extravagant entombing, no worship of the dead with ritual and sacrifice. That the Persian religion did from the outset present to the Jews of Babylonia doctrines of life and of the universe which they were willing at least to consider is apparent from the writings of Deutero-Isaiah ; that in some of the details and phases of its belief regarding the angelic and spirit world it later considerably affected Jewish thought is evident from apocalyptic literature. I am inclined to think that we find in Job a similar trace of Persian influence: that, the author having developed the thought of his predecessors to what seemed an impasse, there came from the Persian belief in the resurrection the suggestion of an explanation of the mystery of evil in life — but, just because the suggestion was foreign, drawn from a foreign religion, he dared not press it, even to himself. Presumably, also, it had come to him in a form too imperfect and too alien to the rest of his thought for him to develop intelligently.

However that may be, the Book of Job gets no further than the bare suggestion, as the solution of the ethical problem of evil, of the possibility of a vindication and a restoration to life of the righteous dead.[1] More clearly Ezekiel's picture of the resurrection of the dead nation had its effect in a little apocalypse, now ordinarily assigned to a fairly late date in the Persian period, embedded in our present book of Isaiah (xxiv–xxvii). The dead shall rise; the inhabitants of the dust shall awake and shout for joy, and " the earth shall bring the shades to life " (xxvi, 19). But these are only the shades of the righteous, who are thus rewarded for their righteousness toward Yahaweh by restoration to life here on earth. The wicked shall be prisoners in the pit, confined in a dungeon, punished after many days, destroyed and their memory blotted out (xxiv, 22 ; xxvi, 14). Here the future life of the individual and the Messianic kingdom of Israel are combined. It is by the restoration to life of the righteous Israelites of past generations that the nation shall be enlarged and strengthened that it may conquer the earth (xxvi, 15–19).

The doctrine of the future life in this apocalypse is still, however, somewhat shadowy as regards the individual; he is yet at

---

[1] There are three cases of resurrection in the historical books, all in the Tales of the Prophets: the son of the widow of Sarepta by Elijah (1 Kings xvii, 9 ff.); the son of the woman of Shunem by Elisha (2 Kings iv, 32 ff.) ; by contact with Elisha's bones at burial (2 Kings xiii, 21). These were not, however, cases of the return of the soul from Sheol. The bodies were not yet buried and hence the souls had not gone to Sheol. With these passages may be compared Is. xxxviii, 18 ; 1 Sam. ii, 6, and many more, where the man is said to be brought down to Sheol, and his restoration to health is a bringing up from Sheol. It is clear, however, that the soul is only on its way to, or arrived at the gates of, Sheol. It has not yet entered in.

least subordinated to the nation. It is with the latter apocalypses of Daniel, after the first triumphs of the Maccabees in the life-and-death struggle with the Syrians, that, following along the two lines originating with Ezekiel, of the retribution of a just and righteous God for the good and evil done by the individual, and the resurrection to life of the dead bones, we first have a certain picture of judgment and resurrection combined. To those who lived so intensely in the issues of that struggle it seemed unjust that they who had suffered and died heroically in the conflict, like Judas and his father and his brothers, should not also participate in the triumph; and that they who had shamefully betrayed their nation and their faith should not be punished by something more than the sleep in Sheol. The god of justice and of right must surely reward at least the distinguished righteous and punish the infamous traitors. So the writer presents his revelation: "And many of them that sleep in the dust of the earth shall awake, some to everlasting life, and some to shame and everlasting contempt. And the teachers shall shine as the brightness of the firmament; and they that turn many to righteousness as the stars forever and ever." [1]

This doctrine of a resurrection of selected and conspicuous righteous and sinners speedily develops in the subsequent apocalyptic literature into a belief in the general resurrection of the dead. So in 2 Esdras iv, 41, we read: "In the grave the chambers of souls are like the womb; for like as a woman that travaileth maketh haste to escape the anguish of the travail, even so do these places haste to deliver those things that are committed unto them from the beginning"; and again: "the earth shall restore those that are asleep in her, and so shall the dust those that dwell therein in silence, and the chambers shall deliver those souls that were committed unto them"; [2] Enoch xli, 1 is of the same import: "In those days shall the earth give back those that are gathered in her, and Sheol shall restore those it has received, and Abaddon shall render up what has been intrusted to it." In Apoc. Baruch, xxi, 23

---

[1] Dan. xii, 2 f. Apparently the return of Elijah mentioned in Mal. iv, 5, and a similar idea attached to Enoch through the interpretation of Gen. v, 24, contributed to this doctrine.　　　　　[2] vii, 32.

we have a similar deliverance of the dead, accompanied with the idea that there shall be no more death: "May Sheol be sealed up henceforth, that it receive no more dead ; and may the chambers of souls restore those that are shut up in them." The end has been reached, when God's purpose is fulfilled, and birth and death shall be no more.

Sometimes the judgment and the retribution take place, partially at least, before the resurrection. So in Enoch, chaps. i–xxxvi, Sheol is represented as containing four divisions : (1) for the souls of the wicked who have received their punishment in this life, who shall not be raised at the last day ; (2) for the spirits of the wicked, not punished in this life, awaiting in great pain the day of judgment; (3) for the souls of the moderately righteous, free from pain, awaiting in a sort of negative condition their reward at the day of judgment; (4) a paradise where the great saints dwell, drinking the water of life until the resurrection. Here Sheol has become a hell, a purgatory, and a paradise. Elsewhere in Enoch, however (chaps. xxxvii–lxxi), the righteous pass at once into the presence of God, to be guarded in the heavenly places by the pre-existent "Son of Man," to be raised to life at his coming, that they may share in the Messianic Kingdom.[1]

These doctrines are a development of the idea of retribution and reward, applied first to the nation and then to the individual. They reflect also in a new form the old belief in the Day of Yahaweh, now become a day of judgment for the individual Israelite. But while they may be said to be a logical outcome of previous Jewish doctrines and beliefs, they also show evidence of Persian influence too unmistakable to be denied. It would seem that the Persian belief acted as a stimulant and a clarifier in bringing the Jewish belief to a definite form.

It was not only Persian belief, however, which helped to form the Jewish doctrine of a future life. In the apocryphal literature originating in or influenced by Egyptian Judaism the Platonic idea of the future life as an inherent immortality of the soul was to some extent grafted on the Jewish doctrine of the life hereafter. According

[1] Enoch xxxviii, 1 ; xl, 5 ; xliii, 4 ; xlix, 3 ; li, 1 ; lx, 6 ; lxi, 12 ; lxx, 4.

to this view there was no need of a resurrection. The judgment, for punishment or reward, was executed at death, and there was no day of judgment at which the final rewards of life should be meted out. Nor, for another reason, can there be a resurrection — the bodies of men are a clog upon the spirit, birth is a fall from a higher existence, and death a release from imprisonment. Man was created for incorruption, and is an image of God not in his bodily part but in the spirit imprisoned within the body. At death the spirits of the righteous, released from their bodily prisons, go to their immediate reward in the blessedness of God. This is the teaching of the Book of Wisdom with regard to the nature of the soul and with regard to the future life of the righteous.

In the Platonic doctrine the soul is eternal and uncreated, confined in the body because of a fall from the life of pure reason in a previous state of existence. This life is for it a species of purgatory. If here it resist the temptations of the flesh, it shall pass to the fellowship of the gods. If it succumb to those temptations, it shall be born again on earth, and if after repeated trials it fail to reform, then it shall be cast into Tartarus.[1] This doctrine of metempsychosis and rebirth in the flesh does not, however, appear in the Book of Wisdom. As Wisdom promises immediate passage after death to the felicity of the heavenly kingdom for the souls of the righteous, so for the wicked it denounces the eternal torment of hell.[2]

[1] This is the view presented in *Phædo*, which depends in its turn upon Orphism. The body hinders thought, and therefore death, as the separation of soul from body, is a consummation to be desired by the philosopher. Plato accepts the old tradition of many successive births, the soul departing to Hades and returning again, so that in fact the living are born from the dead. Only those souls which true philosophy has purified depart to the invisible world and the presence of the Gods. Orphism taught that the soul is entombed in the body. It may attain perfection through a connection with a series of bodies. When thus completely purified, it will be freed from the circle of generation and again become divine, as it was before entrance into this mortal body.

[2] Similar is the picture of the future life presented by the Fourth Book of Maccabees, where Abraham, Isaac, Jacob, and the other patriarchs dwell with God, to be joined at their death by the righteous, especially those who have died for the faith; the wicked presumably going into eternal torment. The picture here, however, is much less spiritual than in the Book of Wisdom, and much closer in its presentation of the future of the righteous to the Pharisaic and common Palestinian view.

This doctrine of the future life abolishes Sheol entirely, except as a place of torment. It is based on a very high conception of man's spiritual and a very low conception of his bodily life. It looks to no return of the souls of the righteous in bodily form to this earth, and no establishment here of a glorious kingdom in which they shall rule triumphant over their foes. It has adopted, moreover, a more philosophical view of immortality, as against the vaguer Jewish view of a very long period, ages upon ages. This Platonic-Jewish doctrine of the future life profoundly affected Christian and post-Christian Jewish theology, especially as adopted and expounded by Philo.[1] In Palestinian Jewry it had little effect. According to Josephus (*Ant.* i, v; *Bell. Jud.* ii, viii, 11) it was held by the Essenes; presumably also by Grecian Jews.

The common doctrine of the future life held among the Jews of Palestine at the commencement of our era, the doctrine of the Pharisees, taught in the schools and synagogues, is fairly represented in various passages of the New Testament. After death the righteous were with the patriarchs (in Abraham's bosom)[2] in a paradise of feasting and joy; and the wicked in a place of torment. Here both awaited the Day of Judgment, when, raised from the dead, they should be rewarded or punished according to the deeds done on earth.[3] Righteous Israelites, for they only were contemplated in the Jewish doctrine, were then restored to rule in a new-made earth triumphant over all their foes, part of a regenerate Israel, an incarnate expression of the Law of God.

While, however, this was the common, it was far from being the universal, view. The conservative, priestly party continued to the last to resist foreign innovations and cling to the older pre-apocalyptic and in some regards pre-prophetic view of the solidarity of the family and nation, of retribution and reward for the individual only in

---

[1] Philo's doctrine was substantially Plato's dualism. The body is a prison, coffin, or grave for the soul, which seeks to rise again to God. Even in this life the truly wise and virtuous may be lifted above his sensible existence, and enjoy in ecstasy the vision of God. Beyond this ecstasy lies one further step, namely entire liberation of the soul from the body, and its return to God. Death brings this consummation, but only to those who have kept themselves free from attachment to things of sense. All others must at death pass into another body.

[2] Luke xvi, 19-31.   [3] Matt. xxv, 31-46.

this life, and of immortality as existing only in the family and the nation. Sheol to them is an "eternal house" (Eccles. xii, 5), in which "the dead know not anything, neither have they any more a reward" (ix, 5). "There is no work, nor device, nor knowledge, nor wisdom in Sheol" (ix, 10).[1] This division of view, which ultimately coincides with the sectarian division of Sadducees and Pharisees, begins to show itself clearly about 200 B.C. In Hebrew literature, as we have seen, the Pharisaic view finds expression in the Apocalypses; the Sadducean view in the Wisdom literature[2] and the Psalter.[3] The former was the doctrine of the Pharisees, the Synagogues, and the people as a whole; the latter, or Sadducean, doctrine was held by an aristocratic, conservative minority, in control of the Temple and the priesthood.[4]

[1] This view is, however, tempered with agnosticism in Ecclesiastes, so iii, 21 : "Who knows the spirit of the sons of men, whether it ascends upward, and the spirit of beasts, whether it descends downward to the earth?"

[2] Ecclus. xxx, 18 f.; xxxviii, 20–23; Bar. ii, 17.

[3] A considerable number of psalms in the first book treat of, or refer to, death and the after state, and in three of these (xvi, xvii, xxxvi) commentators have found indications of a hope of personal immortality. In the Korahite Psalter a similar hope has been recognized in xlix; in the Prayers of David, in lxi and lxiii; and in the Psalter of Asaph in lxxii. Later than this in the Psalter there is no glimmer of such a hope. The theory of the last two books is that with death existence ceases, and that the blessings of God and the rewards of good and evil are to be expected here. The last two books belong to the Temple as the earlier books do not. They represent specifically the priestly view, and belong to the period and the sphere of the spiritual predominance of the priestly aristocracy, which, when the Pharisees developed into a party, became the Sadducees.

[4] For much in this chapter I am indebted to Professor L. B. Paton's *The Hebrew Idea of the Future Life*, reprinted from *The Biblical World*, vol. xxxv, nos. 1–5.

CHRONOLOGY

(The dates in this table are largely approximate only)

1300 B.C.	Moses.
1000 B.C.	David.
950 B.C.	Solomon's Temple. Commencement of the Yahawist Narrative.
925 B.C.	The Great Schism: Israel and Judah.
875 B.C.	Commencement of the Elohist Narrative.
850 B.C.	Elijah, and the beginning of the war against Baal.
840 B.C.	The Yahaweh party triumphs in Israel under Jehu; and in Judah by the overthrow of Athaliah. Completion of Yahawist Narrative.
800 B.C.	Tales of the Prophets.
775 B.C.	Completion of Elohist Narrative, including Book of the Covenant.
750 B.C.	Amos and Hosea.
721 B.C.	Fall of Samaria.
720–692 B.C.	Isaiah and the Renaissance in Judah.
692–640 B.C.	The Reaction under Manasseh and Amon.
628–586 B.C.	Jeremiah.
623 B.C.	Deuteronomy and the Reformation under Josiah.
597 B.C.	Beginning of the Exile.
593–560 B.C.	Ezekiel.
586 B.C.	Destruction of Jerusalem.
538 B.C.	Restoration under Cyrus. Commencement of Persian period.
516 B.C.	Dedication of the second Temple.
440 B.C.	Rebuilding of the walls of Jerusalem under Nehemiah, reforms of Nehemiah, and commencement of the Samaritan schism.
380 B.C.	The adoption of the Law as Bible and religion under Ezra.
350 B.C.	Completion of Samaritan schism.
333 B.C.	Greek conquest, and commencement of Hellenistic period.
242 B.C.	First mention of the Synagogue, showing synagogal system as well and long established.
250–200 B.C.	The Canon of the Prophets.
168 B.C.	Desecration of the Temple by Antiochus Epiphanes.
165 B.C.	Rededication of the Temple by Judas Maccabæus.
142 B.C.	Simon appointed High Priest and prince of the Jewish people.
40 B.C.	Herod appointed King of Judæa by the Roman Senate.

SELECTED BIBLIOGRAPHY

GENERAL

GALLOWAY, GEORGE. The Philosophy of Religion (New York, 1914).

JASTROW, MORRIS, JR. The Study of Religion (London, 1901).

TOY, C. H. Introduction to the History of Religions (Boston, 1913).

JEVONS, F. B. An Introduction to the History of Religion (London, 1896).

KUENEN, ABRAHAM. National Religions and Universal Religions (New York, 1882).

MOORE, G. F. History of Religions, 2 vols. (second volume not yet published) (New York, 1913).

ERMAN, BEZOLD, GOLDZIHER, etc. Die Religion des Orients (in Die Kultur der Gegenwart) (2d ed., Leipzig, 1913).

SMITH, W. R. Lectures on the Religion of the Semites (2d ed., London, 1894).

LAGRANGE, MARIE-JOSEPH. Études sur les religions sémitiques (2d ed., Paris, 1905).

JEREMIAS, FRIEDRICH. Semitische Völker in Vorderasien (in Lehrbuch der Religionsgeschichte, edited by Chantepie de la Saussaye, vol. i, 3d ed., pp. 246–383) (Tübingen, 1907).

BAETHGEN, FR. Beiträge zur semitischen Religionsgeschichte (Berlin, 1888).

BAUDISSIN, WILHELM WOLF VON. Studien zur semitischen Religionsgeschichte, 2 vols. (Leipzig, 1876–1878).

BLISS, F. J. Religions of Palestine (New York, 1912).

MONTEFIORE, C. G. Origin and Growth of Religion as illustrated by the Religion of the Hebrews (London, 1893).

SMITH, H. P. The Religion of Israel (New York, 1914).

LOISY, A. The Religion of Israel (New York, 1910).

MARTI, KARL. The Religion of the Old Testament (New York, 1907).

ADDIS, W. E. Hebrew Religion (New York, 1906).

OTTLEY, R. L. The Religion of Israel (New York, 1905).

KUENEN, ABRAHAM. Religion of Israel to the Fall of the Jewish State (English translation by D. H. May), 3 vols. (London, 1882).

KÖNIG, EDUARD. Geschichte der alttestamentlichen Religion (Gütersloh, 1912).

VALETON, J. J. P., JR. Die Israeliten (in Lehrbuch der Religionsgeschichte, edited by Chantepie de la Saussaye, vol. i, 3d ed., pp. 384–467) (Tübingen, 1907).

SMEND, RUDOLF. Alttestamentliche Religionsgeschichte (2d ed., Freiburg, 1899).

SELLIN, ERNST. Beiträge zur israelitischen und jüdischen Religionsgeschichte, 2 vols. (Leipzig, 1896–1897).

BUDDE, KARL. Religion of Israel to the Exile (New York, 1899).

CHEYNE, T. K. Jewish Religious Life after the Exile (New York, 1898).

TOY, C. H. Judaism and Christianity (Boston, 1891 .

DAVIDSON, A. B. The Theology of the Old Testament (New York, 1904).

STADE, BERNHARD. Biblische Theologie des Alten Testaments (2d ed., Tübingen, 1905).

SMEND, RUDOLF. Alttestamentliche Theologie (Tübingen, 1899).

KAYSER, A. Die Theologie des Alten Testaments in ihrer geschichtlichen Entwickelung (3d ed. by Karl Marti, Strassburg, 1897).

DILLMANN, AUGUST. Handbuch der Alttestamentlichen Theologie (edited by Rudolph Kittel, Leipzig, 1895).

McCURDY, J. F. History, Prophecy, and the Monuments, 3 vols. (New York, 1894–1901).

PETERS, J. P. Archæological History of Hither Asia (in The Universal Anthology, vol. xxxii, pp. 270–420).

MERCER, S. B. Extra Biblical Sources for Hebrew and Jewish History (New York, 1913).

BARTON, G. A. A Sketch of Semitic Origins (New York, 1902).

MEYER, EDUARD. Geschichte des Altertums, vol. ii (2d ed., Berlin, 1909). (In course of publication.)

MEYER, EDUARD. Die Israeliten und ihre Nachbarstämme (Halle, 1906).

GRESSMANN, HUGO (with ARTHUR UNGNAD and HERMANN RANKE). Altorientalische Texte und Bilder, 2 vols. (Tübingen, 1909).

SMITH, H. P. Old Testament History (New York, 1903).

KENT and RIGGS. A History of the Hebrew People, 2 vols.; A History of the Jewish People, 2 vols. (New York, 1896–1900).

KITTEL, R. Geschichte des Volkes Israel (2d ed., Gotha, 1912).

GUTHE, H. Geschichte des Volkes Israel (2d ed., Tübingen, 1904).

WINCKLER, H. Geschichte Israels, 2 vols. (Leipzig, 1895–1900).

WELLHAUSEN, JULIUS. Israelitische und jüdische Geschichte (2d ed., Berlin, 1894).

STADE, BERNHARD. Geschichte des Volkes Israel, 2 vols. (Berlin, 1887–1888).

Encyclopædia Biblica, edited by T. K. Cheyne and J. S. Black, 4 vols.

Dictionary of the Bible, edited by James Hastings, 5 vols.

Encyclopædia of Religion and Ethics, edited by James Hastings. (In process of publication.)
Encyclopædia Britannica, 11th ed.
Jewish Encyclopedia.
Catholic Encyclopedia.

The first two of these six great encyclopædias deal exclusively with Biblical themes, and cover practically all that is discussed in this volume. Some of the articles are monographs of very great value. The former is radical, the latter moderate. The Encyclopædia of Religion covers a wider field; its articles dealing with the matter of this volume are not in general so extended as those in the two preceding, but the broader treatment enables the student to compare the usages and doctrines of other religions. The Biblical and oriental articles in the Encyclopædia Britannica are as a rule extremely valuable. The titles of the last two works suggest their special usefulness to the student of the " Religion of the Hebrews." Both contain material of value.

In German the best dictionaries of the Bible are : (1) Riehm, Handwörterbuch des biblischen Altertums, 2d ed., F. Baethgen, 2 vols. (Leipzig, 1893); (2) H. Guthe, Kurzes Bibelwörterbuch (Tübingen, 1903); and (3) the comprehensive Protestantische Realencyclopädie (3d ed., Leipzig). As a general dictionary of religion : Die Religion in Geschichte und Gegenwart, edited by Fr. M. Schiele, 1909.

In French the best general Bible Dictionary is F. Vigourony's Dictionnaire de la Bible, 5 vols. (Paris, 1895).

(1) The Orientalische Bibliographie, (2) the Zeitschrift für Alttestamentliche Wissenschaft, (3) the American Journal of Theology, (4) the Orientalistische Litteraturzeitung, and (5) the Journal of Theological Studies contain in each issue full bibliographical details.

CHAPTER I. SOURCES AND METHODS OF STUDY

JASTROW, MORRIS, JR. Hebrew and Babylonian Traditions (New York, 1914).

ROGERS, R. W. Cuneiform Parallels to the Old Testament (New York, 1912).

CLAY, A. T. Light on the Old Testament from Babel (Philadelphia, 1907).

HARPER, R. F. The Code of Hammurabi (Chicago, 1904).

JOHNS, C. H. W. Babylonian and Assyrian Laws, Contracts, and Letters (New York, 1904).

HILPRECHT, H. V. Explorations in Bible Lands (Philadelphia, 1903).

BALL, C. J. Light from the East (London, 1899).

NICOL, T. Recent Archæology and the Bible (Edinburgh, 1899).

SCHRADER, EBERHARD. Keilinschriftliche Bibliothek, 6 vols. (Leipzig, 1889–1900).

FOWLER, HENRY T. A History of the Literature of Ancient Israel (New York, 1912).

CORNILL, C. H. Introduction to the Canonical Books of the Old Testament (New York, 1907).

KAUTSCH, EMIL. The Literature of the Old Testament (London, 1898).

DRIVER, S. R. Introduction to the Literature of the Old Testament (6th ed., New York, 1897).

KENT, C. F. Students' Old Testament, 4 vols. (New York, 1905–1910).

CHARLES, R. H. Apocrypha and Pseudepigrapha of the Old Testament, 2 vols. (Oxford, 1913).

BUDDE, KARL, und BARTHOLET, A. Geschichte der Althebräischen Litteratur (Leipzig, 1906).

ORR, JAMES. The Problem of the Old Testament (New York, 1906).

PETERS, JOHN P. The Old Testament and the New Scholarship (London, 1901).

SMITH, W. R. The Old Testament in the Jewish Church (2d ed., London, 1892).

EERDMANNS, BENNO. Alttestamentliche Studien (Giessen, 1908–1910).

For the individual books of the Old Testament: The International Critical Commentary, edited by Briggs, Driver, and Plummer, is the best general commentary in existence.

Other recent series of commentaries covering the Old Testament are: (1) The Sacred Books of the Old Testament (Hebrew and English) (edited by Paul Haupt, Leipzig, 1893, not completed); (2) Göttingen Handkommentar zum Alten Testament (edited by W. Nowack, Göttingen, 1896); (3) Kurzer Hand-Commentar zum Alten Testament (edited by Karl Marti, Tübingen, 1898); (4) Kommentar zum Alten Testament (edited by Ernst Sellin, Leipzig, 1913).

CHAPTER II. LAND AND PEOPLE

Baedeker's Palestine and Syria (5th ed., Leipzig, 1912).

SMITH, GEORGE ADAM. The Historical Geography of the Holy Land (London, 1898).

SMITH, GEORGE ADAM. Jerusalem from the Earliest to the Latest Times, 2 vols. (London, 1907–1908).

HUNTINGTON, ELLSWORTH. Palestine and its Transformation (Boston, 1911).

ROBINSON, EDWARD. Biblical Researches in Palestine, 3 vols. (London, 1867).

VINCENT, H. Canaan d'après l'exploration récente (Paris, 1907).

GUTHE, H. Bibelatlas (Leipzig, 1911).

GUTHE, H. Palästina (Bielefeld, 1907).

THOMSON, PETER. Kompendium der palästinischen Altertumskunde (with full bibliographical data) (Tübingen, 1913).

THOMSON, PETER. Palästina und seine Kultur in fünf Jahrtausenden (Leipzig, 1909).

BENZINGER, I. Hebräische Archäologie (2d ed., Freiburg, 1907).

NOWACK, F. Lehrbuch der hebräischen Archäologie (Freiburg, 1894).

JASTROW, MORRIS, JR. Egypt and Palestine, 1400 B.C. (in *J. B. L.*, xi, pp. 95–124).

DELATTRE, A. J. Le Pays de Chanaan (in *Revue des questions historiques*, July, 1896, pp. 5–94).

For more detailed study of the land, and records of excavations and discoveries, the publications, and especially the great maps and memoirs, of the Palestine Exploration Fund should be consulted. The quarterly statements of the Fund, which began to be published in 1868, constitute a current history of exploration and discovery in and about Palestine since that date. In 1911 the Fund commenced the publication of an Annual, of which two numbers have appeared to date.

Special bibliographies of Palestine literature are published by Peter Thomson, in Systematische Bibliographie der Palästinaliteratur, vol. i (Leipzig, 1895–1904); vol. ii (Leipzig, 1905–1909); vol. iii (Leipzig, 1910–1914, to appear in 1915).

CHAPTER III. PRIMITIVE RELIGION OF THE HEBREWS

FRAZER, J. G. The Golden Bough (3d ed., 1911–1914): vol. i, Magic Art and the Evolution of Kings, 2 parts; vol. ii, Taboo and the Perils of the Soul; vol. iii, The Dying God; vol. iv, Adonis, Attis, Osiris; vol. v, Spirits of the Corn and of the Wild; vol. vi, Scapegoat; vol. vii, Balder the Beautiful, 2 parts.

TYLOR, E. B. Primitive Culture, 2 vols. (3d ed., New York, 1889).

TRUMBULL, H. C. The Blood Covenant (2d ed., New York, 1885).

TRUMBULL, H. C. The Threshold Covenant (New York, 1896).

TRUMBULL, H. C. The Covenant of Salt (New York, 1899).

COOK, S. A. The Religion of Ancient Palestine (Chicago, 1909).

PATON, L. B. The Early History of Syria and Palestine (New York, 1902).

PETERS, J. P. Early Hebrew Story (New York, 1904).

BACON, B. W. Genesis of Genesis (Hartford, 1892).

GORDON, A. R. The Early Traditions of Genesis (New York, 1907).

CURTISS, S. I. Primitive Semitic Religion To-day (Chicago, 1902).

TOY, C. H. Polytheism in Genesis as a Mark of Date (in Essays on Modern Theology and Related Subjects, pp. 1–12) (New York, 1913).

CURTISS, S. I. The Tribes of Israel (in Historical and Critical Contributions to Biblical Science) (New York, 1901).

JASTROW, MORRIS, JR. The Men of Judah in the El-Amarna Tablets (in *J. B. L.*, xii, 61–72).

WELLHAUSEN, JULIUS. Reste arabischen Heidenthums (Berlin, 1887).

KNUDTZON, J. A. Die El-Amarna Tafeln (Leipzig, 1910–1913).

WOLF, WILHELM, GRAF VON BAUDISSIN. Adonis und Esmun (Berlin,1911).

BUDDE, KARL. Die biblische Urgeschichte (Giessen, 1883).

GUNKEL, H. Genesis (2d ed., Göttingen, 1913).

GUNKEL, HERMANN. Schöpfung und Chaos (Göttingen, 1895).

PROCKSCH, OTTO. Das Nordhebräische Sagenbuch (Leipzig, 1906).

GRÜNEISEN, KARL. Der Ahnenkultus und die Urreligion Israels (Halle, 1900).

MEYER, EDUARD. Die Entstehung des Judentums (Halle, 1896).

STADE, BERNHARD. Die Entstehung des Volkes Israel (in Ausgewählte akademische Reden und Abhandlungen, pp. 97–121).

MEYER, E. Der Stamm Jakob und die Entstehung der israelitischen Stämme (in *Z. A. T. W.*, vi, 1–16).

GRESSMANN, H. Sage und Geschichte in den Patriarchenerzählungen (in *Z. A. T. W.*, xxx, 1–34).

GALL, AUGUST VON. Altisraelitische Kultstätten (in *Z. A. T. W.*, Beihefte, iii).

WESTPHAL, GUSTAV. Jahwes Wohnstätten (in *Z. A. T. W.*, Beihefte, xv).

CHAPTER IV. THE RELIGION OF MOSES

GRESSMANN, H. Mose und seine Zeit (Göttingen, 1913).

BACON, B. W. The Triple Tradition of the Exodus (Hartford, 1894).

BARTON, G. A. Yahweh before Moses (in Studies in the History of Religions) (New York, 1912).

BREASTED, J. H. Development of Religion and Thought in Ancient Egypt (New York, 1912).

BUDGE, E. A. W. The Book of the Dead, 3 vols. (London, 1898).

JASTROW, MORRIS, JR. Palestine and Assyria in the Days of Joshua (in *Z. A.*, vii, pp. 1–7).

MEYER, E. Kritik der Berichte über die Eroberung Palästinas (in *Z. A. T. W.*, i, 117–145).

CHAPTER V. THE RELIGION OF CANAAN AND ITS INFLUENCE ON THE HEBREWS

MACALISTER, R. A. S. The Excavation of Gezer, 3 vols. (London, 1912).

BÖHL, F. Kanaanäer und Hebräer (Leipzig, 1911).

BUHL, FRANTZ. Geschichte des alten Palästina (Tübingen, 1896).

Chapter VII. Development of the Priesthood

Baudissin, W. Wolf von. Die Geschichte des alttestamentlichen Priestertums (Leipzig, 1889).

Maybaum, Sigmund. Die Entwickelung des altisraelitischen Priestertums (Breslau, 1880).

Paton, L. B. The Use of the Word *Kohen* in the Old Testament (in *J. B. L.*, xii, 1–14).

Walker, D. A. The Levitical Priesthood (in *J. B. L.*, xix, 125–131).

Gates, O. H. The Relation of Priests to Sacrifice before the Exile (in *J. B. L.*, xxvii, No. 1, pp. 67–92).

Chapter VIII. Development of Ritual

Kittel, R. Studien zur hebräischen Archäologie (Leipzig, 1908).

Foote, T. C. The Ephod (in *J. B. L.*, xxi, 1–47).

Langdon, Stephen. The History and Significance of Carthaginian Sacrifice (in *J. B. L.*, xxiii, 79–93).

Chapter IX. Effects of the National Schism

Peters, J. P. The Two Great Nature Shrines of Israel: Bethel and Dan (in Studies in the History of Religions, pp. 231–241) (New York, 1912).

Chapter XII. Early Codes

Carpenter, J. E., and Battersby, G. H. The Hexateuch, 2 vols. (London, 1900).

Addis, W. E. The Documents of the Hexateuch, 2 vols. (New York, 1893–1898).

Paton, L. B. The Original Form of the Book of the Covenant (in *J. B. L.*, xii, 79–93).

Chapter XIII. Writing Prophets and their New Doctrines

Batten, L. W. The Hebrew Prophet (New York, 1905).

Cornill, C. H. Prophets of Israel (Chicago, 1897).

Smith, W. R. The Prophets of Israel (London, 1882).

Ewald, H. Die Propheten des alten Bundes, 3 vols. (Göttingen, 1867–1868) (translated by J. F. Smith, Commentary on the Prophets of the Old Testament, 5 vols., London, 1875–1881).

Kuenen, Abraham. The Prophets of Israel (English translation by A. M. May, 3 vols., London, 1875).

Smith, George Adam. The Book of the Twelve Prophets, vol. i (New York, 1896).

SELLIN, ERNST. Der Alttestamentliche Prophetismus (Leipzig, 1912).
MAYBAUM, SIGMUND. Die Entwickelung des israelitischen Propheten-thums (Berlin, 1883).
DUHM, B. Theologie der Propheten (Bonn, 1875).
NOWACK, W. Die kleinen Propheten (Göttingen, 1897).
WELLHAUSEN, JULIUS. Die kleinen Propheten, übersetzt mit Noten (2d ed., Berlin, 1893).
BAUMANN, EBERHARD. Der Aufbau der Amosreden (in Z. A. T. W., Beihefte, vii–viii).

CHAPTER XIV. THE FALL OF ISRAEL AND THE RENAISSANCE IN JUDAH

SMITH, GEORGE ADAM. The Book of Isaiah, vol. i (London, 1889).
DUHM, B. Jesaia (Göttingen, 1892).

CHAPTER XVI. THE REFORMATION

DAY, E. The Promulgation of Deuteronomy (in J. B. L., xxi, 197–213).
TOY, C. H. The Triumph of Yahwism (in J. B. L., xxiv, No. 2, pp. 91–106).

CHAPTER XVII. THE FALL OF JERUSALEM AND THE PROPHECIES OF THAT PERIOD

DRIVER, S. R. The Book of the Prophet Jeremiah (New York, 1906).
GIESEBRECHT, FRIEDRICH. Das Buch Jeremia (Göttingen, 1907).
MITCHELL, H. G. The Theology of Jeremiah (in J. B. L., xx, 56–76).

CHAPTER XVIII. EZEKIEL THE THEOLOGIAN

CORNILL, C. H. Das Buch des Propheten Ezekiel (Leipzig, 1886).
SMEND, RUDOLF. Der Prophet Ezekiel (Leipzig, 1880).

CHAPTER XIX. HOLINESS

PATON, L. B. The Original Form of Leviticus XXI–XXII (in J. B. L., xvii, 149–175).
PATON, L. B. The Original Form of Leviticus XXIII–XXV (in J. B. L., xviii, 35–60).

CHAPTER XX. THE EXILE

HAUPT, PAUL. Babylonian Elements in the Levitic Ritual (in J. B. L., xix, 55–81).
FISCHER, O. Die Chronologie des Priesterkodex und ihre Umgestaltungen (in Z. A. T. W., xxxi, 241–255).

CHAPTER XXI. THE RESTORATION

BENNETT. The Post-exilic Prophets (New York, 1907).

HUNTER, P. H. After the Exile, 2 vols. (Edinburgh, 1890).

SMITH, GEORGE ADAM. The Book of Isaiah, vol. ii (London, 1889).

SMITH, GEORGE ADAM. The Book of the Twelve Prophets, vol. ii (New York, 1898).

MEYER, EDUARD. Der Papyrusfund von Elephantine (Leipzig, 1912).

SACHAU, EDUARD. Aramäische Papyrus und Ostraka (Berlin, 1911).

CURTIS, E. L. The Return of the Jews under Cyrus (in Essays in Modern Theology and Related Subjects, pp. 33–40) (New York, 1911).

BRIGGS, C. A. An Analysis of Isaiah 40–62 (in Old Testament and Semitic Studies in Memory of W. R. Harper, vol. i, pp. 65–112) (Chicago, 1908).

TORREY, C. C. The Edomites in Southern Judah (in *J. B. L.*, xvii, 16–20).

COBB, W. H. Where was Isaiah XL–LXVI written? (in *J. B. L.*, xxvii, No. 1, pp. 48–64).

SELLIN, ERNST. Studien zur Entstehungsgeschichte der jüdischen Gemeinde nach dem babylonischen Exil, 2 vols. (Leipzig, 1901).

CHAPTER XXII. THE PROBLEM OF EVIL

CHEYNE, T. K. Job and Solomon (London, 1887).

JASTROW, MORRIS, JR. A Babylonian Parallel to the Story of Job (in *J. B. L.*, xxv, 135–191).

CHAPTER XXIII. THE LAW

KENT and SANDERS. The Growth of Israelitish Law (in Historical and Critical Contributions to Biblical Science) (New York, 1901).

BEWER, J. A. The Original Significance of the Rite of the Red Cow (in *J. B. L.*, xxiv, 41–44).

CHEYNE, T. K. The Date and Origin of the Ritual of the "Scapegoat" (in *Z. A. T. W.*, xv, 153–156).

ADLER, S. Der Versöhnungstag in der Bibel, sein Ursprung und seine Bedeutung (in *Z. A. T. W.*, iii, 178–184).

BENZINGER, J. Das Gesetz über den grossen Versöhnungstag (in *Z. A. T. W.*, ix, 65–88).

COUARD, L. Die religiös-nationale Bedeutung der Lade Jahves (in *Z. A. T. W.*, xii, 53–90).

BUDDE, K. Die ursprüngliche Bedeutung der Lade Jahwe's (in *Z. A. T. W.*, xxi, 193–197).

BRANDT, WILHELM. Jüdische Reinheitslehre und ihre Beschreibung in den Evangelien (in *Z. A. T. W.*, Beihefte, xix).

CHAPTER XXIV. THE NEW RELIGION

TORREY, C. C. Ezra Studies (Chicago, 1910).

MONTGOMERY, J. A. The Samaritans (Philadelphia, 1907).

BROWN, FRANCIS. The Decline of Prophecy (in Essays in Modern Theology and Related Subjects, pp. 65-82) (New York, 1911).

TORREY, C. C. The Prophecy of Malachi (in *J. B. L.*, xvii, 1-15).

TORREY, C. C. The Composition and Historical Value of Ezra-Nehemiah (in *Z. A. T. W.*, Beihefte, ii).

LÖHR, MAX. Sozialismus und Individualismus im Alten Testament (in *Z. A. T. W.*, Beihefte, x).

CHAPTER XXV. THE TEMPLE

FULLERTON, KEMPER. The Anti-Sacrificial Psalms (in Essays in Modern Theology and Related Subjects) (New York, 1911).

PETERS, J. P. The Sons of Korah (in Essays in Modern Theology and Related Subjects, pp. 41-48) (New York, 1911).

TOY, C. H. On some Conceptions of the Old Testament Psalter (in Old Testament and Semitic Studies in Memory of W. R. Harper, vol. i, pp. 1-24) (Chicago, 1908).

PETERS, J. P. Notes on some Ritual Uses of the Psalms (in *J. B. L.*, xxix, No. 2, pp. 113-125).

CHAPTER XXVI. THE SYNAGOGUE AND THE SCRIBES

OESTERLEY, W. O. E., and BOX, G. H. The Religion and Worship of the Synagogue (New York, 1907).

SCHÜRER, EMIL. The Jewish People in the Time of Jesus Christ, 5 vols. (Edinburgh, 1890-1891).

CHAPTER XXVII. PERSECUTION AND NATIONAL REVIVAL

JOSEPHUS. Antiquities of the Jews (English translation by William Whiston, many editions). (The best translation is that into French, under the direction of Theodor Reinach, Paris, 1900-1904; the best critical edition of the original is that by B. Niese, Berlin, 1887-1894, 6 vols. and index.)

BEVAN, E. R. Jerusalem under the High Priests (New York, 1904).

BEVAN, A. A. A Short Commentary on the Book of Daniel (Cambridge, 1892).

PRINCE, J. D. Critical Commentary on the Book of Daniel (Leipzig, 1899).

Chapter XXVIII. The Messianic Hope

CHARLES, R. H. The Book of Enoch (Oxford, 1912).

CHARLES, R. H. Eschatology, Hebrew, Jewish, and Christian (London, 1899).

GREENSTONE, J. H. The Messiah Idea in Jewish History (Philadelphia, 1906).

STANTON, V. H. The Jewish and Christian Messiah (London, 1886).

BRIGGS, C. A. Messianic Prophecy (New York, 1886).

DRUMMOND, JAMES. The Jewish Messiah (London, 1877).

DAY, T. F. Man and the Messianic Hope (in Essays in Modern Theology and Related Subjects, pp. 83–92) (1911).

BARTON, G. A. Pre-existence of the Messiah (in *J. B. L.*, xxi, 78–91).

BALDENSPERGER, W. Die messianisch-apokalyptische Hoffnung des Judentums (3d ed., Strassburg, 1905).

HILGENFELD, A. Jüdische Apokalyptik (Jena, 1857).

STADE, BERNHARD. Die messianische Hoffnung im Psalter (in Ausgewählte Reden und Abhandlungen, pp. 37–76) (2d ed., Giessen, 1907).

HARRIS, J. R. The Odes and Psalms of Solomon (New York, 1909).

RYLE, H. E., and JAMES, M. R. The Psalms of Solomon (1891).

KITTEL, GERARD. Die Oden Salomos (Leipzig, 1914).

FRANKENBERG, WILHELM. Das Verständnis der Oden Salomos (in *Z. A. T. W.*, Beihefte, xxi).

FRANKENBERG, WILHELM. Die Datierung der Psalmen Salomos (in *Z. A. T. W.*, Beihefte, i).

Chapter XXIX. The Future Life

BURNEY, C. F. Israel's Hope of Immortality (Oxford, 1909).

CHARLES, R. H. A Critical History of the Doctrine of a Future Life (London, 1899).

LODS, A. La Croyance à la vie future et le culte des morts dans l'antiquité israélite (Paris, 1906).

TORGE, PAUL. Seelenglaube und Unsterblichkeitshoffnung im Alten Testament (Leipzig, 1909).

FREY, J. TOD. Seelenglaube und Seelenkult im alten Israel (Leipzig, 1898).

SCHWALLY, F. Das Leben nach dem Tode nach den Vorstellungen des alten Israels (Giessen, 1892).

PORTER, F. C. The Pre-existence of the Soul in the Book of Wisdom and in the Rabbinical Writings (in Old Testament and Semitic Studies in Memory of W. R. Harper, vol. i, pp. 205–270) (Chicago, 1908).

STAVE, E. Über den Einfluss des Parsismus auf das Judenthum (Leipzig, 1898).

CUMONT, FRANZ. Les Mystères de Mithra (2d ed., Brussels, 1902) (English translation by T. J. McCormack, The Mysteries of Mithra, Chicago, 1903).

CUMONT, FRANZ. Astrology and Religion among the Greeks and Romans (New York, 1912).

KRAUSS, SAMUEL. Talmudische Archäologie, 3 vols.

WEBER, F. Jüdische Theologie (2d ed. by Franz Delitzsch and G. Schnedernan, 1897).

BOUSSET, WILHELM. Religion des Judentums im neutestamentlichen Zeitalter (Berlin, 1903).

GRESSMANN, HUGO. Der Ursprung der israelitisch-jüdischen Eschatologie (Göttingen, 1905).

BRANDT, WILHELM. Die jüdischen Baptismen (in Z. A. T. W., Beihefte, xviii).

PATON, L. B. The Hebrew Idea of the Future Life (in Biblical World, 1910, pp. 8–20, 80–92, 159–171).

INDEX OF NAMES AND SUBJECTS

INDEX OF BIBLE PASSAGES

OLD TESTAMENT

GENESIS

EXODUS

LEVITICUS

NUMBERS

DEUTERONOMY

2 SAMUEL

1 KINGS

2 KINGS

1 CHRONICLES

2 CHRONICLES

EZRA

NEHEMIAH

JOB

PSALMS

PROVERBS

ECCLESIASTES

ISAIAH

EZEKIEL

DANIEL

HOSEA

BARUCH

1 MACCABEES

2 MACCABEES

ENOCH

APOCALYPSE OF BARUCH

SIBYLLINE ORACLES

PSALMS OF SOLOMON

EPISTLE OF JEREMIAH

JUBILEES